MARKETING RESEARCH
A management information approach

MARKETING RESEARCH

A management
information approach

DANNY N. BELLENGER

and

BARNETT A. GREENBERG

both of the
School of Business Administration
Georgia State University

1978

RICHARD D. IRWIN, INC.   Homewood, Illinois   60430
Irwin-Dorsey Limited   Georgetown, Ontario   L7G 4B3

First Printing, January 1978

ISBN 0-256-01990-8

Library of Congress Catalog Card No. 77–79385

Printed in the United States of America

To
Judy Bellenger and Marti Greenberg

Preface

This text provides an introduction to the area of marketing research. It is intended for use in the first undergraduate course in marketing research but may also be of value at the M.B.A. level. The treatment in the text assumes the student to have had courses in principles of marketing and principles of statistics.

Two basic approaches can be taken in a marketing research course. First, an attempt can be made to train the student as a researcher. Heavy emphasis is placed on research techniques and methods, such as sampling, questionnaire design, and experimentation. This has been the traditional approach in marketing research courses, but since most marketing students will not become professional researchers, a strong argument can be made for a more managerial approach. This second approach, with a managerial focus, attempts to train the student as an intelligent user of information. The first approach seems more appropriate for elective courses designed for those students whose career plans will require them to design and implement marketing research projects. A user or managerial orientation, however, seems better for the typical marketing major. Thus, a managerial approach has been adopted in this text.

The managerial orientation is developed by stressing such topics as the informational needs of marketing managers, decision models and concepts, and the applications of research in marketing management. An attempt has been made to demonstrate the close relationship between the information provided by research and the decision making of marketing managers. Some understanding of research techniques is necessary, of course, for the marketing manager to evaluate the quality of the information he receives. The emphasis of the text is not on research methodology, however. The sections on data collection and analysis present an overview, but do not attempt an in-depth treatment of these areas. Rather, the text stresses marketing information from the manager's point of view and should provide the future manager with a better understanding of the interaction of research and decision making.

The text consists of 14 chapters gathered into three parts. Part I (Chapters 1–3) examines marketing decision-making activities which give rise to the need for research. Such topics as problem definition, the specification of information needs, and decision-making models are covered in this section. Part II (Chapters 4–10) deals with the research process. Data collection, basic analysis, and research reporting are discussed along with qualitative and quantitative research in marketing. Part III (Chapters 11–14) explores the application of marketing research in selected marketing decision areas along with the management of research activities. Management information needs for analyzing market opportunities and making product, pricing, distribution, and promotion decisions are examined. Illustrations of research which provide information in selected decision areas are also presented. The final chapter discusses some basic concepts and principles related to managing the marketing research program within a firm.

The text material makes extensive use of the systems framework to add structure to the discussion. An assortment of cases is also provided as a supplement to the text. An attempt was made to include cases with sufficient variation in length, type of organization, and subject area to allow the professor considerable flexibility in their use. Case topics include problem definition, decision analysis, research design, data analysis, and managerial interpretation of research.

The authors are indebted to a number of people. Specifically, we wish to thank David W. Cravens of the University of Tennessee and James Littlefield of the University of North Carolina for their excellent criticisms and suggestions. Several others have made very helpful suggestions. Among them are Kenneth L. Bernhardt, Jac L. Goldstucker, Dan H. Robertson and Wilbur S. Wagman, all of Georgia State University; Charles F. Steilen at the Chinese University of Hong Kong; and Jerry E. Wheat at the University of Miami.

We also want to acknowledge the kindness of all the individuals and companies who provided us with the illustrations that are an integral part of this book. Individual acknowledgments accompany several illustrations.

Additionally, we wish to thank our assistants and typists for their invaluable support. These include Bill Adcock, Susan Baylen, Brenda

Hemperley, Elizabeth Hirschman, Ruth Otte, Ravi Parameswaran, Ugur Yavas, and Susan Logan.

Finally, we wish to thank our families whose contributions are beyond measure.

December 1977   DANNY N. BELLENGER
                                                  BARNETT A. GREENBERG

Contents

search would exceed its value. When there is an insufficient budget to do a technically adequate job. When time is an enemy. When conducting research would tip your hand to a competitor. When research findings would not be actionable. When research is politically motivated. When the problem is not clear and the objectives not well defined. When a test does not represent later reality. When the findings are intended for use in legal proceedings. When what is to be measured changes slowly. When the information already exists.

Cases for part one

Part two
Conducting marketing research

Steps in the research process: *Defining the marketing decision and determining information needs. Research problems. Review the literature. Formulating research hypotheses. Categorize and operationally define the variables. Design research. Collect data. Analyze data. Report/ evaluate findings.* An illustration of the research process. The value of the research process: *Systematic. Logical. Empirical. Replicable.*

General data requirements. Internal secondary data: *Securing internal secondary data. Converting accounting data to marketing information.* External secondary data: *Securing external secondary data. Sources of external secondary data. An illustration of external secondary data. Evaluating external secondary data.* Commercial data: *The nature of commercial data. Types of commercial data. An illustration of commercial data*

Measurement: *Types of variables. Scaling. Questionnaire construction. Nonmetric multidimensional scaling. Reliability and validity in measurement. Alternative contact methods.* Sampling: *Sampling decisions. Sample size. Sampling techniques. Probability samples. Nonprobability samples.*

Introduction. Focus group interviews: *Description. Dynamics and the role of the moderator. Advantages and uses. Disadvantages and mis-*

uses. Depth interviews: *Description. Advantages and disadvantages of depth interviews. Using depth interviewing: Some examples.* Projective techniques: *Description. Type of projective techniques. Advantages and disadvantages of projective techniques. Using projective techniques: Some examples.* Other considerations in qualitative research: *Sampling in qualitative research. Analyzing qualitative data. Limitations of qualitative research. Trends in qualitative research.*

8. Quantitative research in marketing 199

Survey research: *The nature and use of survey research. Illustrative applications of survey research.* Experimental research: *Experimental designs. An illustration of experimental research.* Simulation in marketing: *The basic concept of simulation. An illustration of simulation.* Other considerations in quantitative research: *Sampling and analysis. Limitations of quantitative research. Trends in quantitative research.*

9. Basic analysis 228

Sorting and summarizing by cross tabulation. Selecting statistical techniques. Measures of central tendency and variability: *Mean. Median. Standard deviation. Confidence intervals.* Tests of significance: *The t test. The chi-square test. Analysis of variance.* Correlation and association: *Simple regression. Multiple regression. Multiple discriminant analysis. Factor analysis.* Marketing models as analytical techniques: *Defining models. An example of a general marketing model. An example of a tailor-made marketing model. Appendix.*

10. Communicating and evaluating research results 263

Research reporting as a communication process: *Encoding and decoding. Feedback. Noise. Transmittal (media channels).* System for research reporting: *Determine report parameters. Plan report. Develop report. Deliver report.* Evaluating research results: *Internal evaluation. External evaluation.*

Cases for part two

Part three
Applying and managing market research

Part one

Deciding when to conduct marketing research

chapter

1

Marketing information and decision making

THE DECISION ENVIRONMENT

The task of management within the modern corporation is extremely complex. Firms have many goals which are usually pursued simultaneously. Some of the more apparent ones are profits, market share, geographic expansion, growth, dominance, satisfied customers, social responsibility, and in this era, a desire to conserve scarce resources. The goals which are emphasized at any given time depend on a number of internal and external factors and how management reacts to them. The marketing strategies of a firm have become increasingly significant elements in goal attainment. Marketing managers have a major responsibility toward that end since they are concerned with the problems and decisions which shape marketing strategies.

Marketing management as a unit must assume responsibility for such diverse areas as: product development, pricing, sales, market research, advertising, promotion development, physical distribution, and channel structure. In doing this, the managers must develop answers to questions such as the following related to advertising.

1. Out of your total budget for daytime TV spots, should you divert $1 million to nighttime network television . . . and if you do, what changes will you make in your pattern of daytime TV?
2. Results of new advertising copy run in three test markets are satisfactory, but not outstanding. What will increase its effectiveness and how will you test the changes in time for national expansion a year from now?

3. You expect to have an improved product ready for distribution in six months. What ideas should the agency creative people be developing now to generate a strong positive consumer reaction to the product change?[1]

The answers to such questions will help determine the degree to which the firm is able to meet its goals. Marketing managers are responsible for making appropriate decisions. The kinds of decisions they make are influenced by a number of factors such as:

1. The volatile nature of buyers.
2. The geographic dispersion of markets.
3. The variability of people in the marketing organization.
4. The dependency on people outside the organization.
5. The diversity of alternatives in terms of marketing mix and promotion mix.

These factors and many others contribute to the risk and uncertainty associated with marketing decision making. Decisions concerning new-product development, advertising campaigns, pricing strategies, and market research all contain a great deal of risk and uncertainty. Costly research efforts, expensive advertising campaigns, and expenditures for new-product research represent significant drains on the resources of the firm. When these costs are coupled with risk and uncertainty, it becomes obvious that the quality of decisions made by the marketing manager is critical in determining the firm's success. How can marketing managers function effectively in this highly complex decision environment?

The answer lies, at least in part, in the effective application of scientific methods to marketing decision making. Decision making is predictive in nature. In making a decision, the manager is predicting both the outcome of a number of alternative solutions, and that the course of action chosen represents the optimum among the available alternatives. When selecting among alternative advertising campaigns, there is an implicit prediction as to which will be most effective in stimulating sales. The decision to use a particular marketing mix implies a prediction about future profitability resulting from the particular alternative selected.

The aim of science is to facilitate more accurate decision making by providing more nearly perfect knowledge. The ability to predict the outcomes of particular alternative courses of action more accurately reduces the risk associated with uncertainty. Of course, perfect knowledge is not a practical reality. However, the more nearly perfect the

---

[1] See "Procter and Gamble Brand Management," Procter and Gamble Company, p. 10.

knowledge, the less uncertainty in the decision-making process and hence the less risk in predicting outcome. Harper W. Boyd and William F. Massey point out that, ". . . Many years will pass before enough is understood about marketing factors and their interrelationships to permit the making of nearly perfect predictions whenever they are needed for problem-solving."[2] Nevertheless, important advances have been made in problem solving in marketing, and the use of scientific methods can facilitate marketing decision making.

The purpose of this chapter and the others in Part I is to establish a conceptual framework for treating marketing decision making/information generating in a scientific fashion. A more detailed discussion of selected areas of this framework will be presented in later chapters.

Today's business organizations need highly structured methods to cope with the significant increases in size, complexity, and diversity of operations. These factors are moving management away from the art that has existed into a new arena. What management needs today is an underlying science, or at least a very structured approach, to decision making. This approach has been given the name "systems." The systems approach provides a means for accommodating increasing organizational complexity. It provides a framework for visualizing both internal and external environmental factors in an integrated fashion. In short, the systems approach is a structured way of thinking about managing.

THE SYSTEMS CONCEPT

The word system can be defined in many ways depending upon the purpose for the definition. For our purpose the following definition seems best: *a system is a structure which implements an ongoing process*. The structure may be formed by many diverse parts, but the parts work together toward a common objective. The word system connotes order, a plan, a method, or arrangement.

A dictionary definition of a biological system can serve in explaining the concept: "An assemblage of parts or organs of the same or similar tissues, or concerned with the same function; e.g., the nervous system, the digestive system."[3] Similarly, a marketing system consists of diverse parts (a structure) which are concerned with the same function—the process of generating the desired quantity and type of transactions.

---

[2] Harper W. Boyd, Jr. and William F. Massey, *Marketing Management* (New York: Harcourt Brace Jovanovich, Inc., 1972), p. 21.

[3] Joel E. Ross, *Management by Information System* (Englewood Cliffs, N.J.: Prentice-Hall, 1970), p. 2.

Figure 1–1
The systems concept

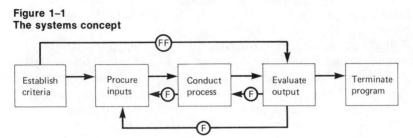

A system can be thought of as having certain basic aspects (see Figure 1–1). Any system whether mechanical, biological, or behavioral can be viewed in these terms.

1. The central focus of a system is the *internal parts or components* which carry out the process. Seymour Tilles defines a system as "a set of interrelated parts."[4] These parts must work together to efficiently carry out the desired process. The parts of the system and the relationship between them are controllable elements for a manager. The managerial role within a system is as a coordinator of controllable factors. A manager must monitor and control the operation of the functional parts and system's inputs in such a way as to achieve the desired results.

2. *Inputs* are the other controllable elements of a system. The inputs flow into the central processing unit and either act as support in building or developing the functional parts or act as raw material for the process. Inputs can include people, money, equipment, information, and many other elements depending upon the nature of the process being performed by the system.

3. *Outputs* are the end products of the process. The outputs of a total marketing system are the transactions of specified type and quantity, generated by the system. The output of a gasoline engine is generally some type of motion. The nature of the outputs and whether they accomplish the goals of the system depend on the manager's skill in arranging the functional parts of the system and in securing needed inputs.

4. *Feedback* keeps the manager informed about the results obtained by the outputs of the system. It helps control the system by monitoring results. If results are not in line with system goals, the manager can alter the inputs, change the goals, or rearrange the

---

[4] Seymour Tilles, "The Manager's Job: A Systems Approach," *Harvard Business Review*, 41 (1963), pp. 73–81.

functional parts of the system to bring goals and results into harmony.

5. The *environment* of the system consists of all uncontrollable factors which affect the process. The nature of the environment depends upon the specifications of the particular system being used. As narrower areas of the firm's total activity are viewed as comprising a system, the number of uncontrollable variables increases. Corporate goals may be uncontrollable for a new product development manager and thus, they must be viewed as a part of the environment. They are external constraints on the activities of the system.

This notion of uncontrollable factors in the environment is the key to understanding the limits of a system model. For example, a firm may be engaged in the marketing process for a particular product which is subject to rigid governmental certification procedures. The firm cannot control the certification process, thus a relevant decision process model would not include it. References would be made, however, to such activities as *monitor certification process*. Thus, the firm would use information about the procedure in its decision-making process.

SYSTEM LANGUAGE

In this text, systems will be represented through the LOGOS language.[5] In LOGOS, systems are represented by rectangles and identified by an action phrase of two to five words. When a system is actually a wholly contained element of a larger system, it is called a *subsystem*. Figure 1–1 contains five subsystems. These five subsystems and their interrelationships constitute a *suprasystem*. Illustrating the suprasystem with these five subsystems, each of which represents the same level of activity, is known as defining the system at the first level of detail.

Flows into a system or subsystem are illustrated in LOGOS by a *signal path*. In Figure 1–1, for example, there is an incoming signal path to "Procure inputs" from "Establish criteria." In this particular case the incoming flow is a signal to proceed with the procurement of inputs as well as some parameters for the procurement process. Note that there are no signal paths into "Establish criteria." This does not imply that no signals exist. Rather, these signals have simply remained undefined in this model. A strong case can be made for the univer-

---

[5] The material in this section is adapted from Leonard E. Silven, *Systems Engineering Applied to Training* (Houston, Tex.: Gulf Publishing Company, 1972), chap. 2.

sality of all systems, thus requiring the analyst to arbitrarily limit his model at some point. In this case, no signals to or from the larger suprasystem have been defined.

Flows from a system or subsystem are illustrated in LOGOS by an *outgoing signal path*. The *incoming signal path* to "Procure inputs" from "Establish criteria" in Figure 1–1 is an outgoing signal path from "Establish criteria." It is largely through the use of signal paths that the interrelationships of subsystems are illustrated.

Feedback is illustrated in LOGOS by a signal path labeled with an Ⓕ. These paths are not the same as other signal paths. As mentioned earlier, feedback helps in controlling the subsystem to which it is transmitted. For example, a process is conducted which requires inputs. If the process is initiated, but problems arise, it may be desirable to immediately require a change in the inputs. Thus, the feedback path from "Conduct process" will control the inputs procured to improve the implementation of the process. Similarly, the output of the process may be evaluated in terms of the criteria for successful implementation of the process. It may be determined in "Evaluate output" that changes are required in the inputs and/or the process. Thus, feedback from evaluation helps in controlling the inputs and the conduct of the process.

Notice the action verb, "Evaluate." Students of decision making are constantly confronted with the task of evaluation. All too frequently, however, no provision is made for the formal criteria upon which evaluation is based. In Figure 1–1, in the signal path labeled with ⒻⒻ is a feedforward and serves the vital function of providing criteria for evaluation. A feedforward is used when one subsystem produces a vital ingredient for some subsystem positioned further along in the suprasystem. The value of the feedforward will become clearer as the decision process is discussed further.

The benefits of the systems approach

What are the major advantages to the systems approach? The systems approach provides a framework for the manager to organize his thoughts relative to the implementation of a given process. It helps him to see the essential elements in a situation and the relationship between these elements. It provides a structure for analyzing, planning, and controlling a given set of activities. In short, the systems approach provides a means for understanding highly complex situations and thereby improving managerial decision making. The systems approach gives organization and structure (a scientific method) to managerial activities and therein lies its major benefit.

THE INFORMATION-DECISION INTERACTION

The decision-making process

Making decisions is the basic responsibility of management. The manager must make decisions relative to planning, organizing, and controlling the operation. Where and how are these decisions made? Decisions are usually mental in nature and are made within the mind of the manager. The individual is required to think and exercise judgement relative to a given situation. The process starts with the recognition of a problem in some specified area. Perhaps a new product has been developed, and a base price must be established. This represents a problem which must be solved by deciding on a price. In any decision environment the manager must consider the controllable variables, the uncontrollable variables, and the relationship between them. He or she can manipulate the controllable aspects of the situation within the constraints of the uncontrollable environment in an attempt to solve the problem. With a thorough understanding of the problem and the variables involved, the manager must develop alternative solutions and project the outcomes of each possible course of action. Based upon an evaluation of the projected outcomes and related goals, the manager must select the best alternative; that is, he or she must make the decision.

It is helpful to look at decision making in a systems framework, even though the process is often carried out in the manager's mind. What are the inputs into the process? The basic input is information; two types are needed. First, information about the various aspects of the decision situation is needed. What is the problem? What variables are concerned? What alternatives are available? What is the best alternative given the goals of the manager? Secondly, information is needed relative to the useful frameworks for organizing and understanding the relationships between variables. These frameworks will be referred to as decision models. All of these parameters are formalized as criteria in "Establish criteria" in Figure 1–2. These criteria direct the acquisition of information and provide the basis for evaluat-

Figure 1–2
The decision-making system

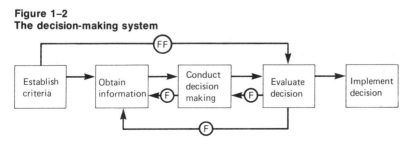

ing decisions. Decision models are utilized to convert information into decisions. The decision is evaluated using the criteria that have been established. The decision-making process and the managerial system designed to carry out the process will be discussed more fully in Chapters 2 and 3.

The research process

As noted, information is the basic input for the decision-making system. A decision maker must have some means for obtaining vital decision information. The process of generating such information can be termed the *research process*. This process includes the activities of collecting data, processing data to transform it into useful information, and transmitting the processed information to the manager. This process can also be viewed in a systems context. In this way, we can see that raw data is the basic input into the system and information is the output (see Figure 1–3). A fuller discussion of the research process is presented in Chapter 4.

Figure 1–3
The information management system

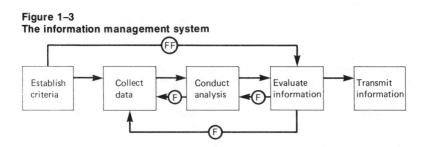

The interaction of information and decision making

Information is the common denominator of both the decision-making system and the information management system. The information management system generates an output (information) which is the vital input for decision making. Viewing the information system in isolation can produce a distorted result. The only objective of an information management system is to improve the decisions which are outputs of the decision-making system. The raw data inputs and the structure of the functional parts of the information system must be designed to meet the informational needs of management. Feedback from the ultimate decision should control the type of information going to the manager, and the information required should dictate the data collection and processing activities (see Figure 1–4).

Figure 1–4
The interaction of decision making and information management

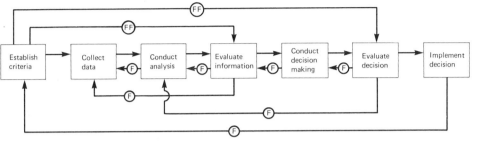

To summarize the interaction, data is collected for processing by the information management system. Processing transforms the data into useful information which is then transmitted to the manager. The manager uses the information to arrive at decisions in his or her area of responsibility. Feedback from these decisions dictates the modifications needed in either of the joint systems.

For example, sales records may be collected and processed to form sales forecasts for future periods. These forecasts are delivered to the sales manager for use in the planning process. A sales manager might use the forecasts to make decisions relative to the allocation of sales-people to various territories and to set sales quotas. The results of this decision in the form of feedback, provide a basis for modifying, if necessary, the information management and/or decision-making systems.

Thus, information and decision making are inseparable if the organization is to be managed effectively, and a basic understanding of marketing decision making is a prerequisite for understanding research and information management activities. With this thought in mind, the remainder of this chapter and of Part One is devoted to a review of marketing decision making and decision-making techniques.

THE NATURE OF MARKETING ACTIVITIES AND DECISIONS

Marketing decision areas

The successful management of the marketing function is based upon the ability of the firm to match its products and services with existing markets. By developing a framework for the total marketing process, we can identify the critical decision areas. The reason for developing marketing information within an organization is to improve marketing decisions. Thus, we must clearly define the nature of marketing activities and decisions as a starting point for developing marketing information. Developing information without first knowing for what it is to be used is a futile but all-too-common practice. In most cases knowing exactly what information you need is half the battle. Without a strong orientation toward the needs of the manager, the information system is likely to fail. The decisions which are uniquely marketing related can be conveniently grouped into two areas: (1) Market analysis and (2) Formulating the marketing mix. (See Figure 1–5.)

Figure 1–5
The conduct marketing decision-making subsystem

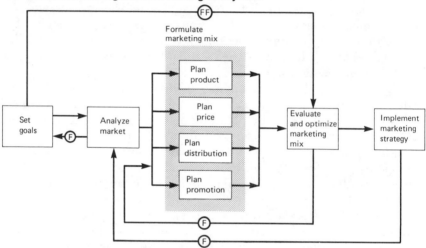

Analyze market

Market analysis is the first important decision area which is uniquely in the realm of the marketing manager. Marketing management is responsible for investigating the nature and structure of the market in order to locate market opportunities for the firm. Relative to this area the marketing manager must first make decisions involving market segmentation. Market segmentation means breaking the total market into homogeneous submarkets. Markets can be segmented based on geography, socioeconomic variables, or buyer behavior (shopping patterns, usage rates, or buying motives). A basis for segmentation must be established which will effectively subdivide the total market into groups which are internally similar. This allows groups to be appealed to with a single marketing program. After the segmentation is complete, a profile must be developed for each segment. This profile should provide the basic characteristics of the consumers and the major means of competition used by each competitor. The potential for each segment can then be forecast and the segment evaluated. A target segment or segments can then be selected based on this evaluation. Many customer and market considerations must be taken into account in the market analysis process. These include:

1. The nature of the market.
   a. Number of potential buyers.
   b. Characteristics of buyers—age, income, occupation, education, sex, size of family, race, life style, psychographics, etc.
   c. Characteristics of users if users are different from buyers.
   d. Where users and buyers live.
   e. Where buyers buy.
   f. Size of purchases.
   g. When buyers buy.
   h. How buyers buy—brand specification or not; impulse or planned; cash or credit.
   i. Why buyers buy—attitudes and motivations.
   j. Who influences buying decisions.
   k. Uses for product or service.
   l. Indications of changes in buying habits.
2. The structure of the market.
   a. Number of competitors.
   b. Market share of each competitor.
   c. Characteristics of leading products or services.
   d. Differentiation of our product or service from the leaders.
   e. Policies and procedures used by the principal competitors.

After the target market has been selected and the nature of the target segments described, programs must be developed to reach the target.

Formulate marketing mix

To put the development of a marketing program into perspective it is important to understand the notion of the marketing concept. The marketing concept stresses the integration and coordination of many functional decision areas within marketing. In addition, the concept argues that the needs, wants, and values of consumers should be the focal point of marketing. This focal point gives a direction to the formulation of an effective and profitable marketing program. Information from market analysis thus becomes an input into other marketing decisions.

The formulation of a marketing program typically involves the integration of four major areas. These include product, price, distribution, and promotion; jointly they are called the marketing mix. These variables are usually controllable to some degree for marketing management. Decisions must be made relative to each of the four areas in an attempt to formulate a mix which will attract and hold the desired type of customers. The nature and extent of the decisions made in each area are summarized in the following list

1. Product decision areas
    a. Nature of the physical product
        Quality; materials, workmanship, design, method of manufacture.

        Models and sizes.

        Essential or luxury.

        Convenience, shopping, or specialty.
    b. The package
        Attributes of protection, convenience, attractiveness, identification, adaptability, economy, material, size, construction, label design, color, copy, closure, competitive value.
    c. The brand
        Adequacy with reference to memory value, suggestiveness, pleasingness, family expansion, legal protection, and good value.
    d. Service—kind, quality and quantity
        Installation.

        Education in use.

        Repair.

        Provisions of accessory equipment.

        Delivery.
2. Price decision areas
    a. Base price
        At factory.

        To wholesalers.

        To retailers.

        To ultimate consumers.
    b. Price alterations
        Discounts—trade, quantity, cash, other.

        Allowances.

        Service charges.

        Price maintenance.
    c. Transportation charges
    d. Credit terms

3. Distribution decision areas
   a. Distribution channels
   Number of retailers.
   Number of wholesalers.
   Percent of retailers and wholesalers by type.
   Degree of aggressive retailer cooperation.
   Degree of channel integration.
   b. Physical distribution
   Modes of transporation.
   Storage facilities.
   Inventory control procedures.
4. Promotion decision areas
   a. Personal selling
   Recruiting and selection methods.
   Training procedures.
   Supervision procedures.
   Stimulation devices.
   Compensation plan.
   b. Advertising
   Media selection and mix.
   Appeals and themes.
   c. Sales promotion
   Types of activities—premiums, bulletins, etc.
   Cooperative arrangements.
   d. Publicity
   Volume and nature—releases, clippings, mentions.[6]

The problem facing the marketing manager is organizing and arranging these elements in order to achieve optimal efficiency. The objective is to develop an integrated and workable marketing program. To do this the manager must have decision information related to each of the decision areas.

LEVELS OF DECISION MAKING

There is another critical dimension to decision making in addition to the delineation of decision areas. This is a definition of decision levels. All decisions within the advertising area, for example, cannot be viewed in the same way. Deciding to aggressively use advertising as a competitive weapon does not have the same implications or require

---

[6] Parts of this summary were adapted from A. W. Frey, *The Effective Marketing Mix* (Hanover, N.H.: Amos Tuck School, Dartmouth College, 1956).

the same information as deciding on the copy for a given ad. Robert N. Anthony in *Planning and Control Systems* presented a very useful hierarchy of decision levels.[7] Anthony noted that it is "apparent that mistakes with serious practical consequences have been made when techniques and generalizations found valid for one class of activities (level of decision) have been applied to the other."[8] He established three decision levels—Strategic planning, Management control, and Operational control. The first two of these deal with management decision making and the third with operating procedures. Anthony also breaks Management control into two divisions: planning and control.

Since this text deals with information for marketing management we will consider only the first two levels of Anthony's hierarchy. For the purpose of description we have labeled the levels of decision making with which we will deal as follows:

1. Strategic planning
2. Management planning
3. Management control

These correspond approximately to Anthony's Strategic planning, Management planning, and Management control. Before defining our three levels of decision making, certain terms should be clear: planning, control, strategic, and operational. The term *planning* means deciding what to do or how to do it. *Control* means assuring that desired results are obtained. To do this, the manager must set performance standards, measure actual results, and take corrective action when necessary. *Strategic* decisions are those that establish the firm's general position relative to the external environment and the competition. *Operational* decisions deal with the ongoing administration of the internal organization.

With these concepts in mind, we can define *strategic planning* as *policy formulation* with respect to the various decision areas. At this level management is deciding what to do in terms of market analysis and formulating the marketing mix. Policies are strategy-type statements which establish long-term goals or thrusts. For example, a firm may establish an overall marketing policy of seeking market positions through segmentation. This implies corollary policies in each area of decision making, such as policies of style innovation and price discrimination in the product and price areas respectively. Note that strategic planning does not lead immediately to implementation, but lays the groundwork for more specific planning.

---

[7] The basis for this section of Chapter 1 was derived from Robert N. Anthony, *Planning and Control Systems: A Framework for Analysis* (Boston: Harvard Business School, Division of Research, 1965).

[8] Ibid., p. 17.

Management planning involves the process of establishing *programs* to implement the policies established at the strategic level. These programs specify procedures and budgets designed to obtain and use resources in such a way as to accomplish the organization's policies. For example, a firm might set the following specific objective:

During the next model year, model B will be introduced and attain monthly sales of 1,000 units by the end of the third quarter.

Objectives at the management planning level of decision making provide measureable criteria for evaluating short-term performance. These objectives lead to specific strategies through which the objectives can be attained. For example, the introductory objectives for model B may call for penetration pricing. Finally, a specific operating plan and budget can be developed. At this point the actual program for model B would be set.

Management control requires decisions to insure that the programs are, in fact, continuing to implement the policies. Thus, the outputs of management control are corrective actions designed to keep the organization on the desired course. In the case of model B, for example, management control would monitor implementation to insure that operational plans were being carried out, evaluate the success of management planning, and compare long term performance to policies.

In order to make a clear distinction between the three levels of management decisions it may prove helpful to compare them on a number of dimensions. Table 1–1 presents for each decision level: the level of management typically involved, the nature of the activity, the characteristics of the activity, the tempo, the inputs, the type of information needed, and the output of the given decision level. By breaking each decision area into these three levels, the manager can more clearly define the nature of the decisions involved and thus the type of information needed.

The marketing decision matrix

Marketing management must deal with many different decision areas on different levels. By looking at these various areas and levels of decisions in conjunction, a marketing decision matrix is formed. (See Table 1–2.) This matrix provides the manager with a framework to organize his activities and determine the types of information he needs. In order to effectively manage the firm's marketing activities, it is necessary to clearly define the nature of the decisions in each cell of the matrix and to develop useful information for use in each area. This decision matrix is a starting point for developing effective marketing

Table 1–1
The three basic levels of managerial decision

	Decision level		
	Strategic planning	*Management planning*	*Management control*
Level of .... management	Top management	Middle management	Middle management and Lower management
Activity	Policy formulation	Programming	Correction
Characteristics	External perspective Staff oriented	Internal perspective Line oriented	Internal perspective Line oriented
Tempo	Irregular	Regular Periodic	Daily
Inputs	Staff studies External situation Internal achievements	Policy statements Operational summaries	Performance criteria Performance measurement
Information	Special "one time" reports Inquiries (unrestricted)	Regular reports Inquiries (restricted)	Exceptions as they occur
Outputs	Policies	Programs	Corrective actions

information. Several illustrations of the interaction between information and selected marketing decisions are presented in Part Three, but a brief illustration at this point may help in understanding the concept. In reading the illustration, note the research inputs into the target market selection, product design, pricing and promotion decisions.

Table 1–2
The marketing decision matrix

Decision areas / *Level of decision*	*Strategic planning*	*Management planning*	*Management control*
Market analysis			
Product			
Price			
Distribution			
Promotion			

GRANADA/MONARCH: AN ILLUSTRATION OF THE INFORMATION/DECISION-MAKING INTERACTION

On September 27, 1974, Ford Motor Company introduced two new car lines to the public: Ford Granada and Mercury Monarch, two of the first domestically-produced luxury small cars. At a time when economic conditions were adversely affecting all new car sales, Granada broke Ford Division first-day sales records for a new car with 5,254 units sold. Monarch first day sales of 1,702 units were the best for a new car introduced by Lincoln-Mercury in 14 years.[9]

Ford product planners had earned the right to celebrate these success stories. Granada and Monarch were the result of nearly five years of market studies, consumer surveys, design trials, plans made and changed. Their development actually grew out of two separate new car programs launched in 1970. One of these was an examination of the growing luxury, high-priced compact car market and the possibility of a successful entry into that market by Ford. Cars in this market include Audi, BMW and Volvo. The other program was a redesign of the Maverick, Ford's economy compact introduced in 1969. (Its Lincoln-Mercury counterpart is Comet.)

Maverick was produced to compete with the growing number of foreign-built autos sold in the United States. With a long sloping hood and short rear deck, its primary appeals were low initial and operating costs and ease of maintenance—it was a basic machine. While Maverick first-year sales were impressive, the car did not stem the tide of the increasingly popular imports.

In 1970, however, Ford introduced a more suitable competitor for the imports, the subcompact Pinto. In addition to its competitive role, the economy Pinto had an immediate effect on Maverick sales. It became clear that Pinto was actually cutting into the sales of its "big brother" in the Ford line-up. Maverick sales also were affected by competition at the upper price range of the compact market. The Valiant, Dart, and Nova—while sharing the compact class with Maverick—were roomier, offered larger engines and more options. Caught between the two competitive forces, Maverick needed a change, and the direction of that change was up—to compete with the heavier, roomier compacts and to move clearly out of Pinto's product range.

With the two new car programs in mind. Ford's design studios began to produce design concepts for the Maverick "X" and Comet "X" and the new luxury compact.

---

[9] Illustration from Educational Affairs Department, *Granada/Monarch* (Dearborn, Mich.: Ford Motor Company, 1975).

Research: The luxury car

Initial research on the luxury model was conducted in Santa Monica, California, in June 1970, with a consumer sample (where consumers were invited to examine and comment on proposed vehicle designs). Ford market researchers wanted to determine the potential of a Ford product in the Mercedes or Audi category, and to get an idea of the features such a car should have. They learned from the sample that consumers would want the car to be small but solidly built, with a high level of luxury and substantial interior room. A relatively high price for the car would be acceptable.

In April 1972, another major study was conducted in San Diego, this time to test three actual prototype models, as well as two European Ford cars. The consumers selected for the sample either owned 4-door cars or were considered prospective buyers.

The results were decisive, but not promising for Ford's interests in the luxury car market: The consumers did like the cars themselves, but considered the planned price of $6,000 (in 1972 dollars) too high. The response indicated that a Ford entry into the luxury compact market would not be successful, and company management decided to abandon the program. However, the design features regarded favorably by the consumers were later incorporated into the development and planning of prototypes being considered as future Maverick and Comet replacements. The luxury car program, though not followed through to production, made its contribution.

Maverick and Comet: A new approach

During the first half of 1971, marketing researchers began testing the appeal of new design concepts for Maverick and Comet to small car owners and prospective buyers.

Results of this research, too, were not heartening; none of the design concepts developed for the new cars scored as a show-stopper with the consumers. But some helpful information did come out of the first study. The cars that did receive some favorable attention were the 4-door prototypes. These were considerably more "boxy-looking" than the existing sloping lines of Maverick and Comet and carried a more formal image. The 2-door prototypes had styling touches quite similar to the existing compacts and were not perceived as improvements.

In the summer of 1972, consumers in Toledo and Chicago reviewed a new group of 2-door and 4-door designs. The 2-door concepts again were not perceived as improvements over the existing car, but a 4-door styling theme produced by the Lincoln-Mercury Design Studio was received favorably. The consumers considered it a formal style—a family car, but definitely not in the lower price range.

The success of the 4-door Lincoln-Mercury entry directed designers toward adapting the formal appeal to the 2-door car, dropping at that stage nearly all the existing Maverick and Comet characteristics. A Dayton study conducted early in 1973 with Maverick, Comet, and Nova owners confirmed that this more formal styling approach was on the right track.

Another significant result of this research was that the participants regarded the new formal approach as substantially different from the traditional compact car with its basic economy and sometimes downright sparse interior—the new models had a definite air of luxury and "foreignness."

After further studies, final design touches were made on the 2-door and in the spring of 1973, company management approved both the 2-door and 4-door designs.

One of the chief characteristics of the cars was "package efficiency"—that is, maximum use of the functional space available with its wheelbase of 109.9 inches. Hip and shoulder room were increased over the standard compact interior dimensions, and entry and exits were improved with the use of tilted door hinges and wider doors. The boxy shape of the car allowed improved visibility, while trunk space and fuel tank capacity were enlarged. Ford's interior designers added luxury touches to give the car the traditional big-car "feel" of comfort and quality.

However, the research indicated that these cars were so different in style and image from the basic, economy Maverick and Comet that the existing car names were no longer considered appropriate by the consumers sampled. Just as the product itself had moved away from the original economy compact concept, the name, too, would have to be brought up to date. But, then, what of the Maverick and Comet lines? Did the introduction of this newly developed luxury car signal the end of the economy compact or should both cars be maintained?

In August of 1973, a study was conducted in Atlanta to try to resolve the issue. Prospective buyers of compact, intermediate, and standard-size cars examined the new car along with other Ford and General Motors Corporation cars of all sizes. The new styling carried a definite appeal across the spectrum of prospective buyers who participated in the research, and was considered to equal intermediate size cars in roominess and to surpass them in luxury. Also, 33 percent of the respondents estimated the sticker price to be much higher than the prices finally established for the Granada and Monarch.

More significantly, one third said there was no other car on the road like the new car. It was clearly too distinctive simply to serve as a substitute for the existing Maverick and Comet lines. Also, 1973 marked the beginning of serious fuel shortages and the resulting increase in small car popularity and sales. These considerations all influenced the solution of the issue—the Maverick and comet would be retained as compact economy entries and the new car, in Ford and Lincoln-Mercury versions, would be a completely new product offering.

Several possible names for the new cars were researched to find names that consumers considered appropriate for a luxury small car. In the tradition of Mustang and Pinto, Stallion was tested along with Fairmont, Lucerne, Eagle and others. However, test participants favored Granada and Monarch as indicating excellence and suitability.

Advertising: Right to the point

Association with a luxury car, as confirmed by the research, would prove helpful in developing merchandising and positioning strategy, the next step for company management. The functional approach to car design, clearly in demand according to the studies, also became a key part of the advertising for the cars.

Research had shown that the greatest sales potential for the Granada and Monarch was among car buyers looking for functional benefits. These buyers made up 54 percent of the compact market and 34 percent of the intermediate and standard size car markets, the largest attitudinal segment of buyers. They were interested in value, and the advertising that would get their attention would have to offer that value in straight-forward terms.

In the past, a touch of humor and emphasis on the fun of driving a Ford Motor Company product have been successful advertising approaches, but the practical thinkers that made up the potential Granada and Monarch market would not be so attracted. Three elements were selected as key points of emphasis: the availability of low-priced but well-equipped models, good gas mileage provided by the standard six-cylinder engine, and the value of the cars for their price.

Test print advertisements were prepared and presented to consumer panels. Subheadings broke up the copy and highlighted the practical appeals of the car—The Design, The Economics, The Comforts, The Construction—and photographs and diagrams appeared throughout. Results indicated that this was an effective format. Headlines making big promises, such as "Ford Presents the Unexpected," fared poorly; the panelists wanted the facts. Car size comparisons in the copy proved particularly effective when the Mercedes was included.

Consumer samples in Los Angeles, reviewing print advertisements that stressed price and fuel economy, described the material as blunt—but that was the kind of frankness they appreciated.

One of the studies included an examination of the car after the advertisement review, to ensure that the actual product would not be a disappointment in the dealers showroom after the potential customer had read the advertisement in the morning newspaper. The reactions were reassuring, as some of the respondents found the car even more impressive than indicated in the advertising.

Introduction time

Plans for the introduction of the new cars were next on the marketing agenda. While the customary aim of new car advertising is to zero-in on the potential buyers of the particular car model—the "target market"—Ford Motor Company management wanted to make an impact on all car buyers with the Granada-Monarch message. Television commercials announcing the arrival of the new cars were prepared, and during introduction week, these commercials ran in each U.S. TV household an average of three times.

A newspaper insert was developed to introduce the entire 1975 Ford line, but featured Granada on the cover and prominently inside. Over 70 million copies were distributed during the announcement week in Sunday, daily, and weekly newspapers. Monarch appeared in Sunday supplements such as *Parade*. Preannouncement advertisements appeared in the major national magazines.

In all, the average American family saw, read, or heard about Granada 16 times during the three weeks before and four weeks after the announcement.

In keeping with the direct, factual advertising approach for the car, the company dropped the customary "tease" aspect of car advertising prior to actual introduction; preintroduction Granada and Monarch advertisements dealt frankly with the car's features (except for photographs or art), and that included price.

Pricing information caused some headaches since suggested retail prices weren't determined until the last minute before the print advertisements went to press. But early advertising studies had shown that consumers appreciated such information, and making that favorable impression was worth the extra effort involved in making the figures available.

Merchandising aids for Ford and Lincoln-Mercury dealerships were prepared and distributed to the dealers for their introduction day activities. For greater exposure after introduction, Granadas and Monarchs were displayed at major shopping plazas throughout the country and at the major airport terminals.

Direct mail advertisements were sent to owners of Ford, Lincoln, and Mercury cars as well as owners of competitors' products. Participating Lincoln-Mercury dealers held a "Day of the Cat" sweepstakes, with a 1975 Monarch as grand prize, to promote the Lincoln-Mercury version of the new car with the popular "Sign of the Cat" theme. Ford and Lincoln-Mercury sales districts planned additional programs and displays for the remainder of the model year.

In addition, Granadas and Monarchs were test driven and given highly favorable reviews by the top car-buff-magazine writers. The first domestically produced luxury compacts in the United States were clearly in the public eye. And, as the first day sales results indicate, marketing and advertising efforts for the cars were "on target."

The buyer points the way

Granada and Monarch make up an important car marketing story in their own right, and for the trends they indicate for car marketing in upcoming years. Their development involved their own appeal to today's car buyer and their positioning in the total Ford Motor Company car lineup. The company's move into the luxury small car market—previously believed to have only low sales potential—was an undoubted success.

Input from the consumer research performed throughout the development of the new cars was critical in shaping their design and image, and in determining the future of the Maverick and Comet lines. The advertising themes and approaches were geared to the interests and concerns of the potential buyers. Even the names for the Ford and Lincoln-Mercury versions of the car were settled on only after careful testing with consumers.

Clearly, the consumers themselves provided the guideposts for the company's design, engineering, and marketing staffs, and Ford Motor Company firmly believes consumer research to be the key to successful car marketing for the future.

SUMMARY

In this chapter the development of a framework for generating marketing information was begun. Additional aspects of the framework will be discussed in later chapters. The systems concept was presented as a basic way of looking at this highly complex area. The information/decision-making interaction involves two systems and two processes. The research process, aimed at generating information, is carried out by a structure which may be called an information management system. The output of this system is information which is an input into the decision-making process. The decision-making process is implemented by a structure which can be referred to as a management or decision-making system.

To develop an effective research and information management network, the nature of marketing decisions as well as the decision-making process and system must be understood. Marketing decisions may be classified by area and level. The two areas which are uniquely related to marketing management are market analysis and formulation of the marketing mix. Each of these decision areas can be subdivided into the strategic planning, management planning, and management control levels. The categorization of marketing decisions is a good starting point for information planning.

AN OVERVIEW OF THE TEXT

So far we have been concerned with the information/decision making interaction as an introduction to the first of three major parts into which this book is divided.

Part One (Chapters 1–3) examines the decision making/research interaction within the business environment. Such topics as problem definition, the specification of information needs, and decision models are covered in this section. This material is intended to provide a basis for understanding when to conduct research and for evaluating the value of research as a support activity for decision makers.

Part Two (Chapters 4–10) presents an overview of the research process and research methodology. Data collection, basic analysis, and research reporting are discussed in this section, along with qualitative and quantitative research in marketing. A thorough understanding of the research process and the techniques used in marketing research allow the manager to make effective inputs into the design of research and to evaluate the quality of information he receives.

Part Three (Chapters 11–14) explores the applications of marketing research and the management of the research process. Information needs for various types of decisions are examined along with illustrations of research designed to produce such information. This material is designed to provide the future manager with some insights on how marketing research can be of use in many decision-making activities. The final chapter discusses the basic concepts and principles related to managing the marketing research program within a firm.

DISCUSSION QUESTIONS

1. Define a system and a process and discuss the ways in which they are related.

2. What are the basic elements of a system? How can the systems concept help in the study of marketing management and research?
3. Define decision making and research in a marketing management context. Describe both in a systems framework.
4. Discuss the relationship between decision making and research.
5. Discuss the basic decision areas and levels of decision making in marketing.
6. Select at least three cells in the marketing decision matrix and discuss the general nature of information needs in each.
7. Discuss the following statement—"the foundation of effective marketing research is a clear understanding of the decision-making process and system."

SELECTED REFERENCES

Anthony, Robert N. *Planning and Control Systems: A Framework for Analysis*. Boston: Harvard Business School, Division of Research, 1965.

Boulding, Kenneth E. "General Systems Theory—The Skeleton of a Science," *Management Science* (April 1956), pp. 197–208.

Emery, James C. *Organizational Planning and Control Systems: Theory and Technology*. New York: The Macmillan Company, 1969.

Ross, Joel F. *Management by Information System*. Englewood Cliffs, N.J.: Prentice-Hall, Inc., 1970.

chapter

2

Decision analysis and information value

Marketing managers, as discussed in Chapter 1, must be concerned with two areas unique to marketing. These areas are analyzing the markets and formulating the marketing mix. The major responsibility of marketing management is to make decisions relative to these two areas. The degree of their success in making good decisions will materially affect the overall success of the organization. Managers must make these decisions in an environment filled with risk and uncertainty. The systems concept can provide a logical and systematic framework to aid managers in dealing with their complex decision environment. The systems concept encourages the manager to think in terms of processes and structures to implement those processes. The basic process involved here is decision making, and the structure to carry out the process might be called a decision-making system or management organization.

STEPS IN THE DECISION-MAKING PROCESS

The decision process itself can be defined as a series of actions or steps needed to make a decision and the desired sequence for these steps. This provides a logical and systematic method to approach the decision-making activity which can help to minimize the risk associated with the process. The following list presents a brief description of the steps in the decision-making process. (See diagram in Figure 2–1.) Each step in the process may give rise to specific information needs.

The first logical step in the decision-making process is to recognize

Figure 2–1
A model of the decision-making process

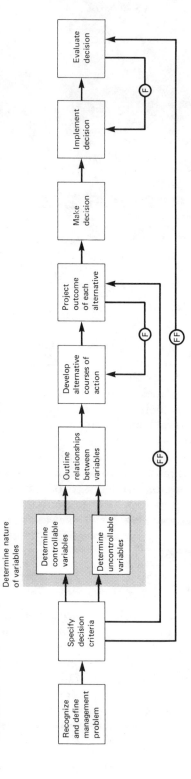

and clearly define the managerial problem. This is often the most difficult step in the process. It is critical that the real problem and not just symptoms of the problem be isolated. A managerial problem in the context used here would involve a situation within the organization requiring some manager to make a decision. The decision might relate to analysis of markets or to the formulation of some aspect of the marketing mix. For example, the company may have developed a new product and a decision must be made relative to the base price to be charged. Deciding on the base price would constitute a marketing management problem. Problem definition through "situational analysis" is discussed further in Chapter 3.

After the problem or decision has been recognized and clearly defined, the decision criteria must be specified. What is the objective or objectives that need to be considered in attempting to arrive at the best decision? Should the decision lower cost, increase market share, conserve resources, or accomplish some mix of objectives? The major objective or objectives to be considered in arriving at a decision comprise the decision criteria. The criteria for each decision should be derived from the overall marketing department goals.

Next, the important variables in the environment of the decision under consideration should be determined. These variables can be divided into controllable and uncontrollable categories. In general, the controllable category includes marketing goals, the basis used for market analysis, the selection of a target market, and the formulation and implementation of the various elements in the marketing mix. The positioning of these variables may comprise alternative solutions to the managerial problem. The uncontrollable variables involve the structure and decisions in other parts of the organization and the external environment. The corporate goals, production capacity, and other elements of the organizational system will influence the decisions of the marketing managers, but may be uncontrollable from his point of view. Likewise, the external environment comprised of the legal and political structure, the state of the economy, the social and cultural structure, the state of technology, and basic level and determinates of demand are usually uncontrollable variables. When some specific uncontrollable variable can be identified as having a major effect on the outcome of a given decision, and the probability of the variable being in various different positions estimated, the variable can be treated as a state of nature in *decision analysis* (to be discussed in this chapter).

After the major controllable and uncontrollable variables have been determined for a given decision, it is then important to outline the relationship between the variables. Are the variables independent of each other or will manipulating one variable affect the state of another variable? How will the outcome of positioning one variable (perhaps price) in a specific way be affected by the state of another variable or variables (such as demand)? This type of question can be answered only if the relationships between variables are known. Such information can prove to be a critical input into making a good decision. Techniques which can be useful in structuring these relationships are also discussed later in the chapter. Such a relationship, when clearly defined, can be called a decision model. This model allows the decision maker to project the expected outcome of various alternative courses of action in terms of the decision criteria.

Now the decision maker is in a position to examine alternative courses of action which may solve the problem at hand. The alternatives comprise a series of possible decisions. Three different prices may be considered for a new product relative to a base price decision, or two different distribution channels relative to a distribution decision. These alternatives can be derived from the controllable variables which are relevant for the decision in question.

In order to evaluate these alternatives and arrive at a logical decision, the outcome of each alternative must be projected in terms of the decision criteria. The outcome of three alternative prices might be projected in terms of market share if this has been established as the decision criterion. These projections form the basis for making the decision. The decision itself is simply the alternative chosen for implementation. After a course of action is decided upon, the next step is to put the decision into operation—set up the distribution channel, establish the base price, or take whatever actions are necessary to implement the decision. Making one decision may give rise to additional managerial problems which require other decisions. This may set off a sequence of decision making relative to some area of the marketing activities of the organization. Normally, the sequence would start with *strategic planning* decisions which would generate the need for *management planning* decisions which would in turn create a need for *management control* decisions. After a decision at any level has been set in motion, it must be monitored so that necessary adjustments in implementation can be made.

Carrying out the various steps in this decision-making process gives rise to information needs. Information is needed to isolate the problem, to determine the relevant variables, to build the decision model, and so forth. In addition, the organizational context in which the decision process is conducted can alter the information needs.

DECISION ANALYSIS

The area of study referred to as decision theory has produced several techniques or tools which can be of use to the manager in carrying out the decision-making process. These techniques are particularly helpful in summarizing the relationships between variables in the decision environment so as to form decision models. Such models can in turn be used to project the expected consequences of various possible alternative courses of action and to estimate the value of additional information in a specific decision setting. A major set of these techniques can be grouped under the heading of Bayesian Analysis.

Bayesian decision analysis divides the decision-making process into three basic stages: prior analysis, preposterior analysis, and posterior analysis. Prior analysis gives the decision maker a set of techniques (which includes decision trees) to select among alternatives based on existing information. Prior analysis allows the decision setting to be structured into a decision model based on presently available information. This information consists of the prior judgments of the decision maker. Preposterior analysis gives the decision maker a set of techniques to aid in answering the question—is additional information worth the cost of securing it? The primary use of these techniques is in assessing the value or benefit of information. Finally, posterior analysis provides the decision maker with a set of techniques for revising the prior decision based on new information. Traditionally posterior analysis (and in some cases, preposterior analysis) makes use of Bayes' Theorem in the revision process, but in a broader sense, posterior analysis can be used to include any procedure for data analysis which leads to a revised decision.

Prior analysis

Prior analysis through the use of decision trees can be most easily explained by the use of an example. Before going into an example, however, some basic terms and concepts should be clear.

Alternatives. Alternatives are the possible courses of action open to the decision maker. He must choose one alternative as a solution to his managerial problem. The alternatives must involve controllable variables for the manager.

States of nature. States of nature are relevant uncertainties. They are variables beyond the control of the decision maker but whose position or state will affect the outcome of selecting a specific alternative. For example, whether or not it will rain today is a relevant uncertainty in a decision regarding carrying an umbrella. The rain cannot be controlled but its likelihood can be estimated thus it is a state of nature for the umbrella decision.

Consequence. A consequence is the outcome of a given alternative and state of nature in terms of some specific decision criterion. If profit is the decision criterion, then what profit or loss will a specific alternative coupled with a certain state of nature yield?

Subjective probability. A probability is the likelihood that something will occur. It can be quantified in an index ranging from 0 to 1, with 0 indicating no possibility and 1 indicating a certainty. Probabilities may be either objective or subjective depending upon how they are derived. An objective probability is based on the relative frequency with which something occurs. If a fair coin is tossed an infinite number of times, the relative frequency of heads is .5, thus the objective probability of getting a head on any one toss is .5. Objective probabilities are not available in most decision-making environments thus the decision maker must rely on his rational beliefs about the likelihood that certain things will occur. Probabilities derived in this way are called subjective probabilities. Various states of nature can have subjective probabilities assigned to them. For example, if market share were an important state of nature, the manager might rationally believe that there is a .5 chance of a 40 percent market share and a .5 chance of a 60 percent market share.

Expected value. The expected value of a specific alternative is the average consequence of selecting the alternative an infinite number of times. For example, if you could toss a coin and call either heads or tails, receiving $5 for a correct call and losing $5 for an incorrect call, the expected value from calling heads would be $0. This is the average monetary consequence of calling heads on an infinite number of tosses. It can be computed by adding the products of all possible consequences multiplied times the probability of getting that consequence. In the coin tossing example there are two possible consequences from calling heads, +$5 if the coin lands on heads and −$5 if the coin lands on tails. The probability of landing on heads is .5 and the probability of landing on tails is .5. Thus the expected value from calling heads is $[.5 \times (+\$5)] + [.5 \times (-\$5)] = 0$. If risk is not considered, the decision maker would select the alternative with the best expected value (highest expected profit, lowest expected cost, and so forth).

The decision tree. Now to explain the decision tree technique, suppose that you are a manager with a company that has decided to expand into a new territory. You are assigned to select the most profitable channel of distribution. The alternatives are to use a wholesaler or to set up your own sales offices. The wholesaler would cost 30 percent of your sales and your own office would cost a fixed $30,000. All other costs are equal to 65 percent of sales. The most profitable alternative would depend on the sales volume. You subjectively estimate that there is a .5 probability of having sales of $90,000 and a .5 probability of having sales of $120,000.

To arrive at the best alternative using a decision tree, start by stating the alternatives (use a wholesaler or set up our own office) on the first two branches of the tree working from left to right (see Figure 2–2).

Figure 2–2
Building the decision tree
Work from left to right ────────────────────────────────►

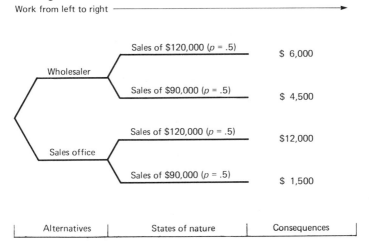

| Alternatives | States of nature | Consequences |

Next, add the states of nature which will affect the consequences of each alternative. These should be added on branches to the right of the alternatives. The probability associated with each state of nature should be placed in parentheses on the same branch. In this case, sales of $120,000 (probability = .5) or sales of $90,000 (probability = .5) will affect the outcome of both alternatives, thus these two states of nature should be added to each alternative. Next, compute the consequence of each alternative–state of nature set in terms of the decision criterion (profit in this case). This means four consequences are to be computed: (1) wholesaler with sales of $120,000 [$120,000 revenue − ($36,000 distribution cost [.30 × $120,000] + $78,000 other cost [.65 × $120,000]) = $6,000 profit]; (2) wholesaler with sales of $90,000 [$90,000 revenue − ($27,000 distribution cost [.30 × $90,000] + $58,500 other cost [.65 × $90,000]) = $4,500 profit]; (3) sales office with sales of $120,000 [$120,000 revenue − ($30,000 distribution cost + $78,000 other cost [.65 × $120,000]) = $12,000 profit]; and (4) sales office with sales of $90,000 [$90,000 revenue − ($30,000 distribution cost + $58,500 other cost [.65 × $90,000]) = $1,500 profit]. The consequence in terms of dollar profit should be placed at the end of each alternative–state of nature set. This completes the building of the decision tree.

To determine the best alternative, the expected monetary value must be calculated for each alternative. This is done by adding the products of the consequences times the probabilities for the state of nature for each alternative (see Figure 2–3). For the wholesaler alter-

Figure 2–3
Solving the decision tree

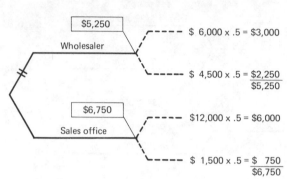

Sales office is the best alternative based on expected monetary value.

native the expected value is $(.5 \times \$6,000) + (.5 \times \$4,500) = \$5,250$. The \$5,250 expected value is placed in a box at the end of the wholesaler alternative branch. For the sales office alternative the expected value is $(.5 \times \$12,000) + (.5 \times \$1,500) = \$6,750$. This value is placed in a box at the end of the sales office alternative. The expected values of the two alternatives are then compared and the alternative with the best expected value (highest profit in this case) is chosen. The sales office would be chosen in this example. Thus to build the decision tree, one should work from left to right placing alternatives, states of nature, and finally consequences. To solve the tree, one works from right to left computing expected values.

In building the decision trees we have in effect constructed a decision model which we then use to project the expected consequence of the various alternatives. The decision tree defines the relationship between the controllable variable (alternatives) and the uncontrollable variable (states of nature) which were relevant in the specific decision in question. Thus this tool of decision analysis can aid the manager in structuring the decision-making process discussed earlier. This is, of course, no substitute for thinking, which is the essence of decision making, but it can assist in developing a rigorous approach to managing.

To firmly grasp the decision tree technique and to understand its value, another example may be helpful:

Artex Computers is interested in developing a tape drive for a proposed new computer. Artex does not have research personnel available to develop the new drive itself and so is going to subcontract the development to an independent research firm. Artex has set a fee of $250,000 for developing the new tape drive and has asked for bids from various research firms. The bid is to be awarded not on the basis of price (set at $250,000), but on the basis of both the technical plan shown in the bid and the reputed technical competence of the firm submitting the bid.

Boro Research Institute is considering submitting a proposal (i.e., a bid) to Artex Computer to develop the new tape drive. Boro Research management estimated that it would cost about $50,000 to prepare a proposal; further, they estimated that the chances were about 50–50 that they would be awarded the contract.

There was a major concern among Boro Research engineers concerning exactly how they would develop the tape drive if they were awarded the contract. There were three alternative approaches that could be tried. One approach involved the use of certain electronic components. The engineers estimated that it would cost only $50,000 to develop a prototype (i.e., a test version) of the tape drive using the electronic approach, but that there was only a 50 percent chance that the prototype would be satisfactory. A second approach involved the use of a certain magnetic apparatus. The cost of developing a prototype using this approach would be $80,000 with a 70 percent chance of success. Finally, there was a mechanical approach with a cost of $120,000, but the engineers were certain they could develop a successful prototype with this approach.

Boro Research could have sufficient time to try only two approaches. Thus, if either the magnetic or electronic approach were tried and failed, the second attempt would have to use the mechanical approach in order to guarantee a successful prototype.

What action would you recommend if the desire is to maximize the expected value of profits?

This example carries the decision environment to a more complex level and points out one of the major advantages of the decision tree technique. The technique encourages a logical and systematic approach which is invaluable in decision making. To implement the technique, the decision maker is forced to think in terms of controllable alternatives, relevant states of nature, and probable consequences.

This decision environment involves two related sets of alternatives and three sets of states of nature. The first set of alternatives relate to making the bid or not making the bid and the second set involves the choice of approach to try first if the bid is made and Boro gets the contract. The first set of states of nature is getting the contract or failing to get the contract; the second is the electronic approach working or failing; and the third set is the magnetic approach working or failing. The construction and solution of the decision tree are shown in Figure 2–4.

Figure 2–4
The Boro Research Institute decision tree

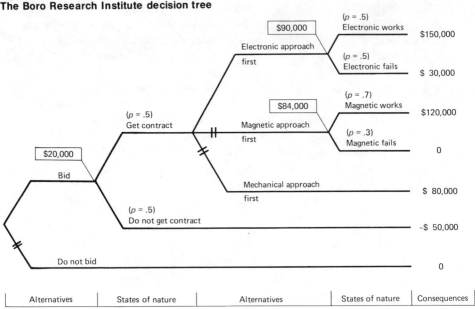

First the decision maker must decide to bid or not bid. If the bid is made, the company will either get the contract or lose the contract. If Boro gets the contract, they must then decide whether to try the electronic, the magnetic, or the mechanical approach first. If the electronic approach is tried and fails, then the time constraint forces the use of the mechanical approach which will definitely work. The company must get a prototype that will work and they have time to try only two approaches. If the magnetic approach is tried and fails, then the mechanical approach must again be used.

Based on expected value, the electronic approach should be tried first if the bid is made and the contract won. This alternative will yield an expected value of $90,000. The $90,000 becomes the consequence of making the bid and winning the contract. This gives an expected value of $20,000 for making the bid. Using expected value as the basis for the decision—the company should make the bid—and if it receives the contract, try the electronic approach first. If the electronic approach fails, the mechanical approach must then be used.

This example illustrates several important concepts. First, there may be more than one set of alternatives and one set of states of nature for a given decision. If so, the decision tree technique can accommodate this complexity with little difficulty. Secondly, expected value may not be an adequate basis for making a decision. The decision maker must also consider the risk involved in taking a given course of action. He may be adverse to choosing alternatives with higher expected values if they involve greater risk. For Boro, a decision to bid involves the risk of losing $50,000 if the bid does not result in a contract. There is a .5 probability of not getting the contract; thus, the risk is substantial. The decision maker is faced with a trade-off between lower risk and higher expected value. This trade-off can be made subjectively by the manager, or the manager's risk aversion can be quantified by the use of preference curves[1] and incorporated into the tree analysis. Given the risk involved in the Boro decision, the manager might well decide not to make the bid.

Preposterior analysis

Before deciding to do research, an assessment should be made of the cost of the research effort and the benefit or value of the information to be produced. Only if the probable value of the information exceeds its probable cost should research be undertaken. Preposterior analysis, in this context can be defined as a set of concepts and problems associated with estimating the cost and value of information.

In considering the concept of information cost and value, it is convenient to reduce the nature of information to a single concept, quality. The notion of information quality for a single research effort might be translated as quality of the research design. This is obviously an over simplification since information has many facets, such as subject matter, accuracy, age, and so forth. The distillation of all these facets into a single characteristic, however, allows the examination of several critical concepts related to preposterior analysis. The exact relationships between information quality and its cost and values can often not be determined. The general nature of the relationship can, however, be very enlightening. The following discussion of information quality is thus conceptual rather than empirical.

As the quality of information increases, its value tends to increase, first at an increasing rate, while the quality is relatively low; but after some point, starts to increase at a decreasing rate. The incremental value of improved quality slows as perfect information is approached. Information value could not exceed the value of perfect information which would simply imply 100 percent of the possible quality for a given decision situation. The functional relationship between information value and quality is shown in Figure 2–5.

---

[1] See Robert Schlaifer, *Analysis of Decisions under Uncertainty* (New York: McGraw-Hill Book Company, Inc., 1969), chapter 3.

Figure 2–5
The relationship between information quality and value

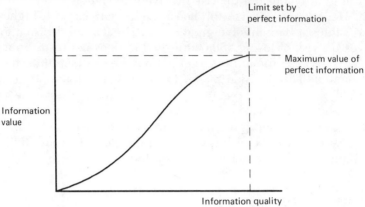

Figure 2–6
The relationship between information quality and cost

The cost of information is also related to quality. Figure 2–6 shows this functional relationship. As quality increases, it would be expected that cost would increase first at a decreasing rate to some point, then at an increasing rate up to the level of perfect information. At low levels of quality, improvements can be made at lower incremental cost, but at some point this increasing design efficiency will be lost. Any point on the curve represents an efficient design for a given level of quality. An inefficient design will yield costs above the curve for a given quality, as represented by *B* in Figure 2–6. This might result from too elaborate a design, too large a sample, or any number of other problems. Changes in the research design can also shift the research along

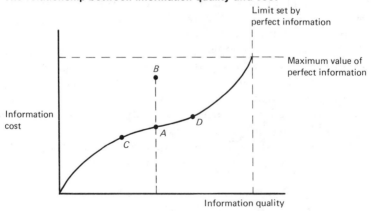

the curve to C or D. Any design that leads to other than optimum information quality, whether it has a cost on the curve or not, is also inefficient. This optimum level of quality, and thus research design, can only be determined when cost and value are considered together. If the optimum point is A, then a design which puts the research at C or D would be inefficient, just as point B is inefficient.

To find the best level of information quality, (as represented by alternative research designs) the cost and value should be considered together as shown in Figure 2–7. The optimum quality occurs when the value exceeds the cost by the largest amount.

In practice, information quality is usually translated into one or more alternative research designs. A single cost point and a single value point is then computed for each alternative. In considering whether or not to undertake a single project the rule would be to do

Figure 2–7
Balancing cost and value

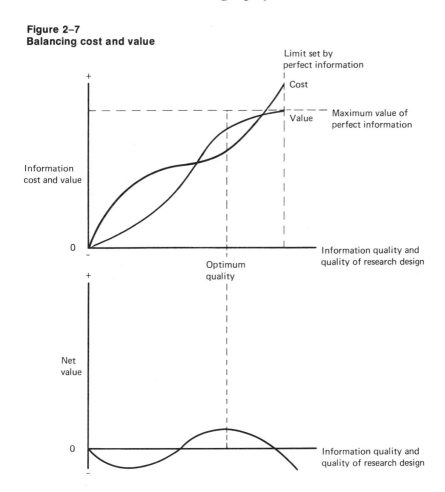

the research only if the expected value exceeds the expected cost. This is illustrated in Figure 2–8A. If only one design is under consideration, this rule (accept a project with a positive net value) would apply whether the design provides optimum quality or not. Where a series of alternative designs are under consideration, the one with the highest net value should be selected. In Figure 2–8B proposed design *B* should be selected since it gives the largest net value. In many cases,

Figure 2–8
Operationalizing the concept of information quality

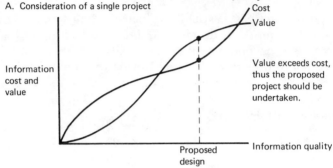

A. Consideration of a single project

Information cost and value

Cost

Value

Value exceeds cost, thus the proposed project should be undertaken.

Proposed design

Information quality

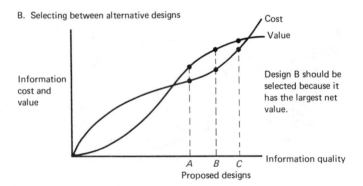

B. Selecting between alternative designs

Information cost and value

Cost

Value

Design B should be selected because it has the largest net value.

A   B   C
Proposed designs

Information quality

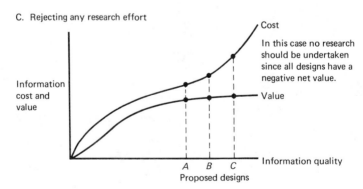

C. Rejecting any research effort

Information cost and value

Cost

In this case no research should be undertaken since all designs have a negative net value.

Value

A   B   C
Proposed designs

Information quality

cost and value considerations will make any research undesirable. This is the case if the net value for all possible quality levels is negative. That is, the cost exceeds the value for all possible designs. This is illustrated in Figure 2-8C.

Information value

The most difficult problem in preposterior analysis is the estimation of the value of information. The cost associated with designing and implementing a given research project can usually be estimated with some precision. Researcher time, interviewing cost, computer usage, and the like can often be quantified and reduced to dollar figures. Estimating information value is much more difficult because the primary benefit of information is to improve decision making at the managerial level. In estimating information value, its managerial implications must be examined. The key question is "How much will the information improve the managerial decision"? The major factors affecting the value of information are the nature of the decision it is intended to improve and the accuracy of the information. This, of course, is assuming that the information is timely in nature. If the manager receives information after the decision is made, it has no value at all. The benefits of information which give it value in decision making can be classified as tangible and intangible.

Tangible benefits.   Tangible benefits are those that relate to decisions which cause clearly quantifiable changes in costs, sales, investments, and the like. A decision about which of two alternative distribution systems to employ might be clearly related to cost, (as shown in the illustration starting on page 32). The cost of the two systems might vary as the sales volume changes. Thus, the most profitable system could depend on the level of sales. A sales forecast would, therefore, have tangible benefit. It would relate to a decision that has a clear quantifiable impact on cost and profit. In a case like this, the benefit or value of the information can be computed rather precisely using the procedures discussed later in this section. This assumes that subjective estimates based on current information can be developed for the probability of various sales levels and the level of accuracy of the forecast. A much more difficult task is encountered when one considers intangible benefits.

Intangible benefits.   Intangible benefits are those that are especially difficult to translate into monetary value. Tangible benefits are often difficult to estimate, but a clear relationship to some variable which can be measured in dollar terms does exist. With intangible benefits the relationship to costs, sales, profits and so forth is complex and unclear. Suppose, for example, U.S. Steel is considering which of three advertising campaigns to run to improve public goodwill. Though some relationship may exist to monetary values, the key intent of the decision is improved goodwill. How much this will increase sales or reduce cost would be very difficult to calculate. Thus, the benefit of information to be used in making the decision may have to be determined in a rather subjective fashion. All the important considerations that can be quantified, should be; but the final estimation of benefits must be essentially subjective. This makes a conceptual understanding of the factors contributing to information value critically important.

James Emery has suggested that a good way to approach the subjective estimation of information value is to consider its potential for "surprise content." The greater the potential of the information for giving the decision maker something surprising that will alter his decision, the greater its potential benefit. He suggests several questions which may be helpful in subjectively assessing the value of information:

Can the information tell the decision maker something he does not already know or strongly suspect?

In how many cases would this type of information be expected to provide a significant surprise?

Is the information selective enough to provide significant insights?

Would less sophisticated research have as much surprise potential?

Can a surprise cause a different course of action to be selected?

What are the potential benefits from a change in action?

How sensitive are the benefits to changes in action?[2]

Such questions may help to direct the manager and researcher in a critical evaluation of subjective benefits. Now let us turn our attention to some relatively simple techniques which can be used in preposterior analysis.

Techniques for preposterior analysis

Preposterior analysis gives the decision maker a set of techniques which can be helpful in answering the question—is additional information worth the cost of securing it? This question can be answered, as just discussed, by comparing the cost and value of information. If the value exceeds the cost, then the answer is to secure the new information. The cost of research or of purchasing information from outside sources can usually be estimated with acceptable precision. The major problem is to determine the value of the information.

---

[2] James C. Emery, "Cost/Benefit Analysis," as cited in D. J. Couger and R. W. Knapp, eds., *System Analysis Techniques*, (New York: John Wiley and Sons, Inc., 1974), p. 424.

The information in question may be either perfect information (1.0 probability of being correct) or imperfect information (less than 1.0 probability of being correct). Information of value in a given decision would relate to the position of the state of nature; the exact level of sales if this is the state of nature. The value of perfect information can be computed by the use of an opportunity-loss matrix. Knowing the value of perfect information gives an upper limit to the amount which should be paid for any additional information in a specific decision.

Going back to the distribution example starting on page 32, what would be the value of knowing, with certainty, the exact level of sales which will be achieved in the new territory? As you will recall, two alternative distribution channels were under consideration for a new territory, and sales was the key state of nature. The decision tree for this situation is shown in Figures 2–2 and 2–3. To determine the value of perfect information related to sales, an opportunity-loss matrix can be computed (see Figure 2–9). The lost opportunity with the best decision is the expected value of perfect information. All that perfect information about sales can possibly do is to eliminate the lost opportunity; thus, this is the upper limit of its value.

Figure 2–9
An opportunity loss matrix for the distribution decision

State of nature	Probability	Use wholesaler	Expected value	Use sales office	Expected value
		(A)	(1)	(B)	(2)
Sales of $90,000	.5	0	0	3,000	1,500
		(C)	(3)	(D)	(4)
Sales of $120,000	.5	6,000	3,000	0	0
		Σ =	3,000	Σ =	1,500

Expected value of perfect information (EVPI) = minimum opportunity loss = $1,500.

To construct an opportunity-loss matrix, start by placing the states of nature and their probabilities down the left side. Then place the alternatives across the top with a column to the right of each for the expected value for that alternative. The expected value column is used to add the total expected opportunity loss for each alternative. To determine the appropriate values for cells (A) and (B), assume that sales of $90,000 actually occur. Given this assumption, what is the best alternative? The wholesaler will yield $4,500 profit and the sales office $1,500 (see Figure 2–3). Thus, the wholesaler is best, and selecting it would yield no lost opportunity. This is the best possible decision under the $90,000 sales assumption. The appropriate value for cell (A) is 0 opportunity loss. If the decision maker incorrectly selects the sales office, he would have $1,500 profit, $3,000 less than with the best possible decision. Thus, the opportunity lost by selecting the sales office under the $90,000 sales assumption is $3,000. This value is placed in cell (B). An identical procedure is used to compute the values for cells (C) and (D) with the assumption of $120,000 sales.

The value for cell (1) can then be derived by multiplying the probability of $90,000 sales ($p = .5$) times the value in cell (A). The values for cells (2), (3), and (4) are obtained by an identical procedure. The expected opportunity loss of each alternative is then computed by adding the expected value column for that alternative. Use a wholesaler = 0 + $3,000 = $3,000; Use a sales office = $1,500 + 0 = $1,500. The best alternative will always have the lowest opportunity loss. In this example the sales office has the lowest with $1,500. This value, the expected opportunity loss for the best alternative, is the expected value of perfect information. In no case should the cost of additional information be allowed to exceed this limit.

The value of imperfect information can also be computed if the probable accuracy of the information can be subjectively established. Determining the value of imperfect information may be accomplished via procedures involving the use of Bayes' Theorem, which are beyond the scope of this discussion, or by adding an additional alternative branch to the decision tree. The decision tree approach takes both cost and value into account at the same time.

Suppose that in our distribution example we are presented with the opportunity to buy, for $1,000, a sales forecast that would tell us either that sales will be $120,000 or $90,000. The probability of the forecast being correct is .9. Should we purchase the sales forecast information or not?

This can be decided by adding an additional alternative branch to our original decision tree (see Figure 2–10). The additional alternative is to buy the sales forecast. Two states of nature will affect this alternative; the forecast says that sales will be $120,000 or the forecast says that sales will be $90,000. Based on our current information the probability of each state of nature is .5. If the forecast says sales will be $120,000, then we will use the sales office because this would yield $12,000 profit as opposed to $6,000 for the wholesaler. If the forecast says sales will be $90,000, then we will use the wholesaler because the profit will be $4,500 as opposed to $1,500 for the sales office. If we use the sales office and the forecast is correct, we will have $11,000 profit ($12,000 original profits − $1,000 cost of the forecast). If we use the sales office and the forecast is not correct, then profits would fall to

Figure 2–10
The decision relative to purchasing imperfect information

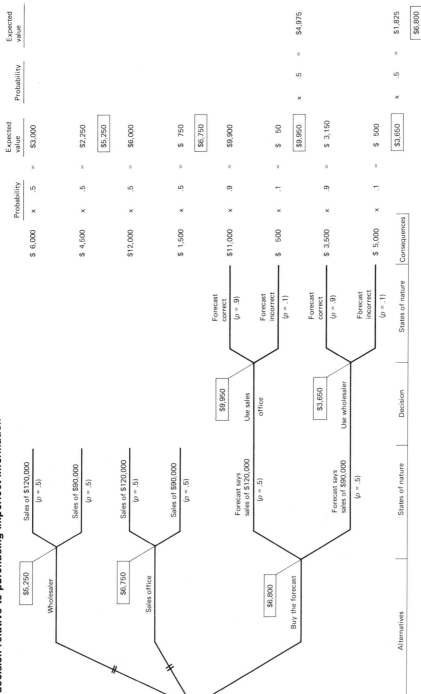

$500 ($1,500 original profit − $1,000 cost of the forecast). If we get a forecast that says sales will be $90,000, we will use the wholesaler. Given this decision if the forecast is correct, we will have $3,500 profit and if it is incorrect, $5,000 profit. The expected value from the sales office decision is $9,950 and from the wholesaler decision $3,650. These values become consequences for computing the expected value of buying the forecast. The expected value from buying the forecast and basing the decision on the additional information is $6,800. This is higher than the expected value for the other alternatives, thus the decision based on expected value would be to buy the additional imperfect information.

This is only a very limited sampling of the techniques available for preposterior analysis, but they serve to illustrate the basic procedures and the value of the approach. Much more detailed treatments can be found in the Selected References provided for the chapter.

Posterior analysis

Posterior analysis involves the process of revising decisions based on new information. Confining the definition to the strictly Bayesian approach, posterior analysis is a set of techniques, using Bayes' Theorem, for revising prior probabilities based on new information. Such revisions in probabilities may lead to revised decisions. A detailed treatment of the Bayesian approach to revising decisions is beyond the scope of this text. In a more general sense, however, posterior analysis can be used to mean any form of data analysis which may generate information leading to revised decisions. In this context the analysis of data by the use of models or statistical techniques can be considered as a part of posterior analysis. This more general meaning appears to hold greater promise for developing a comprehensive and integrated approach to decision making.

BENEFITS AND MANAGERIAL APPLICATIONS OF DECISION THEORY

One of the primary benefits of Bayesian analysis to the practical decision maker is the structure which it brings to the decision-making process. It encourages a logical and systematic consideration of alternatives, relevant uncertainties, and probable consequences. This added element in the decision-making process has the potential for generating more thoroughly considered and thus improved managerial decisions.

In addition, the Bayesian approach provides a framework for evaluating information needs and estimating the value of information.

This is, of course, a critical concept in the relationship between information and decision making.

A study was conducted in the early 1970s by Rex V. Brown to explore the uses business was making of decision theory. This survey uncovered many interesting applications and problems in the use of such techniques. The following discussion of his findings is from *Marketing Applications of Personalist Decision Analysis* published by the Marketing Science Institute.[3]

Application at DuPont

Substantial decision analysis is going on throughout the DuPont organization, stimulated by staff groups in the Development department and elsewhere. Managers in the various departments have shown increasing interest in the staff groups' services (which are supplied for a fee) during the past ten years. Yet, even after all this time, Dr. Sig Andersen, manager of one of the consulting groups and perhaps the most prominent figure in the application of decision analysis, says he feels that it has not yet reached the point where it really has a major impact at the general manager level in DuPont. J. T. Axon, Manager of the Management Science Division, says:

> I think [Andersen and his colleagues] have indeed been pioneers and missionaries on behalf of . . . (Decision Analysis) within DuPont, and I share with them the conviction that their work has improved the quality of numerous decisions around the company. Their impact has been seriously limited, however, by the absence of appropriate educational efforts aimed at the decision makers. Even at this date, we have in DuPont, in my judgment, very few key decision makers who are 'alive' to the possibilities of . . . (Decision Analysis) and comfortable in its use. It is this lack that has dragged down the DuPont effort.

At DuPont, middle and even senior managers increasingly will take action or submit recommendations that include decision analysis along with more conventional analyses, but the presentation to top management is likely to be supported by more informal reasoning, not decision analysis.

For example, in the case of a new product which had just reached the prototype stage at DuPont, the question before management was: On what scale should initial pilot production be carried out? Critical uncertainties involved the reliability of the military demand for which the prototype had been originally designed, and the amount of supplementary commercial business that would be generated.

---

[3] From Rex V. Brown, *Marketing Applications of Personalist Decision Analysis* (Cambridge, Mass.: Marketing Science Institute, 1971), pp. 6, 9–20.

Decision analysis was performed on a computer to produce "risk profiles" of return on investment for various plant sizes and pricing strategies. The inputs included probability assessments of demand for each possible end-use of the product (based on market research), as well as assessments of cost and timing. The analysis indicated that, on the basis of the assessments used, a certain price was optimal, and a $3-million pilot plant would have the highest expected rate of return.

When this conclusion was transmitted to top management, it was couched in the language of informal reasoning, not of decision analysis. Management opted for a smaller, $1-million plant, but adopted—unchanged—the pricing recommendation of the study. It appears that top management, without explicitly disagreeing with the assumptions underlying the analysis, possessed an aversion to risk which was not assumed in the analysis.

Pillsbury's approach

James R. Petersen, vice president of The Pillsbury Company and general manager of the Grocery Products Company, uses decision trees regularly in evaluating major recommendations submitted to him. More than a dozen marketing decisions a year are approved by him on the basis of the findings of detailed decision analysis. (Many more decisions in his divisions are rendered after first using a skeletal decision tree to clarify the key problem issues.)

Typically, a middle manager in the Grocery Products Company will spend a week or so developing a decision analysis approach often with the help of a staff specialist. When the middle manager's recommendation comes to be considered by Petersen, this analysis is the vehicle for discussion.

For instance, in one case, the issue before management was whether to switch from a box to a bag as a package for a certain grocery product. Petersen and his sales manager had been disposed to retain the box on the grounds of greater customer appeal. The brand manager, however, favored the bag on cost considerations. He supported his recommendation with a decision analysis based on his own best assessments of probable economic, marketing, and other consequences. Even when the sales manager's more pessimistic assessments of the market impact of a bag were substituted for the brand manager's, the bag still looked more profitable. Petersen adopted the recommendation, the bag was introduced, and the profits on the product climbed substantially.

During the course of discussions, some Pillsbury executives urged that the bag be test-marketed before management made a firm decision. The original decision analysis showed, however, only a one-in-ten chance that the bag would prove unprofitable—and if that occurred, it would probably be not too unprofitable. A simple, supplementary analysis showed that the value of making a market test could not remotely approach its cost. Accordingly, no test marketing was undertaken. Management's confidence in the analysis was later confirmed by the bag's success.

Uses of GE

At General Electric, there has recently been a formal head office requirement that all investment requests of more than $500,000 be supported by a probabilistic assessment of rate of return and other key measures. In the wake of this requirement, and largely in the area of plant appropriations, more than 500 instances of computerized decision analyses have been recorded over the past four years.

Heavy use is made of a library of special decision analysis programs developed largely by Robert Newman, manager of Planning Services, who works with managers in other GE operations on a consulting basis. The consulting relationship, no doubt enhanced by Newman's own experience in line management, often has an impact on issues beyond the scope of the originating inquiry, as this example shows:

One GE division was faced with a shortage of manufacturing capacity for a mature industrial product. Using the information and assessments supplied by the division manager (including a suspicion that the product was obsolescent), Newman spent a few hours on a decision analysis which suggested that the division should not increase capacity, but raise prices. Both the consultant and the manager felt uneasy about this conclusion.

Further discussion yielded new but confidential information that the division was developing a product which promised to supplant the old one. This intelligence, plus various estimates of the probability of success and related matters, led to a new analysis employing GE's prepackaged computer programs. This study pointed to the conclusion that research and development expenditures on the new product should be increased by a factor of 20. The recommendation was adopted, the new product went into production two years later, and it achieved highly profitable sales of some $20 million a year.

SUMMARY

Several decision techniques are available to marketing managers which can bring structure to the process of decision making. The major set of these decision techniques can be grouped under the heading Formal (Bayesian) Decision Analysis.

Bayesian decision analysis breaks the decision-making process into three phases: prior analysis, preposterior analysis, and posterior analysis. Prior analysis allows the manager to make use of decision trees in selecting between alternative courses of action based on existing information. Preposterior analysis is an important ingredient in the research process. It should be initiated before research is designed and refined based on the details of the design. The essence of this activity is to answer the question "Is additional information worth the cost of generating it?" To answer the question, the cost and value of the information must be estimated. If the value exceeds the cost, then the decision should be to develop the additional information. In considering the conceptual foundation of preposterior analysis, it is useful to reduce the many facets of information to the single dimension of quality. This can be roughly equated to the sophistication and breadth of the research design. As the quality of information improves, the cost and value increase in a functionally related fashion. These functional relationships provide a conceptual basis for considering the cost and benefit of information under varying conditions. The value of information, in a managerial sense, is related to its managerial use. How much does it improve the decision for which it is an input? Both tangible and intangible benefits must be dealt with to get a true picture of information value. Certain procedures can be of great use in operationalizing preposterior analysis. These procedures are numerous and include both the opportunity loss matrix and the decision tree. Finally, posterior analysis involves the revision of prior decisions based on new information. This revision may be made via Bayes' Theorem or in a broader sense by any procedure for data analysis. These techniques, although still in limited use, are becoming more widely accepted by modern business with the passage of time. They appear to hold great promise for improving decision making through the addition of increased structure to the process.

DISCUSSION QUESTIONS

1. Define decision analysis. What are the major techniques used in such analysis? Discuss the benefits of this approach to the marketing manager and the marketing researcher.

2. Assume that you are a retailer who is considering a new item for resale. To include the new item in your store an old item must be removed which has consistently returned $500 profit per year. You calculate that if the new item does well you will make $1,500 profit from it this year; if it does moderately well you will make $500 profit; but if it sells poorly you will lose $500 this year on the new item. You estimate the chances of success of the new product as follows: to do well .4; to do moderately well .3; and to

do poorly .3. What should you do based on expected value? What part should risk aversion play in making this decision?

3. You must establish a system to handle order processing for a new product. You can buy a computer to do the job, rent computer time, or do the job by hand. Either method will handle the processing effectively. The cost of each system would vary according to the volume of new orders. The cost estimates (per year) are:

Buy	High volume	$15,000
	Medium volume	14,500
	Low volume	14,000
Rent	High volume	$16,000
	Medium volume	14,000
	Low volume	12,000
Hand	High volume	$20,000
	Medium volume	15,000
	Low volume	10,000

Based on sales forecasts the probability of a high volume is .3, a medium volume .4, and a low volume .3.

Which system would be best, based on expected value?

4. Explain the basic concept of preposterior analysis. What is the purpose and use of this type of analysis in marketing research?

5. Suppose that a retailer is currently using a particular display area for cigars and averaging $500 profit per year on them. A map salesman approaches the retailer with a proposal to remove the cigars and put a map display in their place. It is estimated if the maps do well they would return a profit of $2,000 per year; if they do moderately well the profit will be $500, but if they do poorly they will yield a $1,000 loss. The retailer supposes the probability of doing well to be .3, of doing moderately well .3, and of doing poorly .4.

   a. What is the best decision based on current information?
   b. What is the maximum amount that any information on sales can be worth?
   c. How can knowing the maximum value of information be of help to the decision-maker/researcher?

6. In the decision described in (5), if a sales forecast for maps can be developed for $400 and has a .8 probability of being correct, should the retailer buy the forecast?

SELECTED REFERENCES

Brown, Rex V., Kahr, Andrew S., and Peterson, Careron R. *The Applied Art of Analyzing a Decision*. Cambridge, Mass.: Marketing Science Institute, 1973.

Brown, Rex V.   *Decision Analysis in the Organization.* Cambridge, Mass.: Marketing Science Institute, 1974.

Day, Ralph L.   "Optimizing Marketing Research through Cost-Benefit Analysis," *Business Horizons* (Fall 1966), pp. 45–54.

Emery, James C.   "Cost/Benefit Analysis," as cited in D. J. Couger and R. W. Knapp, eds., *Systems Analysis Techniques* New York: John Wiley and Sons, Inc., 1974, pp. 397–425.

Enis, Ben M. and Broome, Charles S.   *Marketing Decisions: A Bayesian Approach.* Scranton, Pa: International Textbook Company, 1971.

Green, Paul E. and Tull, Donald S.   *Research for Marketing Decisions,* 2d ed. Englewood Cliffs, N.J.: Prentice-Hall, Inc., 1970, chapter 2.

Schlaifer, Robert   *Analysis of Decisions under Uncertainty.* New York: McGraw-Hill Book Company, Inc., 1969.

Wentz, Walter B.   *Marketing Research: Management and Methods,* New York: Harper and Rov⸱ Publishers, 1972.

chapter

3

Determining information needs

The purpose of the marketing research process is to generate information which will help management answer questions related to decision areas of current interest. The informational activities inside the marketing division of an organization play a major support role for marketing management. Information is needed to improve marketing decisions. If informational activities within the marketing system lose their managerial orientation, they become pointless and without direction. Planning for research to generate either a continual flow of information or one specific set of information should start with an evaluation of the decision-making system.

The first step in the process of providing information must involve an assessment of the decision areas, problems, and decision makers within the organization. The activities involved in such an assessment can be called a marketing information audit.

THE MARKETING INFORMATION AUDIT

A marketing information audit is a comprehensive review and evaluation of the complete decision making and information-producing activities within the organization.[1] It should include all basic decision areas and levels. The objectives of the audit are:

1. To determine the exact nature of the marketing decisions considered within the organization.

[1] See R. L. Ackoff, "Management Misinformation Systems," *Management Science* (December 1967), pp. B-147–B-156.

2. To determine who in the decision-making system is responsible for each of the required decisions.
3. To define the exact information needs of each decision maker.
4. To locate the sources of the data required to develop the needed information.
5. To determine the type of processing (analysis) needed to transform the data into usable information.
6. To locate inefficiencies within the existing system.

The marketing information audit can be divided into three major phases: (1) demand audit, (2) supply audit, and (3) information management audit. The demand audit looks at the decision making side of the organization. This effort should be directed at isolating the marketing decisions, decision makers, and information needs. The information needs should be specified in terms of type, form, and amounts of information for each decision maker. The supply audit deals with locating the sources of data from which the needed information can be generated. The information planner needs to be familiar with the organizational units and their ability to supply data internally. If the data is not available internally, then it must be developed from external sources. This may involve either tapping secondary sources or designing procedures to collect primary data. Finally, the management audit investigates the efficiency of operation within the information management system. Do the components of the system adequately carry out the functions of data collection, data processing, and information transmission? This is the equivalent of asking can the system efficiently carry out the research process?

The focus of this chapter is the *demand audit* portion of the total marketing information audit. Elements of the *supply* and *information management* audits are discussed in later chapters. One of the vital outputs of the demand audit is a comprehensive statement of information needs within the organization. This can be conveniently organized by use of the marketing decision matrix discussed in Chapter 1. After the demand audit, the researcher should be able to fill-in each cell of the matrix with the information needed to make the decisions in that decision area and on that decision level. Data requirements can then be derived from the information needs.

In order to understand the information demand audit, two facets must be explored. First, the conceptual nature of the decision-making process must be understood along with the modifications necessitated by the organizational structure. The decision-making process was discussed in considerable detail in Chapter 2 but the impact of organizational structure on information needs is still to be examined. Secondly, operationalizing the audit through situational analysis must be considered. These areas will be discussed in turn, followed by a discussion of when information needs do and do not call for marketing research.

THE IMPACT OF ORGANIZATIONAL STRUCTURE ON INFORMATION NEEDS

The decision-making process occurs in the context of a decision making or organizational structure. According to one source, "An organizational structure may be defined as a vertical pattern of work, people, and physical resources that contributes to the attainment of the enterprise missions."[2] It is not enough to know what decisions are to be made or how to make a decision. An analysis of information requirements is incomplete without a knowledge of where (by whom) decisions are made. Regardless of its size, virtually every organization has a structure which determines which members make specific decisions. In this section, some basic considerations in organizational structure and their impact on decision making and information needs are examined.

Basic considerations

Regardless of the size or complexity of an organization someone is ultimately responsible for making each specific decision. Along with this responsibility, the individual assumes a position of authority which enables him or her to perform in the organization. The organization exists because one person is not able to make all the decisions required in a particular enterprise. While retaining primary responsibility, the top manager must delegate many decisions to others. This delegation process generates many basic requirements for information in terms of both decision making and reporting. The persons responsible for each decision must have information on which to base their judgments and their superiors must also have information to evaluate their performance. Thus, delegation causes a decentralization of information needs throughout the organization.

Although the terms centralization and decentralization are used in varying contexts, most writers concur that the terms refer to "the degree of delegation of duties, power, and authority to lower levels of an organization."[3] Since the degree of centralization and decentralization

---

[2] B. Hodge and H. J. Johnson, *Manpower and Organizational Behavior* (New York: John Wiley and Sons, Inc. 1970), p. 158.

[3] H. Y. Hicks, *The Management of Organizations* (New York: McGraw-Hill Book Co., 1967), p. 349.

is a function of delegation, it is not necessarily reflected in the organization chart. Furthermore, the degree of delegation in different departments and functions of an organization may vary. For example, if a large consumer goods company is organized by product lines, the marketing staff functions may also be decentralized. On the other hand, the marketing staff functions could be centralized.

There is nothing intrinsically good or bad about decentralization. On the positive side one may argue that decentralization allows participation by lower levels of management in decision making. On the other hand, however, centralization allows top management to exercise more direct control over the organization and also provides uniformity and integration of inputs for planning purposes. No organization would be meaningful if centralization were carried to the extreme. Similarly, a completely decentralized organization would have no central leadership and poor coordination of efforts. Although most authorities agree that every firm operates at some point along a continuum between extreme centralization and extreme decentralization, there is considerably less agreement as to which direction is more popular.

Although a positive correlation between information technology and centralization is an intriguing possibility, it is only fair to point out arguments to the contrary. It can be argued, for example, that delegation is more a function of the need for specialized decision-making talent than for information. That is, getting better information to the decision maker is of no use if the decision maker is not capable of utilizing it.

Luthans points out:

. . . organizational centralization-decentralization is much broader than mere information flows. Growth, homogeneity of personnel, and . . . the environment may all play a role in the eventual organization structure. Whether the computer is of such significance that it can override these other variables is yet to be seen. But one conclusion seems certain. The computer *will* have an impact on structure as on all other areas in organization and management. The only question is *when* and *how much*.[4]

Regardless of the influence of information technology and the computer on organization structure, the degree of centralization does affect the information requirements of an organization. For example, the span of control in a highly centralized organization is narrower than that of a highly decentralized organization. In the decentralized organization management control decisions are made at lower levels in the organization structure. Therefore, information related to these de-

---

[4] Fred Luthans, *Organizational Behavior: A Modern Behavioral Approach to Management* (New York: McGraw-Hill Book Company, 1973), p. 144.

cisions flows upward through relatively few levels of management. On the other hand, in a highly centralized organization this information is frequently transmitted to the highest levels of management. Since it is often difficult to determine the degree of centralization by examining an organization chart, one must be aware of the informal organization structure. That is, the formal structure is revealed through the organization chart, but the informal structure reveals the manner in which decision making actually takes place. The information planner must take both into account.

In addition to delegation, the type of organizational structure adopted by the firm will have a significant impact on the structure of information needs. There are two widely used organization structures: the line and staff structure, and the matrix structure.

The line and staff structure was developed to accommodate the need for specialized support services within organizations. Basically, the distinction between line and staff is that of decision making versus support. Marketing research, for example, is usually a staff activity, while sales management is a line activity. Note that the distinction between line and staff generally conforms to the separation of the decision-making and research processes discussed in Chapter 1.

The matrix organization structure includes both functional departments (vertical lines) and a project orientation (horizontal lines). Obviously, this structure violates the unity-of-command principle. Assigning specialists to projects, while retaining their places in functional departments, creates an environment in which confusion easily arises. The difficulties involved in coordinating personnel and resolving problems are the primary disadvantages of the matrix structure. On the other hand, the concentration of specialized talent in project ventures constitutes the primary advantage. According to Luthans, "Many modern organizations which are facing tremendous structural and technical complexity have no choice but to move to such an arrangement."[5]

Information needs in a matrix organization are complicated by the lack of unitary upward accountability. That is, a member of a project group is accountable to both the project manager and the manager of the department from which he is assigned. The assignment of specialists to the project, however, provides a more direct link for the interaction between research and decision making. Assume for example that a researcher is accountable to both the project manager and his immediate superior in the marketing department. If this relationship problem is handled well, the commitment of research staff to the project insures the availability of information as it is needed for decision making.

---

[5] Luthans, *Organization Behavior*, p. 177.

Marketing organization structures and information needs

Discussion in the preceding section was devoted to fundamental considerations in organization structure as they relate to information needs. These fundamentals must also be considered in the light of specific structures which are common in marketing organizations. The most typical marketing organizational structures are: (1) functional, (2) territorial, (3) product-based, and (4) customer-based. Each of these forms will be discussed briefly in terms of its informational implication.

Marketing organization based on functions. In the functional organization, decision making is departmentalized along activity lines such as promotion, distribution, new product development, and so forth. Functional organization is most appropriate when a firm's activities are highly centralized (geographically), the product line is relatively narrow, and the target market is not segmented. When these conditions exist, each functional department is able to service the entire marketing operation with its repective contribution.

Functionalized departments suffer from one primary disadvantage. That is, they tend to be myopic in their view of the company. Specialists in promotion tend to concern themselves primarily with the problems of their own department or, at best, their own contribution to narrow measures of corporate performance. This problem is particularly difficult to overcome since the chief marketing administrator is the only executive with a multifunctional perspective. A considerable amount of horizontal information flow, both formal and informal, is required to attain effectiveness from this type of organizational structure.

Marketing organization based on geographic area. Firms with widespread geographic markets are frequently faced with the necessity of organizing along territorial lines. Generally, this orientation is the result of building the organization up from the lowest field unit— the salespeople. In some cases, however, even those firms without extensive personal sales efforts find it desirable to organize along geographic lines if there are noticeable differences in their buyers among two or more geographic regions.

In the geographically-based organization, information tends to be gathered in its most disaggregate form at the sales level. As the information proceeds up through district and region management, it is aggregated and changed to meet the needs of decision makers at each level. In terms of the levels of decision making discussed in Chapter 1, sales people, and possibly district managers, are concerned primarily with management control decision making. District managers and/or regional managers tend to be concerned with management planning. The region manager and/or marketing administrator tend to be primarily concerned with strategic planning. Information at the sales level needs to be current and extensive in terms of individual customers within each territory. The district manager, however, requires a more aggregate report in order to anticipate any needed changes in operating strategy. The marketing administrator requires summary information about the entire marketing operation, usually broken down by region. This information is then used in conjunction with information provided to other top level administrators to evaluate and revise corporate policy.

Marketing organization based on products. In discussing both functional and territorial organizations, key assumptions were made concerning the nature of the firm's products. In each case the firm was assumed to have a single product line or, at least, relative homogeneity among products. In many firms, however, product offerings are sufficiently diverse to require specialized treatment. An organization which proves to be effective for one product line might prove ineffective for a different product line. When this situation arises, the marketing organization is usually built around products.

In a relatively decentralized line and staff organization based on products—advertising, distribution, product development, and cost and price analysis are all line-oriented functions which produce decisions relative to the implementation of marketing strategy for the product. Although information does flow between departments at the product level and the corporate level, the information needs are very specific to individual departments. Thus product-based organization structures usually generate highly segmented information requirements.

Marketing organizations based on customers. A number of situations exist which cause many firms to organize their marketing decision making based on customers. For example, a firm may sell its product lines to different customer types. The marketing manager assigned to a consumer-oriented market would probably not do a good job of simultaneously managing marketing strategy in an industrial market. Thus a separate organization is created for each type of buyer.

The information requirements of organizations based on customers are often quite unique. They may require a high degree of cooperation between customers and sellers in order to maintain a meaningful flow of information. The manufacturer must be aware of the needs of the customer in order to provide the highly technical and/or specialized products which lead to the seller-client relationship. Similarly, the customer must be provided with a sufficient amount of information about the manufacturer's goods or services in order to assess their inadequacies. This situation may lead to a cooperative relationship in which information is exchanged on a frequent basis. It is not uncommon under these conditions for manufacturers to develop entirely new products, or make substantial alterations in existing products, in order to meet the specifications of a single customer.

OPERATIONALIZING THE INFORMATION DEMAND AUDIT

Now that we have discussed some of the conceptual and organizational considerations which influence the information demand audit, let us turn to basics of actually conducting such an investigation.

Situational analysis

The most critical aspect of a demand audit lies in the interface between a manager's problem and the development of a clear and relevant statement of information needs. This interface provides the source of direction for research. From the manager's perspective a need for solutions is the most important view of the situation. The researcher's view, however, is different but related. The researcher must translate the manager's problem situation into a specific set of information needs. At the point where the researcher attempts to aid in the delineation of the managerial problem and information needs, he or she is involved in *situational analysis*.

Situational analysis deals with the definition and structuring of problems which require a decision by management. The key term is "problem." What is a problem, and particularly, what is a marketing problem? The lack of emphasis in business studies on problem definition may lead one to believe that real management problems are usually obvious and that solving all of these problems would result in business success. To the contrary, problems only become real when they are defined, and the difficulties of problem definition are among the most serious faced by managers and researchers.

For the purpose of this discussion we will use the following definition:

A management problem is any business or administrative situation in which the difference between the desired state of affairs and the actual state of affairs is of sufficient magnitude to warrant action.

Upon closer examination this definition can be used to cover every area of marketing decision making. Thus, while the definition may fall short of the desired level of scientific rigor, it does reflect the state of the art in marketing today. Notice that the key to problem identification is a difference between the actual and the desired states of affairs.

A state of affairs, such as a market share level, exists in reality. In and of itself, this state of affairs has no particular meaning. Only when compared to some desired state of affairs, such as market share objective, can a problem come into existence. Furthermore, it is only when this difference is "of sufficient magnitude to warrant action" that we technically recognize a problem. For effective problem definition, management must specify both the desired state of affairs and the amount of difference which would warrant action.

It is important to note that our ability to determine a difference between actual and desired states of affairs is usually limited to the measurement of symptoms. When a problem is recognized, however, the action which results must relate to the underlying causes rather than those symptoms. Thus, we can view a management problem in terms of two major components: (1) the symptoms through which the existence of a problem is recognized, and (2) the true cause of the problem, or that area of activity in which a decision must be made to arrive at a solution.

Symptoms and the symptom syndrome. Symptoms are further described by two characteristics: (1) they must be expressed in terms of management needs, goals, or objectives; and (2) they must be observable, preferably empirically measurable. Therefore, the need for a product development plan qualifies as a symptom. The underlying problem is the absence of a vehicle through which management can attain meaningful product development. Thus, a need exists. Furthermore, the plan itself is observable, and management can determine when the need has been satisfied. The quality or success of the plan is another matter. Similarly, a sales chart which illustrates actual performance and an established objective could produce a symptom of a problem. The chart indicates the current sales levels as well as a sales target; in reviewing the chart, management may see the symptom of a problem. Notice that in both of these cases the symptom itself does not lead directly to problem definition.

One of the most common difficulties faced by both the manager and the researcher is the "symptom syndrome." That is, managers and analysts all too easily fall into the trap of approaching a problem in terms of its symptoms, rather than its underlying causes. The single symptom which is most frequently cited is some measure of sales. Sales may be decreasing, unchanged, increasing at too slow a rate, or otherwise failing to meet some criteria for success. In every case, however, the mere knowledge that sales performance is off the mark does not constitute the definition of a problem. Rather, sales performance is an indicator through which management can become aware of problems. Obviously, there are as many indicators as there are performance criteria. Other common indicators include various measures of profit and market share.

When any performance measure deviates from the desired pattern, the result is a symptom of a potential problem. As a personal analogy, assume that you are not feeling well and discover that you have fever. Normal body temperature for most people is 98.6 degrees Fahrenheit. Thus, a reading of 98.6 degrees on a thermometer becomes a performance criterion. When a reading above or below the criterion is registered, we are alerted to the presence of a potential problem. Just as a physician considers high body temperature as a symptom of a potential health problem, the manager should consider poor sales performance as a symptom of a potential marketing problem. It should be noted that symptoms are not always cast in a negative context. We are also interested in symptoms of unexpectedly good performance; e.g., the medical profession's interest in unusually healthy, elderly individuals, or a marketing manager's interest in sales or profit performances which significantly exceed the criteria for success.

If the physician is able to diagnose symptoms of an illness correctly, and at an early onset, the probability of a serious health problem is reduced. The same principle holds for the marketing analyst. If an information system is well conceived and implemented, symptoms of potential problems are discovered and diagnosed before a crisis develops. Management's ability to incorporate such safeguards into its information system is an indication of good problem definition techniques and system design.

Problem causes and decision areas.   The second major component of a problem, the underlying causes, is much less familiar territory. A potential problem exists for every marketing-related variable. Problems can be caused by changes in consumer perceptions or attitudes, a change in the legal environment, the action of a competitor, and numerous other external factors as well as the internal decision making of management. There is no simple procedure for defining a problem. Marketing management includes components of both science and art. Thus the marketing practitioners must strive for an effective blend of creativity along with the scientific method.

The "scientific method" is the distinguishing feature of science as we know it today. While science itself refers to a body of knowledge, the scientific method refers to the manner in which that body of knowledge is changed. Carlos Lastrucci has defined science in terms of scientific method as follows:

An objective, logical, and systematic method of analysis of phenomena, devised to permit the accumulation of reliable knowledge.[6]

Notice that the first part of this definition is concerned with the manner in which the accumulation of reliable knowledge will occur.

---

[6] Carlos Lastrucci, *The Scientific Approach: Basic Principles of the Scientific Method* (Cambridge, Mass.: Schenkman Publishing Company, Inc., 1967), p. 6.

Thus, if our work is objective, logical, systematic, and replicable, it is scientific. Obviously, the business person is frequently forced to make decisions under conditions which do not meet these criteria.

Scientific methods are more readily used in later stages of the marketing research process. We are concerned here, however, with the delineation of a marketing decision area for which a problem is deemed to exist. We could be relatively scientific at this point only if an extensive body of knowledge were available from which to draw solutions to recurring problems. This is generally not the case. In fact, attempts to emulate science at this stage can often be undesirable.

The scientific method by its very nature has distinct advantages and disadvantages. On the plus side it provides the framework for the orderly accumulation and analysis of data to produce information. On the other hand, it is all too easy for the scientific method to lead to rigidity in the way various situations are viewed. This phenomenon is described by Kuhn[7] in his paradigm theory of the evolution of science. Scientists in the days of Copernicus, for example, maintained a paradigm which was currently accepted than it would have been to universe. It was easier for an astronomer of that day to expand upon the paradigm which was currently accepted than it would have been to break away from the trend of thought. Therefore, if a problem arose which related to the earth's position relative to the planets and stars, the existing theory would be the basis for problem definition. Copernicus questioned that paradigm at great personal and professional risk.

As an analogy in marketing, assume that a retailer is interested in relocating his store. If marketing were a fundamental discipline, a body of knowledge supported by research findings would exist. From these findings the retailer could draw a decision as to the best location. Since this is not the case, the retailer can at best hope to gain some insight from the body of knowledge that exists and to explore his problem with an open mind. In order to be meaningful, problem definition frequently requires imagination and creativity which break away from commonly accepted thinking. "Pat" definitions and stereotype solutions based on particular symptoms should be avoided. Creativity is the watchword for effective problem definition.

An illustration of information needs

After the problem has been creatively defined, the information needed to make a decision can be determined. To illustrate the specification of information needs, let us examine an airline case. The airline is not in trouble, but recent shifts in economic conditions have

---

[7] T. S. Kuhn, *The Structure of Scientific Revolution*, 2d ed. (Chicago: University of Chicago Press, 1962).

resulted in a reassessment of policies and strategies for the next two to five years. One of the decision areas facing top level executives of the airline concerns the allocation of resources and effort between business and pleasure travel market segments. Management is well aware from experience of the distinct differences in operating characteristics and profitability of service for these two segments. They discovered, however, that a study of these two segments in the airline's system of routes has not been conducted for several years. The uppermost cells of the decision matrix in Table 3–1 illustrate information needs relating to this problem. For example, management will need to know the difference in profitability between business and pleasure travel, expressed in revenue-passenger-miles (RPMs). They will also need to know the projected level of RPMs in the business and pleasure segments of the market. Furthermore, management will need a summary of operating statistics, such as load factors and share of RPMs for both business and pleasure segments throughout the airline's system. This type of information would ultimately lead to strategic planning decisions related to the market. Management might then adopt a policy of seeking market share penetration in business travel segments. Similarly, this part of the analysis may result in a policy of maintaining a systemwide return on investment of 5 percent (after taxes and expressed as a percentage of gross sales).

In the context of the overall decision problem, further information needs for market analysis at management planning and management control levels of decision making are illustrated. For example, district managers would need summaries of activity by major account clients in their district as well as new account activity. This might be required on a monthly basis to detect seasonal or cyclical trends. In addition to the summaries, the district manager would probably request projections of business travel within the district. Anticipating the types of decisions to be made, both district managers and station managers would request information concerning penetration goals by segment for their corresponding responsibilities, as well as reports of penetration performance, probably on a quarterly basis.

Notice that the nature of information needs at each of the three levels of decision making is different. For example, information needs at the management control level of decision making are ongoing as opposed to one-time at the strategic planning level. Also, keep in mind that these are not intended to be exhaustive lists of information needs for this type of decision-making problem. You will recall from Chapter 1 that the levels of decision making, while associated in general with levels of management, may be carried on at all levels of management. That is, management control information needs may exist at the corporate level, the district level, as well as the field level. The information

Table 3–1
Illustration of information needs in a decision matrix

Decision areas / Level of decision	Strategic planning	Management planning	Management control
Market analysis	1. Profitability of business versus pleasure RPMs 2. Projections of business travel 3. Operating summaries in business and pleasure segments–systemwide	1. District major account summaries (monthly) 2. District new account summaries (monthly) 3. District business travel profile and projections (monthly)	1. Penetration goals/ Segment 2. Penetration performance/ Quarter
Product	1. Important product features for business travelers 2. Alternatives for product enhancement	1. Desired departure times/route segment 2. Competitor departures/route segment	1. System schedule 2. On-time performance/ route segment 3. Operation confirmations
. . .	. . .	. . .	. . .

needs discussed thus far all pertain to market analysis. Decisions resulting from this type of information might narrow the scope of alternatives available in remaining decisions. For example, the policy stated earlier concerning market share penetration in business segments might require a high priority for allocations of product and distribution to those segments. At the management planning level, decisions might be made classifying specific route segments as "business" or "pleasure." This would result in a different treatment for each of those routes in an allocation of the marketing mix at the district level. Finally, at the management control level, the task may become one of refining penetration policy based on market performance over time.

A clear statement of information needs is the starting place for effective marketing research. Providing information which can improve the decisions made by marketing managers is how research gains value. Even when information is thought to be needed, however, research may still not be justified.

DECIDING WHEN TO CONDUCT MARKETING RESEARCH

Before proceeding with research, the marketing manager and researcher should be confident that certain basic conditions are present. Perhaps the best way to approach the question—to research or not to research?—is by considering situations where research should *not* be conducted. Lee Adler provides an excellent list of such situations in *A "Dissident" View on Marketing Research.*[8]

When the cost of research would exceed its value

This concept was discussed in Chapter 2. Each proposed research effort, whether it is designed as a one time project or for ongoing implementation, should be subjected to a cost/benefit analysis. Only if the benefit (value) of the information exceeds the cost should research proceed. For example, the research department of a large chemical firm developed a new coating for aluminum window the door frames which could prevent stains from concrete during construction. It was estimated that a study of market potential using depth interviews with a sample of 100 firms would cost approximately $12,000. The production cost of the product was very low, however, and would require no extra equipment. Management estimated that going into limited production for one year and including the product in the existing line would cost only $15,000. Since the market potential study was intended only for use in deciding whether to enter limited production or not, it was dropped as too expensive relative to its potential value.

---

[8] Lee Adler, *A "Dissident" View on Marketing Research*, (Princeton, N.J.: Center for Marketing Communications, 1975).

When there is an insufficient budget to do a technically adequate job

Technical problems may arise with research relating to inadequate sample size, lack of pretesting, lack of trained interviewers, and so forth. When budget limitations prevent a reasonable level of accuracy in a research project, it is better to avoid research and the false impressions that can be created. A common problem arises in the case of industrial marketing research where personal interviews are often required to get the technical data and careful diagnosis needed. Personal interviews can be very expensive per interview, thus the size of the sample may be restricted. This is acceptable if there is no need for conclusive results. Some very useful hypotheses may be developed, but the need is often to project to the total market. This may not be possible when the sample is too small due to budgetary constraints.

When time is an enemy

Information, however accurate, has no value if it is not timely. If the decision must be made before the research can be completed, then no research should be undertaken. Time is a particularly serious enemy in highly competitive fashion markets. The decision to introduce a new product may be urgent if the product life cycle is known to be short and a competitor is on the brink of introducing a similar product.

When conducting research would tip your hand to a competitor

This problem is most often encountered in relation to new product testing. Open-field testing in test markets may give important product information to competitors before the actual product introduction. This would allow them to formulate a competitive response more quickly than would otherwise be the case. Such a possibility should not be allowed to prevent necessary data collection, but it presents a very real risk. One way to avoid the problem is to conduct tests in controlled distribution systems or in computer simulated markets. Testing products with friendly customers should also be considered, particularly in industrial markets where trial use under normal working conditions is often required for effective evaluation.

When research findings would not be actionable

If for any reason the information produced through research could not be acted upon, it would have no value. Information gains value as an input to managerial decision making, thus, if the decision cannot be affected by specific information, research should not be undertaken to produce the information. Many factors, physical and mental, can lock management into a specific course of action. Where this occurs, research is useless. For example, the advertising group for pool chemicals with a rather large company did an extensive study of customer attitudes toward one of the company's products. The intent was to provide a basis for deciding on the copy appeals for proposed advertising. After the study had already been completed, it was discovered that the new product development department was almost finished with the design of a new product which had a totally different dispensing system and chemical base. The consumer attitude survey was thus wasted, since advertising of the old product was dropped. The key to overcoming this general problem is to get agreement from the decision makers, before doing research, as to the courses of action to follow, assuming various research results. If such an understanding is not possible prior to the design and implementation of research, both the researcher and the manager should exercise caution.

When research is politically motivated

Marketing management is a competitive game. Different managers are trying to advance their careers, to win others to their way of thinking, and in some cases, to boost their egos. In this environment it is quite possible that pseudoresearch will be proposed for political rather than decision-making purposes. The manager of a sporting goods store in a downtown urban area wanted to relocate in a newer building in the same area. His company had several other stores located in the suburbs. In order to support his position, he commissioned a study of the "higher" sales potential at the new site. His mind was made up, and he had to convince top management. If the study had not supported his position, he would have discredited the results by finding fault with the sample, questionnaire, or analysis. The research was clearly not intended to improve objective decision making.

When the problem is not clear and the objectives not well defined

Both managers and researchers often contribute to this situation. Managers tend to emphasize symptoms rather than problems, a most common statement as mentioned earlier being that "sales are down." This is only a visible symptom of some deeper problem. The researcher must probe the situation and the decision maker to uncover the real issues and problems. This requires that the manager and researchers work closely; particularly in the early stages of the research process. Many researchers seem to be tempted to substitute their own judgements for those of the decision maker or to cast the problem in a mold that fits their particular methodological expertise. The specialist trained in experimental design may want to conduct an experiment, whatever the problem. This can lead to waste, inefficiency, and information which is not relevant to the decision maker. No research should proceed without a clearly stated managerial decision as its point of departure. This managerial decision must be defined with ample and meaningful management input.

When a test does not represent later reality

This can be a very serious problem in experimental research. Favorable experimental results in product or advertising copy testing may not project to the marketplace. Advertising research often shows copy, graphics, and so forth, doing well in isolated tests, but doing poorly when combined into a total ad. The parts do not harmonize when used together. In such cases, researching isolated parts does not get the desired results. The total ad must be tested. When the controls used in experimental research remove the environment too far from reality, the value of the research may be questioned.

When the findings are intended for use in legal proceedings

Attempting to use marketing research as legal evidence has many potential pitfalls. For example, what constitutes good research from a technical or a management point of view may not be acceptable from a legal standpoint. Also, research results may be subpoenaed for use by the adversary.

In a recent survey by an advertising agency, 90 percent of the sample correctly understood an ad. The FTC argued that this was proof that some portion of the audience was deceived and that ads with the "capacity to deceive" are unlawful. In this case, the research proved very damaging.

When what is to be measured changes slowly

Some variables change very slowly over time. For example, corporate image studies on an annual basis for large companies are generally not necessary because their images are very resistant to change. An appropriate time span between such studies is usually five years or so, unless some major event has occurred which may cause the image to change.

Many facets of consumer behavior are also reasonably stable. The average percentage of the family food dollar spent on various categories of food for home consumption has changed very little over the last ten years, for example. When behavior patterns are this stable, there is little need to research them on a regular basis.

When the information already exists

Reinventing the wheel may be great fun at times, but it has very little value. When data already exist in the corporate data bank or in external secondary sources, there is no need for primary research. Searching secondary data can be extremely tedious work, but is an essential element of an effective information program.

In summary, proposals to conduct research should be carefully evaluated before serious design efforts are undertaken. This can avoid considerable waste and enhance the potential for research to have significant benefits when it is undertaken. Research should not be designed or implemented when any of the conditions described above exist.

SUMMARY

The need for marketing research is an outgrowth of the information needs of marketing management. Research has value only as a support activity for decision making. Given this fact, research must have a managerial orientation to be effective. This means that (1) the managerial problem or decision, (2) who is responsible for making the decision, and (3) the information needed to arrive at an intelligent decision must be specified as a basis for initiating research. This is accomplished through a marketing information audit or more specifically through the information demand portions of this audit.

The marketing information demand audit involves a careful definition of marketing decisions in an organization, who makes those decisions, and what information they need to carry out their tasks effectively. An understanding of the basic nature of the decision-making process and the impact of variations in organizational structure on information requirements form a critical underpinning for the demand audit. The first step in actually conducting an information demand audit is a situational analysis. In this analysis an attempt is made to define the true nature of the problem or decision as opposed to the surface symptoms. The information needed to arrive at an intelligent decision can then be specified.

Whether or not a perceived information need justifies research must also be considered. Certain conditions such as high information cost, relative to value or lack of time, may make research questionable even when a need for information exists. Thus the starting point for marketing research is the perceived informational needs of marketing management when those needs do not violate certain basic conditions.

DISCUSSION QUESTIONS

1. Why is it important that research be preceded by careful analysis of managerial information needs?
2. Discuss the steps in the decision-making process and give an illustration of the type of information that may be needed at each step.
3. What impact do variations in organizational structure have on information needs?
4. What is the intent of situational analysis? Discuss the problems which may arise in such an analysis.
5. Assume that you are concerned with deciding what price to set for a new plastic coffee cup developed by your company. Develop a list of information that would be needed to make the decision.
6. Develop a list of questions that should be asked in determining whether or not an information need justifies research.

SELECTED REFERENCES

Edwards, M. O. "Solving Problems Creatively," *Systems and Procedures Journal* (January-February 1966), pp. 16–24.

Goldstucker, Jac L.; Greenberg, Barnett A.; and Bellenger, Danny N. "How Scientific Is Marketing? What Do Marketing Executives Think?" MSU Business Topics, vol. 22 (Spring 1974), pp. 35–43.

Hodge, B. J., and Johnson, H. J. *Management and Organizational Behavior* New York: John Wiley and Sons, Inc., 1970.

Newman, Joseph W. "Put Research into Marketing Decisions," *Harvard Business Review* (March-April 1962), pp. 105–12.

Osborn, Alex F. *Applied Imagination*, 3d rev. ed. New York: Charles Scribner's Sons, 1963.

Cases for part one

Valley Center Family Market: Using marketing research*

The Valley Center Family Market was established in 1948 in a growing area of a mountain state city. Its first building was 50 by 75 feet. In this space the store had its reserve stock, its open merchandise, and two check-out stands. Shrewd buying, good store displays, and weekly house-to-house distribution of promotional material made the store successful almost from the first. However, the building was situated on a lot 75 feet wide and 125 feet deep, with a 25-foot setback, allowing only 50 by 75 feet for parking. It was soon apparent that the business available to the store could not be handled in the space it had.

Within a year and a half, it bought the adjacent hardware store building on the west, thus increasing the enclosed space to an area of 75 feet by 75 feet, with a little more area for customer parking. With this change, the owners bought a strip of residential property 50 feet

---

* From *Cases in Marketing* by Lawrence C. Lockley, Charles J. Dirksen, and Arthur Kroeger (Boston: Allyn and Bacon, Inc., 1971).

deep, immediately in back of the area already owned by Valley Center Family Market. They also bought the three pieces of residential property immediately to the east of their original plot of land. Two houses were removed from this property, and the land black topped for additional parking. In 1960, the owners of Valley Center Family Market improved their main store building by adding another 40 feet in width, and a 37 foot by 75 foot second story at the back of the main selling floor. The remaining dwelling to the east was razed and parking space provided for 22 more customer cars. In 1961, sales reached a level of 625 percent of the first year's volume. From that year to the last part of 1970, sales rose slowly but steadily, until the store building seemed perpetually crowded. Toward the end of 1970, several large discount stores, selling groceries as well as a full line of clothing, tools, garden supplies, drugs, furniture, and housewares, were opened in the community. Sales started to slow down. The owners of Valley Center Family Market ran more weekend and mid-week specials, broadened the area in which their promotional material was distributed, and made every effort to improve the appearance and convenience of their store. Nevertheless, the sales volume for 1971 was 25 percent below that for 1970.

The owners decided to investigate to find out what course they should follow to regain their former sales volume. In talking with other store owners, they learned that all wholly self-service stores in the general neighborhood had lost business, in varying amounts, when the discount stores were opened. The one exception was a small store in a strictly residential neighborhood which had carried a credit and delivery business accounting for three quarters of its sales volume.

When one of the owners of Valley Center Family Market "shopped" several of the discount stores and examined prices in the food departments, he found that Valley Center's prices were at least as low for manufacturers' brands, and that, in some cases, Valley Center was actually underselling the discount stores on these standard items. The discount stores, however, had various job lots of merchandise the brands of which were unfamiliar to the representative of Valley Center. Prices of these products were very low. The Valley Center man bought a number of cans and packages of the low-priced merchandise. That night, the owners of Valley Center Family Market carefully compared the merchandise bought at the discount stores. Most merchandise they compared seemed to them to be noticeably inferior to that carried in Valley Center.

In the attempt to learn more about the proportion of their customers doing some of their trading at the discount stores, Valley Center passed out a questionnaire to each customer who came through the check-out stands. The customer was promised 25 trading stamps when he or she returned the questionnaire filled out. Since there was no place on the questionnaire for the customer's name or address, the customer did not have to identify himself. The questions were as follows:

1. How many times a week do you usually shop at Valley Center Store? _____
2. In what other food stores have you stopped during the past week? _____

3. Have you shopped in any of the new discount stores?
   _____Yes _____No
   If you have, in which one or ones? _____

4. What proportion of your food purchases do you estimate that you make with Valley Center? _____
5. How many blocks do you come to travel from your home to Valley Center? _____

These questionnaires were passed out to every customer for a full week. A month afterward, only 43 percent of the questionnaires had been filled in and returned. Virtually none of the customers who returned questionnaires said that they had ever shopped at the discount stores, and few of them that they ever shopped anywhere but at Valley Center Family Market. Although the owners of the store did not know what was wrong with their research approach, they were confident that the results of the questionnaire were misleading.

They discussed the possibility of a house-to-house survey in what they believed to be their normal trading area, but after their experience with the questionnaire they did not feel confident that they could get valid answers to their questions.

A local marketing research consultant was asked for recommendations. He suggested that the questionnaires turned-in be used to roughly lay out the territory from which Valley Center drew most of its business. He believed that the unwillingness of customers who now did some of their shopping at the discount stores to return the questionnaire had biased the returns with respect to that question, but he felt that the location of those customers who returned completed questionnaires was probably typical of Valley Center customers as a whole. He suggested that automobile license numbers of all cars using the parking lots of the discount stores be listed by an observer, that the names of the owners and their street addresses be looked up at the state capitol, and a list made of those visitors to the discount stores who lived within the normal trading area of Valley Center Family Store. Then he suggested an interview at the homes of those families living within the normal trading area of Valley Center who had used the discount stores' parking lots.

The consultant estimated that the cost of such a marketing research project would be around $4,000. He believed that an adequate and complete questionnaire would supply a solution to the Valley Center problem, if a solution was to be found. On the other hand, the owners of Valley Center Family Market believed that since they had operated for a year at a reduced sales volume, they should not spend money unless they were reasonably certain that they would get their money's worth.

QUESTIONS

1. Point out the strengths and weaknesses of the marketing research study made by Valley Center Family Market.
2. What should be the objectives of this marketing research study?
3. Comment on the statement by the consultant. Do you think his proposed research project would supply the solution to the Valley Center problem?
4. What research program should Valley Center Family Market follow?

---

case
2

Quaker Oats Company: The 100% natural cereal decision*

The Quaker Oats Company has been a major factor in the cooked and ready-to-eat cereal market for many years. The company's brands were sold in retail outlets which accounted for at least 85 percent of all retail food sales in the United States, as of summer 1972. Earnings in that year were projected to be $2.65 per share, about $55 million on sales of about $770 million.[1]

---

* Case by Philip Burger from *Cases in Marketing Research*, ed. by Walter B. Wentz, pp. 16–19. Copyright © 1975 by Harper & Row, Publishers, Inc. Reprinted by permission of the publisher.

[1] All data contained in this case are obtained from publicly available sources including *Standard & Poor's Stock Guide*, March 1974, a number of articles in *Advertising Age*, and *Fortune*, June 1973. The market plan and distribution data are fictitious.

Quaker corporate headquarters are in the Merchandise Mart in Chicago. The firm has its own in-house advertising agency called Ad-Com. Quaker spends about $60 million annually for advertising, mostly in television and in color print ads. The company has a reputation for being conservative and careful in its marketing decisions. New product entries and withdrawals are kept to a minimum.

A NEW PRODUCT

The research and development group had been working on a new health cereal based on the granola concept. Granola had been made by individuals and small companies for years. Fundamentally, the product is made by mixing rolled wheat, honey, oats, nuts, and other materials mixed at the discretion of the maker. Various concoctions may have a wide variety of flavors with only a slight manipulation of the ingredient levels. The product was thought to appeal to natural food faddists, consumers who bought "health" cereals, and elderly persons who might wish large amounts of natural bulk in their diets.

The Quaker research and development (R&D) laboratory had created a formula that had a distinctive sweet taste together with a pleasant crunch. In blind taste tests, marketing research subjects stated that they definitely preferred the new Quaker formulation to formulations offered by competitors. Most of the competitors' flavors tended to have a bitter taste.

The R&D laboratory devised manufacturing control methods that would guarantee uniform production quality. The cost of production was estimated to be 20 cents per one-pound box or $4.80 per case. Competitive conditions dictated that the retail selling price be in the neighborhood of 59 cents. Since Quaker sold directly to large chains that maintained an average markup of 14 percent, the price would yield about 51 cents per box, or $12.18 per case, to the manufacturer.

TENTATIVE MARKETING PLAN

Total U.S. cereal sales are approximately $900 million annually. Quaker markets variations of Quaker Oats cereal which account for an 8 percent market share of the total cereal market. The bulk of the cereal market is held by the Kellogg Company, General Foods Corporation (Post Cereals), General Mills, and Pillsbury. These firms, which have a large stable of brands serving various market segments, dominate the industry. They make mainly ready-to-eat products which, unlike Quaker Oats, require no cooking.

The new-product marketing team planned on the following costs to get Quaker 100% Natural Cereal into national distribution:

Advertising	$ 5 million
Salesmen	3 million
Trade allowances	3 million
Total	$11 million

In addition, the development and testing of the product totaled $7 million, for a grand total of "funds to be recovered" of $18 million. Annual spending, not including the introductory period, was estimated to be:

Advertising	$2 million
Salesmen	1 million
Trade allowances	2 million
Total	$5 million

Given these figures, the new-product planners felt that a market share of 2 percent was the absolute minimum needed to justify the new product's entry. Less than that would mean trouble. They felt that a 2.5 percent annual market share would sustain the brand and yield a profit. The planners said that market share estimates of less than 2 percent would be sufficient to kill the product, while 2.5 percent or more would justify commercialization.

Since the health food segment of the ready-to-eat cereal market amounted to 6 percent of the total market, it was felt that there was a reasonable chance of achieving the 2 percent minimum. The health food segment then contained only local brands, although the trade papers had rumors that Pet Foods was working on a granola called "Heartland," and Colgate-Palmolive was improving a new brand called "Alpen." The taste and texture of the new brands were unknown. None of the major cereal makers was known to have a satisfactory formula.

MARKET RESEARCH

A prominent Chicago marketing research agency approached the Quaker planners with a proposal to perform some in-home use tests of the new product. The results of the tests would be used in a computer model to generate a forecast of sales. In past tests of the system, highly accurate forecasts of new product sales had been made. The agency's clients included a large analgesics manufacturer, a prominent food product manufacturer, and one of the nation's largest toiletries firms. The cost of the in-home use test and forecast, using a sample of 500 housewives in the Chicago area, was about $20,000, and the results would be available in six weeks. The Quaker new-product planners asked the market research account representative if the system could differentiate between a 2 percent and 2.5 percent market share, with a 90 percent level of confidence. The market researcher answered that this was not possible without a very large and costly sample. The Quaker planners demurred and considered buying the tests and forecasts. Concurrently, top management authorized the allocation of sufficient production capacity in Quaker factories to serve 2.5 percent of the total market.

QUESTIONS

1. Should the market research be purchased? What are the possible outcomes, and what are their probabilities?
2. Analyze the product attributes. Are the market-use assumptions correct? How easily is the product duplicated?
3. How can a new-product planner operationally define new-product success and failure?
4. Can you design a probabilistic decision model to help make this decision for Quaker?
5. Was the decision on allocation of production made at the proper time?

---

case
3
Plastic Products, Inc.*

Plastic Products, Inc. is a relatively small but aggressive manufacturer of industrial plastics located in Chicago. They produce and sell plastic products for industrial uses across the United States as well as in Canada and Japan. The company was established in 1962 by John Adams, a chemical engineer who is currently the president and major stockholder. Mr. Adams is considered a creative genius in the industry and has been personally responsible for the development of several new and innovative products. This success in product development allowed the company to reach a sales level of $11 million in 1977. Operational aspects of the business, however, have not been nearly as

---

* This case was prepared by Danny Bellenger, Georgia State University.

effective as the company's research efforts. A net loss of $77,000 was experienced in 1977.

To improve the production and marketing operations of the business, Mr. Adams hired a new vice president in September of 1977 to head the operational aspects of the company. Mr. Adams intended to continue in the research and development area while Ed Field, the new vice president of Operations, ran the day-to-day business affairs of the company. Mr. Field had extensive experience in this area. He had been with a competitor for 12 years in a similar post before Mr. Adams persuaded him to join Plastic Products.

A NEW PRODUCT

Late in 1977 Adams' research team made another technical breakthrough. A new porous plastic sheet with ultra-high molecular weight polyethylene. This new material could be used to fluidize materials for powder coating and air bearings. Products produced with the new material had certain significant technical advantages over existing products. Mr. Adams was extremely excited about the new process. A patent on the equipment used in the new process was applied for to protect the company; however, the secrecy of the complex details of the process was considered the best protection. Adams wanted to start production at once to make 1978 a "big year." Field was not quite so sure. He started to investigate the alternatives and discovered that a large competitor was interested in purchasing the process. This seemed a very attractive alternative to him. Adams, however, wanted to keep the process and go into production. A meeting was set to discuss the situation. Adams and Field agreed to give all the details to Charles Johnson, a young staff assistant who headed market research, and listen to his conclusions and recommendations before making a decision. The meeting was set for the following Monday.

INFORMATION ON THE PENDING DECISION

Johnson was provided with the following facts and estimates to consider:

1. The process had cost $175,000 to develop.
2. We can sell the process for a fee of $50,000 per year plus 1 percent of sales.
3. If we decide to go into production, the annual fixed cost is estimated at $200,000 with a variable cost of 90 percent of sales revenue.
4. Estimated sales, based on Adams' and Field's collective judgements are:

Annual sales	Probability
$2,000,000	.2
$2,500,000	.3
$3,000,000	.3
$3,500,000	.2

5. A sales forecast can be purchased for $20,000. The forecast would be developed by an outside research firm using an intention-to-buy survey of prospective customers. Based on past experience, it is estimated that there is a .6 chance that the forecast will be essentially accurate; a .2 chance that it will be high by 5 percent; and a .2 chance that it will be low by 5 percent.

Johnson is charged with:

1. Determining the best course of action based on current information.
2. Deciding whether the forecast should be purchased.
3. Pointing out any additional factors that should be considered in making these decisions.

Part two

Conducting marketing research

chapter

4

The marketing research process

Research is the process of generating useful information. All the activities involved in planning the strategy to secure information, collecting data from various sources, processing or analyzing this data, and transmitting the resulting information to the appropriate decision makers are a part of research. In a broad sense, this is true whether the information is generated on a regular, periodic, or one-time basis. Thus, any systematic attempt to produce information which will help answer questions of current interest can be considered research. If the questions of interest are theoretical in nature the investigation may be called *basic research*. When the questions relate to a concrete managerial decision within some institution the investigation is called *applied research*. Applied research is of most concern to the marketing manager and is the topic of concern here. For example, a manager might be attempting to decide on a base price for a new product produced by his firm. In order to arrive at a decision he may need to know the price of competing products. Research could be conducted to answer the question: What is the current competitive price structure in the market for our product? By finding an answer to this question, the manager can make a better pricing decision.

STEPS IN THE RESEARCH PROCESS

The research process consists of a series of actions or steps necessary to effectively carry out research and the desired sequencing of these steps. The intent of such a process is to provide a logical and systematic (scientific) method for conducting, understanding, and evaluating research. The following list presents a brief description of the steps in the research process. These steps are illustrated in Figure 4–1.

Defining the marketing decision and determining information needs

As a basis for beginning the research process, a marketing management problem or decision must be defined based upon a set of symptoms. Correct identification of potential causes of the problem and the resulting information needs have already been described in Chapter 3 as requiring insight and imagination. In the airline example from Chapter 3, the analyst cannot proceed directly from a statement of information need to the collection of data. The need must first be translated into a specific research task. For example, the airline management may request information concerning important product features for the business air travel segment. Without further elaboration, the researcher does not know whether management requires this information in the form of tests of states of nature or relationships between variables. It is not clear whether product characteristics should be expressed in trade terms or consumer perceptions. These and other questions require further elaboration.

As was the case with problem identification and the specification of information needs, these next steps tend to be creative—as opposed to procedural. The researcher is still involved in a process of translation between a need and the manner in which the need can be met. Students whose experience and exposure to research techniques is limited to introductory courses in quantitative methods may be confused by the unstructured nature of the process. Typically, introductory textbooks on statistical procedures and mathematical techniques present problems for which all of this identification is complete. The exercises tend to pick up from there and emphasize the application of particular techniques. Those portions of the research process (techniques) are covered in later chapters concerning data collection and analysis. The early steps in the research process, if properly conducted, should reduce the effort to the measurement of specific variables and tests of relationships or estimation.

Research problems

In translating the management decision and information needs into research, we must be concerned with maintaining continuity and logic in the research process. To accomplish this our first task is to translate

Figure 4–1
The research process

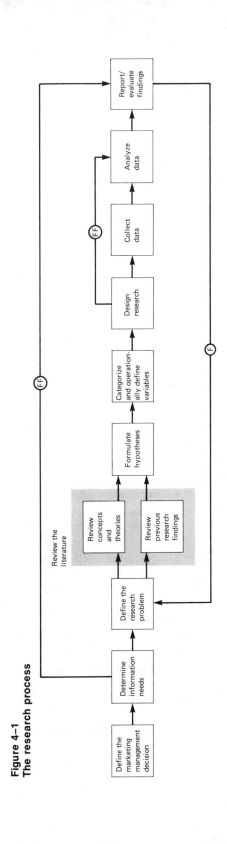

the information need into a research problem or problems. There are two types of research problems: (1) those questions which relate to states of nature and, (2) those questions which relate to relationships between variables. Management problems exist when there is a discrepancy between a desired and the actual state of affairs. Therefore, the discrepancy which arises must lead to questions which can be formulated in terms of a states of nature or relationships between variables.

For example, the information needs may concern the important product features of airline service for business travelers. These needs may lead to a research problem stated in the following form:

What service features are most highly valued by business travelers?

This particular question emphasizes measurement to estimate states of nature. That is, for a given definition of service features, business travelers may be asked to provide rankings. This would indicate those features which are particularly important. On the other hand, the problem does not lead to an investigation of the relationship between service features and consumer behavior. A problem statement relating to such an interaction might be worded as follows:

What is the relationship between business traveler's perceptions of service features by various airlines and the airline selected by these travelers?

Finally, it should be noted that these two problem statements are not mutually exclusive. That is, they may both be part of the same decision related research task.

Note the difference between the management decision problem, information needs, and the research problems. Originally, management perceived a potential problem through the existence of certain symptoms. In the airline case, this may have been the result of unsatisfactory profit performance which led management to consider the possibility of changing its approach to the market place. The creative process of problem definition led management to investigate, as underlying causes, their treatment of business and pleasure travel segments. This management problem subsequently led to the identification of information needs including important product features for business travelers. The research problem became one of defining features which are of importance to people in business and of determining which of those features relate to the purchase of air travel. Once research problems are specified, they must be further refined into specific hypotheses.

If research is to remain relevant to a management problem, it must be (1) properly structured, (2) elaborated through well-conceived hypotheses, and (3) completed with meaningful definitions of the variables which appear in the hypotheses. These activities are all within the creative realm of the research process. The process tends to become increasingly "mechanistic" as the problem is reduced to one of technique application.

Review the literature

After the research problem or problems have been clearly stated, any secondary information available on the topic should be reviewed. This review should include two basic areas. First, theories and concepts related to the research problem should be explored to discover any generalizations which apply to the decision under consideration. Second, relevant research findings from previous studies should be examined. This type of review serves several useful functions: (1) in many cases the research question can be answered based on past work, thus eliminating the need for additional research, (2) past efforts may provide hypotheses for testing in the current study, (3) techniques and procedures may be discovered which prove useful in designing the current research, and finally (4) sources of usable secondary data may be uncovered which lessen the need to collect generally more expensive primary data. Thus, a literature review early in the research effort can save considerable time, money, and effort.

Assume that the researcher in the airline example mentioned earlier decided to search the literature for insight into the problem. He may find a number of studies which have some bearing on the problem; however, none may provide suitable answers. The researcher discovered that most studies concerned the demand for air travel, but none specifically addressed the question of market share. Two variables affecting the demand for air travel in past studies were found to be on-time performance and time-of-departure. With this additional information, the research must proceed to specify hypotheses which may involve these variables.

Formulating research hypotheses

The manner in which research hypotheses are formulated is particularly important since they provide the focal point for research. They also affect the manner in which tests must be conducted in the analysis of data and indirectly the quality of data which is required for the analysis. This section will deal both with a definition of hypotheses and a delineation of the types of hypotheses which can be formulated with their impact on later steps in the research process. A useful definition of a research hypothesis is:

A research hypothesis is a statement which specifies a state of nature or a relationship between variables which is (1) related to a research problem; (2) can be expressed in symbolic notation; (3) is testable; and (4) remains relevant to the management decision problem.

The following three statements are examples of research hypotheses which relate to the research problems suggested in the preceding section:

1. On-time performance is an important product feature for business travelers.
2. Time-of-departure is an important product feature for business travelers.
3. Market share is related to on-time performance and time-of-departure.

Each of the three statements meets at least two of the criteria set forth in the definition of research hypotheses. They are statements concerning states of nature or relationships between variables related to a research problem and relevant to a management decision problem. They are not research hypotheses, however, if they cannot be reduced to symbolic notation and tested.

Each of the statements would require some further refinement to provide the researcher with a clearly testable proposition. For example, the first hypothesis asserts that on-time performance is an important part of an airline's product. Assume that 50 percent of all business people interviewed responded positively to such a question. Is 50 percent significant? That is, what proportion would indicate that on-time performance, in fact, is an important feature? Furthermore, it is not clear just how the hypotheses could be represented in symbolic notation. Consider, therefore, the following revisions:

1. On the average, business travelers will rate on-time performance as an important product feature.
2. On the average, business travelers will rate time-of-departure as an important product feature.
3. An airline's market share of business travelers is a function of relative on-time performance and departure time relative to ideal departure time.

Notice how each of these new statements further elaborates on the nature of the key variables. The researcher now understands that product features are to be rated by businessmen in a manner which would produce a test of importance. Furthermore, market share has been defined in terms of business travelers and related to relative measures of on-time performance and departure time. The three hypotheses can now be stated in symbolic notation as follows:

$H_1: O > S$ O = a rating of on-time performance as a product feature

S = a minimum rating for important features

$H_2: T > S$ T = a rating of time-of-departure as a product feature

S = a minimum rating for important features

$H_3: M = f(O, D)$ M = share of market in business travel markets

O = relative on-time performance

D = departure time relative to ideal departure time

Once hypotheses have been stated correctly and reduced to symbolic notation, decisions can be made concerning operational definitions for the variables which appear in the hypotheses. Before discussing operational definitions, however, further elaboration of symbolic notation is needed.

By symbolic notation we mean the use of letters, numbers, and other symbols to represent variables and the relationships between variables. In the example just presented, the symbol O was used to represent the on-time performance variable. Similarly, the symbols S, T, D, and M were used to represent other variables. Symbolic notation is particularly useful in that it presents a concise form of a statement and clearly illustrates the nature of the hypothesis. The nature of a hypothesis affects the manner in which analysis is conducted at later stages of the research process.

In stating research hypotheses, we are concerned with three types. (Examples of each type are illustrated in Table 4–1.) The first type of

Table 4–1
Types of hypotheses

Type	Illustration
1. Differences	$H_o: x \neq y$ $H_o: x = y$ $H_o: x \neq k$ $H_o: x = k$ where x and y are variables and k is a constant
2. Magnitudes	$H_o: x \leq y \leq z$ $H_o: x < k < y$ $H_o: x > k$ $H_o: x > y > z$ $H_o: x < y$ $H_o: x < k$
3. Relationships	$H_o: x = f(y)$ $H_o: x = kf(y)$ $H_o: x = f(y, z)$ where x, y, and z are variables and k is a constant

hypothesis concerns differences between two variables, one of which may be a constant value, in the range of interest. With this type of hypothesis there are two possibilities. That is, the variables may be equal or not equal. Hypotheses of differences relate to states of nature.

A hypothesis of differences in the context of the airline example might be: the importance ratings of on-time performance and time-of-departure as product features in business travel markets are equal. In symbolic notation the hypothesis would be: $O = T$.

The second type of hypothesis is concerned with magnitudes. There are numerous possibilities involving inequalities and/or equalities between two or more variables. The first two hypotheses in the airline example were of this type. In each case, one variable (on-time performance or time-of-departure) was hypothesized to be greater than another variable (a minimum rating for importance). As is the case with hypotheses of differences, hypotheses of magnitudes relate to states of nature. Furthermore, hypotheses of magnitudes have an important relationship with statistical tests and analysis. That is, hypotheses of magnitude involving two variables lead to "one-tailed tests" and hypotheses involving three variables lead to "two-tailed tests." If an information need is satisfied by simply establishing that one variable is greater than (or less than) another variable, a one-tailed test will be adequate. On the other hand, it may be necessary to establish that a variable exists within a range between two other variables. In this case, the two-tailed test is required. If research hypotheses are not properly stated at this point in the research process, improper tests might be applied later and the research may fail to satisfy information needs.

The third type of hypothesis concerns the relationship between variables. The symbolic notation used here is known as "functional notation." The symbol f is used in the equation to indicate that there is a relationship by which the variables in parentheses on the right hand side determine the value of the variable on the left hand side of the equal sign. The first illustration in Table 4–1 of a hypothesized relationship would be read as follows: "X is a function of Y." In the airline example the third hypothesis is of this type. Market share is hypothesized to be some function of on-time performance and time-of-departure. Before this hypothesis can be tested by a specific technique, further elaboration of the nature of the functional relationship must be provided. This aspect of the process will be discussed further in the following section.

Categorize and operationally define the variables

Research hypotheses deal with various types of variables. Before designing research to test these hypotheses, the variables need to be categorized and operationally defined. Relative to categorization, there are many different types of variables. Four basic types are independent variables, dependent variables, control variables, and intervening variables.

Independent variables may either be primary or secondary in nature. A primary independent variable is a factor which is measured by the researcher to determine its relationship to some selected phenomenon. The selected phenomenon is the dependent variable. For example, the researcher may measure time-of-departure to determine its relationship to airline market share. Time-of-departure would be the primary independent variable, and airline market share would be the dependent variable.

Another type of independent variable is of a secondary nature. These secondary independent variables are factors which are measured by the researcher to determine whether they modify the relationship between the primary independent variable and the dependent variable. For example, on-time performance might affect the purchase of air travel regardless of time-of-departure. Thus, on-time performance could modify the relationship between time-of-departure and market share. If this is thought to be the case, then on-time performance should be measured to determine whether it modifies the relationship and if it does, how this modification changes the basic relationship under study.

An additional possibility is to control on-time performance so as to cancel out its effect on market share. In this case on-time performance would become a control variable. Control variables are those factors which are controlled by the researcher to neutralize any effect they might otherwise have on the dependent variable.

Finally, there are intervening variables. These are factors that may affect the dependent variable but cannot be directly measured. Their presence must be inferred from the effects of the independent variables on the dependent variable. Learning is such a variable in many research settings. A researcher may investigate the relationship between time-of-departure as an independent variable and market share as a dependent variable. Share may rise as scheduling improves. The researcher knows that learning on the part of the consumers must have taken place, but he may not be able to measure the learning directly. It must be implied from the relationship between the independent and dependent variables.

The relationship between the various types of variables is summarized in Figure 4–2.

Primary independent, secondary independent, and control variables can hopefully be constructed so as to be causal forces and the dependent variables thus become effects. The control variables are potential causes which are cut off from affecting the dependent variables. Intervening variables are inferred relationships which exist between the independent and dependent variables.

The criteria stated earlier for hypotheses included testability. A research hypothesis is of little use if we cannot conduct some test to

Figure 4–2
The relationship between variables

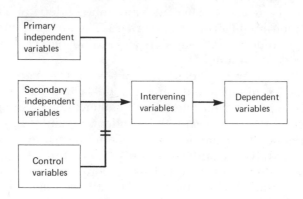

Causes ──────────▶ Relationships ──────▶ Effects

accept or reject a position. As yet, however, we have only required that a test be feasible. After the variables have been decided upon and categorized it is necessary to operationally define each of them so as to make a hypothesis test possible. An operational definition of a variable must accomplish two things: (1) it must specify what is to be measured; and (2) it must produce measures which are consistent with the management problem. Consider, for example, the variable "O" in the third hypothesis of the airline example [$M = f(O, D)$]. The symbol O has been defined as "relative on-time performance." While this definition may be relevant to the management problem, it is not specific enough for the measurement task. A more correct operational definition of this variable might be stated as follows:

Relative on-time performance is the ratio of the proportion of on-time (CAB definition) flights operated by the subject carrier to the proportion of on-time flights operated by competitors.

If O_s is the percentage of the subject carrier's flights which operated on-time and O_c is the percentage of competitors' flights which operate on-time, O in the third hypothesis could be expressed as the ratio O_s/O_c. If the subject airline and its competitors operate the same proportion of flights on-time, O would equal 1. The value of O would range between zero and 1 if competitors are on-time more often and between 1 and infinity if the subject carrier has the advantage.

Note that O is an independent variable in the original hypothesis, but may become a dependent variable at another stage of research. According to the definition of O, two proportions must be calculated and expressed as a ratio to give O a value. In symbolic notation:

$$O = f(O_s, O_c),$$

or
$$O = \frac{O_s}{O_c}$$

where O is relative on-time performance when O_s and O_c are the percentage of on-time flights operated respectively by the subject and competitor carriers.

With this definition, O is clear to the researcher and the measurement task is clear. Furthermore, since O is involved in a functional relationship, the researcher can speculate about the nature of the relationship between O and M. That is, M should increase as O increases, a positive correlation. Regardless of the manner in which O is calculated, it is an independent variable in the hypothesis.

Design research

After the information needs of the marketing decision-making system have been identified, a decision has been made to do research, and the information needs have been translated into a research task; research can then be designed to develop the information and the information management system structured so as to carry out the research process. A brochure published by the American Marketing Association makes the following observation regarding research design.

"A research 'design' might be described as a series of advance decisions that, taken together, comprise a master plan or model for the conduct of the investigation." These decisions can be made only after the problem is defined and the objectives of the research are specified, and should generally precede embarking on the project. Appropriate design requires careful consideration of the problem and objectives to be met in relation to the time and resources available for the study.

The design, or plan, of a research investigation is best put in writing. It will ordinarily cover the following aspects:

1. Objective(s) of the investigation, including, perhaps, first a statement of general aim and then one of operational objectives in as specific a form as possible.
2. The relation of these objectives to the problem at hand.
3. The form in which results will be obtained and how they may be used.
4. The methods to be used in attaining each of the objectives of the investigation with perhaps an appendix or two on the more technical aspects.
5. A time schedule for the entire operation, including tentative deadlines for specific phases of the work.
6. Personnel and administrative setup, with duties specified for each person working on the project.
7. A budget with breakdowns by type of expenditure; if the project is to

require several years, estimates may also be desirable of year-to-year expenditures.
8.   Form and scope of final report.[1]

A design has also been defined as a "specified framework for controlling the collection of data in a . . . (scientific way),"[2] and "the specification of methods and procedures for acquiring the information needed to structure or to solve problems."[3]

Generally, then, a research design can be considered a blueprint to guide the data collection, data processing, and information transmission. It is developed before the process is put into action. The design should anticipate what needs to be done and specify exactly how and when it is to be accomplished. In addition to acting as a master plan to guide the effort, the research design allows for refinement in the calculation of the feasibility and cost of the research. It can help in refining the answers to the question posed in Bayesian preposterior analysis—is additional information worth collecting? The basic function is thus to "insure that the required data are collected accurately and economically."[4]

Prior to designing the research, the information needs, research problems, hypotheses, and variables should have been clearly established. These are prerequisite steps in the research process prior to research design. The technical questions that should be answered in a research design itself include the following:

1.   What data are required to develop the needed information?
2.   What secondary data are available either from internal or external sources? Secondary and commercial data will be discussed in the following chapter.
3.   Do gaps exist between the data requirements and available secondary data? If so, the gaps must be filled with primary data.
4.   If secondary data will fill all data requirements, then how will the data be analyzed? That is, what logical structures will be used to transform the raw data into the desired information? This may be accomplished by the use of statistical methods, models, or a combination of the two as discussed in Chapter 9.
5.   *a.*   If data gaps do exist which need to be filled by primary data, then what type of research will be performed? Various alterna-

---

[1] Robert Feber, Sidney Cohen, and David Luck, *The Design of Research Investigation* (Chicago, Ill.: American Marketing Association, 1958), p. 5.

[2] Harper W. Boyd, Ralph Westfall, and Stanley F. Stasch, *Marketing Research*, 4th ed. (Homewood, Ill.: Richard D. Irwin, Inc., 1977), p. 41.

[3] Paul E. Green and Donald S. Tull, *Research for Marketing Decisions*, 3d ed. (Englewood Cliffs, N.J.: Prentice-Hall, Inc., 1975), p. 68.

[4] Boyd, Westfall, and Stasch, *Marketing Research*. p. 41.

tive approaches and purposes exist in research; these will be reviewed in this chapter and developed more fully in Chapters 7 and 8.

b. How will the variables in the research be measured? Will observation, questioning, or mechanical means be used to do the measuring? What types of measures are needed? What scales are to be generated? If attitudes are to be measured, what techniques will be used? If a questionnaire is to be used, what form will it take (structured or unstructured), what specific questions will be asked, and how will the respondents be contacted (telephone, mail or in person)? See Chapter 6.

c. What population has the data required in the research? Should the data be secured from the total population or from a smaller sample? If a sample is to be taken, what sampling frame will be used, how large should the sample be, and what sampling technique should be used? See Chapter 6.

d. Again, as with secondary data, what methods will be used to analyze the data after they have been collected?

6. How will the information be presented after it has been developed? The reporting of research results is discussed in Chapter 10.

7. What will be the cost of carrying out the research and how long will it take from collection of the data until delivery of the information to the manager?

The important technical considerations in research design are illustrated in Figure 4–3. The research design is based on the results of the steps in the research process which have been completed previously. As just noted, in designing the research, the researcher should first determine the total data needs and the secondary data which are available. By comparing these, any gaps which exist can be located. These

Figure 4–3
Expanded model of research design subsystem

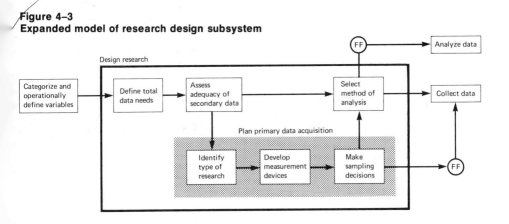

gaps must be filled by collecting primary data. If no gaps exist, methods for analyzing the secondary data can be selected. If gaps do exist, four basic areas need design decisions: (1) the type of research appropriate to the problem must be decided; (2) after the type of research is determined, measurement devices must be developed; (3) another design decision area is sampling; and finally, (4) methods to transform the data into useful information must be selected. A complete consideration of all these areas prior to implementing research activities of either an ongoing or one-time nature can save considerable effort and result in improved information for decision making at a reduced cost. A fuller discussion of measurement, sampling, and methods of analysis will follow in subsequent chapters. After all the decisions needed to form a blueprint for carrying out the research have been made, the cost and benefit of the information should again be assessed. Cost estimates can be refined based on the details of the research design, thus giving a more accurate answer to the question— Is the additional information worth collecting? If the answer is still yes; then the information is worth the cost and the research process should continue.

At this point, a discussion of the various types of research may be helpful. Research and research designs can be classified or typed in many different ways. Two basic methods are classifications by purpose and classification by approach.

Research purposes.　Research may be undertaken for three basic reasons: to develop hypotheses, to test hypotheses about states of nature, or to test hypotheses about relationships between variables. Research aimed at developing hypotheses can be called *exploratory research.* Exploratory research may be needed when there is a lack of relevant marketing theory, a lack of ongoing research programs to provide specific direction and/or a lack of knowledge about the market place and its potential reactions to marketing stimuli. Exploratory research can help in discovering problems, hypotheses, and potential explanations which can then be investigated with more conclusive work. Since the objective is not to test hypotheses but to develop new ideas, exploratory research often uses approaches with limited structure which are characterized by flexibility and ingenuity. To illustrate the concept of exploratory research, assume that the manufacturer of a car wax had been experiencing a decline in sales. The reason for this decline was not apparent to the managers of the company. Thus, research was designed to uncover possible explanations for the decline. The outputs of the research effort were hypotheses as to the causes of the sales decline; such research can be described as exploratory in nature.

Research may also be directed at testing hypotheses about states of nature or relationships between variables. Such research can be described as conclusive in nature. It is designed to solve a specific, well-defined problem; to test a stated hypothesis. If the hypothesis relates to a state of nature, then the research designed to test it can be called *descriptive research*. This is the case since in order to accomplish such a test the state of nature must be described. The description of the actual state of nature serves as a benchmark for testing the hypothesized state. A crayon manufacturer may hypothesize that the average retail price paid for a box of crayons is 25 cents. This may be an important bit of information for a pricing decision. As a basis for testing this hypothesis, research is designed to describe the current average retail price. The results would provide a basis for evaluating the 25-cent hypothesis. This would be descriptive research. Descriptive studies are generally more rigorous than exploratory research and provide a more accurate and complete description of a situation. They do not, however, establish cause-effect relationships. This is not their purpose. They simply provide descriptions and thus benchmarks for testing the state of nature hypotheses.

Conclusive research may also be directed at testing hypotheses about the relationship between variables. Such research can be classified as *causal research*. The relationship between consumer income and the consumption of beer may be in question. Whether such a relationship exists and the form of the relationship if it does exist, may be important informational inputs for a market analysis decision. If research is designed to test the hypothesis that a relationship exists between income and beer consumption, it can be described as causal research.

Research approaches.   Research may also be classified by approach. Two basic approaches are quantitative and qualitative. Each approach has unique attributes and applications in marketing research which will be discussed in Chapters 7 and 8. The quantitative approach can be further subdivided into inferential (primarily survey), experimental, and simulation.

The quantitative approach involves the generation of data in quantitative form which can be subjected to rigorous quantitative analysis. Inferential designs are constructed so as to form a data base from which to infer characteristics or relationships to a population. This usually means survey research where a sample of a population is questioned or observed to determine its characteristics, and it is then inferred that the population has the same characteristics or relationships. Survey research might be used to describe the age, sex, and income of the users of a specific brand of toothpaste. This would likely involve taking a sample of the population, measuring the variables for each person in the sample, and using a statistical method for a summary description. The state of nature found in the sample is then inferred for the population with some defined level of accuracy.

Experimental   Experimental research is characterized by much greater control over the research environment by the researcher than is present in inferential research. Variables are manipulated to observe their effect on other variables. This approach allows the researcher to establish cause-effect relationships which can only be inferred in survey approaches. For example, the relationship between alternative advertising materials and consumer retention may be established in a controlled experiment. Various experimental designs will be presented and discussed in Chapter 8.

Simulation   The simulation approach involves the construction of an artificial environment within which data is then collected. Survey research is often used to build the environment, and then the research proceeds in an experimental mode. Simulation allows the manipulation of variables and the observation of results that would be too disruptive to allow in the real environment. Research can thus be conducted without the potential adverse effects that result from actual field experiments. The variables are then manipulated in reality, only after their impact is better understood. Simulation can also be useful in building models of future conditions which cannot yet be dealt with directly. A fuller discussion and an illustration of simulation research is also provided in Chapter 8.

Qualitative Research   It is not difficult on an intuitive basis to understand the meaning of qualitative research (as contrasted to quantitative research) as being those types of research which generate results either in nonquantitative form or which are not subjected to rigorous quantitiative analysis. The techniques used most frequently in qualitative research are focus group interviews, projective techniques, and depth interviews. These techniques and their application are discussed extensively in Chapter 7. The quantitative approach is more widely accepted among marketing researchers than the qualitative approach. Quantitative research can generally be designed to attempt to accomplish any of the basic purposes which may be under consideration. The use of the qualitative approach must be more selective. No absolute guidelines can be given as to when, or in what situations, to use qualitative research; however, a number of usages appear to be reasonable.

1. Hypothesis formulation—to develop hypothesis for later quantitative testing is a valid use of this approach.
2. Questionnaire design—to define variables or attributes which should be examined, to specify ranges for checklists, and to indicate form or wording for specific questions.

3. Complex topic—where demonstration or interviewer explanations are needed for the respondent to understand a new or complicated product or service.
4. Embarrassing topics—where the topic may present mental barriers which the interviewer can overcome.
5. General understanding—where the researcher is seeking a general "feel" for consumer attitudes or concerns for ideas to test as advertising copy, promotional themes, or product features.
6. Postsurvey elaboration—to attempt to discover some of the reasons behind the findings of the study.

In reviewing this list, it is apparent that qualitative research is not appropriate in all situations. In fact, its use should be restricted to situations where broad generalization is not required. The best use of the qualitative approach is in conjunction with quantitative research. When designing a given project, the researcher should feel free to select from each area those techniques and procedures which best meet his needs. By doing this, an optimum research design can be constructed.

Paul Diesing has stated persuasively that the gap between quantitative and qualitative research can be bridged by techniques such as content analysis and computer modeling. The ability to better measure and to quantify findings that can now only be presented as imprecise qualitative results will be major progress. However, Diesing acknowledges that this progress may be slow in coming.[5]

Collect data

Data may be collected from either secondary or primary sources as called for by the research design. The measurement devices and sampling procedures to be used in collecting primary data should also have been specified in the design. Data collection is the heart of the research process and gives it an empirical characteristic. The data collection may be either a continual or one-time operation depending upon the type of decision for which the information is to be used (see Chapters 5 and 6).

Analyze data

After the data have been collected, they must be transformed into usable information. This data manipulation is called analysis. Analysis

---

[5] Paul Diesing, "Objectivism versus Subjectivism in the Social Sciences," *Philosophy of Science*, vol. 33 (March–June 1966), p. 129.

allows for the testing of the research hypotheses and for the transformation of raw data into information of use to management. Any number of logical frameworks may be used to achieve this transformation. The appropriate method depends on the type of data which have been generated and the use to be made of the information (see Chapter 9).

Report/evaluate findings

Finally, the results of the research must be transmitted to the decision maker. This requires the development of some type of final report. The report should do two basic things. First, it should present the findings and show how they relate to the original problem under consideration. Second, the methods used to generate the findings should be outlined in a fashion consistent with the manager's expertise. This will allow the manager to evaluate the research results and assess their value in a particular decision environment (see Chapter 10).

AN ILLUSTRATION OF THE RESEARCH PROCESS

An illustration of a research effort showing the steps in the research process may be helpful in clarifying the various concepts involved.

1. *The marketing decision.* A local bakery was considering a package change for its coffee cakes. (Note: Certain modifications have been made to protect the confidentiality of the firm, but the process presented here represents an actual research effort.) The old package was made of aluminum foil and a new paper container was being considered. Cost reduction was the major reason for considering the change. The alternatives under consideration were to keep the old package or change to the new, lower cost, paper design.

2. *Information needs.* Information on several different topics might prove helpful in making the decision. Principally, how much cost reduction is involved, and what impact would the change have on sales revenue. If the cost reduction is larger than the negative influence on sales, then the new package would be adopted assuming no other adverse considerations exist. To judge the impact on sales, information on consumer reaction to the new package would be helpful. Information on the cost savings was already available, thus the value of the information on sales impact would relate to the extent of cost reductions. After considering potential costs and benefits a decision was made to design a research project.

3. *Research problem.* The research problems developed from these information needs were: *(a)* What is consumer reaction to the new package? and *(b)* Is consumer reaction related to usage rate of the product? The impact of an adverse reaction from heavy users would be more detrimental to sales than an adverse reaction from light users.

4. *Literature review.* No specific secondary data on this topic could be found. In general, it was found that package changes for established products had met with adverse reaction.

5. *Formulate hypotheses.* Based on the research problems, two hypotheses were formulated: *(a)* Consumer reaction to the package change will be negative and *(b)* Consumer reaction will not be related to usage rate.

6. *Categorize and operationally define the variables.* The dependent variable in this research situation is consumer reaction to the package change and the primary independent variable is usage rate. Several secondary independent variables might act to distort or modify the relationship between the dependent and primary independent variable. The reaction to the package change might relate to household income, social class, number of children, and several other variables without regard to usage rate. A decision was made to treat household income, occupation of the head of the household, marital status, number of children, and education of the homemaker as secondary independent variables for the purposes of the study. Reaction to the product was operationally defined in terms of the consumer's expressed intent to stop buying the product if the package is changed. Usage rate was defined as "how often do you purchase this product?" A screening question was used to insure that all respondents had used the product.

7. *Design research.* It was first determined that secondary data were not adequate to develop the needed information. Thus primary data were needed. A survey of homemakers appeared to hold the greatest potential for assessing general consumer reaction to the package change. A focus group session was planned to aid with the questionnaire design. (This technique is discussed in Chapter 7.) The population of interest in the survey was defined as all homemakers in the metropolitan area who had tried the product. A sample size of 600 was computed as necessary to give the desired level of accuracy. Since the packages (old and new) would need to be shown as a part of the interview, personal interviews were essential. In order to conduct the survey in an efficient manner with personal interviews, an area sampling technique was selected. (This procedure is discussed in Chapter

6.) The metropolitan area was broken into blocks, and a sample of blocks randomly selected. Interviews were planned with all homemakers living in each block. Interviewer instructions and call-back procedures were also carefully prepared. In designing the measurement device (questionnaire) a focus group session was first conducted. This session provided insights into the terminology used by homemakers in discussing the product. It also indicated that the two major concerns the homemakers had with the new package were that the coffee cakes could not be heated in the package and that the paper might cause the cakes to dry out over time by absorbing the moisture. Based on the original research problem, operational definitions, and focus group results, a questionnaire was designed. Some of the questions were:

a.   Screening question—Have you ever tried this product? (the product was shown to the homemaker) Yes_____ No_____ If the response was No, the interview was not conducted since this homemaker was not in the defined population.

b.   On the average, how often do you buy _____ coffee cakes?

Once a week	_____
Once every two weeks	_____
Once a month	_____
Once every two months	_____
Less than once every two months	_____

c.   If the product came in this package (new package was shown), would you continue to buy it? Yes_____ No_____

d.   If no, why? _____

e.   Do you think the paper package would cause any problems?
             Yes_____   No_____
If yes, what problems? _____

_____

f.   Marital status?   Married_____
                    Single _____

g.   Your education?

Some high school	_____
High school graduate	_____
Vocational training	_____
Some college	_____
College graduate	_____

h.   Occupation of the household head?_____

_____

    i. Approximate annual household income (before taxes):

Under $5,000	_____
$5,000–$9,999	_____
$10,000–$14,999	_____
$15,000–$19,999	_____
$20,000–$25,000	_____
Over $25,000	_____

Tabulations and cross tabulations were planned as the basic form of analysis. Chi-square was to be computed for each cross tabulation. (These procedures are discussed in Chapter 9.) At this point the cost estimates for the study were refined and again compared with the expected value of the information. A decision was made to implement the study.

8. *Collect data.* After the design was finished, the survey work was undertaken. The sample was selected and the interviewers briefed and sent into the field. Procedures were set up to check the interviewers' work by calling a small number of respondents for each interviewer. The survey yielded 487 usable interviews.

9. *Analyze data.* Tabulations and cross tabulations were then prepared and chi-square statistics computed. It was found that 43 percent of the respondents said no, they would not continue to purchase the product if the package was changed. Most of these negative responses were frequent purchasers. The major reason given was that they always heat the product before serving it and that the foil made this much more convenient. Many said that they would switch to a competitive product with the foil tray if the change was made. This pattern of responses held throughout the various demographic categories.

10. *Evaluate and report the findings.* Based on the analysis, it was concluded that the package change would have a major negative effect on consumer acceptance of the product. This could translate into a sizable loss in sales. It was recommended that the new package be test-marketed in an experimental setting to determine the extent to which adverse consumer reactions translated into actual lost sales. Due to the strong negative reaction to the package change, however, management decided to drop the idea without further testing.

THE VALUE OF THE RESEARCH PROCESS

In conducting research the researcher should strive to achieve validity so that reliable managerial decisions can be reached. Validity in its simplest form refers to the absence of bias. Validity in research is of

[handwritten margin notes: "2 types of validity - internal - external"]

two types: internal validity and external validity. Internal validity means that the outcome of the investigation is a result of things being dealt with in the research. This indicates that outside forces did not distort or materially alter the basic results of the study. External validity means that the results obtained in the investigation apply in the "real world" to similar types of situations. For example, relationships found in highly controlled experimental settings may not exist when the controls are removed. The manager must make decisions in an open environment subject to many uncontrollable forces. Thus research, to have practical value, must be externally valid and apply in the manager's real decision environment.

The researcher may attempt to insure the needed validity by following a scientific method in his work. "The scientific method encourages a rigorous, impersonal mode of procedure dictated by the demands of logic and objective procedure."[6] This implies an objective, logical, and systematic method. Objective refers to attitudes which are free from personal bias or prejudice and to methods whose purposes are to ascertain the demonstrable qualities of a phenomenon. Objectivity demands that in any speculative argument the ultimate resolution comes from observations or experiences that can be verified by trained observers. Logic is also essential to the scientific method. A logical method implies that the researcher is guided by the rules of logical reasoning. Systematic means that the investigation proceeds in an orderly manner in its organization of a problem and in its method of operation. Systematic also implies internal consistency.

The scientific method, which is necessary to insure validity in research, can be made operational by adopting an established marketing research process. The marketing research process as previously defined, is simply a set of actions or steps which are necessary to carry out research and the sequence in which the steps should be performed. There are several reasons for translating the scientific method into a set of steps for marketing research: (1) It provides a procedure and, more specifically, ensures careful selection of specific methods for obtaining and analyzing data; (2) The steps act as a reminder to check the work; and (3) The research is more readily explained when broken into steps.[7]

Good research follows some defined pattern as set down in a research process. The exact steps and sequence may vary from researcher to researcher, but good research tends to follow a similar

---

[6] Carlos L. Lastrucci, *The Scientific Approach: Basic Principles of the Scientific Method* (Cambridge, Mass.: Schenkman Publishing Company, Inc., 1967), p. 7.

[7] See Lyndon O. Brown and Leland L. Beils, *Marketing Research and Analysis,* 4th ed. (New York: The Ronald Press Company, 1969).

format (such as the one described in the previous section) and thus to have certain common characteristics, including those described below.

Systematic

Good research is systematic. This means that it is structured with specified steps to be taken in a specified sequence. It has a set of rules for carrying out the process. These rules include procedures and techniques for defining problems, stating testable hypotheses, labeling and operationally defining the relevant variables, designing a study to collect data which can be used to test the hypotheses, testing hypotheses, and presenting the final results. The systematic nature of the process does not rule out creative thinking but it does reject the use of guessing and intuition in arriving at conclusions.

Logical

Good research is also logical. The rules of logic are used to develop internal consistency and in generalizing to the decision-making environment. Both the logical processes of induction and deduction can be of value in structuring and carrying out research. *Induction* is the process of reasoning from a part to the whole or from individual cases to a universe. *Deduction* is the mental process of reasoning from some premise or relevant theories and concepts to a conclusion which follows necessarily from the premise. The logic of good research makes it much more valuable for effective decision making than casual observation or intuition on the part of the decision maker.

Empirical

Good research is empirical in nature. This means that research is related to some specific aspect or aspects of a real situation. The collection and manipulation of data in such a way as to derive useful information identifies the research process. Dealing with concrete data gives research a basis for external validity. The extent to which external validity is achieved depends upon the degree of similarity between the sample environment being investigated and the usually larger, more complex decision environment. The empirical nature of research differentiates it from other equally logical aspects of decision making.

Replicable

Finally, good research is replicable. This is a product of having carefully followed design procedures in carrying out the investigations and, of having recorded these procedures. This allows research results to be verified by replicating the study and thereby building a sound basis for decisions. Careful recording also allows research results to be used in other similar decision situations. Information generated by research is generally one of the least transitory elements in the decision-making process.[8]

SUMMARY

In summary, the research process is a set of steps which are necessary for carrying out research and the desired sequence for these steps. This process starts with a marketing management decision which must be made and goes through the activities in generating information to aid in making the decision. The findings from the research process should help to answer the question or questions posed in the research problem. Answering these questions provides at least a part of the information needed to solve the managerial problem which gave rise to the research.

This chapter has outlined a structure for research which can include many different techniques and procedures. Sound structure is the essence of good research. The specific techniques can vary greatly in type and level of sophistication without affecting general validity; but the logic and systematic nature of the scientific method provided by following a sound research process are vital to effective research.

When a decision is made to design and conduct research, a plan of action must be formulated. This plan, or blueprint, is called a research design. The research design should provide the details of what is to be done in the research and how it is to be accomplished. It should incorporate advance decisions on such topics as the type of research to conduct, the measurement devices to be used, the sampling procedures to be followed, and the methods to be used in analyzing the data. The design should not be allowed to become a straitjacket, however. As the research progresses, unforeseen circumstances may arise which require modifications. Flexibility must be maintained, but a carefully thought-out research design still provides major benefits by providing organization, goals, and direction to the research effort.

Subsequent chapters in this section will provide additional elaboration on various aspects of the research process. Particular emphasis is on the design, implementation, and reporting of research efforts. Part Three will then concentrate on applying and managing marketing research.

---

[8] See Bruce W. Tuckman, *Conducting Educational Research* (New York: Harcourt Brace Jovanovich, Inc., 1972), pp. 10–12.

DISCUSSION QUESTIONS

1. Discuss the steps in the research process. What is the advantage of following such a process in doing research?
2. Define the following terms and give an example of each.
   a. Hypothesis.
   b. Research problem.
   c. Operational definition.
   d. Dependent variable.
   e. Independent variable.
3. Distinguish between a managerial problem and a research problem.
4. Discuss the first six steps in the research process for each of the following managerial decisions:
   a. A local sporting goods retailer is trying to decide between three different potential store locations. Only one can be selected.
   b. A national manufacturer of packaged foods is considering whether or not to introduce a new dinner "Noodles with Mushrooms." It has beef flavored vegetable protein chunks as a meat substitute.
   c. A soft drink manufacturer is trying to select the best advertising media for the teenage market.
5. Suppose that you are the manager of a large cabinet company considering the introduction of a new line of plastic kitchen cabinets for mobile homes. Your marketing research director suggests a market survey to determine the extent of demand and the style preferences. What questions should you ask as a basis for determining whether the research is needed or not?
6. List and discuss the advance decisions that should be included in a research design. What is the purpose of such a design?
7. Suppose that Procter & Gamble is developing a revised marketing strategy for Pringles potato chips. The intent is to gain additional market penetration. It has been determined that a profile of the characteristics of consumers preferring each available brand is among the information needed. Discuss the design of research to secure this information.
8. Discuss the different types of research and the advantages and disadvantages of each.

SELECTED REFERENCES

Boyd, Harper W., Jr., Westfall, Ralph and Stasch, Stanley F. *Marketing Research: Text and Cases*. 4th ed. Homewood, Ill.: Richard D. Irwin, Inc., 1977.

Diesing, Paul. "Objectivism versus Subjectivism in the Social Sciences," *Philosophy of Science* vol. 33 (March–June 1966), pp. 124–33.

Kerlinger, F. N. *Foundations of Behavioral Research*. New York: Holt, Rinehart & Winston, 1965.

Lastrucci, Carlos L. *The Scientific Approach: Basic Principles of the Scientific Method.* Cambridge, Mass.: Schenkman Publishing Company, Inc., 1967.

Luck, David J.; Wales, Hugh G.; and Taylor, Donald A. *Marketing Research,* 4th ed. Englewood Cliffs, N.J.: Prentice-Hall, Inc., 1974.

Tuckman, Bruce W. *Conducting Educational Research.* New York: Harcourt Brace Jovanovich, Inc., 1972.

chapter
5

Secondary and commercial data

The mainstays of most marketing information programs are secondary data and commercial data. This is true because these types of data are often less expensive than internally produced primary data.

Secondary data are data that have been produced by someone else for purposes other than making the specific decisions called for in our marketing organization. In contrast, primary data are produced for our specific needs. Secondary data may be either internal or external. Internal secondary data are data produced within our firm for purposes other than marketing decision making. The accounting activities within the firm are usually the major source of this type of data. External secondary data are produced outside of the firm. They are collected and initially processed by outside organizations either for their own or for public use. Data collected and categorized by the U.S. government for public use would be external secondary data for a business enterprise.

Commercial data and/or information are those which can be purchased from outside suppliers. Note that commercial data can be either primary or secondary. Many firms produce and sell information as their business. It may be advantageous to use these organizations when our own firm lacks the necessary expertise or when, by spreading certain technical cost over a large number of clients, they can provide information at less expense than would be required for primary data. Commercial information may be either syndicated or custom-made. Syndicated information is produced to meet the needs of a large number of similar users. Copies of general reports are available for purchase. Custom-made information is tailored to the needs of one specific firm. The extent to which the outside firm processes (analyzes) the data to transform them into the needed information is a subject for negotiation. The information is, of course, produced for the confidential use of one firm. Many research firms offer both types of services.

The alternative data sources are shown in Figure 5–1. This chapter will concentrate on secondary and commercial data with specific emphasis on sources, illustrations, and evaluation of these types of data.

Figure 5–1
Alternative data sources

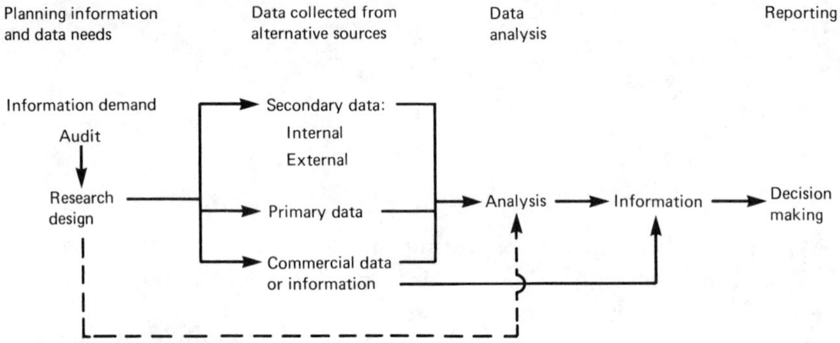

Both secondary and commercial data may be used for either ongoing decisions or for special one-time problems. Securing and managing this type of data are often very routine operations; nevertheless, they are vital and fundamentally important. The successful marketing information/decision-making system must be able to take advantage of these types of data. They are the basis of sound information programs. Thus, the manager must be familiar with and able to evaluate this kind of data.

GENERAL DATA REQUIREMENTS

Before moving to a discussion of securing and evaluating secondary and commercial data, it may prove helpful to examine the general data requirements for most businesses. The data required to generate the needed information vary greatly from organization to organization. In general, however, the marketing information needed by most organizations require data at least on:

1. The consumers.
2. The markets.

3. The competition.
4. The continuing products or services.

Data requirements are, of course, not confined to these areas.

An infinite amount of data could be generated from each of the four areas listed. Some of the data are public and can easily be drawn from secondary sources while other data are more specifically related to the company and may need to be developed from primary sources. Data relative to each area would include, but not be confined to, the following:

The consumer

Number of current and potential consumers.

Consumer characteristics (age, income, life style, etc.).

Where the consumers live.

Where the consumers buy.

When the consumers buy.

The size of purchases.

How the consumers buy (relative importance of brand, cash or credit, etc.).

Why the consumer buys (attitudes and motives).

Who influences the consumer.

What changes in buying behavior are taking place.

The markets

The general business conditions.

Market size (dollar volume of the industry).

Market trends.

Market potential.

Geographical sales and relative profitability of different markets.

Economic factors affecting sales volume.

Seasonal and cyclical fluctuations.

Changes in consumer group importance.

The competition

Number of competitors.

Market share of each competitor.

Shifts in market share.

Characteristics of leading competitive products or services.

Differentiation of our product or service from competitors.

Policies and procedures used by the principal competitors.

The continuing products or services

Sales volume (by geographic area, type of consumer, etc.).

Market share.

Shifts in market share.

Brand repeat purchases and switching rate.

Cost.

Contribution to profit/unit.

Consumer satisfaction with the product or service.

Channel structure.

Base price and alterations.

Sales force effectiveness.

Advertising effectiveness.

Both secondary and primary sources would be needed to generate the needed data. For example, relative to the market, a statement of general business conditions might be developed from government publications, Moody's, Standard and Poor's, and/or the Survey of Buying Power. These are all secondary data sources. Changes in consumer group importance might be determined from panel data, consumer profile analysis, consumer typologies, and/or psychographic analysis. These would all involve the collection of primary data.

INTERNAL SECONDARY DATA[1]

Securing internal secondary data

Internal secondary data can come from any of the records kept by the firm. The firm's accounting records are a major source of such data particularly as related to sales (revenue) and costs. The basic accounting system of the firm is designed to produce financial information for use by financial decision makers, both inside and outside the firm. This information is aggregate and historical in nature, found in the form of corporate income statements and balance sheets. The financial participants in the firm and the management are concerned with evaluating how well the resources of the firm have been used in some recently past time period. The emphasis is on depicting the performance of the firm in terms of total revenue, total investment, and total cost. The basic accounting system of the firm is shown in Figure 5–2.

---

[1] Adapted from Wilbur S. Wayman, Jr., "A Management Information System Perspective for Developing Logistics Cost Information," John R. Grabner, ed., *Perspectives in Logistic Research* (Transportation and Logistics Research Fund: The Ohio State University, 1973), pp. 423–36.

Figure 5–2
Financial accounting system

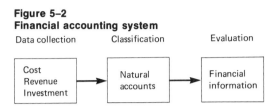

Data collection   Classification   Evaluation

A major purpose of the financial accounting system of the firm is to make a determination of income. This is achieved by calculating the revenue for the period, a relatively easy procedure, and subtracting from this revenue the costs for the period. Costs are collected and classified into *natural* accounts, such as salaries, wages, cost of goods sold, rent, and so forth. After income has been determined, the asset and liability position can be calculated and presented in the balance sheet. The financial accounting system of the firm produces financial information suited to the needs of the financial decision maker. It does not, however, produce information for the marketing manager to make decisions. The marketing manager must have the data reclassified to put them in a form which meets his or her decision-making needs.

The ideal condition for producing cost and revenue data for the marketing manager would be to have an accounting system solely for that purpose. Then as products flow from the firm to specific customers in specific geographical locations, revenue and marketing costs could be accumulated. This would permit an evaluation of the revenues and cost (including marketing cost) by products, customers, and geographical areas under the particular conditions existing in the firm at that time. Then the marketing manager would be in a position to better control the existing marketing program and plan a program for implementation in the future. Such separate accounting systems for marketing do not exist within most companies and it is unlikely that they will exist in the near future because of the cost of such an organization.

A less-than-ideal condition for producing cost and revenue data for the marketing manager is to utilize the data collected and classified to produce financial information. This requires that the data be reclassified into a form suitable for producing marketing information. This is not a procedure that the marketing manager can leave to the accountant. It is a procedure that the marketing information specialists and managers must participate in and ultimately control. The accountants in the firm typically have the only cost and revenue data available for the marketing manager to use, but it is the marketing manager who is familiar with the operations of the marketing system. The marketing manager knows what kind of information he needs to make his decisions, therefore the burden rests on him to guide the accountant in constructing from the financial classifications new classifications relevant to marketing system decision making.

The construction of marketing system cost and revenue information may proceed as a two-step process. First, the cost data from the financial cost classifications are reclassified into marketing functional accounts. Typical functional classifications for marketing might be transportation, sales, advertising, research, and so forth. The number of functions would vary from company to company depending on a number of factors such as size, operational procedures, and internal structure. All other cost and revenue would be placed in two other separate accounts. This reclassification and allocation process is shown in Figure 5–3.

Figure 5–3
Marketing accounting system

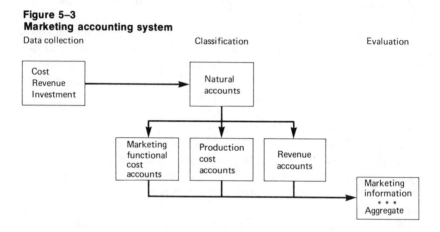

The reclassification and allocation of cost data from natural accounts to marketing functional accounts pose some of the most difficult problems in accounting. Cost data collected for one purpose must now be used for another purpose. It may be very difficult to break out marketing costs from production costs especially in those cases where costs are joint or common. There have been many texts and articles written which consider this problem, but regardless of the sophistication of the techniques used, the results are in some measure arbitrary. This is one reason why it is essential that the marketing manager be the final judge of how marketing system costs are to be constructed.

With marketing cost data organized into functional accounts and production cost and revenue available, the marketing manager can have information developed on the marketing system in aggregate terms. While helpful for judging the magnitude and major components of marketing system costs and contribution to total profitability, this aggregate information does not allow the marketing manager to evaluate differences between products, customers, or geographic areas. The second step in the process of constructing marketing system information is to further classify and allocate the total bundle of cost and revenue into significant marketing activity categories: product, customer, and geographic area. This second step is shown in Figure 5–4.

Again a major problem is cost allocation. All costs cannot be directly associated with either a product, customer, or geographic area. In certain cases the relationship is indirect and some costs occur jointly or in common. There are techniques available for allocating costs, but as mentioned, they are to some extent arbitrary. For the marketing manager to make better decisions the information produced should reflect the actual workings of the marketing system. The more arbitrary the determination of costs, the less likely it is that these figures will reflect the true conditions of marketing system performance. If the marketing manager cannot obtain the true costs of marketing system performance, then it is imperative that he understand thoroughly what kind of cost information he is getting. Then with the exercise of judgement he can make up for any known deficiencies in the cost information.

Figure 5–4
Marketing accounting detailed system

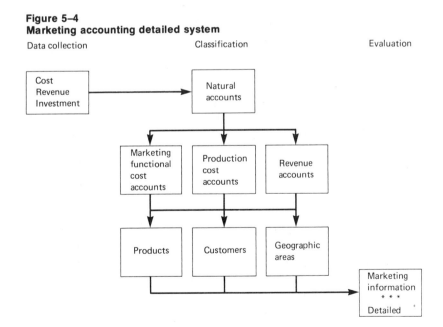

Thus far, the discussion has considered cost and revenue information needed primarily for management control decisions. This information can be produced by reclassifying and evaluating historical accounting data. Strategic and management planning decisions are made, however, with a view to the future. Yet all of the marketing system information produced thus far by the marketing accounting system has been derived from the past. Marketing information needed for planning decisions presents additional problems in construction.

Past or historical cost and revenue can be calculated with some degree of certainty, whereas future cost and revenue represent forecasts which are uncertain. This means that to produce cost and revenue information for planning decisions, we must employ tools and techniques other than those of typical responsibility accounting. The accountant is the custodian of the raw cost and revenue data available within the firm, but in the case of producing cost and revenue information for planning decisions, it is often necessary to employ the services of not only the accountant, but also the operations researcher or decision scientist.

The major problem in developing cost and revenue information for planning is to convert what is known about the past into what will occur in the future. The planner needs information on the costs and revenues associated with alternative courses of action; he or she is not as concerned with totals as with incremental differences between alternatives.

The marketing manager, accountant, and decision scientist have available to them many forecasting techniques that can be used to produce information for planning. The major concern of the marketing manager should be that the forecasts reflect as nearly as possible the true nature of future conditions. Since these conditions are uncertain someone will have to assess the probabilities associated with the forecasts. This is the responsibility of the marketing manager who is the one most knowledgeable of the marketing system and the underlying relationships involved. For this reason, the marketing manager must be familiar with the components of the costs and revenues being forecast and with the forecasting techniques. Certain basic techniques of analysis which can be used in forecasting will be discussed in later chapters.

If the decision environment is relatively stable, then forecasts based on past data will be reliable. If the decision environment is dynamic, the forecasts based on past data will be very unreliable; here is where the marketing manager must play a most significant role in producing cost and revenue information for marketing planning decisions. Where the interrelationships of the marketing system are changing, the manager must assess the value of forecasts and determine the final figures to be used in planning. No one else can assume this responsibility for the marketing manager.

Converting accounting data to marketing information

To illustrate the conversion of accounting data to marketing information a regional shoe wholesaler had the following profit and loss statement for last year.

Profit and Loss Statement

Sales		$1,800,000
Cost of goods sold		1,500,000
Gross Margin		300,000
Expenses		
Salaries	$200,000	
Rent	40,000	
Office supplies and equipment	20,000	
		260,000
Net Profit		$ 40,000

Management was concerned about increasing the company's profitability. The sales manager says that it cost more to service some types of accounts than others and that the adult shoe line is more profitable than the children's line. He says the main problem, however, is the high cost of selling to department stores, one of the firm's two types of customers. He believes that they take too much of the sales force's time and says that the company should concentrate on discount houses. There is a need to evaluate the relative profitability of the different types of customers so that decisions can be made to improve profitability. The firm now sells adult and children's shoes to both department stores and discount houses. The natural accounts in the profit and loss statement are not adequate for an effective evaluation.

The first step in converting the accounting data to marketing information is to reallocate the natural accounts to functional marketing accounts. The functional accounts might be sales, inventory control, and billing costs. The allocation would be in accordance with the functional reason for incurring the expenses. If salespeople's salaries are $130,000 in total, then this amount goes from the salaries natural account to the sales functional account. The problem, as previously noted arises when common or joint costs, such as the manager's salary, must be allocated. Thus, the allocations tend to be somewhat arbitrary. Rent could be allocated on a floor space basis, and office supplies and equipment based on the extent of their use for each activity. The natural accounts might be reallocated as follows:

Reallocating natural accounts to functional accounts

	Natural accounts	Sales	Inventory control	Billing costs
Salaries	$200,000	$150,000	$35,000	$15,000
Rent	40,000	5,000	30,000	5,000
Office supplies and equipment	20,000	5,000	5,000	10,000

The next step in developing a profit and loss statement for each customer type is to allocate the functional marketing accounts along with the sales and cost of goods sold to each customer type. Some basic data are needed for this purpose such as cost, selling price, and number of units of each type of shoe sold; number of units sold per customer type; and the number of orders per customer type. These data are shown below:

Basic data for profit analysis

Product	Cost/unit	Selling price/unit	No. of units	Sales for period
Children's	$12.50	$15.00	40,000	$ 600,000
Adult	16.66–2/3	20.00	60,000	1,200,000

Customer type	No. of sales calls	No. of orders	Sales of children's shoes	Sales of adult shoes
Department Stores	3,000	800	$400,000	$500,000
Discount Houses	1,000	400	200,000	700,000

Marketing functional cost allocation

Sales expense	4,000 calls	$160,000 cost	$40/call
Billing cost	1,200 orders	30,000 cost	$25/order
Inventory control cost	100,000 units	70,000 cost	$.70/unit

With this data base a profit and loss statement can be developed for department stores and for discount houses. These statements will aid in an evaluation of the two customer types.

Profit and loss statements for two customer types

	Department stores		Discount houses	
Sales				
Children's shoes	$400,000		$200,000	
Adult shoes	500,000		700,000	
Total sales		$900,000		$900,000

	Department stores		Discount houses	
Cost of goods sold				
Children's shoes	$333,333		$166,667	
Adult shoes	416,667		583,333	
Total cost of goods sold ...		750,000		750,000
Gross Margin		$150,000		$150,000
Expenses				
Sales	$120,000		$ 40,000	
Inventory control	35,000		35,000	
Billing......................	20,000		10,000	
		$175,000		85,000
Net Profit or Loss		($ 25,000)		$ 65,000

These profit and loss statements by customer type give additional information to the decision maker. The discount houses have a much lower marketing cost than the department stores, thus, the profits from this customer type are higher. In fact, a loss is incurred with the department stores. This may cause management to shift more sales emphasis to the discount houses. It may be, however, that the cost could not be reduced significantly in this way if they have certain fixed components. The higher sales volume generated by keeping the department stores may also help to generate economies of scale. Several considerations might lead management to retain their current level of marketing effort directed to the department stores. However, the comparative data provide very useful bits of information.

This example illustrates how accounting data can be reformulated to provide marketing information. Similar procedures can be used to produce comparisons of products and geographic areas in terms of profit, cost, investment, sales volume, and numerous other important variables.

EXTERNAL SECONDARY DATA

Securing external secondary data

External secondary data has certain unique characteristics which should be kept in mind in the searching and securing process. The data were not produced with the firm's particular needs in mind. Rather they were collected and processed by someone else according to their specifications. Thus in securing external secondary data the researcher and manager must be careful to insure that the data fit their special decision-making needs.

The major problem in collecting secondary data is in finding the appropriate source. The mass of potential sources must be filtered to locate useful data. In primary data collection the focus is on sampling and measurement, but these are of concern only in the process of evaluating secondary data. The sampling and measurement decisions have already been made by the original researcher. To be able to effectively find secondary data the researcher should maintain an index of sources which contain previously used and potentially needed data. When needs arise the index can then be consulted. If the needed data cannot be located in the index, other sources can be searched.

In conducting such a search the subject area should first be identified. Then with the subject in mind, bibliographies or indexes can be consulted. Selected bibliographies and indexes of particular use in business and marketing are presented in the next section of this chapter. After a possible source has been identified the researcher can move on to an evaluation of the data in terms of specific needs.

The well-grounded marketing manager must be familiar with the basic sources of secondary data. This knowledge will allow the manager to better direct the information activities of the firm and to evaluate the information received.

Sources of external secondary data

As noted, the biggest problem in the use of external secondary data is locating appropriate sources. The need may be for theories and concepts or for empirical marketing data. The following annotated bibliography[2] presents a series of selected sources which may prove to be useful to the marketing information planner.

Bibliographies and indexes

1. *Business Periodicals Index*
    New York: H. W. Wilson Company. Monthly annual accumulation.
       A detailed unannotated bibliography of articles in business periodicals. It presents specific subject articles from most major business publications and journals. For marketing, it includes: *Advertising Age, Marketing/Communications, Sponsor, Sales Management,* and others.
2. *Public Affairs Information Service*
    New York: Public Affairs Information Service, Inc. Weekly, with four accumulations and a yearly volume.
       A listing by subject of current books, pamphlets, periodical articles, government documents, and other useful library materials in

---

[2] Adapted from Charles F. Steilen and Roley Altizer, *A Guide to Marketing/Advertising Information* (Atlanta, Ga.: AdMar Books, 1972).

the field of economics and public affairs. Includes English language publications of all types, with emphasis on factual and statistical materials in these publications.

3. *Funk and Scott Index of Corporations and Industries*
Cleveland: Predicasts, Inc. Weekly with semiannual and annual accumulations.

Enables the marketer to locate and keep abreast of analyses, opinions, and newsworthy items appearing in a wide variety of publications and relating to specific industries and corporations. Includes articles appearing in all major business, financial, and trade magazines, key newspapers, analytical reports of investment advisory services, and bank newsletters. Information is initially arranged by specific industry under a coding system. Secondly, company information is presented alphabetically by company name.

4. *Catalog of United States Census Publications*
Washington, D.C.: U.S. Department of Commerce, Bureau of the Census, quarterly issue.

Designed to aid in locating data available from the Census Bureau. Each issue describes reports and other material becoming available during the period covered and is divided into two basic parts—one dealing with publications; the other with data files and special tabulations. Each area is broken down into appropriate categories depending upon new information made available.

5. *Monthly Catalog of U.S. Government Publications*
Washington, D.C.: U.S. Government Printing Office. Monthly with annual index issue in December.

A catalog of current publications published by the various departments and agencies of the U.S. government. Descriptions are arranged by number and are listed by subject headings and titles in an alphabetical index. Each issue contains materials which are of potential value to marketers.

6. *Marketing Information Guide*
Washington, D.C.: U.S. Department of Commerce, monthly.

An annotated bibliography of current governmental and nongovernmental materials designed to serve the domestic and foreign marketing information needs for those concerned with the sale or purchase of industrial products and services. Breaks information down into marketing functions, areas and markets, and industries and commodities. Lists also the addresses of the publishers of the articles, studies, and other materials as well as the cost. Each issue includes a subject index for that month, and the December issue includes a yearly subject index.

7. *Tables of Contents of Selected Advertising and Marketing Publications*
   Princeton, N.J.: Marketing Communications Research Center, bimonthly.
   A compilation of current tables of contents from over 25 bimonthly, monthly and quarterly marketing and advertising publications from the United States, Canada, and England.

8. *ICP Quarterly*
   Indianapolis: International Computer Programs, Inc., quarterly.
   A catalog of computer programs available for purchase. Covers software for practically any area of concern for marketing management. Includes programs for sales analysis, forecasting and management, mailing lists, computer letter writing, market research, simulations, models and games. Each listing gives specific information concerning the program in addition to the seller's address and price information.

Contemporary theories and concepts

1. *Journal of Marketing*
   Chicago: American Marketing Association, quarterly.
   Publishes general and original research articles dealing with all phases of marketing. Includes with each issue a section reporting on recent legal developments in marketing, a marketing abstract section reporting on recent articles and papers from other sources, and a book review section.

2. *Journal of Marketing Research*
   Chicago: American Marketing Association, quarterly.
   Features articles in the field of marketing research. Focus of attention is on methodology and the philosophical, conceptual, and technical problems in marketing research. Serves as a means for exchanging ideas and keeping abreast of current developments in the field.

3. *Harvard Business Review*
   Boston: Graduate School of Business Administration, bimonthly.
   A management oriented publication dealing with important aspects and events of all phases of business. Good source of trend and in-depth information on marketing operations.

4. *The Journal of Business*
   University of Chicago Press, Chicago.
   A quarterly journal dedicated to professional and academic thinking and research in all functional areas of business.

5. *Sales and Marketing Management*
   New York: Sales Management, Inc., twice monthly except April, June, and November—three issues monthly during these periods.

Feature magazine for all aspects of marketing. Covers current trends and important occurrences in marketing with implications for sales managers. "The Survey of Buying Power" is presented in one of the June issues.

6. *Industrial Marketing*
   Chicago: Crain Communications, Inc., monthly.

   Covers the field of industrial marketing with news and feature articles. Often deals with business publication advertising, both in terms of articles and statistics on volume.

7. *Advertising Age*
   Chicago: Crain Communications, Inc., weekly.

   The national newspaper of marketing. Primarily concerned with news of the field but is also a good source of other market data. Publishes advertiser expenditures on media along with other information on the top 125 advertisers, U.S. agencies, market data available from outside sources. Includes other feature articles.

8. *Fortune*
   Chicago: Time, Inc. monthly.

   A general business magazine reporting, on an in-depth basis, information relating to the field. Also includes some general feature articles, current trends in marketing, and an analysis of specific industries.

Statistical market data

1. *City and County Data Book*
   Washington, D.C.: Department of Commerce, Bureau of the

   As a supplement to the Statistical Abstract, this book presents a variety of statistical information for county, Standard Metropolitan Statistical Areas, and cities. For each county, SMSA, and city with 25,000 or more population, information is presented which relates to some 144 statistical items. These include: population, retail trade, wholesale trade, manufactures, and other vital statistics. Also includes totals for states, divisions, regions and the entire United States.

2. *United States Census*
   Washington, D.C.: Department of Commerce, Bureau of the Census.

   The reporting pattern for the latest census is as follows:
   Vol. I: Characteristics of Population
   Vol. II: States and Small Areas (Housing)
   Vol. III: Block Statistics
   Contents: Total population count by counties, states, urban-rural classifications. Details are given in terms of sex, age, marital status, etc. Housing census contains data about housing units by

number of rooms, persons per room, number of basements, plumbing facilities, contract rent, etc.

3. *Survey of Current Business*
Washington, D.C.: Department of Commerce, Office of Business Economics, monthly with weekly statistical supplement.

Each issue updates some 2,500 pieces of statistical information relating to such areas as: general business indicators, employment, population, domestic trade, commodity prices, transportation, communications, and specific raw materials industries. Also included is a review of the current business situation, feature articles, and a brief summary and analysis of significant economic developments.

4. *Business Statistics*
Washington, D.C.: Department of Commerce, Office of Business Economics, biennial (in odd years).

This is a supplementary part of the *Survey of Current Business.* It is a comprehensive compilation of a historical series of statistics for the past 30 years. Covers the same business and market indicators as the *Survey,* but puts them in a more historical perspective.

5. *Statistical Abstract of the United States*
Washington, D.C.: Department of Commerce, yearly.

The standard summary of statistics of the social, political, and economic organization of the United States. A convenient volume for statistical reference and a guide to other statistical publications and sources. Primarily national data but many tables broken down by region or state. Includes data on population, other vital statistics and information on business enterprise, income and expenditures, prices, communications, transportation, housing, manufacturing, distribution, and services.

6. *Survey of Buying Power*
New York: Sales Management, Inc.
An edition of *Sales and Marketing Management* magazine providing detailed breakdowns of consumer income, population, and retail sales. Includes national and regional summaries; metropolitan area, county, and city rankings; metropolitan area data by state; in addition, it provides potential marketing applications of the survey data.

7. *Rand McNally Commercial Atlas and Marketing Guide*
Chicago: Rand McNally Company, annually with monthly supplements on business conditions.

A single-volume world atlas with over 500 pages of maps and statistics on every part of the world. Also includes an index of over

100,000 cities and towns plus marketing tables containing over 40 statistical items for each U.S. county. Provides population figures for over 6,000 U.S. localities usually not available elsewhere.

8. *A Graphic Guide to Consumer Markets*

New York: National Industrial Conference Board, yearly.

A compact publication with basic statistical information frequently used by marketers of consumer goods and services. Material is divided into six sections: population, income, expenditures, markets, advertising, prices, and production. Gives trends, basic distributions and detailed breakdowns for each section in graphic form.

An illustration of external secondary data

To illustrate the types of secondary data which are available from external sources, suppose that a furniture retailer is trying to decide between two cities for a new store location. His two potential sites are in Gibson County, Indiana, a part of the Evansville Metropolitan Area; and Adams County, Indiana, a part of the Fort Wayne Metropolitan Area. To secure data for an initial comparison of these two sites, he might go to the *Survey of Buying Power*. From this source the following statistics might be selected for comparison:

	Gibson County	*Adams County*
Total county population	31,100	25,800
Total metro area population	290,200	373,700
No. of households in the county	11,100	8,200
Total net income (EBI), county	$ 127,808,000	$ 111,760,000
Total (EBI), metro area	$1,195,538,000	$1,838,637,000
Average EBI/household, county	$11,514	$13,629
Percent of households by cash income groups:		
$0–$2,999	16.3	8.9
$3,000–$4,999	10.1	7.2
$5,000–$7,999	13.2	11.5
$8,000–$9,999	9.7	8.2
$10,000–$14,999	22.6	28.1
$15,000–$24,999	23.0	28.7
$25,000 and over	5.1	7.4
Buying power index, county	.0127	.0109
Buying power index, metro area	.1297	.1885
Furniture sales–Home furnishings, county	$ 1,657,000	$ 2,601,000
Furniture sales–Home furnishings, metro area	$22,802,000	$42,029,000

Source: Data from the July 1975 issue of *Survey of Buying Power.*

The *Buying Power Index* is one of the most often used figures from this source. It is a weighted index that combines population, effective buying income and retail sales into a measure of the market's ability to buy and expresses it as a percentage of the U.S. potential.

Based on a review of this data, the retailer might favor Adams County since its income level is higher even though it is somewhat smaller than Gibson County. The size differential gives the edge to Gibson County in *Buying Power* but Adams County has a much higher volume of furniture sales. Several other factors such as growth patterns, site costs, extent of competition, and so forth, would need to be investigated before making a decision, but these data provide the retailer with a good starting point.

Evaluating external secondary data

Before they can be used effectively, external secondary data must be evaluated to insure that they meet the needs of the research involved. The two key areas to consider in this context are: (1) Are these the data that are required, in the format that is needed and (2) Was the research which generated the data technically sound? Both of these questions must be answered in the affirmative for the secondary data to be of use.

Given the wide range of secondary sources and the diversity of uses for this type of data, it is very difficult to generalize about the relative merits of alternative sources. Some guidelines can be provided, however, for carrying out an evaluation of specific secondary data from some known source. Certain of the technical aspects of such an evaluation may not be clear at this point, but these will be explained in later chapters of the text.

1. Do the data meet our needs?
    a. Is the subject matter consistent with our research?
    b. Is the time period consistent with our needs?
    c. Do the secondary data appear in the correct units of measurement?
    d. Do they cover the subject of interest in adequate detail?
    e. If the data are not in the desired format, how difficult will it be to make necessary alterations?
2. Is there any suspected bias in the research due to the environment in which the study was conducted?
    a. Who sponsored the research?
    b. What organization designed and implemented the research?
    c. Are they qualified?
    d. Do either the sponsor or the researcher have any vested interest in the outcome of the research?
    e. Is the time period when the data were collected significantly different in any way from the average?
    f. When were the data published?
3. Was the research design technically sound?
    a. Is the methodology and terminology adequately explained?

     b. What type of research was conducted—survey, experimental, focus groups, etc.?

     c. Was the type of research conducted consistent with the objectives of the study?

     d. Was the measurement device properly constructed?

     e. Was the population for data collection correctly defined?

     f. Are estimates of reliability and validity provided?

     g. If a sample was taken, were the sample size and sampling technique acceptable?

     h. Is the level of accuracy provided by the sample sufficient for the purpose at hand?

     i. Were correct techniques selected for analyzing the data produced in the research?

4. Was the research correctly implemented?

     a. Were questionnaires pretested?

     b. Was interviewing or other data collection properly supervised?

     c. Was the sample selection adequately controlled?

     d. Are nonsampling biases such as nonresponse present in the data?

     e. Were the raw data properly edited, sorted, summarized, and analyzed?

     f. Are the raw data available for review?

     g. Is the statistical analysis consistent with the quality of the data? For example, were parametric procedures used on nonparametric data?

5. Are the findings properly reported?

     a. Are the presentation and description of the data clear?

     b. Do charts and tables appear to be accurate?

     c. Are statistical procedures adequately explained?

     d. Does the report appear to exaggerate the findings?

By answering these questions, the researcher should be in a better position to evaluate the data for his purposes. The answers should allow him to judge how well the data fit his needs and how accurate they are.

COMMERCIAL DATA

The nature of commercial data

Commercial data or information has been defined as data or information available for purchase from sources outside the firm.[3] Commer-

---

[3] For an excellent discussion of this topic, see Chapter 7 of Bertram Schoner and Kenneth P. Uhl, *Marketing Research: Information Systems and Decision Making*, 2d ed. (New York: John Wiley & Sons, Inc., 1975).

cial research services may also be purchased, such as interviewing and statistical analysis. Such services along with data and/or processed information are needed by most firms at some point in their operations. Some firms rely almost exclusively on such commercial data and others to a very limited extent. In evaluating the need to use commercial research organizations, several factors should be considered.

First, there is the cost consideration. Can the commercial organization do the needed work at less expense to our firm than it would cost for internal primary research? This is a very difficult question to answer even in dollar cost terms. The real problem, however, comes in evaluating the relative value of the information produced. Can the outside firm produce more reliable and valid results? This will in part depend on the size and sophistication of the information system within our firm. In general, we might expect that cost/revenue analysis and other ongoing information needs might be better met internally while special project types of research for one-time decisions might need to be purchased outside. Also, it may be less expensive to purchase highly specialized services such as field interviewing from commercial organizations. Few firms are large enough to maintain the specialized personnel needed for such tasks.

Finding commercial firms is another problem after a decision has been made to seek outside assistance. A list of research and consulting firms may be developed from the Yellow Pages of the telephone directory, from the suggestions of associates, and/or from the American Marketing Association Directory. Indexes which describe the specific services offered by each firm are not possible due to the rapidly changing nature of the industry.

In selecting a research firm, an attempt should be made to assess several factors:

1. What is the firm's track record, who have they worked for in the past, and are they willing to give the names of clients from whom recommendations can be solicited? Usually there are no examples of their finished work available since most research reports are confidential; thus, reputation must be relied upon.

2. How long have they been in business? Does it look as if they are in business for the long run?

3. What types of people do they have in their organization, what are their backgrounds? You should visit their offices if possible and talk with as many people as possible, not just the salesperson.

4. Is the organization made up primarily of sales people or are they research people (who are often poor sales people)?

5. What volume of business do they have and what types of projects have they conducted?

6. Do they seem to understand your firm's problem?
7. Do they think about the problem or do they always seem to have quick answers to every question?
8. Are they willing to prepare a formal proposal stating what should be done to solve the problem and how much it will cost?
9. What is their price and how does it compare with other proposals and with the cost of making a bad decision? The firm shouldn't necessarily get the cheapest research it can, but the cheapest research that adequately meets the needs.
10. Can they give a good presentation to management at the company? Research is worthless unless it affects management decision making in some way.

Types of commercial data

Commercial data and services can be secured in infinite variety. However, a sizable percentage of such data are produced in four basic ways: panels, store audits, field censuses, and surveys.

Panels. Panels are ongoing groups organized by firms so as to collect data over a period of time. Each member of the panel is asked about his behavior, attitudes, opinions, and so forth at periodic intervals. Some panels simply report on their activities while others are asked to react to specific products, advertisements, and so forth. Panel data have the particular advantage of presenting a picture of consumer behavior over time. This time element is also the major disadvantage of the panel approach. As time passes, some members leave and others must be added. There is also aging as time passes; extraneous variation may be created by the simple passage of time.

An example of an ongoing panel is the Market Research Corporation of American Panel. They maintain a panel of 10,000 families classified by various demographic characteristics. Each family keeps a diary which is mailed in weekly. In this they record their purchase behavior. Market Research then prepares monthly reports for its clients on brand loyalty and other market considerations. This allows the client to evaluate various promotional strategies, price alterations, and so forth.

Store audits. Store audits are periodic checks of selected retail outlets to determine the sales of each product. This can be done by taking previous inventory plus purchases minus present inventory. The data is then aggregated to form sales figures for the total sample of stores. Such data can provide a very accurate estimate of sales at the retail level. This may be very helpful in making channel decisions and in evaluating product success, particularly in the early stages of the introduction of a new product.

The *Nielsen Review of Retail Drug Store Trends* is produced from store audits. It is a report on recent developments and future projections in the drug industry. It presents drug store sales trends in total and by geographic area, store type and size, and share of total U.S. retail sales. Also included are similar information on health and beauty aid sales and prescription drug volume. In addition the report includes trends in the U.S. economy and their relation to the drug business, along with highlights of recent research studies relating to the industry.

Field census.   Some companies have extensive field forces who collect data on various topics from all possible sources who will cooperate. For example, Dun and Bradstreet has a field force of over 2,000 employees across the United States. Through this organization they collect data on over 300,000 manufacturing firms. The data include among other items basic identification, type of activity, number of employees, and sales volume. A client of Dun and Bradstreet can get the data on each firm in the census by paying a certain fee. Such data may be very helpful in evaluating competitive behavior, relative market shares, and the like.

Surveys.   A final commonly used method is the independent survey. In this type of effort a new separate sample is selected as a data base for each new study. The data is collected from the sample, but the respondents are not maintained as a continuing group (such a continuing group would be a panel). This approach is used by almost all commercial organizations when certain unique data are desired or when a highly selective population is involved. The procedures used by commercial firms in doing surveys are the same as those used by an internal corporate research department. Such procedures will be discussed in the following chapters.

An illustration of commercial data

Consumer Mail Panels conducted by Market Facts, Inc.[4] provides a good illustration of commercial data and their usefulness to marketing management. The Consumer Mail Panels are national in scope with 45,000 households matched to the characteristics of the total United States. The panels are balanced with national statistics in terms of geography, income, population density, degree of urbanization, and age. The panel is rebalanced every two years based on data of the U.S. Census and the *Survey of Buying Power.*

A very detailed summary of household characteristics is maintained on the panels. This allows subgroups to be easily selected for data

---

[4] This illustration was developed from material supplied by Market Facts, Inc., Chicago, Illinois.

collection purposes. In addition to demographics, such factors as type and ownership of dwelling units, automobile ownership, vehicle ownership, and the ownership of specific items such as kitchen appliances, laundry equipment, pets and so forth, are known for each panel member. Specific data are secured from panel members by mail questionnaires.

The potential uses of the panel are many and varied. A few examples can prove enlightening.

The case of the miserly brand manager

Problem. A strong established brand in a promotion sensitive grocery category required a special promotion to offset new competitive entries. The brand manager was anxious to minimize the size of the price-off to be offered in a coupon without decreasing its effectiveness.

An unidentified coupon mailing was made to matched samples of panel reserve households. A study was made on usage of brands in the product category before and after the coupon mailing to determine conversion rates to the couponed brand. Conversion at 13 cents off was found to be substantially greater than at 7 cents off, and 18 cents was not appreciably better than 13 cents. The 13 cent coupon was selected as the optimum performer in terms of cost-value benefits.

The result. A brand share improvement was achieved at an efficient promotion and redemption cost.

The case of the fussy flyer

Problem. A major airline was interested in improving its load factor on several highly competitive major routes. Management needed to know the scheduling needs and attitudes toward airline performance—theirs and competition's—among travelers on these routes. In-flight surveys would miss competitive flyers.

Frequent flyers on these routes were identified through a mail panel screening. Alternative schedules were evaluated by mail interview, along with an examination of customer airline performance needs. The indicated changes were made and the effect on travel behavior measured with a second wave of panel questionnaires.

The result. A substantial increase in load factors for the routes studied.

The case of the rare bird

Problem. A cross-country ski manufacturer with a limited marketing research budget needed an improved marketing strategy for his fast-growing market. Management needed to learn a great deal about the attitudes and characteristics of recent buyers and current prospects for cross-country skis: What magazines do they read, where do they

plan to buy their skis, what price range are they interested in, and with
what brand names do they identify high quality and performance?

A personal interview survey would have been very costly because
less than 1 in 50 households owned cross-country skis. A low-cost
screening of 20,000 Consumer Mail Panel households was followed by
an illustrated mail questionnaire to an adequate sample of owners and
prospects. This produced marketing planning information at a reasonable cost.

The result.   Efficient media buying and distribution planning that
contributed to market share growth.

SUMMARY

Secondary and commercial data are the cornerstones of most corporate information programs. In order to do a job well, the manager must
be able to effectively evaluate and use such data.

Secondary data may be secured from either internal or external
sources. Internal secondary data can come from any corporate files or
records but accounting data are the primary source of sales, cost, and
investment data. These accounting data must often be reformulated to
generate the kind of information needed by the marketing manager.
Such a reformulation usually starts with an allocation of the accounting
"natural" accounts to "functional" marketing accounts. These functional accounts are then allocated, along with production cost and
sales, to specific types of customers, products, and/or geographic areas.
This allows comparisons of cost, profit, sales, rate of return and so forth
by customer, product, and geographic area which are typically more
helpful to the marketer than the traditional accounting records.

External secondary data can come from numerous sources outside
the firm. These are data collected for use by someone else or for the
general public. The marketer must be careful with such data to insure
that the way they were collected and analyzed meet the firm's specific
needs.

Commercial data or information is purchased from an outside
supplier. Such data may either be tailor-made for a specific firm or
collected and analyzed for a group of similar organizations. In securing
a research firm to do work for the company, a manager should attempt
to evaluate several factors such as the firm's reputation, the quality of
its staff and the details of its research proposal.

DISCUSSION QUESTIONS

1.   Discuss the procedures involved in converting accounting data to marketing information. What are the major problems encountered in such a task?

2. Assume that you are a member of the research staff for a company that makes pocket-sized calculators. Management is interested in launching an advertising campaign to stimulate sales in the college market. You are assigned to the project and asked to develop a preliminary report based on secondary data, which will help in selecting the best advertising media.

3. Develop from secondary sources, an estimate of the total demand this year for automobiles in your state. Prepare an evaluation of the secondary data that you used to develop this estimate.

4. Discuss the factors that should be considered in evaluating external secondary data.

5. Your company manufacturers women's dresses for a regional market. Management is considering a market segmentation study which will aid in more clearly defining their target market. You are asked to develop a list of research firms in your state which could potentially do the study and to evaluate the relative merits of each firm. You are also asked to recommend a firm in your report and give the basis for the recommendation.

6. What are the major advantages and disadvantages to using research firms? In what situations do the advantages generally outweigh the disadvantages?

SELECTED REFERENCES

Bennett, John B., and Weiher, Ronald L. "The Well-Read Manager." *Harvard Business Review* (July–August 1972), pp. 134–46.

Schoner, Bertram, and Uhl, Kenneth P. *Marketing Research: Information Systems and Decision Making*, 2d ed. New York: John Wiley and Sons, Inc., 1975.

Steilen, Charles F., and Altizer, Roley. *A Guide to Marketing/Advertising Information*. Atlanta, Ga.: AdMar Books, 1972.

chapter

6

Basic concepts of primary data collection

Primary data has been defined as data generated by the researcher for his own use. Collecting primary data is an outgrowth of earlier stages in the research process. After the information needs are defined, the data required to produce this information can be specified. The first place to seek the needed data is secondary sources since this is typically a less expensive approach. If gaps exist between the data needs and the secondary data available, then they must be filled with primary data. To meet the need for primary data the researcher may select from among the variety of approaches available: qualitative approaches (focus group interviews, depth interviews, projective techniques), quantitative approaches (surveys, experimentation, simulation), or some combination of these approaches. Regardless of the approach selected, certain basic concepts still apply. These concepts relate to measurement and sampling. Both measurement and sampling are typically involved in primary collection using any of the basic approaches. Thus these two areas will be discussed before moving on to qualitative and quantitative research in marketing in Chapters 7 and 8 respectively.

MEASUREMENT

Measurement is essentially the act of quantification. (Note that quantification as used here may apply to either quantitative or qualitative research.) The variables of interest in a research effort must be quantified so that their state of nature can be determined or the relationships between them investigated. Measurement of relevant variables provides a data base for analysis. If a firm is interested in determining the income distribution of users of its product, then some quantification of income must take place. This quantification is measurement. Measurement can relate to any variable of interest in a given study. The variable or variables of interest are quantified for whatever unit of observation is relevant to the research being conducted. The unit of observation may be individuals, households, stores, businesses, cities, or any number of other possibilities. Thus, the process of measurement involves the quantification of key variables for those units of observation relevant to the study. One study may require the quantification of personality characteristics for individuals while another requires the quantification of shelf space for retail stores. Both represent the act of measurement.

The term measure refers to a unit of data. Quantification is done in these units. For example, length may be measured in feet. A foot is a measure of length. Sales can be quantified in dollar units. A dollar is thus one measure of sales.

Measurement is usually carried out in one of two basic ways: observation or interviewing. The researcher may either observe a situation to secure data or ask questions in a written or oral form. Asking questions in an interview situation tends to be the most often used measurement method in marketing research; however, observation also has many valuable applications. For example, physical product counts in retail stores are a regularly used observational method in store audits. This discussion will center on the interrogative method as it has found considerably wider use.

Types of variables

Measurement in marketing research is generally concerned with one or more of three types of variables. These three variable types are (1) states of being, (2) states of mind, and (3) behaviors. States of being include such things as age, income, and sex as well as less clear-cut variables like social class and personality. States of being are situations that exist in the environment and can be quantified based on some objective external criteria. States of mind are variables that relate to the mental state within an individual. Thus, they tend to be more difficult to measure. These are such variables as awareness levels and attitudes. Behaviors are actions rather than states. A purchase, for example, is a critical behavior in marketing. Quite often marketing research will attempt to relate behaviors to either states of being or states of mind so as to better understand the behaviors. This permits forecasting of behaviors and profiling of particular behavior types in terms of the other variables. An understanding of the type of variables involved in the research is a prerequisite for effective measurement.

Scaling

Another important consideration in the area of measurement is scaling. The scale that is produced in the measurement process reflects the degree of precision or quality achieved in quantification. This is important in evaluating the data produced in research and in selecting methods of analysis to use in processing the data. The relationship between scaling and methods of analysis will be discussed later in Chapter 9.

There are four basic types of scales: (1) nominal, (2) ordinal, (3) interval, and (4) ratio. The nominal scale is the weakest of the four and the ratio scale, the strongest. A nominal scale provides only for the naming of the items being measured. There are categories with names, and each item can be placed in one discrete category. In Figure 6–1A

Figure 6–1
Basic scales

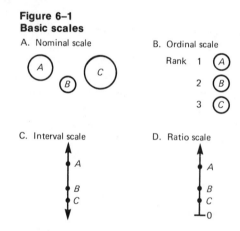

an item can fall in either A, B, or C, but there is no implication of one category being higher or lower than another. They are equivalent classes. For example, sex can be measured using the categories of male and female. Each individual can be placed in one of these two equivalent categories; thus, this would be a nominal measurement of the variable sex.

The next highest order scale is the ordinal scale. Here we add the property of ranking to that of naming. With an ordinal scale one item can be said to be higher, lower, or the same as another item in terms of the variable being measured. This notion is illustrated in Figure

6-1B. An item in A is higher in terms of whatever is being measured than an item in B. We cannot say how much higher only that A is higher than B and C, and that B is higher than C. Assume that a group of shoppers are asked "How good is the quality of meats found in this supermarket relative to meat found in other supermarkets?" and ask to respond in one of three ways: (1) better than other supermarkets, (2) about the same as other supermarkets, or (3) worse than other supermarkets. In this situation an ordinal scale has been created. Shoppers' perceptions of meat quality has been measured on a three point scale. A shopper responding "better than other supermarkets" has a higher perception of quality than one responding with either of the other options. A great deal of the measurement in marketing provides ordinal scaling. This has a considerable impact on the methods of analysis used in marketing research as will be seen in Chapter 9.

An interval scale, which is the third highest in order of precisions, has not only the properties of naming and ranking, but also adds a known interval between points on the scale. With an interval scale we not only know that one item is higher or lower than another, but also how much difference there is between them. In Figure 6-1C, we see that an interval scale is a continuum. The distance between A and B on the scale can be seen to be greater than the distance between B and C. The exact distance from A to B can be quantified. An example of an interval scale is Fahrenheit temperature. The difference between 40° and 80° can be quantified but it is incorrect to say that 80° is twice as high as 40°. The zero on the scale is not really the absence of heat, but an arbitrarily defined reference point. Thus, ratios between points cannot be computed. The scale is a continuum with no absolute zero as a benchmark.

A ratio scale, the strongest basic scale, provides such an absolute zero. This allows differences between points on the scale to be expressed in ratios as well as simply quantified. Figure 6-1D illustrates this concept. A is approximately twice as high on the scale as C. All of the relationships between points on the scale can be expressed in ratios. Income, age, sales, and cost are all variables which can be easily measured on ratio scales. This is because they all have absolute zeros which provide a benchmark.

Some variables can be measured on more than one scale. For example, income has been described as a variable which can be measured on a ratio scale. In designing a data collection instrument, however, it may be expedient to measure income on an ordinal scale. If respondents are asked to state their annual income, they may refuse or deliberately provide a false figure. On the other hand, the same respondents might be more willing to indicate a category, or range of incomes. In this case the researcher faces a trade off between the quality of measurement for a variable and the quantity and validity of responses.

This issue is common in the design and construction of questionnaires. Questionnaires are developed to operationalize the measurement task, and certain basic principles should be followed in the design of such a measurement device.

Questionnaire construction

Questionnaire construction is a part of the research design phase of the research process. Six steps in the research process should have been completed prior to entering this design activity. One critical step in the research process prior to research design must be effectively carried out as a basis for good questionnaire construction. This step is operationally defining the variables to be researched. Operational definitions as previously discussed are definitions in measurable terms. Since the questionnaire must be constructed so as to measure the relevant variables, the researcher must know what the variables are in an operational sense. Thus, a questionnaire is an instrument through which the researcher communicates information needs to a group of potential respondents, stimulates an accurate response, and renders data in a form which is meaningful for analysis.

Types of questionnaires. The general form of the questionnaire may take one of three directions: (1) structured, (2) semistructured, or (3) unstructured. A single questionnaire or interview form may, of course, have elements of each approach. Generally, in a structured questionnaire the answers available to the respondent are specified by the researcher. This provides essentially a multiple choice format. Figure 6–2 provides numerous examples of structured questions (e.g., questions 1–8).

The semistructured form provides specific questions but allows for open ended responses. Something of a "fill in the blank" or "discussion question" approach. This allows the respondent more flexibility in answering the question, but it also complicates the analysis. With the semistructured form, the responses must be categorized after the fact so that they can be sorted and summarized. Questions 9–11 in Figure 6–2 are illustrations of semistructured questions.

Structured and semistructured questionnaires are easily produced in written form and require a minimum of interviewer skill and training. Frequently, semistructured questions are used in the early stages of questionnaire development. Then, structured questions are developed based on the results of pretesting. In the preparation of the questionnaire illustrated in Figure 6–2, for example, question 6 was

Figure 6–2
Sample of structured/semistructured questions

1. *Your sex*
   Male _____
   Female _____

2. *Age*
   Under 18 _____
   18 to 20 _____
   21 to 24 _____
   25 to 34 _____
   35 to 44 _____
   45 to 54 _____
   55 and over _____

3. *Marital status*
   Single _____
   Married _____
   Divorced _____
   Other _____

4. *Last school you attended*
   Grade school _____
   High school _____
   Trade school _____
   College _____
   Post graduate _____

5. *Approximate annual family income*
   (include all wage earners in family)
   Under $5,000 _____
   $5,000 to 7,499 _____
   $7,500 to 9,999 _____
   $10,000 to 14,999 _____
   $15,000 to 19,999 _____
   $20,000 to 24,999 _____
   $25,000 and over _____

6. *Your occupation*
   (check best description)
   Labor _____
   Semiskilled/skilled _____
   Service worker _____
   Technical _____
   Sales _____
   General office/clerical _____
   Management/proprietors _____
   Professional _____
   Student/full time _____
   Retired _____
   Homemaker _____
   Not employed _____

7. Counting yourself, please indicate the number of men, women and children living in your household who are in each of the following age groups:

	No. of males	No. of females
Adult (60 and over)	_____	_____
Adult (45–59)	_____	_____
Adult (30–44)	_____	_____
Adult (18–29)	_____	_____
Children (7–17)	_____	_____
Children (6 or younger)	_____	_____

8. *Do you own or rent your residence?*
   Own _____
   Rent _____

9. Your height _____

10. Your weight _____

11. Has your weight changed more than 5 pounds (either gain or loss) during the last 12 months? If yes, please indicate whether you are concerned about this change and why.

    Yes: _____ No: _____
    If concerned, why? _____
    _____
    _____
    _____
    _____
    _____

originally a semistructured question. The pretest responses resulted in the selection of specific answer categories.

The unstructured format provides neither specific questions nor answers. Rather, a general topic or topics are discussed in a free flowing interview session. This requires that the data collection method be either personal or telephone interviews. The unstructured approach is much more subjective than the others. A great deal of dependence is placed on the interviewer to probe and uncover relevant data. Thus, the need for highly trained interviewers is increased. Such an interview might start out with a statement from the interviewer such as "Let's talk about cars," and proceed with a discussion of that topic.

Whether a questionnaire is structured or unstructured, it may also be disguised or nondisguised. If the respondent is aware of the real purpose of the survey and of his role in the study, the questionnaire is nondisguised. Obviously, "disguised" corresponds to those situations in which the respondent is deliberately deprived of such information. Sometimes the researcher feels that respondents would be less willing to participate, or less accurate in their responses if a nondisguised questionnaire is used. Unstructured questionnaires are often disguised to allow the respondent maximum flexibility in answering questions. There is evidence favoring either approach, and the final decision rests with the judgement of the researcher.

Sequencing.   The questionnaire should start with a concise introduction. The introduction should typically tell who is conducting the research, what the purpose is, and give instructions for answering the questions. The introduction may also indicate the time required to complete the interview and insure the respondent that all responses are confidential if this is indeed the case. The time required and confidentiality are important factors to mention since taking too much time and/or invasion of privacy are the most often cited reasons for refusal to fill out questionnaires or give interviews.

Figure 6–3 is the introduction which accompanies the questionnaire illustrated in Figure 6–2. As the questionnaire turns to the actual questions, the earlier questions should be those that are less difficult, less intimate, and less boring. This will get the interview in motion and flowing well. Few respondents will terminate the interview before completion after it has gotten underway. Such questions as income should not be used as lead questions for this reason. Note in Figure 6–2 that the first four questions relate to typical classifying variables which respondents usually answer without hesitation. The questions concerning weight are reserved for later in the questionnaire. These questions might be sensitive issues for some respondents. A logical flow of questions should be sought in the questionnaire. Questions relating to a given topic should generally be

Figure 6–3
Illustrative questionnaire introduction

> Hello, I am *Dan Roberts* conducting a survey for *The Health Institute*. In our research we are attempting to identify the characteristics of people with weight problems. The questions are intended to give us a general view of your individual characteristics. This information will be kept strictly confidential; we are in no way interested in tying your response back to you personally.

grouped together so that all the data required on one topic can be secured while the respondent's attention is directed to that area. It is also helpful where possible to intersperse hard questions requiring more thought with simpler, less difficult questions. This can provide a mental break for the respondent.

Question formulation. When formulating the actual questions, every attempt should be made to be clear and straightforward. Make them easy to understand with no unfamiliar words. If the respondent misinterprets or misunderstands the question, the answer will be distorted. Technical terms should thus be avoided, and the language selected with the educational level of the respondents in mind. Pretesting the questionnaire can be invaluable in uncovering language that does not communicate the desired meaning. To accomplish this, the pretest should include a discussion with the sample respondents as to their interpretation of the questions. Another important point with respect to question formulation is that memory is limited. A question should not require the respondent to recall attitudes and behaviors from the distant past. Such a request will undoubtedly lead to distorted results. Also, when long questions are asked or complicated instructions given, some aids to memory may be needed.

Quite often in marketing research, some of the questions relate to measuring attitudes. Several generally accepted formats have been developed for this purpose. Before turning to a discussion of attitude measurement techniques, however, it may be helpful to briefly consider some of the basic theory of attitudes.[1] Attitudes are predispositions to behave in certain set ways to given stimuli. A more favorable attitude toward brand X than brand Y indicates a predisposition to purchase brand X when the need for the product arises. Attitudes are thus mental states that influence behavior. These states of mind are

---

[1] For an excellent discussion of attitude measurement, see G. David Hughes, *Attitude Measurement for Marketing Strategies* (Glenview, Ill.: Scott, Foresman and Company, 1971).

affected by a person's beliefs, values, and the stimuli received from the marketplace. The attitude towards a particular object (product, brand, institution, and so forth) is a function of two things: first, the relative importance of the attributes which the person used to evaluate the item (salience) and second, the person's assessment of the item in terms of those attributes (valence). A shopper's attitude toward BIC pens is thus a function of the relative importance to her of such product attributes as price, durability, and style, and her assessment of BIC in terms of these attributes. A consumer may consider price and durability to be extremely important while attaching less importance to style. She may evaluate BIC as very good on price and durability giving her a favorable attitude toward the product. Another consumer may consider style to be the most important attribute in a pen. If an individual evaluates BIC as being low on this attribute relative to other pens, that person's attitude toward the product will tend to be less favorable.

The researcher is then faced with four related facets in attitude measurement. He must consider (1) what are the relevant attributes? (2) how important is each to the individual? (3) what is the individual's assessment of the items under consideration on each of the attributes? and (4) how do all these considerations fit together to form an attitude? Some research is aimed at discovering relevant attributes, some at determining the relative importance of various attributes, but most often the intent is to measure the overall attitude. Thus a good measurement device must take into account both salience and valence. The relevant attributes must also be discovered as a basis for constructing a good questionnaire. Several different attitude measurement techniques are available which allow the researcher to deal in an orderly fashion with the complexities of attitude measurement. This discussion will be confined to three of the most commonly used techniques: (1) the semantic differential, (2) the Likert-type scale, and (3) paired comparisons.

The semantic differential.   The semantic differential version of an attitude measurement device is constructed by developing pairs of antonyms (adjectives or phrases) with cues placed between the antonyms. Antonyms are opposites such as hot versus cold, old versus new, and expensive versus inexpensive. Thus, the technique can be called a bipolar scale. One or more pairs of antonyms should be selected for each of the attributes considered relevant to the attitude. The cues placed between the antonyms may be either numeric, verbal, graphic or some combination of the three. The number of cues varies from as few as two to as many as eleven. Six or seven is the typical number. Most studies suggest that there is little increase in information gained beyond six or seven cues. The best number would depend on the purpose of the measurement and the type of analysis to be conducted on the data. If the researcher wishes to assume the scale to be interval, then more cues are required.

Figure 6–4 is an illustration of some semantic differentials which could be used to measure consumer attitudes toward brands of toothpaste. Scales are shown for taste, decay prevention, and availability—three common attributes used by consumers in evaluating toothpaste. The cues in this case are spaces above a line which are separated by pairs of dots. There are seven cues including the end points.

Two other decisions which must be made by the researcher in constructing semantic differentials are whether to make a balanced or unbalanced scale and whether the scale should be forced choice or not. A balanced scale would have the neutral position in the center of the scale while the unbalanced has it positioned off center with more cues to either the positive or the negative side. The unbalanced scale has the greatest value where the researcher expects the majority of responses to fall on the same side of the neutral point. With the unbalanced scale more cues and thus more precision can be placed where most of the responses fall. Unbalanced scales are rarely used in marketing research. The forced choice/nonforced choice decision relates to whether or not to give the respondent a "no opinion" category. Such a category may be necessary where a large percentage of the respondents lack awareness or knowledge of the subject involved. This prevents a distortion of the results with uninformed answers.

A typical semantic differential scale would ask each respondent to place an x in the cue that best represents his or her attitude for each pair of antonyms. The mean score for different groups can then be computed for each scale item and a profile developed. This allows differences in attitudes to be isolated and related to specific attributes. For example, a group of shoppers might be asked to evaluate a given

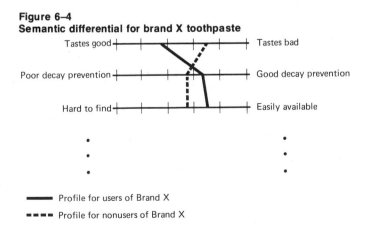

Figure 6–4
Semantic differential for brand X toothpaste

Tastes good | | | | | | Tastes bad

Poor decay prevention | | | | | | Good decay prevention

Hard to find | | | | | | Easily available

———— Profile for users of Brand X

■ ■ ■ ■ Profile for nonusers of Brand X

brand of toothpaste on the semantic differential in Figure 6–4. A profile can then be developed for users and nonusers of the brand which may shed light on the attitudinal reasons for the differing brand behavior. The results would resemble the lines connecting the scales in Figure 6–4. Based on these profiles, the biggest gap between the two groups appears on the taste attribute. It might be suggested that the taste of brand X is a key factor and might be changed to attract nonusers.

The Likert-type scale. The Likert-type scale is formed by a series of statements related to the topic under consideration. One or more statements can be included to represent each attribute considered relevant to the attitude. These statements may be either positive or negative. The respondent is asked to indicate a level of agreement or disagreement with each statement. Five opinions are generally provided: (1) strongly agree, (2) agree, (3) uncertain, (4) disagree, and (5) strongly disagree. Weights are then assigned to the cues for each statement with the most positive response typically having a weight of 5 and the most negative a weight of 1. The weights on all statements can then be summated to produce the final scale value for each individual. The higher the total score for the individual, the more positive his attitude and the lower the score, the more negative the attitude.

Suppose that a researcher wishes to measure attitudes toward State Bank. He might make the following statements and ask the respondents to indicate their level of agreement with each by underlining one of the five options.

1. State Bank has friendly personnel.

Strongly agree	Agree	Uncertain	Disagree	Strongly disagree
(5)	<u>(4)</u>	(3)	(2)	(1)

2. State Bank is a progressive institution.

Strongly agree	Agree	Uncertain	Disagree	Strongly disagree
(5)	(4)	<u>(3)</u>	(2)	(1)

3. State Bank is not concerned about people.

Strongly agree	Agree	Uncertain	Disagree	Strongly disagree
(1)	(2)	(3)	<u>(4)</u>	(5)

An individual responding as above would get a score of 11. Another person with a score of 6 would have a less favorable attitude toward State Bank while a person with a score of 12 would have a more favorable attitude.

A problem with the summation is that the unique evaluations of each attribute are lost. A score of 11 can be achieved in several different ways. For this reason Likert-type questions are often used in marketing research with no summation.

The paired comparison technique. Both the semantic differential and the Likert-type scale produce ordinal measurements of attitude. The paired comparison technique is somewhat more sohpisticated and produces an interval measurement. This technique actually produces an aggregate measurement of the items of interest (products, brands, stores, and so forth) for a group of respondents rather than a score for each respondent as with the two previously mentioned techniques. Rather than producing an attitude score for respondents A, B, C, . . . relative to product X, the paired comparison technique produces an aggregate score for products X, Y, Z, . . . for a group of respondents.

Assume, for example, that three department stores (A, B, and C) are to be scaled on the basis of merchandise quality. With the semantic differential and the Likert-type scales we would ask each respondent to express an opinion about the merchandise quality of each store. The paired comparison approach would, however, produce an aggregate score of merchandise quality for stores A, B, and C.

To construct a paired comparison scale the items to be scaled are all paired and the respondents are asked to choose one item from each pair on some specified basis, such as merchandise quality.[2] The number of pairs required is equal to $n(n - 1)/2$, where n is the number of items to be scaled. In the example of store merchandise quality, three stores would require 3 pairs $[3(3 - 1)/2]$.

Now suppose that the three department stores are to be scaled by 78 respondents on the basis of merchandise quality. First, the stores are paired, and the pairs presented to each respondent. One store is selected from each pair by each respondent. These responses are then grouped in a frequency table with the three stores listed on both axes (see Figure 6–5A). The number of respondents selecting the store listed at the top over the store listed at the side is placed in each cell. When the store is compared with itself in the matrix, half the sample is placed in the cell. Next the table is proportioned (see Figure 6–5B). This matrix of proportions is then converted to a Z matrix in which the cell values are the normal deviates Z corresponding to the deviation of the proportion from .500 (see Figure 6–5C). That is, the cell values are the number of standard deviation units from the cell proportions to an even distribution of responses (.500). This means that the diagonal will have .000 in each cell. The Z for proportions less than .500 will be negative, and positive for those over .500. The exact value for each cell is determined from a standard normal deviate (Z) table.[3]

---

[2] For a detailed description of the paired comparison technique, see A. L. Edwards, *Techniques of Attitude Scale Construction* (New York: Appleton-Century-Crofts, 1957), pp. 20–29.

[3] The calculation of Z in this case is accomplished by subtracting .500 from each cell value. This operation produces a fraction which is treated as a proportion of a distribution. For example, store B was selected over store A in a proportion of .371 (see Figure 6–5B). Subtracting .500 from .371, we get a proportion of −.129 in the left tail of a normal distribution. Referring to any table of the area under the normal curve, we find that .129 of the curve corresponds to a Z value between .32 and .33. Through extrapolation we can calculate the Z value and thus derive the −.329 in Figure 6–5C for the corresponding cell in the Z table.

Figure 6–5
Steps in developing paired comparison scale

A. Frequency table *preference of B to A*

Stores	A	B	C
A	39	29	47
B	49	39	44
C	31	34	39

B. Proportions table

Stores	A	B	C
A	.500	.371	.602
B	.629	.500	.564
C	.398	.436	.500

C. Z table

Store	A	B	C
A	.000	−.329	259
B	.329	.000	.161
C	−.259	−.161	.000
Sum	.070	−.490	.420
Mean	.023	−.163	.140
Score	.186	0	.303

After the Z value for each cell has been determined the columns are summed and the mean taken. The scale value for each column is then determined by chainging the lowest mean to zero and making an equal addition or subtraction from the other means. Store B thus has the lowest perceived merchandise quality (scale value 0), store A is higher than B, and store C has the highest value. We can also see that the difference between A and B (.186 − 0 = .186) is greater than the difference between A and C (.303 − .186 = .117).

This technique has found greatest application in brand preference studies, pretesting advertisements, and in gaining similarities' measures for multidimensional scaling (to be discussed in the next section). Paired comparison is a relatively simple task for the respondent who is asked to compare two items at a time and select one on some specified basis. This simplicity can also create a significant problem because it is achieved by making all possible pairs of items. As the number of items increases, the number of pairs grows rapidly. For example, 20 items would require 190 pairs. This can cause respondent fatigue which may bias the results.

Nonmetric multidimensional scaling

The procedures discussed thus far have dealt with measurement in one dimension. Multidimensional scaling allows the researcher to measure an item in more than one dimension at a time.[4] These procedures in one operation identify the basic dimensions and place the objects within these dimensions. The basic data required to generate a multidimensional scale is between ordinal and interval in nature. The term nonmetric refers to the fact that the data is not interval quality. It is actually ranks of intervals between objects. These ranks of intervals can be secured from a sample of respondents in several different ways. Two of the more common methods are: (1) to form all possible pairs of pairs of objects and ask the respondents to identify the more similar pair AB or CD, and (2) to form all possible pairs of objects and ask the respondents to rate each pair of objects in terms of similarity (e.g., highly similar, somewhat similar, dissimilar).

After the basic data is secured from the sample on perceived similarities between objects, the objects are placed in n- dimensional metric space "whose interpoint-distance ranks, best preserve the rank order of the starting interpoint proximities."[5] These points can be mapped in space as illustrated in Figure 6–6. Objects which are perceived as similar appear in clusters. Competing brands, products, or stores will exhibit this characteristic. Blank spaces may indicate market opportunities if enough consumers' ideal points are located in that space. The dimensions are usually interpreted and labeled by the researcher after the mapping has been completed. The dimensions in Figure 6–6 were labeled as "sporty" and "luxurious" based on the positioning of the cars along each dimension.

---

[4] Multidimensional scaling is a relatively sophisticated subject. It is not possible to explain this approach to attitude measurement in these few pages. Rather, a simple summary discussion is provided, and interested readers are encouraged to pursue the suggested readings.

[5] P. E. Green and F. J. Carmone, "Multidimensional Scaling: An Introduction and Comparison of Nonmetric Unfolding Techniques," *Journal of Marketing Research*, vol. 6 (August 1969), pp. 330–41.

Figure 6–6
A multidimensional mapping of cars

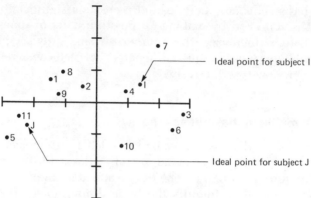

1. Ford Mustang 6
2. Mercury Cougar V8
3. Lincoln Continental V8
4. Ford Thunderbird V8
5. Ford Falcon 6
6. Chrysler Imperial V8
7. Jaguar Sedan
8. AMC Javelin V8
9. Plymouth Barracuda V8
10. Buick LeSabre V8
11. Chevrolet Corvair
    Source: From P. E. Green and F. J. Carmone, "Multidimensional Scaling: An Introduction and Comparison of Nonmetric Unfolding Techniques," *Journal of Marketing Research,* vol. 6 (August 1969), pp. 330–41, published by the American Marketing Association.

Reliability and validity in measurement

When developing any measurement device an attempt should be made to insure or at least measure its reliability and validity.[6] Both of these concepts relate to specific scales rather than to approaches and procedures. The reliability and validity of the semantic differential technique cannot be determined, but these concepts can be explored for a specific semantic differential questionnaire.

A questionnaire can be said to be *valid* when it measures what it is intended to measure. Validation of attitude measurement instruments is particularly difficult because of the elusive and changing nature of these states of mind. A measurement device can be said to have *predictive validity* when the behavior predicted from the attitude measure correlates highly with the actual observed behavior. When the attitudes and behaviors are measured at the same point in time the

---

[6] Readers interested in pursuing the subjects of validity and reliability should examine the suggested readings at the end of this chapter.

correlations indicate what is called *concurrent validity*. *Construct validity* involves the degree to which a specific attitude fits into the person's total mix of attitudes or personality dimensions. This can be measured by correlating the attitude score of interest with other related attitudes or characteristics. *Content validity* relates the relevance of items in the questionnaire to the total attitude being scaled. Does the item measure an attribute of importance in the attitude? This is usually a subjective judgement of the researcher or of experts selected by the researcher.

A measurement device is *reliable* if it gets similar results over time. Are the measurements at different points in time consistent for the same respondent? The three commonly used methods for estimating reliability are (1) test-retest, (2) equivalent-form, and (3) split-half. Test-retest involves correlating the attitudes measured for a group of respondents at one point in time with the attitudes of the same group at another point in time. The same measurement device is used at both times. If the correlation is high, then the instrument can be said to have test-retest reliability. Equivalent-form reliability correlates the attitudes of a group of respondents measured with two different measurement devices that are considered to be equivalent forms. That is, the two forms of the instrument are intended to measure the same thing. Both forms are administered to the same group of respondents at approximately the same point in time. The split-half approach correlates the attitudes measured by half the items that comprise the instrument with the attitudes measured by the other half. Since all the items are aimed at measuring the same total attitude the correlation should be high if the questionnaire is reliable. Both the equivalent-form and split-half approaches are actually measures of internal consistency within the measurement device. They do not measure stability over time, thus they are not true measures of reliability by the standard definition.

The construction of a valid and reliable measurement instrument requires considerable time and effort. The importance of accurate measurement to effective marketing research, however, justifies the effort required. This typically means extensive pretesting before a questionnaire is put into actual use.

Alternative contact methods

After the questionnaire has been designed and its validity and reliability evaluated in pretest, a method for contacting respondents must be selected. The three common contact methods are personal, telephone, and mail. Each of these has certain advantages and disadvantages which should be considered in the selection process.

Personal contact allows immediate feedback and adjustment by the interviewer. Probing, open-ended type questions, and general topic discussions (unstructured form) are best handled with the personal interview. Structured questionnaires can also be used very effectively with personal contact. Personal contact is usually the most expensive contact method, however, and is often restrictive in geographic coverage. It requires highly trained interviewers and field supervision to be effective.

One of the key problems in personal interviewing is the establishment of a good relationship, or rapport, between parties.[7] Interviewers should be able to detect a dishonest respondent in order to insure maximum validity in survey data. It has been shown that most interviewers are capable of sensing this problem when it is present.[8] The electronic era has provided researchers with valuable aids for in-depth analysis of interviews. Specifically, audio and video recording devices enable the interviewer to concentrate more directly on questioning the respondent then recording results. Unfortunately, the presence of such devices may be an inhibiting factor on the respondent. This problem is apparently not significant, although members of some social class groups respond differently when interviewed in the presence of recording devices. The researcher is concerned with achieving an open and honest rapport with the respondent and should be attentive to any element of the interview environment which might be distracting.

Telephone contact is less expensive but must be limited in length. The questions must be concise and are usually open-ended since giving a list of possible responses over the telephone can be very cumbersome. The telephone approach gives the respondent little time for thought and reevaluation. His responses are usually first impressions.

The rapport sought in personal interviews is even more difficult to achieve over the telephone. Certainly, the ease with which the respondent can refuse to answer and terminate the interview is discouraging. The refusal of respondents to provide certain types of information is a problem in any survey, but some unique problems exist in the telephone interview. Although probing is not as easily done as in the case of personal interviews, some limited probing can be accomplished by telephone. It was found, for example, that respondents who refused to answer questions concerning income were prone to indicate whether their income fell above or below a "critical"

---

[7] S. G. Trull, "Strategies of Effective Interviewing," *Harvard Business Review*, vol. 42 (January 1964), pp. 89–94.

[8] W. A. Belson, "Tape Recording: Its Effect on Accuracy of Responses in Survey Interviews," *Journal of Marketing Research*, vol. 4 (August 1967), pp. 253–60.

income.[9] Thus, instant feedback allowed the researcher to gain more income data by telephone than might have been feasible with a mail survey.

Mail contact usually requires a more structured questionnaire but allows the respondent added time for contemplation. The coverage area can also be more expansive than with personal contact assuming a set budget exists. A major problem with mail contact is the typically high nonresponse rates. One key factor affecting response rates is the respondents' level of interest in the subject under investigation. Nonresponse can easily run into the 80 to 90 percent range.

Nonresponse raises serious questions of bias in survey findings and typically increases the cost of obtaining sufficient information. One technique, which has generated a mixture of success, is the use of monetary inducements. Although the promise of monetary rewards proved to be of little help in one study, respondents who were offered a reward were more thorough in completing the questionnaire than other respondents.[10] Evidence also suggests that monetary inducements do increase response rates when they actually accompany the questionnaire. Another technique which has proven useful in increasing response rates in mail surveys is prior contact.[11] Although telephone contact appears more effective, improved rates were also achieved through prior contact by mail.

The best contact method for any given research depends on the type of measurement device to be used and the nature and location of the respondents. Time and cost constraints can also figure heavily into the decision. The nature and location of respondents moves the discussion into another area of consideration—sampling.

SAMPLING

The second major decision area in primary data collection is sampling. Sampling refers to the selection of a limited number of respondents from the total group of those with the data that is needed. The reason for selecting a percentage of the total rather than attempting a complete census usually relates to cost. If a firm is interested in the attitudes of current users of its product toward product durability, and it has 500,000 users, a complete census may be too expensive. Thus, a small part of the 500,000 is selected, and their attitudes measured.

---

[9] V. C. Skelton, "Patterns behind Income Refusals," *Journal of Marketing*, vol. 27 (July 1963), pp. 38–41.

[10] T. R. Woltruba, "Monetary Inducement and Mail Questionnaire Response," *Journal of Marketing Research*, vol. 3 (November 1966), pp. 389–400.

[11] J. E. Stafford, "Influence of Preliminary Contact on Mail Questionnaires," *Journal of Marketing Research*, vol. 3 (November 1966), pp. 410–11.

These attitudes are then projected to the larger group. The total group that we're concerned with is called the population. The smaller part of this group from which data is sought is the sample. An intermediate group of interest is the sample frame. The sample frame is an operational definition of the population; the group or lists from which sample respondents can actually be selected. If the population is all residents of Denver, the sample frame might be the Denver telephone directory. This list is an approximation of the population, but would not include all the residents. Some do not have telephones and others have unlisted numbers; thus, the frame is typically smaller than the population.

The fact that a large portion of the population is omitted from the sample respondents, introduces the potential for error. Much of the need for order and precision in selecting a sample results from attempts to minimize this potential error. The potential error resulting from omitting some population elements from the frame is called frame error. Errors generated by the sample being smaller than the frame can be called random error. Most of the standard statistical procedures for estimating confidence intervals, testing hypotheses, and determining sample size relate only to overcoming random error with some specified degree of confidence. Other potential errors are too often neglected in primary data collection. The potential error due to some sample elements failing to respond is called nonresponse error. These three sources of sampling related errors are illustrated in Figure 6–7. Together with measurement error they comprise the total error in

[margin notes: frame error, random error, nonresponse error]

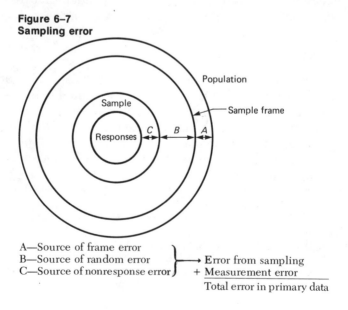

Figure 6–7
Sampling error

A—Source of frame error
B—Source of random error   ⎫→ Error from sampling
C—Source of nonresponse error ⎭ + Measurement error
                                   ———————————————
                                   Total error in primary data

measurement
error.

primary data collection. Measurement error is any distortions in the
data occuring in the act of quantification.

Sampling decisions

After a decision has been made to use sampling in primary data
collection, certain other decisions must be made. These decisions relate to sample size and sampling technique. Before such decisions can
be made, however, some basic questions must be answered.

1. What data must be collected?
2. Who has the needed data? This allows the researcher to define the
   sample population and to select a sampling frame.
3. Where are the population elements located, and how is the data
   distributed within these elements? That is, what are the geographic bounds of the population, and do some elements have
   more data than others? This has an impact on the desirability of
   alternative sampling techniques to be discussed later in the
   chapter.
4. What level of accuracy is needed from the sample? How close
   must the sample statistics be to the population parameter? This
   depends in part on the risk associated with getting incorrect results, and in part on the practical limitations expressed in number
   5 below. The level of accuracy needed has a significant impact on
   the sample size.
5. What are the time and cost limitations on the sample? How soon
   the data are needed and the budget for the research effort place
   very real practical constraints on the sampling operation.

Based on the answers to questions 1–4, the researcher is able to
construct the ideal sample (size and technique). The answer to question 5 tells the researcher whether he has sufficient time and
money to construct the ideal sample. Quite often some practical modifications are required in the sample to meet the constraints imposed
by the internal research environment.

Sample size

The standard statistical method for determining the appropriate
sample size is based on the standard error statistic. The standard error
formula is filled in with the predetermined information and solved for
n, the sample size. Many different formulas are available, the correct
one depending upon the type of statistic to be computed from the
sample—percentage, mean, difference between means, and so forth.

For example, with a study aimed at estimating a percentage and using a simple random sample, the formula is:

$$s_p = \sqrt{\frac{P \cdot Q}{n}} \quad \text{for infinite population}$$

where,

  s_p = the standard error of the percentage
  P = the percentage of the sample processing the attribute
  Q = the percentage of the sample not possessing the attribute
  n = the sample size.

Suppose that a study is being conducted to estimate the percentage of households in the United States that plan to buy a new washing machine next year. The desired level of accuracy is a .95 probability that a range of 5% (± 2.5%) around the estimate from the sample will contain the true percentage. Based on past experience, it is estimated that the percentage will not exceed 30%. To compute the needed sample size:

  P = .3
  Q = .7

.95 confidence level = 1.96 s_p from the standard normal deviate table

1.96 s_p = 2.5% to conform to the desired accuracy level

Thus

$$2.5\% = (1.96)(s_p) \quad s_p = \frac{2.5\%}{1.96} = 1.27\%$$

$$.0127 = \sqrt{\frac{(.3)\,(.7)}{n}}$$

$$n = \frac{P \cdot Q}{s_p{}^2} = \frac{(.3)\,(.7)}{(.0127)^2} = 1{,}302$$

The required sample size for the desired level of accuracy is 1,302. With this sample size the researcher can say that there is a .95 probability that the true population percentage falls within a range of ±2.5% around the sample percentage. This, however, takes into account only random error. Anyone reviewing research results should remember that frame error, nonresponse error, and/or measurement error could make the stated accuracy level incorrect.

A similar procedure can be used to determine sample size when dealing with different types of statistics, assuming the correct standard error formula is selected. The above illustration assumed an infinite population. When the population size is finite ánd known, the following formula[12] can be quite useful:

$$n = \frac{P(1-P)}{\dfrac{h^2}{z^2} + \dfrac{P(1-P)}{N}} \qquad \text{for finite population}$$

where,

n = the sample size

N = the population size

P = the percentage of the sample possessing the attribute, .3 in the above illustration

h = the allowable error, 2.5% in the above illustration

z = the confidence level in standard normal deviate units, 1.96 in the above illustration

Note that the sample size is largest when P is equal to .5. Thus, if the researcher has no knowledge about the percentage of the sample possessing the attribute, P can be set at .5 to insure the desired level of accuracy.

To illustrate the use of the formula, suppose that there is a need to estimate the percentage of residents in a small town that have used the public library in the past year. The population size is 30,000, nothing is known about the probable percentage, so P is set at .5, the allowable error (h) is $\pm 5\%$, and the desired confidence level is .95 ($z = 1.96$). The needed sample size for this level of accuracy is:

$$n = \frac{.5(1-.5)}{\dfrac{(.05)^2}{(1.96)^2} + \dfrac{.5(1-.5)}{30,000}} = 385$$

Tables are available in several statistics books which give sample size for specified levels of accuracy and population sizes. Given this information, the researcher can simply look up the appropriate sample size for a particular project.

This discussion has not gone into great detail on statistical procedures. Excellent and much more extensive discussions of the methods and formulas used to determine appropriate sample sizes, or to estimate sampling error from a given sample result, can be found in numerous basic statistics textbooks.

Sampling techniques

The sampling technique refers to the way in which the desired number of elements are to be selected from the sampling frame. The two basic approaches are probability sampling and nonprobability

---

[12] See John Neter and William Wasserman, *Fundamental Statistics for Business and Economics*, 2d ed. (Boston: Allyn and Bacon, Inc., 1962), p. 411.

sampling. With a probability sample each element in the frame has a known probability of being selected for the sample. This probability is not known with a nonprobability sample. Probability samples are thus more scientific and usually preferred over the nonprobability approaches.

Probability samples

Simple random sampling.   With a simple random sample every element in the population has an equal chance of being selected for the sample. This implies that the selection process has been left strictly to chance. Such a sample is generally drawn with the aid of a random numbers table. Suppose a department store wishes to sample its credit card holders. It has issued 12,000 customers one of its cards. The sample size is to be 300. Of course, all the card holders' names or numbers could be placed on slips of paper and a physical lottery conducted but this is very time consuming. The process is simplified with the random numbers table.

To select the sample, each card holder is assigned a number from 1 to 12,000. Then three hundred, five-digit random numbers are selected from the table. To do this some random starting point is selected and a systematic pattern is used in proceeding through the table. We might start in the second row, fifth column and proceed down the column to the bottom of the table and then move to the top of the next column to the right. When a number exceeds the limits of the numbers in the frame, in this case over 12,000, it is simply passed over and the next number selected that does fall within the relevant range. Since the numbers were placed in the table in a completely random fashion, the resulting sample is random. This gives each card holder an equal probability of being selected.

Systematic sampling.   Another frequently used probability sampling technique is the systematic sample. This procedure is very useful when the sampling frame is available in a random list. With this approach, the selection process starts by picking some random point in the list. Then every nth element is selected until the desired number is secured.

With the credit cards the sampling interval would be 40, or $12,000 \div 300$. First, the card holders would be placed in a list; this would likely be readily available from a computer printout. Next, a card holder from the first 40 on the list would be randomly selected. From this point every 40th name in the list would be selected.

This is easier than using the random numbers table to select each separate card holder and will probably yield just as accurate a result except where the list contains some type of order bias. For example, if the department store had been giving a special gift to every 20th person to receive a card; if the list had the card holders in the order they received their card; and if the sampling interval happened to coincide with the special gift recipients, a bias could be introduced. Those who had received special gifts might have a more favorable attitude toward the store, might use their card more frequently, and so forth. The order bias in this illustration is easily apparent, but care must be taken with systematic sampling to avoid situations where the order bias is not obvious. Where care is taken systematic sampling can be very helpful.

Stratified random sampling. The basic concept of stratified sampling is that different subgroups or strata within the population may be different. If strata can be identified that are homogeneous internally but different between strata, then a subsample can be selected from each strata and combined for the total sample. The selection of the subsamples within each strata would be random. The approach will yield a more representative sample from a population with well defined subgroups than the simple random sample.

Suppose that the behaviors and attitudes being researched in the credit card study are suspected to vary by income level. Since the department store has income figures on each card holder from the application forms, the population could be subdivided on the basis of income and a simple random sample selected from each income strata. The results are then combined to form a total sample for the population.

Another possible reason for taking a stratified sample is to obtain data on specific strata within the population as well as the total group. With a stratified sample of card holders, each separate income stratum can be analyzed without the need for asking income in the questionnaire. The researcher is also more likely to get enough respondents in each stratum for meaningful analysis; a problem which may arise with a simple random sample when some strata are relatively small.

A stratified sample may be either proportional or disproportionate in nature. A proportional stratified sample has the sample elements distributed among strata in the same proportion that the population elements are distributed. If 30 percent of the population is in the over $25,000 income stratum, then 30 percent of the sample is from this stratum. With a disproportional stratified sample some strata get disproportional representation in the sample. This may be because they are thought to have more relevant data, they are of more interest to the researcher, or they are a particularly small percentage of the total population. To illustrate, the attitudes and behaviors of low income credit card holders may be of particular interest to the department store mentioned above. If this is the case, 50 percent of the sample might be taken from the low income stratum while this stratum contains only 20 percent of the population. Such a procedure would result in a disproportionate stratified sample.

Cluster sampling.   Cluster sampling involves grouping the population and selecting clusters or groups rather than individual elements for inclusion in the sample. With the credit card illustration the list could be formed into 120 clusters of 100 card holders each. Three clusters might then be selected for the sample. This procedure still yields a probability sample, but the potential for order bias and other sources of error is accentuated. The sample size must often be larger than the simple random sample to insure the same level of accuracy. The clustering approach can, however, often make the selection process much easier and increase the efficiency of field work if personal interviews are to be done.

Area sampling.   One type of cluster sampling that is particularly useful is called area sampling. This is where the clusters are geographic subdivisions such as counties or city blocks. Area sampling is particularly helpful where no list of the population is available. It also makes field interviewing more efficient since the interviewer does several interviews at each location, a city block for example.

Suppose that a researcher wishes to do personal interviews with residents of a large city. The interviews relate to attitudes concerning shopping in the central business district. To take an area sample, the city might first be divided into blocks. A series of blocks would then be randomly or systematically selected. All of the residents living in the chosen blocks would be interviewed. When geographic clustering is used, it is likely that the respondents in each cluster will be more like each other than would be the case if a simple random sample were selected. Thus, a larger sample is needed to get the same level of accuracy as with nonclustering techniques. The cost savings in the field work is likely, however, to more than offset the expense of the increased sample size.

Nonprobability samples

Nonprobability samples are sometimes called "researcher controlled." This is because the selection process is based on the subjective decisions of the researcher or ease of access to the respondents rather than probability theory. Such samples, although less scientific than probability samples, can sometimes be justified for a given situation.

Convenience sampling.   With a convenience sample, population elements are selected for inclusion in the sample based on ease of access. Getting data from elements that are convenient can create a very biased result unless the population is homogeneous. If the population elements are all very much alike with respect to what is being measured, however, then a convenience sample may be acceptable.

If a researcher wished to secure data from gasoline purchasers, ten convenient stations might be selected and interviews conducted at the pumps. This would constitute a convenience sample of gasoline purchasers.

Judgment sampling.   Mayer and Brown state that:

> In a judgment sample, the researcher's judgment is used in selecting items from the frame which are in some sense more "representative" of the population than a randomly selected sample.[13]

Rather than using a probabilistic means of obtaining the sample, only those elements that appear to be typical with respect to the variables under consideration are chosen. The resulting sample is generally less costly, and random error may actually be reduced. According to Mayer and Brown:

> For a judgment sample, the random sampling error is normally smaller than for a probability sample. The sampler will usually select items that are closer to the average.[14]

This technique thus provides a concentration of "representative" units rather than a random distribution of elements. Mayer and Brown point out that, "under certain circumstances the advantages of objectivity are surpassed by increased accuracy."[15] Of course, frame, nonresponse, and measurement error may be present as in any primary data collection.

Judgment sampling is used quite often in qualitative research where the desire is to develop hypotheses rather than to generalize to larger populations. For example, a judgment sample of "typical housewives" might be taken to secure reactions to a new rug cleaner.

Quota sampling.   This form of nonprobability sampling may appear to be quite scientific. It is often quite elaborate and resembles a stratified random sample. With this approach the population is divided into strata based on some characteristic thought to be releated to the variable being measured in the primary data collection. A certain number or quota of elements is then selected from each strata. The selection of elements within each strata is typically left to the judg-

---

[13] Charles S. Mayer and Rex V. Brown, "A Search for the Rationale of Non-Probability Sample Designs," *Proceedings, American Marketing Association*, Fall Conference, 1965 (Chicago, 1966), pp. 295–96.

[14] Ibid., p. 306.

[15] Ibid., p. 308.

ments of the interviewers. With quota sampling the population is often subdivided by more than one variable. A two variable stratification would yield a cross-classification arrangement with quotas assigned by cell. The size of the quota for each strata is generally proportionate to the size of that strata in the population.

To illustrate quota sampling, suppose that there is a need to sample apartment residents. Apartments are divided into strata based on number of bedrooms and the presence of tennis courts. A certain number of interviews (quota) is assigned to each type, and the interviewers are instructed to seek out apartments meeting the criteria. The selection of the exact residents is left to the interviewers.

SUMMARY

Two fundamental concepts or decision areas are involved in primary data collection. These are measurement and sampling.

Measurement is the act of quantifying the variables of interest in the research. This quantification typically involves the development and use of a questionnaire or interview form. In constructing such a device the researcher must be careful to give adequate instructions to the respondents, to develop a logical sequencing of questions, and to use wording that conveys the desired meaning to all respondents. One important type of variable in marketing research, which can be very difficult to measure, is an attitude. Several standard questionnaire formats have been developed for measuring attitudes, including: the semantic differential, the Likert-type scale, and the paired comparison technique. The overall quality of measurement achieved by a measurement device is indicated by the basic scale obtained: nominal, ordinal, interval, or ratio. The type of scale generated influences the method of analysis appropriate in any given research. Two important considerations in the measurement activity are validity (does the instrument measure what it is supposed to measure?) and reliability (are the measurements consistent over time?). Careful pretesting is required to insure a valid and reliable questionnaire.

Sampling relates to the selection of elements in a population from which to seek data. The population is all elements (individuals, households, stores, firms, and so forth) that have the data of interest. In order to take a sample, which is usually done to reduce the cost of primary data collection, first the population must be operationally defined. This operational definition of the population, which can actually be contacted by the researcher, is called a sample frame. After the frame is determined, two decisions must be made: (1) How large should the sample be? and (2) What sampling technique should be used? Procedures for determining the appropriate sample size are based on the standard error concept. Sampling techniques are procedures for actually selecting the desired number of elements from the frame. These techniques can be divided into two broad groups: probability and nonprobability samples. With probability samples each element has a known probability of being included in the sample. The nonprobability techniques do not allow the researcher to determine this probability. Probability techniques include simple random sampling, systematic sampling, stratified sampling, cluster sampling, and area sampling. Nonprobability techniques include convenience sampling, judgment sampling and quota sampling.

DISCUSSION QUESTIONS

A bank in a metropolitan area of 1,500,000 residents is interested in women's attitudes toward discrimination by banks. Specifically the bank wishes to determine: (1) whether a nondiscrimination market segment exists that can be identified by attitudinal data, and (2) if such a segment exists, what are their characteristics? The accompanying questionnaire was developed for use in the study.

1. How should the sample frame be defined?
2. How large should the sample size be?
3. Discuss the advantages and disadvantages of various sampling techniques for the research. What sampling technique would you recommend? Why?
4. What contact method would be best?
5. What problems do you see with the questionnaire? What changes should be made to improve the instrument?
6. Discuss the scaling achieved in the various parts of the questionnaire.

Questionnaire

Hello, I am conducting a banking survey for a local bank. I would appreciate it very much if you would take three or four minutes to answer the following questions. The information from the survey will be kept confidential; you need *not* give your name.

Part I: How important do you consider the following factors in choosing a bank? (Circle one number for each.)

	Of little importance					Very important	
1. Convenience	1	2	3	4	5	6	7
2. Offers full range of services	1	2	3	4	5	6	7
3. Drive-in facilities	1	2	3	4	5	6	7
4. Good reputation	1	2	3	4	5	6	7

		Of little importance					Very important	
5.	Do not discriminate against women in offering service	1	2	3	4	5	6	7
6.	Helpful and pleasant personnel	1	2	3	4	5	6	7
7.	They know me	1	2	3	4	5	6	7
8.	Where my husband banks	1	2	3	4	5	6	7
9.	I know them	1	2	3	4	5	6	7
10.	Parking facilities	1	2	3	4	5	6	7

Part II: Please respond to the following statement by indicating your level of agreement or disagreement with the statement. (Strongly agree, Agree, Neutral, Disagree, or Strongly disagree)

		Strongly agree	Agree	Neutral	Disagree	Strongly disagree
1.	Banks presently serve the needs of female customers effectively.	——	——	——	——	——
2.	Most banks apply the same rules to both men and women in granting loans.	——	——	——	——	——
3.	Most banks discriminate against women in offering service.	——	——	——	——	——
4.	If I found out about a bank that did not discriminate against women, I would switch my account to that bank.	——	——	——	——	——

	Strongly agree	Agree	Neutral	Disagree	Strongly disagree
5. I would drive across town to do business with a bank that did not discriminate against women.	____	____	____	____	____

Part III:

1. Marital status: Single   ____
                    Married   ____
                    Divorced   ____
                    Other (specify) ____

2. If married, how long?   _____

3. How many children do you have?   0 ____   4 ____
                                         1 ____   5 ____
                                         2 ____   6 ____
                                         3 ____   over 6 ____

4. Age: Under 18   ____
             19–24   ____
             25–34   ____
             35–44   ____
             45–54   ____
         55 or over   ____

5. Do you have a bank credit card in your own name? Yes ____ No ____

6. Occupation: Secretarial/Clerical   ____
                   Medical   ____
                   Professional/Technical ____
                   Homemaker   ____
                   Other (specify):   _____
       How many hours per week are you employed outside the home? ____

7. Education: Some high school   ____
                High school graduate ____
                Vocational training   ____
                Some college   ____
                College graduate   ____
                Graduate degree   ____

8. What percentage of the household income do you earn?
                   0% ____
                1–20% ____
              21–40% ____
              41–60% ____
              61–80% ____
            81–100% ____

9. Household Income: Under 5,000_____
                                5,000–8,000_____
                                8,001–11,000_____
                              11,001–15,000_____
                              15,001–20,000_____
                              20,001–30,000_____
                                over 30,000_____

SELECTED REFERENCES

Axelrod, J. N. "Attitude Measures That Predict Purchase," *Journal of Advertising Research*, vol. 8 (March 1968), pp. 3–17.

Churchman, G. W. and Ratoosh, P., eds. *Measurement: Definitions and Theories*. New York: John Wiley & Sons, Inc., 1959.

Dommermuth, William P. *The Use of Sampling in Marketing Research*. Chicago: American Marketing Association, 1975.

Hughes, G. David *Attitude Measurement for Marketing Strategies*. Glenview, Ill.: Scott, Foresman and Company, 1971.

Kanuk, Leslie and Berenson, Conrad. "Mail Surveys and Response Rates: A Literature Review," *Journal of Marketing Research*, vol. 12 (November 1975), pp. 440–53.

Mendenhall, William; Ott, Lyman; and Scheaffer, Richard L. *Elementary Survey Sampling*. Belmont, Calif.: Wadsworth Publishing Co. Inc., 1971.

chapter

7

Qualitative research in marketing*

INTRODUCTION

The purpose of this chapter is to introduce the techniques of qualitative research and their applications in marketing. The value of using such techniques has become increasingly evident over the past several years, as more and more researchers have used qualitative research methods in their effort to generate information on which to base marketing decisions.

Intuitively, one can with little difficulty define qualitative research, particularly if it is contrasted with quantitative research. By quantitative research we mean research which provides information to which numbers can be applied. For example, we can determine how many people there are between the ages of 35 and 50 inclusively. We can count each one of these individuals and arrive at a number. Of course, we usually find it impossible to count each individual; therefore, typically we take a sample of people, determine how many people ages 35 to 50 are contained in the sample, then generalize to the entire population. We can similarly measure how many people drink brand X cola or use brand Y deodorant soap. We have objective information (numbers) on which to base decisions.

Qualitative research, on the other hand, involves finding out what people think and how they feel—or at any rate, what they say they think and how they say they feel. This kind of information is subjective since it involves feelings and impressions, rather than numbers.

---

* This chapter is adapted from Danny N. Bellenger, Kenneth L. Bernhardt, and Jac L. Goldstucker, *Qualitative Research in Marketing* (Chicago: American Marketing Association, 1976).

Sampson defined qualitative research by describing its characteristics, purposes, and techniques:

> Qualitative research is usually exploratory or diagnostic in nature. It involves small numbers of people who are not usually sampled on a probabilistic basis . . . In qualitative research no attempt is made to draw hard and fast conclusions. It is impressionistic rather than definitive.[1]

Two key arguments can be made which support the belief that in many situations qualitative research provides a reasonable approach in carrying out some part of the marketing research tasks. First, marketing research can be considered to be an applied behavioral science (which is indebted to the behavioral sciences for many of the concepts and techniques which they have adopted). While marketing research has borrowed heavily from the concepts, theories, and techniques of the behavioral sciences, it has also inherited a major limitation of those fields—the lack of accurate measurement systems. Hays indicates the general awareness of the problem as follows:

> In some of the older scientific fields we take for granted such procedures, which give precise, succinct, and numerical specifications of the scientists' observations. How to devise similar measurement procedures is still a major problem for psychology and her sister behavioral sciences. The modern psychologist knows that he is only at the frontier of the true application of scientific method to the study of behavior.[2]

There are many social and behavioral scientists who share this kind of concern about the development of better and more accurate measurement systems in their fields. Past history suggests that any improvements will be quickly incorporated into applied fields such as marketing research. However, it is also true that the search for more advanced measuring instruments may be slowed by the resistance of many practitioners who oppose quantification on philosophical grounds. As an example, Nicosia and Rosenberg have expressed concern for attempts to quantify what may best be left qualitative:

> We are also aware that the blind research for quantifiable regularities in society can lead to ignorance of those aspects of man—the most important ones—that are intrinsically nonquantitative.[3]

---

[1] Peter Sampson, "Qualitative Research and Motivational Research," in *Consumer Market Research Handbook*, ed. Robert M. Worcester (London: McGraw-Hill Book Company (UK) Limited, 1972), p. 7.

[2] William L. Hays, *Quantification in Psychology* (Belmont, Calif.: Brooks/Cole Publishing Company, 1967), p. 2.

[3] F. H. Nicosia and Barr Rosenberg, "Substantive Modeling in Consumer Attitude Research," *Attitude Research in Transition*, ed. Russell I. Haley (Attitude Research Committee of the American Marketing Association, 1972), p. 246. Also, see M. H. Gopal, *An Introduction to Research Procedure in Social Sciences* (Bombay: Asia Publishing House, 1970), p. 205 and Donald P. Robin, "A Philosophical Evaluation of Predicting Human Behavior through the Inductive Process," *Southern Journal of Business*, vol. 6 (April 1971), p. 25.

The argument by Nicosia and Rosenberg, as well as by many others, suggests that the progress of measurement in marketing research may be slow. Much marketing research, and virtually all qualitative research, is directed at subjective aspects of consumer behavior and opinion. These types of concerns must necessarily rely on the behavioral sciences for the theories and techniques of research and analysis. Clearly, the behavioral sciences have not yet developed either a tradition or a framework for totally precise quantitative measurement or analysis.

Because of the various measurement problems, applied quantitative research has certain practical limitations. First, quantitative researchers have had many successes, but quantitative research techniques have not yet achieved a level of reliability in predicting consumer behavior that is fully satisfactory to marketing management.[4] This can, of course, be in part explained by the cost and time limitations which are inherent in applied research, but the lack of a firm theoretical basis for measurement must also be considered a contributing factor.

Other researchers see problems with possible overemphasis on quantitative research and analysis. Demby pointed out that "Blind belief in computer programs has led to some mindless research and senseless analysis . . . "[5] Einhorn expressed concern that the proliferation of computers and packaged programs is having at least one adverse effect on the quality of research because of a ". . . temptation to substitute immediate empirical analysis for more analytical thought."[6]

Many other criticisms of quantitative marketing research could be pointed out. However, it is not our intention to indict quantitative research but to show that there is no clearly correct choice to be made between purely quantitative and purely qualitative research. The payoff in business research is improved information for decision making. To the extent that either quantitative or qualitative research achieves this objective, each merits consideration.

The key argument supporting the use of qualitative research is that the research process and the decision-making process retain major subjective elements. The initial steps in the research process, that is,

---

[4] Alvin A. Achenbaum, "The Gresham's Law of Research," *Attitude Research in Transition*, ed. Russell I. Haley (Attitude Research Committee of the American Marketing Association, 1972), p. 25, and Albert V. Bruno and Edgar A. Pessemier, "An Empirical Investigation of the Validity of Selected Attitude and Activity Measures," *Proceedings, Third Annual Conference*, ed. M. Venkatesan (Association for Consumer Research, 1973), p. 456.

[5] Emanual H. Demby, "From the Qualitative to the Quantitative and Back Again," *Attitude Research in Transition*, ed. Russell I. Haley (Attitude Research Committee of the American Marketing Association, 1972), p. 94.

[6] Hillel J. Einhorn, "Alchemy in the Behavioral Sciences," *Public Opinion Quarterly*, vol. 36 (Fall 1972), p. 368.

defining the problem and the informational needs, formulating the hypotheses, and defining variables, are essentially subjective in nature. In addition, much of the research design stage, such as determining the type of research, sampling procedure, and designing the measurement instrument, are also qualitative. Quantitative precision is meaningless if the wrong hypothesis is tested, the wrong variables are measured, or if the wrong instrument is chosen for a given problem. Even when these failings are avoided, the research results are subject to the judgmental interpretation of the researcher and of the ultimate decision maker. Clearly, the theoretical precision and objectivity of quantitative research can be substantially diluted by this array of subjective or qualitative factors. Thus the qualitative approach will still have merit in various subjective areas of marketing research even if the problems of accurate measurement can be overcome.

A final point should be made here concerning questions about the validity of the nonquantitative procedures which are now available and the determination of the situations where their use would be most appropriate. Many questions can be raised about specific qualitative techniques, even when used in clinical situations. Dohrenwend has found that ". . . there is no evidence that open questions possess the advantage of being more productive of depth."[7] Yoell stated that "The TAT Test has been found to measure only the condition or situation immediately preceding a given activity and not the general characteristics of the individual, not the personality."[8] Qualitative techniques are subject to further question when transferred from the clinic to the marketplace. It was noted by Boyd, Westfall, and Stasch that ". . . these techniques were developed to obtain information from a single individual over a long period of time."[9] The criticisms of the research techniques used by qualitative researchers raise legitimate concern and will be discussed later in this chapter. It does not appear, however, that these questions are very much more serious than those raised about the techniques and measuring devices of quantitative research.

From the discussion thus far, we see that qualitative research has both advantages and limitations. Marketing researchers are thus faced with a need to exercise judgment when determining which type of research technique to use in solving a specific problem. In the re-

[7] Barbara Snell Dohrenwend, "Some Effects of Open and Closed Questions," *Human Organization* (Summer 1965), p. 183.

[8] William A. Yoell, "Determination of Consumer Attitudes and Concepts through Behavioral Analyses," *Attitude Research at Sea*, ed. Lee Adler and Irving Crespi (Attitude Research Committee of the American Marketing Association, 1966), p. 23.

[9] Harper W. Boyd, Jr. and Ralph Westfall, and Stanley F. Stasch, *Marketing Research: Text and Cases* (Homewood, Ill.: Richard D. Irwin, Inc., 1977), p. 632.

mainder of this chapter the application of three qualitative techniques will be discussed—focus group interviews, depth interviews, and projective techniques.

FOCUS GROUP INTERVIEWS

Description

The focus group interview, or group interview, is a technique which grew out of the group therapy method used by psychiatrists. The concept is based on the assumption that individuals who share a problem will be more willing to talk about it amid the security of others sharing the problem. It offers a means of obtaining in-depth information on a specific topic through a discussion group atmosphere which allows an insight into the behavior and thinking of the individual group members. Rather than using a structured question-and-answer methodology, the procedure is to encourage a group to discuss feelings, attitudes, and perceptions about the topic being discussed. One researcher has described the technique as "A chance to 'experience' a 'flesh and blood' consumer . . . to go into her life and relive with her all of the satisfactions, dissatisfactions, rewards, and frustrations she experiences when she takes the product into her home."[10] In spite of being one of the most frequently used techniques in marketing research today, there are no prescribed guidelines for focus group interviews, no book of rules, no formulas, and no strategies."[11]

Merton, Fiske, and Kendall distinguish the focus group as following these criteria:

Persons interviewed are known to have been involved in a particular situation; . . . The hypothetically significant elements, patterns, processes, and total structure of the situation have been provisionally analyzed by the social scientist. . . . On the basis of this analysis he takes the third step of developing an interview guide, setting forth the major areas of inquiry and the hypotheses which provide criteria of relevance for the data to be obtained in the interview. Fourth and finally, the interview is focused on the subjective experiences of persons exposed to the pre-analyzed situation in an effort to ascertain their definitions of the situation.[12]

The groups are generally conducted with women, especially homemakers, but can be conducted with any homogeneous group of

---

[10] Myril Axelrod, "Marketers Get an Eyeful When Focus Groups Expose Products, Ideas, Images, Ad Copy, etc. to Consumers," *Marketing News* (February 28, 1975), p. 6.

[11] Ibid.

[12] Robert K. Merton, Marjorie Fiske, Patricia L. Kendall, *The Focused Interview* (Glencoe, Ill.: The Free Press, 1956), p. 3.

consumers. For example, Dr. Alfred Goldman has conducted focus group sessions for National Analysts with computer engineers, personnel managers, heads of manufacturing companies, paper-making chemists, retailers, models, doctors, lawyers, and persons whose net worth exceeds a half million dollars.[13]

Focus group interviews typically last one and a half to two hours, which gives the moderator sufficient time to develop a good rapport with respondents and thus get very candid answers. Often the moderator is able to get below the conscious level, and the respondents reveal their personalities, emotions, and true feelings. This technique thus allows the researcher to handle sensitive areas more effectively via the group method than with individual interviews.

The technique is particularly suited for new product prototype testing, studying package changes, advertising strategy changes, and advertising copy formulation. It is a very flexible technique, and the interview session can be used to show various products, demonstrations, ads, and commercials or even to conduct taste tests or product usage tests as part of the group interview.

The ideal group is 8 to 12 people. Fewer than 8 is likely to burden each individual, while more than 12 tends to reduce each member's participation. With respect to group member selection, Merton et al. state:

> It appears that the more socially and intellectually homogeneous the interview group, the more productive its reports . . . . Interviewees of widely differing social status often make comments or refer to experiences which are alien or meaningless to the rest. . . . Some continue to be interested in what is being said, but others become restless and ultimately withdraw their attention.[14]

The number of group sessions conducted depends on the topic being considered, the number of segments to be studied, and expense and time considerations. Covering every possible segment is almost impossible, so the research must concentrate on the few segments most useful to the specific purposes of the study. For example, if the study requires interviews with broad spectrums of age groups from teenagers to retired people, and heavy users and light users are separated, a large number of group interviews will have to be conducted. The objective, of course, is to try to have as few groups as possible, while at the same time realizing the necessity to replicate the focus group interviews for each segment being studied. If there are two with

---

[13] "Coffee Klatch Research: A New Look at Focus Groups," *Ad Day* (March 15, 1975).

[14] Merton et al. *The Focused Interview* p. 3.

any one age group and they go in totally different directions, a third session should be conducted.

It is essential to get as much commonality in a group as possible so that the numerous interacting demographic variables do not confuse the issues; to be most productive, all the participants must be on the same wave length. For example, Young and Rubicam, which conducts approximately 600 focus group interviews per year, almost never puts married full-time homemakers with children at home in the same group as unmarried, working women because their life-styles and overall goals and needs are completely different. They also break teen-age and child groups carefully and rarely interview men and women together.[15]

A number of researchers think age is the most important break after sex, being a better means of separating the group than occupation or income. Great extremes on any of these are bad, however. This is usually not a problem since researchers are typically looking at the middle class only, tending to avoid the extreme of income categories.

Some researchers argue that groups can easily be racially integrated while others feel that separate groups should be conducted with each race. Even those that argue for integration, however, say that one token black may be worse than no blacks at all; it is usually better to have two to three blacks out of ten.

There is much disagreement about the importance of good recruiting to obtain the group members. A minority of researchers feel that because the interview is so subjective and the sample so small and unrepresentative, it does not really matter how you obtain the individuals. A majority of the researchers, however, feel strongly that proper recruiting is essential to the success of the focus group interview. First, it is necessary for the members to have had experience with the product being studied. It is impossible to elicit valuable comments from individuals with no background upon which to draw. Second, people who have participated in group interviews previously (some research firms use a six month limit, some one year, and a very few have no restrictions) should not be allowed to participate. They know what to expect and are too ready to respond, and "show off" for the other participants. As one researcher has put it, "I've heard every excuse and rationalization for repeat respondents, but I will never accept that a repeat respondent can possibly contribute to a session in the same way as a new respondent. . . . the only kind of respondent who can make a contribution to my qualitative work is a fresh, spon-

---

[15] Myril Axelrod, "Ten Essentials for Good Qualitative Research," *Marketing News* (March 14, 1975), p. 10.

taneous, involved, honest respondent who has not pre-thought her answers."[16]

Many researchers believe that an individual should not be allowed to participate in a group containing a friend, neighbor, or relative; they will tend to talk to each other and not to the group as a whole. For that same reason, church groups or organizations should not be asked to send people because the people that arrive in these groups have already established relationships, with some being leaders and some being followers.

The physical environment is very important to the success of the focus group interview. The atmosphere should be as relaxed as possible to encourage informal, "off the cuff" discussion. An impressive large table in a big corporate conference room may inhibit many participants and should be avoided. The environment should encourage the individuals to give their opinions and feelings, not their judgments; it is imperative to avoid giving the group members the impression that they are experts and you want their intellectual opinions, and the setup of the room is important in this regard.

Most researchers feel it is important for the client or manager to observe the focus group session. This can be done by having him or her actually participate as a group member, or much more commonly, by watching from behind a two-way mirror. It is usually much better to observe from a detached position where there is no danger of disrupting the normal functioning of the group and where the observer can take notes. A short break may be desirable during the session so that the observer can specify to the moderator other things which he or she would like probed in more detail.

Dynamics and the role of the moderator

The one thing on which everyone agrees with respect to focus group interviews is that the moderator's role is of prime importance to success. Rapport, level of verbal ability, relevancy, and direction of the discussion are important responsibilities of the moderator. There have been several good articles written telling the moderator how to carry out these responsibilities effectively.[17]

The moderator's skill in achieving interaction among a group of participants who have never met each other before and probably never will meet each other again determines the kinds and the importance of

---

[16] Ibid.

[17] See for example A. E. Goldman, "The Group Depth Interview," in *Marketing Research: Selected Readings*, eds. Joseph C. Seibert and Gordon Wills (New York: Penguin Books, 1970), pp. 266–71; or Donald A. Chase, "The Intensive Group Interview in Marketing," *MRA Viewpoints*, 1973.

emerging data. Therefore, the moderator, often a trained psychologist, must be thoroughly knowledgeable about the category under study and must know when to probe the group members and when to remain quiet. This special talent can be developed only by specific training and by learning from a great deal of trial and error.

A few of the key qualifications are:

1. *Kind but firm.* He must simultaneously display a kindly permissive attitude toward the participants, encouraging them to feel at ease in the group interview environment, while insisting that the discussion remain germane to the problem at hand.
2. *Permissiveness.* While an atmosphere of permissiveness is desirable, the moderator must be at all times alert to indications that the group atmosphere of cordiality is disintegrating. Before permissiveness leads to chaos, the moderator must re-establish the group purpose and maintain its orientation to the subject.
3. *Involvement.* Since a principal reason for the group interview is to expose feelings and to obtain reactions indicative of deeper feelings, the moderator must encourage and stimulate intensive personal involvement.
4. *Incomplete understanding.* A most useful skill of the group moderator is his ability to convey lack of complete understanding of the information being presented. Although he may understand what the participant is trying to express, by carefully inserting noncommittal remarks, phrased in questioning tones, the respondent is encouraged to delve more deeply into the sources of his opinion.
5. *Encouragement.* Although the dynamics of the group situation facilitate the participation of all members in the interaction, there may be individuals who resist contributing. The skillful moderator should be aware of unresponsive members and try to break down their reserve and encourage their involvement.
6. *Flexibility.* The moderator should be equipped prior to the session with a topic outline of the subject matter to be covered. By committing the topics to memory before the interview, the moderator may use the outline only as a reminder of content areas omitted or covered incompletely.
7. *Sensitivity.* The moderator must be able to identify, as the group interview progresses, the informational level on which it is being conducted, and determine if it is appropriate for the subject under discussion. Sensitive areas will frequently produce superficial rather than depth responses. Depth is achieved when there is a substantial amount of emotional responses, as opposed to intellectual information.[18]

Advantages and uses

When used properly, the focus group interview technique offers a number of advantages over other techniques. John Hess has described

---

[18] This section is adapted from Donald A. Chase, "The Intensive Group Interview," *MRA Viewpoints,* 1973.

some of the potential advantages of the technique as follows:

Synergism—combined group effort produces a wider range of information, insight and ideas.

Snowballing—random comments may set off a chain reaction of responses that further feed new ideas.

Stimulation—the group experience itself is exciting, stimulating.

Security—the individual may find comfort in the group and more readily express his ideas.

Spontaneity—since individuals aren't required to answer each question, the answers given become more meaningful.[19]

In addition, the company whose products are being discussed may benefit by:

Serendipity—key items or concepts unthought of may be discovered.

Specialization—the use of highly trained interviewers can be condensed through group interviewing.

Scientific scrutiny—sessions may be analyzed in detail after the interviews are completed.

Speed—the use of groups speeds up the interview process and the data accumulation.

Structure—group structuring is not so obvious and leading arrangements can be used that are unavailable in individual interviewing.[20]

Major benefits accrue from focus group interviews. These interviews provide the researcher with an opportunity to learn directly from consumers, in their own terms, their reasons for buying a product, their expectations of its performance, and the rewards which they hope to reap from using it. "No one has done the original thinking for the woman. No one has locked her into little boxes by 'prethinking' her reactions and responses. She isn't forced into categorizing her spontaneous and uninhibited reactions so she gives them to you as they happen."[21]

Eugene L. Reilly points out an additional advantage of focus group interviewing. He states that "Our own work in traditional focus group inquiry had caused us to respect the ability of consumers (especially in the early stages of ideation), to assess (through reaction) new product ideas, new concepts, new strategies, etc."[22]

---

[19] John M. Hess, "Group Interviewing," in *Scientific Marketing*, eds. Gerald S. Albaum and M. Venkatesan (Glencoe, Ill.: The Free Press, 1971), pp. 231–33.

[20] Ibid.

[21] Myril Axelrod, "Markets Get an Eyeful When Focus Groups Expose Products, Ideas, Images, Ad Copy, etc. to Consumers," *Marketing News* (February 28, 1975), p. 6.

[22] Eugene L. Reilly, "Bringing Together the Needers and Providers: A New Rule for Qualitative Research," in *Attitude Research in Transition*, ed. Russell Haley (American Marketing Association, 1972), p. 108.

Marketing researchers use the focus group technique in many different ways. The greatest uses appear to be:

1. To generate hypotheses that can be further tested quantitatively.
2. To generate information helpful in structuring consumer questionnaires.
3. To provide overall background information on a product category.
4. To get impressions on new product concepts for which there is little information available.
5. To stimulate new ideas about older products.
6. To generate ideas for new creative concepts.
7. To interpret previously obtained quantitative results.

To generate hypotheses. A researcher has indicated that when you purchase focus group interviews, you are not buying consumer research. "You are really buying the head of the person who will do the research—the key question is can the person organize information and help you define problems?" With focus groups you are really looking for definitions of problems rather than for solutions. You have a loosely defined problem area and you want the researcher (moderator) to give you a hand with it. The group sessions give him the guidance to help define the particular problems involved. The researcher and client draw up a discussion guide together, and when the focus groups are done, what you have is a good operational definition of what the problems are and how they can be stated in the form of hypotheses which can be analyzed via quantitative research.

Because of the qualitative nature of the technique, focus groups are most successful when they allow the researcher to design a better subsequent research study using experimental design or other quantitative techniques. In many major consumer research-oriented companies, any time a major quantitative study is to be conducted, focus groups will be used first to help define the issues and generate appropriate hypotheses for testing.

With sample sizes typically smaller than 100, data which are only directional in nature, and numbers which are not projectable, it is important to recognize that the conclusions generated from focus groups are only hypotheses and that quantitative research must be used to confirm the results before they can be used for decision making.

Several examples can be cited to indicate how focus groups have been used to generate hypotheses. A major gasoline producer, concerned about the future growth of sales of gasoline through service stations, wanted to find out what consumers felt about the gasoline station of the future. It wanted to identify possible opportunities for sales of alternative products and services through its retail network, and used 12 focus group sessions in five cities throughout the country to select some possibilities which would be worth investigating in some detail, eventually testing the best ideas with test markets and other quantitative techniques.

Another example of the successful use of focus groups for hypothesis generation concerns research on consumer reactions to bank automated tellers. A series of focus group sessions were conducted with potential users, the results indicating that people found the automatic tellers very impersonal and were afraid of losing their money to the machine. The results of the group meetings indicated that the machines should be personalized, the required secret codes should be easy to remember, and an incentive should be given to the consumer to try out the machine. The hypotheses developed were further tested and confirmed, and a program was created which gave the machine a name and personality all its own. Consumers were allowed to create their own secret code, and free McDonald's hamburgers were given as incentives for using the tellers. The machines now experience the highest usage rate of any automatic tellers in the country, with 30 percent of the bank's customers using them, twice the national average.

A third example concerns the use of focus groups to study why women were rejecting vegetable protein products. The quantitative studies found that women said they did not like the taste, but other research showed women could not taste the difference between these products and equivalent meat products. The focus group sessions found that a possible important reason was that the women did not want to deprive their families of meat.

To structure questionnaires.   Focus groups are used to help researchers learn and understand the consumer language associated with specific product categories or brands. The language consumers use often may not be at all similar to company technical phrases or buzzwords. One researcher offered semimoist dog food, porous-tipped pens, and demand deposits as represenative of corporation words not very relevant to consumers. A major use of focus groups is often to find out the key phrases or words used by consumers in talking about the particular product or service.

As an example, a soft drink company, before doing a major study on brand positioning, needed to define the needs people are seeking to satisfy with soft drinks. They know it is not just thirst ("when you see a kid down four cans of cola, you know it can't just be thirst") or a craving for sweets. Such things as social facilitation and escape are also important needs, and 20 focus groups sessions were conducted throughout the country to identify a complete, all encompassing set of needs which were then incorporated into a questionnaire which was used in a quantitative study.

Focus groups are also used to determine new areas to investigate in a quantitative study. For example, a soft drink company used focus groups to examine consumer reaction to several different package changes, including a new wide mouth bottle. The participants indicated that they were concerned with the loss of carbonation in the new package, something that the researchers had not been sensitive to previously. Without the focus groups, the quantitative research would not have investigated this important aspect of the package change.

It is sometimes hard for the researcher to know how to structure a particular question, and focus groups can be helpful in this regard. For example, in studying frequency of use of a laundry product, should the question be put in terms of number of times per month, or in terms of proportion of wash loads?

To provide overall background information. Focus groups are often used by advertising agencies before making a new business presentation to a potential client. The creative and account personnel are thus able to hear first hand what consumers feel about the product category, the potential client's product, their likes, dislikes, and level of satisfaction with existing products. They are able to hear directly from consumers how they buy and how they use the product, together with their reasons for buying and using it.

In a similar manner, companies considering a merger, acquisition, or product line extension into an unknown category may conduct focus group interviews with consumers and/or distributors to determine the attractiveness of the expansion and factors they should consider in their evaluation. In short, what is the product to consumers, how do consumers talk about the category, and how do they judge and evaluate the product.

The wealth of information generated is of great value in introducing someone to a new product category, and as a result, advertising agencies often will conduct focus group interviews when new account teams are assigned to an account.

To get impressions on new product concepts. One of the most common uses of the focus group technique is the examination of new product concepts to check out ideas at an early stage. As one researcher put it, "So many times the people who work on a project and intellectualize about it almost day and night get so caught up in their reasoning that they no longer can 'see' it clearly. As a result, they can miss the most obvious red flags."[23]

The following examples show how focus groups can be used to help new product personnel understand how their product fits with consumer needs. First, Texize Chemicals, producers of a wide line of

---

[23] Myril Axelrod, "Marketers Get an Eyeful When Focus Groups Expose Products, Ideas, Images, Ad Copy, etc. to Consumers," *Marketing News* (February 28, 1975), p. 6.

household products including Fantastik,® used a series of focus groups for a new product called Glass*Plus.® Quantitative research had shown that housewives were using Fantastik® to clean glass, a use for which the product was not recommended. The company conducted some focus groups to guide their product development effort and found that there appeared to be a need for a product between Fantastik,® a heavy duty cleaner, and glass cleaners like Windex.® Such a product would be one which could clean glass and also be used as a household cleaner. As a result of the initial concept, they were able to develop Glass*Plus,® which after a great deal more consumer research, both qualitative and quantitative, was successfully introduced, advertised as an all-purpose light duty spray cleaner. Texize, which has been very aggressive in the new products area, uses focus groups to make preliminary examinations of as many as four to five new product concepts each month, conducting over a hundred group sessions each year.

The focus group technique can also be used effectively by industrial products companies to examine the impressions of dealers toward a new product concept. Owens-Corning Fiberglas is one company which has conducted research of this type. The company's Transportation Marketing Division conducted a series of focus group interviews with mass merchandise, oil company, and private label tire dealers. The research objective was to see what key benefits and merchandising aids would best help dealers sell glass radials. Previous research had shown that consumers would buy fiber glass radials provided they cost less than steel ones. Owens-Corning marketing personnel watched from behind a one-way mirror as a researcher got groups of 3 to 15 dealers talking about the tire business in general and fiber glass radials in particular. The marketers were very surprised by what they saw as they were convinced that product acceptance would be smooth sailing. But dealers talked about the problems they had when glass bias-belted tires were introduced eight years previously. Even though the bias-belted tires had become big sellers, the dealers were worried that they would have similar initial problems with the glass radials. As a result, the marketing team was able to rework sales themes and promotional copy, with a much higher probability of a successful introduction of the new product.[24]

To stimulate new ideas about older products.   Focus groups can also be used to get consumer impressions of existing products. Such things as consumer satisfaction with what is available now, usage

---

[24] This example is taken from "Owens-Corning Listens to Dealers," *Sales Management* (March 3, 1975), p. 23.

habits, which of several forms or package types are best, possible line extensions, and potential product improvements can all be studied with the focus group technique.

To cite an example, a Texize product, Grease relief,® whose original concept came out of focus groups, was studied using groups to examine some of the above questions. The quantitative research the company had conducted had not indicated any packaging problems, but some focus group participants were found to have a strong underlying distaste for the package. The focus group interviews indicated that the housewives did not like to handle it (pick it up off the shelf). Analysis indicated that the phallic shape of the package was responsible. The company then conducted a series of focus group sessions in Atlanta, a strong Grease relief® market, to determine what type of package might be attractive to the consumers. By the end of each session, respondents had made it clear that a dish detergent-type bottle would be best. In spite of this, participants were sent home with a spray package Texize had developed. Another group session with the individuals was planned for one week later. During these follow-up sessions the participants said the new spray package was a super package and thoughts of a dish detergent package were generally downrated. Because members of the group are sometimes so far removed from reality in these sessions, the results are not necessarily indicative of how the product will do in the store, so the company decided to do further testing. The final result was the successful introduction of a spray package to attract new users and a large economy sized dish detergent-type package without a spray for heavy users. This example shows how qualitative research can be used most effectively, that is, in conjunction with quantitative research, with each type making important contributions. The qualitative focus groups, were able to identify a problem area which quantitative research was unable to uncover. The groups also identified a possible solution, which was then verified and adjusted via a quantitative followup study.

To generate ideas for new creative concepts. In addition to helping orient new account teams and gathering information useful for new business presentations, a great number of focus group interviews are conducted by advertising agencies to obtain ideas for new creative strategies for their clients. Myril Axelrod of Young and Rubicam states that:

Group sessions are, for instance, a most valuable way of letting a copywriter know, hopefully before he has become too emotionally committed to an idea, whether his copy is indeed saying what it is intended to say; whether the consumer is "reading" it in the way he wants her to read it; whether it has meaning to her that is relevant to the way she uses the product and to her needs in the category.[25]

Most large scale quantitative studies are concerned with the majority, the numbers, and not the single interesting idea that might emerge. For example, during one series of group interviews designed to select a slogan for a new service system the moderator threw open the discussion for the participants' own ideas. One was particularly succinct and clear, even in perfect rhyme. The phrase was tested further, and now is on General Electric trucks all over the country.[26] While this type of experience is admittedly rare, the group sessions often will provide the creative personnel with a wealth of ideas to pursue in their creative process.

Another use of focus groups in advertising is to pretest advertising. The Marketing Workshop in Atlanta, and undoubtedly other research firms as well, conduct short focus group sessions as part of their normal process of testing advertising. They hold a 20- to 30-minute focus group interview after they have administered a quantitative questionnaire to evaluate the effectiveness of the commercials. The purpose of the short group sessions is to provide further insights into why the individuals feel the way they do about ads and to get more detailed information on how respondents interpret the ads.

To interpret previously obtained quantitative results. Although not one of the more frequent uses for focus groups, it is one which offers much promise for producing valuable information. This can be demonstrated, using as an example a product of a major soft drink company. The product, a 10 percent fruit juice carbonated soft drink, had an acceptable taste, a price which was a little high, and was oriented toward that segment of the soft drink market which was concerned with nutrition.

In the test market, the soft drink started strong, held up for a while, and then dropped off rapidly. Some 30 percent of the market had tried one of the three falvors in a very short time period. The quantitative research which had been conducted had not predicted the falloff in sales and slow death of the product, and the company wanted to know why this had happened.

The panel data they had been gathering showed that repeat purchase was slow, but because of the six to eight week lag for the panel data, it did not tell them "why" the product did not experience a high degree of repeat purchase. They did some focus group interviews and found that the product had a taste that sated very easily, but was a

---

[25] Myril Axelrod, "Marketers Get an Eyeful," p. 6.

[26] "Coffee Klatch Research: A New Look at Focus Groups," *Ad Day* (March 15, 1975).

taste that people described as a kind of thing that you would "have at a wedding." When asked if that was good or bad, people responded, "It's OK for weddings." In other words, people liked it but thought of it as being only for special occasions. When asked why they were not buying it, they responded, "Because we've already had it." It seemed that one dose every eight weeks or so was enough. If people wanted to get nutrition in what they drank, it turned out they would buy straight juice or vitamins. If they wanted a soft drink, they did not care about the nutrition at all, and they certainly were not willing to pay extra for it.

Disadvantages and misuses

Some of the advantages of the focus group technique also lead to disadvantages and misuses. For example, focus groups apparently are occasionally used merely as evidence to support a manager's preconceived notions, largely because studies using the techniques are usually cheaper to conduct than quantitative studies using surveys or experimental designs.

Focus group interviews are easy to set up, difficult to moderate, and difficult to interpret, and are therefore very easily misused. Often one can find evidence in the interviews to support any position, a reason why many managers use them to support their preconceived ideas. It is obviously very important that extreme care be used in the interpretation, necessitating a highly skilled moderator. This is one of the major disadvantages of the technique, especially since there is an extremely limited number of highly qualified moderators.

In addition, the data are not at all projectable because (a) the sample is so poor with respect to the way in which the individuals are recruited (seldom are they recruited randomly), and (b) because everyone does not have an equal say. The quiet person in the corner may be the heaviest user of your product, yet may not say much during the focus group session.

The environment in which focus groups are conducted leads to other limitations. For example, it is difficult to test pricing in focus groups. People are overly sensitive to pricing questions and the participants are only able to respond to relative type questions such as, "Is this worth more or less than this?" Because of this, store tests must be used for pricing studies. A related disadvantage is that the participants are not in their kitchens or homes during the focus groups, and they are therefore outside the environment in which they would normally use the product. This may cause some difficulty in responding to some of the discussion topics.

Another disadvantage is the difficulty in recruiting participants for focus group sessions. This, of course, depends on how many groups are actually conducted and the difficulty in recruiting participants; for specialized sessions this may run as high as $1,500. Focus groups are thus not a cheap method, although the total investment is smaller than most quantitative research projects.

A final disadvantage of focus groups is that there are many charlatans in the business of conducting focus groups, and the marketer must exercise great care in selecting a research firm to conduct the interviews. Some factors to consider in this regard were discussed in Chapter 5.

DEPTH INTERVIEWS

Description

The depth or unstructured interview is a one-to-one interview, organized to encourage the respondent to talk freely and to express his ideas on the subject being investigated. As with other qualitative research techniques, this method is used to identify consumer attitudes, motives, and behavior, and to measure their relative importance. As Boyd, Westfall, and Stasch indicate, "The objective of these interviews is to get below the respondent's surface reasons for particular marketing decisions and to find the underlying or basic motives."[27]

The depth interview often lasts for an hour or longer. The interviewer usually has an outline of topics to cover, but does not use a set of specific questions. In fact, he merely identifies the general field of interest, intermittently making appropriate comments to encourage the respondent to discuss his views. He stimulates the respondent with occasional questions that may emphasize a particular point, which can serve to lead the respondent in various directions. Although the interviewer is not a vocal participant in the discussion, his role is of great importance. The interviewer must create an environment in which the respondent feels absolutely free to discuss his feelings without fear of disapproval or loss of status.

Advantages and disadvantages of depth interviews

An advantage of the depth interview over focus group interviews is that one can pin down every piece of information to an individual, whereas with group interviews it is sometimes difficult to determine who said what. Another advantage is that under a one-to-one free ex-

---

[27] Harper W. Boyd, Jr., Ralph Westfall, and Stanley F. Stasch, *Marketing Research* 4th ed. (Homewood, Ill.: Richard D. Irwin, Inc., 1977), p. 111.

change environment, the respondent often reveals motives and attitudes which he will not or cannot express in a group setting.

Disadvantages apparently outweight the advantages to such an extent, however, that depth interviewing is seldom used any longer. The problems in implementing it are almost overwhelming. One must have highly trained and skilled interviewers because the validity and reliability of the analysis depends upon the interviewer's evaluation and interpretation of the information which has been gathered. Furthermore, subjective analysis makes it difficult to compare results or to verify them statistically.

There are few adequately qualified interviewers. Therefore, the fee of those who are qualified are usually very high, making this technique among the most costly. Since there is a lack of trained interviewers, there is a need to structure questions and provide greater structure to the interview itself. This defeats the purpose of the depth interview. Open-ended questions are occasionally interspersed within a structured framework to accomplish some of the objectives of the depth interview.

Another disadvantage concerns the length of the interview. It requires from one to two hours to get the kind of information needed from the depth interview. The length coupled with the cost usually means that on any one project the number of interviews is limited. Hence, small samples are the rule rather than the exception, limiting the validity of the findings.

In industrial marketing research, however, where the number of potential respondents is often small, depth interviews are viable and frequently used. To be successful with this type of research, the key respondents must be identified, access to them must be arranged and the interviews must be carefully interpreted to derive a knowledgeable concensus.

Using depth interviewing: Some examples

Even though the disadvantages are great, there are, nevertheless, situations where the depth interview technique can be used beneficially. One example of a recent study using this technique involved research for a medical film production firm. The people interviewed were physicians in training, post graduates at hospitals, hospital administrators, and chief residents. The company wanted to know what the interviewee thought about the films, what the films were used for, the desirability of a library of films and the like. The interview lasted three hours with each doctor, and centered on the whole medical film library program.

One problem with depth interviews is the length of time it takes to code, edit, and interpret the interviews. For this study, 52 interviews were attempted and 48 were completed. It took over two months to arrange the interviews, and then took three months to interpret the tapes. The research firm charged the company $175 per interview and still lost money. They later determined they should have charged $500 per interview. The results of this study indicated that the physicians liked the idea of a medical film library, but actually had very little need to use the films. They felt the usage rate did not appear to justify the high cost of the films, and the company dropped the program as a result of the study.

Another study using depth interviews concerned travel agents' perceptions of travel clubs and airline package travel programs. The questions investigated were: How did the travel agents perceive the various steamship and airline package plans? How did they promote these plans to their customers? How did they decide which ones to promote? and What incentives were needed to encourage travel agents to promote a specific package plan?

The researchers felt it would be extremely difficult to do these interviews in groups because many of the travel agents were competitors and might not reveal the information needed. It was thus felt that much better information would be obtained through individual depth interviews.

The sample was 50 travel agents in Philadelphia and New York. The sample size is quite small, of course, which is one of the limitations of depth interviewing. The depth interviews were very useful in this case, and a number of hypotheses were developed. These were then investigated by a followup study using a quantitative research design.

PROJECTIVE TECHNIQUES

Description

Projective techniques, as used in marketing research to attain information about consumers' attitudes, have been adapted from clinical psychology. While a number of projective techniques are used in psychological research, only a few are common to market research, and they are used primarily because they can be easily administered and evaluated. Marketing researchers most often employ visual stimulus techniques, free expression methods, or role playing techniques. Whether the stimulus is a picture, word, image, or sentence, the aim in each is to provide an environment which encourages the respondent to project his feelings and unconsciously to express them in his response.

Standard structured questionnaires presume that the consumer knows what he thinks, wants, and believes. Therefore, the consumer is able to respond with facts which the researcher can collect and analyze. This is not always the case, however. Projective techniques attempt to gain answers to the "whys" of buying behavior by using indirect psychological testing. The respondent unconsciously projects his feelings, attitudes and opinions about the stimulus into his responses, which provides the basis for the researcher's analysis.

Rather than interpreting research data on the basis of peoples' answers, projective tests change the process by asking people to interpret the actions of others. In so doing, they project their own personality, experiences, outlooks, and thus show something of their real attitudes and motivations. In commenting on responses obtained through projective techniques, Boyd and Westfall state, "The emphasis is on his perception of the material, the meaning he gives to it, the way in which he organizes or manipulates it."[28]

Because projective techniques utilize indirect investigation methods, there are no right or wrong answers, and the respondent is generally unaware of the tests' purposes. Therefore, interviewer-respondent tension is decreased, and there is less approval-seeking bias in the responses.

Projective techniques are sensitive to unconscious or latent aspects of personality. The ambiguity of the stimulus presented evokes a profusion and richness in the responses generated. By permitting multiple responses, the data exhibit multidimensionality and provide further insights into the interrelationships of attitudes, personality and behavior. Projective techniques can thus be especially helpful when approaching buyer behavior from a holistic, or total person, point of view.[29]

Types of projective techniques

Projective techniques naturally vary according to the problem being studied, the environment, and other circumstances surrounding their use. Each of the various techniques is designed so that it will provide an opportunity for the respondent to express freely his opinions and feelings. The stimulus should be interest-arousing and should encourage discussion, yet not disclose the nature of the research project.[30]

Thematic apperception tests. The technique used most often in market research is the Thematic Apperception Test, or TAT. In this

---

[28] Boyd and Westfall, *Marketing Research*, 3d ed. (1972), p. 629.

[29] Garner Lindzey, *Projective Techniques and Cross-Cultural Research* (New York: Appleton-Century-Crofts, 1961), pp. 42–43.

[30] Dietz Leonhard, *The Human Equation in Marketing Research* (New York: American Management Association, Inc., 1967), p. 73.

type of test, a visual stimulus depicting a social situation or series of situations is presented to the respondent. He is asked to explain the situation, tell what might have gone on before and what will occur as a result of the situation.

The assumption is that the respondent's story about the stimulus is based on personal experiences and observations from conscious and unconscious images, even though he is relating a story about the people in the picture. Thus, the pictures serve to encourage projection and delve into important attitudes and motivations.

A series of pictures or even actual demonstration of a product may also be used to provide continuity and more encouragement in developing the story. The pictures themselves give few clues as to positive or negative feeling and expressions. This makes it easier for the respondent to identify with the situation and leaves him free to provide the emotions and feelings as he understands them.

Analysis of TATs involves looking for recurring motives, opinions and attitudes, but single remarks may also provide insights. In addition, the analyst compares the story's content with what could have been said but was left unsaid. He notes expressions of pleasure or displeasure, comments about the product's appearance and use, and family reactions, since each of these may help explain the respondent's attitudes and beliefs about the product.

Role playing. Role playing is another projective technique which can be used in market research. This technique may use either a verbal or visual stimulus which is presented to the respondent. Rather than being asked his own opinion, the respondent is asked to relate the opinions or attitudes of other people—neighbors, friends, or typical members of a group for example. In supplying an answer, it is hoped that the respondent will disclose his or her own preferences, prejudices, and purposes.

In a role-playing situation the interviewer might explain that she is trying to get opinions about her new product, a new brand of soup, for example. When the respondent has been exposed to the product, perhaps he has sampled the soup and examined pictures of the labels showing flavors available, he would then be asked, how do you think your friends or neighbors will react to this product? How will housewives react to its preparation and taste?

Another situation where role playing is often used is to determine company images or perceived personality traits of users of a product. The respondent may be asked to describe the characteristics of the user or to choose words from a list that would best describe the company, the product or the purchaser. For example, role playing might be used to determine what sort of women purchase certain brands of cosmetics.

Cartoon completion. Another projective technique that utilizes visual stimuli is the cartoon completion test. In this instance the respondent is asked to complete a cartoon caption in response to the comment of another cartoon character or an obvious action depicted in the sketch. Cartoon completions are often used to solicit reactions to frustrating situations—the cap does not come off a can, a sales clerk is inattentive or does not have a particular brand, a newly purchased product breaks before one gets it home.

Association techniques. Word association tests ask the individual to say the first word which comes to mind in response to words read by the interviewer. The words selected as stimuli are chosen to reveal motivations about the subject of the research. They are carefully ordered so that the responses become automatic. A variation of this technique asks the respondent to give as many single words as he can in response to the initial stimulus.

Word association tests are analyzed according to the frequency with which a particular response occurs, the amount of hesitation in responding, and by the number of respondents who cannot give any response to a particular word. Hesitation or nonresponse is assumed to indicate comparative emotional involvement.

A word association test of attitudes about breakfast meat products might begin with the following words:

breakfast _____

family _____

warm _____

eggs _____

meat _____

flavor _____

Sentence completion tests extend the word association idea by asking the respondent to finish a sentence. The meaning of the initial phrase is disguised so there is no right or wrong answer. The respondent is free to answer as he pleases, and there is no time limit. Since more thought is involved, the responses are considered to give better results than word associations. Other association tests that are used in market research are those that measure recall of trademarks, symbols, and brand awareness.

Advantages and disadvantages of projective techniques

As a qualitative research method, projective techniques assist the marketing organization in answering subjective questions such as, what is a product, what is a brand, and what is a consumer?[31] Their greatest advantage lies in providing an insight into why buyer behavior occurs as it does, an inference that can be made from looking at the consumer's underlying attitudes and opinions.

As is the case with depth interviews, projective techniques are not being used as much as they once were. This too is related to the disadvantages of the technique.

Disadvantages center around the subjective results and analyses that are required when using projective techniques. Analysis is quite difficult and often is too clinical. It does not tell the marketing manager what he should do. For example, with respect to media, what media should be bought to reach the type of audience identified by the projective technique? Should the brand manager use a coupon or not? The data from projective techniques may not help in answering these questions.

William A. Yoell, a critic of projective techniques, comments that they are misunderstood, misapplied, prescientific, and the results are often misused. He questions whether the phenomenon of projection actually occurs in all cases, and whether the tests in fact measure "personality rather than culture and social awareness."[32] His point has been countered by Robert G. Largen who asserts that Yoell's criticisms can be applied to survey research as well.[33]

Most researchers agree that an effort should be made to discover more valid technologies. In the use of projective techniques, researchers resign themselves to trading statistical validity for quality of information because they create supplementary results rather than substitutes for statistics.[34]

A recent experiment aimed at improving projective techniques by improving their validity and methodology was conducted by Dan H. Robertson and Robert W. Joselyn.[35] In this study, projective techniques were used in conjunction with a more traditional methodology which facilitated quantitative analysis. Robertson and Joselyn conclude that while projective techniques can contribute to understanding consumers' psychological perceptions, the market researcher must be convinced of their methodological validity and reliability before he will make consistent use of them.

---

[31] Herta Herzog, "Behavioral Science Concepts for Analyzing the Consumer," in *Readings in Marketing: The Qualitative and Quantitative Areas,* ed. Philip R. Cateora and Lee Richardson (New York: Appleton-Century-Crofts, 1967), pp. 188–93.

[32] William A. Yoell, "The Fallacy of Projective Techniques," *Journal of Advertising,* vol. 3 (1974), pp. 33–35.

[33] Robert G. Largen, "Critique" to William A. Yoell's article, "The Fallacy of Projective Techniques," *Journal of Advertising,* vol. 3 (1974), pp. 36–37.

[34] Dietz Leonhard, *The Human Equation in Marketing Research.*

[35] Dan H. Robertson and Robert W. Joselyn, "Projective Techniques in Research," *Journal of Advertising Research,* vol. 14 (October 1974) pp. 27–30.

Using projective techniques: Some examples

One of the foremost examples of using projective techniques is Mason Haire's classic study of consumer attitudes about instant coffee. Although survey research indicated that people did not use instant coffee because they disliked the flavor, Haire's projective testing found that instant coffee represented a departure from "homemade" coffee and traditions about caring for one's family. Instant coffee was perceived as being indicative of the housewife's being lazy and a poor wife. Haire's technique involved presenting two shopping lists to housewives and asking them to describe the purchaser. The lists were identical, except that one list included Nescafe Instant Coffee and the other list Maxwell House Coffee. As anticipated, the housewives projected their opinions and concepts of instant coffee into their description of the person using each shopping list.[36]

Several more current examples can be cited. For example, in one study using projective techniques a cartoon was used in which two women, in their backyards separated by a picket fence, were talking. The first said, "I've been using _____ product for some time now." The other woman had a blank cartoon-like balloon over her head. The interviewee was asked by the researchers, "What is this other woman thinking? Do not give us your opinion but what you think others think."

Another technique involved the use of a stock photograph catalog to get pictures of people at different socioeconomic levels. Pictures of "skidrow" residents, street cleaners, janitors, dirty blue collar workers, clean blue collar workers, white collar workers, and professional managers were selected. They were put together in a set of $2'' \times 2''$ photographs. Interviewees were asked which of the people in these photographs were most likely to use an automatic bank teller, to drink a particular brand of beer, and so on. From this, the researcher was able to develop a consumer profile of the product being researched.

Projective techniques have also been used to analyze soft drink consumers. People were asked what animals come to mind when they think of Pepsi (a cheetah, a swanky cat; quick, agile, nonpredatory cats), Coke (lion, elephant, a dog of fine breeding), and RC Cola (mouse or ardvaark). The important findings resulted when the respondents are asked to expound on why they chose the animal they did for the particular brand.

Another example of the use of projective techniques to study soft drinks involved the use of celebrities. People were asked what celebrities came to mind when various soft drink brands were mentioned.

---

[36] Mason Haire, "Projective Techniques in Marketing Research," *Journal of Marketing*, vol. 14 (April 1950), pp. 649–56.

Coca-Cola reminded people of John Wayne and Johnny Carson, the Pepsi reminded them of female celebrities. Again, the follow up questions asking why they chose that celebrity provided important insights.

The reason for using projective techniques in this way is that it is fun for the respondents, and as a result they give the researcher a wealth of information in their answers that would not otherwise be generated. Nevertheless, projective techniques are not used extensively today for many of the reasons mentioned.

OTHER CONSIDERATIONS IN QUALITATIVE RESEARCH

Sampling in qualitative research

Although qualitative research makes some use of probability sampling techniques, the most common technique is judgmental sampling where the respondents are selected according to the judgment of some person knowledgeable in the area being studied or who is involved in the particular project. This sampling technique was discussed in Chapter 6.

Analyzing qualitative data

In addition to its unique psychological measurement techniques, qualitative research is characterized by subjective or nonquantified analysis and interpretation. In the first place, the actual data collected from depth interviewing, projective techniques, and focus group interviews are dependent on the interviewer's subjective observations. Since the opinions and attitudes observed in response and actions are multidimensional and difficult to discern, the evaluation is also difficult. Content analysis of what transpired involves verbal and written responses plus direct observations. There is no completely objective scheme of analysis; instead, interpretation generally relies on the judgment, ability, and experience of the interviewer to glean important responses from the interviews.

Formal content analysis was developed in the 1940s in the field of communications research. It was defined by Berelson as ". . . a research technique for the objective, systematic, and quantitative description of the manifest content of communications."[37] Communications can be taken to mean any linguistic expression and thus applies to the data generated in qualitative research. Most content analysis in

---

[37] Bernard Berelson, *Content Analysis in Communications Research* (Glencoe, Ill.: The Free Press, 1952), p. 18.

qualitative research is informal in nature and lacks extensive structure. This may be desirable in many cases since it avoids any implications of quantitative precision. If this danger can be avoided, however, formal content analysis appears to hold considerable untapped potential.

The specific steps in formal content analysis can be summarized as follows:

1. *Specify needed information.* This is the first step in any type of analysis —qualitative or quantitative.
2. *Map out plans for tabulation.* How will the answers to various questions be categorized? (perhaps favorable toward our product, neutral, or negative) How will each category be coded? (1-favorable, 2-neutral, and 3-negative)
3. *Lay out the skeleton of the outline.* List important variables, how they are to be classified, and how the variables relate to the specific questions and answers. Many types of variables may be considered in content analysis with most relating to the two broad categories, "What is said" and "How it is said." The following list by Berelson illustrates several types of variables that may be usefully employed:
   a. What is said

   Subject matter: What is the communication about?

   Direction: Is the treatment favorable or unfavorable toward the subject?

   Standard: What is the basis (or grounds) on which the classification of direction is made?

   Values: What goals are explicitly or implicitly revealed?

   Methods: What means or actions are employed to realize goals?

   Traits: What characteristics of persons are revealed?

   Actor: What characteristics of persons are revealed?

   Authority: In whose name are statements made?

   Origin: What is the place of origin of the communication?

   Target: To whom is the communication particularly directed?
   b. How it was said

   Form of communication: Is it fiction, news, television, etc.?

   Form of statement: What is the grammatical or syntactical form of the unit of analysis?

   Intensity: How much strength or excitement value does the communication have?

   Device: What is the rhetorical or propagandistic character of the communication?
4. *Fill in categories for each variable.* The systems of categories for each variable should be exhaustive and mutually exclusive. This step involves filling out the skeleton outline with exactly defined categories.
5. *Establish procedure for unitizing the material.* To be recorded on the analysis outline the interview must be broken into units. The most com-

mon unit is the answer to a single question. A communication may also be unitized by words, themes, values, persons, groups, institutions, products, and so forth. The proper unit would depend on the information needed.

6. *Try out the analysis outline and unitizing procedure.* This amounts to a pretest of the analytical design.

7. *Use the analysis outline and interpret the results.*[38]

It is apparent from the above format that highly trained interviewers are needed since they not only record responses but serve as the focal point for analysis of the data. A basic understanding of the research project, the area being studied, plus a thorough background in human behavior is required.

Analysis of qualitative data depends on two inferences, one a part of the underlying psychological theory, and the other inherent in the sampling and research process itself. The initial inference occurs during testing or interviewing. Responses are inferred to be indicative of the respondent's attitudes and opinions. Analysis of the data is, of course, predicated on the validity of this inference. Information resulting from the sample data and subsequent analysis are later presumed to be an insight into the behavior of larger groups of people. Both quantitative and qualitative research utilize this sampling premise. Here again the use of judgmental samples makes questionable any inference from the sample to a larger population. The counter-argument here is that qualitative research does not test hypotheses in search of facts and empirical information; rather it generates hypotheses that can be further tested with quantitative research methods. As such, sample information provides only hints about population behavior, and the sampling inference from qualitative data can either be loosely made, or it may not be required at all.

Limitations of qualitative research

Limitations and ensuing criticisms are inherent in the very nature of qualitative research. The fact that it is often described as nonquantitative, nonobjective and judgmental indicate where its limitations lie. Qualitative research techniques aim at measuring subjective opinions and attitudes, and in order to do so, the methodology involved is also subjective. Questions regarding reliability, that is, would the same results be observed if the research was repeated; and validity, does the technique actually measure what the researcher thinks is being measured, are often raised with respect to qualitative research.

---

[38] This format was derived from Darwin P. Cartwright, "Analysis of Qualitative Material," in *Research Methods in Behavioral Sciences*, ed. Leon Festinger and Daniel Katz (New York: The Dryden Press, 1953), pp. 454–67.

The lack of established norms for use of projective techniques, depth interviews, and focus groups, and the fact that analysis and results are not quantified or readily understood, result in a lack of confidence by many researchers and marketers. Rather than producing numbers and statistics, qualitative research provides hypotheses about behavior, an elusive subject at best.

The interviewer/moderator's role also creates limitations. Because he or she is responsible for gathering relevant data as well as analyzing and interpreting it, the interviewer must be highly trained. The interviewer's role is central in qualitative research, but this may in fact induce a personal bias which is not easily discerned and can only be diminished by using experienced personnel or by checking results with other professional opinions. Such expertise is not only expensive but difficult to locate and acquire.

The samples used in qualitative research are often small and judgmental; this in itself may be viewed as a limitation. Precise inferences cannot be made from such a sample to a larger more diverse population. Since the techniques themselves were designed originally for clinical use, there is also some question about using them effectively in the marketplace.

Each of these limitations has generated criticism of qualitative research, and they are in some sense justified. However, criticism of qualitative research must be evaluated in view of the purpose of this type of research. Qualitative research does not answer quantitative questions relating to population behavior. Instead, it is a systematic exploration that generates well-defined hypotheses, or questions, for further study. Qualitative and quantitative research are most effectively used in conjunction with each other. In view of this role, the limitations described here appear to be at least as acceptable as those inherent in any research methodology.

Trends in qualitative research

Marketing research, like any process, is continually changing to reflect trends in methodologies as well as those in the marketplace. Although qualitative research has suffered at the hands of its critics, the need for qualitative data has long been recognized. More and more marketers are recognizing qualitative research as one means of quickly and effectively analyzing today's ever-changing market and of gaining insights into buyer behavior.

There is a trend toward merging qualitative research with other techniques and approaches. The research cycle has progressed from early qualitative research using small samples, through a quantitative orientation using large samples, to the current situation where qualitative and quantitative are used together with both large and small samples.[39] Qualitative intelligence and quantitative data together can improve research results.

In addition, techniques are being developed so that qualitative data can be quantified and subjected to a more systematic analysis. The recent work of Robertson and Joselyn in improving projective techniques through quantitative methods shows that qualitative research can be made more objective and still provide insights into consumer attitudes and opinions.[40]

While less use is being made of depth interviewing and projective techniques (because extensive training is required and the analysis is expensive and time-consuming), focus groups have become recognized as an effective and efficient way to assess consumer views about a product, service, or institution. Focus groups provide consumer feedback that is necessary to the "marketing approach," and as such they are used as part of many research studies. For example, in the development of advertising campaigns, at least one advertising agency always begins the process by conducting focus group interviews.[41]

In summary, the use of qualitative approaches, particularly in the form of focus groups, is on the upsurge. When coupled with appropriate quantitative procedures, qualitative techniques can be increasingly useful items in the marketer's kit of research tools. Various quantitative procedures and approaches are presented in the following chapter.

SUMMARY

Qualitative approaches to primary data collection are designed to probe the thoughts of a selected group of people for impression, ideas, or language concerning a given product, service, or institution. No hard and fast conclusion should ever be drawn from qualitative data, but important insights can be gained. The basic purpose of qualitative research is to generate hypotheses in the exploratory phase of a research effort. These hypotheses can then be tested through more rigorous quantitative study.

Three qualitative approaches are used in varying degrees in marketing research. These are focus group interviews, depth interviews, and projective techniques with focus groups being used much more

---

[39] Emanuel H. Demby, "From the Qualitative to the Quantitative and Back Again," in *Attitude Research in Transition,* ed. Russell Haley (Chicago: American Marketing Association, 1972), p. 94.

[40] Robertson and Joselyn, "Projective Techniques in Research," pp. 27–30.

[41] David B. McCall, "What Agency Managers Want from Research," *Journal of Advertising Research,* vol. 14 (August 1974), pp. 7–10.

frequently. With the focus group technique a series of groups with 8 to 12 consumers are interviewed by a moderator. The moderator encourages a free flowing discussion of some specified topic. The group discussions are then reviewed for important ideas and concepts which may be translated into relevant, testable hypotheses. With depth interviews the interviewer conducts a series of one-to-one discussions with a sample of respondents. The discussion centers on the general topic of interest but is not structured with specific questions. The interview is free flowing and the quality of data as well as the analysis depends on the skill of the rsearcher. Projective techniques are used to encourage the respondent to reveal his attitudes and opinions in an indirect fashion. He is presented with a stimulus (words or pictures) and asked to describe how some other person would react to this situation. The assumption is that he will "project" his own personal thoughts into his description of how others would react.

Due to their subjective nature and typically small sample sizes the output of qualitative techniques should never be projected to larger populations. This is the job of quantitative research.

DISCUSSION QUESTIONS

1. Define focus group interviews, depth interviews, and projective techniques. Compare and contrast these three qualitative approaches.

2. Discuss the limitations of qualitative approaches in marketing research.

3. What are the legitimate uses of qualitative approaches in marketing research? Describe some research situations where qualitative techniques might be useful and some others where they should not be used.

4. What is the role of the moderator in the focus group interview? Discuss the characteristics which a good moderator should have.

5. Assume that you are doing research on records and tapes for the college market. Develop a discussion guide for a focus group session. Try a short interview with a group of students.

6. Based on the group session conducted in question 5, develop a set of hypotheses for testing with quantitative approaches.

7. Ask a friend to draw a department store and label the departments. Then based on the picture try to develop hypotheses about your friend's attitudes, opinions, and shopping behavior relative to department stores. What problems do you see in extending this approach to a larger study?

SELECTED REFERENCES

Axelrod, Myril D. "Marketing Get an Eyeful When Focus Groups Expose Products, Ideas, Images, Ad Copy, etc. to Consumers." *Marketing News* (28 February 1975), pp. 6–7.

Axelrod, Myril D. "10 Essentials for Good Qualitative Research." *Marketing News* (14 March 1975), pp. 10–11.

Brown, Lyndon O., and Beik, Leland L. *Marketing Research and Analysis,* 4th ed. New York: Ronald Press, 1969.

Goldman, A. E. "The Group Depth Interview." *Journal of Marketing* (July 1962), pp. 61–68; also reprinted in *Marketing Research: Selected Readings.* Ed. Joseph Seibert and Gorden Wills. New York: Penguin Books, 1970, 266–71.

Green, Paul E.; Wind, Yoram; and Jain, Arun K. "Analyzing Free Response Data in Marketing Research." *Journal of Marketing Research* (February 1973), pp. 45–52.

Robertson, Dan H., and Joselyn, Robert W. "Projective Techniques in Research." *Journal of Advertising Research* (October 1974), pp. 27–30.

Stebbins, Robert A. "The Unstructured Research Interview as Incipient Interpersonal Relationship." *Sociology and Social Research* (January 1972), pp. 164–77.

chapter

$202 - 207$

8

Quantitative research in marketing

Quantitative research in marketing is designed to generate concrete information about population characteristics and behaviors; it tends to deal with more objective measurement and analysis than does qualitative research. It differs from qualitative research in that qualitative approaches are concerned with subjective assessments of attitudes, opinions, and behavior. The measurement and analysis in qualitative research is a function of the individual researcher's insights and impressions. In quantitative research, measurement and analysis are detached from the researcher's judgement and are performed in a more formal, rigid fashion. Thus, quantitative research has applications beyond hypothesis formulation. Quantitative approaches can be used to describe larger populations and to test hypotheses.

The basic quantitative research approaches used in marketing research are surveys, experiments, and simulation. These approaches will be discussed in the following sections of this chapter with illustrations provided to aid in understanding both the approach and its value to marketing management.

SURVEY RESEARCH

The nature and use of survey research

The purpose of survey research is primarily inferential. An attempt is typically made to secure data from a sample of a total population and then, after analyzing this data, to infer or project these findings to the large group. The intent may be simply to describe the population (perhaps as a basis for testing hypotheses about states of nature); or alternatively the intent may be to test hypotheses about relationships between variables, to describe these relationships, and to infer that such relationships exist within the total population.

The steps in the typical survey are outlined in Table 8–1. Relative to the requirements of the survey, certain factors should be clear as a basis for developing the survey. First, what information is desired, and what data are needed to produce the information? Second, who has the data that are being sought; what is the population for the survey? Next, how accurate does the survey data need to be in reflecting the true population values? Finally, what time and cost constraints exist in achieving the survey goals?

Table 8–1
Steps in the typical survey

1. Determine the requirements of the survey
2. Determine the sampling plan
   a. Sample size
   b. Sampling technique
3. Prepare a measurement device
   a. Questionnaire or interview form
   b. Instructions to the interviewer
4. Collect the data
5. Analyze the data
   a. Sort and summarize
   b. Develop additional hypotheses
   c. Use statistical procedures and/or models to process the data
6. Develop the final report
   a. Translate the information into managerial terms
   b. Transmit the information to the proper decision maker

The answers to the first three questions allow the design of an optimum survey. Based on these answers, a sample can be planned to secure the desired level of accuracy, appropriate questions constructed to get the needed data from the respondents, and methods of analysis selected to convert the data into useful information. The answer to the last question tells the researcher whether he will have sufficient time and resources to conduct the optimum survey. The time and cost limitations may force modifications which result in a less than perfect, but more practical design.

Based on the requirements of the survey, a sampling plan can be designed and a measurement device constructed to collect the needed data. The principles of sampling and measurement were discussed in

Chapter 6. Designing the sampling plan would typically involve determining the sample size and sampling techniques, while the measurement tasks would concern constructing the questionnaire or interview form and developing instructions to the interviewers. After the data collection procedures have been devised, the field work can be done. Careful control of the field work is needed to minimize the nonresponse and measurement error present in the data. When the data collection is finished, the analysis process starts. The process of analysis and selected basic analytical procedures are discussed in Chapter 9. The first step in the analysis is typically to sort and summarize the data. Then additional hypotheses which were not apparent at the start of the study might be developed. Finally, the data are processed using appropriate statistical procedures and/or models to extract the desired information. The final step is to develop a report for management use which would translate the information into managerial terms and transmit it to the proper decision makers.

It can be seen from this description that typical survey research is a relatively straightforward application of the research process. The specific techniques vary greatly from survey to survey, but the basic intent is the same—to gain insights concerning some defined population.

Illustrative applications of survey research

Survey research can be used to produce many different types of information of value in managerial decision making. This information may relate to demographics, psychographics, life styles, behaviors, or any number of other variables. In order to illustrate the structure and potential value of surveys, two studies will be presented. The first deals with attitudes and the second with life styles.

An attitudinal survey. A large bank in a metropolitan area was considering the possibility of using a nondiscrimination theme in a new promotion campaign directed at the female market. Before undertaking this type of campaign, however, management wanted to be sure that a significant segment of the female population actually had a concern for nondiscrimination. A study was thus proposed to answer two important questions: (1) Do women feel that they are being discriminated against and (2) if so, can the bank use nondiscrimination as an effective marketing strategy?

Based on these questions, two general hypotheses were developed: (1) A female nondiscrimination segment exists and can be identified from attitudinal data; (2) This segment's attitudes are related to selected profile variables. If these hypotheses were supported by research, a segment profile could be developed.

To test the hypotheses, an area sample of 600 adult females was selected. Three hundred and ten usable responses were obtained. The questionnaire for the survey contained several questions including five statements dealing directly with bank discrimination against women. (See the Discussion Questions at the end of Chapter 6.) The respondents were asked to strongly agree, agree, remain neutral, disagree or strongly disagree with each statement. These statements were:

1. Banks presently serve the needs of female customers effectively.
2. Most banks apply the same rules to both men and women in granting loans.
3. Most banks discriminate against women in offering services.
4. If I found a bank that did not discriminate against women, I would switch my account to that bank.
5. I would drive across town to do business with a bank that did not discriminate against women.

Ten questions were also asked as a basis for profiling any nondiscrimination segment. These included marital status, years married, number of children, age, bank credit card ownership (in the woman's own name), occupation, hours per week employed outside the home, education, percentage of household income earned, and household income. The data were analyzed using cross-classification and chi-square. (These procedures are explained in Chapter 9.)

Table 8–2 summarizes the responses to the attitudinal questions. These responses indicate a significant nondiscrimination segment among the female population. In order to determine the nature of this nondiscrimination segment, the responses to each attitudinal question were cross-classified with each of the ten profile variables and a chi-square statistic computed. This analysis revealed that nondiscrimination attitudes were significantly related to several characteristics, allowing the development of the profile shown in Table 8–3. This is a profile of what could be described as an economically independent woman.

The results of the survey suggested that a nondiscrimination segment did exist which could be identified from attitudinal data. Also, the attitudes toward discrimination could be related to selected profile variables. From these results, the bank management concluded that a nondiscrimination policy and promotional campaign were viable marketing strategies. The survey also provided a basis (in the form of a segment profile) for selecting media to communicate with this segment.

Life style research. Life style research and psychographics (measuring psychological traits) is perhaps the fastest growing new

Table 8–2
Attitudes toward bank discrimination against females in offering services

Statement	Strongly agree	Agree	Neutral	Disagree	Strongly disagree	N
Banks presently serve the needs of female customers effectively.	7%	36%	26%	21%	10%	305
Most banks apply the same rules to both men and women in granting loans.	2	10	21	43	24	305
Most banks discriminate against women in offering services	11	27	33	23	6	300
If I found a bank that did not discriminate against women, I would switch my account to that bank.	9	21	32	27	11	306
I would drive across town to do business with a bank that did did not discriminate against women.	4	16	19	40	21	307

Source: Danny N. Bellenger and Jac L. Goldstrucker, "Discrimination against Women: An Opportunity for Bank Marketing," *Journal of Bank Research* (Summer 1975), p. 157.

trend in market analysis. The reason is that social and market researchers know that consumer behavior is rapidly changing, and the old demographic measures—income, education, occupation, sex, age, and so forth—fall short of explaining these changes. A series of studies have shown that consumer behavior is related much more closely to life style than to demographics and can thus be understood much better in these terms. An understanding of consumer behavior is basic to developing products and services that meet customer needs, and successfully marketing those products and services.

Life style research is generally aimed at measuring three groups of factors: (1) activities, (2) interests, and (3) opinions. This is typically

Table 8–3
A profile of the nondiscrimination segment of the female bank market

Characteristics	Profile
Marital status	Single or divorced
Age	Young (19–34)
Bank credit card ownership	Has a bank credit card in her own mane
Occupation	Employed outside the home in a professional, technical or medical job
Percent of household income earned	Earns a large percent of the household income

Source: Danny N. Bellenger and Jac L. Goldstucker, "Discrimination against Women: An Opportunity for Bank Marketing," *Journal of Bank Research* (Summer 1975), p. 159.

Figure 8–1
Life-style segments developed through survey research

Attitude Group

Activity Group

Traditional Values
(44% of Toronto adults subscribe to these)

Those who believe in one of these values are more apt than others to subscribe to the rest of them. . .

I think the law should come down hard and control all drug traffic.

I believe God is the foundation of religion.

I believe a person should have sexual relations only with the married spouse.

I think work is important for a constructive life.

I believe our metro government is completely honest.

I believe our provincial government is completely honest.

I believe acquiring money is a useful social goal.

I trust the news reporting in our Toronto daily papers.

In general, traditional value people are satisfied with mass media, their church, their housing and their family . . .

> . .but to some extent they feel things are changing too fast these days.

On the Water
(28% participate actively)

Water skiing
Power boating
Snowmobiling
Sailing
Fishing

House & Garden
(40% participate actively)

Home decorating
Gardening
Home projects
Picnicing
Bar BQ
Bird watching
Community & social service projects

Life is Good
(43% of Toronto adults think Positively that it is)

Those who say my life is full rather than empty, also find:

My life is friendly.

My life is interesting.

The quality of my life — the things I do, the kind of life I lead — has gotten better in the past 5 years.

My family's income is better than it was 5 years ago, and so is my job and my housing.

I'm satisfied with what's happening in my own family.

Games
(35% participate actively)

Bowling
Bingo
Checkers

Dissatisfaction with Government
(Some degree of dissatisfaction is expressed by 36% of Toronto adults)

Those who are dissatisfied with provincial government feel more than others that:

I'm dissatisfied with metropolitan government.

I'm dissatisfied with federal government.

I don't think metro government is honest.

I don't think provincial government is honest.

Young at Heart
(32% participate actively)

Tennis
Biking
Ping pong
Chess
Hiking
Playing music

Dissatisfaction with mass media
(32% of Toronto adults are dissatisfied to some extent with their media)

Those who are dissatisfied with local schools also tend to feel:

I'm dissatisfied with television.

I'm dissatisfied with radio.

I'm dissatisfied with newspapers in this area.

Figure 8–1 *(continued)*

Spectator Group

Sports Fan

(36% are avid watchers)

Watch professional football
Watch baseball
Watch amateur football
Watch professional hockey
Watch basketball
Watch amateur hockey
Watch boxing
Watch lacrosse
Watch curling
Watch soccer
Watch tennis
Watch sportscar racing
Watch stock car racing
Watch trotting races

Culture

(32% are enthusiasts)

Listen to symphony
Watch ballet
Watch opera
Watch theatre
Watch tennis
And like/read
the *Globe & Mail*

Kitsch

(36% share this popular taste)

Watch rodeo
Watch circus
Watch horseshows
Watch ice shows
Listen to folk
country-western concerts

Young Entertainment

(35% participate)

Listen to rock music
Attend movies (not on TV)
Listen to jazz
Like/read the *Sun*

Interest Group

History/Books/Politics

(Shared by 33%)

History
Book collecting
Antiques
Museums
Poetry
Fine art
Politics
Auctions
Military history
Artcrafts

Fashion/Needlework

(Shared by 35%)

Fashion
Needlecrafts
Artcrafts

Gourmet

(Shared by 39%)

Drinking fine wines
Eating fine cheeses

Conservation

(Shared by 34%)

Conservation of land
Conservation of animals

Adapted from survey by Fredrick P. Currier, Barbara Bryant, and Andrew Morrison, in "Attitude and tivity Life-Styles Make New Way to Segment Marketing," *Market Opinion Research News* (Detroit, Mich.: arket Opinion Research, 1974), pp. 4–6.

done by providing the respondent with an extensive list from each group and asking for a reaction to each in terms of level of interest, participation, agreement, or whatever is appropriate. Items that tend to be strongly related based on the responses are then grouped together by a statistical procedure known as *factor analysis*. Each respondent is then given a summary score on each factor. These factors are the life-style variables, and people who behave in different ways usually have significantly different scores on at least some life-style variables. This allows differing consumer behavior patterns to be profiled and understood. Such an understanding allows the marketer to develop marketing strategies that are more in tune with the market and are thus more successful.

An example of life-style analysis may be helpful in seeing its value as well as illustrating the survey nature of such research.[1] A large metropolitan newspaper was interested in gaining a fuller understanding of its market and of various behaviors related to newpaper readership within its public. To do this a life-style survey was conducted with a sample of 1,100 city residents. The 16 life-style factors developed from the survey and factor analysis are shown in Figure 8–1. Each of the 1,100 respondents was given a score on each factor which was the sum of the responses on the questions included in the factor. These 16 factors then provided 16 life-style variables to be used in describing and understanding the market and its behavior.

Individuals can fall into more than 1 of the 16 groups—in fact, every individual has a score on each of the 16 variables though it may range from a high positive score through the neutral range down to a negative score. Whereas the psychographic researchers have divided their market segments into mutually exclusive groups (given such names as Forerunners, New Conformists, Retreaters, or Drudges, Achievers, and High Speeders), here a respondent can be high on the "Life is Good" variable and at the same time, high on "Home and Garden"; a high participant in "Kitsch" spectator activities may fall into a neutral or negative (nonparticipant) range on other activities.

The analysis of the data produced many interesting insights. Demographically, the "Traditional Value" group tends to be older people, parents, from blue collar households. "The Life is Good" group is the upward mobiles—those with at least some university education, with professional, managerial, and white collar jobs, or students who expect to hold such jobs some day. They were younger and many have reached upper income levels while still under 45.

[1] The description of this survey by Frederick P. Currier, Barbara Bryant, and Andrew Morrison is adapted from "Attitude and Activity Life Styles Make New Way to Segment Marketing," *Market Opinion Research News* (Detroit, Mich.: Market Opinion Research, 1974), pp. 4–6.

The "On the Water" and "Young at Heart" groups at first appear similar—young, single, mid-to-upper income and more male than female. However, on closer inspection they have some differences. Those who like biking, hiking, tennis and chess (the "Young at Heart") were more apt to be university graduates or have some college education. Those who liked boating and snowmobiling were more blue collar.

The 16 groups varied greatly by market segments, whether one looks at product market segments or demographic segments of a life cycle type. As examples, when the 18–35 year old market segment was looked at first for singles and then for married, proportions in the 16 groups change dramatically. Among the singles, only 18 percent subscribe to "Traditional Values" and only 15 percent are in the "House and Garden" group. However, 65 percent participate in "Young at Heart" (tennis, hiking, etc.) and 70 percent in "Young Entertainment" (rock and jazz music, attending movies). Once married, this same age group shifted—more into "Traditional Values" (36 percent), highest of all life-cycle groups on "Life is Good" (56 percent), 45 percent enjoyed "House and Garden," while "Young at Heart" and "Young Entertainment" dropped 40 percent. Obviously, the fact of marriage—according to comparisons on these group measures—demonstrates a big shift in allocation of discretionary income.

Since this study was sponsored by a newspaper, the groups were looked at by newspaper readership. Here again the 16 variables proved distinctive measures. Readers of the three newspapers in the market showed distinctively different profiles on the 16 variables. With this information marketing managers for the newspaper could develop strategies to expand their readership by appealing to different life-style types.

EXPERIMENTAL RESEARCH

The experimental approach to marketing research involves data collection and analysis in a more controlled setting than is the case with survey research. The researcher exercises control over the test variable and often over various other aspects of the research environment. The test variable, which is generally the primary independent variable in the study, is called a treatment. Only aspects of the research environment which may alter the results of the experiment are called extraneous variables. These are secondary independent variables which the researcher may attempt to control in such a way as to remove their impact or at least separate it from the impact of the primary independent variable. The treatment is injected into the experimental setting, and the resulting movements of some other variable are observed. This variable is the dependent variable in the research. The result of the treatment is observed with respect to its impact on specified test units. These test units are the entities which respond to the experiment, i.e., households, firms, individuals, or whatever the subjects of the experiment happen to be.

The basic concept and components of an experiment are summarized in Figure 8–2. The concept is to manipulate some variable or variables in a controlled environment and observe the effect on some other variable or variables. This allows the researcher to establish cause-effect relationships, assuming the research has been properly conceptualized and controlled. The components of an experiment can be summarized as follows:

1. Treatment; primary independent variable in the research.
2. Observations; dependent variable.
3. Extraneous variables; secondary independent variables.
4. Test units; entities which respond to the treatments.
5. Analysis; measurement of the relationships between variables in the study.

Figure 8–2
Basic concept and components of an experiment

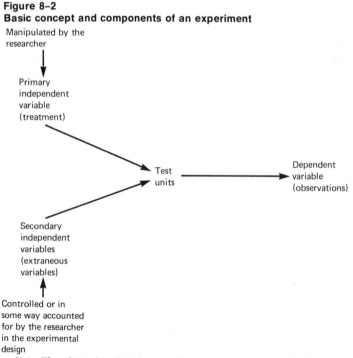

Note: The relationships between variables are determined either by observing the magnitude differences or by analysis of variance.

The framework or structure of the experiment is called the experimental design. These designs may be either formal or informal. Banks explained the purpose of experimental designs as follows: "the goal of experimental design is the confidence that it gives the researcher that his experimental treatment is the cause of the effect he measures."[2] The design adds an element of control which can increase the validity of the findings. A brief discussion of alternative experimental designs is presented in the following section.

It should also be noted that experiments can be classified as either laboratory or field. Actually, most experiments are somewhere between these two extremes. The term field experiment implies that the experimental environment is natural or realistic. This would provide the experiment with external validity. The absence of controls would, however, damage the internal validity of the research. As more controls are added to increase internal validity, we move to an increasingly artificial environment and sacrifice some external validity. By adding such controls, the experiment becomes more laboratory in nature. The researcher should attempt to reach an acceptable balance which provides reasonable control while maintaining the "real world" applicability of the results.

Analysis of variance is the statistical procedure typically used to process the data resulting from formal experimental designs. This type of analysis is performed by a technique, or actually a group of techniques, used to measure the effects of the treatment on the dependent variable. It results in one or more F-ratios which can be evaluated to see if the treatment has a statistically significant impact on the dependent variable. Analysis of variance will be discussed in more detail in Chapter 9. Informal designs use a less sophisticated form of analysis based on differences in magnitudes.

Experimental designs

Informal designs.   Informal experimental designs include a wide range of structures with the *before-and-after without control, after-only with control,* and *before-and-after with control* being three of the more commonly used.

Before-and-after without control design.   In this design a single test group or area is selected. The dependent variable is measured before the introduction of the treatment, the treatment is then introduced and the dependent variable is measured again after the treatment has been introduced. The effect of the treatment is determined

---

[2] Seymour Banks, "Designing Marketing Research to Increase Validity," *Journal of Marketing* (October 1964), pp. 32–40.

by subtracting the original value of the dependent variable from the value after introduction of the treatment.

For example, a firm selling popcorn might be interested in the impact on sales on a package change. To determine the effect of the new package, a test city might be selected. The sales level for a specified time period before introduction of the new package would be determined. The new package would then be introduced into the market and the sales level measured for a comparable time period after the change. The impact of the new package would be the sales with the new package minus the sales with the old package.

Test area: Sales with old package (A) $\xrightarrow{\text{Treatment introduced}}$ Sales with new package (B)

Treatment effect = B − A

The major problem with this design is that considerable extraneous variations can be introduced with the passage of time. This time induced variation is not controlled in the before-and-after without control design.

After-only with control design. With this design two groups or areas are selected; a test area and a control area. The treatment is introduced into the test area but not the control area. The dependent variable is then measured in both areas at the same time. Data can thus be collected without the problems introduced with passage of time. The impact of the treatment is evaluated by subtracting the value of the dependent variable in the control area from its value in the test area.

For the popcorn firm to use this design in evaluating their package change, two cities could be selected—a test city and a control city. The new package would be introduced in the test city while the old package was retained in the control city. Sales would then be measured in both cities for the same time period. The impact of the new package can be determined by subtracting the sales in the control city from the sales in the test city.

Test area: $\xrightarrow{\text{Treatment introduced}}$ Sales with new package (B)

Control area: Sales with old package (D)

Treatment effect = B − D

The assumption here is that the two cities are identical with respect to their behavior toward popcorn. To the extent that this assumption is not true, extraneous variation is introduced.

Before-and-after with control design.   This design helps to avoid extraneous variation resulting both from the passage of time and from the noncomparability of the test and control areas. With it, two groups or areas are selected; one test area and one control area. The dependent variable is measured in both the test and control areas for an identical time period prior to the introduction of the treatment. The treatment is then interjected into the test area but not the control area and the dependent variable is measured in both for an identical time period after the introduction of the treatment. The impact of the treatment is determined by subtracting the change in the dependent variable in the control area from the change in the dependent variable in the test area.

With this design the popcorn firm might select two cities; a test city and a control city. Sales would be measured in both for some time period with the old package, then the new package would be introduced into the test city. After the introduction, sales would be measured in the control city with the old package and in the test city with the new package. The impact of the new package could be ascertained by subtracting the change in sales in the control city from the change in sales in the test city.

		Treatment introduced	
Test area:	Sales with old package (A)	$\longrightarrow$	Sales with new package (B)
Control area:	Sales with old package (C)		Sales with old package (D)

$$\text{Treatment effect} = (B - A) - (D - C)$$

Where various constraints do not interfere with its use, this would be the preferred informal design. At times, however, due to the lack of historical data, time, or a comparable control area, one of the other informal designs must be selected.

Formal designs.   The formal experimental designs offer more control and a more precise statistical procedure for analysis.[3] Again, a wide variety of formal experimental designs are available. Four which are representative of this group and which have found some application in marketing research are: the *completely randomized design,* the *randomized block design,* the *latin square design,* and the *factorial design.*

Completely randomized design.   With this design the treatments are assigned to test groups or areas on a completely random basis. The

---

[3] For an excellent concise discussion of experimentation in Marketing, see Keith K. Cox and Ben M. Enis, *Experimentation for Marketing Decisions* (Scranton, Penn.: International Textbook Company, 1969).

assumption is that extraneous variation is randomly distributed among the test areas and thus exerts a relatively equal effect on each test area. Therefore, extraneous variables need not be controlled. After the test areas are selected the treatments are randomly assigned to the test areas. The dependent variable is then measured in each test area for a series of time periods or other replications. The result is a matrix of measurements with the test areas on one axis and the replications on the other. This matrix can then be subjected to analysis of variance procedures to determine whether the treatment is significantly related to the dependent variable.

Suppose that a national magazine wishes to determine the impact of three "introductory offer" prices ($5 for the first year, $7 for the first year and $9 for the first year) on the volume of new subscriptions. The company might select three cities and try the alternative prices in the three different cities for four months. The four months would represent different replications. The volume of new subscriptions would be measured in each city for each month and the resulting matrix subjected to analysis of variance.

Month \ City	A	B	C
1	$7 New subscriptions	$9 New sub.	$5 New sub.
2	$7 New sub.	$9 New sub.	$5 New sub.
3	$7 New sub.	$9 New sub.	$5 New sub.
4	$7 New sub.	$9 New sub.	$5 New sub.

The major problem with this design is finding test areas that are identical so that extraneous variables can be assumed to have a relatively equal impact in each test area. When important extraneous variables are present, other designs should be used.

Randomized block designs. This design allows the researcher to isolate and control one extraneous variable. The impact of this variable can be separated and statistically measured.

Suppose that the magazine company feels that the cities selected to test the alternative subscription prices may affect the volume of new subscriptions without regard to the prices. The city would thus be an extraneous variable. To isolate and control the variations caused by the different cities, each price can be assigned to some subdivision within each city. Perhaps the company has been using direct mail, in-store displays, and salesmen to secure subscriptions. In this case a different price could be used with each of the different promotion methods. This would allow all three prices to be tested in each city. New subscription volumes would be placed in a matrix with the cities on one axis and the alternative prices on the other. Each cell in the matrix would represent a different promotional method and would contain the new subscriptions resulting from a specific price, city, and promotional method combination. The analysis of variance procedure appropriate for this design yields two F-ratios; one which can be tested to determine the statistical relationship between price and new subscriptions and one which can be used to determine the relationship between city and new subscriptions. An obvious flaw with the experiment as presented is that new subscriptions may vary for the different promotional methods, without regard to price or city. Promotional method is thus a second extraneous variable.

City \ Price	$5	$7	$9
A	Direct mail New sub.	Display New sub.	Salesmen New sub.
B	Direct mail New sub.	Salesmen New sub.	Display New sub.
C	Salesmen New sub.	Direct mail New sub.	Display New sub.

Latin square design. This design can isolate and statistically account for the variation caused by two extraneous variables. Thus, with this design the magazine company could statistically control the impact of both city and distribution method on the volume of new subscriptions. In this case each treatment (price) would be assigned to each promotional method and to each city. Each promotional method would also be used in each city. This means that the same number of cities and promotional methods must be used in the design. To accumulate the data a matrix is formed with the cities on one axis and the promotional methods on the other. The treatments are then assigned so that each treatment appears in each city and with each promotional method once and only once. The cells in the matrix again contain the volumes of new subscriptions and an analysis of variance procedure can be used to evaluate the impact of the prices, cities and promotional methods on new subscriptions.

The three formal designs discussed to this point all assume that the independent variables interact with the dependent variable, but not

City Promo- tional method	A	B	C
Direct mail	$5 New sub.	$7 New sub.	$9 New sub.
Salesmen	$9 New sub.	$5 New sub.	$7 New sub.
Display	$7 New sub.	$9 New sub.	$5 New sub.

with each other. A fourth design is used particularly to investigate interaction between independent variables.

Factorial designs. This group of designs can be used to determine whether two or more treatments, when used together, produce an impact on the dependent variable which is significantly different from their aggregated impacts when used separately. Suppose that the magazine company is considering two possible actions to increase new subscriptions: a reduction in price from $9 per year to $7 per year for the first year and the gift of a cookbook with the first year's subscription. They feel that these two actions may interact to produce a significantly increased impact and wish to test this hypothesis. To do so, each possible combination of treatment may be tested in selected test areas for a certain number of time periods. In this case, the four combinations ($9 with no cookbook, $7 with no cookbook, $9 with a cookbook, and $7 with a cookbook) could be assigned to four separate cities. The same assumption about extraneous variation is required as in the case of a completely randomized design. Various other versions of the factorial design are available, however, which can account for extraneous variables. With the magazine example, the new subscriptions would be measured in the four cities for a series of replications (perhaps months). The results could then be subjected to a form of analysis of variance which produces three F-ratios; one for each treatment and one for the interaction effect.

Treatments Replications	$9 with no cookbook	$7 with no cookbook	$9 with a cookbook	$7 with a cookbook
1	New sub.	New sub.	New sub.	New sub.
2	New sub.	New sub.	New sub.	New sub.
3	New sub.	New sub.	New sub.	New sub.
4	New sub.	New sub.	New sub.	New sub.

A comparison of alternative designs. Experimentation is differentiated from other research approaches in that it is the only technique that separates cause-effect from mere correlation. That is, the experimental design insures that the computed statistics can be read as depicting causal relationships if the experiment has been properly controlled. Relationships can be identified as cause-effect since one variable (a treatment) was manipulated and the resulting effect measured. The extent of control over the treatments and the environment is the key facet of the experimental approach.

Within this general framework, however, conditions vary and these variations affect the proper selection of design for a given task. In general, the complexity (and thus cost) increases as one moves through the series of designs just described with *the before-and-after without control* being the least complex and *the factorial designs* the most complex. All of the formal designs allow the researcher to measure the experimental error in quantitative fashion. All of the designs discussed, except *the before-and-after without control*, allow the researcher to control for variation over time. The number of variables statistically controlled varies from design to design: with the informal designs none are controlled, with *the completely randomized* only the treatment, with *the randomized blocks* the treatment plus one extraneous variable, with *the latin square* the treatment plus two extraneous variables, and with *the factorial designs* it depends on the exact design selected. Only *the factorial designs* allow the researcher to test for interaction effects. The specific research purpose along with technical and cost considerations should determine whether the experimental approach is desirable and if so, which design is best.

An illustration of experimental research

An example may prove helpful in understanding the concept and value of experimental research. The management of a regional supermarket chain was considering the use of multiple-unit pricing for a specific product in their stores. Before committing the time and money required to convert to multiple-unit pricing on the item, they wanted to feel confident that this approach would increase sales; thus, a decision was made to test consumer reactions to the new policy.

The research staff felt that the impact of the new policy might vary according to (1) the price multiple used, (2) the specific store [since the demographics of their trading areas were not uniform], and (3) the week when the test was conducted. To determine the impact of the multiple-unit pricing concept on sales, an experiment was designed. The standard price for the item was 40¢/unit. Different price multiples formed the treatments for the experiment: $T_1 = 2/79¢$, $T_2 = 3/\$1.19$, $T_3 = 4/\$1.59$, $T_4 = 5/\$1.99$, and $T_5 = 6/\$2.39$. The store and the weeks of the test were extraneous variables in the research. The dependent variable was the percentage change in sales from the average sales of the product in that store. The average was derived from historical records. To test the impact of the treatment on the dependent variable given the two extraneous variables, a *latin square design* was selected. Five stores were chosen which represented the different trading areas of the chain. Each treatment was placed in each store for one week, and the percentage change in sales from the norm measured. The experimental design and the resulting change in sales are shown below:

Week / Store	1	2	3	4	5
A	T_5 −18	T_1 +23	T_2 +2	T_3 +5	T_4 −8
B	T_1 +12	T_2 −3	T_3 −6	T_4 −14	T_5 −22
C	T_2 +6	T_3 +2	T_4 −5	T_5 −12	T_1 +18
D	T_3 −3	T_4 −18	T_5 −24	T_1 +11	T_2 +1
E	T_4 −22	T_5 −26	T_1 +43	T_2 +1	T_3 −10

An analysis of variance indicated that one of the treatments is significantly better than the others relative to its impact on sales. The 2 for 79¢ option showed by far the best results. Based on these findings a decision was made to adopt the new multiple-unit pricing policy at the 2 for 79¢ level in order to move existing inventories of the item. This decision was, of course, monitored over time to determine its longer range impact.

SIMULATION IN MARKETING

The basic concept of simulation

The simulation of marketing systems has evolved as one of the most interesting and potentially powerful tools available for analyzing marketing problems. Through simulation techniques the marketing analyst has the means for observation and experimentation which have long been available only to the physical scientist.

Building and running a simulation model permits observation of the dynamic behavior of a system, or part of a system, under controlled conditions. Experiments can be constructed to test hypotheses concerning the system under study. Simulation provides a means for analyzing marketing problems that otherwise could not be studied due to complexity, lack of control and expense.

As the term is used in business and social science applications, *simulation* refers to "the operation of a numerical model that represents the structure of a dynamic process. Given the values of initial conditions, parameters and exogenous variables, a simulation is run to represent the behavior of the process over time."[4] Simulation then, seeks to duplicate the important operating characteristics of a system over a period of time. Because of the size, complexity and noncontrollability of most marketing systems, simulation techniques have potentially wide and varied uses in the field.

In a thorough and well-documented paper, Kotler and Schulz[5] summarized the significant work in simulation modeling in marketing prior to 1970. They divide this work into three basic areas: computer models of the behavior of marketing system components, computer models of the effect of different marketing instruments on demand, and human-machine interactive marketing simulation (marketing games).[6]

Marketing system simulations are designed to reproduce the behavior of distributors, customers, and competitors. Marketing-instrument simulation models have been constructed to describe the effects on demand created by price, advertising, personal selling, new product development, and marketing research. The third major area of marketing simulation work is in human-machine interactive models or marketing games. These models do not attempt to imitate the actual decision behavior of marketing executives, but rather to allow "players" to take a role in the outcome of marketing results. More recent simulation research has been in the areas of constructing models of consumer behavior,[7] scenario building for short- and long-range marketing planning,[8] and in the simulation of entire markets.[9]

[4] Robert C. Meir, William T. Newell and Harold L. Dazier, *Simulation in Business and Economics* (Englewood Cliffs, N.J.: Prentice-Hall, 1969), p. 1.

[5] Phillip Kotler and Ronald L. Schulz, "Marketing Simulation: Review and Prospects," *Journal of Business*, (July 1970), pp. 237–95.

[6] Ibid., p. 239.

[7] Victor J. Cook and Jerome D. Herniter, "Nomad or How Consumers Behave," *Sloan Management Review*, (Spring 1971), pp. 77–97.

[8] Frank Schulz, "A Practical Model for Short- and Long-Range Planning," *Management Adviser*, (March–April 1973), pp. 17–26.

[9] M. R. Lavington, "A Practical Microsimulation Model for Consumer Marketing," *Operation Research Quarterly*, (1970), pp. 25–45.

Lipson, Darling, and Reynolds pointed out the existence of an "interface gap—the lack of symbolic understanding that exists between the executive and information specialist."[10] This interface gap is particularly wide between marketing managers and marketing simulation-model builders. In order to build a realistic and useful model representing a marketing system, the model builder must have the financial support and personal commitment of the decision makers within the marketing system.

It is in the area of applied simulation models that past marketing simulation research has been most lacking. A case study illustrating the development of a simulation model should be helpful in understanding the construction, use, and potential value of simulation models in marketing.

An illustration of simulation

When it was announced that a new subway system was to be constructed within the metropolitan area, a large department store became concerned about the system's impact on sales.[11] The system was to be built using the "cut and cover" method. Construction involved the partial or total closing of three streets adjacent to the store. In addition, one "feeder" street was to be made one-way.

In an attempt to assess the effects of subway construction on traffic flows and sales levels for their store, management requested that a model simulating the construction impact be developed. The model is part of a long-range planning strategy for the store, which also looked at the expected sales levels and the customer-mix after the construction is completed and new buildings have been erected near the store.

The conceptualization stage.   Preliminary work on the model was a difficult task. First, it was discovered that almost a total vacuum of usable information existed. In initial efforts at information gathering, several sources were consulted; however, no data was available on traffic flows and sales patterns from similar stores in other locations which had undergone major construction.

Next the administrators of the local and other subway systems were contacted. They could supply only aggregate information on retail sales drop-off during construction, such as a 10–20 percent figure. The

---

[10] Harry A. Lipson, John R. Darling, and Fred D. Reynolds, "A Two-Phase Interaction Process for Marketing Model Construction," *MSU Business Topics*, (Autumn 1970), p. 34.

[11] Illustration adapted from Elizabeth C. Hirschman, Danny N. Bellenger and Dan H. Robertson, "An Application of Simulation in Retail Management," *Simulation* (January 1977), pp. 185–88.

great majority of studies carried out by these agencies on the effects of construction dealt with "environmental impact" and not with retail sales.

Since the road to developing an "analogous model" was effectively blocked due to the nonexistence of a prior model, the "logical model" route was chosen. It was decided to "think through" those factors which would logically affect sales levels during the construction period. These factors would then be measured, if possible, and built into a simulation model.

The development stage.   After a period of consultation with both store officials and subway systems personnel, several salient factors were distilled for inclusion in the model. These factors include:

1. The location and duration of each phase of construction around the store.
2. The current traffic entering the store, broken down by each of the store entrances.
3. The proportion of sales to traffic for each door; how many of the people who came in the door bought something.
4. The average dollar sales per transaction for each door.
5. The proportion of planned versus impulse purchases for each door. It was felt that impulse sales drop off more rapidly than planned sales during periods of inconvenience.
6. Seasonal adjustment factors for both sales and transactions. and most importantly,
7. Estimates as to the relative amount of drop-off in traffic during each phase of construction.

Since it is vital to the validity of any simulation that the area of subjective "unknowns" be made as small as possible, an effort was made to secure accurate data on each factor.

Factor one: The store's planning department, working with subway officials, developed an outline of each proposed construction phase relevant to the store, and attempted to assess the duration and disruptive effects of each phase. Estimates as to maximum, minimum, and expected durations were stated for each construction phase, and the phases were ordered in probable sequence of occurrence. The construction had three, possibly overlapping phases.

Factors two, three, four and five: Information on these factors was gathered using an in-store questionnaire. During a two week period, 1,600 interviews were completed in the store. A proportional sample was taken at each of the store entrances. Interviewing was conducted on a systematic basis throughout each day.

In addition to generating figures on total traffic per door, proportion of transactions per door, planned versus impulse purchases per door, and average dollar value of the transaction per door, other data were collected. These data included information on traffic patterns within the store, types of merchandise purchased, customer satisfaction, mode of transportation to the store and area of residence. These data were applied toward the postconstruction strategy analysis.

Factor six: Using sales and transaction for past years, separate seasonal indices were developed using the ratio to centered moving average method.

Factor seven: Factor 7, the estimate of traffic fall-off for each door during construction, was the factor on which the least amount of objectively derived data was available. It was, therefore, the most subjective and difficult to evaluate.

Based on discussions with subway officials and persons at department stores near construction sites, values of traffic loss for each phase of construction were developed. The value vectors represent estimates as to the proportion between 0 and 1, of people who will *continue to enter* through the door or *transfer* to another door during a particular construction phase.

A more realistic set of values would probably include a stochastic decay function which explicitly takes into account the proportion of impulse to planned purchases, however, the development of these functions was postponed until actual construction when accurate data are available. In the initial model, one value vector was established for each door for each construction phase and was used for every month of the phase duration.

The model construction stage.   Once the information-gathering portion of the project was completed, work began on construction of the model itself.

The model spans the supposed maximum time period for completion of all three phases of construction affecting the store. Within this framework, each construction phase was allowed to stretch from its minimum to maximum length.

For additional flexibility, the total model may be easily extended beyond its current length by increasing the number of iterations desired in the outer loop. Further, the "subjective" door traffic proportion estimates were accessibly located in a separate section of the program for easy alteration. Those values, such as the seasonal indices, which are based on "objective" statistical data were entered as constants in the model.

The model is a simple and straightforward product of the seven logical factor inputs. A flow chart of the model is shown in Figure 8–3.

Using sets of arrays and five calculating subprograms, the model prints out the following values each month:

	Total traffic
	Total transactions
Deterministic	Total sales with construction
	Total sales without construction (potential sales)
	Total sales lost because of construction

	Total traffic mean and standard deviation
	Total transactions mean and standard deviation
Probabilistic	Total sales with construction mean and standard deviation
	Total sales without construction mean and standard deviation
	Total sales lost because of construction mean and standard deviation

Results and validity. The model was executed on three simulation runs. The first run was a simulation of the *minimum* effects of construction on sales at the store. The second simulation run was to show the *maximum* impact and the final run simulated *expected* sales loss. The projected sales loss ranged from 16 percent to 21 percent per year during construction with 18.5 percent being the expected loss.

This figure, if valid, is a sizable amount of money moving in a negative cash flow direction.

Validity of the model can be questioned in two areas. First, the working logic of the model itself and second, the assumptions about the proportion of traffic drop-off. That the workings of the model were valid was attested to by the fact that the potential sales figures generated by the model (what sales would be if there were no construction) were statistically indistinguishable (at .95 confidence level) from actual sales figures for the two previous years.

The validity of the estimates of traffic drop-off due to construction was, of course, undeterminable at the time since no prior studies of this type had been conducted. However, the assumptions made about drop-off percentages did not appear to be unreasonable; and in fact, the dollar value of sales lost given by the model were in line with the 10 percent to 20 percent aggregate drops experienced in other places during similar construction.

An important practical result of the simulation is that it indicated that management should take specific actions now to ease the impact of the upcoming construction. For instance, bus lines could be petitioned to re-route busses serving the store to stop at unobstructed

Figure 8–3
Simulation model flow chart

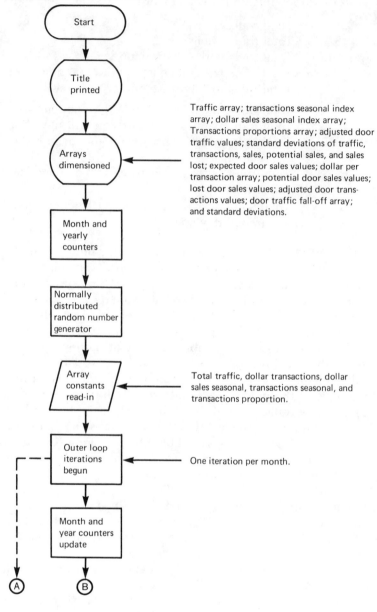

Traffic array; transactions seasonal index array; dollar sales seasonal index array; Transactions proportions array; adjusted door traffic values; standard deviations of traffic, transactions, sales, potential sales, and sales lost; expected door sales values; dollar per transaction array; potential door sales values; lost door sales values; adjusted door transactions values; door traffic fall-off array; and standard deviations.

Total traffic, dollar transactions, dollar sales seasonal, transactions seasonal, and transactions proportion.

One iteration per month.

Figure 8–3 (continued)

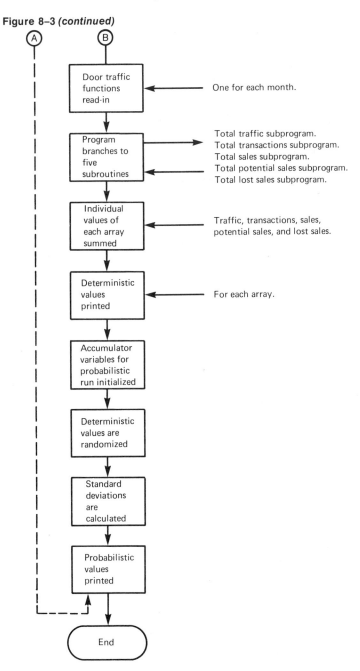

entrances. Promotional efforts could be undertaken to inform customers of the construction progress and to tell them which entrances are closed and which are open; and which streets provide the most convenient access routes. Measures such as these could help hold sales losses to a minimum and maintain customer goodwill as well.

OTHER CONSIDERATIONS IN QUANTITATIVE RESEARCH

Sampling and analysis

In contrast to qualitative approaches, quantitative research makes extensive use of probability sampling. The samples are generally larger and selected in a more scientific fashion than those used in qualitative research. This gives the research results a more conclusive nature and makes them projectable to larger populations. The type of probability sample varies greatly from study to study, but in general the samples are more accurate reflections of the total population than those used for depth interviews or focus groups.

Relative to analysis, quantitative research relies heavily on statistical techniques with increasing use of models. The analysis tends to be more objective with much less reliance on the researchers' subjective judgments than is the case with qualitative research. This type of analysis generally supplies results in numerical form rather than in terms of impressions and opinions.

The rigorous nature of the sampling and analysis as well as the measurement in quantitative research gives it an objectivist character. Thus, quantitative approaches tend to be quite effective when the need is for numerical precision and the purpose is conclusive (either descriptive or causal).

Limitations of quantitative research

Even though quantitative research is very scientific, it does have numerous limitations. Some of these limitations make the joint use of qualitative and quantitative approaches a very attractive research alternative. The following list provides a sample of some of the limitations of quantitative research.

1. For effective quantitative research the effort must start with a well defined hypothesis. Where this is not possible and the research intent is simply to develop hypotheses, qualitative approaches appear to hold more promise.
2. Quantitative approaches are not particularly effective at getting below surface responses and behaviors. When the need is to find "why" certain situations exist, qualitative research again appears

to be the better choice. As quantitative techniques are developed more fully; however, this limitation may become less acute.

3. Another potential limitation is the increasing difficulty in gaining access to consumers. There appears to be a rising concern for privacy among the public at large. This concern may increase the difficulties of gaining a representative sample from the marketplace. This can create external validity problems with experiments and decrease the projectability of survey findings.

4. As we have noted previously, information has value only as it affects managerial decision making. If the outcome of quantitative research is not properly interpreted for managerial use, its value is lost. Problems in interpreting quantitative data and analysis can severely limit the value of quantitative research. In many instances, quantitative techniques appear to have developed more rapidly than management's abilities to interpret and understand such material.

5. Finally, the research environment of marketing has become increasingly complex. This makes the task of reducing the realities of the market to numerical form much more difficult. Numerous variables must be considered at the same time to gain real understanding. This puts additional pressure on the techniques of quantitative research to handle the increased complexity. Perhaps more importantly, it adds to management's difficulties in interpreting and using quantitative findings.

Trends in quantitative research

Several trends are apparent in the realm of quantitative research. Many of these stem from attempts to deal with some of the limitations just listed.

1. New and different variables are being explored in marketing research. Variables that go beyond the standard demographics in explaining behaviors are finding increasing use. These include among others the life style variables.

2. Additional use is also being made of multivariate designs and procedures. These approaches provide more complex and realistic pictures of the environment.

3. More sophisticated analytical procedures are being used to deal with the multivariate research designs. Some of these techniques are discussed in more detail in Chapter 9.

4. Researchers are showing more concern for sampling and measurement error in their work. More attempts are being made to quantify and report such errors.

5. Quantitative research is moving toward more use of longitudinal studies rather than one time projects. Research conducted over time on the same subject can provide a much more realistic picture.
6. Relative to the individual quantitative approaches, there appears to be an increasing use of experimental research though survey methods still dominate. Simulation has yet to make a significant impact in applied research or to reach its full potential.
7. Finally, marketing research is becoming an increasingly multidisciplinary field. Facets of psychology, management science, statistics, and so forth are being integrated to expand the base of the discipline. This increases the need for both researchers and managers with a wide range of knowledge and expertise in many fields.

SUMMARY

Quantitative approaches to primary data collection are typically more objective in nature than the qualitative approaches. In the quantitative approaches, an attempt is made to remove the researchers subjective assessments from the sampling, measurement, and analysis. Stress is placed on concrete numbers rather than the researchers' opinions or impressions. The three major research approaches in the quantitative area discussed in this chapter are surveys, experiments, and simulation.

Surveys typically involve sampling a larger population, measuring selected variables for this sample, analyzing the data, and then projecting the results to the total population. This approach is particularly suited for developing profiles of markets or market segments in terms of demographics, life styles, and behaviors. It can also be used to test hypotheses about states of nature and to establish relationships. The relationships established in survey research cannot, however, be concluded to be of the cause-effect variety. To establish cause-effect relationships, the experimental approach is needed.

An experiment involves data collection in a more controlled environment. The researcher controls the primary independent variable (treatment) and may control a certain number of secondary independent variables (extraneous variables). In this way, a cause-effect relationship between the dependent variable and the primary independent variable can be established if proper controls are maintained. The various alternative structures for such experiments are referred to as designs. These designs range from very simple informal types to highly sophisticated formal designs which allow statistical control of extraneous variables and the testing of interaction effects. The formal designs are analyzed through the use of analysis of variance procedures which will be discussed in Chapter 9.

Simulation is a third alternative in the quantitative area. With this approach, the researcher creates an artificial environment within which certain variables can be manipulated and others observed. Building the environment may require the use of survey or secondary data. After the model is constructed, its operation often resembles an experiment. The distinguishing feature of the simulation approach is the creation of an artificial environment or model within which information can be generated.

DISCUSSION QUESTIONS

1. Compare and contrast the three quantitative approaches to marketing research discussed in this chapter. What are the distinguishing characteristics of each, what are their advantages and disadvantages and in what type of situation should each be used?

2. A local bank wishes to develop a profile of the customers using various banks and savings and loan associations in the area. How could this be accomplished? Be specific concerning the sampling and questionnaire design.

3. Discuss the different experimental designs and their unique features.

4. An advertising agency is trying to determine the impact of three different newspaper ads on the consumer. Carefully define the variables and then discuss the development of an experiment to accomplish this research task.

5. Discuss the potential applications of simulation by marketing management.

6. Assume that you are managing a state controlled liquor distribution system. How could simulation be used as a tool to aid in making the necessary decisions related to store and warehouse location, inventory levels, and so forth?

SELECTED REFERENCES

Banks, Seymour. *Experimentation in Marketing.* New York: McGraw-Hill Book Co., 1965.

Cox, Keith K., and Enis, Ben M. *Experimentation for Marketing Decisions.* Scranton, Pa.: International Textbooks, 1969.

Kotler, Phillip, and Schulz, Ronald L. "Marketing Simulations: Review and Prospects," *Journal of Business* (July 1970), pp. 237–95.

Parten, Mildred. *Surveys, Polls, and Samples: Practical Procedures.* New York: Harper & Brothers, 1950.

Tull, Donald S., and Albaum, Gerald S. *Survey Research: A Decisional Approach.* New York: Intext Educational Publishers, 1973.

chapter
9

Basic analysis

After a group of data has been collected, the meaning must then be determined. Processing data to extract meaning is called analysis. This usually requires that the data be placed in some logical framework so that relative magnitudes and relationships can be determined. Analysis is thus the process of reducing data to relevant and meaningful results. This has been described as finding patterns and relationships that exist in numerical data and reducing these to summaries that can be readily interpreted, used, and communicated; or letting the data speak.[1] The purpose is to derive findings which help to answer the questions developed as the research problem.

Analysis can be broken into three basic steps: sorting and summarizing the data, developing additional hypotheses which were not originally considered, and finally, processing the data through the use of appropriate statistical procedures and/or models. The discussion in this chapter will review both statistics and models as methods of analysis. Based on the results of applying these procedures, inferences may be made about the variables under study.

In sorting and summarizing, appropriate categories are established and the data divided along the lines of these groups. The data falling in each category are then counted and summary measures developed. The categories should be selected in such a way that they have clear relationships to the ultimate information needs. A useful framework for the sorting and summarization task is cross tabulation which allows the simultaneous counting of data related to two or more variables at

---

[1] A. S. C. Ehrenberg, *Data Reduction: Analyzing and Interpreting Statistical Data* (New York: Wiley, 1975).

the same time. The simple tabulation of one variable can also be very useful.

The hypotheses which are to be examined in a study should be stated as clearly and fully as possible early in the study. These statements help to direct the formulation of the research design and affect the success of the study. It is usually not possible, however, to think of every relevant hypothesis in advance no matter how well the research is planned. Thus, new hypotheses may be suggested when the researcher carefully examines the sorted and summarized data. These hypotheses may then form the basis for additional research efforts. The data that generates the new hypotheses should not be used to test them.

After the data has been reviewed in its summary form, the researcher is then ready to select and apply the appropriate statistical methods or models. These should have been predetermined in the research design but they should be reviewed at this point. The statistical procedures are then used to make the estimates or perform the hypothesis testing required in the research.

SORTING AND SUMMARIZING BY CROSS TABULATION

The basic principle of data sorting is to select relevant categories for subdividing the total mass of data. The elements in each category are then counted and the categories compared. A sales manager may have five salesmen under his direct control. One factor he considers important in evaluating their performance is new accounts. He might collect data on new accounts and categorize these by salesman:

Salesman	New accounts	Percent
A	20	29
B	10	14
C	30	43
D	5	7
E	5	7
Total	70	100

This simple tabulation may provide a useful bit of information to the manager in assessing the performance of his salesmen. Based on the tabulation we might conclude that salesman C is doing an outstanding job at developing new accounts while salesmen D and E may need some special direction or incentives.

A cross tabulation allows the researcher to look at two variables at the same time. A matrix is formed with the categories of one variable on one axis and the categories of the second variable on the other. The elements falling in each cell of the matrix would then be summarized. Suppose that the sales manager in the above illustration is concerned not only with the number of new accounts, but also with their size. He feels that larger accounts are generally more profitable on a per unit basis as well as in aggregate profit. Thus the salesman who develops accounts with sizable customers could develop fewer and still add as much or more to company profits as another who solicits a large number of smaller accounts. To include the variable of customer size along with salesmen a cross tabulation could be used.

	Salesman				
Customer sales volume	A	B	C	D	E
Under $1,000,000	80%	10%	100%	0%	0%
$1,000,000 to $10,000,000	20	80	0	20	0
Over $10,000,000	0	10	0	80	100
Total............................	100%	100%	100%	100%	100%
N	20	10	30	5	5

The cross tabulation gives the sales manager new insights. It appears that salesman C is concentrating on small accounts while D and E are going after the over $10,000,000 in sales group. His evaluation of relative performance might now change in favor of D and E.

The cross tabulation permits a two (or three with a three-way table) dimensional look at the data. Thus it is very useful in the sorting and summarizing phase of analysis. When the research objective is to determine relationships between variables the researcher will normally construct a cross tabulation for each combination of dependent and independent variables. Independent variables may also be cross tabulated to investigate their potential relationships.

The primary benefit of the cross tabulation is to give an overview of the data. To aggregate it into a manageable, comprehensible form. The cross tabulation may also permit subjective hypothesis testing. By comparing the distribution of elements in each category certain patterns and relationships may become obvious. If such a relationship was hypothesized, then the observed pattern may be taken to support or refute the hypothesis. Cross tabulations may also aid in the discovery of new hypotheses which were not originally considered. Finally, this technique may allow the researcher to discover hidden relationships in the data. Many variables are related in a nonlinear fashion. Such relationships can escape the more sophisticated analytical techniques because many are based on linear assumptions. In the following cross tabulation age is related to consumption in a very visible way. The relationship is not linear, however. Consumption is low for younger and older consumers and high for the two center age groups. This relationship would not be found with simple regression, for example. Cross tabulations can thus help to locate relationships that might not otherwise be discovered.

Consumption of brand X per month	Age			
	Under 20	20–30	31–40	Over 40
0–2	90%	0%	0%	90%
3–5	10	5	5	5
6–8	0	5	10	5
9–11	0	80	75	0
12 or over	0	10	10	0
Total	100%	100%	100%	100%
N	200	200	200	200

In making cross tabulations certain basic rules should be followed:

1. Carefully define the categories which are used in the table. For example, *high, medium,* and *low* would not be acceptable income categories. A manager reviewing the results might define these categories in a totally different way than the researcher. The meaning of the table is lost without clearly labeled categories.

2. The values in the cells of the table should generally be percentages. This allows ready comparisons of categories with different bases. A category with 173 elements can then be easily compared with another category that has only 85 elements. The direction in which the table should be percentaged depends on the purpose for making the cross tabulation. In general the table should be percentaged so that each category being compared adds to 100. The preceeding table is percentaged so that the age categories can be compared. It is important to interpret the table consistently with the direction of percentaging. The 90 percent in the upper left cell means that 90 percent of the Under 20 age group consumed 0–2 units of brand X per month; not that 90 percent of those consuming 0–2 units are under 20. The percentages are normally rounded to whole numbers when a cross tabulation is presented in a report. This aids the reader in comparing percentages and any additional precision is typically meaningless.

3. The number of observations on which the percentages are based should always be specified. Percentages must represent a significant block of data to have any real meaning. If we were to compare males and females as to their brand preference for soft drinks and 50 percent of the men preferred brand X while only 10 percent of the females preferred that brand, it might be concluded that men are much more likely to prefer brand X than females. If, however, the

percentages are based on a sample of two males and one thousand females the conclusion would clearly be unwarranted. In order to be able to judge what meaning to attach to percentages their bases must be known.

There is a danger in relying too heavily on two-way cross tabulations. At times relationships can appear to exist which are really not present. This can occur particularly where the two variables being cross tabulated are both related to some third variable. Three-way tables are very useful in uncovering such spurious relationships. For example, if we look at the following two-way table we might conclude that the sex of this sample of single people who have full time jobs outside the home is closely related to their brand preference. Females are likely to prefer brand X while males are likely to prefer brand Y. Some other variable might be causing this relationship, however. Perhaps single females with full time jobs outside the home earn lower salaries in general. Thus income might be a key variable. A three-way table may help to locate the true nature of the relationships. If the three-way table produced the result below we might conclude that income is related to brand preference and that sex is related only because it is related to income. Thus the three-way table may have uncovered a spurious relationship between sex and brand preference.

Brand preference	Sex	
	Female	Male
X	90	10
Y	10	90
Total	100%	100%
N	500	500

Brand preference	Female		Male	
	Under $10,000	$10,000 or over	Under $10,000	$10,000 or over
X	100	0	100	0
Y	0	100	0	100
Total	100%	100%	100%	100%
N	450	50	50	450

After the data has been sorted and summarized, the next step is to carefully examine the summaries for additional hypotheses which may be worth further study. These would typically be reported in the final report and may lead to recommendations for additional research. After this review is completed statistical methods and/or models may be selected and applied to extract further information from the data.

SELECTING STATISTICAL TECHNIQUES

Two considerations are important in the selection of statistical techniques: the quality of the data, and the purpose the researcher has in mind. Relative to data quality many factors can be considered. The primary considerations are usually the nature of the distribution and the measurement scale. The four basic scales (nominal, ordinal, interval, and ratio) were discussed in Chapter 6. One group of statistics, called parametric statistics, are designed for use where normal distributions with homogeneous variance among groups can be assumed, and the measurement is at least interval in nature. Nonparametric statistics require fewer assumptions about the distribution; it need not be a normal distribution nor equal in group variances. They are also based on nominal or ordinal measurement which makes them very useful in marketing research, since the data is often less than interval quality.

In selecting statistical techniques the scaling is often taken to reflect the quality of data. Table 9–1 shows statistical techniques which

Table 9–1
Appropriate statistics for different scales of measurement

	Purpose of statistics			
Scale	Measures of central tendency	Measures of variability	Test of significance	Measures of correlation or association
Nominal	Mode	Information H	Chi-square	Contingency correlation coefficient
Ordinal	Median	Percentiles	Sign test Run test Mann-Whitney U test Kruskal-Wallis Friedman's two-way analysis of variance	Spearman correlation Kendall's tau
Interval	Mean	Standard deviation Average deviation	t test F test	Product-momentum correlation Regression Factor analysis Discriminant analysis*
Ratio	Geometric mean Harmonic mean	Percent variation Coefficient of variation		

* Discriminant analysis requires interval independent variables and a nominal dependent variable.

Source: Adapted from S. S. Stevens, "Measurement, Psychophysics, and Utility," in *Measurement: Definitions and Theories*, ed. C. W. Churchman and P. Ratoosh, (New York: John Wiley and Sons, Inc., 1959), pp. 25–27.

are appropriate for given purpose and scale combinations. The statistical procedures listed for nominal and ordinal scales are nonparametric, while those indicated for interval and ratio scales are parametric in nature. A statistic listed for one scale can be used for any higher order of measurement but not for a lower scale. Thus the chi-square could be used with any scale, but the *t* test should be used only with interval or ratio measurements.

MEASURES OF CENTRAL TENDENCY AND VARIABILITY

The most often used measures of central tendency are the mean and the median. The standard deviation is a principal measure of variability. The mean and standard deviation may be used together to form a confidence interval.

Mean

The mean is the average of all the elements in the data base. The values for each element are added and the sum divided by the number of elements. This can be computed using the following formula:

$$\overline{X} = \frac{\Sigma X}{N}$$

where $\overline{X}$ is the mean, ΣX is the sum of the individual items $(X's)$ and N is the number of items.

Suppose that a soup manufacturer is selling through a series of 100 supermarkets and needs an estimate of the shelf space allocated to his product. A sample of 15 stores is taken, and the number of inches of shelf space measured with the following results:

90	79	68
89	76	66
87	74	65
85	73	50
81	71	41

The mean is 73 determined by dividing the total (1,095) by 15.

Median

The median is the value that divides the distribution of numbers in half with 50 percent of the numbers above it and 50 percent below it. In the above shelf space example the median is 74.

The median is not as sensitive to the values at the extremes of the distribution as the mean. The median here is slightly higher than the mean because the mean is pulled down by the very low value at the lower end of the distribution.

Standard deviation

The standard deviation is a measure of variability in the distribution. It can be calculated using the following formula:

$$S = \sqrt{\frac{\Sigma(X - \overline{X})^2}{N - 1}}$$

where S is the standard deviation, $(X - \overline{X})^2$ is the deviation of each value from the mean squared, and $N - 1$ is the number of elements minus one.

In the shelf space illustration the standard deviation is 13.9. The value of this statistic is related to the range between the highest and lowest values; typically the greater the range the greater the standard deviation.

Confidence intervals

In estimating a population value from sample data it is desirable to form a range estimate rather than relying on a single point. In the above example, if the researcher is estimating the average shelf space from sample data, the probability of the sample mean exactly equalling the population mean is very small. Thus taking the sample mean as an estimate can be misleading. A better method is to form a confidence interval as the estimate. The confidence interval is a range that the researcher can assign a probability that the true population mean falls within. The associated probability is called a confidence coefficient. When the population standard deviation is not known (which is generally the case), an approximate confidence interval for a mean can be computed with the following formula:

$$\text{Confidence interval} = \overline{X} \pm Z\, s_{\overline{x}} \quad \text{✓ Standard Error}$$

where $\overline{X}$ is the sample mean, Z is the number of standard deviations from the mean needed to give the desired confidence coefficient and $s_{\overline{x}}$ is the standard error of the sample mean derived from the standard deviation of the sample, S.

Assume that for the shelf space illustration we wish to form a confidence interval that we can say with a .95 probability contains the true population mean. The Z would be 1.96 for a .95 confidence coefficient assuming a normal distribution and the $s_{\overline{x}}$ can be computed as follows:

$$s_{\overline{x}} = \frac{S}{\sqrt{n - 1}} \left(\sqrt{\frac{N - n}{N - 1}} \right) \quad \text{Standard Error}$$

where S is the sample standard deviation, N is the population size and n is the sample size.

$$s_{\bar{x}} = \frac{13.9}{\sqrt{15 - 1}} \sqrt{\frac{100 - 15}{100 - 1}} = 3.46$$

The confidence interval for a .95 confidence coefficient is thus:

Confidence interval $= 73 \pm 1.96\,(3.46) = 66.22$ to 79.78

The researcher can now estimate that the true population mean falls between 66.22 and 79.78 and have a .95 probability of being correct.

TESTS OF SIGNIFICANCE

Tests of significance are used to determine whether values or variables are related to one another. The appropriate test for a given situation depends on the exact purpose and the quality of the data involved.

The *t* test

The t test is appropriate with interval data and can be used for several purposes. One of its major uses is to compare two sample means to determine whether the difference between them is a real (significant) difference or is just due to chance. The following procedure can be used to perform a t test where the samples are independent.

Steps

1. Calculate group variance for sample number 1.

$$S_1^2 = \frac{N_1 \Sigma X_1^2 - (\Sigma X_1)^2}{N_1(N_1 - 1)}$$

2. Calculate group variance for sample number 2.

$$S_2^2 = \frac{N_2 \Sigma X_2^2 - (\Sigma X_2)^2}{N_2(N_2 - 1)}$$

3. $\dfrac{(N_1 - 1)S_1^2 + (N_2 - 1)S_2^2}{N_1 + N_2 - 2} = \underline{\hspace{2cm}}$

4. $\dfrac{N_1 + N_2}{N_1 N_2} = \underline{\hspace{2cm}}$

5. Step 3 $\times$ Step 4 $= \underline{\hspace{2cm}}$

6. $\sqrt{\text{Step 5}} = \underline{\hspace{2cm}}$

7. $\overline{X}_1 - \overline{X}_2 = \underline{\hspace{2cm}}$

8. $t = \dfrac{\text{Step } 7}{\text{Step } 6}, df = N_1 + N_2 - 2$

9. Look up the critical value of t in a t table for the appropriate df and the desired level of significance.

10. If the computed t exceeds the critical t from the table then the null hypothesis (which says that the means are equal) can be rejected at level of significance used to find the critical t.

The chi-square test

A more often used test of significance, in marketing, is the chi-square (χ^2) test. It can be used with even nominal measurement to test for significant relationships between variables. The normal case is two variables; the chi-square is often used in conjunction with a two-way cross tabulation. The data in the two variable case are put in a contingency table as a starting point. For example, assume that a researcher wishes to test for a relationship between brand preference and sex in the contingency table below:

Brand preference

Sex	X	Y	Total	
Male	466	169	635	$646 \times \dfrac{635}{844}$
Female	180	29	209	
Total	646	198	844	

The χ^2 value for this table can be computed using the following formula:

$$\chi^2 = \sum \left[\frac{(o - e)^2}{e} \right]$$

where o is the observed frequency in each cell of the contingency table (466, 169, 180, and 29 in our illustration) and e is the expected frequency for the corresponding cells that would exist if the variables were not related. In computing the expected frequency for each cell, if all column and row totals were the same, the total frequency in the matrix could simply be divided by the number of cells. Since this is usually not the case, the expected frequencies can be calculated by dividing the product of the column and row totals for the specific cell by the total frequency in the matrix. In the example, the cell with the observed frequency of 466 would have an expected frequency of $(635 \times 646) \div 844$ or 486.

The χ^2 for the contingency table is thus:

$$\chi^2 = \frac{(466 - 486)^2}{486} + \frac{(169 - 149)^2}{149} + \frac{(180 - 160)^2}{160} + \frac{(29 - 49)^2}{49} = 14.171$$

The degrees of freedom are equal to the rows minus one times the columns minus one, or 1 for this example. With the degrees of freedom and the desired level of significance a critical value of chi-square can be looked up in a chi-square table. If the desired level of significance is .01, then the critical value is 6.63. If the computed chi-square (14.171) exceeds the critical value (6.63), which is the case here, then the null hypothesis (that the variables are not related) can be rejected at the level of significance used to select the critical value.

 Note that when calculating chi-square, the actual frequencies, not percentages, should be used in the contingency table. As rules of thumb it is also desirable to have a total frequency of at least 50 and no more than 20 percent of the cells with expected frequencies of less than 5. This last rule often requires that some columns or rows be combined.

Analysis of variance

Analysis of variance is actually a set of techniques designed to test for relationships between variables using the F test. A slightly different procedure is used to analyze the results of each of the different formal experimental designs. The F test is basic to each variation, however, and the one-way analysis of variance used with the completely randomized design illustrates the basic concept.

Suppose that the impact of package color (red, green, and blue) on sales of a consumer product is to be tested. The packages are assigned to three different cities, and the sales volume in number of cases is measured for six months. The results are shown in the following matrix:

City Month	A Red	B Green	C Blue	Total
1	94	80	92	
2	89	75	76	
3	86	90	81	
4	95	85	85	
5	97	83	86	
6	99	85	86	
Total	560	498	506	1,564
$\overline{X}$	93	83	84	87

The F statistic can be computed in the following way:

Source of variation	Sum of squares	Degrees of freedom	Mean squares	F
Among the treatment means	SSA	DF_1	$MSA = \dfrac{SSA}{DF_1}$	$\dfrac{MSA}{MSW}$
Within the treatment groups	SSW	DF_2	$MSW = \dfrac{SSW}{DF_2}$	
Total	SST	DF_3		

where, SSA, indicates sum of squares among treatment means, SSW, sum of squares within treatment, SST, sum of squares total, MSA, mean squares among, and MSW, mean squares within.

The SSA is the product of the number of rows times the sum of the squared differences between the column means and the total mean.

$$SSA = 6[(93\text{-}87)^2 + (83\text{-}87)^2 + (84\text{-}87)^2] = 366$$

The SSW is the sum of the squared differences between the value in each cell and the mean for the column containing that cell.

Month	City A Red $(Xi_1 - \overline{X}_1)^2$	City B Green $(Xi_2 - \overline{X}_2)^2$	City C Blue $(Xi_3 - \overline{X}_3)^2$
1................	1	9	64
2..............	16	64	64
3..............	49	49	9
4..............	4	4	1
5..............	16	0	4
6..............	36	4	4
Total	122	130	146

$$SSW = 122 + 130 + 146 = 398$$

DF_1 is equal to the number of columns minus one, or 2 in this example. DF_2 is the columns times the rows minus one, or 15. DF_3 is $DF_1 + DF_2$, or 17.

To compute the F statistic:

SSA = 366	$DF_1 = 2$	MSA = 183	$F = \dfrac{183}{26.53} = 6.9$
SSW = 398	$DF_2 = 15$	MSW = 26.53	
SST = 764	$DF_3 = 17$		

Assume that the management would like to test the relationship between package color and sales at the .05 level of significance. From the F table for a .05 level of significance with $DF_1 = 2$ and $DF_2 = 15$ the critical value of F is 3.68. Because the computed F (6.9) is greater than the critical value (3.68), the null hypothesis should be rejected. The experimental evidence indicates that there is a significant difference in at least two of the treatment means; that package color is related to sales. From the analysis thus far we cannot specify which treatment means are significantly different. Additional procedures are available to make this determination. A subjective assessment of the original data suggests that the red package yields significantly higher sales than the others.

CORRELATION AND ASSOCIATION

The cross tabulation procedure discussed earlier is one way to look at the association between variables. Other more sophisticated techniques are also available which allow the researcher to measure the extent and nature of such relationships and to quantify the results. One technique often used for this purpose in marketing research is regression analysis.

Basically regression allows the researcher to estimate the relationship between a dependent variable and one or more independent variables in the form of an equation. Simple regression is used with one independent variable and multiple regression with two or more. This analysis provides coefficients which can be used as a measure of the extent of association between the variables. These coefficients are the coefficient of correlation and the coefficient of determination. One of the primary uses of regression is in building forecasting models. If there is a need to forecast some variable which can be quantitatively related to other more easily accessible variables, then a regression model may prove very useful.

Simple regression

The first step in doing a simple regression is to develop a basic model. To do this the variables must be selected, operationally defined, and categorized into dependent and independent. The management of a wire manufacturer was interested in forecasting the annual potential demand by state for a specific type of wire used for right of way fences on interstate highways. The forecasts were needed as informational input for geographic market analysis, production scheduling, and distribution decisions. The research staff knows that the demand for wire is closely related to the number of miles of highway constructed each year. However, the waste factor, the fact that fences run in irregular patterns, and other similar considerations make the relationship less obvious. The researchers decided to build a forecasting model using simple regression. The dependent variable is rolls of wire sold per year in a given state (Y), and the independent variable is number of miles of interstate highway constructed in the state for the year.

To complete the decision relative to the model the form of the relationship must be decided. A linear relationship is usually assumed; however, other types of functions may also be selected. The linear function can be expressed as

$$Y = a \pm b\ (X)$$

where Y is the dependent variable, X is the independent variable, a is the Y intercept of the function and b is the slope.

The second step is to collect data on the variables and to fit the model to the data. From various secondary sources the number of miles of interstate highway constructed per state per year can be ascertained. The sales of wire per state per year can also be secured from trade publications. Such data were secured for the 50 states for a three year period. This gives 150 observations or data points to fit the model to. The computational technique typically used in simple regression is the "least squares" method. This procedure estimates the coefficients of the equation that minimize the sum of the squared differences between the actual values of the dependent variable for each data point and the values predicted by the equation. This can be computed by hand but the high-speed computer makes the task relatively simple.

The third step is to interpret the results of the regression. Several bits of output are possible with simple regression analysis, but the most important are usually:

1. Estimates of the coefficients of the equation, a and b. These are used to build the forecasting model.
2. The coefficient of correlation (r) which is a measure of the degree of association between the variables. It can vary from -1 to $+1$, with -1 indicating a perfect fit of the model to the data in an inverse fashion, $+1$ indicates a perfect fit in a direct fashion, and 0 would mean no association.
3. The coefficient of determination (r^2) which measures the percent of variation in the dependent variable explained by the independent variable.
4. The standard error of the estimate (s_{est}) which can be used to translate forecasts made using the equation into range rather than point estimates. The narrower the range the more valuable the model is as a forecasting tool.

The results of the simple regression might look as follows:

$$a = 0$$
$$b = +17$$
$$r = .99$$
$$r^2 = .98$$
$$s_{est} = 12$$

The forecasting model would be $Y = 0 + 17 (X)$. By inserting a value for X the value of Y can be predicted. The r^2 indicates that 98 percent of the variation in sales is accounted for by variation in miles of construction. Given that this is almost all of the variation it might be concluded that this single variable is adequate for forecasting demand. The s_{est} is relatively small which also indicates that the model is a good forecasting tool. Suppose that the firm finds that a given state is planning 60 miles of new interstate construction next year. To form a range estimate of the total demand for wire, that can be said with .95 confidence contains the true demand, the first step is to insert the 60 miles into the predictive equation.

$$Y = 0 + 17 (60) = 1020$$

Assuming a normal distribution, $1.96\ s_{est}$ will yeild the desired level of confidence. The conficence interval is

$$\text{confidence interval} = Y \pm 1.96\ s_{est}$$
$$= 1020 \pm 1.96\ (12)$$
$$= 996.5 \text{ to } 1,043.5$$

The researcher can now say that there is a .95 probability that the true demand will fall within this range. This is, of course, assuming that the 60 miles of construction is accurate.

Multiple regression

Multiple regression is quite similar to simple regression with the exception that multiple regression is used with two or more independent variables. The steps in carrying out multiple regression are the same as those for simple regression: develop a model, fit the model to collected data, and interpret the results.

Again many different functions may be used as the basic model in multiple regression; a linear equation is most common, however.

$$Y = a \pm b_1(X_1) \pm b_2(X_2) \pm \ \cdots$$

Y is the dependent variable, the X's are independent variables, and a, $b_1, b_2, \ldots$ are coefficients of the equation.

Data are fitted to the model using a computer and the results then interpreted. Among the more important outputs of the multiple regression analysis are:

1. Estimates of the coefficients of the equation $(a, b_1, b_2, \ldots)$ which can be used to form a predictive model.
2. Partial coefficients of determination (r_i^2), one for each independent variable. These measure the percent of variation in the dependent variable explained by that particular independent variable. This is the same as the coefficient of determination in a simple regression.

3. The coefficient of multiple determination (R^2) which indicates the percent of variation in the dependent variable explained by all of the independent variables taken together. Note that this is not necessarily the sum of the coefficients of partial determination due to possible correlation between the independent variables.
4. The standard error of the estimate (s_{est}) which is used in translating predictions into range estimates.

A test of significance (an F test, for example) may also be performed in the regression analysis. This allows the researcher to test for statistically significant relationships between the variables. One must be careful in interpreting statistical significance in relation to predictive value, however. Relationships may be statistically significant and still lack any real predictive ability.

To illustrate the application of multiple regression, suppose that a life insurance company wishes to build a model to predict the success of applicants for sales positions. They interpret success in terms of sales volume for the first year with the company. The research staff believes that years of formal education, years of previous selling experience, and age may be key variables in predicting the sales volume generated in the first year by the new salesman. The dependent variable is thus sales for the first year with the company (Y), and the independent variables are years of formal education (X_1), years of previous selling experience (X_2) and age (X_3). Data may be collected on these variables for all current salesmen in the firm. The data would relate to their first year's sales volume adjusted for inflation, their age when starting with the company, and so forth.

The model would then be fitted to the data and the results interpreted. Assuming the following output:

$$a = 100{,}000$$
$$b_1 = +2{,}000$$
$$b_2 = +5{,}000$$
$$b_3 = +1{,}000$$
$$r_1^2 = .08$$
$$r_2^2 = .12$$
$$r_3^2 = .02$$
$$R^2 = .16$$
$$s_{est} = 90{,}000$$

It might be concluded that these variables do not form the basis for a good predictive model. They account for only 16 percent of the total variation in first year sales and the standard error of the estimate is very large. For an applicant with a college degree (16 years of education), five years of previous selling experience, and 30 years of age, the point estimate is $187,000. But when this is converted to a confidence interval with a .95 confidence coefficient the estimate becomes

$187,000 \pm 1.96$ ($90,000) or between $3,600 and $363,400. Thus the predictive power of the model is very weak.

A variation of multiple regression, called step-wise regression, performs the analysis on a variable by variable basis. The model is built by adding the most important independent variable first, the second most important next, and so forth. The results are provided after each step so that the relative importance of the variables can be evaluated. As a technical point it should be noted that regression analysis generally requires interval data. The exception being that two category, nominally scaled independent variables can be used. These are called "dummy" variables.

Multiple discriminant analysis

When the researcher wishes to perform regression analysis but has a nominally scaled dependent variable, multiple discriminant analysis can be used. For example, suppose that brand preference (brand X or Y) is the dependent variable of interest, and its relationship to income and age is being investigated. Regression analysis would be ruled out because the dependent variable is not intervally scaled.

A multiple discriminant analysis could be carried out to determine which independent variables are most useful in predicting whether the consumer uses brand X or Y. Like regression, the analysis provides a predictive equation, measures of the relative importance of each variable, and a measure of the ability of the equation to predict actual brand preference.

Different variations of discriminant analysis are available which can be used with two or more categories in the dependent variable.

Factor analysis

In some instances a researcher may have a large number of related variables that need to be reduced to a smaller number of basic factors. This often occurs in multiple regression where a large number of highly correlated independent variables can lead to distorted results. The technique for making this type of data reduction is called factor analysis. It allows the researcher to group variables into factors based on the correlation between variables. The factors may then be treated as new variables and their value derived by summing the values of the original variables which have been grouped into the factor. The meaning and name of the new variable is usually determined subjectively by the researcher based on which original variables have been grouped into the factor. Note that this technique, along with the other multivariate analytical procedures discussed in this chapter, are explained in more detail in the appendix for those who wish to explore the topic more fully.

MARKETING MODELS AS ANALYTICAL TECHNIQUES

Defining models

Marketing models provide the researcher with another set of analytical devices. A model can be defined as "a simplified representation of the relevant aspects of an actual system or process."[2] The system or process would normally be reduced to the essential variables with relationships between these variables specified. A marketing model which can provide useful information should involve two sets of variables. First, a variable or variables whose position or state is an important informational input into the decision-making process. Secondly, variables for which data can be secured and which are related in some specified way to the important decision variable. This allows the model to be used to transform raw data into useful decision information.

There are many types of models which can prove useful for marketing decision makers. Certain models can be identified in each of the marketing decision areas. Most of these models are symbolic in nature. Symbols are used to represent the essential variables within the process under consideration. Symbolic models may be subdivided into mathematical and verbal. Mathematical models use the language of mathematics to denote the variables in the model and the relationships between variables. Verbal models use words or phrases for this purpose. Both mathematical and verbal models may be further subdivided into descriptive and normative. Descriptive models describe a process as it actually exists, while normative models present the process as it should be. Both normative and descriptive models may be either deterministic or stochastic. Deterministic implies that probability plays no role in the model while stochastic models incorporate probabilities.

Any of these various types of models may be either tailor-made for a specific management situation or a general marketing model which has application to some problem under consideration. In order to construct a tailor-made model, the variable whose state is a key informational input must be identified, the variables for which data are available and that can be related to the informational variable must be

---

[2] James H. Donnelly, Jr. and John M. Ivancevich, *Analysis for Marketing Decisions* (Homewood, Ill.: Richard D. Irwin, Inc., 1970), p. 13.

specified, and the relationships between the variables defined. In many decision situations, a general marketing model, such as a transportation model or break-even model, already exist which can be used to transform data into useful information. This is, of course, possible only if the data needed to establish the parameters of the model can be collected.

Effective analytical models are in many cases the necessary bridges between research and decision making. A great deal of research is designed either to build a tailor-made model by locating the essential variables and specifying the relationships between variables or to determine the positions of variables (states of nature) which set the parameters for general or previously built models. Examples of a general and a tailor-made model may help to clarify their position in the information-decision making interaction.

An example of a general marketing model

Assume that a manager is attempting to decide whether or not to introduce a new product. He wants all new products to at least break-even in the first year. To make his decision he needs to know the anticipated sales and the break-even level for the new product. Thus, one vital informational input is the break-even sales volume. A general model exists which can be used to estimate the position of this variable if specific data can be secured. A break-even model is shown in Figure 9–1. The data necessary to determine the break-even sales in units is: (1) the total fixed cost (x_1), (2) the average variable cost per unit (x_2), and (3) the average revenue per unit (x_3). Research can be designed and implemented to secure this data. The data can then be fitted to the general model to determine the position of the break-even point (y_1). This flow may be summarized as follows:

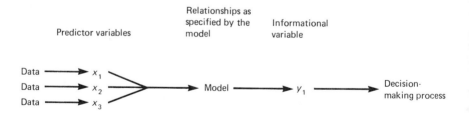

Data are secured to establish the position of each predictor variable which is necessary to set the parameters of the model. The data are fitted to the model so as to ascertain the position of the informational

Figure 9–1
Break-even model

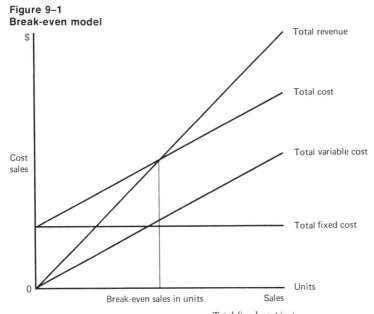

$$\text{Break-even sales in units}\,(y_1) = \frac{\text{Total fixed cost}\,(x_1)}{\text{Average revenue per unit}\,(x_3) - \text{Average variable cost per unit}\,(x_2)}$$

variable. The position of this key informational variable then becomes an input into the decision-making process. In many cases the analytical model provides a vital link in the information decision-making chain.

An example of a tailor-made marketing model

With some decisions no general model exists which will provide the needed link. In these cases research may be undertaken to build a tailor-made model for use in a specific decision environment. For example, the manager of a state liquor distribution system must decide the volume of shipments to each store within the state. To be able to make a sound decision he needs to know the demand in the geographic areas surrounding each store. A model is needed to provide a forecast of demand for each area. Research may be needed to build a model which can produce the necessary forecasts.

To build the model variables for which data can be secured and which are related to liquor demand must be determined. Then the relationship between the predictor variables and the informational variable (demand) must be specified. In research of this type in Ohio, it was discovered that the demand for specific types of liquor could be closely related to the Index of Buying Power.[3] The demand for type A liquor in a given geographic area (y_1) was found to be a function of the Index of Buying Power for that area (x_1). Thus, a separate model $(y_1 = f[x_1])$ was developed for each type of liquor. Since the Index of Buying Power is available from secondary sources for each county within a state, this model proved very valuable for forecasting demand. Such forecasts provided a valuable informational input for making the needed distribution decisions.

In summary, both general and tailor-made models can be of considerable value to decision makers with any organization. There is a need to identify models which can be of use for specific types of marketing decisions. This topic is explored in several excellent texts.[4]

SUMMARY

Analysis can be considered to be the process of extracting the desired information from a body of data. To accomplish this task the data must be reduced to some logical framework. The steps in this reduction process are to sort and summarize the data, develop additional hypotheses, and finally apply statistical procedures and/or models. Sorting and summarizing can be accomplished by the use of various tabulation and cross tabulation procedures.

Relative to statistical analysis, four categories of statistics are available to the researcher based on his purpose: measures of central tendency, measures of dispersion, tests of significance, and measures of correlation and association. Several procedures can be grouped in each category with the appropriate technique depending on the quality of the data on which it is to be used. Data quality can in part be determined by the measurement scale that has been achieved. In addition to statistical procedures the marketing analyst has models which can be used to transform data into the desired information. These models may be either general marketing models like the break-even model, or they may be tailor-made for the specific situation. Often statistical procedures and models are used in conjunction to carry out the desired analysis.

---

[3] Wilbur S. Wayman, Jr., "A Comprehensive Logistics System Decision Model for a State Controlled Liquor Distribution System" (unpublished Ph.D. dissertation, The Ohio State University, 1973).

[4] See for example Phillip Kotler, *Marketing Decision Making: A Model Building Approach* (New York: Holt, Rinehart and Winston, Inc., 1971) or David B. Montgomery and Glen L. Urban, *Management Science in Marketing* (Englewood Cliffs, N.J.: Prentice-Hall, Inc., 1969).

APPENDIX

This appendix is provided for those who desire a more extensive treatment of multivariate analysis in Marketing.

The multivariate revolution in marketing research
Jagdish N. Sheth

Can the current multivariate methods revolution in marketing research be explained? What is the role of computer technology in the rapid diffusion of multivariate methods? This article defines multivariate analysis and discusses the reasons for the probable continuing increase in its use in marketing research.

Many would agree with the statement that the computer has produced significant advances in the natural and social sciences. However, this general observation overlooks the fact that these two areas have applied computer technology in different ways.

The current diffusion of computer technology is occurring at a time when most of the natural sciences possess several well-developed and invariant laws based on deductive reasoning. Under these circumstances the computer has provided opportunities for model building and for programming a complex network of constructs which enables large-scale testing of physical laws. The most outstanding example of these applications has been provided by the successful exploration of outer space.

However, the social sciences, including marketing, have yet to develop invariant laws. The result is that most of the research in this area is empirical. Attempts are made to explore realities in order to understand the basic nature of the disciplines. Thus, since much of marketing research is empirical and exploratory, the computer has been primarily used to analyze, sort, process, and compact standard commercial data into manageable data banks.

Perhaps computer utilization for model building in the natural sciences and for data analysis in the social sciences provides the best indication of the anticipated rapid adoption of multivariate methods in marketing research. In addition, two facilitating conditions have emerged which ensure large-scale diffusion of multivariate methods in the future.

Source: Reprinted from the *Journal of Marketing*, vol. 35, (January 1971) p. 13–19. Published by the American Marketing Association.

The first condition refers to the fact that after three decades of systematic data-gathering, marketing research has learned the art of data collection. For example, procedures exist for drawing accurate samples from populations, training interviewers and respondents, receiving cooperation from respondents, designing structured questionnaires, and coding and tabulating collected data. In this respect, the marketing discipline may be more advanced than some of the other social sciences such as political science. In fact, the increasing accumulation and storage of market research reflects the validity and usefulness of the information collected. Today it is difficult to find a large-scale enterprise which has not been affected by the information explosion.

Second, the market place is a complex phenomenon. A multitude of factors intervene between the marketing activities of companies and market responses. A simple input-output approach does not seem to provide satisfactory answers to marketing problems. Therefore, attempts are constantly made to examine intervening factors and how they mediate between marketing activities and market responses. This has resulted in the collection of information which corresponds to the complexity of the phenomenon.

The capability of the computer to process these complex, large-scale data banks has resulted in the increased use of multivariate methods in marketing research. The extent of this "multivariate revolution" in marketing research is indicated by several factors. For example, a vast number of canned computer programs for these techniques are already developed and available.[1] In addition, several reviews on the usages of multivariate methods in marketing have been written.[2] A third indication is provided by the increasing number of articles in such journals as the *Journal of Marketing, Journal of Marketing Research*, and *Journal of Advertising Research* which treat applications of multivariate methods to marketing problems.

Inevitably, some questions may be raised about this revolution: How long will it last? Is it not just another fad which will fade away as soon as a new one is introduced? What will be the consequences on future marketing research if multivariate methods are here to stay? Which techniques will be the most relevant and important? However,

---

[1] Kenneth M. Warwick, "Computerized Multivariate Methods," paper presented at AMA Workshop on Multivariate Methods in Marketing, Chicago, January 21–23, 1970.

[2] Jagdish N. Sheth, "Multivariate Analysis in Marketing," *Journal of Advertising Research*, vol. 10 (February 1970), pp. 29–39; Ronald E. Frank and Paul E. Green, "Numerical Taxonomy in Marketing Analysis: A Review Article," *Journal of Marketing Research*, vol. 5 (February 1968), pp. 83–98; and Paul E. Green, Frank J. Carmone, and Patrick J. Robinson, "Nonmetric Scaling Methods: An Exposition and Overview," *Wharton Quarterly*, vol. 2 (Winter-Spring 1968), pp. 159–73.

before these questions can be answered, existing multivariate methods should be understood and classified.

WHAT IS MULTIVARIATE ANALYSIS?

Although Kendall gives a more technical definition,[3] it is possible to characterize multivariate analysis as all statistical methods which simultaneously analyze more than two variables on a sample of observations. As such these methods are extensions of univariate analysis (all known distributions including binomial, poisson, and normal distribution as well as probability system and Bayesian approaches to the analysis of one variable), and bivariate analysis (including cross-classification, correlation, and simple regression used to analyze two variables).

Figure 9A–1 presents a classification of most of the multivariate methods. It is based on three judgments the marketing researcher must make about the nature and utilization of his data: (1) Are some of the variables dependent upon others, thereby requiring special treatment? (2) If yes, how many are to be treated as dependent in a single analysis? and (3) What are the presumed properties of the data? Specifically, are the data *qualitative* (nonmetric) in that the marketing reality is scaled on nominal or ordinal scales, or *quantitative* (metric) and scaled on interval or ratio scales? The technique to be utilized will depend upon the answers to these three questions.

Multiple regression, including several of its variants such as step-wise regression and simultaneous regression, is the appropriate method of analysis when the researcher has a single, metric dependent variable which is presumed to be a function of other independent variables. The objective of multiple regression is to predict the variability in the dependent variable based on its covariance with all the independent variables. This objective is then achieved by the statistical rule of least squares.

Whenever the researcher is interested in predicting the level of the dependent phenomenon, he would find multiple regression useful. For example, sales are predicted from the knowledge of their past relationship (covariance) with marketing efforts; market shares have been predicted based on consumer preference, retail structure, and point-of-purchase advertising and promotion; and consumer buying behavior is predicted from the knowledge of personality and socioeconomic profiles.

If the single dependent variable is dichotomous (e.g., male-female)

---

[3] Maurice G. Kendall, *A Course in Multivariate Analysis* (London: Charles Grifflin & Company, 1957).

Figure 9A–1
A classification of multivariate methods

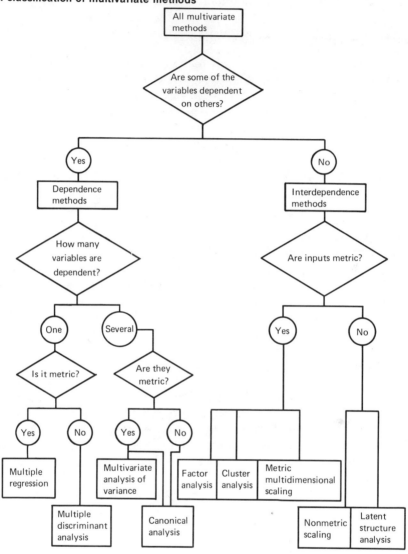

or multichotomous (e.g., high-medium-low), and therefore nonmetric, the multivariate method of *multiple discriminant analysis* is appropriate. The primary objective of discriminant analysis is to *predict* an entity's likelihood of belonging to a particular class or group based on several predictor variables. For example, discriminant analysis has been widely used in marketing to predict whether (1) a person is a good or poor credit risk based on his socioeconomic and demographic profile, (2) innovators can be distinguished from noninnovators according to their psychological and socioeconomic profiles, and (3) private label buyers can be separated from national brand buyers based on socioeconomic and purchasing differences.[4]

The primary objective of multiple discriminant analysis is to correctly classify entities into mutually exclusive and exhaustive classes or groups. This objective is achieved by the statistical decision rule of maximizing the ratio of among-group to within-group variance-covariances on the profile of discriminating (predictor) variables. In addition to the prediction of class membership based on the profile, discriminant analysis reveals which specific variables in the profile account for the largest proportion of intergroup differences.

Multivariate analysis of variance (multi-ANOVA) is an extension of bivariate analysis of variance in which the ratio of among-groups variance to within-groups variance is calculated on a *set* of variables instead of a *single* variable. As such, multi-ANOVA is useful whenever the researcher is testing hypotheses concerning multivariate differences in group responses to experimental manipulations. For example, he may be interested in using one test market and one control market to examine the effect of an advertising campaign on sales as well as awareness, knowledge, and attitudes.

The objective in *canonical analysis* is to simultaneously predict a *set* of dependent variables from their joint covariance with a *set* of independent variables. Both metric and nonmetric data are acceptable in canonical analysis. The procedure followed is to obtain a set of weights for the dependent and independent variables which provides the maximum simple correlation between the composite dependent variable and the composite independent variable.

Canonical analysis appears very useful in marketing because the multitude of marketing and environmental factors tend to produce a variety of market responses. The writer, for example, is currently investigating the "hierarchy of effects" (awareness-interest-attitude-conviction-action) as multiple consequences of advertising and promotion.

Thus far the discussion has focused on multivariate methods applied to data which contain both dependent and independent variables. However, if the researcher is investigating the interrelations, and therefore the interdependence, among all the variables, several other multivariate methods are appropriate. These include factor analysis, cluster analysis, and metric multidimensional scaling if the variables are presumed to be metric, and nonmetric multidimensional

---

[4] Sheth, "Multivariate Analysis in Marketing," p. 29.

scaling and latent structure analysis if they are presumed to be nonmetric.

Factor analysis is based on this proposition: If there is systematic interdependence among a set of observed (manifest) variables, it must be due to something more fundamental (latent) which creates this commonality. One can even consider all the manifest variables as simply *indicators* of this fundamental factor. What is this factor? Can it be extracted from the observed data and their relationships? Is it unidimensional or multidimensional? For example, can an individual's income, education, occupation, and dwelling area be considered as indicators of his social class? How can this factor be extracted? Conversely, factor analysis is also used as a data-reduction method which summarizes the commonality of all the manifest variables into a few factors.

The statistical approach utilized in factor analysis is to maximally summarize all of the variance (information), including the covariance (interdependence), in as few factors as possible, while retaining the flexibility of reproducing the original relationship among the manifest variables.

Factor analysis has been widely used in marketing. It has been used to (1) extract latent dimensions of relative liquor preferences such as sweetness, price, and regional popularity; (2) cluster a series of nighttime television programs or magazines based on their relative viewership and readership; and (3) systematically search for powerful predictors of a phenomenon under investigation.[5]

In *cluster analysis,* the objective is to classify a population of entities into a small number of mutually exclusive and exhaustive groups based on the similarities of profiles among entities. Unlike discriminant analysis, the groups are not predefined. In fact, two major objectives are to determine *how many* groups really exist in the population, and what is their composition.

Cluster analysis seems useful for market segmentation on personality, socioeconomic and demographic, psychological, and purchasing characteristics of the consumers. However, several other applications have been made in marketing. Examples include the clustering of test market cities in order that they may be selected and controlled for experimentation, and grouping a variety of computers based on their objective performance characteristics.[6] Most of the clustering methods are judgmental, however, and devoid of statistical inferences. In fact, judgment is needed in selecting and coding attributes, in obtaining

---

[5] Ibid.

[6] Frank and Green, "Numerical Taxonomy in Marketing Analysis," p. 83.

indices of resemblance or similarity, in choosing among various clustering algorithms, and in naming and testing derived clusters.

Both *metric* and *nonmetric multidimensional scaling* methods, unlike all other multivariate methods, start with a single piece of information. This information relates to perceived relative similarities among a set of objects, such as products, from a sample of respondents. The basic assumption in both metric and nonmetric multidimensional scaling methods is that people perceive a set of objects as being more or less similar to one another on a number of dimensions (usually uncorrelated with one another) instead of only one. However, it may be impossible to directly obtain this multidimensional map from the respondents. One reason for this difficulty is that the respondent may not be consciously aware that he is judging similarities among objects based on these dimensions. A second reason is that he is unwilling to reveal factors (dimensions) that enter into his judgment on similarities. Given this impossibility of directly obtaining the dimensions, reliance is placed on statistical methods of multidimensional scaling to infer the number and types of dimensions that presumably underlie the expressed relative similarities among objects. Therefore, multidimensional scaling methods are applicable in those areas of marketing research where *motivation research* is currently used.

In both metric and nonmetric multidimensional scaling, the judged similarities among a set of objects (e.g., products, suppliers) are statistically transformed into distances by placing those objects in a multidimensional space of some dimensionality. For example, if objects A and B are perceived by the respondent as being most similar compared to all other possible pairs of objects, these techniques will position objects A and B in such a way that the distance between them in multidimensional space is shorter than that between any two other objects.

Despite the similarities between metric and nonmetric multidimensional scaling, there are two important differences. First, metric multidimensional scaling extracts the dimensionality of metric similarity data, whereas the input to nonmetric multidimensional scaling is nonmetric (ordinal) similarities. The metric similarities are often obtained on a bipolar similarity scale on which pairs of objects are rated one at a time. The nonmetric similarities are obtained by asking respondents to rank order (on the basis of similarity) all possible pairs that can be obtained from a set of objects. Various procedures such as dyadic or triadic combinations or rating scales can be used. Second, metric multidimensional scaling attempts to reduce the observed similarities to be represented in a space of minimum dimensions from the trivial representation in n-1 dimensions, where n is the number of objects. In nonmetric multidimensional scaling, the objective is to metricize the nonmetric data by transforming nonmetric data into a metric space, and then by reducing the dimensionality. This is done by a decision rule of monotone transformation in which the observed rank orderings of pairs of objects are reproduced as closely as possible in an arbitrary metric space of some specified dimensions. This metric space is usually Euclidian, although non-Euclidian spaces can be created by the computer.

Although metric multidimensional scaling has not been applied to any large extent in marketing, nonmetric multidimensional scaling has become very popular in the last three years under the pioneering efforts of Paul Green. It has been applied to the dimensionality of similarities among automobiles, magazines, graduate schools, and several other sets of objects.[7]

Latent structure analysis shares both of the objectives of factor analysis: to extract latent factors and express relationship of manifest variables with these factors as their indicators, and to classify a population of respondents into pure types. Traditionally, nonmetric data have been the input to latent structure analysis, although recently metric data have also been used. In marketing, the only applications of this method have been by Myers and Nicosia.[8] One of the main reasons for this has been the lack of computer programs to handle the tedious calculations inherent in this method.

IS MULTIVARIATE REVOLUTION A FAD?

A number of compelling reasons suggest that the rapid use of multivariate methods in marketing is not a fad. Instead, these methods are so important that they will be used more frequently in the future.

First, let us examine the anatomy of several behavioral and operations research methods (e.g., pupil dilation, Markov chains) that degenerated into fads. This was due to three factors. First, some operations research methods clearly proved to be ahead of their times. They presumed (through model building) considerable knowledge about the response functions to marketing efforts at a time when no one actually understood how the marketing mix is related to market reactions. These research methods may prove useful once some laws of market behavior have been established. Second, other behavioral and operations research methods took a normative posture of how markets

---

[7] Green, Carmone, and Robinson, "Nonmetric Scaling Methods," p. 159.

[8] John G. Myers and Francesco M. Nicosia, "New Empirical Directions in Market Segmentation: Latent Structure Models," in *Changing Marketing Systems: Consumer, Corporate and Government Interfaces,* Reed Moyer (ed.) (Chicago: American Marketing Association, 1967).

may or should behave at a time when the empirical inductive approach of descriptive research was considered more appropriate. Third, some methods, particularly in the behavioral area, proved to be genuine fads because they created the illusion that market complexity can be easily described by simple "buzz word" models.

None of these factors seems to be present in multivariate methods. Multivariate methods are largely empirical, deal with the market reality by working backward from reality to conceptualization, and easily handle the complexity presumed to be inherent in marketing research.

Second, multivariate methods as "innovative methods" seem to be consistent with modern marketing concepts of focusing on marketing research needs. And the most pressing need of marketing research is the ability to analyze complex data. This is clearly indicated by the following statement: "For the purposes of marketing research or any other applied field, most of our tools are, or should be, multivariate. One is pushed to a conclusion that unless a marketing problem is treated as a multivariate problem, it is treated superficially."[9]

As discussed earlier, this need for complex analysis is manifested today since data collection is a well-developed and standardized art, and computer capabilities are easily accessible.

Finally, a number of multivariate methods are simply extensions of univariate and bivariate analysis of data. Also, there exist a great variety of multivariate methods. Both of these factors contribute toward inhibiting their degeneration to fadism, because fads generally involve highly specialized research tools. However, some specific multivariate techniques may become fads due to overselling. Also we should expect the usual problems of coordinating the man-machine interface which are inevitable in the use of multivariate methods.

However, none of these factors is likely to deter the progress of the multivariate revolution primarily because all the facilitating conditions are present today.

ROLE OF THE COMPUTER IN MULTIVARIATE REVOLUTION

Perhaps the most important factor in the rapid diffusion of multivariate methods in marketing research is the availability of computer programs. In fact, we can assert that the lack of computer programs has been a major factor in the imbalance between the extensive data banks in existence today and their weak statistical analysis in most marketing research activities. It would seem that a union between multivariate

---

[9] Ronald Gatty, "Multivariate Analysis for Marketing Research: An Evaluation," *Applied Statistics,* vol. 15 (November 1966), p. 158.

methods and the computer will provide excellent opportunities for more scientific approaches to marketing problems.

What are the effects of this union on the development of marketing information systems? At present, marketing information systems in most companies basically consist of large data banks. However, a truly useful marketing information system requires an integrated approach between data banks and their retrieval and analysis in accordance with the needs of marketing management. Since most management decisions are complex, a truly multivariate analysis is needed that can be undertaken only if computer facilities are readily available. For example, a recurring decision in marketing management will involve budget allocation among several marketing forces, including advertising, direct mail, promotion, and personal selling. Ramond and Sheth have developed a marketing information system for budget allocation in which time-series audit data on market responses and marketing activities are analyzed by multivariate regression.[10] In essence, changes in shares of market responses such as sales are regressed on changes in shares of several marketing forces including advertising, direct mail, and promotion. Their relative weights and signs are then used by the marketing manager to choose one of the following alternatives given that his objective is to increase the profitability of marketing forces: (1) Maintain the present budget allocation policy. (2) Increase the total budget by a certain amount to reach the optimum level of profitability. (3) Reallocate the budget among marketing forces proportionate to their relative weights. (4) Reduce the total budget by a certain amount to bring expenditures to the optimum level. (5) Phase out the product. This type of marketing information system could not be achieved without a complete interface between the computer and some multivariate method.

A second area benefiting from this interface is testing and estimating parameters of complex and comprehensive theories of the market place. Two specific examples may illuminate this point. First, in the area of advertising effectiveness, a number of researchers[11] have conceptualized a "hierarchy of effects" of advertising and promotion. This hierarchy usually begins with awareness and ends with purchase behavior; in between, several other effects such as interest, knowledge, preference, liking, and conviction are sequentially arranged. It is also presumed that advertising will have, in general, less impact as we move from awareness to action. It would seem that despite numerous

---

[10] Charles Ramond and Jagdish Sheth, "Controlling Marketing Performance: Two Case Examples," paper presented to the Workshop on Marketing Information Systems, Association of National Advertisers, August 20, 1970.

[11] Robert C. Lavidge and Gary A. Steiner, "A Model for Predictive Measurement of Advertising Effectiveness," *Journal of Marketing*, vol. 25 (October 1961), pp. 59–62.

empirical studies, no study has as yet attempted to validate the hierarchy by using an appropriate multivariate method.[12] Since the theory
presumes a number of effects, canonical analysis appears most appropriate to test the theory and estimate parameters of relative relationships between the hierarchy of effects and a set of advertising variables such as media and copy. Unless such a complex multivariate
analysis is done, it is not possible to either support or reject the theory
of multiple advertising effectiveness. Much of the inconclusive support currently found in the research literature is perhaps due to this
lack of multivariate analysis. Such multivariate analysis, however, was
impossible without the appropriate computer capabilities.

Another example comes from an outstanding effort by Farley and
Ring to fully test the Howard-Sheth theory of buyer behavior through
the use of simultaneous linear equations and the computer.[13] Howard
and Sheth have developed a comprehensive and complex theory of
buyer behavior in which a large number of psychological constructs,
such as attention, overt search, attitude, motives, and satisfaction,
intervene between the marketing stimuli and the buyer's responses.
In addition, a number of exogenous factors, such as social class, culture, and reference groups, also determine a buyer's responses via
their influence on the psychological constructs. Finally, several of the
constructs are dynamically interdependent on one another because of
the theory's information processing framework. Farley and Ring operationally defined these interdependencies in terms of a set of eleven
simultaneous equations; then, using the panel data collected as part of
the Columbia Buyer Behavior Project on a sample of more than 900
respondents, they tested the theory. Although they were only
moderately successful in validating the theory, their effort represents
one of the best examples of how the union between the computer and
multivariate methods facilitates the testing of complex theories.

There are several areas of marketing research in which only univariate data have been collected, although the phenomenon is recognized to be complex. In these areas, the combination of multivariate
methods and the computer may be most beneficial in furthering systematic and scientific analysis to possibly generate some invariant
laws. An example is the research on durable appliances, particularly
related to purchasing plans of households. Despite the recognition
that purchasing plans are determined by a composite of several important factors, most attempts at measuring them have remained uni-

[12] Kristian S. Palda, "The Hypothesis of a Hierarchy of Effects: A Partial Evaluation,"
Journal of Marketing Research, vol. 3 (February 1966), pp. 13–24.

[13] John V. Farley and L. Winston Fling, "Deriving an Empirically Testable Version of
the Howard-Sheth Theory of Buyer Behavior," paper presented at the Third Annual
Buyer Behavior Conference, Columbia University, May 1969.

variate. A single scale is used on which the degree of certainty of buying intentions within a specified time period is obtained from the respondents. It is very probable that this univariate scale is used as a surrogate for more complex factors and has not represented the construct well enough to either predict or explain subsequent purchasing behavior. With the use of multivariate methods such as factor analysis, it is conceivable that buying intentions may indeed prove to be a multidimensional concept.

CONCLUSION

A number of facilitating factors suggest that multivariate methods may rapidly diffuse in marketing research, and may become a way of life in the statistical analysis of marketing data. These include (1) the empirical, inductive tendency in conducting marketing research due to lack of discovery of marketing laws; (2) collection of large-scale data on marketing problems; (3) confidence in data banks in terms of their reliability and validity; and (4) availability of computers and canned computer programs. The last factor is certainly the most important one in enhancing the diffusion of multivariate methods.

The role of the computer in furthering the maturity of the marketing discipline is thus immense. By diffusing multivariate methods, it is likely to enable marketing researchers to attempt large-scale marketing information systems in which an integrated marketing approach can be undertaken. It will enable researchers to test and estimate parameters of complex generalized theories and models. With the use of multivariate methods, the computer is likely to generate a sudden increase in in-depth scientific empirical research on well-known issues in marketing.

DISCUSSION QUESTIONS

1. Discuss the process of analysis; its steps, its purpose and its relationship to the total research process.
2. Suppose that you are employed by a toothpaste company. They are interested in looking at any possible relationship between age and the brand of toothpaste used. First, operationally define the variables, then conduct a small survey in your area and finally put your results into a cross tabulation. What would you conclude about the relationship between brand used and age?
3. The following values reprsent the sales of our product last month in a sample of 20 cities.

$ 8,000	$ 7,000	$ 5,000	$ 8,000	$ 9,000
10,000	15,000	12,000	8,000	8,000
7,000	6,000	9,000	10,000	7,000
6,000	11,000	13,000	11,000	13,000

What is the mean sales, what is the median sales, and what is the standard deviation of the sample? Assume that we are correctly selling our product in 100 cities. What would you estimate the average sales to be in the 100 cities assuming that a confidence coefficient of .95 is desired?

4. Given the following cross tabulation:

| Product | Sex | |
used	Male	Female
Yes	60	70
No	40	30
Total.................	100%	100%
N	200	300

Compute a chi-square statistic. Are the two variables related at the .05 level of significance?

5. Discuss the interpretation of regression analysis results. How can the predictive power of a regression model be judged?

6. Discuss the concept of an analytical model and the application of models in marketing research and decision making.

7. Assume that you are a member of the management team for a major league baseball franchise. In order to plan for personnel needs, concessions, and so forth, daily attendance forecasts are needed. Discuss the development of a tailor-made model for this purpose.

SELECTED REFERENCES

Buzzell, Robert D.; Cox, Donald F.; and Brown, Rex V. *Marketing Research and Information Systems*. New York: McGraw-Hill Book Co., 1969, chapters 5 and 6.

Clover, Vernon, and Balsley, Howard. *Business Research Methods*. Columbus, Ohio: Grid, Inc., 1974, chapters 8, 9, and 11.

Donnelly, James H., and Ivancevich, John M. *Analysis for Marketing Decisions*. Homewood, Ill.: Richard D. Irwin, Inc., 1970, chapter 2.

Ehrenberg, A. S. C. *Data Reduction: Analyzing and Interpreting Statistical Data*. New York: John Wiley & Sons, Inc., 1975.

Greenberg, Barnett A.; Goldstucker, Jac L.; and Bellenger, Danny N. "What Techniques Are Used by Marketing Researchers in Business?" *Journal of Marketing* (April 1977), pp. 62–68.

Kotler, Philip. *Marketing Decision Making: A Model-Building Approach.* New York: Holt, Rinehart and Winston, Inc., 1971.

Langhoff, Peter, ed. *Models, Measurement and Marketing.* Englewood Cliffs, N.J.: Prentice-Hall, Inc., 1965.

Montgomery, David B., and Urban, Glen L. *Management Science in Marketing.* Englewood Cliffs, N.J.: Prentice-Hall, Inc., 1969.

Tull, Donald S., and Albaum, Gerald S. *Survey Research: A Decisional Approach.* New York: Intext Press, 1973, chapters 8 and 9.

chapter
10

Communicating and evaluating research results

In Chapter 4 the marketing research process was described in ten steps. All but one of those steps have been discussed in the preceding pages. If research were conducted solely for the benefit of the researcher himself, there would be little need to proceed past the ninth step of data analysis. In most cases, however, research is conducted in support of a larger decision-making process. It is, therefore, necessary to communicate the results of research to those who will utilize the information in making decisions. The process by which research results are communicated is the major focus of this chapter.

Since the reporting of research findings is fundamentally a communication process, the first part of the chapter is devoted to a communication model. This model points out the elements of communication which affect research reporting. It also points out the importance of reporting research results in a manner which will be meaningful to the audience of the report. Report preparation and evaluation of the research are covered in subsequent sections of the chapter.

RESEARCH REPORTING AS A
COMMUNICATION PROCESS

Research reporting is, essentially, the task of translating research results and communicating the translation. The term "translating" may appear to be out of place since we are not immediately concerned with communicating in different languages, e.g., English, French, or German. The researcher is usually a specialist, however, with a different technical language, or jargon, than that used by the manager. Thus,

Figure 10–1
Interactive communication model

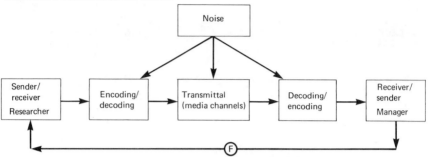

the researcher must successfully translate from his terminology into that of the manager.

The model illustrated in Figure 10–1 is a basic "dyadic" interactive communication model. In the case of research reporting, the "Sender/Receiver" is the researcher and the "Receiver/Sender" is the manager. Translation takes place in the encoding, decoding, and transmittal phases of communication. For the time being, the researcher will be referred to as the sender, who must encode a message which can be transmitted and decoded by the manager, or receiver. Feedback and noise will be discussed later.

Encoding and decoding

The researcher has defined a problem, designed his research, implemented the study, and analyzed results. All of this activity is performed and recorded in the researcher's own language. Formal logic, statistical hypothesis, experimental designs, and mathematical analysis are among the many tools used by researchers to produce answers to the manager's questions. The problem is to convert these language elements into symbols which the manager can decode and comprehend correctly.

Assume, for example, that a consumer goods manufacturer is faced with several marketing strategy alternatives dependent upon the size of a certain age group in its market. That is, if the percentage of customers of age 40 and older is greater than 50 percent, one strategy would be implemented. If the proportion is smaller, a different strategy would be required. The strategy alternatives are clearly understood, but the firm's management cannot afford to select the wrong one. Therefore, the marketing research staff is asked the following question:

Is the percentage of consumers of product *x* who are 40 years of age and older greater than 50?

An analyst has attacked the problem and completed his study. The following notations appear in his records:

$$H_0 : \P \geq .50$$
$$H_1 : \P < .50$$

Where

$\P$ = proportion of customers of age 40 and older.

$$n = 200, p = .46$$

For $\alpha = .05$; $B = .10$, reject H_0 if $z < -1.65$.

In his first attempt to provide a response for management the analyst drafted the following remarks:

Memorandum to: Marketing Management
From: Marketing Research Staff
Subject: Proportion of product x customers of age 40 and older

Between May 1 and May 15, interviews were conducted with 200 randomly selected purchasers of product x. Each respondent indicated his or her age, and a frequency distribution by age was developed from the data. The proportion of the sample of age 40 or older was .46.

Although the sample proportion (p) of .46 is less than the indicated .50, we cannot necessarily conclude that the true population proportion $(\P)$, is in fact less than .50. Rather, we tested the hypothesis that $\P$ is at least .50.

$$H_0 : \P \geq 0.50$$
$$H_1 : \P < 0.50$$

It is common in these tests to use an *alpha* of .05 which gives us a critical z value of -1.65 for the left-tail test. Using the standard formula for calculating the standard normal deviate (z) we tested the null hypothesis for the following decision rule:

If z is less than (a greater negative value) -1.65, reject H_0.
The calculation of z is:

$$z = \frac{p - \P}{s_p} = \frac{p - \P}{\sqrt{\dfrac{pq}{n-1}}} = \frac{.46 - .50}{\sqrt{\dfrac{.46 \times .54}{199}}} = \frac{-.04}{.0353} = -1.13$$

Since the calculated z in the test is greater than the critical value $(-1.13 > -1.65)$, our decision rule might lead us to accept the null hypothesis. That is, the finding of the survey $(p = .46)$ could occur if $\P = .50$, and this should not be attributed to random chance.

It is important to note at least one limitation of the study as conducted. Since the question which we addressed focused on a proportion of at least .50, we did not concern ourselves with estimating the true proportion. In using the customary *alpha* risk of .05, we have simply decreased the possibility of stating in error that ¶ is less than .50. It is reasonable to assume, therefore, that ¶ could be greater, perhaps substantially greater, than .50. If a ¶ greater than .50 changes the nature of management's problem, we suggest further research to more accurately estimate ¶.

If any further information concerning the study is required, please address your inquiries directly to Mr. A.

Sincerely,
Mr. B

If the party to whom this memorandum is addressed is familiar with hypothesis testing, statistical inference, and the Central Limit Theorem, then encoding may not be a problem. While the existence of a technically sophisticated manager is conceivable, it cannot be assumed. Casual references to *"z"* values, *"alpha,"* "null hypothesis," and other elements of research jargon have not been translated by the sender into a different symbolic code.

Imagine, for a moment, that you are a marketing executive who "came up through sales" and graduated from college 15 years ago. You have asked the research staff to answer a question regarding customers who purchase product *x*. The researcher has encoded a message (the memorandum) and you must now decode it. Since your college education included some exposure to mathematics and statistics, most of the words, symbols, and numbers are at least vaguely familiar. You do not, however, get an answer to your question. Nowhere in the memorandum do you find a clear "yes" or "no."

If the researcher had properly anticipated the needs of the manager he might have encoded the following message:

Memorandum to: Marketing Management
From: Research Staff
Subject: Proportion of product *x* customers of age 40 and older

In response to the question you raised concerning the age of customers of product *x*, we have conducted a brief study. The results of a survey of 200 customers indicate that approximately 46 percent are 40 years of age or older. However, we cannot rule out the possibility that the actual percentage is 50 percent or greater.

Please note that the particular research design used does not allow us to specify the precise proportion. We can only state that it appears to be approximately 46 percent.

If you desire further inquiry into this matter, or more detail on the study, please let me know.

Respectfully,
Mr. B

Feedback

Note that the second memorandum says essentially the same thing as the first. More important, however, it probably answers the manager's question to his satisfaction. The researcher has included all of the necessary precautions and conditions for interpreting the findings. If any further questions arise, the manager will initiate feedback to the researcher. When this happens, the manager becomes a sender, and the researcher is a receiver.

Suppose, for example, that the manager decides to pursue the age question further. He informs the researcher that he would like a more accurate estimate of the age of product x customers. The additional information must not cost much money, but a certain amount of additional funds are available. The message is encoded and transmitted as a memorandum to the researcher. Since the manager is faced with the task of encoding, he is careful to reference the researcher's earlier remarks concerning the limits of the research design. He further notes the dollar constraint to indicate that a major new research effort is not warranted.

The role of feedback in an interactive communication system is to bring the output of the system in line with system objectives. In the current example the researcher responded to the initial request with a unit of output represented by the memorandum. In the eyes of the manager, this output did not adequately meet the objective of the system. Through feedback, the manager is able to alter the subsequent output of the researcher. If successful, this further action will improve the manager's ability to make a decision.

To complete the illustration, we simply note that the researcher used his sample data to estimate a confidence interval for the proportion of product x customers 40 or older. He encoded a second response to the manager which satisfied the information need. Although highly simplified, this example illustrates the principles of encoding, decoding and feedback in research reporting. The production of more sophisticated reports is treated later in the chapter.

Noise

Throughout the previous example, research reporting is treated as a simple process of encoding, transmitting, and decoding. While these steps constitute the main functions in communication, the additional feature of *noise*, or interference, makes communication an even greater challenge. It can not be concluded that perfect encoding and decoding will insure faultless communication. The researcher's inability to encode a message precisely in the terms required for perfect understanding by the manager is, of course, a form of noise. That is, a sender must encode his message with both an incomplete understanding of the receiver's knowledge and language, and also a limited inventory of encoding symbols (words, signs, and numbers).

In addition to the sender's limitations, communication must take place in spite of numerous sources of external interference. This type of external noise exerts the least impact in personal, two-party, face-to-face communication. As the number of parties involved increases, and/or the medium becomes less personal, the opportunity for external interference increases. When a researcher reports in person to an individual manager, the effect of noise is minimized. The manager may be distracted by telephone calls, a bad cold, or other interruptions, but has the opportunity to request immediate review, elaboration, or revision of the researcher's messages. The potential impact of noise is minimized by immediate feedback and the interactive nature of face-to-face communication.

The written memorandum creates additional opportunities for noise, such as misspelled words, misplaced decimal points, time pressures on the reader, and others. Again, if the parties involved are in close physical proximity, good feedback and interaction can remedy the problem. The problem of noise is discussed further in the sections on media and procedures.

Transmittal (media channels)

The processes of encoding and decoding are shown in Figure 10–1 with the intermediate step of transmittal. Here we are concerned with the movement of an encoded message from a sender to a receiver. The subject of transmittal necessarily focuses on the various media available for communication. While there is no such thing as a simple medium, we are more familiar with some than with others. Speech, for example, is an auditory medium with which most people are quite familiar. Effective speech, however, is not easy to achieve. The researcher must choose media for transmitting his report which, within practical limits, enhance the total effectiveness of communication.

Media selection is a complex problem, and there is no simple solution. The approach to media selection offered in this chapter is oriented to the needs of individuals who merely seek a few guidelines which, more often than not, will result in effective and efficient reporting. The first principle to be followed in media selection concerns the preferences of the receiver. Second, the sender should select the simplest media available, given the communication task. Finally, media must not be called upon to do much more than carry a message. A brief discussion of each of these points follows, those seeking a fuller understanding of the subject should consult additional sources.

The receiver's cognitive style.   Each individual receiver has a particular manner, or style, in which he seeks meaning in the world which surrounds him. This behavioral feature is called cognitive style. Cognitive style has already been discussed in one context in the section on encoding and decoding. There we were concerned with meanings and the selection of a proper language. Regardless of the meaning of a message, however, cognitive style is also reflected in our preferences for media. Five obvious components of cognitive style are the senses through which we receive stimuli. A written message is visual; a spoken message is auditory; the "feel of mink" is tactile; and so on. Messages can range from a presentation of a real object, to a set of words and/or numbers which represent that object.

If the researcher knows that the manager prefers to see and feel a real object (as opposed to reading a description), arrangements might be made for the manager to participate in some portion of the research as part of the report. A memorandum alone might prove to be relatively inefficient in this case. When the researcher knows that a manager prefers to hear, touch, smell, or taste, media selection becomes a positive factor in the communication effort. In any event, the researcher should avoid selecting media which are known to be in conflict with the manager's cognitive style.

Keeping it simple.   As new, more sophisticated devices for communication appear, many senders are tempted to apply the innovations in the hope of becoming more effective in reaching receivers. Examples of recent media-related innovations include multimedia presentations, highly portable film and videotape equipment, and portable computer terminals. The researcher, as any other sender, should approach media selection with an eye for efficiency. The guiding force should be what is the simplest medium required for the desired results.

A well-planned and carefully written report may be just as effective as a multimedia presentation involving audio tapes and slide projectors. Keep in mind, however, that the multimedia presentation may be the most efficient means for reaching certain managers. As audio and visual components are added, costs generally increase. The more sophisticated media, such as motion picture films or videotape, incur the greatest expense and should be used only when the combination of sound, sight, and motion are all required. In light of these guidelines it is obviously no accident that the vast majority of reporting involves written or spoken words accompanied by simple visual aids.

The limits of media.   In and of themselves, media have no strange powers over receivers. One of the most dramatic media tools developed in recent history is electronic data-processing hardware. Laymen must be reminded constantly that computers are capable of doing only what they are made to do by their users. The same is true of other communication media. When properly used, however, any medium can be impressively effective relative to a poor application of the same medium. If a picture is worth a thousand words to one manager, but fails to carry sufficient meaning to another, it is the manager's cognitive style, not the medium itself, which determines success.

One must also consider the problem of noise when assessing the effectiveness of a medium. Audio channels, for example, are highly vulnerable in that receivers may be distracted and miss part of the message. In such cases, selected visual supplements, which serve as a more permanent record may be desirable. In any event, the wise sender accepts the multitude of limitations inherent in communication and attempts to select media which provide maximum message transmittal within desired levels of time and cost.

Figure 10–2
Procedure for producing a research report

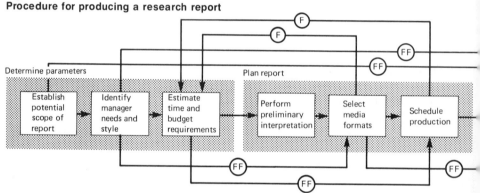

SYSTEM FOR RESEARCH REPORTING

The foregoing discussion provided some insight into the general nature of the communication task in research reporting. In this section a step-by-step procedure for producing reports is presented.

Although some helpful hints on writing and other production activities are included in the discussion, the reader should consult some of the suggested readings at the end of the chapter for further assistance.

Gallagher has summarized the futility of seeking a simplistic approach to reporting by stating:

The search for a magic formula for preparing effective reports quickly and easily has been as endless and intensive as the search for the fountain of youth, and the results have been about the same. . . . One harmful side effect, however, is that these easy remedies encourage motion without much progress, for when the writer becomes disillusioned with one, he discards it in favor of another that is easy but equally ineffective. . . . Let's be realistic then. Preparing reports is more than applying the seat of the pants to the seat of the chair. It takes time, thought, empathy, technique, and work . . .'

Many people are shocked to learn that they cannot take communication for granted. Most have been well prepared to read literature or express thoughts *to their own satisfaction*. The objective of reporting, however, is effective and efficient communication in which success is measured by the receiver's or manager's satisfaction. This focus on the needs and style of the manager was discussed earlier in the chapter. It serves now as the starting point of a system for producing reports which, if properly applied, will help the user avoid the pitfalls de-

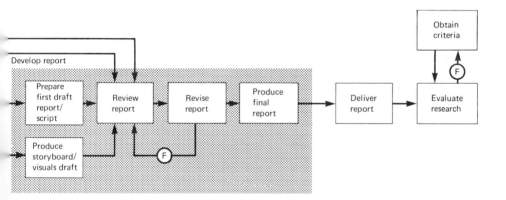

scribed by Gallagher. A model of the system is illustrated in Figure 10–2.

Determine report parameters

The point at which reporting becomes a formal process is sometimes overlooked. That is, most reports are written by the person who has conducted the research. It is important, therefore, that the researcher is able to recognize when the research has ended and reporting has begun. For this reason, a logical first step in the reporting procedure is to determine the parameters of the report. In this step the researcher must sit back and view the completed research, the audi-

---

' W. J. Gallagher, *Report Writing for Management* (Reading, Mass.: Addison-Wesley Publishing Co. Inc., 1969), p. 13.

ence, and the resource parameters within which a successful report can be developed.

First, the potential scope of the report is determined. The researcher reviews (1) the original problem, (2) the intended research design, (3) the results of analysis, (4) additional questions which arose during the study, and (5) areas where further inquiry is desirable. This review establishes the total range of content which the report could conceivably encompass. It is important to perform the review before determining parameters which delimit the scope. Properly conducted, this step prevents the researcher from overlooking seemingly unimportant elements of the research which may prove relevant later.

The second parameter is the manager. As pointed out earlier in the chapter, successful reporting is oriented to the needs and style of the manager, whose background, interest, and experience in research will set the tone for the style of the report. An understanding of the manager's business operations and information needs will enable the researcher to place meaningful limits on the scope of the report. Finally, the manager's location, the nature of the report presentation, and the manager's cognitive style all have an impact on the format which will be used for reporting.

Last, but not least, the resources available for producing a report should be estimated. Obviously, some steps in the procedure are not necessary when a simple written memorandum is intended. The researcher knows that he or she must spend time and use the necessary support to complete the task. In many cases, however, a rather lengthy, well-illustrated document or presentation is called for. In these cases the amount of time and money devoted to report preparation can run into weeks and thousands of dollars. In order to plan such a task, the researcher must establish the limits of available resources.

Plan report

Given the potential scope, the manager's needs and style and resource constraints, the researcher moves into report planning, the first step of which involves a preliminary interpretation of research findings. Some readers may question a procedure in which research results are interpreted after the manager's needs and style are examined. The questions might arise, "Doesn't prior consideration of the manager bias the interpretation?" Hopefully, the answer is "No!" The key to understanding this procedure is the meaning of interpretation.

In properly conducted research the researcher strives for objectivity through the use of scientific methodology. Unfortunately, complete objectivity is seldom achieved in applied research. Recall the earlier example concerning the age of product x customers. Management requested a specific answer to their question, but the researcher knew that the customers' ages could not be determined with certainty. That is, some probability of error inevitably prevents an absolutely certain statement of findings. In light of this predicament, the researcher must make an intelligent statement of these findings, which fully conveys existing uncertainties. The conversion of research findings into meaningful statements for management decision making can be referred to as interpretation. (Note that interpretation is a component of encoding in the communication process.) When completed, the report plan should include a content outline (including notes on the tone of the report), notes on the media for transmittal, and a production schedule. (A sample production schedule is shown in Table 10–1.) Recall the feedback in Figure 10–2. This points out the needs to adjust resource constraints or plans when the two do not match.

Table 10–1
A report production schedule

			Dates
I.	General organization		
	A.	Organization meeting	———
	B.	Task and approach agreement	———
II.	Development of scenarios		
	A.	Initial themes	———
	B.	Draft and circulate papers	———
	C.	Debate and consolidation	———
III.	Review and reassessment		
	A.	Interface with management	———
	B.	Specialty counseling	———
IV.	Finished report		
	A.	Drafts	———
	B.	Final report	———

Note: This is a production schedule developed to produce a research report from a project dealing with the consumer environment and life styles in the 1970s and 1980s. A research team had undertaken the project for the Whirlpool Economic and Marketing Research Department at the request of Sears. The production schedule represents an attempt to develop a consolidated report from the efforts of a series of research teams.

Source: Adapted from *CEL–80 A Report on Consumer Environments and Life-Styles of the Seventies*, (Benton Harbor, Mich.: Whirlpool Corporation, 1971) pp. 6–7.

Among the components of report planning, the outline has probably received the greatest attention. Regardless of the medium, a written outline with distinctive categories and hierarchy of subdivisions is the preferred starting place. One author discusses outlining in terms of: (1) isolating the findings of content segments through arrangement, analysis, and interpretation; (2) identifying coverage, sequence, and typography of the outline; (3) descriptive wording of the captions; and (4) criteria for evaluating the final outline draft.[2]

Having determined the potential scope of the report, the researcher should now attempt to identify the findings of each content area and arrange them in order of the outline. Pending the nature of the research, content areas may be isolated based upon time periods in a historical development, geographic distribution, market segment, consumer characteristics, or some other criteria. It is important to develop content areas which are related to each other through the major research issue or hypothesis. These content areas subsequently serve as the body of the report. At this stage of outlining, the researcher should decide the actual scope, or coverage, of the final report.

According to Dawe:

"The finished outline will show three things: (1) the coverage; (2) the sequence; and (3) the relative importance of the parts. In the final draft, page numbers will be added so that the outline becomes the Table of Contents."[3]

The coverage and sequence are traditionally illustrated in the outline with the following major headings:

I. The letter of transmittal.
II. The title page.
III. Table of contents.
IV. The synopsis.
V. The body of the report (one or more content chapters or sections).
VI. The addenda (bibliography, footnotes, appendices).

The relative importance of the parts of the outline is illustrated by the use of subdivisions and successive number and letter designations. Generally speaking, it is best to use descriptive terms in headings as opposed to generic headings. Furthermore, a minimum of two subdivisions are required to break down a section. Regardless of the style adopted, the reporter should maintain the same rules throughout the report. A number of excellent sources are available which describe outlining and writing styles. An illustrative content outline is shown in Table 10–2.

Finally the outline draft should be evaluated. The following suggestions provide a partial list of evaluative criteria:

1. The content chapters or divisions of the report should be arranged in the best sequence for its development. If the chapters or divisions grow logically out of each other in an interdependent relationship, then they will be presented in this way. If they assume varying degrees of im-

---

[2] Jessamon Dawe, *Writing Business and Economics Papers, Theses and Dissertations* (Totowa, N.J.: Littlefield, Adams & Co., 1965), p. 75.

[3] Ibid., p. 79.

Table 10–2
A content outline: From the Whirlpool study on consumer environments and life-styles of the 1970s and 80s

Contents

I. Project scope and approach
    General objectives
    Criteria for CELS–80
    CELS–80 members
    Project approach and methodology
II. Demographics of the 70s
    Population trends
    Productivity
    Income and expenditures
    Families and households
    Work force
    Urbanization and geographic distribution
    Education
III. Life-styles and values of the 70s
    Where's the revolution
    Consumer choices
    The youth culture
    Women's lib and the women's place
    Will families survive
    The family scene
    Mobility
    Services
    Affluence and values
    New poverty of time
    An old poverty of space
    Ecology and environment
IV. Summary of findings and significant implications
    Summary of factors and forces
    Business relevancies

Source: *CEL–80 A Report on Consumer Environments and Life-Styles of the Seventies*, (Benton Harbor, Mich.: Whirlpool Corporation, 1971), p. 2.

portance to the accomplishment of the major purpose, a descending order of significance is likely the best sequence.

2. The Roman divisions should separate the report into fairly equal, comparable segments. It is poor form to put all the report findings under a single Roman number. Each of the major discussion areas will make up at least a single chapter or part with a Roman-number designation of its own.

3. The captions should be mutually exclusive. If the same sort of item appears more than once in the outline, an overlap is indicated and a revision is called for.

4. All captions on the same level should carry the same grammatical form, to indicate parallelism in emphasis. If one item at a certain level is a phrase,

then all items should be phrases. If one is a sentence, then all should be sentences. The noun-phrase construction for all captions is generally preferable for formal research papers.

5. Synonyms and rearrangement of wording should be employed to avoid monotonous repetition.
6. Every item included in the outline should represent at least a single paragraph in the paper. Several paragraphs may be used to elaborate a single outline entry; but if the material discussed is not important enough to occupy a paragraph of discussion, the outline entry is probably unnecessary.
7. The interrelationship of discussion areas should be apparent.
8. The captions at any level should be of approximately equal importance.
9. Phrasing should cover all the material discussed under a caption.
10. One-item subdivisions are illogical. If two subdivisions are not possible, there is no need to subdivide.[4]

Develop report

The next sequence of steps involves report development. Development is more than the simple act of writing or producing. It implies an interactive process of production, review, and revision which ultimately yields a finished product. The first step is preparation of a first draft, or script. Using the outline and other inputs the researcher makes a first attempt to encode his message. If visual materials are involved, a storyboard or draft of visual aids is also produced in this step.

Visual aids (graphics) play a particularly important role in reporting. They include "tables, charts and graphs, and pictorial illustrations such as photographs, maps and diagrams."[5] Graphics are concise and dramatic. They act as focal points and convey large amounts of information. R. L. Shorter offers the following cautions in using graphics:

1. *Don't use so many charts that they overwhelm the rest of the report.* The reader will either ignore everything else, or—if he doesn't like charts— ignore the entire report.
2. *Use charts to explain or support the major points in the report.* The fewer charts you use, the more attention each gets; so if you use only one or two it is doubly important that they relate to the main facts you are trying to convey.
3. *Don't try to convey too much information on one chart.* If you do, it will be cluttered and hard to understand. It's better to put the information in two simple charts than to crowd it into one complex one.

---

[4] Ibid., p. 86.

[5] Leland Brown, *Effective Business Report Writing*, 3d ed. (Englewood Cliffs, N.J.: Prentice-Hall, Inc., 1973), p. 121.

4. *Design the chart to focus on the meaning you are trying to convey.* Don't merely convert figures into graphic form and expect this to tell the reader what you want him to know.
5. *Keep it simple.* Leave out all unnecessary frills and trimmings. Don't add technical notes and other details that are not needed to *understand* the chart.
6. *Tie it in with your written presentation* by referring to it in the written text and by placing it as close as possible to the section of the text where you discuss it. This will spare your reader the annoyance of holding his thumb on page 4 when you refer him to a chart on page 45.[6]

Figure 10–3 illustrates the type of simple tables and charts that are most effective in research reports. When the draft text and visuals are completed, the report is ready for review. Review is an evaluation in which the report is tested against criteria developed in earlier steps. Is the content complete? Are the needs and style of the manager accommodated? Can a finished version of the report be produced within resource parameters? Finally, is the report grammatically and otherwise technically sound? The review usually results in revisions which are subjected again to review. When no further revisions are necessary, a final version is produced and delivered to the manager.

Production may simply involve the skills of a typist and the use of a copying machine. On the other hand, television production could involve casting, taping on location, and editing. Proper planning, particularly production scheduling, is essential for more sophisticated production efforts. Poor planning inevitably results in cost overruns as unanticipated problems arise. If the researcher himself is to produce the report, simplicity is the rule. Elaborate media productions (television, motion pictures, and other audio-visual formats) should be implemented by professionals, either within the researcher's firm or in the media industry. Note that production is the final step of encoding.

An illustrative section of a finished report is shown in Table 10–3.

Deliver report

Delivery is the equivalent of transmittal in the communication process (Figure 10–1). Delivery begins when the message leaves the sender. In the case of a personal oral presentation, encoding ends with the selection of the words which form a message, and delivery begins when the words are actually spoken. The message is in transmittal as sound waves move from the speaker toward the receiver. Delivery can be a frustrating experience since the sender has relatively little control

---

[6] R. L. Shorter, *Written Communication in Business,* 3d ed. (New York: McGraw-Hill Book Co., 1971), p. 404.

Figure 10–3
Effective tables and charts: An illustration

Table AA
Growth pattern for consumer good industries

Industry classification	Expected rate of growth in the 1970s
1. Radio, television, records	8.1%
2. Toiletries	6.7%
3. Foreign travel	6.5%
4. Automobiles	6.4%
5. Higher education	6.0%
6. Drugs	5.8%
7. Gas, electricity	5.7%
8. Medical services	5.5%
9. Appliances	5.5%
10. Shelter	5.4%

Source: *The Consumer of the Seventies,* The Conference Board, p. 67.

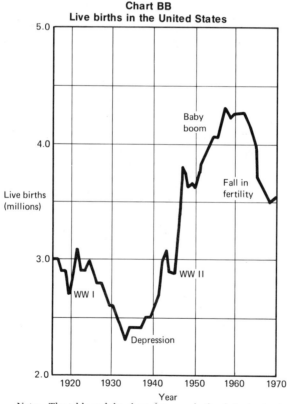

Chart BB
Live births in the United States

Note: The table and the chart above are both relatively simple, but they convey a great deal of information. The key is to achieve sharp focus on a specific topic in the simplest fashion possible.

Source: *Cel–80 A Report on Consumer Environments and Life Styles of the Seventies,* (Benton Harbor, Mich.: Whirlpool Corporation, 1971), p. 11 and p. 40.

Table 10–3
The final report: An illustrative section from the Whirlpool consumer environments and life-styles report

IV. Summary of findings and significant implications
Summary of factors and forces

1. Urbanization
The trend to the development of a more urban society will continue. The results will be further congestion of the cities, the growth of megalopolises, and the continuing growth of suburban areas. A further decline of the cores of cities and the development of ring areas will occur. No larger extension is anticipated in the creation of new cities which will attract large populations. The reduction of a rural emphasis will result in significant changes in life-styles. Urban concentrations will heighten the desire for privacy and the "need to get away from it all." Mass housing and mass transportation requirements will be stimulated.

2. Cosmopolitanism
Travel, affluence and leisure will foster more cosmopolitan tastes and life styles. The effect will be that our life styles will reflect the tastes and products of the world. Broader exposure of consumers will result in even more favorable images of international products. The world will be brought into American homes. The results will be both an uplifting of tastes and a broader acceptance of different life styles. Consumers will be exposed to an increasing number of product alternatives and choices will become more difficult. Markets will be segmented on psychological and sociological as well as the usual demographic and geographic bases.

(Other sections follow in sequence).

Source: *CEL–80 A Report on Consumer Environments and Life-Styles of the Seventies,* (Benton Harbor, Mich.: Whirlpool Corporation, 1971), p. 32.

over the message while it is in transmittal. This problem, as mentioned earlier in the chapter, increases as communication becomes less personal. In any event, the researcher's ability to alter a transmitted message is negligible. Most subsequent changes in the report will originate with a request from the manager.

The most common delivery problems facing researchers arise in oral presentations. A few specific points should be noted on this important problem area. Bonner provides a simple list of things to do:

1. Simplify the data.
2. Make the report concise.
3. Get the listener's attention early.
4. Present the information in a logical order.
5. Use visual aids effectively.
6. Choose your words carefully.
7. Enunciate clearly and naturally.

8. Give easiest-to-understand information first.
9. Exhibit self-confidence.
10. Talk to your listeners.[7]

EVALUATING RESEARCH RESULTS

After the report has been delivered, the researcher has an opportunity to evaluate the project. Evaluation involves a comparison of the research objectives against the research process and output. Thus, there are two types of evaluation to consider: (1) internal, or evaluation of the specific decisions and strategies adopted in the course of the project, and (2) external, or manager satisfaction. Obviously, these two elements overlap to some degree. If we examine the sources of information upon which evaluation is based, however, the two are clearly different.

Internal evaluation

Once a problem is defined and the researcher begins to design a study, questions immediately arise which require professional judgment. For example, a decision might be made concerning the sample frame, in which one source is chosen and others are eliminated. Upon completion of the study, the researcher can review his decision in light of its results. If the sample frame, say a directory of manufacturers or telephone directory, proved difficult to work with, a note to that effect might prevent the same problem from arising in a similar future study.

Every step in the project should be reviewed to identify strong as well as weak features. If the project was conducted by several analysts, or if the researcher works in a staff group, peer review is a particularly useful technique for evaluation. Colleagues are thus in a position to share in the benefits of the evaluation. Peer evaluation is conducted in some companies before the report is delivered and/or in a "debriefing" session upon completion of the project.

Again, internal evaluation is largely a function of professional judgment by researchers, and focuses on technical aspects of the study. Sample design, hypothesis construction, data collection, and analytical techniques are subjects which rarely attract critical review on the part of the manager. Rather, the technical expertise of the researcher provides the source for this evaluation. After all, it is the researcher who enjoys the benefit of the time and cost-saving limits produced by internal critique.

---

[7] William H. Bonner, *Better Business Writing* (Homewood, Ill: Richard D. Irwin, Inc., 1974), pp. 279–80.

External evaluation

External evaluation is provided largely by the manager and is based on the extent to which his or her needs are met. A point was made earlier in the chapter along these lines. That is, the needs of the manager include good, well-conceived answers to his questions. The researcher meets this need with a properly conducted, well-communicated study, *regardless of the results.* In other words, "manager satisfaction" does not mean providing the manager with the specific answer he would like to see. While that particular outcome may be emotionally gratifying, it is not a basis for evaluation. Rather, did the manager receive the information that was needed in order to make a better decision?

Because the manager may not view this evaluation in the objective manner described above, the researcher must be aware of the nature of manager feedback. Is the manager actually providing information which serves as a basis for evaluation; or simply expressing pleasure or displeasure with the results? An example of the former might be:

Although I am generally pleased with the outcome of your study, I am concerned that the sample was not divided in some way to account for differences in demand between age groups.

In this case a manager has raised a point which should cause the researcher to review the sample design. Was the design consistent with the problem and hypothesis? Was this aspect of the problem clearly communicated by the manager? Is additional information available for the manager on this point? What steps might be taken to avoid the problem in the future?

While the preceding example clearly serves to assist the researcher, the following is of little use:

I was pleased to see the outcome of your study. As you know, I have strong interest in this project and will be able to proceed largely as a result of the study.

Obviously, the manager is pleased. Unfortunately, the researcher does not know if his work has been critically reviewed.

Research is a dynamic and challenging process. The researcher is constantly faced with decisions which require judgment. Only through thoughtful internal and external evaluation can this process improve over time. Finally, proper evaluation requires dedicated objectivity on the part of the researcher.

SUMMARY

Marketing research does not end with the completion of a study. Rather, the final step is the communication of research activity and findings to the manager. As a communication process, research reporting involves encoding, transmittal, and decoding, each of which is subject to interference (noise). Effective communication requires a receiver, or manager orientation in which encoding and channel selection are based upon manager needs and style.

The simplest task in reporting involves personal, two-party communication, such as a face-to-face conversation between researcher and manager. Feedback is readily available to the researcher in these dyadic, interactive situations. Thus, the researcher is able to alter his presentation immediately and enjoys the best opportunity for successful communication. As the parties become more distant and/or the medium becomes less personal, the communication task becomes more difficult.

The researcher should adhere to a system for research reporting. The first function is parameter identification. At this point the researcher establishes the potential scope of the content, identifies manager needs and style, and estimates resources requirements. These parameters set the stage for the second function, report planning. The planning function produces an outline and notes based on preliminary interpretation of research findings and the selection of media. Regardless of the size or complexity of the report, a well developed outline is an important aid. The plan should also include a production schedule.

The third function of the reporting system involves report development. Development is an iterative process in which drafts are produced, reviewed, and revised. When an acceptable version is reviewed, a final report is produced. The report is then delivered to the manager in the fourth function of the system.

Finally, the study is evaluated to provide useful information for future research, as well as assess the value of the study itself. Internal evaluation is conducted by the researcher(s) and serves the primary purpose of aiding future efforts. External evaluation is largely dependent upon feedback from the manager. This type of evaluation is important both to future efforts and to the evaluation of the study. Unfortunately, managers often fail to provide the meaningful feedback upon which external evaluation is based.

DISCUSSION QUESTIONS

1. Researchers are often frustrated by the apparent lack of understanding of managers and the need to explain again items covered in detail in research reports. Give several possible reasons for this problem in terms of reporting as a communication process.

2. The use of sophisticated techniques and media in reporting can be very effective but is often avoided in favor of simple written or oral presentations. Discuss the reason for the use of simplified procedures.

3. Why is it critical that the reporting phase of the research process be managerially oriented?

4. *a.* Discuss the basic steps in report development.

   b. Develop a list of "do's" and "don'ts" which might serve as a guide to the report writer and as a basis for evaluating a report for the manager.

5. The success of a study is often determined through external evaluation. A study may be successful, however, even though the manager is disappointed in the outcome. Explain.

6. From a manager's point of view, what makes a "good" report?

SELECTED REFERENCES

Dawe, Jessamon. *Writing Business and Economics Papers, Theses, and Dissertations.* Totowa, N.J.: Littlefield, Adams & Co., 1965.

Kemp, Jerrold E. *Planning and Producing Audiovisual Materials,* 2d ed. San Francisco, Calif.: Chandler Publishing Co., 1968.

Lesikar, Raymond V. *Report Writing for Business,* 5th ed. Homewood, Ill.: Richard D. Irwin, Inc., 1977.

Wolf, P. M. and Aumer, R. R. *Effective Communication in Business,* 6th ed. Cincinnati, Ohio: South-Western Publishing Co., 1974.

Cases for part two

The location of a playground*

Using census data for small areas

Situation. A city Parks and Recreation Director was recently appointed in a metropolitan area of about 100,000 people; the central city, Middletown, has about 65,000. The immediate task of the park director is to present a plan to the city manager for locating a new city playground in a neighborhood with a large number of children from low-income families where there is currently a lack of play areas. The playgrounds are used most regularly by children aged 5–14. The plan must be presented to the city council with documentation for the recommendation.

What does the park director need to know?

Where in the city are the playground users?

Where are the existing playgrounds?

---

* This case was prepared by Cynthia Murray Taeuber, Data User Services Division, Bureau of the Census, Washington, D.C.

Where is land available for a playground?

Where are the neighborhoods with a large number of children from low-income families?

Where should the park director go to get her information?

Some is available from her own office (e.g., location of existing playgrounds). She has a large map of the city and draws in the boundaries of the existing parks.

To determine where land is available, the park director goes to the city planning office and discusses the problem with the director who shows her a map of all existing vacant land sites. The two identify several possible locations which they map onto a cellophane sheet to overlay on the map of other park locations (see Exhibit 1).

Exhibit 1
Existing playgrounds, parks, and possible land sites: 1971 (census tracts in Middletown and vicinity)

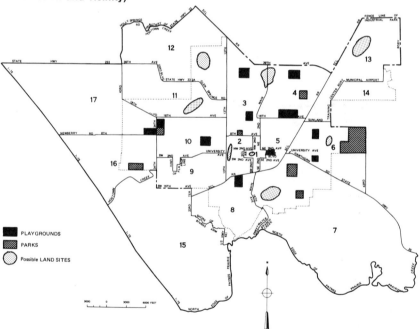

Source: U.S. Department of Commerce, Bureau of the census, 1970 Census of Population and Housing Census Tracts, Standard metropolitan statistical area Final Report PHC(1).

The park director still needs to know the location of low-income families with children. The city planner suggests she consult 1970 Census data to obtain the information. Age and income data are available for neighborhood-like areas in SMSA's called "census tracts."[1] The planner explains that SMSA stands for "standard metropolitan statistical area," which in 1970, comprised a county with a central city (or twin cities) of 50,000 or more persons plus contiguous counties which were socially and economically integrated with the central county. Census tracts are subdivisions of SMSA's. For a more complete definition, they refer to the *1970 Census Users' Guide*, "1970 Census Geography: Concepts, Products, and Programs" (*Data Access Description* #33),[2] and the statistical publications themselves. The planner explains that Middletown is part of an SMSA so there is a printed publication with the needed data which is referred to as a Census Tract Report. The top left corner of the report has the code "PHC(1)" which is another way to refer to this series of Census reports. The P and H together in the code indicate that the report has data from both the population and housing censuses.

They open the PHC(1) report and look at Table 1 (reproduced on pages 288–93) which gives age data for both males and females (referred to as "age by sex") for the entire county, the city, and the remainder of the county ("balance"), and for the individual census tracts. Studying the table further, they see the lines are marked "Male, 5 to 9 years" and "Male, 10 to 14 years" and the equivalent lines for females. If she uses these data, she can add the columns on the office adding machine to obtain the total number of children aged 5–14.

They then turn to the back of the report where there is a map showing the boundaries of the census tracts and the tract numbers corresponding to the numbers in the table (shown on the map on page 302). From the table of contents they identify Table 2 titled "Income Characteristics of the Population: 1970" (reproduced on pages 294–99). This table shows the income distribution and data for "income below the poverty level." The poverty index provides a range of low-income cutoffs adjusted by factors such as family size, sex of the family head, number of children under age 18, and farm and nonfarm residence. (See Appendix B.)

There are a number of choices among the types of data which might be used to describe the income characteristics of each tract:

1. An income distribution.
2. The mean or median income.

---

[1] Small-area data are also available outside SMSA's. See Appendix A for a discussion of small-area data availability.

[2] 1970 Census Users' Guide, Part I, is available for $2.35 from the Superintendent of Documents, Government Printing Office, Washington, D.C. 20402. Copies of Data Access Description #33 are available by writing to the Data User Services Division, Bureau of the Census, Washington, D.C. 20233.

Table 1
General characteristics of the population: 1970

[For minimum base for derived figures (percent, median, etc.) and meaning of symbols, see text]

Census Tracts	Total	Middletown	Balance	Tract 0001	Tract 0002	Tract 0003	Tract 0004	Tract 0005	Tract 0006	Tract 0007	Tract 0008	Tract 0009	Tract 0010
RACE													
All persons	104 764	64 510	40 254	593	6 136	5 951	5 560	4 940	4 016	5 997	4 628	8 535	5 809
White	82 665	52 048	30 617	410	3 274	5 700	5 507	4 827	906	1 093	4 537	8 324	5 718
Negro	21 563	12 041	9 522	178	2 807	210	36	94	3 105	4 900	42	94	36
Percent Negro	20.6	18.7	23.7	30.0	45.7	3.5	0.6	1.9	77.3	81.7	0.9	1.1	0.6
AGE BY SEX													
Male, all ages	52 217	32 372	19 845	267	2 895	2 822	2 741	2 371	1 850	2 847	2 504	4 744	3 058
Under 5 years	4 518	2 569	1 949	12	172	224	337	167	233	356	69	314	162
3 and 4 years	1 732	969	763	7	84	82	126	69	103	155	20	66	56
5 to 9 years	4 809	2 643	2 166	17	163	206	373	188	280	428	38	90	192
5 years	878	488	390	1	39	37	61	48	54	82	11	33	32
6 years	957	534	423	6	25	40	87	37	51	89	11	21	43
10 to 14 years	4 791	2 529	2 262	13	134	174	329	170	272	395	48	27	203
14 years	791	488	426	4	25	33	52	40	51	59	11	27	45
15 to 19 years	6 546	4 659	1 887	29	343	214	212	206	170	306	146	2 067	292
15 years	939	494	445	8	31	30	63	33	26	78	10	—	51
16 years	866	446	420	8	34	42	43	38	41	51	7	2	36
17 years	884	499	375	5	40	48	38	42	45	69	13	21	52
18 years	807	485	322	7	56	48	39	40	29	60	20	1 011	58
19 years	2 050	725	1 325	7	182	48	29	53	29	48	96	1 032	95
20 to 24 years	9 159	1 261	7 898	68	925	496	155	423	160	228	479	1 691	803
20 years	2 171	820	351	11	212	85	27	111	26	62	329	671	184
21 years	2 264	867	397	14	245	120	20	111	38	47	475	437	207
25 to 34 years	7 640	4 803	2 837	33	399	520	498	357	212	327	449	508	430
35 to 44 years	4 628	2 556	2 072	8	165	246	395	210	152	245	83	4	246
45 to 54 years	4 178	2 371	1 807	36	197	294	262	244	154	238	71	42	294
55 to 59 years	1 718	865	853	16	82	117	71	117	50	83	31	—	139
60 to 64 years	1 492	771	721	8	110	109	38	86	54	99	38	—	128
65 to 74 years	1 853	931	922	17	139	159	50	136	79	109	35	—	120
75 years and over	885	414	471	10	66	63	21	67	34	33	19	—	49
Female, all ages	52 547	32 138	20 409	326	3 241	3 129	2 819	2 569	2 166	3 150	2 122	3 791	2 751
Under 5 years	4 267	2 361	1 906	16	148	215	268	157	240	358	92	230	138
3 and 4 years	1 659	893	766	3	56	70	121	65	87	148	27	63	54
5 to 9 years	4 588	2 420	2 168	8	161	197	326	163	263	386	54	94	177
5 years	871	467	404	3	40	39	60	31	45	84	12	25	37
6 years	925	497	428	2	31	43	66	60	53	88	8	21	29
10 to 14 years	4 673	2 506	2 167	29	163	220	332	184	238	393	34	20	221
14 years	940	493	447	5	40	50	55	37	52	80	5	2	43
15 to 19 years	6 074	4 285	1 789	34	408	246	255	212	216	333	173	1 587	247
15 years	856	481	375	1	31	42	55	52	51	72	7	—	43
16 years	886	471	415	7	36	42	60	28	54	72	7	3	43
17 years	846	493	353	4	27	44	62	45	36	78	9	17	48
18 years	1 632	1 316	316	9	71	46	49	39	35	53	14	816	47
19 years	1 854	1 524	330	14	243	70	29	48	40	68	104	750	62

RELATIONSHIP TO HEAD OF HOUSEHOLD

20 to 24 years	8 519	6 492	2 027	57	1 022	497	207	360	227	279	1 195	1 464	442
20 years	2 148	1 812	356	13	364	79	40	75	46	54	307	622	85
21 years	2 087	1 648	439	14	324	120	29	77	53	53	384	355	106
25 to 34 years	7 135	4 338	2 797	22	274	453	526	309	288	420	279	359	313
35 to 44 years	5 041	2 845	2 196	21	186	308	404	245	216	312	79	20	276
45 to 54 years	4 711	2 680	2 031	34	230	339	258	285	184	295	75	8	355
55 to 59 years	1 927	1 067	860	14	128	157	73	140	67	112	32	1	167
60 to 64 years	1 766	1 016	750	16	141	168	53	149	91	88	29	1	146
65 to 74 years	2 348	1 311	1 037	38	216	211	65	228	86	121	29	1	179
75 years and over	1 498	817	681	37	164	118	51	137	50	53	41	—	90

RELATIONSHIP TO HEAD OF HOUSEHOLD

All persons	104 764	64 510	40 254	593	6 136	5 951	5 560	4 940	4 016	5 997	4 628	8 535	5 809
In households	95 176	55 219	39 957	580	5 364	5 933	5 554	4 877	4 003	5 899	4 513	2 650	5 537
Head of household	31 115	18 777	12 338	268	2 188	2 284	1 544	1 832	1 146	1 563	747	958	2 056
Head of family	23 729	13 571	10 158	149	1 034	661	1 430	1 314	941	318	699	931	408
Primary individual	7 386	5 206	2 180	87	154	623	114	518	205	245	048	27	648
Wife of head	20 147	11 384	8 763	166	659	436	1 283	121	640	868	629	914	276
Other relative of head	39 091	20 897	18 194	59	608	955	2 671	660	2 144	331	488	773	770
Not related to head	4 823	4 161	662	13	909	258	56	264	73	137	649	5	435
In group quarters	9 588	9 291	297		772	18	6	63	13	98	115	5 885	272
Persons per household	3.06	2.94	3.24	2.16	2.45	2.60	3.60	2.66	3.49	3.77	2.58	2.77	2.69

TYPE OF FAMILY AND NUMBER OF OWN CHILDREN

All families	23 729	13 571	10 158	119	1 034	1 661	1 430	1 314	941	1 318	699	931	1 408
With own children under 18 years	13 252	7 416	5 836	31	431	756	1 034	567	577	862	218	535	645
Number of children	29 137	15 694	13 443	85	926	1 377	2 225	1 166	513	2 326	368	767	334
Husband-wife families	20 147	11 384	8 763	87	659	1 436	1 283	1 121	640	868	629	914	1 276
With own children under 18 years	11 318	6 205	5 113	22	272	649	941	489	377	552	195	519	596
Number of children	24 632	12 917	11 715	63	563	1 193	2 023	1 003	954	1 470	324	746	1 257
Percent of total under 18 years	74.8	72.1	78.1	51.2	49.4	80.3	88.5	79.2	53.6	53.9	82.0	91.0	91.8
Families with other male head	594	299	295	5	65	32	24	31	27	46	20	2	24
With own children under 18 years	218	95	123	1	9	6	11	12	9	27	2	2	4
Number of children	470	179	291	2	19	6	18	24	18	64	4	2	5
Families with female head	2 988	1 888	1 100	27	310	193	123	162	274	404	50	15	108
With own children under 18 years	1 716	1 116	600	8	150	101	82	66	191	283	21	14	45
Number of children	4 035	2 598	1 437	20	344	178	184	139	541	792	40	19	72
Percent of total under 18 years	12.3	14.5	9.6	16.3	30.2	12.0	8.0	11.0	30.4	29.1	10.1	2.3	5.3
Persons under 18 years	32 923	17 922	15 001	123	1 140	1 486	2 286	1 267	1 779	2 726	395	820	1 370

MARITAL STATUS

Male, 14 years old and over	39 013	25 119	13 894	229	2 451	2 251	1 754	1 886	1 116	1 727	2 362	4 315	2 546
Single	15 742	12 004	3 738	98	1 406	622	385	606	336	562	1 608	3 373	1 152
Married	21 600	12 170	9 430	105	857	1 510	1 312	1 164	706	1 027	674	939	1 333
Separated	634	336	298	6	112	33	4	15	39	80	19	1	13
Widowed	763	401	362	10	101	50	20	38	30	77	16	—	25
Divorced	908	544	364	16	87	69	37	78	44	61	64	3	36
Female, 14 years old and over	39 959	25 344	14 615	278	2 809	2 547	1 948	2 102	1 477	2 093	1 947	3 449	2 258
Single	12 052	9 452	2 860	69	368	522	349	187	397	551	1 158	494	613
Married	22 052	12 530	9 522	111	870	1 539	349	444	803	1 180	667	932	333
Separated	982	651	331	17	146	48	27	32	126	208	10	10	10
Widowed	3 892	2 209	1 683	81	419	335	111	322	172	243	53	10	226
Divorced	1 703	1 153	550	17	152	151	100	149	105	119	69	13	86

Table 1 (continued)

Census Tracts	MIDDLETOWN – Con.						Balance of County							
	Tract 0011	Tract 0012	Tract 0013	Tract 0014	Tract 0016	Tract 0017	Tract 0006	Tract 0007	Tract 0008	Tract 0011	Tract 0012	Tract 0014	Tract 0015	Tract 0016
RACE														
All persons	2 027	2 313	2 095	58	3 515	2 337	125	2 407	16	1 475	1 036	2 358	3 988	334
White	2 016	2 303	1 604	21	3 485	2 323	125	2 381	16	1 459	1 018	1 927	3 754	257
Negro	2	8	486	37	5	1	–	22	–	4	10	430	213	74
Percent Negro	0.1	0.3	23.2	63.8	0.1	–	–	0.9	–	0.3	1.0	18.2	5.3	22.2
AGE BY SEX														
Male, all ages	993	1 130	1 167	54	1 783	1 144	58	1 185	9	727	509	184	2 096	155
Under 5 years	92	127	15	–	157	132	7	140	–	88	67	123	173	12
3 and 4 years	38	37	10	–	65	57	3	49	1	40	25	59	53	3
5 to 9 years	109	109	103	–	184	163	5	137	–	103	73	149	130	22
5 years	14	27	10	–	31	31	1	21	1	15	13	30	28	4
6 years	22	23	12	1	35	33	2	31	–	26	14	27	23	4
10 to 14 years	133	92	211	2	190	136	4	137	1	57	37	137	114	18
14 years	33	20	55	–	33	24	1	21	–	21	10	28	22	3
15 to 19 years	106	71	258	2	133	104	8	98	–	76	33	95	151	13
15 years	30	19	48	–	39	27	–	23	–	19	5	31	25	3
16 years	31	11	51	1	28	31	2	21	–	16	8	15	27	2
17 years	20	12	52	2	27	21	–	21	–	19	7	15	26	2
18 years	15	14	58	–	26	32	3	19	–	14	5	18	30	3
19 years	10	15	49	1	26	22	3	22	–	8	8	18	43	3
20 to 24 years	54	210	222	15	284	18	2	141	–	21	29	88	663	6
20 years	15	30	47	2	33	6	3	13	–	8	6	14	117	2
21 years	8	42	46	1	48	15	3	29	–	5	4	11	163	2
25 to 34 years	126	239	208	16	302	179	13	211	–	123	145	205	408	18
35 to 44 years	166	78	42	13	233	179	8	142	3	132	57	139	125	22
45 to 54 years	137	96	17	5	170	127	5	77	–	69	39	105	145	19
55 to 59 years	29	26	11	–	54	33	1	34	1	13	15	45	43	10
60 to 64 years	28	18	7	–	29	14	2	26	–	8	7	37	35	6
65 to 74 years	9	28	1	–	26	21	1	28	–	2	4	43	60	3
75 years and over	4	19	–	–	21	8	–	14	–	2	3	18	49	3
Female, all ages	1 034	1 183	928	4	1 732	1 193	67	1 222	7	748	527	174	1 892	179
Under 5 years	76	162	6	–	130	125	7	135	1	79	66	138	138	9
3 and 4 years	33	58	4	–	55	49	1	51	1	43	18	56	43	5
5 to 9 years	112	115	64	–	169	131	12	128	–	109	74	144	94	33
5 years	28	21	9	–	26	27	6	28	–	19	18	34	18	9
6 years	28	27	13	–	25	25	2	28	–	24	16	27	23	9
10 to 14 years	124	81	172	1	165	128	6	145	–	74	47	137	110	25
14 years	24	12	38	2	28	20	5	31	–	15	13	27	27	9
15 to 19 years	108	64	168	2	128	106	–	132	–	59	25	96	154	16
15 years	30	10	39	–	28	21	1	27	–	15	11	19	13	5
16 years	29	13	26	–	27	22	–	28	–	15	9	29	23	3
17 years	24	11	33	–	32	25	3	26	–	15	4	17	27	5
18 years	17	16	32	–	24	19	–	23	–	9	2	19	31	5
19 years	8	14	38	1	17	19	6	28	–	6	5	12	60	1
20 to 24 years	59	220	144	1	260	59	2	151	–	19	39	85	528	9
20 years	10	41	25	–	38	13	1	21	–	4	6	15	84	2
21 years	8	44	32	2	40	12	–	29	–	3	3	15	121	1

RELATIONSHIP TO HEAD OF HOUSEHOLD — TYPE OF FAMILY AND NUMBER OF OWN CHILDREN — MARITAL STATUS

	(1)	(2)	(3)	(4)	(5)	(6)	(7)	(8)	(9)	(10)	(11)	(12)	(13)	(14)
25 to 34 years	143	229	195	—	295	232	12	202	—	154	149	187	321	20
35 to 44 years	182	97	79	—	237	183	6	132	2	131	58	144	136	25
45 to 54 years	143	97	53	—	187	137	5	97	—	86	39	88	144	21
55 to 59 years	27	30	36	—	52	57	1	23	—	11	4	45	45	7
60 to 64 years	26	46	13	1	37	19	5	35	2	11	3	50	40	5
65 to 74 years	24	12	7	—	40	21	2	29	—	7	5	49	78	5
75 years and over	10	12	1	—	32	21	2	13	—	8	8	11	94	4

RELATIONSHIP TO HEAD OF HOUSEHOLD

	(1)	(2)	(3)	(4)	(5)	(6)	(7)	(8)	(9)	(10)	(11)	(12)	(13)	(14)
All persons	2 027	2 313	2 095	58	3 515	2 337	125	2 407	16	1 475	1 036	2 358	3 988	334
In households	2 027	2 302	137	4	3 513	2 326	125	2 407	16	1 475	1 033	2 281	3 837	334
Head of household	565	779	51	2	1 149	645	40	710	5	396	305	647	562	87
Head of family	523	642	36	2	905	608	33	616	4	379	287	570	1 084	80
Primary individual	42	137	15	—	244	37	7	94	1	17	18	77	478	7
Wife of head	483	577	30	2	824	555	30	558	4	353	276	510	960	75
Other relative of head	955	881	55	—	332	108	55	104	7	718	442	24	1 083	170
Not related to head	24	65	—	—	208	18	—	35	—	8	10	77	232	2
In group quarters	—	11	1 958	54	2	11	—	—	—	—	3	—	151	—
Persons per household	3.59	2.96	2.69	...	3.06	3.61	3.13	3.39	3.20	3.72	3.39	3.53	2.46	3.84

TYPE OF FAMILY AND NUMBER OF OWN CHILDREN

	(1)	(2)	(3)	(4)	(5)	(6)	(7)	(8)	(9)	(10)	(11)	(12)	(13)	(14)
All families	523	642	36	2	905	608	33	616	4	379	207	570	1 084	80
With own children under 18 years	365	374	27	—	553	441	22	414	2	286	193	374	466	52
Number of children	779	722	48	—	1 123	935	41	915	3	619	393	889	846	122
Husband-wife families	336	577	30	2	824	555	30	558	4	353	276	510	940	75
With own children under 18 years	720	330	24	—	497	408	21	376	2	268	184	339	400	49
Percent of total under 18 years	88.9	85.4	5.0	—	88.3	91.1	82.2	87.2	60.0	91.4	93.5	85.9	79.9	83.3
Families with other male head	3	8	—	—	9	3	2	9	—	1	3	12	35	—
With own children under 18 years	1	5	—	—	4	2	—	3	—	—	2	6	11	—
Number of children	2	7	—	—	6	2	—	5	—	4	5	13	15	—
Families with female head	37	57	6	—	72	50	1	49	—	25	8	48	89	5
With own children under 18 years	28	39	5	—	52	31	—	35	—	17	7	29	55	3
Number of children	57	64	7	—	85	56	4	68	—	39	12	58	112	7
Percent of total under 18 years	7.0	8.4	0.9	—	7.3	5.8	8.9	7.0	—	6.2	3.0	6.1	12.4	5.1
Persons under 18 years	810	762	820	6	1 169	963	45	966	5	630	402	952	900	138

MARITAL STATUS

	(1)	(2)	(3)	(4)	(5)	(6)	(7)	(8)	(9)	(10)	(11)	(12)	(13)	(14)
Male, 14 years old and over	692	822	893	53	1 285	737	43	792	7	478	342	803	1 701	105
Single	191	207	855	34	402	167	8	174	2	112	57	205	615	21
Married	488	594	35	18	845	563	33	576	5	363	283	564	1 004	80
Separated	7	3	—	—	10	—	2	—	—	—	—	2	16	3
Widowed	7	6	2	1	14	5	—	15	—	2	—	9	34	3
Divorced	6	15	1	—	24	5	2	27	—	—	2	25	48	1
Female, 14 years old and over	746	837	724	4	1 296	829	42	845	5	501	353	782	1 577	114
Single	183	122	671	2	297	173	3	158	—	94	50	141	311	25
Married	495	606	36	2	851	569	31	585	5	368	281	540	1 024	79
Separated	4	11	2	—	7	2	—	3	—	—	—	10	—	2
Widowed	43	59	10	—	82	43	4	54	—	28	12	68	166	9
Divorced	25	50	7	—	66	44	4	48	—	11	10	33	76	1

Table 1 (concluded)

Census Tracts	Balance of County—Con.						Totals for split tracts							
	Tract 0017	Tract 0018	Tract 0019	Tract 0020	Tract 0021	Tract 0022	Tract 0006	Tract 0007	Tract 0008	Tract 0011	Tract 0012	Tract 0014	Tract 0016	Tract 0017
RACE														
All persons	2 397	9 079	3 814	3 628	971	7 626	4 141	8 404	4 444	3 502	3 349	2 416	3 849	4 734
White	2 200	5 736	2 697	2 441	1 346	5 260	1 031	3 474	4 553	3 475	3 321	1 948	3 742	4 523
Negro	168	3 338	1 111	1 180	618	2 354	3 105	4 922	42	6	18	467	79	169
Percent Negro	7.0	36.8	29.1	32.5	31.4	30.9	75.0	58.6	0.9	0.2	0.5	19.3	2.1	3.6
AGE BY SEX														
Male, all ages	1 190	4 396	1 910	1 797	940	3 649	1 908	4 032	2 515	1 720	1 639	1 228	1 938	2 234
Under 5 years	111	438	196	165	74	354	240	496	70	180	194	123	169	243
3 and 4 years	44	177	76	69	30	134	106	204	21	78	62	59	68	101
5 to 9 years	156	501	204	196	78	411	285	565	39	212	182	149	206	319
5 years	33	68	43	36	20	78	48	103	5	29	40	30	35	65
6 years	180	94	31	43	24	70	56	120	5	29	37	27	39	66
10 to 14 years	37	567	246	236	95	412	276	532	12	48	129	139	208	316
14 years	113	99	39	49	22	75	52	80	48	212	30	29	35	61
15 to 19 years	30	423	194	192	101	389	178	404	11	54	104	97	146	217
15 years	41	87	35	58	25	103	27	101	147	182	24	31	42	57
16 years	17	91	44	41	24	77	43	72	10	49	24	15	27	72
17 years	14	84	44	35	22	77	32	88	8	47	19	15	30	39
18 years	11	62	36	27	14	74	43	82	13	39	19	18	18	32
19 years	52	289	124	31	16	325	163	61	20	18	23	103	290	17
20 to 24 years	11	68	24	98	59	45	27	369	96	75	239	16	35	100
20 years	12	56	25	19	13	66	38	88	329	20	36	12	50	26
21 years	195	508	198	18	9	501	225	76	475	10	46	221	320	20
25 to 34 years	175	441	207	202	109	360	160	538	450	249	384	152	255	374
35 to 44 years	120	434	153	170	94	360	199	387	83	298	152	110	189	354
45 to 54 years	45	221	83	156	122	191	52	315	74	206	135	45	64	247
55 to 59 years	14	199	102	88	63	152	54	117	31	42	41	38	35	78
60 to 64 years	20	249	141	88	41	154	81	125	39	41	25	43	32	28
65 to 74 years	9	126	62	137	69	80	35	137	36	17	32	18	24	41
75 years and over					35			47	19	6	22			17
Female, all ages	1 207	4 683	1 904	1 831	1 031	3 937	2 233	4 372	2 129	1 782	1 710	1 178	1 911	2 490
Under 5 years	128	440	155	148	79	383	247	493	93	155	228	138	139	253
3 and 4 years	54	171	76	61	26	157	91	199	28	76	76	56	60	103
5 to 9 years	155	487	208	193	95	435	275	514	55	221	189	144	202	286
5 years	28	90	41	37	12	82	51	111	12	35	39	34	29	55
6 years	23	103	33	33	22	77	55	116	8	52	43	27	34	48
10 to 14 years	160	527	206	206	120	404	244	538	34	198	128	139	190	288
14 years	27	106	47	50	13	89	52	111	5	39	25	29	30	47
15 to 19 years	86	450	142	149	88	387	221	465	173	167	89	96	144	192
15 years	18	118	24	33	18	77	51	90	7	45	21	19	37	39
16 years	27	95	24	43	28	99	55	99	9	44	16	29	37	49
17 years	18	82	35	33	18	76	36	104	14	38	19	17	33	43
18 years	12	87	27	22	16	59	38	76	39	26	18	12	17	31
19 years	73	354	149	17	19	76	41	96	104	14	19	85	269	30
20 to 24 years	15	69	30	126	78	409	233	430	196	78	259	15	40	26
20 years	18	75	36	23	21	93	51	82	384	11	47	15	41	30
21 years														

RELATIONSHIP TO HEAD OF HOUSEHOLD

25 to 34 years
35 to 44 years
45 to 54 years
55 to 59 years
60 to 64 years
65 to 74 years
75 years and over

All persons
In households
  Head of household
    Head of family
    Primary individual
  Wife of head
  Other relative of head
  Not related to head
In group quarters
Persons per household

TYPE OF FAMILY AND NUMBER OF OWN CHILDREN

All families
  With own children under 18 years
    Number of children
Husband-wife families
  With own children under 18 years
    Number of children
    Percent of total under 18 years
Families with other male head
  With own children under 18 years
    Number of children
Families with female head
  With own children under 18 years
    Number of children
    Percent of total under 18 years
Persons under 18 years

MARITAL STATUS

Male, 14 years old and over
  Single
  Married
  Separated
  Widowed
  Divorced
Female, 14 years old and over
  Single
  Married
  Separated
  Widowed
  Divorced

Table 2
Income characteristics of the population: 1970

Census Tracts	County			MIDDLETOWN									
	Total	Middle-town	Balance	Tract 0001	Tract 0002	Tract 0003	Tract 0004	Tract 0005	Tract 0006	Tract 0007	Tract 0008	Tract 0009	Tract 0010
INCOME IN 1969 OF FAMILIES AND UNRELATED INDIVIDUALS													
All families	23 871	13 689	10 182	122	1 004	1 657	1 419	1 437	926	1 309	705	952	1 445
Less than $1,000	1 782	422	360	7	72	28	5	23	69	88	24	47	20
$1,000 to $1,999	1 738	572	566	10	123	46	6	35	82	106	14	44	45
$2,000 to $2,999	1 252	697	555	6	111	61	28	56	88	135	20	106	23
$3,000 to $3,999	1 587	878	709	10	97	97	36	77	68	154	29	129	65
$4,000 to $4,999	1 736	987	749	20	94	146	29	77	117	96	48	176	53
$5,000 to $5,999	1 684	922	762	—	90	142	84	100	104	70	20	160	48
$6,000 to $6,999	1 538	835	703	18	89	150	104	73	81	76	54	91	52
$7,000 to $7,999	1 690	954	736	22	80	179	140	96	87	75	60	73	80
$8,000 to $8,999	1 607	882	725	7	60	107	172	105	76	92	49	42	36
$9,000 to $9,999	1 486	787	699	5	11	68	215	89	60	119	48	28	42
$10,000 to $11,999	2 436	1 426	1 010	—	62	220	281	193	37	75	57	34	115
$12,000 to $14,999	2 734	1 622	1 112	11	78	212	204	208	40	50	89	17	222
$15,000 to $24,999	3 112	1 954	1 158	11	67	186	215	217	17	75	85	5	345
$25,000 to $49,999	934	665	269	6	20	15	281	204	—	50	89	—	275
$50,000 or more	155	86	69	—	—	—	6	26	—	3	19	—	24
Median income	$8 329	$8 655	$7 933	$7 444	$5 056	$7 885	$10 200	$9 219	$5 375	$5 016	$9 719	$4 852	$13 939
Mean income	$10 155	$10 443	$9 768	$7 977	$6 682	$8 829	$11 125	$10 060	$5 734	$6 150	$13 856	$5 150	$16 826
Families and unrelated individuals	42 878	29 900	12 978	254	3 808	2 538	1 579	2 169	1 231	1 661	3 450	6 845	2 790
Median income	$4 308	$3 250	$6 474	$4 100	$1 793	$6 232	$9 834	$6 355	$4 409	$4 373	$1 764	$923	$6 073
Mean income	$6 622	$5 903	$8 279	$5 446	$3 244	$7 008	$10 423	$7 726	$4 987	$5 365	$4 596	$1 468	$10 266
Unrelated individuals	19 007	16 211	2 796	132	2 804	881	160	732	305	352	2 745	5 893	1 345
Median income	$1 243	$1 131	$1 839	$1 941	$1 320	$2 599	$2 167	$2 399	$946	$1 667	$1 318	$868	$848
Mean income	$2 184	$2 069	$2 855	$3 106	$2 012	$3 582	$4 195	$3 145	$2 718	$2 444	$2 218	$873	$3 218
TYPE OF INCOME IN 1969 OF FAMILIES													
All families	23 871	13 689	10 182	122	1 004	1 657	1 419	1 437	926	1 309	705	952	1 445
With wage or salary income	21 426	12 453	8 973	104	864	1 469	1 369	1 273	831	1 155	662	894	1 335
Mean wage or salary income	$9 021	$9 209	$8 760	$7 245	$6 047	$8 250	$9 983	$8 937	$5 476	$6 203	$11 202	$4 408	$13 435
With nonfarm self-employment income	2 584	1 550	1 034	11	96	172	158	159	74	63	56	41	326
Mean nonfarm self-employment income	$5 594	$5 627	$5 543		$5 227	$4 346	$6 676	$5 950	$3 211	$3 309	$2 294	$724	$7 120
With farm self-employment income	868	136	732	—	10	13	20	14	6	4	—	—	23
Mean farm self-employment income	$7 738	$394	$9 102										
With Social Security income	3 629	1 863	1 766	25	205	312	112	277	145	211	81	31	183
Mean Social Security income	$1 417	$1 430	$1 403	$660	$1 214	$1 724	$1 510	$1 602	$452	$1 261	$844	$255	$393
With public assistance or public welfare income	1 432	815	617	27	186	59	39	31	139	171	14	10	39
Mean public assistance or public welfare income	$785	$815	$677	$585	$863	$625	$522	$595	$891	$978			$783
With other income	8 990	6 109	2 881	39	277	648	587	674	156	222	481	575	964
Mean other income	$2 410	$2 654	$1 893	$3 578	$2 028	$1 827	$1 546	$2 402	$1 168	$1 087	$4 295	$1 589	$3 875

RATIO OF FAMILY INCOME TO POVERTY LEVEL[1]

Percent of families with incomes:													
Less than .50 of poverty level	5.8	5.6	6.2	5.7	11.8	2.5	0.7	2.3	15.9	14.4	4.7	7.2	3.3
.50 to .74	4.4	3.9	5.2	8.2	11.6	2.3	0.4	1.5	6.7	9.8	1.3	7.5	1.5
.75 to .99	5.1	4.5	5.8	9.0	11.4	2.7	1.8	5.2	6.7	12.4	0.7	6.2	0.8
1.00 to 1.24	5.1	4.3	6.0	8.2	5.4	4.4	4.7	5.2	8.4	9.0	2.8	6.5	2.0
1.25 to 1.49	5.4	4.8	6.1	8.3	7.8	4.4	3.0	6.3	8.2	6.3	2.1	7.9	1.7
1.50 to 1.99	12.2	11.8	12.7	17.2	12.0	13.0	11.6	13.6	18.0	13.9	8.8	24.9	5.9
2.00 to 2.99	20.5	20.5	20.4	4.9	14.9	30.4	25.1	20.6	19.7	21.1	18.3	23.6	13.9
3.00 or more	41.6	44.5	37.6	43.4	25.3	40.4	52.8	48.2	13.5	13.1	61.3	13.2	70.8

INCOME BELOW POVERTY LEVEL[1]

Families	**3 660**	**1 917**	**1 743**	**28**	**348**	**123**	**41**	**130**	**289**	**478**	**47**	**199**	**82**
Percent of all families	15.3	14.0	17.1	23.0	34.7	7.4	2.9	9.0	31.2	36.5	6.7	20.9	5.7
Mean family income	$1 982	$1 942	$2 025	$1 675	$1 994	$1 888	$2 363	$1 985	$2 091	$2 314	$1 022	$1 771	$1 556
Mean income deficit	$1 507	$1 549	$1 460	$1 056	$1 411	$1 282	$1 067	$1 130	$1 803	$1 664	$1 983	$1 444	$1 454
Percent receiving public assistance income	20.3	20.6	20.1	60.7	33.0	17.9	14.6	11.5	33.9	22.2	2.94	3.28	2.93
Mean size of family	2.48	3.77	4.04	2.54	3.59	3.20	3.68	3.05	4.41	4.43	2.94	3.28	2.93
With related children under 18 years	2 478	1 365	1 113	10	221	70	35	77	231	391	33	159	39
Mean number of related children under 18 years	2.88	2.71	3.08	...	2.65	2.49	3.68	2.12	3.46	3.21	1.82	1.60	1.85
With related children under 6 years	1 513	876	637	.5	118	19	16	61	137	245	23	155	23
Mean number of related children under 6 years	1.55	1.50	1.63	...	1.62	...	...	1.15	1.53	1.71	...	1.31	...
Families with female head	1 164	761	403	.10	161	47	14	61	169	260	21	4	.15
With related children under 18 years	970	640	330	.10	117	34	14	32	153	231	16	4	9
Mean number of related children under 18 years	2.94	2.89	3.03	...	2.68	1.97	...	1.94	3.24	3.25	...	...	...
With related children under 6 years	546	363	183	.5	59	8	...	22	89	152	.11	...	.5
Percent in labor force	63.0	64.2	60.7	...	49.2	...	...	...	59.6	73.7	...	...	...
Mean number of related children under 6 years	1.60	1.59	1.62	...	1.80	...	...	...	1.60	1.66	...	...	...
Family heads	**3 660**	**1 917**	**1 743**	**28**	**348**	**123**	**41**	**130**	**289**	**478**	**47**	**199**	**82**
Percent 65 years and over	19.6	13.8	25.9	17.9	23.9	4.1	14.6	8.5	18.3	15.3	6.7	20.9	7.3
Civilian male heads under 65 years	1 955	986	969	13	125	71	21	93	900	184	26	195	62
Percent in labor force	66.9	60.6	73.3	...	69.6	70.4	...	60.2	72.2	69.6	34.6	54.4	46.8
Unrelated individuals	**6 911**	**5 482**	**1 429**	**63**	**1 323**	**332**	**57**	**297**	**145**	**203**	**1 796**	**368**	**583**
Percent of all unrelated individuals	54.1	54.9	51.1	47.7	60.0	37.7	35.6	40.6	47.5	57.7	66.2	79.3	49.4
Mean income	$772	$758	$798	$798	$843	$845	$765	$685	$946	$926	$760	$309	$747
Mean income deficit	$1 715	$1 143	$1 009	$1 015	$1 045	$1 038	$1 089	$1 204	$872	$912	$1 162	$1 616	$1 179
Percent receiving public assistance income	8.0	5.3	18.2	38.1	7.0	10.2	...	6.7	36.6	24.6	0.3	...	1.9
Percent 65 years and over	15.4	9.8	36.9	46.0	14.1	23.2	26.3	16.5	40.7	39.9	0.5	...	3.1
Persons	**21 179**	**12 706**	**8 473**	**134**	**2 574**	**725**	**208**	**694**	**1 420**	**2 321**	**1 934**	**1 021**	**823**
Percent of all persons	22.1	22.7	21.2	31.0	46.9	12.2	3.7	13.7	35.6	39.3	42.6	33.5	14.6
Percent receiving Social Security income	11.0	8.8	14.1	29.1	11.4	14.8	16.3	11.2	9.3	9.8	5.8	1.7	3.5
Percent 65 years and over	10.6	7.6	15.2	29.1	12.2	13.5	13.5	10.5	9.8	7.8	0.5	...	3.5
Percent receiving Social Security income	63.8	68.5	60.3	100.0	67.5	71.3	71.4	52.1	61.9	71.4	.59	265	79.3
Related children under 18 years	7 114	3 683	3 431	23	616	169	77	146	768	1 259	$59	265	70
Percent living with both parents	48.9	44.8	53.4	...	40.4	62.1	54.5	51.4	31.1	33.8	42.4	94.3	62.9
Households	**5 999**	**4 034**	**1 965**	**65**	**1 003**	**288**	**72**	**254**	**371**	**570**	**617**	**214**	**309**
Percent of all households	22.4	22.3	22.7	35.5	47.6	13.8	4.8	14.5	34.8	38.5	35.7	21.7	14.9
Owner occupied	2 107	947	1 160	12	239	103	52	66	146	210	—	—	48
Mean value of unit	$9 000	$10 700	$7 500	...	$8 200	$500	$14 900	$15 200	$900	$500	—	—	$22 100
Renter occupied	3 892	3 087	805	53	764	185	20	188	225	360	617	214	261
Mean gross rent	$108	$118	$70	$82	$108	$135	...	$92	$54	$63	$192	$69	$111
Percent lacking some or all plumbing facilities	17.9	7.6	39.0	9.2	8.8	6.9	...	2.8	17.5	16.7	—	—	8.4

[1]Excludes inmates of institutions, members of the Armed Forces living in barracks, college students in dormitories, and unrelated individuals under 14 years.

Table 2 (continued)

Census Tracts

	MIDDLETOWN – Con.						Balance of County							
	Tract 0011	Tract 0012	Tract 0013	Tract 0014	Tract 0016	Tract 0017	Tract 0006	Tract 0007	Tract 0008	Tract 0011	Tract 0012	Tract 0014	Tract 0015	Tract 0016
INCOME IN 1969 OF FAMILIES AND UNRELATED INDIVIDUALS														
All families	500	663	38	—	913	599	32	608	...	371	282	565	1 148	79
Less than $1,000	—	22	—	—	12	5	—	26	...	—	—	4	39	—
$1,000 to $1,999	—	22	—	—	26	—	—	32	...	5	—	15	53	7
$2,000 to $2,999	—	33	—	—	24	6	—	39	...	5	9	18	49	7
$3,000 to $3,999	—	52	—	—	7	—	—	30	...	10	5	33	98	—
$4,000 to $4,999	4	23	4	—	24	6	5	52	...	—	6	25	98	8
$5,000 to $5,999	5	44	—	—	17	11	—	51	...	5	9	44	94	4
$6,000 to $6,999	17	58	—	—	44	26	5	63	...	5	10	33	109	—
$7,000 to $7,999	6	64	—	—	61	36	—	49	...	5	35	70	100	—
$8,000 to $8,999	22	67	6	—	49	40	3	62	...	20	50	53	47	—
$9,000 to $9,999	24	53	17	—	124	122	9	72	...	48	54	42	67	6
$10,000 to $11,999	86	82	6	—	160	73	9	81	...	116	91	82	129	21
$12,000 to $14,999	227	75	5	—	245	231	—	47	...	137	33	102	146	22
$15,000 to $24,999	98	55	—	—	80	32	—	11	...	11	5	44	92	16
$25,000 to $49,999	11	—	—	—	16	5	—	4	...	9	—	—	16	6
$50,000 or more	—	—	—	—	5	—	—	—	...	—	—	—	11	5
Median income	$18 789	$8 007	$11 059	—	$12 834	$13 705	$10 444	$8 224	...	$14 263	$11 556	$8 764	$7 340	$14 071
Mean income	$19 757	$8 274	$11 096	—	$14 477	$15 108	$10 392	$8 824	...	$15 519	$11 305	$8 897	$8 941	$16 341
Families and unrelated individuals	583	864	93	—	1 338	697	32	697	...	394	314	705	1 824	79
Median income	$17 267	$7 257	$9 192	—	$9 802	$12 244	$10 444	$7 638	...	$13 966	$11 148	$7 921	$5 343	$14 071
Mean income	$17 683	$7 404	$7 650	—	$11 215	$13 960	$10 392	$8 328	...	$14 801	$10 587	$7 773	$6 785	$16 341
Unrelated individuals	83	201	55	—	425	98	—	89	...	23	32	140	676	—
Median income	$1 464	$931	$4 219	—	$2 337	$6 667	—	$5 227	...	—	$1 000	$2 556	$1 862	—
Mean income	$5 186	$4 537	$5 269	—	$4 206	$6 939	—	$4 941	...	—	$4 259	$3 240	$3 123	—
TYPE OF INCOME IN 1969 OF FAMILIES														
All families	500	663	38	—	913	599	32	608	...	371	282	565	1 148	79
With wage or salary income	455	613	38	—	837	554	32	560	...	366	266	516	1 074	68
Mean wage or salary income	$15 451	$8 012	$11 096	—	$12 707	$13 707	$9 716	$8 332	...	$12 814	$10 670	$8 713	$7 780	$18 019
With nonfarm self-employment income	89	60	—	—	138	107	—	47	...	66	30	42	106	—
Mean nonfarm self-employment income	$12 362	$2 597	—	—	$6 030	$3 837	—	$3 971	...	$6 528	$5 553	$3 436	$7 501	—
With farm self-employment income	5	23	—	—	13	5	—	16	...	—	5	3	15	—
Mean farm self-employment income	...	87	—	—	75	87	—	57	...	25	...	72	127	11
With Social Security income	32	87	—	—	75	87	—	57	...	25	—	72	127	11
Mean Social Security income	$1 750	$1 054	—	—	$1 435	$1 199	9	$1 573	...	$1 180	—	$824	$1 329	—
With public assistance or public welfare income	5	22	—	—	13	—	—	10	...	—	—	38	37	7
Mean public assistance or public welfare income	—	—	—	—	—	—	9	—	...	—	—	—	—	—
With other income	302	298	—	—	559	327	7	116	...	183	136	553	853	18
Mean other income	$5 613	$992	—	—	$3 105	$2 869	—	$1 306	...	$3 295	$1 011	$1 362	$1 694	...

RATIO OF FAMILY INCOME TO POVERTY LEVEL[1]

Percent of families with incomes:							
Less than .50 of poverty level	—	—	1.0	1.3	0.8	—	8.9
.50 to .74	5.9	3.2	3.6	—	3.2	4.8	10.1
.75 to .99	4.4	2.2	5.1	—	2.2	3.2	—
1.00 to 1.24	3.3	0.9	4.3	4.0	0.9	3.9	—
1.25 to 1.49	3.3	0.9	8.7	1.3	0.9	5.6	—
1.50 to 1.99	6.6	1.4	17.3	—	1.4	7.2	1.8	—
2.00 to 2.99	13.0	5.7	26.6	14.6	5.7	11.2	15.6	4.0	17.4	5.1
3.00 or more	26.8	16.9	33.4	78.7	16.9	20.4	25.0	76.0	75.9
	36.7	68.9			68.9	43.6	59.4	73.7
	1.2						10.5
	1.0						15.8
	8.8						
	89.0						

INCOME BELOW POVERTY LEVEL[1]

Families	**90**	**57**	**59**	**5**	**137**	**7**	
Percent of all families	13.6	6.2	9.7	0.8	11.9	8.9	
Mean family income	$1 559	$1 167	$2 562		$1 738		
Mean income deficit	$1 657	$2 055	$795		$217		
Percent receiving public assistance income	6.7	5.3	6.8		22.8		
Mean size of family	3.60	3.39	3.30		5.49	2.88	
With related children under 18 years	.51	.43	2.57		4.33	.49	
Mean number of related children under 18 years	2.76	2.00	2.57		4.33	2.27	
With related children under 6 years	.45	.24	.20		.22	.32	
Mean number of related children under 6 years	1.38					1.56	
Families with female head	.12	.16	.05		.12	.18	
With related children under 18 years	.7	.13	.05		.12	.14	
Mean number of related children under 18 years							
With related children under 6 years	.7	.05	.05		.05	.05	
Mean number of related children under 6 years							
Percent in labor force							
Mean number of related children under 6 years							
Family heads	**90**	**57**	**59**	**5**	**137**	**7**	
Percent 65 years and over	25.6	41	39.0		24.1		
Civilian male heads under 65 years	60		31		36		
Percent in labor force	48.3	56.1	83.9		72.2	53.3	
Unrelated individuals	**49**	**62**	**194**	**5**	**16**	**347**	
Percent of all unrelated individuals	59.0	30.8	45.6	9.1	18.0	42.9	51.3
Mean income	$807	$973	$592			$918	
Mean income deficit	$1 047	$925	$1 314			$876	$1 024
Percent receiving public assistance income				5.1		30.0	2.6
Percent 65 years and over	24.2					65.0	2.0
Persons	**49**	**386**	**387**	**25**	**219**	**741**	**14**
Percent of all persons	16.1	10.9	9.5	1.1	9.5	15.6	19.2	4.3
Percent receiving Social Security income	11.1	1.0	24.2		24.2	26.8	7.4
Percent 65 years and over	14.0	1.0	20.1		20.1	16.4	7.2
Percent receiving Social Security income	68.5		88.6	12	88.6	100.0	94.3
Related children under 18 years	128	91	73		73	186	104
Percent living with both parents	90.6	73.6	74.0		74.0	76.3	56.7
Households	**13**	**126**		**5**	**63**	**90**	**204**	**7**
Percent of all households	2.4	16.8	11.1	0.8	11.6	15.2	20.3	8.9
Owner occupied	43	23	41		41	35	30	7
Mean value of unit	$11 300		$11 000		$11 000	$8 300	$19 800	
Renter occupied	84	103	22		22	55	174	
Mean gross rent	$128	$206				$82	$125	
Percent lacking some or all plumbing facilities			9.5		9.5	21.1	3.9	

[1]Excludes inmates of institutions, members of the Armed Forces living in barracks, college students in dormitories, and unrelated individuals under 14 years.

Table 2 (concluded)

Census Tracts

	Balance of County — Con.									Totals for split tracts				
	Tract 0017	Tract 0018	Tract 0019	Tract 0020	Tract 0021	Tract 0022	Tract 0006	Tract 0007	Tract 0008	Tract 0011	Tract 0012	Tract 0014	Tract 0016	Tract 0017
INCOME IN 1969 OF FAMILIES AND UNRELATED INDIVIDUALS														
All families	584	2 203	942	871	546	1 951	958	1 917	705	871	945	565	992	1 183
Less than $1,000	—	91	60	71	15	80	69	88	24	—	22	5	12	5
$1,000 to $1,999	—	160	60	52	52	136	82	132	14	5	35	15	33	—
$2,000 to $2,999	6	144	63	86	46	102	88	167	20	—	42	18	24	12
$3,000 to $3,999	9	161	98	50	10	196	68	193	29	10	57	33	7	9
$4,000 to $4,999	43	163	63	73	62	178	117	200	48	—	29	25	32	49
$5,000 to $5,999	25	211	76	87	14	136	109	148	20	9	53	44	28	31
$6,000 to $6,999	22	153	87	45	25	143	81	121	54	5	63	33	17	33
$7,000 to $7,999	11	180	89	75	55	107	87	139	60	22	74	70	44	37
$8,000 to $8,999	22	139	95	83	23	171	87	124	49	11	102	53	61	58
$9,000 to $9,999	35	149	60	66	38	134	79	154	48	42	73	42	49	75
$10,000 to $11,999	62	181	93	66	49	163	66	191	57	72	136	82	130	184
$12,000 to $14,999	64	214	35	62	25	175	46	156	89	202	166	102	181	137
$15,000 to $24,999	241	207	50	33	53	170	49	97	89	364	88	44	267	472
$25,000 to $49,999	44	36	8	26	68	49	17	3	85	109	5	—	86	76
$50,000 or more	—	14	5	—	10	11	—	4	19	20	—	—	21	5
Median income	$14 672	$7 103	$6 586	$6 367	$7 731	$7 042	$5 505	$6 252	$9 719	$16 580	$8 956	$8 764	$12 978	$14 157
Mean income	$14 609	$10 445	$7 122	$7 689	$11 682	$8 667	$5 889	$6 998	$13 856	$17 952	$9 179	$8 897	$14 626	$14 862
Families and unrelated individuals	615	2 851	1 175	1 142	665	2 480	1 263	2 358	3 455	977	1 178	705	1 417	1 312
Median income	$14 218	$5 629	$5 526	$5 043	$6 373	$5 710	$4 536	$5 377	$3 768	$15 362	$8 301	$7 921	$10 064	$13 172
Mean income	$14 261	$8 597	$6 170	$6 492	$9 956	$7 423	$5 123	$6 241	$4 599	$16 521	$8 253	$7 773	$11 501	$14 101
Unrelated individuals	31	648	233	271	119	529	305	441	2 750	106	233	140	425	129
Median income	$5 900	$584	$533	$853	$214	$963	$946	$995	$322	$500	$792	$556	$337	$423
Mean income	$7 697	$2 316	$2 320	$2 644	$2 038	$2 834	$2 718	$2 948	$2 226	$758	$4 498	$3 240	$4 206	$7 121
TYPE OF INCOME IN 1969 OF FAMILIES														
All families	584	2 203	942	871	546	1 951	958	1 917	705	871	945	565	992	1 183
With wage or salary income	541	1 884	806	671	447	1 742	863	715	662	821	879	516	905	1 095
Mean wage or salary income	$13 858	$7 869	$6 850	$7 920	$10 317	$8 181	$5 633	$6 898	$11 202	$14 276	$8 816	$8 713	$13 040	$13 781
With nonfarm self-employment income	83	215	53	111	65	216	74	110	56	155	90	42	138	190
Mean nonfarm self-employment income	$4 480	$5 346	$3 163	$3 421	$13 337	$4 966	$3 211	$3 592	$2 294	$9 878	$3 582	$3 436	$6 030	$4 118
With farm self-employment income	6	258	72	44	42	262	6	20		14	28	3	13	11
Mean farm self-employment income		$20 721	$5 287	$3 893	$2 950	$1 181					$2 161			
With Social Security income	38	507	215	254	103	337	154	268	81	57	98	72	86	125
Mean Social Security income	$693	$434	$399	$376	$535	$257	$433	$327	$844	$500	$991	$824	$465	$350
With public assistance or public welfare income	5	61	88	98	35	136	148	181	14	5	22	38	20	5
Mean public assistance or public welfare income		$564	$897	$609	$256	$788	$858	$001				$553		
With other income	301	486	137	212	149	240	163	338	481	485	434	169	577	628
Mean other income	$1 956	$576	$2 074	$2 020	$3 853	$1 692	$1 169	$1 162	$4 295	$4 738	$998	$1 362	$3 084	$2 431

RATIO OF FAMILY INCOME TO POVERTY LEVEL[1]

Percent of families with incomes:									
Less than .50 of poverty level	1.0	8.8	9.8	9.3	5.9	7.5	15.3	10.1	4.7	0.6	4.1	2.7	2.9	0.4
.50 to .74	3.6	5.9	4.6	7.7	9.3	7.2	6.5	7.8	1.3	—	3.1	3.7	2.7	0.5
.75 to .99	3.4	6.4	10.0	10.4	2.7	6.2	8.4	10.1	0.7	1.7	3.3	4.1	0.6	1.8
1.00 to 1.24	3.4	7.9	6.7	6.8	2.7	6.2	7.9	7.5	2.8	0.7	3.0	4.6	1.3	1.7
1.25 to 1.49	2.4	6.7	7.9	5.1	6.3	6.6	7.9	7.1	2.1	1.1	5.7	4.6	1.3	2.1
1.50 to 1.99	3.8	13.5	10.3	14.0	14.5	15.0	18.0	15.0	8.8	1.1	11.1	17.5	5.2	3.9
2.00 to 2.99	19.2	21.6	20.8	18.6	17.0	19.5	19.8	22.8	18.3	11.3	24.2	26.2	15.9	18.3
3.00 or more	66.6	29.1	25.9	28.1	40.7	31.4	15.0	19.6	61.3	84.6	45.5	37.5	69.5	71.3

INCOME BELOW POVERTY LEVEL[1]

Families	**27**	**467**	**229**	**239**	**98**	**409**	**289**	**537**	**47**	**5**	**99**	**57**	**44**	**32**
Percent of all families	4.6	21.2	24.3	27.4	17.9	21.0	30.2	28.0	6.7	0.6	10.5	10.1	6.5	2.7
Mean family income	$4,259	$2,034	$2,125	$1,885	$1,764	$1,911	$2,091	$2,342	$1,022		$637	$2,483	$209	$2,039
Mean income deficit	$783	$1,489	$1,489	$424	$522	$566	$803	$569	$983		$556	$870	$904	$1,242
Percent receiving public assistance income		27.6	20.1	21.3	13.3	21.3	33.9	20.5			6.1	22.8	15.6	
Mean size of family	6.44	4.43	4.03	3.59	3.66	4.11	4.41	4.32	2.94		3.55	5.49	3.23	6.06
With related children under 18 years	21	342	140	138	50	286	231	421	33	.5	60	43	43	26
Mean number of related children under 18 years		3.21	3.09	2.74	3.28	3.01	3.46	3.16	1.82		2.50	4.33	2.00	4.08
With related children under 6 years	21	178	82	56	33	184	137	265	23	.5	49	22	24	26
Mean number of related children under 6 years		1.53	1.76	1.48	2.09	1.77	1.53	1.67			1.35			1.00
Families with female head	.6	147	43	60	15	97	169	265	21	—	12	12	16	6
With related children under 18 years	.6	118	38	42	15	80	153	236	16	—	7	12	13	6
Mean number of related children under 18 years		2.94	3.16	2.12		3.60	3.24	3.25		—				
With related children under 6 years	.6	58	33	11	8	52	89	157	11	—	.7	.5	.5	.6
Mean number of related children under 6 years		62.1	60.6			59.6	59.6	74.5	—	—				
Percent in labor force		1.52	1.52			1.88	1.60	1.64						

Family heads	**27**	**467**	**229**	**239**	**98**	**409**	**289**	**537**	**47**	**5**	**99**	**57**	**64**	**32**
Percent 65 years and over	22.2	22.3	30.6	32.6	32.7	21.3	18.3	17.9	6.7	.5	23.2	21.1	10.9	18.8
Civilian male heads under 65 years	21	247	116	113	51	250	90	215	26	.5	69	36	41	26
Percent in labor force		81.0	73.3	63.7	70.6	74.8	72.2	71.6	34.6		47.8	72.2	56.1	100.0

Unrelated individuals	**11**	**378**	**132**	**138**	**55**	**243**	**145**	**219**	**47**	**62**	**78**	**60**	**194**	**16**
Percent of all unrelated individuals	35.5	58.3	56.7	50.9	46.2	49.7	47.5	49.7	66.1	58.5	33.5	42.9	45.6	12.4
Mean income		$836	$740	$946	$470	$777	$946	$953	$760	$741	$773	$918	$592	
Mean income deficit		$966	$1,037	$845	$1,328	$1,039	$872	$886	$1,162	$1,108	$1,132	$876	$314	
Percent receiving public assistance income		29.4	22.0	22.5	7.3	19.8	36.6	22.8	0.3			30.0	—	
Percent 65 years and over		51.1	50.8	56.5	36.4	42.6	40.7	39.3	0.5		19.2	65.0	—	

Persons	**185**	**2,447**	**1,056**	**997**	**414**	**1,946**	**1,420**	**2,540**	**1,934**	**87**	**429**	**373**	**401**	**210**
Percent of all persons	7.7	27.0	27.7	27.5	21.2	25.7	34.7	30.9	42.6	2.5	12.5	15.6	10.3	4.5
Percent receiving Social Security income	6.5	13.8	14.2	20.2	13.5	11.6	9.3	11.0	5.8	6.9	10.0	26.8	2.7	5.7
Percent 65 years and over	6.5	14.6	16.8	25.0	15.9	13.1	9.8	8.9	0.5		12.6	16.4	4.5	5.7
Percent receiving Social Security income	.74	50.4	48.0	65.1	77.3	50.8	61.9	74.8	.59	.16	68.5	100.0	.91	86
Related children under 18 years		1,086	494	422	792	792	768	1,332	617		136	186		
Percent living with both parents	83.8	49.8	56.5	53.6	61.9	42.4	31.1	36.0	42.4		91.2	76.3	73.6	86.0

Households	**33**	**539**	**224**	**260**	**129**	**397**	**371**	**633**	**617**	**18**	**141**	**90**	**133**	**38**
Percent of all households	5.6	27.9	31.6	36.4	26.7	29.6	34.1	31.2	35.6	2.0	13.5	15.2	11.0	3.0
Owner occupied	19	325	168	180	75	261	146	251	—	.5	57	35	30	24
Mean value of unit		$6,700	$6,200	$5,600	$4,900	$9,700	$7,900	$9,700			$11,500	$8,300	$17,500	
Renter occupied	.14	214	56	80	54	136	225	382	617	.13	84	55	103	.14
Mean gross rent		$44	$56	$55	$55	$47	$54	$65	$192		$128	$82	$206	
Percent lacking some or all plumbing facilities	57.6	46.9	44.2	33.8	56.6	50.9	17.5	16.0	—		—	21.1	—	50.0

[1]Excludes inmates of institutions, members of the Armed Forces living in barracks, college students living in dormitories, and unrelated individuals under 14 years.

3. The number of families whose incomes are from public assistance or public welfare.
4. Percent of families with a given ratio of family income to the poverty level less than 1.0 (the standard definition of poverty used in 1970).
5. The number of families with incomes below the poverty level; or
6. The number of families with incomes below the poverty level with related children under 18 years.

Similar data are available for the black and Spanish-language population in Tables P-5 through P-8 for tracts with at least 400 members of the specified group. (These tables are not reproduced in this report.)

The park director studies each possibility in light of her particular needs. She must first decide on a definition of low-income. She can use the 1970 census poverty index or her own operational definition using the income data in options 1 or 2. Even doing that, however, with options 1–5, she can find areas with a concentration of low-income families but she won't know if children were present (a recommendation to place a playground in a predominantly low-income elderly neighborhood would not win the park director a promotion!). Option 6 is a count of families with children under 18 *and* whose family income is below the poverty level. She cannot directly determine the number of 5–14 year olds from this summary. Thus she has the following choices:

1. Use counts of low-income families with children under 18 (Table 2) and the counts of children aged 5–14 (Table 1) from all families.
2. Approximate the number of 5–14 year olds in low-income families. An approximation can be made by using Table 2 to compute the number of related children under age 18 in low-income families (multiply the mean number of such children by the number of low-income families with children). Then, using the age data for the total population from Table 1, compute the proportion of the under age 18 population which is 5–14 years old and apply that to the number of children in low-income families. Appendix C of this case study illustrates the method of approximating. Note that the mean number of children in the families varies considerably and it is not sufficient to make a decision based solely on the number of families.
3. Get the data in the exact form desired by a "special tabulation" from the Census Bureau. The park director called the Census Bureau for a rough estimate and found that a special tabulation would cost about $3,000.

She decided that in this particular case it was not worth the expense of a special tabulation. With the aid of a calculator, she filled in the computation sheet shown in Exhibit 2 to estimate the number of children aged 5–14 in low-income families. While developing the computation sheet, she noticed that tracts 6, 7, 8, 11, 12, 14, 16, and 17 have data listed in three places: under "Middletown," the "balance of county," and "totals for split tracts." These split tracts, as shown on the tract maps, cross the city boundaries (broken line), and thus separate data are given for the part of the tract in the city of Middletown, the part outside the city (balance columns), and the total for the entire tract. For this study she used only the data for the Middletown section of the tracts.

Exhibit 2
Computation of an approximation of the number of children aged 5–14 in low-income families in Middletown: 1970

Tract No.	*(1)* Number of children under 18 in low-income families*	*(2)* Total no. of 5–14 yr. olds	*(3)* Total no. under 18 yrs.	*(4)* Pop. aged 5–14 / Pop. under 18	*(5)* Estimated no. of children aged 5–14 in low-income families
Total SMSA	7,137†	18,861	32,923	0.57	4,068
Middletown	3,699	10,098	17,922	0.56	2,071
0001					
0002					
0003					
0004					
0005					
0006					
0007					
0008					
0009					
0010					
0011					
0012					
0013					
0014					
0016					
0017					

* These do not add to 3,699 because of suppression in tracts 0001 and 0017.
† Middletown plus the balance do not add to 7,137 because of rounding.

The city planner discussed some aspects of the data the user should be aware of:

The census was taken April 1, 1970. After several years, the characteristics of the population change, especially for small geographic areas, as people age and move in and out of the area. Lacking a source of more recent data, the park director can only assume that the relationship among the tracts are relatively the same as they were in 1970.

Census data can never be viewed as exact. In any mass statistical operation such as a decennial census, human and mechanical errors occur although efforts are made to keep these nonsampling errors at an acceptably low level. Also, some data are based on a sample and thus subject to sampling variability. (See Appendix D for a more complete discussion.)

Sometimes data are omitted and replaced by ". . ." in the data tables. This occurs when (1) the number of people in a certain category is so small that it might be possible to identify them if the information were released and thus the data are withheld to maintain confidentiality; or (2) when the base of a derived figure (such as median or percentage) is too small to provide reliable data, the statistics are not computed to maintain data quality.

The park director reviewed the data with others in the community who worked in the tracts she picked as possible location sites and then she wrote her report for the city council.

EXERCISES

1. Compute an approximation of the number of children aged 5–14 in low-income families in Middletown. Duplicate Exhibit 2 on a separate sheet

Exhibit 3
Census tracts in the Middletown SMSA (inset map—Middletown and vicinity)

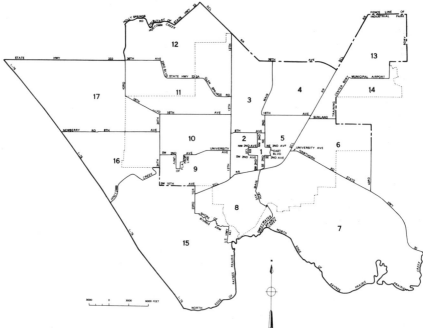

Source: U.S. Department of Commerce Bureau of the Census, 1970 Census of Population and Housing Census tracts, Standard metropolitan statistical area Final Report PHC(1)-77.

of paper for your work. (An illustration of the computation is in Appendix C of this case study.)

2. Trace the map in Exhibit 3 and enter onto the map the figures for the approximate number of related children aged 5–14 in low-income families in the census tracts of Middletown.

3. Make a second map showing the number of all children aged 5–14 in the census tracts of Middletown.

4. Write a report for the city council recommending a location site for the playground in a tract with a relatively large number of children from low-income families with limited playground facilities. Consider in your recommendation the supplementary information on the total number of children aged 5–14 in the tracts as this will impact on the total demand for play space and equipment.

APPENDIX A—DATA FOR SMALL AREAS

I. SMSA's—Standard Metropolitan Statistical Areas

The population residing in SMSA's constitutes the "metropolitan" population. Except in the New England States, a standard metropolitan statistical area is a county or group of contiguous counties that contains at least one city of 50,000 inhabitants or more (or "twin cities" with a combined population of at least 50,000). Contiguous counties are included in an SMSA if, according to certain criteria, they are socially and economically integrated with the central county. In the New England States, SMSA's consist of towns and cities instead of counties. An SMSA includes at least one central city (there is one exception to this) and the complete title of an SMSA identifies the central city or cities. In the 1970 census, there were 233 SMSA's. The boundaries of an SMSA may change over time as the area grows. The metropolitan population is further classified as "in central cities" and "outside central cities."

Census tracts in metropolitan areas. For statistical purposes each SMSA is divided into census tracts. These were initially designed to be small, relatively homogeneous and permanent areas with an average population of about 4,000. Data about tracts from the decennial censuses are published in Census Tract Reports, Series PHC(1). Tract boundaries are established cooperatively by a local committee and the Bureau of the Census so that the tracts tend to be uniform with respect to population characteristics, economic status, and living conditions, although sometimes the more dynamic, growing areas may not be homogeneous in terms of characteristics. Because the tract boundaries are generally maintained over time, historical comparisons can be made, although in 1970 some major boundary changes were made in some SMSA's. Sometimes the boundaries are changed because of a revised physical feature (a new freeway for example), subdivided because of a large population increase, or because some old boundaries have lost their significance. Tables A and B in the Census Tract Report show the comparability of tracts between 1960 and 1970. The Census Tract Reports, one for each SMSA, also have tabulations of population and housing information for each census tract and maps to show the areas.

Other small area data in SMSA's.   Complete count and sample population and housing data are also available on computer tape and microfilm for enumeration districts (ED's) and block groups (BG's). ED's and BG's are subdivisions of census tracts, places, and MCD's/CCD's. While these data have a number of limitations, they can be used as building blocks for geographic areas not tabulated by the Census Bureau. Their small size allows users substantial flexibility when aggregating to create data for user-defined areas.

Block data (identified in the urbanized areas of all SMSA's) may also be used as building blocks although only complete count data are available. Block statistics are published in HC(3) reports and are on computer tape.

II. Nonmetropolitan tracted areas

The population living outside SMSA's constitutes the nonmetropolitan population. Some nonmetropolitan counties also had census tracts designated because it was expected that they would eventually become a part of an SMSA. A few other isolated areas were also tracted if a local committee was willing to draw tract boundaries. While SMSA tracted areas have data published in PHC(1) reports, nonmetropolitan tracted areas remain unpublished but are available for less than $10 from the Customer Services Branch, Data User Services Division, Bureau of the Census, Washington, D.C. 20233.

III. Nonmetropolitan untracted areas

Most nonmetropolitan areas do not have census tracts. Data are published for cities and towns and, on computer tapes and other unpublished forms, are available for county subdivisions called Minor Civil Divisions (MCD) or Census County Divisions (CCD), and for still smaller Enumeration Districts (ED), and places.

Minor Civil Divisions are primary political and administrative subdivisions of counties in 29 States. The most common type of MCD is the township but there are also towns, precincts, magisterial districts, etc. In the 1970 census there were 28,130 MCD's.

In 21 States, MCD's are not suitable for presenting census data, primarily because of frequent boundary changes. Over 7,000 Census County Divisions have been established as relatively permanent statistical areas by the Bureau of the Census in cooperation with State and local authorities. States containing CCD's are: Alabama, Arizona, California, Colorado, Delaware, Florida, Georgia, Hawaii, Idaho, Kentucky, Montana, New Mexico, North Dakota, Oklahoma, Oregon, South Carolina, Tennessee, Texas, Utah, Washington, and Wyoming.

Tabulations are available for MCD's and CCD's on computer tapes (First, Second, Fourth, and Fifth Count, File C) and on microfilm (about $8/reel—and most States are one reel), or by paper printout ($10/county). These can be purchased from the Census Bureau. Limited published data for MCD/CCD's are in PC(1)-B.

Enumeration Districts are further subdivisions of MCD's and CCD's and another source of small area data for nonmetropolitan untracted areas. They are geographic areas delineated for administrative convenience in controlling and directing the conduct of the Census. These data are available on computer tape and microfilm.

APPENDIX B—POVERTY INDEX

The poverty index provides a range of low-income cutoffs adjusted by the factors shown in table A.

Table A
Weighted average thresholds at the poverty level in 1969, by size of family and sex of head, by farm and nonfarm residence

		Nonfarm			Farm		
Size of family	*Total*	*Total*	*Male head*	*Female head*	*Total*	*Male head*	*Female head*
All unrelated individuals ..	$1,834	$1,840	$1,923	$1,792	$1,569	$1,607	$1,512
Under 65 years	1,888	1,893	1,974	1,826	1,641	1,678	1,552
65 years and over	1,749	1,757	1,773	1,751	1,498	1,508	1,487
All families	3,388	3,410	3,451	3,082	2,954	2,965	2,757
2 persons	2,364	2,383	2,394	2,320	2,012	2,017	1,931
Head under 65 years ..	2,441	2,458	2,473	2,373	2,093	2,100	1,984
Head 65 years and over .	2,194	2,215	2,217	2,202	1,882	1,883	1,861
3 persons	2,905	2,924	2,937	2,830	2,480	2,485	2,395
4 persons	3,721	3,743	3,745	3,725	3,195	3,197	3,159
5 persons	4,386	4,415	4,418	4,377	3,769	3,770	3,761
6 persons	4,921	4,958	4,962	4,917	4,244	4,245	4,205
7 or more persons	6,034	6,101	6,116	5,952	5,182	5,185	5,129

Source: Table A, in Appendix B of *General Social and Economic Characteristics Report*, PC(1)–C, page App. 30.

The index allows only for differences in the costs of living between farm and nonfarm families; differences between cities and regions of the country, for example, are not taken into account. In 1969, the thresholds, for the index ranged from $1,487 for a female unrelated individual over age 65 living on a farm to $6,116 for a nonfarm family with a male head and with seven or more persons. The average threshold for a nonfarm family of four headed by a male was $3,745.

APPENDIX C—COMPUTATION ILLUSTRATION

Data are not always published in the exact form desired but it is often possible to compute what is needed. In this case study, for example, the park director wanted an approximation of the number of 5–14 year olds in low-income families. The description below illustrates a method for doing this if you are willing to assume that the proportion of children aged 5–14 is the same in both the total and the low-income family population. The steps below relate to the columns in Exhibit 2.

1. From Table 2, compute the number of related children under 18 in the low-income families:

    Column 1 = (Mean number of related children under 18 years) (Number of families with income below the poverty level with related children under 18 years)

    For the SMSA, this is: $(2.88)(2,478) = 7,137$

2. From Table 1, compute the total population age 5–14 years:

    Column 2 = (Males 5 to 9 years) + (Males 10 to 14 years) + (Females 5 to 9 years) + (Females 10 to 14 years)

    For the SMSA, this is: $4,809 + 4,791 + 4,588 + 4,673 = 18,861$

3. From Table 1, the number of persons under 18 years is shown not in the "age by sex" stub (although it could be computed from this), but in the last line of the stub "Type of Family and Number of Own Children." Thus it often pays to check other categories.

    For the SMSA, the number of persons under 18 years is 32,923.

4. Compute the proportion of the total 0–17 population which is 5–14 years:

    $$\text{Column 4} = \frac{\text{Column 2}}{\text{Column 3}}$$

    For the SMSA, this is: $\frac{18,861}{32,923} = 0.57$

5. Compute an estimate of the number of 5–14 year olds in low-in-
    come families:

    Column 5 = (Column 4)(Column 1)
    For the SMSA, this is: (0.57)(7,137) = 4,068

APPENDIX D—ACCURACY OF THE DATA

The Census Bureau has shown a continuing concern for the quality
of the data obtained in the decennial censuses. Human and mechanical nonsampling errors occur in any mass statistical operation
such as a decennial census. When estimates are made from sample
tabulations they are subject to both nonsampling errors and sampling
errors.

The Census Bureau has conducted studies of nonsampling errors in
its evaluation and research programs. They cover the accuracy of
selected subject matter (response errors) and the effectiveness of the
enumeration process (coverage errors). These studies are published in
the PHC(E) report series.[1] Most of the information in this series is
applicable to census statistics at the national level; for example, income other than earnings (such as Social Security, public assistance,
interest, dividends, etc.) tends to be underreported which could over-
state the low-income group the park director was most interested in.
On the other hand, there is evidence that low-income people are un-
derenumerated, a fact which could serve to undercount the group of
interest. At best, this information can be only approximately applied to
statistics for small areas.

Some of the data are collected from the entire population ("complete count" or 100 percent items) and some from a sample of the
population. Complete count data in the tract reports are in Tables 1,
H-1, and H-3. The data in the other tables are all based on a sample as
noted in a sentence under the title of the tables (see Table 2 for example) which refers you to the text.

In this case study, for example, the park director can identify income as 20 percent sample data by consulting the listing of sampling
rates for various subjects in Table C of Appendix C in the back of the
PHC(1) report. Since income was collected at a sample of households
rather than at all households, the data is subject to *sampling variability*, which is also discussed in Appendix C of PHC(1).

---

[1] For a list of these reports and an index to the subjects in the reports, see *Data User
News*, volume 10, no. 8 (August 1975), p. 1–2, 8. The reports are also listed in *Data
Access Description* no. 39.

Basically, sampling variability means that sample data tabulated in census reports may be different from the values that would have been obtained if a complete count of the population had been made. In using sample data therefore, the researcher should account for sampling variability by using the data in Tables D through F of Appendix C. These tables enable the researcher to approximate the *standard error* of any sample tabulation in the report.

The standard error can be used to obtain a *confidence interval* before making decisions based on the data. A confidence interval is a range of estimated values with a prescribed confidence of including the value that a full census would have obtained. The procedure for constructing a confidence interval is illustrated below.

The interpretation of a confidence interval may be explained as follows:

If all possible samples were selected, each of these were surveyed under essentially the same conditions, and an estimate and its estimated standard error were calculated from each sample, then—

1. Approximately two-thirds of the intervals from one standard error below the estimate to one standard error above the estimate would include the average value of all possible samples. We call an interval from one standard error below the estimate to one standard error above the estimate a two-thirds confidence interval.
2. Approximately nine-tenths of the intervals from 1.6 standard errors below the estimate to 1.6 standard errors above the estimate would include the average value of all possible samples. We call an interval from 1.6 standard errors below the estimate to 1.6 standard errors above the estimate a 90-percent confidence interval.
3. Approximately nineteen-twentieths of the intervals from two standard errors below the estimate to two standard errors above the estimate would include the average value of all possible samples. We call an interval from two standard errors below the estimate to two standard errors above the estimate a 95-percent confidence interval.
4. Almost all intervals from three standard errors below the sample estimate to three standard errors above the sample estimate would include the average value of all possible samples.

Thus, for a particular sample, one can say with specified confidence that the average of all possible samples is included in the constructed interval.

In relation to this case study, Table F lists age as having a sample rate of 20 percent; but there is also a headnote which reads "Subjects marked with an asterisk were tabulated on a 100 percent basis in Table

1 . . . ." Since the age data in this case are taken from Table 1, they are not sample data and there is no need to estimate the standard errors for the age data in Table 1.

Family *income* and *poverty status* are both 20 percent items and their standard errors should be computed. For each subject, Table F provides a factor by which the appropriate value in Table D or E should be multiplied to obtain the standard error. The values in Tables D and E give approximate standard errors which ignore some aspects of the sample design, sample size, and estimation processes. The factors in Table F adjust the approximate standard errors to account for these effects. For cross-tabulations of more than one subject (for example, race and poverty status use the largest factor.

In Middletown there are an estimated 1,365 families with income below the poverty level and with related children under 18 years old. This number lies between the values of 1,000 and 2,500 shown in Table D; linear interpolation gives a value of 66 as the approximate standard error.[2] Since the factor for poverty status in Table F is 1.0, multiply 66 by 1.0 to arrive at a standard error of 66. It is now possible to construct a confidence interval as follows:

1. To find the upper end of a 95 percent confidence interval, add two standard errors ($2 \times 66 = 132$) to 1,365; thus, the upper end of the 95 percent confidence interval is 1,629.
2. To find the lower end of a 95 percent confidence interval, subtract two standard errors from 1,365; thus, the lower end of the 95 percent confidence interval is 1,233.
3. The 95 percent confidence interval is written (1,233, 1,629). This means that there are 95 out of 100 chances that this range would contain a complete census count. To construct a 99 percent confidence interval, multiply the approximate standard error (66) by 2½ ($66 \times 2½ = 165$); the 99 percent confidence interval is (1,220, 1,530).

The approximate standard error for tabulations by census tract can either be derived from Table D or be computed from a formula. Notice that it is relatively much higher for tracts with a small population. For numbers that fall between those shown in the table, standard errors may be estimated by linear interpolation or by using the formula given below. For example, in Tract 0007 it is estimated that there were 391 low-income families with children under 18 (Table 2). Table D lists

---

[2] Linear interpolation for this example is performed as follows:

$$60 + \frac{(1{,}365 - 1{,}000)}{(2{,}500 - 1{,}000)} (85 - 60) = 60 + 6 = 66$$

the standard errors for 250 or 500. By linear interpolation the estimated standard error would be about 38.[3] Alternatively the approximate standard error can be computed by using the formula:

$$\sqrt{N^2 (1 - f) \frac{pq}{n}}$$

Where

N = total population of the geographic area (in this case, there are a total of 1,309 families in census Tract 0007). Note that "N" is the number of housing units, families, or persons in the geographic area, not those with a given characteristic. In this example, you would not use the total number of families in poverty in the tract as this is a base defined by a particular type of population; rather you use the total number of families in the tract which is 1,309.

f = the sampling fraction $\frac{1}{5}$.

$n = fN$ (in this case: $\frac{1}{5} \times 1,309$)

$p = \frac{X}{N}$ where X is the estimated number—in this case, 391

$q = 1 - \frac{X}{N}$

Thus the problem is:

$$\sqrt{(1,309)^2(1 - \tfrac{1}{5}) \left(\frac{\left(\frac{391}{1,309}\right)\left(1 - \frac{391}{1,309}\right)}{(\tfrac{1}{5})(1,309)} \right)}$$

$$= \sqrt{1,097} \doteq 33, \text{ the approximate standard error}$$

It is common practice to use a 95 percent confidence interval so in this case both add and subtract 66 (two standard errors) to 391; the range for Tract 0007 is then from 325 to 457 low-income families with children under 18.

Tables D–F also enable you to compute standard errors of percentages. For example, in Tract 0007, almost 30 percent (391/1,309) of the families were low-income families with children under 18. To determine the approximate standard error of this percentage, use Table E. Once again, a full range of numbers is not given. You could use 2.7 in this example as this is the closest approximation for the particular

---

[3] Computation:

$$30 + \left[\frac{391 - 250}{500 - 250} \times (45 - 30) \right] = 38$$

estimated percentage and base of the percentage. But you could also interpolate or use the formula:

$$\sqrt{(1-f)\frac{pq}{n}}$$

where the letters have the same meaning they had in the previous formula. In this particular example, the computation is:

$$\sqrt{(1 - \frac{1}{5})\left(\frac{\left(\frac{391}{1,309}\right)\left(1 - \frac{391}{1,309}\right)}{(\frac{1}{5})(1,309)}\right)} =$$

0.025 or 2.5 percent, the approximate standard error, which we multiply by the appropriate factor for the subject involved (1.0 in this case) to get the estimated standard error.

Using the common practice of applying two times the standard error, the chances are 95 out of 100 that between 25 and 35 percent of the families in Tract 0007 were low-income and had children under 18.

Table D
Approximate standard error of estimated number based on 20-percent sample (range of 2 chances out of 3)

Estimated number (persons or housing units)	Standard error	Estimated number (persons or housing units)	Standard error
50	15	1,000	60
100	20	2,500	85
250	30	5,000	100
500	45		

Table E
Approximate standard error of estimated percentage based on 20-percent sample (range of 2 chances out of 3)

Estimated percentage	Base of percentage (persons or housing units)					
	500	1,000	2,500	5,000	10,000	15,000
2 or 98	1.3	0.9	0.6	0.4	0.3	0.2
5 or 95	2.0	1.4	0.9	0.6	0.4	0.4
10 or 90	2.7	1.9	1.2	0.8	0.6	0.5
25 or 75	3.9	2.7	1.7	1.2	0.9	0.7
50	4.5	3.2	2.0	1.4	1.0	0.8

Table F
Factor to be applied to standard errors

Population subjects†	Sample rate (per-cent)	Factor	Housing subjects†	Sample rate (per-cent)	Factor
*Race	20	0.9	*Tenure	20	0.2
*Age	20	0.8	*Rooms	20	1.0
*Household relationship	20	0.5	*Persons per room	20	0.4
*Family composition	20	0.6	*Value	20	1.0
Country of origin (including			Units in structure	20	0.8
Spanish heritage subjects)	15	1.6	Year structure built	20	0.9
Nativity and parentage	15	1.7	Heating equipment	20	0.8
School enrollment	15	1.0	Basement	20	0.9
Years of school completed	20	1.0	Source of water	15	1.0
Residence in 1965	15	2.0	Sewage disposal	15	1.0
Employment status	20	0.8	Air conditioning	15	1.1
Place of work	15	1.3	Year moved into unit	15	1.1
Means of transportation			Gross rent	20	0.9
to work	15	1.3	All other—20 percent	20	1.0
Occupation	20	1.1	—15 percent	15	1.2
Industry	20	1.1			
Class of worker	20	1.1			
Income—persons	20	1.0			
—families	20	1.0			
Poverty status—persons	20	1.9			
—families	20	1.0			
All other—20 percent	20	1.0			
—15 percent	15	1.2			

* Subjects marked with an asterisk were tabulated on a 100% basis for tables 1, H-1, and H-3. Standard errors are not applicable to these tables.

† Tabulations of data for persons of Spanish heritage are based on the 15-percent sample. For subjects shown in this table as based on the 20-percent sample, the factor for persons of Spanish heritage is obtained by multiplying the appropriate factor in this table by 1.2. For subjects shown as based on the 15-percent sample, the factor in this table can be used directly.

case
5

Multipurpose Stores, Inc. (A)*

Multipurpose Stores (MPS) is a regional retail chain stores organization which operates six furniture-appliance type of stores in the state. One of these stores was located in the city of Littlefield, whose population was approximately 33,000. Littlefield, which was surrounded by several smaller towns, and Springdale, with a population of 18,000, formed the hub of economic, social, and cultural activity in the area. The economy grew very fast during the 60s and the twin-city area was declared an SMSA in 1972 (see Exhibit 1). Despite the general economic health of the area, the local MPS experienced declining sales during the past few years. Early in 1974, MPS management appointed a new manager for the Littlefield-Springdale store. He was directed to improve the sales performance of the Littlefield MPS store.

According to the President of MPS, sales of the Littlefield store were suffering because of a poor store image. He thought that there was some confusion in the minds of both actual and potential customers as to the true identity of the stores. It was hypothesized that such confusion resulted in the loss of sales. MPS President felt that the store was not able to attract many buyers of furniture and appliances because they identified the store with various other items of merchandise including hardware. At the same time, the President felt that the company lacked proper information on which to base any systematic marketing strategy aimed at improving the store's image and sales. The President of MPS and the new store manager agreed that a clear understanding of the overall store image was necessary. A clarification of the strengths and weaknesses of the local store would help them to develop an appropriate and creative marketing program.

Within a few months of his appointment, the new store manager decided that his predecessor had projected a "mom-and-pop" type of store image. He also felt that the previous manager gave the impression that he himself was the owner of the store, for the store clientele

---

* This case was prepared by C. P. Rao, and G. E. Kiser, The University of Arkansas.

seemed to have been doing business mainly on the basis of their personal relationship with the store manager. He felt that such lack of corporate image was a deterrent to business. On the basis of his discussions and his own intuitive evaluation of the situation, the new store manager concluded that knowing the nature and dimensions of the store's image would greatly help him to improve sales performance. Additionally, he felt that an independent assessment of the MPS store and its environment would give him an unbiased basis for initiating a constructive marketing program. With these twin purposes in mind, he sought the help of a marketing consulting firm in Littlefield.

The "image" study

After discussing the problem with the consultants, it was agreed that a store "image" study would be carried out to achieve the following objectives:

1. Identify the relative importance of various store features that respondents take into account when selecting or patronizing a furniture-appliance store.
2. Identify respondent's relative preferences for the area's furniture-applicance stores.
3. Identify the respondent's evaluation of MPS store in Littlefield on the basis of those store features mentioned under 1 above.
4. Collect data about the demographic characteristics of the respondents.

A consumer survey would be conducted utilizing a structured questionnaire. (See Exhibit 2 for the questionnaire designed to be used in the survey.) It was also agreed that the data should be gathered from a sample of present and past MPS customers as well as from a more general list of consumers. With this purpose in view, the following research plan was developed by the consultants.

1. Approximately one third of the respondents would be selected from present customers who previously had patronized the MPS stores. These respondents would be selected randomly from a file of sales tickets issued during the past five years.
2. The remaining two thirds of the respondents reached would be selected randomly utilizing the area telephone directory. While it was expected that most of these respondents would be potential customers in the sense that they have not patronized the MPS stores, it was also expected that a few of these respondents would already be patrons of the MPS store.
3. Approximately 20 percent of the sample members in each group

would be interviewed personally; data from the remainder would be collected through mailed questionnaires.

4. For considerations of time and cost, it was decided to reach 150 MPS store customers and 300 potential customers.

5. Following the data collection phase, the marketing consultants would submit a written report consisting of the following two parts:

    a. An independent evaluation of the MPS store by the marketing consultant group.

    b. An interpretation of the data gathered in the field research.

QUESTIONS

1. How do you evaluate MPS management's analysis of the problem? What alternative approach, if any, would you take in such a preliminary diagnosis of the problem?

2. Critically evaluate the research plan agreed between the MPS management and the marketing consultant group.

Exhibit 1
Population–Blount county

Year	Population	Number increase	Percentage increase
1940	41,100	—	—
1950	59,979	8,879	21.6
1960	55,800	5,821	11.7
1970	77,370	21,570	38.7

Incorporated cities	1960	1970
Littlefield	20,274	30,729
Springdale	10,076	16,387
Oak Grove	1,056	1,582
Lincoln	820	1,023
Hampton	216	908
East Fork	350	810
Woodland	127	650
Dunwoody	209	426
Elkins	—	418
Union Springs	238	260
Jackson	—	274
Winslow	183	227

Retail sales estimates–Blount and Benton counties (now Littlefield– Springdale SMSA)

Year	Retail sales ('000 dollars)
1963	130,892
1964	143,510
1965	158,724
1966	181,127
1967	194,059
1968	212,497
1969	228,491
1970	246,862
1971	261,454
1972	280,677

Exhibit 1 (continued)
Selected retail establishments in Blount county

Business category	Number of establishments in January			
	1969	1970	1971	1972
Department stores	3	3	3	4
Furniture and appliances	37	36	41	51
Hardware and machinery	35	38	38	48

Littlefield–Springdale SMSA demographic profile–1973

Demographic characteristic	Littlefield– Springdale SMSA
Total population	140,700
Percent by age:	
0–5 years	9.5%
6–11 years	9.8%
12–17 years	10.4%
18–24 years	14.2%
25–34 years	15.5%
35–49 years	15.0%
50–64 years	13.6%
Over 65 years	12.0%
Total households	48,300
Effective buying income estimates:	
Net total	$485,869,000
Per capita	3,453
Average household	10,059
Median household	7,415
Percent of households by income groups:	
$ 0–2,999	20.1%
3,000–4,999	13.3%
5,000–7,999	20.5%
8,000–9,999	11.2%
10,000–14,000	18.6%
15,000–24,000	11.1%
Over 25,000	5.2%

Exhibit 1 *(concluded)*

Retail sales data	Littlefield–Spring-dale SMSA—1973	Percent change 1972–73
Per household sales:		+35.7%
Furniture/household appliances	$285	+17.9%
Total..................................	$7,192	+18.8%
Department stores sales	$24,073,000	+42.1%
Furniture/household appliance sales	$13,751,000	+63.7%
Furniture/home furnishings sales	$10,129,000	

Bank deposits and savings and loan resources— Littlefield—1965–74

Year	Bank deposits ($s in '000)	Savings and loan resources ($s in '000)
1965	48,422.9	22,488.5
1966	52,065.8	23,006.7
1967	59,346.3	24,852.1
1968	60,672.1	26,206.5
1969	67,871.1	29,713.3
1970	71,968.1	34,134.2
1971	78,580.0	39,038.1
1972	92,481.8	50,947.3
1973	113,780.2	60,374.3
1974	126,832.2	68,362.0

Exhibit 2
Questionnaire proposed by the marketing consultants for use in the proposed store image survey

Please answer the following questions with a check mark and/or a brief remark to express your experience or opinions.

1. Have you purchased any of the following durable items in the last *six months?* Or planning to buy in the next six months? (Please check as many as applicable.)

Type of item	Purchased during the last 6 months		Planning to buy in the next 6 months			
	Yes	No	Yes	No	Not sure	Not planning
Major appliances (refrigerator washing machine etc.,)	—	—	—	—	—	—
T.V., phonograph, tape recorder etc.	—	—	—	—	—	—
Major furniture item(s) costing more than $100	—	—	—	—	—	—
Minor furniture item(s) costing less than $100	—	—	—	—	—	—

Exhibit 2 (continued)

2. Below is a list of desirable features of any furniture-appliance type of store. Please indicate, how important are these features to you in selecting or patronizing such a store for your purchase needs? (If you consider any feature as highly important please check 7. On the other hand, if the feature describes a least important consideration, please check 1. If your importance rating is in between for any statement, please check the number—2, 3, 4, 5, or 6—which comes closest to expressing your opinion.)

High numbers more important—Low numbers low importance

	Most important						Least important
Attractive decor and display	7	6	5	4	3	2	1
Accessibility of store	7	6	5	4	3	2	1
Informative advertising	7	6	5	4	3	2	1
Courteous store personnel	7	6	5	4	3	2	1
Easy credit	7	6	5	4	3	2	1
Competitive prices	7	6	5	4	3	2	1
Quality merchandise	7	6	5	4	3	2	1
Easy to find part place	7	6	5	4	3	2	1
Wide selection of merchandise ...	7	6	5	4	3	2	1
Carry well known brands	7	6	5	4	3	2	1
Well known to our friends	7	6	5	4	3	2	1
Quick delivery service	7	6	5	4	3	2	1
The type of customers patronizing the store	7	6	5	4	3	2	1
Convenient location	7	6	5	4	3	2	1
Well known generally	7	6	5	4	3	2	1

3. Would you please mention as many furniture-appliance type of stores in our town as you can recall in order of your liking for the stores? (If you like store most, please mention first, then the next and so on.)

_____   _____

_____   _____

4. How do you consider the Multipurpose Stores in our town? (Please write the word(s) which comes uppermost in your mind to fill the blank.)
Multipurpose Stores mostly sells_____

5. On the following list of features, how do you evaluate the *Multipurpose Stores* in our town? (If your evaluation is highly favorable please check 7. Alternately, if your evaluation is highly unfavorable please check 1. If your evaluation is in between please check 2, 3, 4, 5, or 6 whichever comes closest to expressing your evaluation.)

Exhibit 2 *(concluded)*

High numbers more favorable—Low numbers less favorable

	Highly favorable						Highly unfavorable
Attractive decor and display	7	6	5	4	3	2	1
Accessibility of stores	7	6	5	4	3	2	1
Informative advertising	7	6	5	4	3	2	1
Courteous store personnel	7	6	5	4	3	2	1
Easy credit	7	6	5	4	3	2	1
Competitive prices	7	6	5	4	3	2	1
Quality merchandise	7	6	5	4	3	2	1
Easy to find parking place	7	6	5	4	3	2	1
Wide selection of merchandise ..	7	6	5	4	3	2	1
Carry well known brands	7	6	5	4	3	2	1
Well known to our friends	7	6	5	4	3	2	1
Quick delivery service	7	6	5	4	3	2	1
The type of customer's patronizing the store	7	6	5	4	3	2	1
Convenient location	7	6	5	4	3	2	1
Well known generally	7	6	5	4	3	2	1

Would you please provide the following information about yourself:

1. Please check your *age group* on the following:

    _____Under 20 years _____30–39 years _____50–59 years
    _____20–29 years _____40–49 years _____Over 60 years

2. Which of the following categories applies to your *total family* income:

    _____Under $5,000 _____$7,500–$9,999 _____$15,–20,000
    _____$5,000–$7,499 _____$10,000–$14,999 _____Over $20,000

3. Person completing the questionnaire: _____Male _____Female

4. Occupation of the head of the household: _____

case
6
Planned Parenthood of Atlanta (A)*

In early May 1974, Ms. Julie Dallas, a summer intern of Planned Parenthood of Atlanta, was trying to determine what actions to take with regard to the increasing problem of unwanted pregnancies among teenagers and the growth of venereal disease for this group. She felt that greater usage of condoms by teenagers would help both these problems somewhat and wanted to develop a case to present to condom manufacturers to convince them to initiate a marketing campaign oriented toward teenagers. Several summer interns would be joining the staff in the next two weeks and would be available to help conduct any research that would be beneficial to this effort. Ms. Dallas had to design a program in the next week to make use of these interns when they arrived.

BACKGROUND ON THE PLANNED PARENTHOOD
OF ATLANTA

The Planned Parenthood of Atlanta (PPA) is one of 190 local affiliates of the Planned Parenthood Federation of America. The first birth control clinic in the United States was opened in 1914 by Margaret Sanger, who later formed the National Birth Control League. Sanger was a nurse by profession, working mainly with underprivileged persons in New York City. Her work stimulated her to become an activist in the early women's rights movement, with emphasis on the right of women to control conception. While her early concern was with individual rights, the scope of the movement has broadened to include the issue of population control on national and international levels.

In 1939, the League evolved into Planned Parenthood Federation

---

* This case was prepared by Kenneth L. Bernhardt and Danny N. Bellenger, Georgia State University.

of America, sometimes also known as Planned Parenthood/World Population. The stated purposes of the Federation are:

1. To provide leadership in
   a. Making effective means of voluntary fertility control, including contraception, abortion, and sterilization available and fully accessible to all.
   b. Achieving a U.S. population of stable size in an optimum environment.
   c. Developing appropriate information, education, and training programs.
2. To support the efforts of others to achieve similar goals in the United States and throughout the world.

Planned Parenthood of Atlanta was formed in 1964 by a group of concerned citizens organized by Mrs. Herbert Taylor. After a period of provisional affiliation, the Atlanta association became a full affiliate of the Federation in 1967. The original intention of PPA was to provide education in the area of birth control for the Metropolitan Atlanta community and to stimulate public agencies to provide birth control services. Reducing the number of unwanted pregnancies is one of the primary goals of PPA, and they have been using a summer intern program for the past few years to conduct programs in this area oriented toward teenagers.

Early in its existence, Planned Parenthood of Atlanta realized that existing agencies for birth control were handling maximum loads, and needs for services were not being met. When Federal funds were made available, PPA opened its own clinic in January, 1966 at the Bethlehem Community Center. By 1973, seven Planned Parenthood clinics were providing service to approximately 9,000 persons annually. In addition to operating these clinics, they distribute literature and provide speakers throughout the area, mostly directed toward the problem of unwanted pregnancies.

Originally, the PPA operating funds came entirely from membership dues and private donations. By 1974, funding was received from United Way and federal and state government family planning programs.

BACKGROUND ON POPULATION PLANNING

As shown in Exhibit 1, the fertility rate (number of children/woman) in the United States has been on the decline since the late 1950s, and had reached 2.4 by 1970. In 1974, the rate was approximately 2.1 children per woman, considered the theoretical rate whereby Zero Population Growth can be achieved.

The annual birth rate (percent of women of childbearing age who

Exhibit 1
Total fertility rate for the United States, 1800–1970

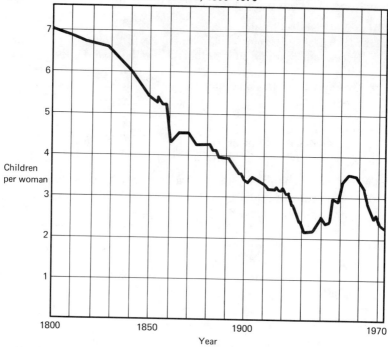

Children
per woman

Year

Notes: Prior to 1917, data available only for white population; after 1917, for total population.

Annual births expressed in terms of implied completed family size, declined until the 1930's, rose, and fell again.

Sources: Prior to 1917—Ansley Coale and Melvin Zelnik, *New Estimates of Fertility and Population in the United States* (Princeton: Princeton University Press, 1963). 1917 to 1968—U.S. National Center for Health Statistics, *Natality Statistics Analysis*, Series 21, Number 19, 1970, 1969 to 1971—U.S. Bureau of the Census, *Current Population Reports*, Series P-23, No. 36, "Fertility Indicators: 1976," 1971. The figure for 1971 is based on an unpublished Census staff estimate.

have a child in that year) was declining as shown in Exhibit 2. The rate dropped between 1961–71 in every age category for both whites and nonwhites. Among nonwhite teenagers, however, the rate only dropped by 16 percent during that period, and only dropped by 3 percent between 1968 and 1971. The greatest disparity between the birth rates of the two racial groups also occurs among teenagers, with the birthrate of nonwhites almost 2½ times that of whites.

Exhibit 3 presents data concerning unwanted fertility in the United States broken down by education and race. The table shows that the overall expected number of births for each woman is 3.0, with the figure being 2.9 for white women and 3.7 for black women. The figure ranges from a low of 2.3 children for a black woman who is a college graduate to a high of 5.2 children for a black woman who never went to high school. The same relationship between education and number of

Exhibit 2
Birth rates by age of mother and color, United States, 1961–1971

	White					Nonwhite				
	1961	*1965*	*1968*	*1971*	*Percent change 1961–1971*	*1961*	*1965*	*1968*	*1971*	*Percent change 1961–1971*
15–19 years	7.9*	6.1	5.5	5.4	−32%	15.3	13.6	13.3	12.9	−16%
20–24 years	24.8	18.0	16.3	14.5	−42%	29.3	24.7	20.1	18.5	−37%
25–29 years	19.4	15.9	14.0	13.5	−30%	22.2	18.8	14.5	13.6	−39%
30–34 years	11.0	9.2	7.3	6.6	−45%	13.6	11.8	9.1	8.0	−41%
35–39 years	5.3	4.4	3.4	2.7	−49%	7.5	6.4	4.9	4.0	−47%
40–44 years	1.5	1.2	0.9	0.6	−60%	2.2	1.9	1.5	1.2	−45%

* Table is read as follows: In 1961, of all white women between 15 and 19 years of age, 7.9 percent gave birth.

Exhibit 3
Unwanted fertility in the United States, 1970*

Race and education	Most likely number of births per women	Percent of births 1966–70 unwanted	Theoretical births per woman without unwanted births
All women	3.0	15	2.7
College 4+	2.5	7	2.4
College 1–3.................	2.8	11	2.6
High school 4	2.8	14	2.6
High school 1–3.............	3.4	20	2.9
Less	3.9	31	3.0
White women	2.9	13	2.6
College 4+	2.5	7	2.4
College 1–3.................	2.8	10	2.6
High school 4	2.8	13	2.6
High school 1–3.............	3.2	18	2.8
Less	3.5	25	2.9
Black women	3.7	27	2.9
College 4+	2.3	3	2.2
College 1–3.................	2.6	21	2.3
High school 4	3.3	9	2.8
High school 1–3.............	4.2	31	3.2
Less	5.2	55	3.1

* Based on data from the 1970 National Fertility Study for currently married women under 45 years of age.

births is very similar for college educated blacks and whites, but black women with a low level of education have a much greater number of children than white women of comparable education. The largest portion of this difference can be attributed to the difference in the percent of births which were unwanted for the two groups.

Column 2 in the table presents data concerning the percent of births which were unwanted. Of children born in 1966–70 to black college graduates, only 3 percent were unwanted, while over half of those born to black women who never went to high school were unwanted. Column 3 in the table presents data concerning the theoretical births per woman eliminating unwanted births. It shows that if unwanted births were eliminated, black women who never went to high school would only have 41 percent more children than black married college graduates (instead of the actual figure of 126 percent more children). Thus it appears the problem is not so much one of motivation differences among the groups as it is a lack of education about and/or availability of contraceptive methods.

Though the birth rates for teenagers have been decreasing as shown in Exhibit 2, the rates of illegitimacy have been drastically increasing. In 1960, 15 percent of births to teenage mothers were illegitimate, while in 1968, this figure was 27 percent. For white teenagers, the percentage in 1968 was 16 percent and for nonwhite it was 55 percent.

Exhibit 4 presents details on illegitimate birth rates by race and age. Illegitimate children are usually unwanted. In 1971, among unmarried teenagers who were pregnant, 83 percent of the white girls and 72 percent of the black girls reported their pregnancies as unwanted. In 1973, 75 percent of the abortions in Georgia were for teenagers, another indicator of the large number of unwanted pregnancies in this age group.

In addition to the problems resulting from unwanted pregnancies, the sexually active person faces the possibility of venereal disease. Over the last decade, the incidence rates of gonorrhea have increased drastically as can be seen from Exhibit 5, particularly for persons under 25. Currently gonorrhea ranks first among reportable communicable diseases in the United States. During fiscal year 1973, 809,681 cases were reported, while estimates of actual occurrence were around 2.5 million cases.

Exhibit 4
Illegitimate live births expressed as percentage of live births, by age of mother and color, United States, 1961–1968

	White			Nonwhite		
Age	1961	1965	1968	1961	1965	1968
Under 15 years	49.9*	57.3	61.0	81.7	86.4	90.8
15–17 years	12.4	17.3	23.4	56.2	62.5	68.8
18–19 years	5.9	9.1	12.8	35.6	38.9	44.3
20–24 years	2.4	3.8	5.1	20.9	23.0	26.4
25–29 years	1.3	1.9	2.0	14.4	16.3	16.8
30–34 years	1.1	1.6	2.0	13.2	14.9	15.5
35–39 years	1.4	1.9	2.5	13.0	14.9	15.7
Over 40 years	1.7	2.2	2.8	12.7	14.0	15.7

* Table is read as follows: in 1961, of all live births to white women under 15 years of age, 49.9% were illegitimate.

While venereal disease is not in the specific domain of Planned Parenthood of Atlanta, it is of concern since one of its prime targets— the sexually active teenager is particularly susceptible. Also, Planned Parenthood of Atlanta is interested in this problem because Atlanta has the highest reported rate of gonorrhea in the United States, with incidence rates approximately three times as high as the national figures presented in Exhibit 5.

A major study concerning unwanted fertility among teenagers was conducted in 1971 by the Institute for Survey Research at Temple University as part of the Commission on Population Growth and the American Future which was established by President Nixon in July 1969. Appendix A presents some data from this study concerning sexuality, contraception, and pregnancy among unwed female teenagers which is based on a national study of 4,611 teenagers.

Exhibit 5
Gonorrhea ratio per 100,000 population by age group, United States, 1960–1972

Age	1960	1970	1972	Percent change 1960–1972
15–19 years	412.7*	782.2	1,035.4	151%
20–24 years	859.2	1,541.5	1,813.5	111
25–29 years	485.5	827.8	921.6	90
30–39 years	192.1	312.9	347.2	81
40–49 years	52.1	80.4	84.6	62

* Table is read as follows: In 1960, for every 100,000 persons between 15–19 years old, 412.7 persons contracted gonorrhea.

CURRENT SITUATION

Each summer for the past few years, one or more interns had joined the PPA staff for the summer. The interns were typically undergraduate and graduate students interested in some aspect of public health. The interns during the summers of 1972 and 1973 had concentrated on a program of distributing free condoms to male teenagers in various recreation centers in low income areas of Atlanta. One purpose of these efforts was to determine how receptive these teens were to this method of contraception.

In May 1974, Ms. Julie Dallas joined the staff of PPA as part of a field internship for her graduate work in Public Health at the University of Michigan. She decided that she wanted to do more with her summer project than had been done in the past. After consultations with top PPA officials, she decided to concentrate on a project which would provide research results useful in convincing condom manufacturers to undertake a marketing education and distribution program oriented toward teenagers.

The immediate problem Ms. Dallas faced concerned what type of research to do to obtain information useful for this objective. She felt that she could obtain the cooperation of the city of Atlanta Recreation Department, and could conduct interviews with teenagers at various parks during the summer. The summer interns, two black students and one white student, who were arriving shortly, would be available to help gather data for the study.

In addition to providing useful campaign information to convince condom manufacturers to promote to this target group, PPA wanted information from the study which would help them develop a strategy to increase their services to best meet the needs of the teenagers. For example, they wondered whether they should open more clinics, distribute more free samples, offer more counseling services, create and distribute more brochures (an example of a PPA information sheet is included in Appendix B)—or what else they could do to help reduce the large number of unwanted pregnancies among this age group.

Two professors at a leading local business school had agreed to help perform any analysis on the data which they collected from their research and also would advise them on the study design. A meeting was scheduled for the next week. Among the questions which she needed to answer before that meeting were the following: *(a)* What should be the objectives of the research; *(b)* How should she define the sample population for the study; *(c)* What type of research to conduct—group interviews, a survey study, an experimental study, or some other type; and *(d)* What specific questions concerning attitudes and behavior should be asked in the research. As the interns would be arriving shortly, it was imperative that she be well prepared for the meeting so that any adjustments necessary could be made quickly.

APPENDIX A

SEXUALITY, CONTRACEPTION, AND PREGNANCY AMONG YOUNG UNWED FEMALES IN THE UNITED STATES

The data

Interviews were completed with females selected in such a way as to represent a national probability sample of the female population, aged 15 to 19, living in households in the United States. In addition to the sample of respondents in housing units, another probability sample was taken of university students living in dormitories. The two samples provided a total of 4,611 interviews, of which 1,479 were with black females and 3,132 were with whites and other races. (Throughout the study, "white" refers to nonblack respondents.) The large proportion of black interviews was the result of a sampling scheme stratified by race.

The sole criterion for eligibility in this study was age, with the provision that only one eligible female could be selected (randomly) from any one household (or any one room in a college dormitory). Women of any marital status were accepted. About 10 percent of the respondents have ever been married; the concern of this paper is with the other 90 percent, those who have never been married.

The never married

Prevalence of intercourse

Table A–1
Never-married females who have had intercourse, by age and race (percent)

	Percent		
Age	Black	White	Total
15	32.3	10.8	13.8
16	46.4	17.5	21.2
17	57.0	21.7	26.6
18	60.4	33.5	37.1
19	80.8	40.4	46.1
Total	53.6	23.4	27.6

Knowledge—Basic biological understanding

Table A–2
Knowledge of onset of fecundity, by age and race, both intercourse statuses (percent)

	"When can a girl first become pregnant?"							
	When period begins		Sometime later		Don't know or no answer		Total	
Age	Black	White	Black	White	Black	White	Black	White
R has had intercourse								
15...............	45.6	46.2	49.7	51.3	4.7	2.5	100.0	100.0
16...............	52.4	55.3	45.9	40.2	1.7	4.5	100.0	100.0
17...............	50.6	64.4	47.7	32.8	1.7	2.8	100.0	100.0
18...............	55.2	71.2	42.3	27.6	2.5	1.2	100.0	100.0
19...............	71.6	63.1	27.8	33.5	0.6	3.4	100.0	100.0
Total	56.4	62.4	41.6	34.8	2.0	2.8	100.0	100.0
R has not had intercourse								
15...............	46.7	48.5	47.4	45.2	5.9	6.3	100.0	100.0
16...............	53.6	53.6	43.4	40.8	3.0	5.6	100.0	100.0
17...............	65.1	62.8	30.7	32.9	4.2	4.3	100.0	100.0
18...............	53.3	64.6	43.7	31.6	3.0	3.8	100.0	100.0
19...............	64.0	67.1	31.2	29.9	4.8	3.0	100.0	100.0
Total	54.1	57.6	41.5	37.5	4.4	4.9	100.0	100.0

Table A–3
Knowledge of pregnancy risk within menstrual cycle by age and race, both intercourse statuses (percent)

| | *When is a girl most likely to . . . :* | | | | | | | |
| | Right before, during, or after period | | About two weeks after | | Any time | | Total | |
Age	Black	White	Black	White	Black	White	Black	White
R has had intercourse								
15..............	43.2	44.6	17.5	41.1	39.3	14.3	100.0	100.0
16..............	53.0	43.8	17.5	43.6	29.5	12.6	100.0	100.0
17..............	49.5	34.7	18.3	51.3	32.2	14.0	100.0	100.0
18..............	55.6	24.1	16.1	62.6	28.3	13.3	100.0	100.0
19..............	34.3	29.6	23.1	59.9	42.6	10.5	100.0	100.0
Total	46.7	33.0	18.8	54.4	34.5	12.6	100.0	100.0
R has not had intercourse								
15..............	51.0	48.8	17.7	30.6	31.3	20.6	100.0	100.0
16..............	46.9	47.0	16.7	36.6	36.4	16.4	100.0	100.0
17..............	44.2	48.2	17.6	40.3	38.2	11.5	100.0	100.0
18..............	49.4	37.0	17.9	49.9	32.7	13.1	100.0	100.0
19..............	47.9	33.1	20.0	55.3	32.1	11.6	100.0	100.0
Total	48.2	44.3	17.6	40.3	34.2	15.4	100.0	100.0

The sexually active

Table A–4
Percent that had first intercourse at each age, by current age and race

| | Current age | | | | | | | | | |
| | 15 | | 16 | | 17 | | 18 | | 19 | |
Age at first intercourse	Black	White	Black	White	Black	White	Black	White	Black	White
<12	17.3*	8.0	3.0	5.5	5.0	1.1	3.3	6.0	0.9	1.4
13	14.2	17.5	6.0	3.7	4.6	1.3	3.7	4.3	2.6	1.2
14	34.7	30.8	21.8	10.4	7.2	6.9	6.6	2.8	4.2	0.6
15	33.8	43.7	31.9	29.8	30.3	14.4	10.8	6.8	8.2	1.3
16	—	—	37.3	50.6	36.9	51.4	29.5	16.6	25.0	11.7
17	—	—	—	—	16.0	24.9	32.8	30.3	34.0	23.7
18	—	—	—	—	—	—	13.3	33.2	23.3	35.7
19	—	—	—	—	—	—	—	—	1.8	24.4
Total ...	100.0	100.0	100.0	100.0	100.0	100.0	100.0	100.0	100.0	100.0

* Table is read as follows: Of black girls currently 15 years old who have had intercourse, 17.3% first had intercourse before age 13.

Table A–5
Percent distribution of frequency of intercourse in "last month" by age and race

	Frequency in last month									
	None		1–2		3–5		6 or more		Total	
Age	Black	White	Black	White	Black	White	Black	White	Black	White
15	45.3*	49.6	34.4	27.4	14.6	13.3	5.7	9.7	100.0	100.0
16	46.4	45.2	30.4	37.1	16.2	2.6	7.0	4.1	100.0	100.0
17	38.6	32.1	40.2	35.4	15.7	18.0	5.5	14.5	100.0	100.0
18	44.6	35.0	33.8	24.9	13.2	21.4	8.4	18.7	100.0	100.0
19	33.6	33.8	25.1	23.1	31.1	18.9	10.2	24.2	100.0	100.0
Total ...	41.0	37.3	32.6	28.6	18.8	18.0	7.6	16.1	100.0	100.0

* Table is read as follows: 45.3% of 15 year old nonvirgins did not have intercourse in the last month.

Contraception

Table A–6
Percent distribution of contraceptive use status, by age and race

	Contraceptive use status									
	Never		Sometimes		Always		No answer		Total	
Age	Black	White	Black	White	Black	White	Black	White	Black	White
15	27.3*	34.1	49.5	44.2	19.6	18.8	3.6	2.9	100.0	100.0
16	21.4	19.5	59.6	56.5	15.2	21.9	3.8	2.1	100.0	100.0
17	10.6	12.4	69.1	68.7	19.5	15.8	0.8	3.1	100.0	100.0
18	10.6	13.1	72.0	68.0	16.4	17.7	1.0	1.2	100.0	100.0
19	10.6	12.1	76.1	59.1	8.6	26.4	4.7	2.4	100.0	100.0
Total ...	14.9	16.0	67.0	61.3	15.4	20.5	2.7	2.2	100.0	100.0

* Table is read as follows: 27.3* of 15 year old black nonvirgins never use any method of contraception.

Table A–7 attempts to show what conjunction there is between first use of contraception and the beginning of sexuality. While there is a looseness of the data since age in years is the only increment, the results do give a clear indication of what percentage do not begin using contraceptives immediately. The summary statistics show that 50 percent of the blacks and about 64 percent of the whites begin using contraceptives at the same age as they become sexually active.

Table A–7
Age of first intercourse by age at first use of contraception, for blacks and whites (percent)

				Age at first intercourse						
Age at first use	<12	13	14	15	16	17	18	19	N.A.	Total
Black										
<12	18.8*									0.9
13		33.6								2.3
14			39.9							5.0
15				44.1						12.5
16					54.1					20.1
17						63.8				18.3
18							71.2			9.1
19								52.0		1.4
N.A. (age) ...										13.3
N.A. (use)/ never used										17.1
Total ...	4.8	5.3	12.3	20.7	26.2	18.3	7.3	0.4	3.2	100.0
White										
<12	31.4									1.2
13		34.2								1.5
14			51.3							4.2
15				58.3						8.8
16					65.0					18.6
17						69.1				16.0
18							72.9			16.6
19								83.6		6.8
N.A. (age) ...										8.7
N.A. (use)/ never used										17.6
Total ...	3.8	4.0	6.9	13.9	25.1	18.8	18.2	6.5	2.8	100.0

* Table is read as follows: 18.8% of black teenagers who had intercourse before age 13 began using contraceptives before age 13.

Table A-8
Percent distribution of most recently used contraception method, by age and race

Method most recently used	15		16		17		18		19		All ages	
	Black	White	Black	White	Black	White	Black	White	Black	White	Black	White
Pills	9.6	2.3	29.4	8.8	21.0	21.4	31.6	25.9	33.4	41.9	26.5	25.0
Foam, jelly, or cream	3.6	2.0	1.8	1.6	3.0	2.7	3.6	4.8	5.0	1.6	3.5	2.7
IUD	3.0	0.0	0.7	0.0	3.4	0.0	4.7	1.3	4.8	0.9	3.6	0.6
Diaphragm	1.0	0.0	0.7	0.0	0.2	0.0	3.0	2.0	1.0	3.9	1.2	1.7
Condom	38.8	25.9	33.4	41.8	32.2	20.1	26.4	16.1	34.3	16.3	32.5	21.8
Douche	7.8	4.3	15.4	4.5	17.7	1.2	7.8	4.0	10.3	1.5	12.1	2.9
Withdrawal	18.5	48.2	5.4	25.3	10.5	41.2	8.6	34.3	4.0	26.2	8.5	33.0
Rhythm	0.0	0.0	0.0	6.2	0.0	2.8	2.2	1.3	0.0	2.5	0.5	2.6
Douche and withdrawal	1.7	7.8	0.7	2.0	3.6	1.9	2.6	2.5	2.4	0.7	2.3	2.2
Condom and other	16.0	9.5	12.5	9.8	8.4	8.7	9.5	7.8	4.8	4.5	9.3	7.5
Total	100.0	100.0	100.0	100.0	100.0	100.0	100.0	100.0	100.0	100.0	100.0	100.0

* Table is read as follows: 9.6% of black 15 year olds who use contraceptives used the "pill" most recently.

Table A–9
Percent giving specified reason for not using contraception, by race

Reason	*Black*		*White*	
Trying to have baby; didn't mind if pregnant	24.2*		12.1	
Too young; infrequent sex; didn't think could get pregnant	27.8 ⎱		16.4 ⎱	
Time of month when couldn't get pregnant	21.4 ⎰ 49.1		42.5 ⎰ 58.9	
Hedonism—heedlessness	7.2		9.6	
Knowledge—logistic	12.7		14.2	
Partner objects; wrong to use	3.0		4.5	
Other	3.8		0.7	
Total	100.0		100.0	

* Table is read as follows: 24.2% of the black teenagers who specified a reason for not using contraceptives said they were trying to have a baby or didn't mind if they got pregnant.

Table A–10
Percent distribution of sources of contraception, by race and age*

Source	15		16		17		18		19		Total	
	Black	White	Black	White	Black	White	Black	White	Black	White	Black	White
Private physician	7.5	0.0	10.6	6.1	8.5	7.6	8.9	12.2	5.2	21.2	7.8	12.7
Drugstore†	60.3	78.1	57.2	67.8	64.0	67.4	61.5	64.6	66.1	58.5	62.8	64.3
Hospital clinic	22.7	0.0	24.6	0.0	17.3	4.2	20.3	5.4	18.5	9.7	19.8	5.5
Other type clinic‡	6.4	7.0	7.6	8.1	7.2	13.0	8.8	10.6	9.7	9.0	8.3	10.0
Other§	3.1	14.9	0.0	18.0	3.0	7.8	0.5	7.2	0.5	1.6	1.3	7.5
Total	100.0	100.0	100.0	100.0	100.0	100.0	100.0	100.0	100.0	100.0	100.0	100.0

*Excludes those who never used contraception, who did not answer the general question on use of contraception, who claimed never to have obtained contraception and those who provided no answer on source.
† Includes those who responded private physician and drugstore.
‡ Includes those who responded hospital clinic and other type clinic.
§ Includes "friends," "relatives," and "commercial establishments other than drugstores."

The relative unimportance of commercial sources other than drugstores may appear surprising in view of the importance of the condom. In cases where the condoms were obtained by the male, there is undoubtedly a considerable amount of doubt about the source.

APPENDIX B

PPA INFORMATION SHEET ON CONDOMS

Planned Parenthood Association
118 Marietta Street, N.W.
Atlanta, Georgia 30303

THE CONDOM (OR THE "RUBBER")

It is wise to know about *more than one method of birth control* in case you stop using the one you are using now.

The *condom,* or rubber, is a method of birth control which many couples have used. It is a good method of birth control. It is also a good way to protect against the spread of infection (V.D.) from a man to a woman or from woman to a man.

HOW TO AVOID MISTAKES

1. The *condom* will work if it is used *every time!*
2. To check for holes you can blow the condom up like a balloon.
3. When the man removes his penis from the woman's birth canal, he should hold the condom so that it does not slip off.
4. If a condom is used several times, be sure to check *EACH TIME* that it has no holes.

Some men do not like to use the condom because they have to stop the loveplay leading up to intercourse to put it on. If the woman puts the condom on for the man, it can become a part of the loveplay and may make the man more willing to use this method of birth control.

Couples should discuss a method of birth control *together* before they use the method. Since we are giving you condoms which you may take home, you may want to show them to your teenagers. Simple, to explain to them how this important method of birth control works.

Condoms can be purchased at any drug store for nominal costs without a prescription or can be secured from the Planned Parenthood Clinics.

No method of birth control is guaranteed 100 percent effective. To increase protection foam may be used by the female partner when the man is using the condom.

A Nurse is always available at the Downtown Clinic for supplies or telephone help. Daily from 2:00 P.M. until 8:00 P.M. and from 9:00 A.M. until 4:30 P.M. Saturdays. *Phone:* 688-9300

case
7

State Apple Association*

In the fall of 1973, the State Apple Association (SAA) had under-taken a co-op advertising campaign with local growers to promote consumption of apples nationwide. Although apple consumption had been increasing over the past 15 years, the association felt that further consumption could be stimulated through a promotional campaign. The advertisements used in the campaign featured scenes depicting a young couple hiking in the Rocky Mountains. They were shown standing by a mountain spring eating the State's apples. The main theme of the campaign was "Eat the Natural Food—Keep Healthy with Apples." This was a variation on the old adage, "An apple a day keeps the doctor away." The SAA had concentrated approximately 50 percent of its campaign efforts in the high population East Coast cities. Research conducted by the association prior to the campaign had de-lineated this as their prime target market based both on potential con-sumption and predisposition toward apples.

In the spring of 1974, the SAA received notification from a United States Federal agency suggesting that some of their recent advertising claims were questionable. The Federal agency had received com-plaints to the effect that SAA advertising was misleading in promoting apples as preventive medicine.

THE GOVERNMENT STUDY

The Federal agency's notification received by the SAA indicated that a study had been commissioned and was currently underway to determine if the complaints of misleading advertising concerning a variety of food products, including apples, was justified. The Govern-ment was undertaking this study partly because of its larger concern with potentially misleading advertising about the health value of cer-

---

* Case by Melanie Wallendorf and Michael Heffring in *Cases in Marketing Re-search*, by Randall J. Schultz, Gerald Zaltman, and Philip C. Burger (Hinsdale, Ill.: Dryden Press, 1975), pp. 144–46. Copyright © 1975 by Dryden Press, a division of Holt, Rinehart and Winston. Reprinted by permission of Holt, Rinehart and Winston.

tain foods. The study would be considered a major input into the decision as to what Government action in the form of trade regulation would result. The Government encouraged the SAA to respond to this notification.

Devon, a suburb of New York City, was chosen by the contracting research agency as the site for its survey. This area consists of 80,000 people, the majority of whom are in the middle and upper income range. The major data collection method was the telephone interview. The research firm felt that systematic random selection was most appropriate for making accurate inferences about the population. They desired responses from 200 qualified participants. This was done in the following manner: a beginning list of 200 people to call was generated by dividing the total population of Devon (80,000) by 200 (= 400). Then from a table of random numbers a starting point for counting was established. From this starting point every 400th name in the local telephone directory was chosen as part of their "first" list. Then such lists of 200 names were generated. Persons on the lists were phoned until 200 qualified participants had been interviewed, using the lists in the order they were selected. For example, if only 100 people recalled the advertisement of the first 200 contacted, then the next step would be to proceed to the second list. This procedure would continue until 200 qualified respondents had been interviewed.

THE SAA STUDY

The apple association, after receiving the details of the government study, decided to conduct a study of their own. The SAA did not believe its ads had been misleading or deceptive. They felt they needed some concrete data to back this belief.

Although the SAA preferred to conduct their study on a nationwide scale, budget limitations forced them to confine their study to one major community area in their home state. The local town selected was Red Deer, a town having approximately 42,000 people in and around its municipal limits. This town is in the heart of the apple belt and is surrounded by agricultural communities. It is also a high apple consumption area. Most people in the area are familiar with the SAA and its promotional campaign.

The SAA hired a local advertising agency they had worked with before to do the study. The advertising agency concluded that if a sample size of 200 was utilized by the government for studying an area of 80,000 people, then a sample size of 100 would be sufficient for the 42,000 people in and around Red Deer. Using local census data the agency divided the town and its surrounding area into five groups based on income levels: low, low-medium, medium, medium-high, and high. They selected 20 people from each area; this was done using a cross-directory in the following manner: the cross-directory was divided into five sections corresponding to the five areas. Then taking each individual area, they would open the book and without looking at the page put a finger on a name. This was done 20 times for each area. After the list was constructed, people were telephoned and asked a variety of questions.

QUESTIONS

Assume the role of a market researcher called in by an independent firm to handle this case.
1. Critically evaluate the sampling procedures of the two studies presented, considering the following points in your discussion:
   Objectives of the two organizations
   Problem definition and its effects on interpretation
   Bias and sampling error
   Population selected for study
   Sample size
   Sampling methods—used and not used.
2. What suggestions would you make for doing the study if the government hired you? If the SAA hired you? What would you do if this was your project for this course and you weren't hired by anyone?

---

case
8

GRAPE Winery, Inc.*

BRIEF LOOK AT GRAPE WINERY

GRAPE Winery is a major producer of New York State wine products, ranking high among wine producers. The major portion of their profits comes from sales of table wines and champagne. The company also bottles Cold Duck, a recently popular beverage which is half champagne, half burgundy.

While all of GRAPE's wines, including their champagne and Cold

---

* This case was prepared by Scott Ward, Harvard Graduate School of Business Administration.

Duck are distributed nationally, the bulk of their wine and champagne sales are in the East—particularly in New York State. Sales of their Cold Duck brands rank behind a few leading brands—there is not much difference between sales of the top brands, however. There are about ten sellers of Cold Duck nationally. Cold Duck seems to be consumed primarily in the East, although sales of all brands are increasing throughout the country. The company maintains a sales force of approximately 60 men, who call on distributors as well as larger retailers in major markets.

Management confessed that it had not predicted the sudden popularity, within the past two years, of all brands of Cold duck. GRAPE produces two brand names of Cold Duck; their John Henry brand is a "premium" Cold Duck selling for approximately $3.25 retail. Their Pierre Lamont brand sells for $2.25. John Henry accounts for approximately two thirds of Cold Duck sales, Pierre Lamont for approximately one third. Retailer margins are high, and, according to management, relatively inflexible. Management is also satisfied with the sales force's penetration of major markets.

Their advertising budget for both Cold Duck brands is small—about $200,000 annually. Management feels other Cold Duck sellers spend comparable amounts. The budget has traditionally been spent on 60-second network television commercials. Additionally, in-store promotional pieces (shelf talkers, etc.) are provided by the sales force.

THE PROBLEM

GRAPE winery is a small company. Major advertising expenditures are out of the question. In fact, major consulting fees are out of the question! You have $8,000 to spend on research.

GRAPE management does not have market research data concerning market segments buying Cold Duck, and so forth. They only know that sales are increasing, although their sales force has not been particularly emphasizing the push of their brands, and their promotional efforts, including advertising, have not increased. In short, they do not know why sales are increasing, if they will continue to increase, if they can drain customers away from other Cold Duck brands, or if they can take action which will increase sales even further. Their question to you, as consultant, was straightforward: "How can we increase sales and share in the Cold Duck market?"

Constraints: $8,000 total fees.

By prior agreement, New York, Hartford and Chicago were selected as key markets for any research to be done. It was felt that these markets would yield results which could be extended to similar markets nationally. Management would interpret your results and recommendations in terms of unique characteristics of liquor distribution and sales in particular markets. You decided that focus group interviews in Chicago would be a good starting point. Reviewing the following transcripts you must now determine what to do next.

Interview Transcript: Group #1/Chicago
Young, Urban, Professional, Single, Male and Female Whites

Group profile

E. David Coolidge, III	Chicago, Illinois
Investment Banker	27 years old
Joanna Smith	Chicago, Illinois
Legal Secretary	24 years old
Bob Barton	Chicago, Illinois
Business Manager	29 years old
Pru Barton	Chicago, Illinois
Assistant to Advertising Manager	22 years old
Kathy Culbertson	Chicago, Illinois
Nurse	25 years old
Doug Gray	Chicago, Illinois
Management Consultant	25 years old
Don Niemann	Chicago, Illinois
Investment Analyst	27 years old
Paul Kimball	Chicago, Illinois
Attorney	27 years old
C. J. DiLaura	Chicago, Illinois
Portfolio Manager	25 years old

Question: How did you first begin drinking Cold Duck?

Dave: I had it served to me at someone's house.

Joanna: It was served at a friend's wedding.

Bob: I had it at home for a Thanksgiving dinner.

Pru: I think it was during the Christmas season and we were having a little party.

Kathy: We used to drink it at college.

Doug: A friend of mine had it at a birthday party.

Don: As I remember it, a group of us got together for an informal evening and someone brought a bottle of Cold Duck along.

Paul: I first had it at a birthday party.

C.J.: We used to serve it at fraternity parties.

Question: When did you first try Cold Duck?

Dave: A couple of years ago.

Joanna: It's been less than a year for me.

Bob: About 10 years ago.

Pru: Last Christmas—So it's been roughly 9 months.

Kathy: Maybe 3 or 4 years ago.

Doug: About a year ago.

Don: I've been drinking it for a year and a half.

Paul: Last fall—About a year.

C.J.: I started drinking it about 4 years ago.

Question: On what types of occasions do you drink Cold Duck?

Dave: I think of it as a dinner drink—either at home or sometimes I'll bring a bottle when I go over to visit a friend. I certainly wouldn't order it at a restaurant or a bar.

Joanna: I'd agree with Dave.

Bob: I almost never have it at home. I usually drink it on informal occasions when we're visiting with friends.

Pru: Let me add to that—Cold Duck isn't bad with dinner.

Kathy: I think of it as going with special occasions. You know—like birthdays, office parties, holiday gatherings and things like that.

Doug: Yes, it's a special occasion drink. I'd say Cold Duck is a replacement for champagne. You know, for weddings and things like that.

Don: I'd drink it anytime—with dinner or television or at a card party—but not for special occasions.

Paul: I expect to drink Cold Duck at parties.

C.J.: Parties maybe, but not for special occasions.

Question: Do you associate Cold Duck drinking with any particular time or season of the year:

Kathy: I'd say it's a winter drink more than anything else.

Paul: I agree.

Others: (Associate with no special time of year)

Question: How often do you buy Cold Duck?

Dave: I almost never buy it—maybe once a year.

Joanna: The same with me. I'll drink it at a party or my date will have a bottle sometimes, but I've never gone out and bought it.

Bob: I buy it a couple of times a year.

Pru: Maybe two or three times a year.

Kathy: I've never purchased any.

Doug: No, never bought a bottle.

Don: A couple of times a year.

Paul: I buy it every three or four months—let's say 5 times a year.

C.J.: Once a year.

Question: What brands of Cold Duck have you tried?

Dave: "X"

Joanna: "X" and I suppose some others, but that's the only name that comes to mind.

Bob: "X"

Pru: "X"

Kathy: I really don't know what brands I've had.

Doug: No, I don't remember any brand names.

Don: I didn't even know that there were different brands of Cold Duck.

Paul: I've had "X".

C.J.: I couldn't tell you.

Question: Of those of you who remember having "X", why did you choose that brand?

Dave: I suppose it's because "X" was being served where I've had Cold Duck. I also think it's cheap.

Joanna: Yes, it's because "X" was around.

Bob: When I've gone in to buy Cold Duck, "X" is usually the one the stores carry.

Pru: Because the stores have it. It is too sweet though.

Paul: The distribution factor plus the fact that I had "X" a couple of times and thought it was alright so there was no reason to switch to another brand.

Question: Have any of you seen any advertising for any of the Cold Duck brands?

Paul: I think I've seen some newspaper ads but I couldn't tell you the brand.

Others: (None had seen radio-television-newspaper-magazine advertising.)

Question: How would you compare Cold Duck with other wine and champagne products?

Dave: I think of Cold Duck as being cheaper than champagne. Also the name is kind of a joke as far as I'm concerned.

Joanna: I think it's kind of a funny name.

Bob: I'd put Cold Duck on a par with cheap champagne.

Pru: But the name makes it an "in" drink.

Kathy: The name appeals to me. It's much different sounding from say Chablis or Bordeaux or other French wines.

Doug: I think of it as being of lesser quality than most wines or champagnes.

Don: Cold Duck sounds to me like a cold towel—it just doesn't make it.

Paul: I'd compare it with a cheap wine.

C.J.: Cheap and a pretty bad hangover.

Question: What kinds of beverages does Cold Duck replace?

Dave: Beer for the most part.

Joanna: I suppose beer or a cheap wine.

Bob: Things like that—social drinks that you feel fast.

Pru: Wine.

Kathy: Wine.

Doug: I think of it as a mixer for punch. You know, instead of champagne or even gin or vodka.

Don: Beer or a dinner wine.

Paul: It replaces wine or champagne.

C.J.: Beer or we use it in a punch—maybe after a football game or something like that.

Question: Where would you be most likely to buy Cold Duck?

Dave: At the supermarket.

Joanna: Supermarket or grocery store.

Bob: I'd buy it at a liquor store.

Pru: Grocery store.

Kathy: Liquor store.

Doug: Liquor store.

Don: Grocery probably, but possibly a liquor store.

Paul: Liquor store.

C.J.: Liquor store.

Question: Have you heard of John Henry or Pierre Lamont wines?

	John Henry	*Pierre Lamont*
Dave:	Yes	No
Joanna:	No	Yes
Bob:	Yes	No
Pru:	Yes	No
Kathy:	Yes	No
Doug:	Yes	No
Don:	No	Yes
Paul:	Yes	Yes
C.J.:	Yes	No

Question: Have any of you seen any ads for any John Henry or Pierre Lamont products?

Paul: I think I've seen some things for Pierre Lamont but I couldn't tell you where.

Others: (No recollection of either brand advertising.)

Question: What would you expect the John Henry and Pierre Lamont Cold Duck to cost?

	John Henry	Pierre Lamont
Dave:	$2.00	$3.00
Joanna:	2.00	2.50
Bob:	2.50	2.50 to 2.75
Pru:	2.40	7.00
Kathy:	2.50	2.00 to 3.00
Doug:	3.00	2.50
Don:	2.00	3.00 to 4.00
Paul:	2.00	2.50
C.J.:	2.00	3.00 to 3.50

Question: From what you know of John Henry and Pierre Lamont what do you think of their products?

Dave: John Henry makes a very good wine. I don't know about Pierre Lamont.

Joanna: Pierre Lamont sounds good and expensive to me.

Bob: I think of John Henry as a cheap wine. I didn't know either of them made a Cold Duck.

Others: (No one was aware of either brand of Cold Duck.)

Pru: I think of champagne when I think of John Henry and it's not bad. Pierre Lamont sounds much better, however.

Kathy: Neither of them mean anything to me.

Doug: John Henry makes very good wines and champagnes.

Don: Pierre Lamont is a pretty good wine, too.

Paul: Of the two, I seem to recall Pierre Lamont as being a superior line to John Henry. However, I think they're both well known and decent wines and champagnes.

C.J.: When I think of John Henry, I think of good champagne—but domestic. Maybe somewhere in between "X" and "Y". Pierre Lamont apparently is the top of the line.

Question: What kinds of people would be most likely to be Cold Duck drinkers?

Dave: I think it's for everybody. Perhaps you'd be most likely to find socially-oriented people drinking Cold Duck because it's kind of an "in-thing" to drink.

Joanna: I think Cold Duck is probably bought by all kinds of people, but the uses probably differ. So you'd have lower class people serving it at weddings because it's cheaper than champagne, while upper class people might drink it with dinner or uniformally.

Bob: Because it seems like a cheaper drink to me, I'd say you'd be most likely to find lower and lower middle-class people drinking Cold Duck.

Pru: I'd expect non-wine drinkers to be Cold Duck drinkers—old ladies, grandmothers and people like that—people who don't like wine but will drink Cold Duck because it's pink and sweet and bubbly.

Kathy: Maybe younger, less educated people. People who are trying to make it, trying to show off to their friends. So instead of having beer they serve Cold Duck. It's got more prestige than beer but it's cheap enough that they can afford it.

Doug: Yes, I'd say younger people also. It's kind of a cheap booze. But I think of it as a middle, not a lower class drink.

Don: I don't see any class distinctions at all. I'd expect to find it as a family drink—something that you can serve to kids as well as adults.

Paul: I'll go along with Pru. Cold Duck is really a drink for nondrinkers.

C.J.: It's everybody's drink—all classes, all ages. I don't see any reason why any one group should be expected to have a monopoly on it.

Question: What do you think or dislike about Cold Duck?

Dave: I think of it as a medium-to-low priced drink which tastes like a medium-to-low priced drink. I'm really indifferent to the taste. I suppose the only think I can really say is that I like the name "Cold Duck," it's unique.

Joanna: I like the bubbles—it reminds me of champagne.

Bob: It really gets into your bloodstream quickly and gets you feeling high awfully fast. If you're looking for that kind of effect, I suppose it's great. I don't really go for it at all.

Pru: The bubbles and the color make it kind of a fun drink, but it definitely tastes too sweet.

Kathy: I like the name. Other than that it doesn't have too much appeal to me.

Doug: I never thought much about it. I think I'd be more likely to drink wine when the occasion calls for it and to drink champagne when the occasion calls for that. What I'm saying, I guess, is that it really doesn't make it as either a wine or a champagne.

Don: It's cheap and when you're just looking for something to drink that's a real asset.

Paul: I like it. It doesn't have a bad taste and you can serve it to anyone. That's an important point, I suppose, anyone will drink it.

C.J.: It tastes good and it's cheap. If you can get by for $2 or $2.50 a bottle, that's pretty good.

Question: From your experience as customers, what would you guess are the most important factors in selling Cold Duck?

Dave: I think you have to have a reasonably priced bottle. Nobody wants to buy the top end of a low priced drink. That's stupid. Even if you come in with a middle priced bottle, you have to differentiate it somehow. "X" is cheap and probably just as good. I'd need a good reason to spend another buck or two for another brand.

Joanna: I agree with that completely. When I think of Cold Duck I think of "X". Somehow you've got to break that association.

Bob: The label is the key. You don't have to be priced low, but you have to change your image. Make it less sweet, push it as a dinner wine and project a high class image.

Pru: In addition to that, I'd change the name. Cold Duck is cheap and sounds cheap. If you're going to charge a high price, you have to make it sound better.

Kathy: My reaction is opposite to Dave's. If I'm buying a cheap type of wine, I feel that the least I can do is to buy a better brand. I see no need to drop the price.

Doug: Yes, I still think it's a good buy at $3.25 or $3.50.

Don: Change the name. Cold Duck sounds like Cold Turkey—it has bad associations for me.

Paul: I don't see anything wrong with the name or the price. I'd leave it as is and just advertise the hell out of it.

C.J.:   I'd push for certain occasions like fraternity parties or birthday parties and I'll leave the name. When I first heard about Cold Duck I thought it was something special. The name will get people to try it—don't change it.

Interview Transcript: Group #2/Chicago *Urban, Black, Blue Collar Workers*

Group profile

Larry A. Schine	Chicago, Illinois
Bus Driver	23 years old—married
J. H. Hawkins	Chicago, Illinois
Bar Porter	45 years old—married
James E. M. Johnson	Chicago, Illinois
Janitor	21 years old—single
George Thomas	Chicago, Illinois
Hotel Banquet Houseman	43 years old—married
Ernest W. Coberson	Chicago, Illinois
Hotel Houseman	22 years old—married

Question: How did you begin drinking Cold Duck?

Larry: I was out in a lounge with some friends and they ordered it.

Hawkins: When it first came out about a year and a half ago I got curious. So I bought a bottle.

James: Some friends of mine had a little party and I tried it there.

George: Everybody was talking about it so I went out and bought some.

Ernest: I had it at a party with some friends.

Question: On what occasions do you drink Cold Duck?

Larry: Whenever some people are around. Sometimes at parties or weddings.

Haskins: When I go out to a bar or a (night) club.

James: Sometimes when I'm at home and want to relax, but not for dinner. I order it when I go out too and it's really best at a party.

George: I had it at a birthday party once and I've tried ordering it at bars but they don't have it. Sometimes at home with the family too.

Ernest: It's a social type drink, so I have it at social gatherings or at home with dinner or TV.

Question: Overall, how often do you buy Cold Duck?

Larry: I've never bought Cold Duck. People just bring it to the house or serve it at parties.

Hawkins: About 3 times a week I get one of those little bottles at the bar.

James: Maybe once every other week.

George: Just about every weekend.

Ernest: I buy a few bottles at once; I guess two or three bottles every couple of weeks.

Question: Do you drink Cold Duck at any special times of year or seasons?

Larry: No, year around.

Hawkins: It's good all the time.

James: I'd say the summer because it's cold.

George: All year.

Ernest: Any time.

Question: When did you first begin drinking Cold Duck?

Larry: Last winter.

Hawkins: About a year and a half ago.

James: June 1970.

George: July 1970.

Ernest: March 1969.

Question: What brands of Cold Duck have you tried?

Larry: Just Cold Duck

Hawkins: I can't remember.

James: Don't know.

George: "M"

Ernest: I like the one in the white bottle but I don't remember the name.

Question: George, why do you like "M"?

George: All "M" products are good and they're medium priced. The store carries "M" Cold Duck, I tried it once and I like it. So I keep buying it.

Question: Have any of you seen advertising for Cold Duck? If so, where?

Larry: Yes, Walgreen had some ads in the newspaper for their brand.

Hawkins: On radio, Rick Ricardo on WBE and WVON. But I don't remember the names.

James: I never saw a Cold Duck ad.

George: "M" has an ad on a billboard in Chicago.

Ernest: I saw some newspaper ads.

Question: How much does Cold Duck cost on the average? What would be an expensive price? An inexpensive price?

	Average	*Expensive*	*Inexpensive*
Larry:	$1.59 to 1.90	$ 4.00	$1.98
Hawkins:	2.00 to 2.50	4.00	.75
James:	2.35	2.89	2.00
George:	2.69	15.00	2.69
Ernest:	1.89	2.89	2.27

(Note: Hawkins is accustomed to purchasing smaller bottles of Cold Duck and his estimates were revised only after clarification. George expected Cold Duck prices to fall in the same range as champagne. I don't believe he made any differentiation.)

Question: What did you drink before you discovered Cold Duck— that is what did Cold Duck replace?

Larry: Beer.

Hawkins: Beer, champagne, champale.

James: Ripple or twist.

George: Rhine wine, but I don't drink it anymore.

Ernest: Champagne.

Question: Why did you switch to Cold Duck?

Larry: It's good at home.

Hawkins: It has more kick than beer or champagne.

James: It's better than Ripple.

George: I just don't like wine anymore.

Ernest: It's more top notch; better for a society-type get together.

Question: What do you like, or dislike, about Cold Duck?

Larry: I like it. It's cool, clean and it has a kick.

Hawkins: It's not strong, kind of mild like champagne.

James: It's a high class drink. You know, It impresses people.

George: I like the taste. It's sweet but not bland. The tartness suits my taste, it's not too sweet.

Ernest: Yeah, the taste is good. The shape of the bottle is also nice. I guess it's "M" that has the nice bottle.

Question: What kind of person would/would not drink Cold Duck?

Larry: A young person. Not somebody who's low class. Maybe high class people.

Hawkins: Ladies mostly; ladies who go out. You know, they drink it on special occasions. All classes would drink it, but probably mostly middle and high class people especially.

James: Anybody could drink it. It fits a lot of occasions.

George: I guess a champagne type drinker. You know, someone who's not a real drinker.

Ernest: I suppose everybody, but especially young people, middle or low class.

Question: When do you make the decision to buy Cold Duck? Who makes it?

Larry: Others buy it. I guess I bought it once and I just went into the store looking for it.

Hawkins: I decide I want some and I just go into the supermarket and buy it.

James: I'm the one who buys it. I do the same thing that Hawkins does.

George: Yeah, I go in looking for it. My wife does the grocery shopping while I go to the liquor counter.

Ernest: I'm like George. I look for it.

Question: How do you decide which brand to buy?

Larry: I just took what brand they gave me.

Hawkins: Yes, I just ask for Cold Duck and they give me a bottle.

James: I guess I like the middle priced one. I don't like anything cheap.

George: I look for "M". The supermarket carries it and I go after it.

Ernest: I buy the most expensive. If it's cheap it's no good. So I buy the best.

Question: Have you ever heard of John Henry or Pierre Lamont? Did you know they both make Cold Duck?

	John Henry	John Henry Cold Duck	Pierre Lamont	Pierre Lamont Cold Duck
Larry:	No	No	Yes	No
Hawkins:	Yes	No	Yes	No
James:	No	No	No	No
George:	No	No	Yes	No
Ernest:	Yes	No	No	No

Question: What do the names John Henry and Pierre Lamont mean to you?

Larry: Marchant sounds good and expensive; the John Henry sounds ok, but not great.

Hawkins: Well, they're both good wines, you know. John Henry is the best in the country, Pierre Lamont isn't bad either.

James: I think John Henry sounds expensive and good. But the other one sounds bad, you know, it sounds like all the others.

George: The one with the fancy name sounds good and expensive. But John Henry—well, I couldn't say.

Ernest: I go along with James. John Henry sounds rich but the other one probably isn't too good.

Question: What would you expect John Henry or Pierre Lamont Cold Duck to cost?

Larry: Pierre Lamont probably costs about $3.50. And John Henry, that sounds cheaper, let's say $1.98.

Hawkins: I'd say they're both about $3.75.

James: John Henry sounds middle-class but I don't know the price.

George: About $3.50 for both.

Ernest: I don't know.

Question: Have you ever seen any advertising for John Henry or Pierre Lamont?

Larry: No.

Hawkins: No

James: It's the one in the red bottle, isn't it?

George: No.

Ernest: No.

Question: If these Cold Duck brands had plastic and regular corks, which would you prefer?

Larry: It doesn't make any difference. All the ones I've tried had plastic tops.

Hawkins: No difference.

James: I like the plastic ones with the silver wire. It's really impressive . . . good for show.

George: Doesn't matter.

Ernest: Plastic cork is best. Really fine drinks come with those plastic tops.

Question: What other alcoholic beverages do you drink?

Larry: Beer.

Hawkins: Everything, but mostly scotch. I still drink scotch every night.

James: Beer, champagne, and some wines.

George: Beer and wine, some scotch.

Ernest: Anything.

Question: (TV board is passed around) What do you think of this television ad?

Larry: I suppose it would make some people curious, but it wouldn't get me to buy it. I think you should fill up a bathtub with Cold Duck and put a girl in it.

Hawkins: It's OK, but that duck has a bad face. The bottle looks nice, nice label.

James: I think it's a bad advertisement. It's stupid. You can't tell that it has anything to do with the drink and that duck is ugly.

George: I don't like animals. I'd rather see a pretty girl.

Ernest: Why do you disguise the product? I drink to feel it, not to see a duck.

---

case
9

Coca-Cola USA*

The division of The Coca-Cola Company that produced and marketed the syrups for Coca-Cola, or "Coke,"[1] and other soft drinks in the United States was named Coca-Cola USA. In January 1972, the manager of the division's Marketing Research Department, in Atlanta, was considering a request from the division's Fountain Division to launch an evaluation of the sales and profit potential of selling a new formulation of syrup in outlets of the BurgerRoyal chain.[2]

The Coca-Cola Fountain Division was engaged in marketing syrups for carbonated beverages, chiefly Coca-Cola, to operators of fountains and vending machines. Its sales representatives had encountered problems in attempting to sell syrups for the new and growing segment of the carbonated beverage industry, commonly referred to as

---

* From David J. Luck, H. G. Wales, D. A. Taylor, *Marketing Research*, (Englewood Cliffs, N.J., Prentice Hall, Inc., 1974), pp. 121–24.

[1] Coca-Cola and Coke are registered trademarks of The Coca-Cola Company.

[2] The name "BurgerRoyal" and the data given in this case are fictitious.

Frozen Carbonated Beverages, through the BurgerRoyal outlets. For brevity we shall refer to these as FCB and BR, respectively.

BR was a prospering firm in the fast food service industry, whose outlets concentrated on hamburgers named, naturally, "BurgerRoyals." A few other types of hot sandwiches, soft ice cream, and french fries comprised the food items. Beverages included coffee, milk, iced tea in season, milk shakes, noncarbonated orange drink, and carbonated soft drinks in three flavors (cola, lemon-lime, and root beer). Carbonated beverage sales at retail averaged around $60 per $1,000 of sales and were quite profitable. BR had been launched in Kansas City, still its headquarters, and spread west to the Rockies and mainly to the Southwest and Southeast—with eventuality of becoming national. During 1972 BR would average around 620 units in operation, and units would average $7,000 sales per month.

BR was possibly the first fast-service food chain to serve frozen carbonated beverages, although they were being adopted widely. BR had developed and patented its own machines to mix and serve FCB, which were considered to be superior equipment. Although BR was renting some of its FCB machines to noncompetitive food outlets, these were few. BR also had researched syrups, for which there were special requirements in FCB machines, and had its own produced secretly by a private brand supplier.

The top management of BR allowed district managers some flexibility in choice of suppliers, and their Oklahoma City district (alone) chose to buy Coca-Cola syrup and sell cola drinks under that trademark. The Oklahoma City manager recently had informed the sales representative of the Fountain Division that higher executives were starting to pressure him to stop buying Coca-Cola syrup and begin using BR's own brand. He was reluctant, as that district had carried Coca-Cola from its beginning, but he also was concerned by the cost differential of $1.80 net per gallon of Coca-Cola syrup versus $1.55 for the BR private brand.

The potentials of FCB syrup sales had been recognized by Coca-Cola USA for over a year, and its research laboratories had been striving to find an ideal formulation for FCB dispensers. That product had been discovered by the laboratories lately, but so recently that its marketing program was just under way. Careful testing indicated that it would produce carbonated drinks fully as palatable as any syrup then in use for FCB and would yield substantially more cups per gallon of syrup. The present syrups being sold by the Fountain Division yielded about 80 cups per gallon. The laboratory technicians estimated that the new FCB syrup would yield 15 to 20 percent more cups per gallon and most likely above the midpoint of that range.

The BR purchasing officials at Kansas City evidenced real interest in this Coca-Cola syrup. The interest was greater in the Coke syrup, but Fountain Division sales representatives believed that once BR could be induced to install the Coke there would be high probability of also buying their root beer and lemon-lime products. The other products would not be branded, but the Division's cola syrup would be retailed as Coca-Cola. The responsible men in BR said that if Coca-Cola syrup could be proven to have so much higher yield than theirs that the cost difference would be clearly offset, they had no doubt that BR would sell Coke.

The Coca-Cola USA sales people also stressed the possibility of the very popular name of their brand, the world's largest selling soft drink, increasing carbonated beverage sales at BR outlets. Of this the BR men were very skeptical and gave the opinion that the Oklahoma City district was not selling appreciably more cola under that brand name than the rest of the units with BR's own supply. However, there had been no promotion of Coke through BR Oklahoma outlets beyond use of the Coke trade mark, and the Fountain Division felt that this brand's profitability for BR would increase also if advertising and point-of-sale merchandising would be exerted by Coca-Cola USA in cooperation with BR.

Discussions between the two companies had reached a stage where BR agreed to have a test conducted to demonstrate whether or not Coca-Cola would be more profitable than BR's own FCB syrup. Further, BR had asked that such a test be conducted in two of its comparable districts with one logically being continuation of Coke in Oklahoma City for the duration of the test. The Wichita area was a logical choice too. Both districts could differentiate between BR units in the main city and those outlying in the district, which numbered as follows:

Oklahoma City—forty units; eighteen in Oklahoma City and others around Oklahoma.

Wichita—thirty units: fourteen in Wichita and balance around central and western Kansas.

Both the average monthly total sales and the carbonated beverage sales per $1,000 sales volume in the units within those districts were about equivalent to the averages for the entire BR system. The average price per cup may be computed at 10 cents, the BR price for small servings, and about 60 percent of FCB sales were of cola flavor. Cost of syrup per cup roughly may be calculated as two cents.

The Coca-Cola USA marketing research manager had his analysts prepare careful cost estimates of a test encompassing all 70 of the units in the Wichita and Oklahoma City districts. This could include testing of the new syrup over a six months' interval that would include both a base and a test period, as well as advertising in one city. Thus the comparative yield of Coca-Cola's syrup, the attraction of its brand name, and effects of advertising might be measured. Altogether such a test would cost around $15,000 inclusive of all overhead items and equipment.

In judging whether or not a project is economically justified, the marketing research manager used a standard that the project must be likely to yield profit to Coca-Cola USA equal to three times its expected costs. (The rate of profit on the syrup was estimated as 10 percent of sales.) This profit must be captured within one year after findings are implemented by management. In our particular case, there is an obvious first consideration: the test's results must so clearly favor adoption of Coca-Cola USA's syrups, in profitability, that BR would adopt them for the entire chain or enough of its outlets to give sufficient payout to Coca-Cola USA.

QUESTIONS

1. On the basis of a payout analysis of anticipated results and costs of the proposed project, should the marketing research manager authorize it? Provide detailed calculations of your analysis.

2. Describe the specific design of the test that you would conduct and the data that it would produce for the decision maker. Include statements on the areas used for testing and control, what would be tested in them, and the time periods of phases of the test.

case
10

The *Atlanta Journal* and *Constitution* (A)*

Mr. Ferguson Rood, research and marketing director for the *Atlanta Journal* and the *Atlanta Constitution*, was still perspiring from the three block walk in the hot August sun back to his office from the meeting he had just been to at Rich's Department Store. At the meeting, he had been told that Rich's, the newspaper's largest advertiser, wanted to test the effectiveness of TV and radio advertising versus newspaper advertising for their upcoming Harvest Sale. He had promised to make his suggestions for the research plan in forty-eight hours, and felt he had much work to do in that short time. He wondered what recommendations he should make for the study, and was concerned that the research design and questionnaire be developed so that the study would represent fairly the effectiveness of the *Atlanta Journal* and the *Atlanta Constitution*. As he began to review his notes from the meeting, he picked up the phone to call his wife and tell her he would be home very late that evening.

BACKGROUND

The *Atlanta Journal* and the *Atlanta Constitution* are a union of two of the largest circulation newspapers in the South. The *Atlanta Constitution*, winner of four Pulitzer prizes for its efforts in the area of social reform, was founded June 16, 1868. The *Atlanta Journal*, founded February 24, 1883, became the largest daily newspaper in Georgia by 1889. Also a winner of the Pulitzer Prize, the *Journal* is the Southeast's largest afternoon newspaper.

In 1950, the *Atlanta Journal* and the *Atlanta Constitution* were combined into Atlanta Newspapers, Inc., a privately held company.

---

* This case was prepared by Kenneth L. Bernhardt, Georgia State University.

The two newspapers maintained independent editorial staffs, and there was very little overlap of readers. Exhibits 1 through 4 present data concerning the adult readership of the newspapers, the gross reader impressions, reach and frequency, and readership over five week days and four Sundays.

To provide the advertisers and potential advertisers with information necessary to help them make their advertising media decisions, the newspaper does a considerable amount of research, often approaching $25,000 in a year. Most of the research is designed to be used in selling advertising to a wide range of advertisers, and includes data on retail trading areas, shopping patterns, product usage and newspaper coverage patterns. In addition to Mr. Rood, the research department had two other trained market researchers and one secretary.

Although there are nine daily newspapers in the Atlanta trading area, all but the *Journal* and the *Constitution* have very small circulations. The principal competition for large advertisers is with radio and TV stations. Exhibit 5 presents information on the circulation of the print media in the Atlanta area. Exhibit 6 contains information on the broadcast media in Atlanta. Although there were 40 radio stations, 28 AM and 12 FM, and 6 TV stations, WSB Radio and TV dominated the market. WSB Radio, for example, was consistently rated among the top six stations in the nation, and had a greater Atlanta audience than the next four stations combined. WSB-TV and WSB Radio, both affiliated with the NBC Network, were owned by Cox Broadcasting Corporation, which also owns television stations in Charlotte, Dayton, Pittsburgh and San Francisco and radio stations in Charlotte, Dayton, and Miami. Cox Broadcasting and WSB-TV and radio stations shared corporate headquarters in Atlanta.

WSB radio was founded in 1922 by the *Atlanta Journal* newspaper. In 1939, former Democratic presidential nominee and Governor of Ohio James M. Cox acquired the newspaper-radio combine. In 1948 WSB-TV was founded, and two years later the newspapers and broadcast media were separated when Atlanta Newspapers, Inc. was established. Today, there is no relationship between the newspapers and WSB radio and TV.

Rich's Department Store was the largest advertiser for the *Journal* and the *Constitution,* accounting for almost five percent of their advertising revenue, and was WSB's largest local advertiser. Founded in 1867, Rich's by 1970 had grown to a company with seven stores distributed throughout Atlanta as shown in Exhibit 7. Sales were approximately $200 million per year with earnings after taxes of almost five percent of sales. The company was classified as a general merchandise retailer, and carried a very wide line of products including clothing, furniture, appliances, housewares, and items for the home. Rich's dominated the Atlanta market, with close to 40 percent of department store sales and approximately 25 percent of all the sales of general merchandise. The merchandising highlight of the year was the annual Harvest Sale, first held in October 1925. The sale typically ran for two weeks, and had become a yearly tradition at Rich's.

BACKGROUND ON THE MEDIA EFFECTIVENESS STUDY

Before preparing his proposal to Rich's for the media effectiveness study, Mr. Rood reflected upon the events of the past 24 hours. The day before, he had received a phone call from the vice president and sales promotion director from Rich's, inviting him to the meeting at Rich's the next day. Having been told that Rich's research director and the research director of WSB–TV and Radio would also be there, Mr. Rood had been a little apprehensive before going. At the start of the meeting he was asked if the Atlanta newspapers would be interested in participating in a cooperative research study aimed at measuring the effectiveness of various advertising media during Rich's September Harvest Sale, their largest annual sales event. It became immediately apparent that the research director from WSB, Jim Land, had met with the Rich's people the week before, and was undoubtedly the source of the idea to conduct the study. A document was then passed out that had been prepared by WSB and was entitled "Suggestions for Rich's Media Research." This document is included in Appendix A, and outlines the objectives of the study, a suggested methodology, together with a questionnaire.

The suggested objectives for the project were: (1) to measure the ability of TV, radio and newspapers to sell specific items of merchandise in Rich's seven Atlanta stores; (2) to determine how each advertising medium complements the others in terms of additional units sold to various segments of the customer population (age, sex, charge account ownership, etc.); (3) to determine what each advertising medium contributed in regard to additional store traffic. Mr. Rood's broadcasting counterpart stated at the meeting that "If Rich's is interested in conducting research to measure the effectiveness of various advertising media, WSB–TV and WSB radio will be happy to assist." Rood had no choice, so he volunteered the support of the newspapers to the study.

The Rich's research manager then asked if the media would participate financially in the study. Mr. Rood suggested that each of the three media participate equally, and committed the newspapers to

$500 for a study that he figured should cost between $2,500 and $3,000 for interviewing. Mr. Land indicated that Cox Broadcasting would be willing to put in $500 each for TV and radio.

They then discussed how the research could be conducted. The WSB proposal suggested in-store surveys, with a separate survey conducted for each item of merchandise tested. The survey would be conducted by Rich's employees working overtime in appropriate store locations during the peak shopping hours. The tabulation of the results could be handled by the broadcast station's computer. Care was to be taken to insure that the TV, radio, or newspaper advertising for the individual items not be "stacked" in favor of one particular medium. The proposed questionnaire (see Appendix) included questions on how the respondents happened to buy the merchandise at Rich's, if they recalled seeing TV, newspaper or radio advertising, and if they bought anything else. Questions were also asked concerning age and ownership of a Rich's charge account.

Mr. Land stated that WSB was not trying to take business away from the newspapers, and that Rood had nothing to fear. His recommendation was that Rich's not take anything away from the newspaper advertising budget. He suggested that the amount of space purchased in the newspapers be the same as the previous year, with additional monies being committed to the broadcast media. The Rich's sales promotion director then discussed some of his thoughts concerning the study. He indicated that Rich's had been sending 400,000 direct mail pieces to announce the Harvest Sale; this year they would send 200,000, diverting the other money to broadcast. This would make $7,600 available for broadcast, and another $12,000 to $15,000 would be made available to purchase broadcast time.

The Harvest Sale was to open with courtesy days on Monday and Tuesday, September 21–22, with the sale beginning the evening of the 22nd and running for 13 days. While decisions concerning which sales items were to be included in the study and the media schedules to be used were not yet available, some progress had been made. Approximately ten items were to be researched, and the newspaper ads on Sunday September 20 would include all or most of the ten items. Newspaper ads for the items would be repeated Monday and Tuesday with emphasis on the *Journal*. The interviews were to be conducted Monday through Wednesday.

On Sunday and Monday, with a possible spillover to Tuesday due to availability, Rich's will run 120 30-second TV commercials on all commercial stations except Channel 17. During the same time they will run 120 radio 30-second commercials on a list of stations which had not yet been determined. With both TV and radio, WSB was to get the lion's share if availability could be arranged. Mr. Rood felt certain in view of the client and the research that WSB would manage to come up with several prime-time commercial openings even if it meant bumping some high paying national advertisers.

Ten items were mentioned as possible subjects for the research. The ten final items selected would come mostly from this list, although one or two other items might be chosen. The items mentioned included (1) color TV console at $499; (2) custom-made draperies; Sterns & Foster mattress at $44; (3) carpeting at $6.99 per square yard; (4) Gant shirts at $5; (5) Van Heusen shirts and Arrow shirts at 2 for $11; (6) women's handbags at $9.99; (7) Johannsen's shoes; (8) pants suits; (9) Hoover upright vacuum cleaner; and (10) GE refrigerator.

Mr. Rood, who had not said very much at the meeting, then asked for 48 hours to review the proposal. Everyone agreed to this, and Mr. Rood promised to present a counterproposal at that time.

Even though it had been rather obvious who initiated the idea for the study and that he at first felt that newspapers were being "set up" by WSB, it had been basically a friendly and relaxed meeting among friends. Mr. Land and Mr. Rood had worked together in the Atlanta Chapter of the American Marketing Association and had a great deal of mutual respect. Mr. Rood thought Land was a tough competitor, and understood that he had been successful using awareness type studies in Cox Broadcastings' other markets to gain additional advertising for broadcast.

When he returned to his office, Rood pulled out some of his files on Rich's. He noticed that the amount of advertising had been fairly constant, approximately 40 pages over the two-week period, during the past three Harvest Sales, and that basically the same products had been promoted. A typical Harvest Sale ad is included in Exhibit 8. He also pulled from the files rate schedules for the *Atlanta Journal* and *Constitution* and WSB (see Exhibits 9 and 10), even though he realized that the exact media schedule would be developed by Rich's advertising agency. Approximately $100,000 would be spent promoting the Harvest Sale, with perhaps a third of this amount being devoted to the sale items.

Mr. Rood decided that he would have to assume confidence in the effectiveness of the newspapers. He felt if the study was done right he would get his share of media exposure and influence. The other decision he quickly made was that in preparing his comments on the proposed research, he would take Rich's point of view rather than that of the *Atlanta Journal* and *Constitution*. He then began to review the events of the day and the WSB proposal in light of what he felt Rich's needed to know. He also knew that whatever he proposed would have to be acceptable to Mr. Land. Noting the lateness in the day, he began work on the counterproposal.

Exhibit 1
Gross reader impressions (delivered by *The Atlanta Journal* and *Constitution* in 15-County Metro Atlanta)

During any five weekdays 864,500 adults read *The Atlanta Journal* or *Constitution* an average of 3.5 times for a total of 3,025,800 weekday Gross Reader Impressions.

During any four Sundays 907,600 adults read The Atlanta Journal & Constitution for an average of 3.4 times for a total of 3,085,800 Sunday Gross Reader Impressions.

These newspapers deliver 3,933,400 adult Gross Reader Impressions when one Sunday is added to five weekdays.

Reach and frequency of newspaper reading

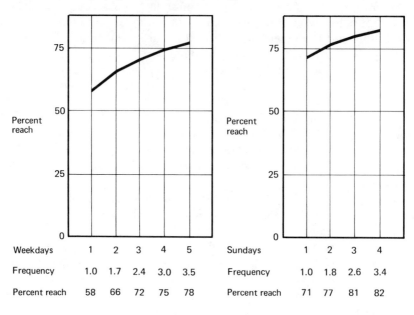

Weekdays	1	2	3	4	5
Frequency	1.0	1.7	2.4	3.0	3.5
Percent reach	58	66	72	75	78

Sundays	1	2	3	4
Frequency	1.0	1.8	2.6	3.4
Percent reach	71	77	81	82

Exhibit 2
Atlanta Journal **and** *Constitution* **readership information**

644,400 Adult Readers   15-County metro Atlanta

Of all metro
Atlanta adults,
644,400 read *The
Atlanta Journal* or
Constitution on
the average week-
day. Of this total,
412,700 read *The
Journal* and
366,100 read *The
Constitution.*
134,400 adults
read both. On the
average Sunday
782,200 metro
Atlanta adults read
*The Atlanta
Journal* and
Constitution.

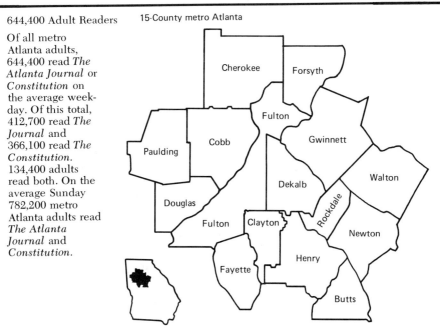

78 percent of all daily circulation is within 15-county metro Atlanta.
66 percent of all Sunday circulation is within 15-county metro Atlanta.

Adult readers of *The Atlanta Journal* **and** *Constitution* **in 15-County Metro Atlanta**

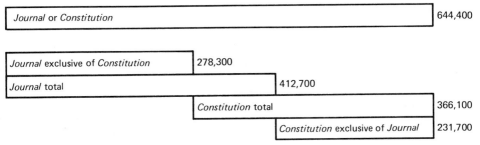

Journal or *Constitution*	644,400
Journal exclusive of *Constitution*	278,300
Journal total	412,700
Constitution total	366,100
Constitution exclusive of *Journal*	231,700

Exhibit 3
Readership of *The Atlanta Journal* **and** *Constitution* **over five weekdays**

644,400 or 58% of all Metro Atlanta adults read either *The Atlanta Journal* or *Constitution* on the average weekday . . . over five weekdays these newspapers deliver 864,900 or 78% of all metro area adults with an average frequency of 3.5 days.

	Total metro area adults	Average 1-day readership		Cumulative 5-weekday readership		Fre-quency
Total adults	1,105,500	644,400	58%	864,900	78%	3.5
Sex						
Female	588,500	331,700	56%	447,600	76%	3.5
Male	517,000	312,700	61	416,800	81	3.5
Household income						
$25,000 and over	104,200	85,900	82%	102,700	99%	4.2
$15,000–24,999	195,300	146,400	75	181,900	93	4.0
$10,000–14,999	241,900	152,800	63	203,900	84	3.7
$5,000–9,999	334,200	170,600	51	241,800	72	3.5
Under $5,000	229,900	88,500	39	133,000	58	3.3
Age						
18–34	470,500	234,500	50%	345,200	73%	3.4
35–49	305,600	197,200	65	250,300	82	3.9
50–64	211,900	145,800	69	184,600	87	3.9
65 and over	116,500	66,700	57	84,700	73	3.9
Race						
White	872,800	528,800	61%	685,100	78%	3.9
Nonwhite	232,700	115,600	50	180,100	77	3.2
Education						
College graduate	173,500	138,000	80%	172,600	99%	4.0
Part college	194,700	137,600	71	174,100	89	4.0
High school graduate	360,500	225,000	62	302,900	84	3.7
Part H.S. or less	365,600	137,000	38	202,200	55	3.4

Exhibit 4
Readership of *The Atlanta Journal* and *Constitution* over four Sundays

782,200 or 71% of all Metro Atlanta adults read *The Atlanta Journal* and *Constitution* on the average Sunday . . . over four Sundays these newspapers deliver 907,300 or 82% of all metro areas adults with an average frequency of 3.4 Sundays.

	Total metro area adults	Average 1-Sunday readership	Cumulative 4-Sunday readership	Number of Sundays frequency
Total adults	1,105,500	782,200	907,300	3.4
Sex				
Female	588,500	418,800	477,800	3.5
Male	517,000	363,400	429,500	3.4
Household income				
$25,000 and over	104,200	89,100	97,200	3.7
$15,000–24,999	195,300	168,800	180,700	3.7
$10,000–14,999	241,900	190,100	216,400	3.5
$5,000–9,999	334,400	215,600	267,300	3.2
Under $5,000	229,900	118,500	145,600	3.3
Age				
18–34	470,500	313,000	390,000	3.2
35–49	305,600	221,300	248,500	3.6
50–64	211,900	167,000	179,900	3.7
65 and over	116,500	80,600	88,500	3.6
Race				
White	872,800	633,100	727,900	3.5
Nonwhite	232,700	149,100	179,100	3.3
Education				
College graduate	173,500	150,200	163,700	3.7
Part college	194,700	157,300	180,200	3.5
High school graduate	360,500	273,900	313,500	3.5
Part H.S. or less	365,600	192,300	240,000	3.2

Exhibit 5
Circulation of print media in Atlanta
METRO ATLANTA NEWSPAPERS: CIRCULATION

Dailies	Edition	Total circulation
Atlanta Constitution	Morning	216,624
Atlanta Journal*	Evening	259,721
Journal-Constitution	Sunday	585,532
Gwinnett Daily News	Evening (except Sat.)	10,111
Gwinnett Daily News	Sunday	10,100
Marietta Daily Journal	Evening (except Sat.)	24,750
Marietta Daily Journal	Sunday	25,456
Fulton County Daily Report	Evening (Mon-Fri)	1,600
Atlanta Daily World	Morning	19,000
Atlanta Daily World	Sunday	22,000
Wall Street Journal	Morning (Mon-Fri)	16,180
Jonesboro News Daily	Evening (Mon-Fri)	9,100
North Fulton Today	Evening (Mon-Fri)	2,300
South Cobb Today	Evening (Mon-Fri)	2,400
New York Times	Morning (Mon-Sat)	500
New York Times	Sunday	3,100

METRO ATLANTA WEEKLY NEWSPAPER CIRCULATION

Atlanta Inquirer	30,000
Atlanta Voice	37,500
DeKalb New Era	16,400
Atlanta's Suburban Reporter	3,900
Lithonia Observer	2,765
Northside News	8,000
Georgia Business News	4,900
Southern Israelite	4,300
Decatur-DeKalb News	73,000
Southside Sun (East Point)	37,700
Tucker Star	10,000
Alpharetta, Roswell Neighbor	6,800
Austell, Mabelton, Powder Springs Neighbor	12,123
Acworth, Kennesaw-Woodstock Neighbor	3,242
Northside, Sandy Springs, Vinings Neighbor	20,836
Smyrna Neighbor	6,872
College Park, East Point, Hapeville, South Side, West End Neighbor	18,813
Chamblee, Doraville, Dunwoody, North Atlanta Neighbor	14,963
Clarkston, Stone Mountain, Tucker Neighbor	15,074
The Journal of Labor (Atlanta)	17,500
Austell Enterprise	1,911
The Cherokee Tribune (Canton)	7,100
Rockdale Citizen	6,031
The Covington News	6,000
The Forsyth County News	4,800
Dallas New Era	4,075
Douglas County Sentinel	7,350
South Fulton Recorder (Fairburn)	4,000
Fayette County News	4,500
Jackson Progress Argus	2,635
The Weekly Advertiser (McDonough)	5,650

The Walton Tribune (Monroe)	5,102
Lilburn Recorder	5,000
Lawrenceville Home Weekly	2,000
The Great Speckled Bird (Atlanta)	7,925
The Georgia Bulletin	14,000
The Covington News (Tues. & Thurs.)	6,200
Creative Loafing in Atlanta	30,000

ATLANTA AREA NEWSPAPERS*

Cobb	28,000
North Fulton	36,000
North DeKalb-Gwinnett	45,000
South DeKalb	44,000
South Fulton-Clayton	53,000

    * These are supplements to the Atlanta Journal, and circulation is to Atlanta Journal subscribers only.

CIRCULATION OF MAJOR MAGAZINES IN GEORGIA

Publication	Circulation
American Home	70,485
Better Homes and Gardens	145,962
Good Housekeeping	114,045
McCall's	139,728
Ladies Home Journal	128,331
Family Circle	106,245
Woman's Day	100,566
Redbook	86,354
National Geographic	103,941
Reader's Digest	331,240
Newsweek	41,070
Time	60,438
U.S. News & World Report	40,417
TV Guide	345,871
Playboy	98,389
Sports Illustrated	38,263
Outdoor Life	25,918
True	18,244
Southern Living	95,000
Progressive Farmer	70,000
Cosmopolitan	25,075
Calendar Atlanta	50,000

Exhibit 6
Broadcast media in Atlanta
METRO ATLANTA AM RADIO STATIONS

Location	Station/ network	Established	Frequency	Power
Atlanta	WSB (NBC)	1922	750 khz	50 kw
	WAOK	1954	1380 khz	5 kw
	WGKA (ABC)	1955	1190 khz	1 kw day
	WGST (ABC-E)	1922	920 khz	5 kw day 1 kw night
	WIGO (ABC-C)	1946	1340 khz	1 kw day 250 w night
	WIIN (MBS)	1949	970 khz	5 kw day
	WPLO	1937	590 khz	5 kw
	WQXI	1948	790 khz	5 kw day 1 kw night
	WXAP	1948	860 khz	1 kw
	WYZE (MBS)	1956	1480 khz	5 kw day
Decatur	WAVO	1958	1420 khz	1 kw day
	WGUN	1947	1010 khz	50 kw day
	WQAK	1964	1310 khz	500 w
N. Atlanta	WRNG (CBS)	1967	680 khz	25 kw day
Morrow	WSSA	1959	1570 khz	1 kw day
East Point	WTJH	1949	1260 khz	5 kw day
Smyrna	WYNX	1962	1550 khz	10 kw day
Buford	WDYX	1956	1460 khz	5 kw day
Austell	WACX	1968	1600 khz	1 kw
Lawrenceville	WLAW	1959	1360 khz	1 kw
Marietta	WCOB	1955	1080 khz	10 kw day
	WFOM	1946	1230 khz	1 kw day 250 w night
Canton	WCHK (GA)	1957	1290 khz	1 kw day
Covington	WGFS	1953	1430 khz	1 kw day
Cumming	WSNE	1961	1170 khz	1 kw
Douglasville	WDGL	1964	1527 khz	1 kw
Jackson	WJGA	1967	1540 khz	1 kw day
Monroe	WMRE	1954	1490 khz	1 kw

METRO ATLANTA FM RADIO STATIONS

Station	Established	Frequency	Power
WSB-FM	1934	98.5 mhz	100 kw
WPLO-FM	1948	103.3 mhz	50 kw
WZGC-FM	1955	92.9 mhz	100 kw
WKLS-FM	1960	96.1 mhz	100 kw
WQXI-FM	1962	94.1 mhz	100 kw
WBIE-FM	1959	101.5 mhz	100 kw
WLTA-FM	1963	99.7 mhz	100 kw
WJGA-FM	1968	92.1 mhz	3 kw
WCHK-FM	1964	105.5 mhz	3 kw
WGCO-FM	1969	102.3 mhz	100 kw
WABE-FM	1948	90.0 mhz	10.5 kw
WREK-FM	1968	91.1 mhz	40 kw

METRO ATLANTA TELEVISION STATIONS

Station	Established	Channel/network	
WSB-TV	9/29/48	2	NBC
WAGA-TV	3/8/49	5	CBS
WXIA-TV	9/30/51	11	ABC
WTCG-TV	9/1/67	17	IND
WETV	1958	30	NET
WGTV	1960	8	NET

Exhibit 7
Map of Atlanta and seven Rich's stores

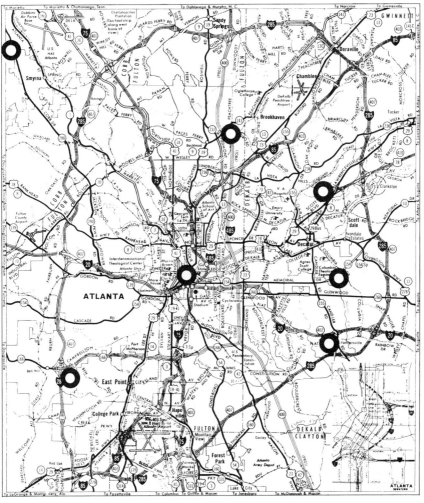

Exhibit 8
Typical Rich's harvest sale ad

Exhibit 9
The Atlanta Journal and The Atlanta Constitution retail display rates

Open rate per column inch

Constitution	$ 8.15
Journal	$11.27
Combination	$14.83
Sunday	$15.56

Yearly bulk space rates

Inches per year per inch	*Constitution*	*Journal*	*Combination*	*Sunday*
100	$6.21	$8.43	$11.09	$11.65
250	6.16	8.35	11.00	11.55
500	6.10	8.28	10.90	11.45
1,000	6.05	8.21	10.81	11.35
2,500	5.99	8.13	10.70	11.24
5,000	5.93	8.05	10.59	11.12
7,500	5.90	8.01	10.54	11.07
10,000	5.87	7.97	10.48	11.01
12,500	5.85	7.93	10.43	10.96
15,000	5.82	7.89	10.38	10.90
25,000	5.70	7.73	10.17	10.68
50,000	5.61	7.69	10.05	10.61
75,000	5.51	7.65	9.93	10.53
100,000	5.41	7.61	9.81	10.46
150,000	5.21	7.51	9.56	10.31
200,000	5.01	7.41	9.32	10.15
250,000	4.81	7.31	9.08	9.99

Exhibit 10
WSB radio and TV advertising rates

WSB–AM radio
Spot announcements—Package plans

Available 5:00–6:00 A.M., 10:00 A.M.–3:30 P.M., and 7:30 P.M.–Midnight, Monday–Saturday; and 5:00 A.M.–Midnight, Sunday. Best available positions in applicable times—no guaranteed placement.

	One minute	*20/30 seconds*	*10 seconds*
12 per week	$40.00	$34.00	$24.00
18 per week	38.00	30.00	21.00
24 per week	32.00	26.00	19.00
30 per week	28.00	24.00	17.00
48 per week	26.00	20.00	15.00

WSB–FM radio
Package plan—52 weeks
   1 minute $16.00
   20/30 seconds 14.00
Quantity discounts available. For example 18 times per week for 52 weeks is one half the above rates.

WSB–TV
Daytime rates
   60 seconds .... $75—235 depending on program
   30 seconds .... 40—140 depending on program
Prime time rates
   60 seconds* .... $540—660 depending on program
   30 seconds .... 390—725 depending on program
   * Very few available.

APPENDIX

SUGGESTIONS FOR RICH'S MEDIA RESEARCH

Objectives

If Rich's is interested in conducting research to measure the effectiveness of various advertising media, WSB–TV and WSB–radio will be happy to assist. As a basis for discussion, here are suggested objectives for this project:

1. Measure the ability of TV, radio, and newspapers to sell specific items of merchandise in Rich's seven Atlanta metro stores.
2. Determine how each advertising medium complements the others in terms of additional units sold to various segments of the customer population (age, sex, charge account ownership, etc.).
3. Determine what each advertising medium contributed in regard to additional store traffic.

How the research could be conducted

The project could consist of a series of in-store surveys. A separate survey would be conducted for each item of merchandise tested. The more items tested, the more reliable the results of the overall research project.

If possible, all seven Rich's stores in the Atlanta metro area should participate in the research.

Each survey could be conducted by placing interviewers (Rich's personnel working overtime) in appropriate store locations during "peak" shopping hours with instructions to complete *brief* questionnaires with customers purchasing the item being tested. (See questionnare attached.)

The interview could cover how the customer got the idea to buy the item, other planned purchases in the store during the same visit, charge account ownership and any other pertinent data. Each interview would last less than a minute and would not bother the customers.

The sample size would vary, depending upon the number of stores participating, the type of merchandise and the sales volume. Interviewers would strive to include all customers purchasing the items during peak hours. Tabulation of the results could be handled by the WSB computer.

Careful attention to items and media schedules

In order to make the research valid and meaningful, the items to be tested must be selected carefully. In addition, care should be taken to insure that the TV, radio, or newspaper advertising for these items is not "stacked" in favor of one particular medium. Close attention to the items being tested and the media schedule for each is necessary.

Questionnaire

The proposed questionnaire is shown below.

POSSIBLE QUESTIONNAIRE FOR RICH'S IN-STORE SURVEY

(All customers purchasing the item advertised are interviewed.)

---

1. *How* did you happen to buy this merchandise at Rich's?

Saw on TV	( )
Heard on radio	( )
Saw in newspaper	( )
TV and radio	( )
TV and newspaper	( )
Newspaper and radio	( )
TV, radio and newspaper	( )
Saw on display	( )
Other:_____	( )

   Asked of customers not mentioning a medium: (2, 3, 4)

2. Do you recall seeing this merchandise advertised on the TV?

Yes	( )
No	( )

3. Do you recall seeing this merchandise advertising in the newspaper?

Yes	( )
No	( )

4. Do you recall hearing this merchandise advertised on the radio?

Yes	( )
No	( )

5. Are you buying *anything else* at Rich's today?

Yes	( )
No	( )
Maybe,	( )
Don't know	

6. Do you have a charge account at *Rich's?*

Yes	( )
No	( )

7. In which group does your age fall?

Under 25	( )
25–34	( )
35–49	( )
50+	( )

Store_____

Time of interview_____

---

case
11

Multipurpose Stores, Inc. (B)*

Multipurpose Stores, Inc., (MPS), a regional retail chain store organization, operated six stores in the state. One of the MPS stores which is located in the city of Littlefield, had experienced declining sales for some time. Early in 1974 the company's top management replaced the Littlefield MPS store manager. The new manager was directed to improve the store's sales. In consultation with the top management, the new store manager speculated that the problem of declining sales was related to the faulty image of the store in the minds of the customers and potential customers (See Case (A), Multipurpose Stores, Inc.). In order to get an objective evaluation of the store's image, the new store manager retained the professional services of a local marketing consulting group. Toward the end of 1974, the marketing consulting group submitted their two-part report. The first part related to an objective evaluation of the store by the marketing consultants while the second part was devoted to presenting the findings emanating from the store "image" study.

MARKETING CONSULTANTS REPORT—PART I

The MPS store in Littlefield is a relatively large furniture, appliance, and hardware store. The store carries a wide variety of brand names in furniture, such as Broyhill, Marflex, Woodward, DeSoto and Twin Oaks. A limited selection of Westinghouse appliances is complemented by a good selection of television sets and stereos. There is also a small hardware department within the same large building.

The MPS store generally projects a "mom and pop" type image and definitely does not give the impression of a store operated by a corporation.

---

* This case was prepared by C. P. Rao and G. E. Kiser, The University of Arkansas.

A professional decor that one would expect to find in a quality full-line furniture and appliance store is lacking. The store does not appeal to visitors and one may generalize by saying it is "lifeless." Upon entering the store, the first impression is that of a wholesale outlet. Although the furniture department is not haphazardly laid out, it lacks originality and does not portray a realistic grouping of the items. There are no partitions between sets or individual pieces. When displaying furniture, attractive arrangement is extremely important, especially in the bedroom layouts, but this is very much missing in the MPS store. Lighting is minimal and makes the decor even more drab. The consultants noted that although the store carries a line of tile and carpeting, there is none either on the floor or on display.

The hardware department is not laid out well and it has a "messy" appearance. The quality of hardware lines, in general, is good though not exceptional. In some merchandise lines, e.g., small appliances, the store carries a good variety. However, this is not true of all merchandise lines.

The area market for furniture and appliance type merchandise consists of two major geographical segments: the city of Littlefield and the outlying areas. The regional economy is growing faster than other areas of the state, and the residents enjoy rising income levels. Despite this healthy environment, the local MPS store is not keeping pace in sales. Although there are some problems with the store's interior and its arrangement; quality furniture, televisions, stereos, and appliances are carried at competitive prices. As an indication of deficient marketing effort, the MPS store lacks exposure to the target market. The vast majority of those respondents included in the survey did not know about the MPS store. Thus, customer awareness of the store's existence and what it has to offer is very limited.

Prestige comes from customers recognizing the high quality of the merchandise carried by the store and the better service that is provided. In this connection, the MPS store suffers not only from a lack of exposure to the target market, but its image is diffused and diluted by multiple lines of diverse merchandise. It is difficult to improve the prestige of the store as a primary furniture-appliance business while the store also tries to sell "nickel and dime" type hardware items. For many potential customers, the esteem associated with a funiture store would be one of the main reasons for purchasing from that store. The customer demands a degree of distinctiveness when purchasing high value items. But a company carrying and selling low value and low prestige items would inflict a damaging effect on the high value and high prestige items. In this sense, the hardware unit of MPS store is quite incongruous with the store's main effort.

Recommendations are:

1. Interior arrangement and decor should be brought to contemporary style.
2. MPS management should make a basic decision regarding the hardware department. The hardware department should be discontinued or, at least, it should be made more compatible with other merchandise in the store.
3. The MPS store should intensify advertising and promotional efforts in order to increase consumer awareness and project an image of a prestigious furniture and appliance store.
4. Specifics concerning the overall marketing strategy in general and promotional strategy in particular should be defered until the "image" study results are available.

MARKETING CONSULTANTS REPORT—PART II

The marketing research consultants submitted preliminary statistical data pertaining to the MPS store customers and potential customers. The data deal with the following aspects of store image and are presented in Exhibits 1 through 5.

1. Relative importance ratings on various furniture-appliance store attributes by the store customers and potential customers.
2. Mentions of the number of the area furniture-appliance stores liked by the respondents.
3. Number of respondents mentioning the MPS as one of their preferred furniture-appliance stores.
4. Evaluative ratings of MPS store on various furniture-appliance store attributes by the store customers and potential customers.
5. Sociodemographic characteristics of the respondents—store customers and potential customers.

QUESTIONS

1. How do you analyze the research data submitted by the marketing consultants in Part II of their report?
2. On the basis of such analysis and the information in Part I of the marketing consultant's report, what conclusions do you draw as to the nature and dimensions of MPS store's image problem?
3. After completing the analysis under 2, what would be your recommendations for improving the sales performance of MPS store in Littlefield?

Exhibit 1
Relative importance of various furniture-appliance store attributes to the store customer and potential customers

Furniture-appliance store attribute	Percent of respondents reporting													
	7		6		5		4		3		2		1	
	I	II	I	II	I	II	I	II	I	II	I	II	I	II
Attractive decor and display	23.1	7.3	10.3	16.4	20.5	16.4	25.6	30.9	7.7	5.5	0.0	5.5	12.9	18.2
Accessibility of store	25.6	25.5	20.5	16.4	25.6	20.0	10.3	23.7	10.3	5.5	0.0	3.6	7.7	5.4
Informative advertising	23.1	10.9	28.2	20.0	20.5	27.3	15.4	14.5	0.0	10.9	2.6	5.5	10.1	10.9
Courteous store personnel	69.2	60.0	15.4	10.9	12.8	16.4	0.0	7.2	0.0	1.8	0.0	0.0	2.6	3.6
Easy credit	5.1	7.3	12.8	14.5	30.8	10.9	15.4	9.1	7.7	10.9	5.1	9.1	23.1	38.2
Competitive prices	56.4	61.8	20.5	21.8	12.8	9.1	7.7	1.8	0.0	0.0	0.0	1.8	2.6	3.6
Quality merchandise	71.8	87.3	20.5	9.1	5.1	1.8	0.0	0.0	0.0	0.0	9.0	0.0	2.6	1.8
Easy to find parking place	30.8	27.3	17.9	7.3	25.6	20.0	12.8	32.7	7.7	3.6	2.6	5.5	2.6	3.6
Wide selection of merchandise	38.5	40.0	28.2	23.6	12.8	21.8	5.1	9.1	5.1	1.8	2.6	0.0	7.7	3.6
Carry well known brands	35.9	34.5	25.6	18.2	12.8	18.2	7.7	21.8	7.7	3.6	5.1	0.0	5.1	3.6
Well known to our friends	12.8	3.6	7.7	7.3	7.7	5.5	15.4	25.5	17.9	10.9	5.1	9.1	33.3	38.2
Quick delivery service	17.9	18.2	5.1	16.4	15.4	18.2	28.2	20.0	15.4	7.3	5.1	3.6	12.8	16.4
Type of customers patronizing the store	5.1	3.6	2.6	3.6	20.5	3.6	17.9	16.4	7.7	9.1	5.1	18.2	41.5	45.5
Convenient location	33.3	21.8	10.3	21.8	20.5	12.7	15.4	21.8	10.3	10.9	0.0	5.5	10.3	5.5
Well known generally	12.8	14.5	12.8	5.5	15.3	25.5	33.3	16.4	7.7	12.7	2.6	3.6	15.4	21.8

Note: Respondent importance ratings were gathered on a seven degree scale—7 representing most important and 1 least important. Under each value of the importance scale, the percentages under I represent the store customer group (N = 78) and under II potential customer group (N = 110).

Exhibit 2
Mentions of the number of area furniture-appliance stores liked by the respondents

	Number of area furniture-appliance stores mentioned				
Respondent group	*1 (percent)*	*2 (percent)*	*3 (percent)*	*4 (percent)*	*5 (percent)*
MPS store customer group (N = 78)....................	12.8	10.3	35.9	28.5	2.5
Potential customer group (N = 110)	36.4	14.5	21.8	27.3	0.0

Exhibit 3
Number and order of mentions of the MPS store as one of respondent preferred furniture-appliance store in the area

	Total number of mentions (percent)	*Order of mentions (percent)*				
Respondent group		*1*	*2*	*3*	*4*	*5*
MPS store customer group (N = 78)	100	30	40	30	—	—
Potential customer group (N = 110)	38	—	9	21	8	—

Exhibit 4
Respondent evaluation of MPS store on various furniture-appliance store attributes

| | Percent of respondents reporting | | | | | | | | | | | | |
| | 7 | | 6 | | 5 | | 4 | | 3 | | 2 | | 1 | |
	I	II	I	II	I	II	I	II	I	II	I	II	I	II
Attractive decor and display	30.8	7.3	17.9	3.6	23.1	12.7	17.9	10.9	5.1	5.5	2.6	0.0	2.6	60.0
Accessibility of stores	33.3	10.9	23.1	9.1	20.5	12.7	15.4	5.5	5.1	3.6	0.0	1.8	2.6	56.4
Informative advertising	17.9	3.6	12.8	1.8	23.1	5.5	28.2	7.3	7.7	12.7	0.0	7.3	10.3	61.8
Courteous store personnel	38.5	5.5	25.6	3.6	17.9	7.3	15.4	9.1	0.0	1.8	0.0	1.8	2.6	20.9
Easy credit	30.8	1.8	25.6	1.8	15.4	1.8	12.8	10.9	0.0	3.6	2.6	3.6	12.8	76.4
Competitive prices	20.5	5.5	23.1	3.6	28.2	10.9	15.4	9.1	2.6	1.8	0.0	1.8	10.3	67.3
Quality merchandise	33.3	5.5	15.6	5.5	20.5	9.1	10.3	5.5	0.0	1.8	2.6	7.3	7.7	65.5
Easy to find parking place	53.8	12.7	17.9	10.9	15.4	7.3	2.6	3.6	5.1	1.8	2.6	3.6	2.6	60.0
Wide selection of merchandise ..	23.1	1.8	23.1	10.9	35.9	1.8	10.3	9.1	2.6	9.1	2.6	3.6	2.6	63.6
Carry well known brands.......	25.6	3.6	33.3	5.5	23.1	9.1	12.8	10.9	2.6	3.6	0.0	1.8	2.6	65.5
Well known to our friends	17.9	3.6	15.4	3.6	25.6	3.6	20.5	7.3	2.6	7.3	5.1	5.5	12.8	69.1
Quick delivery service	23.1	1.8	20.5	3.6	15.4	0.0	25.6	12.7	2.6	5.5	2.6	0.0	10.3	76.4
Type of customers patronizing the store	20.5	3.6	12.8	1.8	28.2	5.5	20.5	14.5	7.6	3.6	0.0	0.0	10.3	70.9
Convenient location	30.8	10.9	23.1	10.9	15.4	9.1	20.5	5.5	0.0	1.8	7.7	7.3	2.6	54.5
Well known generally	33.3	10.9	20.5	5.5	23.1	5.5	15.4	9.1	0.0	3.6	2.6	1.8	5.1	63.6

Note: Respondent evaluation ratings were gathered on a seven degree scale—7 representing highly favorable and 1 highly unfavorable. Under each value of evaluation scale the percentages under I represent the MPS store customer group (N = 78) and II potential customer group (N = 110).

Exhibit 5
Sociodemographic characteristics of respondents

	MPS store customer group (N = 78) (percent)	Potential customer group (N − 110) (percent)
Age:		
Under 20 years	0.0	5.5
20–29 years	35.9	45.5
30–39 years	25.6	23.6
40–49 years	5.1	5.5
50–59 years	17.9	7.3
Over 60 years	15.5	12.6
Total family income:		
Under $5,000	10.3	16.4
$5,000–$7,499	15.4	10.9
$7,500–$9,999	20.5	9.1
$10,000–$14,999	25.6	20.0
$15,000–$20,000	12.8	14.5
Over $20,000	7.7	12.7
No response	7.7	16.4
Sex:		
Male	61.5	36.4
Female	38.5	63.6

case
12

Planned Parenthood of Atlanta (B)*

In September 1974, Ms. Diane Grimes was assigned to evaluate and make use of the data generated from a summer intern research project. Ms. Grimes, a full-time Planned Parenthood of Atlanta (PPA) employee, had been assigned this duty after the first phase of the analysis was complete. The project had been designed and implemented by Ms. Julie Dallas over the summer of 1974. At the end of the summer Ms. Dallas and the other interns had returned to their universities.

---

* This case was prepared by Danny N. Bellenger and Kenneth L. Bernhardt, Georgia State University.

Ms. Dallas joined the staff of PPA as part of a field internship for her graduate work in Public Health at the University of Michigan. She was assigned two black students and one white student to assist with her project.

Past interns, during the summer of 1972 and 1973, had concentrated on a program of distributing free condoms to teenagers in various recreation centers in low income areas of Atlanta. One purpose of these efforts was to determine how receptive these teens were to this method of contraception. Ms. Dallas wanted to do a project with more lasting impact. After consultations with top PPA officials, she decided to concentrate on a project which would provide research results useful in convincing condom manufacturers to undertake a marketing education and distribution program oriented toward teenagers. In addition, the PPA officials wanted information from the study which would help them develop a strategy to increase their services to best meet the needs of the teenagers. For example, they wondered whether they should open more clinics, distribute more free samples, offer more counseling services, create and distribute more brochures—or what else they could do to help reduce the large number of unwanted pregnancies among this age group.

THE RESEARCH PROJECT

Ms. Dallas contacted two professors at a leading local business school who agreed to help perform any analysis on the data which the research group collected and also to advise them on the study design. Together they decided that the best research approach would be a survey of Atlanta teenagers. A judgmental sample of 300 was set as the target with the sample to be equally distributed between black males, black females, white males, and white females. The interviews were to be taken by the interns at local parks, recreation centers, churches, and so forth.

Getting permission to conduct the interviews turned out to be a major problem, particularly in the White community. Due to this problem and the limited duration of the summer internship projects, only 197 interviews were completed; 36 with white males, 67 with black males; 32 with white females, and 62 with black females. The majority of the black respondents were interviewed at parks and recreation centers and the majority of the white respondents were interviewed at YMCA's and recreation centers.

The black teenagers were interviewed by black interns and the white teenagers by white interns. The questions covered a wide range of topics including: knowledge about sex, birth control, and condoms; sexual activeness; magazine reading habits; attitudes toward sex; birth control methods, and the purchase of birth control devices; and social and demographic characteristics. The complete questionnaire is shown in Exhibit 1.

After the data collection was terminated, the data was edited and coded onto computer cards in order to run a series of cross-tabulations. The variable race/sex (categories: white male, black male, white female, and black female) was cross tabulated with other selected variables. Results are shown in the Appendix. Chi square statistics were also computed on several of the tables.

USING THE DATA

Ms. Grimes was faced with several questions and decisions related to the research: (1) How good was the research and is the data reliable? (2) What recommendations should she make for future summer projects; how could this project be extended and improved upon or should such research be dropped? (3) What additional analysis is needed on the data? (4) How should the data be presented to condom manufacturers? What topics should she address and how should she use the research findings in this presentation? (5) Finally, what strategy should PPA follow to increase their services to best meet the needs of teenagers?

Exhibit 1

Planned Parenthood Questionnaire

Hello, I'm _____ . The Planned Parenthood Association of Atlanta is conducting a study of attitudes of teenagers toward birth control. If you are between the ages of 13 and 18, we would like to ask you a few questions.

1. What methods of birth control do you know about? _____

2. What brands of rubbers (also called condoms and prophylactics) can you name? _____

3. How old were you when you first learned about condoms?
   ____6 or less   ____7–9   ____10–11   ____12–13   ____14–15
   ____16 or over

4. How did you first learn about condoms?
   ____Never heard of them before   ____Family Planning Clinic
   ____Father   ____Sex education class
   ____Mother   ____Girlfriend or boyfriend
   ____Other male relatives   ____Other friend
   ____Other female relatives   ____Other: _____

5. Do any of your friends use condoms? ____Yes   ____No   ____Don't Know

6. Have you ever used condoms?   ____Yes   ____No

7. In which of the following places have you obtained condoms? (Check all that apply.)

Exhibit 1 (continued)

————From a friend   ————From a family planning center
————From a drugstore   ————From a pool hall
————From a vending machine   ————Other: (specify)————————

8. Where would you like to be able to buy condoms?————————————

9. What is the advantage of a lubricated condom?————————————

10. What is the difference between a skin condom and a latex condom?————

11. What is the advantage of a nipple end or reservoir end condom?————

12. When is a woman most likely to get pregnant? (Show Card Two)
————During her period   ————15 days after her period starts
————Just before her period   ————Don't know
————Just after her period

For the following statements, please indicate whether you strongly agree, agree, are neutral, disagree, strongly disagree, or don't know. (Show Card)

	Strongly agree	Agree	Neutral	Strongly disagree	Disagree	Don't know
13. Condoms come in different sizes.	——	——	——	——	——	——
14. Condoms come in different colors.	——	——	——	——	——	——
15. Condoms come in different shapes.	——	——	——	——	——	——
16. A pharmacist or druggist is the person who fills prescriptions in a drugstore.	——	——	——	——	——	——
17. Most pharmacists are over 45 years old.	——	——	——	——	——	——
18. Most pharmacists will sell condoms to teenagers.	——	——	——	——	——	——
19. I would feel embarrassed to buy condoms from a pharmacist.	——	——	——	——	——	——
20. I would prefer to buy condoms from a young pharmacist.	——	——	——	——	——	——
21. I would prefer to buy condoms from someone of my own sex.	——	——	——	——	——	——
22. Sex feels as good with a condom as without a condom.	——	——	——	——	——	——
23. I would prefer to buy condoms by mail order.	——	——	——	——	——	——
24. My friends and						

Exhibit 1 *(continued)*

		Strongly agree	Agree	Neutral	Strongly disagree	Disagree	Don't know
	I sometimes talk about other methods of birth control.	___	___	___	___	___	___
25.	My friends and I sometimes talk about condoms.	___	___	___	___	___	___
26.	I would rather buy condoms in a vending machine than in a drugstore.	___	___	___	___	___	___
27.	Condoms provide protection against VD.	___	___	___	___	___	___
28.	Condoms decrease sexual feelings during intercourse.	___	___	___	___	___	___

29. What would you say are the advantages of condoms over other birth control methods? _____

30. What would you say are the disadvantages of condoms over other methods of birth control? _____

31. In what section of the drugstore do you think condoms should be?
    ___Under the counter ___With feminine hygiene
    ___On shelf by prescriptions___With men's toiletries

32. What could manufacturers of condoms do to encourage teenagers to make more use of condoms? _____

33. Have you ever seen any advertisements for condoms?
    ___Yes ___No ___Don't know

34. (If Yes), where did you see these ads? _____

35. Where can people get information about birth control? _____

36. What is your sex? ___Male ___Female

37. What is your age?   ___13 years old   ___16 years old
    ___14 years old   ___17 years old
    ___15 years old   ___18 years old

38. How many years of school have you completed?
    ___6th grade   ___7th grade   ___8th grade   ___9th grade
    ___10th grade   ___11th grade   ___12th grade

39. Which of these best describes where you live?
    ___With both parents   ___With relatives other than parent(s)
    ___With mother   ___Alone
    ___With father   ___With roomate(s) male/female
    ___Other: _____

40. What magazines do you read? _____

41. What is your mother's job? _____

42. What is your father's job? _____

43. What is your religion? _____

44. What is your race? ___Black ___White ___Other: _____

45. Have you ever had sexual intercourse? ___Yes ___No ___Refusal

46. About how often do you have sexual intercourse?
    ___Once a year or less   ___Several times a month
    ___Several times a year   ___Once a week
    ___About once a month   ___Several times a week

47. Have you used condoms in the past month?   ___Yes   ___No

48. (If Yes), where did you get them? _____

Exhibit 1 (concluded)

49. Do you use birth control when you have intercourse?
    ___Always   ___Sometimes
    ___Most of the time   ___No
50. What methods of birth control have you or your partner ever used?
    ___Condoms   ___Pills   ___Diaphragm   ___Foam
    ___Rhythm   ___Withdrawal
51. (Girls) Have you ever thought you were pregnant?   ___Yes   ___No
52. (Girls) Have you ever been pregnant? ___Yes ___No ___No Response
53. (Boys) Have you ever thought you fathered a child?   ___Yes   ___No
54. (Boys) Have you ever fathered a child? ___Yes ___No ___No Response
55. (Girls) At what age did you start having your monthly period _____
56. Did you think you were old enough to get pregnant at that time?
    ___Yes   ___No
57. (Girls) Do you think you are old enough to get pregnant now?
    ___Yes   ___No
58. Do you have any questions or comments?

    Thank you very much for your help. That finishes the interview. We would like to give you a booklet about condoms. And some free sample condoms if you like.
    booklet   condoms
    ___accepted   ___accepted
    ___rejected   ___rejected

Interviewer's comments:

APPENDIX

DATA SUMMARY—TABLES 1–42

Table 1
"Have you ever had sexual intercourse?"

	White male	Black male	White female	Black female	Total
Refused	3%	3%	3%	0%	2%
Yes	67	75	47	36	57
No	30	21	50	64	41
	100%	100%	100%	100%	100%
	n = 33	66	32	58	189

Chi sq = 24.7 with 3 degrees of freedom*

* Chi square computations was made using only the yes and no responses.

Table 2
"About how often do you have sexual intercourse?"

	White male	Black male	White female	Black female	Total
Once a year or less	26%	10%	27%	24%	18%
Several times a year	35	10	40	0	17
About once a month	13	16	13	33	18
Several times a month	9	44	13	29	29
Once a week	4	2	0	0	2
Several times a week	13	18	7	14	16
	100%	100%	100%	100%	100%
	n = 23	50	15	21	109

Chi sq = 28.2 with 9 degrees of freedom*

* Chi square computation was made by collapsing the last three rows (several times/month, once a month, several times/week) into one row.

Table 3
Number of birth control methods mentioned by respondents*

Number	White male	Black male	White female	Black female	Total
None	17%	37%	6%	37%	28%
One	19	9	16	13	14
Two	22	25	19	16	21
Three	25	19	28	26	24
Four or more	17	10	31	3	13
	100%	100%	100%	100%	100%
	n = 36	67	32	62	197

Chi sq = 25.2 with 12 degrees of freedom

* Actual question asked was: "What methods of birth control do you know about?"

Table 4
Methods of birth control mentioned*

Method	White male	Black male	White female	Black female	Total
Condoms	73%	83%	57%	46%	65%
Pill	93	95	97	87	93
IUD	17	24	30	51	31
Diaphragm	20	7	27	5	13
Foams-Jelly	10	21	43	41	29
Rhythm	13	5	17	0	8
Sterilization	17	10	7	8	10
Abortion	7	0	13	0	4
Withdrawal	0	0	7	3	2
Other	7	2	3	5	4
	n = 30	42	30	39	141

* Actual question asked: "What methods of birth control do you know about?" Percentages are the percentage of respondents who named at least one method. Percentages do not cumulate to 100% due to multiple responses.

Table 5
"Do you use birth control when you have intercourse?"

	White male	Black male	White female	Black female	Total
Always	9%	12%	13%	43%	18%
Most of the time	26	16	13	0	15
Sometimes	48	45	13	10	34
No	17	27	61	47	33
	100%	100%	100%	100%	100%
	n = 23	49	15	21	108

Chi sq = 16.6 with 6 degrees of freedom*

* Chi square computation was made by combining "Always" and "Most of the time" responses.

Table 6
"What methods of birth control have you or your partner ever used?"

	White male	Black male	White female	Black female	Total
Condoms	84%	78%	56%	33%	68%
Pills	53	55	22	56	51
Diaphragm	11	3	11	0	5
Foam, jelly	16	8	22	6	10
Rhythm	21	15	22	0	14
Withdrawal	42	18	44	6	23
Other	0	0	0	6	1
	n = 19	40	9	18	86

Note: Percentages may not add to 100% due to multiple responses.

Table 7
"Have you ever used condoms?"

Response	White male	Black male	White female	Black female	Total
Yes	44%	46%	13%	2%	26%
No	56	54	87	98	74
	100%	100%	100%	100%	100%
	n = 36	67	32	62	197

Chi sq = 42.4 with 3 degrees of freedom

Table 8
"Do any of your friends use condoms?"

Response	White male	Black male	White female	Black female	Total
Yes	47%	66%	56%	23%	47%
No	3	6	19	24	14
Don't know	50	28	25	53	39
	100%	100%	100%	100%	100%
	n = 36	64	32	62	194

Chi sq = 33.2 with 6 degrees of freedom

Table 9
Age when respondent learned about condoms*

Age	White male	Black male	White female	Black female	Total
9 or less	23%	23%	9%	15%	19%
10–11	33	27	47	28	32
12–13	36	43	34	46	41
14 or over	3	7	10	11	8
	100%	100%	100%	100%	100%
	n = 36	67	32	61	196

Chi sq = 10.4 with 9 degrees of freedom

* Actual question asked was: "How old were you when you first learned about condoms?"

Table 10
How respondent learned about condoms*

How	White male	Black male	White female	Black female	Total
Father	8%	22%	6%	5%	12%
Mother	3	0	19	13	8
Other Relative	11	10	3	5	8
Sex education class	14	13	13	34	20
Girl/boy friend	3	5	0	18	8
Friend of same sex	50	25	38	16	29
Other	11	19	21	9	13
	100%	100%	100%	100%	100%
	n = 36	67	32	61	196

Chi sq = 62.1 with 18 degrees of freedom

* Actual question asked was: "How did you first learn about condoms?"

Table 11
"In which of the following places have you obtained condoms?"

From	White male	Black male	White female	Black female	Total
A friend	19%	28%	3%	21%	20%
Drugstore	21	60	3	8	19
Vending machine	14	10	0	2	6
Family planning center	3	2	3	0	2
Pool hall	3	2	3	0	2
Other	3	0	0	6	3
Not applicable (never used)	56	46	87	44	54

Note: Percentages do not add to 100% because of multiple responses.

Table 12
"Where would you like to be able to buy condoms?"

Location	White male	Black male	White female	Black female	Total
Don't know	6%	8%	16%	16%	12%
Drugstore	61	42	41	54	49
Everywhere	6	18	16	2	10
No place	8	10	13	18	13
Other	28	24	22	8	20

Note: Percentages do not add to 100% because of multiple responses.

Table 13
"Have you used condoms in the past month?"

	White male	Black male	White female	Black female	Total
Yes	17%	29%	13%	19%	22%
No	83	71	87	81	78
	100%	100%	100%	100%	100%
	n = 23	69	15	21	108

Chi sq = 2.7 with 3 degrees of freedom

Table 14
"Where did you get the condoms (if yes in preceding table)?"

	White male	Black male	White female	Black female	Total
Don't know	0	6%	50%	0	8%
Drugstore	50%	44	50	25%	42
Friend	0	19	0	75	23
Vending machine	25	19	0	0	15
Clinic	0	6	0	0	4
Other	25	6	0	0	8
	100%	100%	100%	100%	100%
	n = 4	16	2	4	26

Chi sq = 17.2 with 15 degrees of freedom

Table 15
Number of brands of condoms mentioned*

Number	White male	Black male	White female	Black female	Total
None	56%	63%	88%	82%	72%
One	19	18	12	13	16
Two or more	25	19	0	5	12
	100%	100%	100%	100%	100%
n =	36	67	32	62	197

Chi sq = 18.9 with 6 degrees of freedom

* Actual question asked was: "What brands of rubbers (also called condoms and prophylactice) can you name?

Table 16
Brands of condoms mentioned*

Brands	White male	Black male	White female	Black female	Total
Trojans	88%	62%	100%	36%	67%
Sheik	6	65	0	64	44
Ramses	6	0	0	0	2
Fiesta	13	8	0	9	9
Sultan	0	8	0	0	4
Prime	0	4	0	0	2
Nuform	0	0	0	9	2
Black Cab	0	8	0	0	4
Tahiti	6	0	0	0	2
Samoa	13	0	0	0	4
Fourex	6	0	0	0	2
Naturalamb	6	4	0	9	6
Other Latex	31	4	0	0	13
Jade	6	0	0	0	2
Frenchster	0	4	0	0	2
n =	16	26	4	11	57

* Actual question asked was: "What brands of rubbers (also called condoms and prophylactics) can you name?" Percentages are the percentages of respondents who named at least one brand. Percentages do not add to 100% due to multiple responses.

Table 17
Advantages of condoms over other methods*

	White male	Black male	White female	Black female	Total
Don't know	47%	53%	21%	66%	51%
None	15	20	7	5	13
Safer	6	8	3	9	7
Easy to get	6	3	14	0	4
Simple to use	21	6	24	4	11
Birth control	9	11	31	13	14
VD protection	3	5	10	7	6
Nonprescription	0	0	3	0	0
n =	34	64	29	56	183

* Actual question asked was: "What would you say are the advantages of condoms over other birth control methods?" Percentages do not add to 100% because of multiple responses.

Table 18
Disadvantages of condoms over other methods of birth control*

	White male	Black male	White female	Black female	Total
Don't know	33%	57%	38%	73%	54%
None	25	13	4	8	12
Less effective, risky	22	15	28	10	17
Decreased sensitivity	8	9	16	2	8
Coitus-connected	8	2	7	5	5
Other	4	4	7	2	4
	100%	100%	100%	100%	100%
	n = 36	67	31	60	194

Chi sq = 27.3 with 9 degrees of freedom.†

* Actual question asked was "What would you say are the disadvantages of condoms over other methods of birth control?"

† Chi square computation used only the first four rows—"Don't know," "None," "Less effective, risky," and "Decreased sensitivity."

Table 19
Percentages giving correct responses to the following questions

Question	White male	Black male	White female	Black female	Total
What is the advantage of a lubricated condom?	28%	12%	32%	8%	17%
What is the difference between a skin condom and a latex condom?	12	14	3	9	10
What is the advantage of a nipple-end or reservoir-end condom?	22	31	9	10	19

Table 20
Percentage agreeing or strongly agreeing with the following statements (1)

Statement	White male	Black male	White female	Black female	Total
Sex feels as good with a condom as without	17%	22%	13%	23%	20%
My friends and I sometimes talk about condoms	47	84	63	50	63
My friends and I sometimes talk about other methods of birth control	59	73	59	77	70
Condoms provide protection against VD	67	100	53	69	77
Condoms decrease sexual feelings during intercourse	36	71	13	23	40

Table 21
Percentage agreeing or strongly agreeing with the following statements (2)

Statement	White male	Black male	White female	Black female	Total
Condoms come in different sizes	50%	79%	53%	43%	58%
Condoms come in different colors	81	89	53	66	74
Condoms come in different shapes	39	86	50	23	52

Table 22
Percentage agreeing or strongly agreeing with the following statements (3)

Statement	White male	Black male	White female	Black female	Total
Most pharmacists will sell condoms to teenagers	42%	62%	41%	70%	58%
I would feel embarrassed to buy condoms from a pharmacist	33	22	50	41	35
Most pharmacists are over 45 years old	14	32	0	10	16
I would prefer to buy condoms from a young pharmacist	36	46	50	49	45
I would prefer to buy condoms from someone of my own sex	48	55	59	47	52
I would prefer to buy condoms by mail order	11	40	22	25	27
I would rather buy condoms in a vending machine than in a drugstore	39	72	28	29	46

Table 23
"In what section of the drugstore do you think condoms should be"

	White male	Black male	White female	Black female	Total
Under counter	36%	32%	34%	24%	31%
Shelf	25	21	22	19	21
Feminine hygiene	0	17	22	18	15
Men's toiletries	36	26	19	37	30
Other	3	4	3	2	3
	100%	100%	100%	100%	100%
n =	36	66	32	62	196

Chi sq = 11.8 with 9 degrees of freedom.

* Chi square computation omitted the "Other" responses.

Table 24
"Where can people get information about birth control?"

	White male	Black male	White female	Black female	Total
Don't know	3%	10%	0%	7%	6%
Planned Parenthood.....	20	13	19	27	17
Clinic	17	30	50	19	27
Hospital	3	19	10	19	15
Doctor	42	36	50	18	34
Media	17	6	16	0	8
Parents	14	19	28	5	15
Friends	14	7	19	6	10
Other	45	40	34	16	32
Family planning clinic	14	2	6	23	11
	n = 36	67	32	62	197

* Percentages may not add to 100% due to multiple responses.

Table 25
"Have you ever seen any advertisements for condoms?"

	White male	Black male	White female	Black female	Total
Yes	50%	17%	22%	18%	24%
No	50	82	75	77	73
Don't know	0	1	3	5	3
	100%	100%	100%	100%	100%
	n = 36	66	32	61	195

Chi sq = 15.6 with 3 degrees of freedom

* Chi square computation omitted "Don't Know" responses.

Table 26
"Where did you see these ads?"

	White male	Black male	White female	Black female	Total
Playboy	11%	2%	0 %	2%	3%
Other girlie magazine	11	0	0	0	2
Other magazine	32	8	16	3	12
Posters....................	4	14	6	9	9
Packaging	0	2	0	0	1
Doubtful answer, e.g., TV, radio	11	0	0	9	5
Not applicable	40	76	75	80	71
	n = 28	49	32	59	168

Percentages may not add to 100% due to multiple responses.

Table 27
Girls—"At what age did you start having monthly periods?"

	White female	Black female	Total
12 or less	74%	53%	61%
13 or over	26	47	39
	100%	100%	100%
n =	15	21	36

Chi sq = 1.6 with 1 degree of freedom

Table 28
Girls—"Did you think you were old enough to get pregnant at that time (when you started having monthly periods)?"

	White	Black	Total
Yes	50%	67%	60%
No	50	33	40
	100%	100%	100%
n =	14	21	35

Chi sq = .97 with 1 degree of freedom

Table 29
Girls—"Do you think you are old enough to get pregnant now?"

	White female	Black female	Total
Yes	93%	95%	95%
No	7	5	5
	100%	100%	100%
n =	14	21	35

Table 30
"When is a woman most likely to get pregnant?"

When	White male	Black male	White female	Black female	Total
During period	11%	24%	9%	27%	20%
Just before her period	28	13	16	23	19
Just after her period	14	13	22	23	18
15 days after her period	33	31	44	18	30
Don't know	14	19	9	9	13
	100%	100%	100%	100%	100%
n =	36	67	32	62	197

Chi sq = 18.7 with 12 degrees of freedom

Table 31
Girls—"Have you ever thought you were pregnant?"

	White female	Black female	Total
Yes	47%	33%	39%
No	53	67	61
	100%	100%	100%
n =	15	21	36

Chi-sq = .65 with 1 degree of freedom

Table 32
Girls—"Have you ever been pregnant?"

	White female	Black female	Total
Yes	13%	14%	14%
No	87	86	86
	100%	100%	100%
n =	15	21	36

Table 33
Boys—"Have you ever thought you fathered a child?"

	White male	Black male	Total
Yes	22%	20%	21%
No	78	80	79
	100%	100%	100%
n =	23	49	72

Chi sq = .17 with 1 degree of freedom

Table 34
Boys—"Have you ever fathered a child?"

	White male	Black male	Total
Yes	5%	7%	6%
No	95	93	94
	100%	100%	100%
n =	23	41	64

Table 35
"What could manufacturers of condoms do to encourage teenages to make more use of condoms?"

	White male	Black male	White female	Black female	Total
Don't know	44%	36%	34%	58%	44%
Nothing	6	8	0	0	4
Advertise	28	28	22	19	24
Educational efforts	25	10	31	8	16
Shouldn't sell	0	2	0	2	1
Other	8	16	22	13	15
n =	36	67	32	62	197

Percentages may not add to 100% due to multiple responses.

Table 36
Age of respondents

	White male	Black male	White female	Black female	Total
13 years	3%	16%	13%	23%	15%
14 years	14	9	19	13	13
15 years	31	18	26	23	23
16 years	14	24	26	23	22
17 years	22	27	16	13	20
18 years	16	6	0	5	7
	100%	100%	100%	100%	100%
n =	36	67	31	62	196

Chi sq = 21.5 with 15 degrees of freedom

Table 37
Education level of respondents

	White male	Black male	White female	Black female	Total
7th grade or less	0	14%	10%	11%	10%
8th grade	19%	9	16	21	16
9th grade	17	19	28	26	22
10th grade	31	21	28	15	22
11th grade	17	30	10	19	21
12th grade	16	7	8	8	9
	100%	100%	100%	100%	100%
n =	36	67	31	62	196

Chi sq = 20.8 with 15 degrees of freedom

Table 38
"Which of these best describes where you live?"

	White male	Black male	White female	Black female	Total
With both parents	66%	51%	66%	52%	56%
With mother	23	28	29	34	29
With father	0	12	—	2	5
With other relatives	6	9	0	11	8
Alone	0	0	5	1	1
Roommate(s)	3	0	0	0	1
Other	2	0	0	0	1
	100%	100%	100%	100%	100%
n =	36	67	31	62	196

Chi sq = 6.2 with 6 degrees of freedom*

* Chi square computation was made using the last 5 rows as one row-"With Father," "With Other Relatives," "Alone," "Roommate(s)," and "Other" responses were aggregated.

Table 39
"What is your mother's job?"

Job	White male	Black male	White female	Black female	Total
Housewife	51%	26%	28%	48%	38%
Lower income— service	6	14	7	12	10
Middle—clerical	31	25	57	23	31
Industrial—labor	0	14	0	3	6
Professional	12	14	8	7	10
Other—deceased, etc.	0	7	0	7	5
	100%	100%	100%	100%	100%
n =	35	65	31	61	192

Chi sq = 26.8 with 9 degrees of freedom

* Chi square computation was made combining the "Lower income-service" and "Industrial-labor" and omitting "Other-decreased, etc."

Table 40
"What is your father's job?"

Job	White male	Black male	White female	Black female	Total
Houseperson	3%	3%	0	8%	4%
Lower income— service	6	10	0	7	7
Middle— clerical	17	18	41%	13	20
Industrial— labor	20	36	16	38	30
Professional	40	13	34	7	20
Other— deceased, etc.	14	20	9	27	19
	100%	100%	100%	100%	100%
n =	35	67	32	61	195

Chi sq = 36.5 with 12 degrees of freedom*

* "Houseperson" was omitted from Chi square computations.

Table 41
Respondent's religion

Religion	White male	Black male	White female	Black female	Total
None	20%	15%	7%	7%	12%
Baptist..............	29	70	13	72	54
Methodist	6	2	7	8	5
Other Protestant	14	6	28	3	10
Catholic	11	6	16	3	8
Jewish	17	0	13	0	5
Other Christian	3	0	16	5	5
Other	0	1	0	2	1
	100%	100%	100%	100%	100%
n =	35	67	31	61	194

Chi sq = 45.5 with 15 degrees of freedom

* Chi square computation was made using the following five rows from above: "None," "Baptist," "Methodist," "Other Protestants," and "Catholic."

Table 42
"What magazines do you read?"

Magazine	White male	Black male	White female	Black female	Total
None	31%	28%	10%	32%	27%
Sports Illustrated	14	25	0	0	11
Playboy	17	12	6	0	8
Other girlie magazine	14	4	0	0	4
Other sports magazine	3	7	0	0	3
Ebony	0	33	0	23	26
Jet	0	21	0	18	13
Other black magazine	0	1	0	16	5
Confessions magazines	0	3	3	13	6
Seventeen	0	0	45	8	10
Glamour, Mademoiselle	3	0	16	0	3
Cosmopolitan	0	0	13	1	2
Ms.	0	0	6	0	1
National Lampoon	5	0	5	0	2
News magazine	0	0	30	3	6
Specialty magazine	22	3	10	2	7
Other	31	13	48	5	19
n =	36	67	31	62	196

Percentages do not add to 100% due to multiple responses.

_____ **Part three**

Applying and managing marketing research

chapter

11

Research for analyzing market opportunities

In this chapter we will focus on research for market analysis, particularly in terms of identification of market opportunities. In Chapter 1, two uniquely marketing decision areas were identified—decisions related to market analysis and decisions related to formulating the marketing mix. The basic decision in market analysis is selection of the target market or market opportunity, but a considerable amount of information is typically needed to do this effectively. This information is not only useful in the target market decision; it also becomes a vital input into decisions related to the marketing mix.

Since it is not possible to cover every aspect of market analysis, this chapter concentrates primarily on information for market segmentation and target market selection. The target market is the group of customers or potential customers that the firm has selected to attempt to do business with. The marketing mix will be designed to meet the needs of this target market. Thus, the nature of the target market holds implications for all marketing decisions. Information, produced through research, must identify and describe the target market in a manner which allows management to formulate a competitive marketing mix and successfully implement its marketing strategy. The identification and selection of target markets is a complex task. In this chapter we use a two-step procedure involving: (1) the identification of alternative market segments and (2) the screening of those alternatives to select the most desirable target.

The thrust of the discussions which follow is the information needed for effective market analysis. These information needs are the link between decision making and research. In order to provide a clearer picture of these information needs, the basic concepts of market analysis will be explored. Illustrations of research designed to produce various types of information for market analysis will also be presented. This union of research methods and decision making through defined information needs is essential if research is to have real value. It should be noted that the majority of the research to be discussed relies on secondary and survey data. This is due to the nature of the market analysis task. Qualitative research also has important applications in this area in discovering directions for quantitative work.

THE STRATEGY OF MARKET SEGMENTATION

Implicit in the concept of market segmentation are the assumptions that (1) the customers in any given market are different and (2) that this heterogeneous group can be divided into two or more relatively homogeneous segments. We must also assume that some of the ways in which the customers differ are related to purchase behavior. It is obvious, for example, that the total group of people who buy hamburgers from fast food franchises contains a wide range of ages, incomes, physical sizes, and political beliefs. Furthermore, subgroups could be formed based on similar ages, incomes, physical sizes, and political beliefs. If none of these characteristics is related to the purchase of hamburgers, however, little is gained by the exercise.

The process of selecting target markets through market segmentation is illustrated in Figure 11–1. Note that the first step involves identifying the bases for segmentation. The bases for segmenting markets must be selected for their relevance to purchase behavior. The various approaches to segmentation are illustrated in Figure 11–2. These approaches are basically one of two types, analysis of consumer characteristics and analysis of consumer response.[1] A meaningful profile of segments usually requires a combination of these approaches.

It would be reasonable to assume, for example, that virtually all of the serviceable market for facial cosmetics (e.g., lipstick, eye liner, powder, etc.) falls within the "female" segment of the population. On the other hand, a particular cosmetic manufacturer might need to identify segments in terms of income, occupation, age, brand image, prod-

---

[1] James F. Engel, Henry F. Fiorillo, and Murray A. Cayley (eds.), *Market Segmentation: Concepts and Applications* (New York: Holt, Rinehart and Winston, Inc., 1972), pp. 10–18.

Figure 11–1
Market segmentation decision process

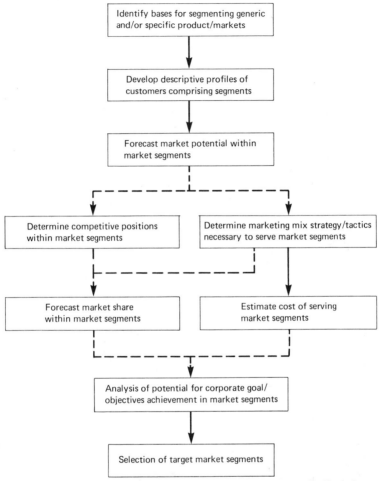

Source: David W. Cravens, Gerald E. Hills, and Robert B. Woodruff, *Marketing Decision Making: Concepts and Strategy* (Homewood, Ill.: Richard D. Irwin, Inc., 1976), p. 246.

uct usage, and price sensitivity in order to select the best target market for a specific product or produce line.

The purpose of identifying segments is to provide better information for planning (and implementing) the marketing mix. The segment is unique in two dimensions which facilitate decision making. First, the needs and wants shared by members of a segment can be satisfied by a marketing mix which is unique from those used for other seg-

Figure 11–2
Basic segmentation classifications

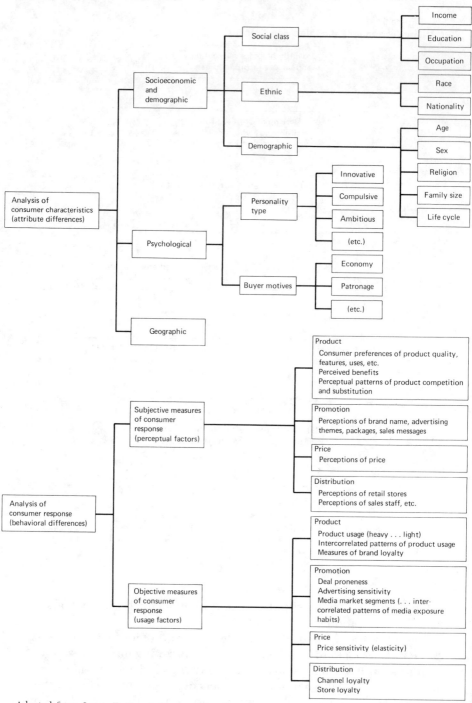

ments. Second, each segment will usually exhibit characteristics or behaviors which prescribe an appropriate marketing mix. The problem facing management, however, is often complicated by the existence of multiple segments, all of which cannot be serviced within the limits of the firm's resources. Strategic planning, therefore, requires that firms select target markets which optimize results in terms of their goals and objectives. Therefore, much of the success of a firm's marketing strategy depends on the care with which target markets are identified and selected.

RESEARCH FOR IDENTIFYING MARKET SEGMENTS

In measuring market segments, it is important to keep three information needs in mind. As mentioned earlier, each segment must be unique in terms of its specific needs or buyer behavior. Second, segments must respond differentially to specific marketing mixes. Finally, segments which meet the first two criteria must also be readily identified.

The first need is usually met by segmenting the total population into various categories of buyers or nonbuyers; regardless of the segmentation classification used, the primary basis for segmentation is actual or potential product usage. The second criterion, differential response to specific marketing strategies, may be met by a number of measures particularly in the area of consumer responses or behavioral differences. Finally, the third criterion is most easily met if segments are identifiable in terms of socioeconomic or demographic measures. Thus, we seldom find meaningful segment identification based on only one type of segmentation classification. When a particular classification is illustrated in the following discussion, it may be in terms of any one or more of the three criteria. Although it is not possible to discuss in detail all of the segmentation classifications illustrated in Figure 11–2, several will be illustrated with emphasis on some of the more important categories. Note that the segmentation basis selected gives direction for researching the market.

SEGMENTATION BASED ON CONSUMER CHARACTERISTICS

Socioeconomic, demographic, and geographic bases

The two earliest bases used for segmenting markets were demographic and geographic. Demography is the study of population, and demographic variables; it includes such measures of a population as the distribution of age, sex, religion, family size, and life cycle categories. These variables are relatively easy to measure, particularly since the advent of the decennial census.

In the past, demographic and geographic variables have been particularly useful in monitoring the changes in population characteristics for large market areas. For example, if a product is known to sell particularly well in urban markets, it is useful to know where new high density population centers are emerging. In recent years marketers of baby food products have been concerned with the declining birth rate in this country. Demographic research provided these manufacturers with new potential market segments in the growing elderly groups with special dietary requirements. Demographic and geographic research may also be combined to point out regional variations in ethnic subcultures. For example, kosher food products have a limited market, primarily among Jews. The density of Jewish population which makes the distribution of kosher products feasible exists only in certain large urban areas. Similarly, the demand for hot, spicy Mexican/Indian dishes is concentrated in southwestern United States.

Socioeconomic data refer to characteristics of a population which have not traditionally been included in demographic studies. The inclusion of socioeconomic variables, such as social class, add more of the behavioral dimension to segmentation research. Social class is normally defined as a composite of income, education, and occupation. Much has been written about social class structure in the United States. It is beyond the scope of this text, however, to provide detailed insight into this subject. The socioeconomic dimension of this first set of segmentation variables is important, however, for two reasons. First, socioeconomic variables tend to be somewhat more difficult to measure than strictly demographic or geographic variables. Second, socioeconomic variables imply smaller group structures and thus, a more finely tuned basis for identifying market segments.

Some studies have shown that the members of the various social class strata in this country have differing media habits and purchasing behaviors. Although it is difficult to generalize that social class strata themselves are large market segments, this information can prove useful in relating other factors to market segmentation. If, for example, the users of a particular product are found to exhibit the socioeconomic and demographic characteristics of a lower class stratum and are restricted to a particular geographic area, this useful information can be brought to bear in devising marketing mixes for the segment. A study of the city of Cincinnati produced the information illustrated in Table 11–1. Obviously, a furniture retailer located in the inner city in Cincinnati would be faced with a different problem in terms of product line strategy and communications strategy, than a similar type of re-

Table 11–1
Socioeconomic and demographic based segments of Cincinnati, Ohio

	Cluster				
Property	I Inner city	II Black ghetto	III Old city	IV Older suburbs	V Newer suburbs
Number of tracts	19	18	60	45	29
Education					
Median years, household head	8.2	9.5	9.2	12.2	11.7
Coefficient of variation	.04	.06	.05	.04	.05
Income					
Median, per household	$3,805	$4,223	$5,649	$8,338	$7,255
Coefficient of variation	.21	.23	.08	.08	.07
Age					
Median years, male head	27.6	28.5	30.2	33.5	25.3
Coefficient of variation	.19	.08	.06	.06	.06
Occupation					
Percent white collar of total	12.3	24.5	28.0	61.6	46.3
Coefficient of variation	.37	.27	.19	.13	.18
Nonwhite					
Percent black of total	53.4	67.5	2.8	1.7	2.1
Coefficient of variation	.73	.25	1.68	2.16	2.52
Housing					
Percent deteriorating of total	40.4	9.3	14.6	3.5	4.2
Coefficient of variation	.17	.55	.50	.73	.65

Adapted from: Jerome B. Kernan and Grady D. Bruce, "The Socioeconomic Structure of an Urban Area," *Journal of Marketing Research*, II (February 1972), p. 17, published by the American Marketing Association.

tailer located in a newer suburb.[2] The former faces a broader geographic market area (29 versus 19 tracts) and a better educated, younger clientele with significantly higher incomes. Residents of the newer suburbs also occupy more white collor jobs and live in homes which are better maintained than inner city residents.

The data for the Cincinnati study were collected from secondary sources, e.g., U.S. Census. The researchers were not concerned with identifying segments which are "better" or "worse" than others, but rather segments which differ in terms of socioeconomic variables. A segment may be more or less appropriate for a particular firm depending on the nature of the products and brands involved.

The discussion of demographic, socioeconomic, and geographic segmentation has thus far centered on the use of these measures as primary segmentation variables. Their value in this regard has decreased in recent years. There is a mounting body of evidence pointing to the need for a more direct analysis of the perceptions and behavior of buyers in segmenting markets. As a result, the role of de-

[2] Jerome B. Kernan and Grady D. Bruce, "The Socioeconomic Structure of an Urban Area," *Journal of Marketing Research*, vol. 11 (February 1972), pp. 15–18.

mographic, socioeconomic and geographic variables has become one of description. That is, these variables are still the most desirable means for describing segments which have already been identified using some other basis.

An excellent example of the use of demographics in segmentation is provided in a study reported by Garfinkle.[3] The purpose of this study was to assist the manufacturer of a brand of toothpaste in devising better media strategy. A national sample of female heads of households was "asked to indicate which brand they buy most often, which brand is their second choice, and then to specify their attitudes toward other major brands of the product category."[4] The respondents were asked to provide information concerning media use and certain socioeconomic and demographic characteristics. Analysis of the findings yielded the following information:

. . . The largest group of new customers came from those who previously considered the brand their second choice. The conversion rate from second choice to regular use was close to 20 percent, as compared to less than 5 percent for people who rated the brand their third choice. Equally significant, the conversion rate from second choice to regular use varied from as low as 10 percent for some brands to as high as 30 percent for other brands in the same product category.

These findings permitted the advertiser to identify his prime targets: *Current customers*, to maintain their loyalty and to keep the switch-away rate to a minimum; and *customers who considered the brand their second choice*, to maximize the conversion rate and thereby gain the largest possible group of customers.[5]

This finding satisfies the first criteria for segmentation. That is, the segments were identified in terms of their purchase behavior and brand preference. This insures that segmentation is based on a factor which might ultimately relate to purchase.

Each of these segments was then analyzed in terms of their state of preferences for 44 television programs and 15 magazines. There was a considerable amount of difference in the preferences for media associated with each of the segments. This finding meets the second criterion for segmentation, the ability to determine varying responses to specific marketing variables. In this case the marketing variable of interest is media.

The prime importance in this section, however, is the application of socioeconomic, demographic, and geographic variables. The same

---

[3] Norton Garfinkle, "A Marketing Approach to Media Selection," in James Arndt (ed.), *Word of Mouth Advertising* (New York: Advertising Research Foundation, 1967).

[4] Ibid.

[5] Ibid.

segments were finally analyzed in terms of these variables. One segment was clearly a higher income, higher class, and more urban market than that associated with the other brands. Another segment appeared to occupy the other end of the spectrum. By identifying the location and type of market in the demographic and socioeconomic data, the marketer can create the right appeals and select appropriate media for reaching the target segment.

Psychological bases

Referring again to Figure 11–2, note that psychological bases for segmentation tend to be related to either personality or motivation. Although an extensive amount of research has been conducted on the basic behavior of buyers, the useful application of psychological studies in segmentation are somewhat limited. These variables tend to be used to satisfy the second criterion for identifying segments. That is, they provide the basis for developing strategies to which a particular segment's response will differ from that of other segments. Since the study of personality differs from the study of motivation, these bases for segmentation will be discussed separately.

Personality and psychographics. Some of the earliest attempts to segment markets in terms of behavioral characteristics involved personality research. Typically, researchers attempted to utilize established personality inventories, such as the Edwards Personal Preference Schedule, the Thurstone Temperament Schedule, and the Gordon Personal Profile, to identify characteristics of market segments.[6] The difficulties encountered in these studies were discussed by Evans in a classic article which pointed out the frustrations involved in personality research.[7] Although researchers found personality to be a difficult basis for segmentation analysis, work in this area has continued. The two basic problems which have confronted researchers in the past involved meeting the first criterion for segmentation and defining personality measurement.

Greno, Sommers, and Kernan claim to have overcome some of these difficulties in a recent segmentation analysis utilizing personality as a basis.[8] They used an area sample with quota controls to insure that the

---

[6] William D. Wells and Arthur D. Beard, "Personality and Consumer Behavior," in Scott Ward and Thomas S. Robertson (eds.), *Consumer Behavior: Theoretical Sources* (Englewood Cliffs, N.J.: Prentice-Hall, Inc., 1973), pp. 141–99.

[7] Franklin B. Evans, "Psychological and Objective Factors in the Prediction of Brand Choice: Ford versus Chevrolet," *Journal of Business,* vol. 32 (October 1959), pp. 340–69.

[8] Daniel W. Greno, Montrose S. Sommers, and Jerome B. Kernan, "Personality and Implicit Behavior Patterns," *Journal of Marketing Research,* vol. 10 (February 1973), pp. 63–69.

racial and social class characteristics of the community were preserved in the sample and that all of the responding housewives would be at the same stage of the family life cycle. Each respondent provided information concerning (1) preferences for 38 product items; (2) the personality traits of *ascendency, responsibility, emotional stability,* and *sociability* as measured by the Gordon Personal Profile; and (3) demographic, socioeconomic, and social-interaction data.

Based on this data, the housewives were divided into six segments labeled: homemakers, matriarchs, variety girls, cinderellas, glamour girls, and media conscious glamour girls. The researchers then determined which personality scores were statistically different between segments. For example, the difference in mean scores for ascendency and sociability between "homemakers" and "matriarchs" is statistically significant. In terms of using personality traits for gaining insight into segment behavior, this finding suggested that matriarchs perceive themselves as on the way up and tend to socialize to a greater extent than homemakers. Combining this information with the product related information in the study, we might conclude that matriarches are interested in expressing their rising place in the world through the acquisition of a variety of material objects. Similarly, promoting these various products to this segment should utilize social themes when possible.

On the other hand, homemakers tend to express themselves through products related to food and food preparation. This is consistent with their view of stable social status and limited social activity. In meeting the third criterion for identifying segments, the researchers provided information on several demographic and socioeconomic variables. Using the same two segments as examples, we note that slightly more homemakers are white than black, of more moderate means, and married to husbands whose occupations are considerably down scale relative to that of matriarchs. Furthermore, homemakers tend to be slightly closer in age to the age of their husbands and, overall, slightly older than matriarchs. Thus, a manufacturer of, say, refrigerators or stoves could use the socioeconomic and demographic information to target his efforts toward the different segments and utilize the personality trait information to vary the theme and approach in marketing to each group.

Although Greno, Sommers, and Kernan were able to satisfy the three requirements for identifying segments, there are still problems in utilizing personality traits to distinguish segment behaviors. A concept which has been developed over the last ten years represents efforts to circumvent some of the problems associated with personality research. The concept is known as psychographics, or life-style analysis. It should be noted that life-style analysis is not wholly de-

rived from the area of personality research. The two are closely related, however, and a detailed examination of their differences is beyond
the scope of this discussion. The reader should consult the list of suggested readings at the end of the chapter for additional sources. Although the terms are sometimes used interchangeably, psychographics is more closely related to the concept of personality, and
life-style analysis is more closely related to measures of activities,
interests, and opinions (see the illustration in Chapter 8 for greater
details).

It is the multifaceted aspect of life-style research that makes it so
useful in segmentation. A prominent life-style researcher, Joseph T.
Plummer, summarizes the concept as follows:

> The new construct, life-style patterns, combines the virtues of de-
> mographics with the richness and dimensionality of psychological characteris-
> tics and depth research.
>
> Life style is used to segment the marketplace because it provides the
> broad, everyday view of consumers . . . life style segmentation can generate
> identifiable whole persons rather than isolated fragments.[9]

A good illustration of life-style segmentation research is provided
by work toward the development of a national advertising campaign
for Schlitz beer.[10] With Schlitz as one of its major accounts, the Leo
Burnett Agency was concerned by the late 1960s that its existing campaign needed revitalizing. At that time, the campaign was built around
the concept line of "When you're out of Schlitz, you're out of beer."
The creative director assigned to the account conducted some informal
life style research by leaving his corporate office and touring taverns
on the street to get a feel for the life style of the heavy beer drinker.

> . . . As the creative man saw him, the heavy beer drinker was, "the man
> who belongs to that 20% of the population that drinks 80% of the beer. A man
> who drinks a case a week or even a case a day . . . he is a guy who is not
> making it and probably never will. He is a dreamer, a wisher, a limited edition
> of Walter Mitty. He is a sports nut because he is a hero worshiper . . . he goes
> to the tavern and has 6 or 7 beers with the boys . . . if we are to talk to this man
> where he lives, in terms he respects and can identify with, we must find for
> him a believable kind of hero he inwardly admires."[11]

A word which Schlitz had used earlier and felt that it "owned"
seemed to represent the life style of the heavy beer drinker. The word

---

[9] Joseph T. Plummer, "The Concept and Application of Life Style Segmentation,"
Journal of Marketing, vol. 38 (January 1974), pp. 33–35.

[10] The Schlitz illustration is adapted from: Joseph T. Plummer, "Life Style and Advertising Case Studies," in Fred C. Allvine (ed.), *1971 Combined Proceedings* (Chicago,
Ill.: American Marketing Association, 1972), pp. 292–94.

[11] Ibid., p. 292.

was "gusto." After conducting a literature search of previous research on the word, it was concluded that "Gusto has been a powerful, hard-working word and has conveyed many relevant meanings to consumers about beer, about taste, and about life."[12] The idea for a new campaign which resulted from the initial research was the "Gusto man, and gusto life" approach.

By the time the campaign idea had been formulated, the results of the Leo Burnett 1968 Life-Style Study was available for male respondents. The agency would feel confident in entering the new campaign if life-style segmentation confirmed the gusto man/gusto life approach. In meeting the first criterion for identifying a segment, the initial segmentation basis was to identify the heavy beer drinker, or heavy user. The relevant life style information is illustrated in Table 11–2. Notice that respondents were segmented as nonusers, light users, and heavy users, as a primary segmentation basis. Life-style data was then used to provide a picture of the heavy beer drinker. The following summary statement confirmed the image of the heavy beer drinker:

. . . The major life style patterns that emerged indicated that the heavy beer drinker was probably more hedonistic and pleasure-seeking toward life than the nondrinker. He seemed to have less regard toward responsibilities of family and job. More than the nondrinker he tended to have a preference for a physical/male-oriented existence and an inclination to fantasize. Finally we found, not surprisingly, a great enjoyment of beer drinking, especially beer which he saw as a real man's drink.[13]

Meeting the third criterion for segmentation, the research also provided demographic data on the heavy beer drinker. The significant demographic features indicated, "that the heavy user is middle class economically, but derives his income from primarily blue-collar occupations. He is young and has at least a high school education."[14] Armed with this rich picture of a target market, the agency produced and successfully implemented the "gusto man" campaign.

Motivation as a basis.   Motivation is a concept which is difficult to define. In fact, the difficulty of defining motives and dealing with motivation in consumer research accounts for the limited application of this basis for segmentation. For the most part, the applicable work in motivation research involves "patronage motives." Patronage motives typically concern the consumer's reasons for shopping at a particular retail outlet. Consumers are classified, for example, as price conscious, convenience oriented, service oriented, or in terms of some other motivating feature.

---

[12] Ibid.
[13] Ibid.
[14] Ibid.

Table 11–2
Life-style patterns of male beer drinkers

	Percent agreement		
	Non-users	Light users	Heavy users
He is self-indulgent, enjoys himself, and likes risks			
I like to play poker	18	37	41
I like to take chances	27	32	44
I would rather spend a quiet evening at home than go out to a party	67	53	44
If I had my way, I would own a convertible	7	11	15
I smoke too much	29	40	42
If I had to choose I would rather have a color TV than a new refrigerator	25	33	38
He rejects responsibility and is a bit impulsive			
I like to work on community projects	24	18	14
I have helped collect money for the Red Cross or United Fund	41	32	24
I'm not very good at saving money	20	29	38
I find myself checking prices, even for small items	51	42	40
He likes sports and a physical orientation			
I would like to be a pro football player	10	15	21
I like bowling	32	36	42
I usually read the sports page	47	48	59
I would do better than average in a fist fight	17	26	32
I like war stories	33	37	45
He rejects old fashioned institutions and moral guidelines			
I go to church regularly	57	37	31
Movies should be censored	67	46	43
I have old fashioned tastes and habits	69	56	48
There is too much emphasis on sex today	71	59	53
— and has a very masculine view			
Beer is a real man's drink	9	16	44
Playboy is one of my favorite magazines	11	21	28
I am a girl watcher	33	47	54
Men should not do the dishes	18	26	38
Men are smarter than women	22	27	31

Source: Joseph T. Plummer, "Life-Style and Advertising Case Studies," in Fred C. Allvine (ed.), *1971 Combined Proceedings* (Chicago, Ill.: American Marketing Association, 1972), p. 294.

A study of bank selection criteria for residents of Austin, Texas revealed different motivations for each of two segments.[15] One group appeared to be convenience oriented, and the other group appeared to be service oriented. The segments were further defined in terms of socioeconomic, demographic, and other variables. The most significant finding in this particular study was that the convenience oriented group perceived all banks to be essentially the same. This

---

[15] W. Thomas Anderson, Eli P. Cox, and David G. Fulcher, "Bank Selection Decision and Market Segmentation," *Journal of Marketing*, (January 1976), pp. 40–55.

segment is therefore, relatively immune to patronage appeals. The service oriented segment, however, does see meaningful differences between banks and their service offerings. Further analysis of this group indicated that it included fewer single persons and more families with young children, slightly higher annual family incomes, a higher percentage of both heads of the household employed full time, and a greater reliance on word-of-mouth promotion in bank selection. Although considerable additional information is required for strategy formulation, banks in Austin and similar communities could benefit from this segmentation research.

Another study of patronage motives in bank selection involved a larger, and perhaps more representative sample, than the Austin study.[16] This study revealed six motive-related segments based on a factor and cluster analysis of the variables in the study. A sample of the descriptive information for the first three of these segments is illustrated in Table 11–3. Again, however, a word of caution is required in interpreting the results of segmentation based on motivation. Motives are such broad and pervasive aspects of behavior that it is difficult to formulate specific strategies without a considerable amount of additional information. Therefore, motivation research may uncover useful information for formulating the major theme of a marketing strategy, but a considerable amount of additional information is usually required to respond to a target segment.

SEGMENTATION BASED ON CONSUMER RESPONSE

Referring again to our earlier discussion of Figure 11–2, recall that the bases for segmentation are divided into two major groups, consumer characteristics and consumer response. The former is most useful in describing general behavior differences between groups of people or listing their attributes. The latter, however, is more directly concerned with the behavior of consumers in direct response to marketing strategies. Consumer response is rapidly becoming the primary basis for segmentation. Several of the research examples cited in the previous section included consumer response as a primary segmentation basis, but also illustrated the use of consumer attributes for completing the segmentation identification process. Similarly, in some of the following illustrations, demographics, socioeconomic variables, and psychological aspects of behavior may be included. It would be difficult within the constraints of this section to illustrate all of the consumer-response research categories. A few have been selected, however, to illustrate the concept.

[16] Dan H. Robertson and Danny N. Bellenger, "Identifying Bank Market Segments," *Journal of Bank Research*, (Winter 1977), pp. 276–283.

Table 11–3
Descriptions of three bank market segments

	Profiles		
	Segment I (10%) *Upper level, white collar*	*Segment II (18%)* *New retiree*	*Segment III (9%)* *New, blue collar*
Most important factors (motive)	Integrity Ego enhancement Expertise	Time convenience Bank philosophy Pricing	Location convenience Time convenience
Least important factors	Time convenience Location convenience	Location convenience	Bank philosophy Ego enhancement
Demographics	45–54 College graduate or better Upper income Professional/management Teachers Farm owners	55+ Newer residents Middle to upper income Retired	Under 35 Lower income Blue collar Renters Newer residents
Financial attitudes	Optimistic Less reliant on savings Do not shop around Not price sensitive Considered heavy credit card users Neutral attitude toward banks	Pessimistic Reliance on savings Not new brand tryers Not heavy users of credit Favorable attitude toward banks	Optimistic No strong need for savings Average users of credit cards Not new brand tryers Not bargain hunters Non-sociable Unfavorable attitude toward banks
Banking habits	Below average use of savings and loans and credit unions Above average in number of savings accounts held Above average in number of loans made Satisfied with banking hours	Above average use of credit unions Satisfied with banking hours	Below average use of all financial institutions except banks Above average number of credit cards Above average in personal loans Dissatisfied with banking hours Drive-in Night depositories
Media habits	Below average in use of radio, T.V. and newspapers	Above average use of radio and T.V.	Below average use of media, especially T.V.

Source: Adapted from Dan H. Robertson and Danny N. Bellenger, "Identifying Bank Market Segments," *Journal of Bank Research*, (Winter 1977), p. 280.

In the complex world within which contemporary marketing decisions are made, the customer's perception of products and marketing strategy is more important than management's perceptions of these variables. A product is defined in terms of the satisfaction of customer needs, regardless of its intended purpose by a manufacturer. Similarly, the success of a brand name is often dependent upon the meaning of the brand as perceived by customers. Assume, for example, that a firm markets a consumer convenience product which competes with a number of brands. The firm is concerned with its general lack of ability to increase and maintain market share. A question arises as to the possibility of identifying market segments for the various brands and then utilizing that information to solidify strategies specifically for a target market segment.

Table 11–4
Toothpaste market segment description

Segment name	The sensory segment	The sociables	The worriers	The independent segment
Principal benefit sought	Flavor, product appearance	Brightness of teeth	Decay prevention	Price
Demographic strengths	Children	Teens, young people	Large families	Men
Special behavioral characteristics	Users of spearment flavored toothpaste	Smokers	Heavy users	Heavy users
Brands disproportionately favored	Colgate Stripe	Macleans, Plus White, Ultra Brite	Crest	Brands on sale
Personality characteristics	High self-involvement	High sociability	High hypochondriasis	High autonomy
Life-style characteristics	Hedonistic	Active	Conservative	Value-oriented

From: Russell I. Haley, "Benefit Segmentation," *Journal of Marketing*, (July 1968), p. 33, published by the American Marketing Association.

Haley introduced a concept known as *benefit segmentation* which may be used as a primary basis for identifying market segments in terms of the benefit which they perceive in products.[17] If in the above example the product happened to be toothpaste, Haley's benefit segmentation approach would have provided some meaningful information at the time of introduction. The information illustrated in Table 11–4 provided summary information for toothpaste market segments. Notice that "principal benefits sought" heads the list. One group of

[17] Russell I. Haley, "Benefit Segmentation: A Decision-Oriented Research Tool," *Journal of Marketing*, vol. 21 (July 1968), pp. 3–8.

respondents to the survey indicated that they seek brightness of teeth as a principal benefit of toothpaste. To complete the other criteria for segment identification, we find that this group is highly sociable and active, and tend to smoke cigarettes. The predominant demographic characteristics of the group is that they are teenagers and young adults whose profile suggests the segment name, "the sociables." Furthermore, we find that this group disproportionately favors Macleans, Plus White and Ultrabright.

Comparing the sociables to other segments identified in Table 11–4, the implications of benefit segmentations become obvious. It is important to note that the same segments may not have been identified on the basis of usage of toothpaste per se, or specific brands purchased. Rather, the groups were primarily formed on the basis of the benefit they seek in the various toothpaste products. With this information, management can formulate more accurate promotional strategies which are aimed specifically at a particular target market.

The preceding examples have focused on the segmentation problems of product manufacturers. In a series of interesting studies, Martineau introduced the concepts of retail store image as a factor in marketing strategy.[18] As the postwar populations shifted from urban to suburban living, the downtown department store was faced with the problem of retaining, and if possible, increasing sales. For the retail store executive, the possibility of store image segments presents opportunities for marketing strategy formulation. Rich and Portis identified three segments for nine major department stores in the New York City area and in Cleveland.[19] Based on the responses from 4,500 randomly selected female shoppers, the researchers identified three types of stores: high fashion, price appeal, and broad appeal. Behavioral differences between the store image segments and descriptive characteristics indicated that members of the high-fashion segment have a relatively high interest in fashion, are less likely to look for bargains, and shop less at discount stores. Furthermore, the high fashion segment tended to have a relatively high income, have no children at home, and live in the suburbs. Although this research did not provide extensive detailed information, the three criteria for segment identification are met. The information can be used to assist retail store managers in designing marketing strategies for their respective target segments.

---

[18] Pierre Martineau, "The Personality of the Retail Store," *Harvard Business Review*, (January–February 1958), pp. 47–55.

[19] Stuart U. Rich and Bernard D. Portis, "The 'Imageries' of Department Stores," *Journal of Marketing*, (April 1964), pp. 10–15.

RESEARCH FOR ESTIMATING MARKET POTENTIAL AND SELECTING TARGET MARKET SEGMENTS

The process of identifying market opportunities involves more than the identification of market segments. Servicing a segment is only an opportunity if it enables the firm to meet its goals and objectives. The opportunity, therefore, is usually measured in terms of the profitability associated with a particular segment. Furthermore, a firm may be faced with resource constraints which force it to select a target market from two or more alternative segments. The basis for selection is usually a financial criterion, such as profit.

In order to assess the attractiveness of a segment as a target market, management must have a projection of the selection criteria (profit, sales, market share, and so forth) and related information upon which it will make a decision. This need usually requires forecasts of sales and costs associated with servicing the segment. The remaining discussion in this chapter will thus be divided into two parts. First, a brief discussion of forecasting will illustrate the techniques and problems associated with this type of research. Second, the use of grids to analyze the profitability of segments will be discussed.

FORECASTING FOR TARGET MARKET ANALYSIS

In the analysis of marketing opportunities the problem of forecasting focuses on the methods to be employed. That is, management should have knowledge of the objectives and criteria upon which decisions will be made. These factors determine the areas of information need. Furthermore, the process of identifying segments provides the researcher with the significant variables or factors which may be relevant to the forecasting problem. Therefore, the major task in forecasting is to determine the appropriate method given the set of known constraints.

Forecasting methods have been classified in a number of ways by various authorities. One, for example, explains that "There are two main approaches in forecasting: . . . (1) noncausal methods; and (2) causal analysis."[20] The former involves analyzing historical data in order to project its pattern of movement through time. The latter involves an analysis of the factor to be forecasted as well as factors which are causally related in an attempt to define that relationship. Using the defined relationship, the factor is forecasted for future time periods.

While it is useful to consider the causal and noncausal nature of

---

[20] Vernon G. Lippitt, *Statistical Sales Forecasting* (New York: Financial Executives Research Foundation, 1969), p. 25.

certain methods, another important classification distinguishes between "objective" and "subjective" forecasting methods. According to Bolt, "Objective forecasts tend to be of a statistical/mathematical nature and subjective forecasts tend to be intuitive, based on the application of experience, intelligence, and judgement."[21] Since the two classifications just discussed are not mutually exclusive, a third one is particularly useful for our limited discussion. In this approach:

. . . We have grouped the techniques into three basic categories; (1) judgmental techniques; (2) time-series analysis and projection, and (3) causal models. The first category uses qualitative data (e.g., expert opinions) and information about special events, and may or may not take the past into consideration. The second focuses entirely on patterns and pattern changes and, thus relies entirely on historical data. The third uses highly refined and specific information about relationships between system elements. It is powerful to take special events formally into account, and it also uses the past as an important input.[22]

It is not possible to discuss all of the forecasting techniques in this single section. Rather, some of the more commonly used techniques are discussed and compared.

Judgmental techniques

Jury of executive opinion. The most common judgmental or subjective technique used in forecasting is the "Jury of Executive Opinion." As the name implies, this technique involves gathering a panel of experienced executives who work together to develop a forecast or the basis for forecasting. The disadvantages of this technique are obvious. It is not scientific and relies solely on individual opinion. Less obvious, but perhaps more important, are the advantages of the jury or panel approach.

If properly conducted, the jury of executive opinion can take advantage of the observations and experience of talented executives. It is not correct to assume that this method is devoid of historical trends or anticipations of the future. The executive's ability to assimilate past experience and a knowledge of a dynamic environment in which the market operates are vital assets in this process.

Forecasts derived from the executive panel tend to decrease in quality with the passage of time. That is, they are most accurate for the short term and least accurate for the long term. Finally, the jury ap-

---

[21] Gordon J. Bolt, *Market and Sales Forecasting—A Total Approach* (New York: Halsted Press, 1972), p. 179.

[22] John C. Chambers, Satinder Mullick and Donald D. Smith, *An Executives Guide to Forecasting* (New York: John Wiley and Sons, Inc., 1974), p. 42.

proach offers the advantage of a forecast which can be developed in a relatively short period of time.

Delphi Technique.   A more structured method for utilizing executive opinion employs the Delphi Technique. As in the case of the jury of executive opinion, a panel of experts is used, but their opinions are collected through a structured questionnaire. Each set of responses is processed and a new questionnaire developed, which is returned to each of the executives. With each new questionnaire the objective is improved closure of opinions by the executives.

In practice the Delphi Technique applied to the panel of executives suffers the same basic disadvantages as the jury of executive opinion. That is, executive opinions as opposed to direct market factors, are the basis for the forecasts. The Delphi Technique offers an additional advantage, however, in that it is more systematic or scientific. The executives do not communicate with each other, and their responses are systematically processed to develop a consensus.

The primary disadvantage of the Delphi Technique is the length of time required to develop a forecast. Whereas a jury of executive opinion can be developed within a matter of days, the Delphi Technique can easily take several months. Although forecasts developed in this manner are still not particularly useful for the long term, the overall quality is usually improved.

Time-series analysis

Regardless of the statistical methods employed, time-series analysis involves attempts to project historical patterns into the future. Time-series generally contain one or more of four types of movements:

1. *Secular trend*—Multi-year general upward or downward movements in a time series.
2. *Periodic movements*—Movements in a time series which recur within a given period of time, such as a year, and generally referred to as seasonal movements.
3. *Cyclical movements*—Movements which are similar to periodic movements but are of longer duration than a year and often irregular in the period of repetition.
4. *Irregular variations*—Movements in a time series which are the result of either a one-time specific event or minor causes which, although they may be repetitious, are of no particular significance.

The most common technique for time-series analysis is the moving average. The purpose of the moving average is to remove cyclical movements, seasonal variations, or irregular movements. This is accomplished by calculating average points from the time-series data.

The average point will tend to provide a smoother time-series plot reflecting the nature of the series without undesired variations. The length of the moving average is arbitrary. In the case illustrated in Figure 11–3 the term must be less than one year since we are concerned with within-season irregularities. Forecasts based on moving averages are obtained by simply extrapolating the moving average for future periods. Moving averages are actually more useful as warning indicators for short-term movements in a time-series. For example, in Figure 11–3, the slight general downward movement of the moving average would help planners anticipate the general direction of the sales curve of the first quarter of the following year.

Figure 11–3
The moving average

Deseasonalized sales
Moving average (seven-term)

Source: John C. Chambers, Satinder K. Mullick, and Donald D. Smith, *An Executive's Guide to Forecasting* (New York: John Wiley and Sons, Inc., 1974), p. 198.

Although time-series analysis has evolved into a fairly sophisticated area of investigation, such forecasts are based on historical data only. This leaves them vulnerable to changes in the underlying conditions of the marketplace. Also note in Figure 11–3 that the calculation of a moving average results in the loss of data at the beginning and end of the series. The months of October, November, and December are not plotted because the following January, February, and March are not available for calculating through the December point. Since the quality of the forecast will deteriorate rapidly over time, the value of moving averages for developing actual forecast figures is questionable. Finally, some of the more recent sophisticated time-series analysis techniques are relatively expensive and highly complicated. Given the inherent problems of using moving averages, it is questionable whether the benefit exceeds the cost in many decision making situations.

Causal methods of forecasting

Both the judgmental and time-series analysis methods dealt directly with the factor to be forecasted. That is, executive opinion or a sales trend were directly examined in order to forecast sales. When using causal methods, the researcher is seeking a better understanding of the relationships between the factor to be forecasted and other factors which cause that behavior. If a tire manufacturer wishes to forecast sales, the question might arise as to the relationship between new car sales and the demand for tires. If the sale of automobiles in an earlier period is known, and if the sale of those automobiles leads to the demand for tires in a later period, tire sales forecasts might be developed based on automobile sales as a causal factor. Although there are a number of causal methods, we will only examine three in this section. These include correlation/regression models, intention-to-buy and anticipation surveys, and leading indicators.

Since the research techniques discussed in this group of forecasting models were all covered in earlier chapters, they will not be redefined at this point. Rather, each will be illustrated in the context of a forecasting problem. It might be useful, however, to review briefly earlier discussions which relate to these methods.

Correlation/Regression methods. Most commonly used, and misused, of the causal methods are the various least squares associative analyses known as correlation and regression techniques. Regression analysis in particular offers many advantages for forecasting. It estimates an equation which can be used to determine the value of a dependent variable (the forecasted factor) given known quantities for the independent variables (the causal factors). An example of a regression line is illustrated in Figure 11–4.

Although the technical restrictions on regression analysis are numerous, it can be a very useful analytical tool. Unfortunately, the use of the term "causal" to describe regression analysis is a misnomer. If the regression results do in fact describe a causal relationship, it is only because the researcher detected the relationship when defining the original model. The line drawn in Figure 11–4 is simply the locus of points for which the sum of squares of the vertical distances between the regression line and the actual data points is minimum. Thus, the regression line is nothing more than a statistical phenomenon. Nevertheless, a well-conceived and carried out regression

Figure 11–4
Regression estimate of relationship between airline market share and quality of service

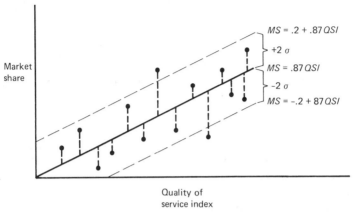

analysis can provide useful forecasts for analyzing market opportunities.

Using the equation for the regression line in Figure 11–4, we can develop a confidence interval for the value of market share in a future period. Since the coefficients in the regression equation are estimates, each of which has a probability distribution, we are able to forecast a range of possible values. This forecast is illustrated in Figure 11–4 by the parallel dotted lines. It remains to be seen whether the forecast is useful given the width of the confidence interval. Since the researcher relies on systematic and logical thought in order to determine likely causal relationships, regression analysis may at times be little more than an extension of the jury of executive opinion. At least, it is always an extension of someone's opinion.

Intention-to-buy and anticipation surveys. Surveys were described in general in terms of quantitative methods for collecting information from respondents. Applied to the forecasting problem as a causal method, surveys are used to determine buyers' intentions and anticipations. That is, the survey would determine estimates of future sales directly from an expression of intentions by potential buyers. This type of forecasting method is most useful as a means of monitoring market conditions. It is relatively expensive and difficult to derive actual forecasts for target market selection.

The primary weakness of the survey approach is the unreliable nature of intentions as predictors of actual behavior. It is not uncommon, for example, for a survey to uncover intentions to purchase, which vastly exceed the actual potential in a market. Frequently, this is a result of the respondent wishing to cooperate with the study, or feeling intimidated if social status is attached to the purchase under study.

Leading indicators.   Frequently, there are factors which relate to the sales or costs associated with a product, but their impact occurs after some period of time. There appears to be such a relationship, for example, between the rate of change in Gross National Product and the demand for air travel. When the domestic economy began to show signs of instability in the late 1960s, it was only a matter of months before the impact was felt in the airline industry. Notice that this approach to forecasting is an application, as opposed to a technique. That is, the techniques included in regression analysis and surveying are frequently used to develop leading indicators.

One of the problems associated with the use of leading indicators is complexity. Single indicators seldom prove to be of much value. A forecast of the demand for steel must take into account not only general economic conditions, but specific trends in a number of industries. Some composite leading indicator indices are published by the Census Bureau and other government and nonprofit agencies. They tend to be of greatest use to primary goods manufacturers and of less value as products approach the consumer stage.

Obviously, the type of forecasting problem, the amount of time available for forecasting, the nature of available data, and the amount of resources all affect the selection of a forecasting method. The brief discussion in this section covers only a few of the many forecasting methods which have been developed. Nevertheless, they illustrate a variety of techniques and the types of trade-offs which the researcher faces in selecting a research approach.

ANALYZING SEGMENT PROFITABILITY

Earlier in the chapter the process of market analysis was described and illustrated in Figure 11–1. The identification of segments and the problem of forecasting have already been discussed. What remains are the other steps in the decision process which ultimately result in the selection of a specific target market. This section deals with the information needs of managers who are faced with this selection decision. The discussion will emphasize the financial analysis of segment profitability. We will assume for the purpose of this discussion that forecasts have been provided for not only market potential, but also competitive positions and market share. Furthermore, analysis of profitability requires assumptions as to the marketing mix strategy and tactics adopted to serve each segment.

The problem of selection is thus reduced to one of estimating the profitability of each alternative segment. This subject is treated in two steps. First, the general subject of assessing segment profitability provides a background for discussing this type of information need. Second, the application of segment profitability analysis to potential markets constitutes the basis for decision making.

The major problem in assessing the profitability of individual market segments is the availability of meaningful revenue and cost information. Usually, cost information is developed for the accounting information system and must be converted for use by marketing managers. This problem was discussed at length in Chapter 5. The following example illustrates the contribution approach to segment profitability, as well as the conversion of account classifications for marketing decision making.[23]

Figure 11–5
Matrix breakdown by products and segments

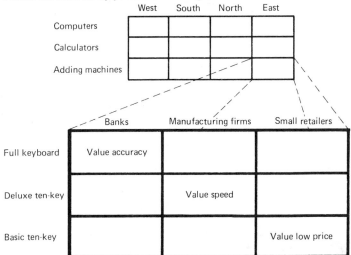

Source: Leland L. Beik and Stephen L. Buzby, "Profitability Analysis by Market Segment," *Journal of Marketing*, 37 (July 1973), p. 50, published by the American Marketing Association.

The first step is to devise a matrix breakdown of the company's market segments. Assume that we are concerned with a manufacturer of computers, calculators, and adding machines. One possible matrix breakdown for this manufacturer is illustrated in Figure 11–5. Notice that the matrices imply that marketing managers are responsible first

---

[23] This illustration is adapted from Leland L. Beik and Stephan L. Buzby, "Profitability Analysis by Market Segments," *Journal of Marketing*, vol. 37 (July 1973), pp. 48–53.

for profitability by product line, and second, by geographic region. This requires the identification of segments which are geographically based and then expressed in terms of customer types by product line. Information for profitability analysis would originate at the region level with details provided for customer type and product type within the product line. This information would then be aggregated to provide company totals.

Table 11–5 illustrates the allocation of costs for each type of adding machine in the product line. Recall from the discussion in Chapter 5 that costs are not necessarily assigned in direct proportion to sales revenues. That is, the assignment of salesmen's salaries and other assignable costs to, say the full-keyboard models, is not in proportion to the sales generated by that model. For example, the full-keyboard model generates half of the adding machine sales, but based on salesmen's effort per unit sold, this model is assigned 48 percent of salesmen's salaries. On the other hand, the full-keyboard model is assigned 67 percent of the product advertising expense based on the actual proportion of advertising devoted to this model.

Table 11–5
Product productivity analysis—contribution approach

	Company total	Full keyboard	Deluxe ten key	Basic ten key
Net Sales	$10,000	$5,000	$3,000	$2,000
Variable manufacturing costs	5,100	2,500	1,375	1,225
Manufacturing contribution	$ 4,900	$2,500	$1,625	$ 775
Marketing costs				
Variable:				
Sales commissions	450	225	135	90
Variable contribution	$ 4,450	$2,275	$1,490	$ 685
Assignable:				
Salaries—salesmen	1,600	770	630	200
Salary—marketing manager	100	50	25	25
Product advertising	1,000	670	200	130
Total	$ 2,700	$1,490	$ 855	$ 355
Product contribution	$ 1,750	$ 785	$ 635	$ 330
Nonassignable				
Institutional advertising	150			
Marketing contribution	$ 1,600			
Fixed-joint costs				
General administration	300			
Manufacturing	900			
Total	$ 1,200			
Net Profits	$ 400			

Source: Leland L. Beik and Stephan L. Buzby, "Profitability Analysis by Market Segment," *Journal of Marketing*, 37 (July 1973), p. 51, published by the American Marketing Association.

Table 11–6
Segment productivity analysis—contribution approach

	Com-pany total	Full keyboard Bank seg-ment	Full keyboard Non-seg-ment	Deluxe 10-Key Manu-factur-ing seg-ment	Deluxe 10-Key Non-seg-ment	Basic 10-key retail seg-ment
Net sales............................	$10,000	$3,750	$1,250	$2,550	$450	$2,000
Variable manufacturing costs	5,100	1,875	625	1,169	206	1,225
Manufacturing contribution	$ 4,900	$1,875	$ 625	$1,381	$244	$ 775
Marketing costs						
Variable:						
Sales commissions	450	169	56	115	20	90
Variable contribution	$ 4,450	$1,706	$ 569	$1,266	$224	$ 685
Assignable						
Salaries—salesmen	1,600	630	140	420	210	200
Salary—marketing manager	100	38	12	19	6	25
Product advertising	1,000	670	0	200	0	130
Total......................	$ 2,700	$1,338	$ 152	$ 639	$216	$ 355
Segment contribution	$ 1,750	$ 368	$ 417	$ 627	$ 8	$ 330
Nonassignable						
Institutional advertising	150					
Marketing contribution.........	$ 1,600					
Fixed-joint costs						
General administration	300					
Manufacturing	900					
Total......................	$ 1,200					
Net profits	400					

Source: Leland L. Beik and Stephan L. Buzby, "Profitability Analysis by Market Segment," *Journal of Marketing*, 37 (July 1973), p. 52, published by the American Marketing Association.

We are now ready to examine the contribution to profits derived from each customer segment. Recall from Figure 11–5 that a particular primary customer-oriented segment has been identified for each model of adding machine. That is, most full-keyboard machines are targeted to banks, deluxe ten-key machines to manufacturing firms, and basic ten-key machines to small retailers. Table 11–6 illustrates the expansion of the information from Table 11–5 to account for customer-oriented segments.

From the table, we can see that sales to the manufacturing and retailers' segments account for virtually all of the profits for the deluxe ten-key and basic ten-key models respectively. In the case of the full-keyboard model, however, over half of the profits are generated from sales outside the bank segment. Although the high profitability of non-segment sales for full-keyboard models can be attributed in part to low salary allocations and the lack of advertising expenditures, the fact that these sales are occurring suggests that additional segments for the model exists. Since the analysis described thus far concerns an existing product line and its historical market segments, we are not necessarily concerned with eliminating existing target markets. This would be the case if we discovered that the profitability of an existing segment falls significantly below corporate objectives. If further research failed to provide information upon which profit performance could be improved, the manufacturer might seek other markets for his products.

In the actual case of the adding machine line, further research should be conducted to determine the nature of nonsegment sales for the full-keyboard models. This could well reveal that those sales are concentrated in another identifiable segment. The new segment would thus constitute an opportunity for expanded sales and profit.

Although the above example concerns a firm and the segments which it already serves, the same form of analysis would be conducted to screen new prospective target markets. That is, the various sales and cost information in Tables 11–5 and 11–6 would be derived from forecasts in previously identified potential market segments. If resource constraints prevent the firm from producing all three adding machine models, this analysis would enable the firm to determine that segment which best meets its criteria for success. Although the full-keyboard model might have the largest sales projection, an analysis of the marketing strategy for servicing those segments might indicate a high cost of entry. On the other hand, the deluxe ten-key model might provide an easier segment entry and still meet the profit objectives of the firm. Although the exact form of the analysis will vary from case to case and firm to firm, this analysis constitutes the final two steps in the process illustrated at the beginning of the chapter in Figure 11–1.

SUMMARY

The process of identifying market opportunities generates numerous information needs. The discussion in this chapter has emphasized the market segmentation approach to target market selection. In general, this approach involves three major components related to information needs. First, market segments must be identified; second, relevant information about market segment potential and marketing costs must be forecasted; and third, each segment must be analyzed to determine which best meet the goals of the firm.

Basically, the concept of market segmentation assumes that any relatively heterogeneous group can be divided into two or more relatively homogeneous groups. Furthermore, segments must respond differentially to varying marketing mix strategies and be identifiable in a manner which allows marketing managers to develop effective strategies. If information identifying market segments is to be used for screening target markets, three criteria must be met. First, it must identify the manner in which a segment is unique in terms of the specific needs of buyer behavior. Second, it should provide insight into the manner in which different segments respond to specific marketing mix strategies. Third, it must provide identification information through which strategies can be devised to reach the members of the segment.

Numerous bases exist for meeting the criteria set forth for segment identification. Socioeconomic, demographic, and geographic measures are traditional approaches to segment identification which most commonly meet the third criterion. That is, these variables are most commonly used today to provide a picture of segment members through which marketing communication can be addressed to the potential customer. Psychological bases, such as personality type and buyer motives, are most useful in meeting the second criterion for segment identification. Measurement of this type helps provide understanding of the manner in which the members of a segment respond differentially to the same marketing mix strategies. Finally, measures of consumer responses, perceptual factors and usage factors, are most useful in meeting the first criterion for segment identification. These bases relate most directly to actual purchase behavior and typically provide the most meaningful distinction between segments.

Once market segments have been identified, it is necessary to project the market potential available within each segment. Marketing strategies and the costs associated with those strategies can be forecasted along with sales to provide the basis for an analysis of segment profitability. In this chapter three types of forecasting techniques were discussed. Judgmental techniques, such as Delphi method and jury of executive opinion, rely on the experience and wisdom of executives or experts as the basis for forecasting. Obviously, these methods tend to be less scientific than quantitative analysis. Nevertheless, they enable the researcher to incorporate a wide range of information into the forecast and prove particularly useful in detecting changes in the environment. Time-series analysis, such as moving averages, use historical records to forecast the future. The primary weakness of these approaches is their total reliance on the statistical analysis of past history. Their usefulness for short-term forecasting, low costs, and the availability of data make these techniques useful in many forecasting situations. Finally, causal techniques (regression analysis, leading indicators, and intention-to-buy surveys) help the researcher better understand the factors which cause changes in the forecasted item. These techniques vary greatly in their accuracy, costs, and data requirements. They are particularly useful, however, in identifying turning points in trends and in helping the researcher to better understand the environment in which forecasts are made.

Given identifiable market segments and forecasts of sales and costs associated with strategies for reaching those segments, target markets can be selected. Screening criteria usually relate to profitability, although other company goals may be involved. Analysis of segment profitability provides better insight into the nature of existing segments as well as the selection of target markets from potential segments. The major problem facing the researcher in this screening process involves the reclassification of accounts to provide useful financial information for marketing decision making.

DISCUSSION QUESTIONS

1. Explain how you would approach the problem of identifying new market segments for each of the following products:
    a. Carbonated soft drinks.
    b. Refrigerator/freezers.
    c. Portable radios.
2. Discuss the advantages and disadvantages of socioeconomic demographic, and geographic factors as bases for identifying market segments.
3. The Kinder Kom Co. produces and distributes 16mm educational films for preschool and early age (grades 1–3) use. Virtually all of Kinder's sales are to educational media centers which service local and regional primary level institutions. Kinder's reputation for quality and service has attracted the attention of several independent producers who are seeking distribution for their films. Two producers have approached the president of Kinder with proposals for joint ventures, one with entertaining materials for libraries and the other with materials which would be used in physicians' offices to explain certain diseases and health care problems. The president of Kinder is impressed with the quality of both producers' work and would like to explore this opportunity. The firm's limited resources, however, would allow them to enter only one of the two markets at this time. Since the markets are institutional in nature, the president of Kinder knows that he would be dealing with public libraries and colleges and universities as one general market segment. The other consists of physicians' practices and clinics which may be approached independently or through professional sources or pharmaceutical firms. (These companies often underwrite such materials as a public relations effort.) The president of Kinder decides to investigate the matter further and allocates $5,000 for the development of forecasts and profitability analyses.

    Assume that you work for Kinder and have been assigned the task of conducting this study. Explain how you might forecast the profitability of the two major segments described earlier using a:

    a. Judgmental technique,

    b. Time-series analysis,

    c. Causal technique.

SELECTED REFERENCES

Chambers, John C.; Mullick, Satinder K.; and Smith, Donald D. *An Executives Guide to Forecasting.* New York: John Wiley and Sons, Inc., 1974.

Cravens, David W.; Hills, Gerald E.; and Woodruff, Robert B. *Marketing Decision Making: Concepts and Strategy.* Homewood, Ill.: Richard D. Irwin, Inc., 1976, chaps. 7 and 8.

Engel, James F.; Fiorillo, Henry F.; and Cayley, Murray A., (eds.), *Market Segmentation: Concepts and Applications.* New York: Holt, Rinehart, and Winston, Inc., 1972.

Furse, David H., and Greenberg, Barnett A. "Cognitive Style and Attitudes as Market Segmentation Variables: A Comparison." *Journal of Advertising,* vol. 4, no. 4 (1975), pp. 39–44.

Greenberg, Barnett A., and Herberger, Roy A. "Is there an Ecology-Conscious Market Segment?" *Atlanta Economic Review,* vol. 23 (March–April 1973), pp. 42–44.

Kotler, Philip. *Marketing Management: Analysis, Planning and Control* (3d ed.). Englewood Cliffs, N.J.: Prentice-Hall, Inc., 1976, chaps. 3–8.

Lippitt, Vernon G. *Statistical Sales Forecasting.* New York: Financial Executives Research Foundation, 1969.

Luck, David J., Wales, Hugh G., and Taylor, Donald A. *Marketing Research* (4th ed.). Englewood Cliffs, N.J.: Prentice-Hall, Inc., 1974, chap. 14.

Still, Richard R., and Cundiff, Edward W. *Sales Management: Decisions, Policies, and Cases* (2d ed.). Englewood Cliffs, N.J.: Prentice-Hall, Inc., 1969, chaps. 13 and 14.

chapter

12

Research for product and pricing decisions

The continued success of the firm is dependent on one factor more than any other—its products. That is, marketing opportunities cannot be explored unless a product is available with which to meet them. Similarly, the other decision areas in marketing strategy formulation depend on the existence of a product and a market for that product. The first part of this chapter, therefore, is devoted to research which meets information needs in product decision making.

Pricing is a somewhat unique marketing mix variable which is often perceived as an integral part of the product itself. Promotion and distribution, which are discussed in the following chapter, are variables which relate more directly to the movement of a product from the seller to the buyer. Pricing, on the other hand, constitutes a decision area which is more immediately tied to product decisions. Given this relationship, the discussion of research for pricing decisions is covered in the same chapter with product related research.

As is true of all areas of marketing decision making, product and pricing decisions are extremely complex and cover a wide range of topics. The discussion in this chapter serves only to illustrate research in a few selected cases. No attempt is made to connect product and pricing decisions directly, and each topic is in fact treated in a separate section of the chapter.

SECTION A: RESEARCH FOR PRODUCT DECISIONS

One of the most commonly used concepts in any discussion of product decisions is the product life cycle. Generally, two points are made which have broad strategy implications. First, profits tend to be

Figure 12–1
Steps in new product development

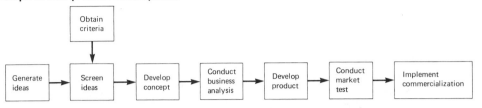

greatest during the period between the introduction of the product and its maturity in the marketplace. Second, the continuous introduction of new products and/or modification of existing products is necessary to insure high rates of profit over time. Food processors, for example, learned this lesson well as "the number of items handled in supermarkets jumped from 6,000 to 7,800" during the boom decade of the 1960s.[1]

A perilous adventure at best, new product development has become a more difficult task with the economic constraints of the early 1970s. Inflation riddled consumers became increasingly cautious and wary of new product proliferation. The number of new products or modifications dropped considerably through the first half of the 1970s. "In fact, fewer than 25 percent of all new products tested each year now reach supermarket shelves."[2]

New product development usually involves a series of decisions and activities, each of which generates information needs. The procedure selected for this discussion is illustrated in Figure 12–1. At each successive step of the procedure additional information is brought to bear which has the effect of first eliminating alternative ideas and then developing the one idea which will best meet the company's objectives in the marketplace. The amount and variety of information required at each step varies considerably depending upon the type of decision being made. The process of screening ideas, for example, tends to be a largely internalized process. On the other hand, the development of a product concept can involve extensive survey research and experimentation. The following discussion offers some elaboration on each of the decision areas.

Generating product ideas

New product ideas are loosely formed concepts which may ultimately be developed into more specific product concepts. Sources of

---

[1] "The Hard Road of the Food Processors," *Business Week*, March 8, 1976, p. 51.

[2] Ibid., p. 52.

information for product ideas include customers, research staff, competitors, salespeople and middlemen, and company employees at every level. As a largely creative process, idea generation should tap every available source. Many firms regularly survey customers in an effort to determine means of improving existing products or discovering new product ideas.

Basic scientific research supported by the government, private foundations, and industry has produced many of the technological innovations which found expression first as product ideas. The development of the memory chip, which has become the nucleus of minicomputers and numerous miniaturized control devices, is an excellent example. It is important, therefore, that the research and development staffs of corporations monitor the reports provided in professional journals and at professional meetings. It should be noted that the inclusion of competitors as sources of information is not meant to imply that industrial espionage is a desired source of product ideas. Obviously, as firms bring products out on the market, those products become idea sources for competitors. It is important for any firm to keep abreast of product development activities on the part of their competitors.

Salespeople and middlemen who handle the company's product should regularly report any ideas which are the result of their encounters with customers. This reporting should be included as a regular feature in the information system. Similarly, some of the techniques described in Chapter 11 (jury of executive opinion and Delphi technique) can be used to extract the best thinking of top management. Managers as sources of ideas are able to consider the complete range of company objectives, past performance, and market activities.

Ideas are rather simple statements and of little value in and of themselves. For example, at one point an idea was generated; someone suggested that eggs without cholesterol might be a good product. Although the idea incorporated intuitive feelings and knowledge of the current state of technology and concern for health in society, it may have appeared as a rather eccentric notion. A food processor or pharmaceutical manufacturer faced with this, and other ideas, should consider them as information inputs at the beginning of a long process of elimination. Customers do not buy ideas. Rather, they buy actual products which can only be marketed if they successfully meet the criteria of the firm.

Screening ideas

If the firm has several product ideas from which to select, it is desirable to have a formal screening process. The term "screening" implies that ideas will be subjected to criteria which will delineate a

Table 12-1
Screening criteria for product ideas

Weight	Criteria
.10	Newness—degree of innovativeness, divergence from existing products in the market.
.15	Compatibility—fit of product idea with existing technical and productive capabilities of the firm.
.20	Investment—size and type of financial requirements versus risk factors.
.20	Competition—probability of creating unique niche in market which is relatively controllable by the firm's marketing strategy.
.15	Company image—ability of firm to maintain or improve image and goodwill through the product.
.20	Marketability—lack of possible problems in the development of a product concept, pricing, promotion, or distribution.

hierarchy of desirability. That is, company criteria for new product ideas will enable management to rank the ideas in order of desirability.

Assume, for example, that the research staff of a company has used the Delphi technique to survey management concerning criteria for screening product ideas. The results of this research might resemble the material illustrated in Table 12–1. Using the six criteria listed in Table 12–1, a form could be developed on which each manager would rate new product ideas. The rating could then be totaled and weighted to provide a quantitative ranking of ideas. A hypothetical summary sheet for five product ideas is illustrated in Table 12–2. If the minimum rating score for a viable idea is .70, only ideas 2 and 5 would be retained for further evaluation. Furthermore, idea 2 would receive priority treatment since its rating value is highest.

The success of this approach is dependent both upon how the pro-

Table 12-2
Idea screening—Summary of management survey

Criteria	Mean scores					Weight	Weighted scores				
	Idea 1	Idea 2	Idea 3	Idea 4	Idea 5		Idea 1	Idea 2	Idea 3	Idea 4	Idea 5
Newness	3.5	4.3	3.3	2.0	4.1	.10	.35	.43	.33	.20	.41
Compatibility	3.6	4.1	3.0	2.5	3.9	.15	.54	.62	.45	.38	.59
Investment	3.3	3.8	3.6	3.0	3.6	.20	.66	.76	.72	.60	.72
Competition	3.0	4.3	3.6	2.3	4.1	.20	.60	.86	.72	.46	.82
Company Image	3.6	4.4	3.5	2.8	4.4	.15	.54	.66	.53	.42	.66
Marketability	3.5	4.1	3.5	2.0	4.0	.20	.70	.82	.70	.40	.80
Totals	20.5	25.0	20.5	15.8	24.1		3.39	4.15	3.45	2.46	4.00
Net Values						÷5	.68	.83	.69	.49	.80

Note: Ideas evaluated on a 1 to 5 scale with 5 being the highest possible rating.

cedure is used and the quality of the criteria. An example of a firm which fails in this respect is provided by a company which experienced phenomenal growth in the 1960s through the introduction of successful advanced technology industrial products. One of the firm's product lines included audiometers, equipment for testing hearing. Although the line included instruments for testing several people at one time, it did not include portable equipment for conducting one test on one individual. Such equipment was available from competitors, but those units did not incorporate the latest technology in the field. The executive in charge of the audiometer line decided to develop the finest portable single-test audiometer known in the industry. The product was actually developed and placed on the market at a price almost four times that of the models offered by competitors. Although the new audiometer was technically superior, it offered little functional advantage over those units available at a significantly lower price. Had this idea been screened against criteria for competition and marketability, it probably would never have reached the concept development stage.

Developing a product concept

Once accepted, a product idea must undergo considerable elaboration to qualify as a useful concept. While a product idea, such as garlic-flavored margarine, connotes the general aspects of a product, the concept must also convey an idea of the target market, its perception of the product relative to other products, and the appeals upon which a marketing strategy can be built for the product to gain an advantage in the market. Yoram Wind has summarized the information requirements in concept testing in the following three questions:

1. What is consumer reaction to the concept? What is the size of the potential market? Which attributes are most important in accounting for consumer reactions to the concepts?
2. How many market segments exist, and what are the characteristics (socioeconomic, demographic, psychographic, and product and brand usage patterns) and reactions to the various concepts?
3. What is the relevant competitive setting of the given concepts, and what is the most desirable positioning for the concept?[3]

Notice that the issues of market segmentation and product identification are interwoven in the preceding questions. Thus, much of the information which is relevant in concept development has already been illustrated in Chapter 11. We will concentrate here on

---

[3] Yoram Wind, "A New Procedure for Concept Evaluation," *Journal of Marketing,* vol. 37 (October 1973), p. 3.

those information needs in concept development which have not been discussed earlier. Those needs are primarily related to question 3 above. That is, the "position" of the product in relation to competitive products. The question of product/brand positioning is a complex research issue which has only recently been successfully approached with the use of multidimensional scaling techniques.

For some time manufacturers have been aware of the multifaceted perceptions with which consumers differentiate various products. Although blind taste tests have pointed out the consumer's difficulty in distinguishing between unmarked brands of beer, strong preferences appear when the brands are known. Whether consumers can tell the difference or not, coffee which is instant, regular grind, or freeze dried elicits strong preferences from different groups of consumers. It is clear, therefore, that the idea posed earlier, garlic-flavored margarine, must be investigated in considerable depth to determine how it might be perceived by potential customers.

Although many people may already enjoy the garlic flavoring on hot French bread and in the preparation of numerous dishes, the success of a new garlic-flavored margarine might depend on the colors of the package, the brand name, the perceived similarities and dissimilarities with other margarine and dairy products, and many other possible variables. We assume that the consumer has a "perceptual map" on which the various products and our concept are positioned along numerous dimensions. The problem is to determine those dimensions which are meaningful and the positions of the various products and concepts within that multidimensional space.

Wind illustrates concept positioning with an example of rum drinks. Assume that a rum manufacturer "is interested in determining the reaction to some new rum mixed drinks. Six concepts—the new rum mixes including rum old-fashioned, rum sour, Hathaway cocktail, Caribe cocktail, rum and iced tea and rum gimlet—and 22 'control' drinks (six of which were rum based) constituted the basic stimulus set."[4] Respondents were informed of the major ingredients of each of the drinks and asked to complete a lengthy questionnaire concerning the perceived benefits of each drink, reactions to the concept, and personal information.

The results of the concept positioning analysis are illustrated in Figure 12–2. This composite "perceptual map" illustrates the positions of the various drinks on the dimensions of popularity and masculinity for the sample group. Notice, for example, that scotch on the rocks is viewed as a relatively popular masculine drink, while pina calada is viewed as a relatively unpopular feminine drink. Further-

---

[4] Ibid., p. 5.

Figure 12–2
Two-dimensional configuration of 22 alcoholic drinks and 6 new rum concepts

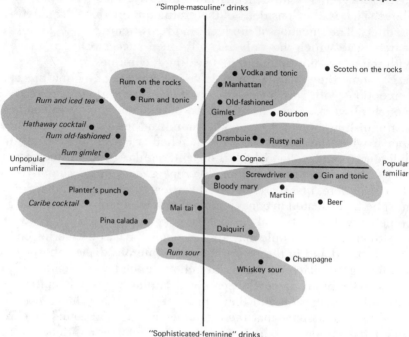

Source: Yoram Wind, "A New Procedure for Concept Evaluation," *Journal of Marketing,* vol. 37 (October 1973), p. 6, published by the American Marketing Association.

more, the masculine/feminine dimension is paralleled by a simple/sophisticated dimension. While the positions of the various drinks in this two dimensional space provide useful information, a cluster analysis proves even more beneficial. The clusters are illustrated by the boundaries drawn around groupings of drinks. Examining the clusters, we would note that only one new rum drink—rum sour—competes with a nonrum drink. Thus, if a manufacturer were interested in expanding the sales of rum, only the rum sour would appear to be a viable means of doing so. Promoting the other rum drinks might simply take some market share away from other existing rum drinks.

The analytical techniques involved in the concept testing described thus far are quite sophisticated and beyond the intended scope of this text. It is useful, however, to know the names of the appropriate techniques and the situations in which they apply. In the case of the rum drinks, further analysis identified market segments based on the perceived benefits derived from drinking. The segments were analyzed in terms of the rum drink products which they found most attractive. Thus, the rum manufacturer would know which drinks are appropriate to each segment. Using the descriptive information of buying behavior in the segments, the rum manufacturer could then proceed to analyze the financial feasibility of serving each segment.

Conducting business analysis

This stage in the development of a product is undertaken to eliminate potentially unprofitable concepts. From the previous stage the firm has some idea of the identity of market segments for each alternative, the potential for the product in that segment, and the company's probable market share. Several additional pieces of information are required to conduct business analysis. Generally, a price must be assigned to the concept in order to estimate dollar sales. Furthermore, a general idea of the costs associated with probable marketing strategies is necessary if the financial feasibility of the concept is to be explored.

This type of analysis was described in some detail in the sections on forecasting and target market selection in Chapter 11. Notice, however, that business analysis is a continuous activity which occurs during product development as well as throughout the life of the product. Financial analysis is first possible at this step in new product development since it requires at least an idea of the product concepts and their relevant market segments. Since the financial feasibility of target markets was discussed in the preceding chapter, and since financial analysis will also be an integral part of the remaining steps of new product development, it is not necessary to elaborate further in this section.

Developing products

Up to this point the development of a new product has been a relatively inexpensive proposition. Idea generation, screening, and product concept development could conceivably cost hundreds of thousands of dollars or as little as a few thousand dollars. Nevertheless, compared to the cost of actually placing a new consumer product on the market, these expenses are small. The development of the product itself frequently involves a serious financial commitment. At this point a physical prototype of the product itself must be produced. Decisions must also be made concerning branding and packaging. Although it is possible for some firms to accomplish this activity with the expenditure of a few thousand dollars, it is more likely to require hundreds of thousands to tens of millions of dollars. Nevertheless, management should never lose sight of the fact that this is still a stage at which it may be more profitable in the long run to abandon a potentially unsuccessful product.

Many of the types of information required in product development have already been discussed in previous sections and chapters. Much of the consumer testing, for example, of a prototype is similar to that used for product concept positioning. Of major concern in selecting a brand name is the perception of brand meaning and position. The primary difference at this point is the availability to the consumer of a physical reality upon which to base judgement. To fully illustrate the complexity and importance of this stage in the development of new products, several examples are offered in the following discussion. These include a concept which is undergoing long-term developments, seemingly good concepts which were developed and subsequently failed, and concepts which proved to be successful.

Although the internal combustion, reciprocating piston engine has predominated as a source of power for the automotive industry, numerous alternatives have come to the surface. One such alternative is the turbine engine. The Chrysler Corporation has pursued its turbine car project since the late 1950s. By 1963 an engine had been developed which the company considered as a viable prototype for testing. In spite of the extensive amount of information which had been gathered in the laboratory and on the proving ground, the researchers on the project felt that they needed additional information concerning the engine's performance in the hands of consumers. This led to a rather novel consumer research project which illustrates the kinds of information which can be produced in product development research.

Chrysler was faced with a number of problems in designing a meaningful consumer research project.

. . . To begin with, there is no such thing as a typical automobile market. Variations in climate alone dictate that a market test for an automobile be conducted in a rather large number of cities. A second drawback in our case was the necessity for us to retain more control over the turbine cars than would have been possible if the cars were offered for sale. If we were to obtain the maximum knowledge from this test, it was essential that we be able to recall any car at any time for study, and we also wanted to be free to make any modifications in the turbine power plant that may have been suggested by our continual program of engineering research.[5]

These problems, coupled with the lack of conveniently dispersed service mechanics for turbine engines, led Chrysler to its consumer

---

[5] Remarks by David T. Miller, Manager of Marketing and Consumer Research, Chrysler Corporation, Detroit Press Conference, April 12, 1966.

evaluation program. The design of the program is described by a Chrysler executive as follows:

. . . We decided, first, to loan out the turbine car for a period of three months. This period of time, we reasoned, would give people ample opportunity to try out turbine power under a variety of driving conditions. With this time interval, we recognized that we could, in a relatively short space of time, obtain the reactions of 200 users.

Our next decision dealt with geographical dispersion of turbine use tests. We wanted to assure a wide dispersion of trials, and therefore work out a plan that allocated trials to a total of 128 areas of population, including at least one area in each state except Alaska and Hawaii. In order to reach the total sample size of 200, we apportioned trials according to car population. By this method, we assigned seven trials to the Los Angeles–Long Beach area, four trials to Pittsburgh, and so on.

The names of people designated to participate in the user program were selected for us by the firm of Touche, Ross, Bailey & Smart. They took nearly 30,000 inquiries which we had received from the public and sorted them by area of the country. They then made the final selections within each area according to the make and model year of cars currently owned, as recorded in a questionnaire which Chrysler asks each applicant to complete.

The sample included owners of both Chrysler and competitive makes of cars of all sizes and model years. The effect of this procedure was to produce a cross section of people representative of the types of consumers who would buy a turbine car if Chrysler marketed such a product.

Once the selection procedure was set, the program went into full swing. The first task of our marketing research group was to decide upon the procedure for "debriefing" turbine users. We considered alternative techniques and eventually settled on an intensive personal interview with each turbine user within two weeks of the conclusion of the use period. These interviews were conducted by members of Chrysler's own marketing research staff. This allowed for more intensive analysis of replies than might otherwise be possible. We also retained an unusual amount of flexibility, since we could change a questioning procedure at any time to reflect what we had already learned in earlier interviews. All conversations with turbine users were tape recorded.[6]

Fifty cars at a time were placed with families. The testing, reworking, and evaluation covered a period of over two years. The results can be grouped into two categories. First, the company was interested in the mechanical and technical feasibility of the turbine engine. Second, Chrysler wanted to know something about consumers' evaluation of the automobile. Basically, the results of the technical aspects of the evaluation were very favorable. Problems, which had not been anticipated, did surface during the test period, but Chrysler was able to solve most of them before the last round of consumer evaluations.

---

[6] Ibid.

One technical problem which arose concerned engaging the gear selector prematurely. With turbine engines, it is necessary to allow the turbine to attain operating idle speed before engaging the transmission.

Regular inspections indicated that some engines have been subjected to temperatures very much higher than those normally allowed by the fuel control . . . It was finally noticed, however, that some drivers would initiate the automatic starting cycle with the ignition key and then very quickly shift the gear selector from the start position before the engine had reached idle speed, thus bypassing the automatic start system . . . Once discovered, the trouble was an easy matter to cure, simply by modifying the automatic start system so that the driver could not over-ride and thus misuse it.[7]

Other problems involved the electrical system, combustion chamber igniters, alloys used in the construction of certain components, and the training of service personnel. Over all, Chrysler felt that the 50-car test provided invaluable technical information at this stage of product development.

The other area of information need concerned consumer reaction. The test results indicated that the consumers were generally impressed with (1) the vibrationless, smooth operation of the turbine, (2) the reduced maintenance requirements, (3) starting ability, (4) good engine power, (5) the instant availability of heat in winter, (6) quietness of operation, and (7) nonstalling characteristics. On the negative side, consumers pointed out (1) the "acceleration lag," (2) disappointment with fuel economy, and (3) lack of fuel availability and lack of service facilities. Generally, however, there was much stronger agreement on the plus side than on the minus side. As one official stated, "The consumer evaluation has uncovered some areas of performance that require improvement. However, if these shortcomings can be overcome, it is evident from this phase of the turbine program that the idea of turbine-powered passenger cars is capable of earning widespread consumer acceptance."[8] Chrysler's turbine car project is now almost 20 years old. The company is currently evaluating the sixth generation of turbine engines for automobiles. This particular illustration of product development is an excellent example of the time and care which must be devoted to the development of a major consumer product. Before Chrysler can introduce a turbine-powered automobile, everything from the automobile itself to the service system which supports it, must be of comparable or superior benefit when compared to the system of conventional powered automobiles.

---

[7] Remarks by George J. Huebner, Jr., Director of Research, Chrysler Corporation, Detroit Press Conference, April 12, 1966.

[8] From remarks by G. J. Huebner, Jr., Detroit Press Conference, April 12, 1966.

In illustrating product development, it is useful to consider cases of failures, as well as successes. The risk of failure is always present, even when product development is based upon good information. One such illustration involves the abortive attempt of Brown-Foreman to introduce its "light whiskey," Frost 8/80.[9] Brown-Foreman produced Early Times and Old Forester bourbons and Jack Daniels whiskey. A brief glance at Table 12–3 reveals the deteriorating market share posi-

Table 12–3
Market share trends of the liquor industry, 1959–1970

	Percent of market		
	1959	*1969*	*1970*
Whiskey types:			
Straights	25.9	22.2	21.2
Spirit blends	32.1	21.2	19.6
Scotch	7.7	12.0	13.4
Canadian	5.0	8.8	8.5
Bonds	4.6	1.8	1.6
Other	0.3	0.3	0.3
Total whiskey................	75.6	66.3	64.6
Vodka............................	7.3	11.5	12.7
Gin..............................	9.2	10.0	10.0
Cordials	3.5	4.6	4.9
Brandy	2.4	3.4	3.5
Rum.............................	1.5	2.8	3.5
Other	0.5	1.4	1.3
Total nonwhiskey	24.4	33.7	35.4
Total consumption (millions of gallons)	228.2	363.9	367.0

Source: *Business Week* Survey and Estimates, as reported in "The Distillers Serve Up New Brands," *Business Week*, March 6, 1971, pp. 80, 81, in Robert Hartley, *Marketing Mistakes* (Columbus, Ohio: Grid, Inc., 1976), p. 83.

tion which the company's products faced at the beginning of the 1970s. That is, among whiskeys, only scotch demonstrated a steady penetration of the market. Furthermore, the total share for whiskey was deteriorating to the rapid gains being made by nonwhiskey beverages—vodka and rum in particular. A concept study was undertaken in a search for the new product. Twenty-four hundred persons were interviewed, both by mail and in person, to provide inputs for the design of a new product. The survey indicated that the "dry, white" whiskey (which had been illustrated in the material provided with the questionnaire) was most desirable. They also indicated that the "whiskey should be priced among the 'upper medium' brands now

---

[9] This illustration is adapted from Robert F. Hartley, *Marketing Mistakes* (Columbus, Ohio: Grid, Inc., 1976), pp. 81–95.

on the market."[10] Furthermore, the segment of respondents which appeared most attracted to the dry, white concept were "affluent, well-educated people in the 25–35 age group, the fun-oriented party-going types."[11]

In developing a prototype, Brown-Foreman purchased whiskey from another distiller which qualified under federal regulations as light whiskey. Brown-Foreman further filtered the color and taste out of the whiskey to provide a clear 80 proof product. Hundreds of names were searched for conflicting trademarks and tested with consumers. The final choice, "frost," seemed to best fit the requirements of the concept. The 8/80, which was added, reflected the eight steps in the product distilling process and its 80 proof. A package was developed which would convey the modern quality image of the product. This was basically a tall slender bottle with a relatively simple black and silver label.

It is at this point, however, that Brown-Forman may have made a mistake. Notice that most of the research upon which product development was based actually involved concept testing. That is, the product, its package, and a marketing strategy were all developed without actual consumer testing in the product development stage. Furthermore, the next stage, test marketing, was also omitted. Thus, in spite of the tremendous amount of research, the $6.5 million which Brown-Forman ultimately invested in the brand could not insure success. In fact, light whiskeys in general have not performed well. It is possible that further research and new brand development might provide a competitor for scotch and the nonwhiskeys. However, the millions of dollars spent to date in an attempt to meet an apparent consumer trend were generally unproductive.

In the cases of both the Chrysler turbine car and the light whiskey, product development involved testing with a sample of consumers. One of the more spectacular success stories in the consumer products market, however, required security during the product development stage as a means of preventing premature competitive entries. The case in point is Gillette Track II Razor and Blade. Several concepts were under consideration when a company employee suggested the Track II concept. Of the double blade configurations under consideration, the Track II seemed most attractive. The company therefore moved into the product development stage.

Since the new product competitive advantage is quickly lost in the razor market, the firm had to test its prototype without revealing it to competitors. This was accomplished by having male company em-

---

[10] Ibid., p. 86.
[11] Ibid.

ployees shave each morning with the new razor when they arrived at work. They shaved in facilities which were equipped with two-way mirrors and microphones. Researchers were thus able to observe the actual reaction of each employee as he used the product. Based on these tests, the company introduced the product, and it ultimately proved to be one of the most successful shaving innovations in the history of the industry. Introduced in October 1971, the Track II shaving system had "captured 50 percent of the razor dollar market and 13 percent of the blade market," by the summer of 1973.[12]

Conducting test markets

One important ingredient has been missing from all of the steps in new product development discussed thus far. None of the activities mentioned thus far expose the total marketing mix to the marketplace. Even though much of the information gathered for new product development comes from consumers and experts in a field, the product and strategy have not as yet been tried together in the market.

As a means of acquiring needed information, test marketing can be used for any strategy question which remains prior to commercialization of the product. Market testing may be used, for example, to experiment with different channels of distribution or different media mixes. Limited markets may be used to test the introduction of a new product in previously untried geographic areas. In general, the idea is to test the market without fully committing the large sums of money required for full scale commercialization.

One of the most important information needs in test marketing concerns the repurchase rate of the product. Lipstein illustrates this problem and a means of solving it in the case of a hypothetical new product, "Electra Oleomargarine."[13] Two possible patterns are illustrated in Figure 12–3. The solid line represents cases in which a high volume of trial purchases is achieved early in the test, but insufficient repeat customers cause a downward sales trend in later months. The dotted line in Figure 12-3 illustrates the case of more gradual acceptance which eventually approaches a stable level.

Unfortunately, most test-market situations do not last long enough to determine which of these two patterns will actually emerge. Assume, for example, that the test market begins on March 1 and ends on April 30 (see Figure 12–3). Assume further that the actual performance of Electra in the test market is indicated by the solid line and that a six

---

[12] "The Idea Man Gillette Picked," *Business Week*, May 5, 1973, p. 60.

[13] Benjamin Lipstein, "Tests for Test Marketing," *Harvard Business Review*, vol. 39, no. 2 (March–April 1961), pp. 74–77.

Figure 12–3
Typical market test brand share for two trends

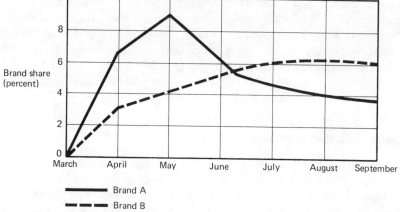

Source: Benjamin Lipstein, "Tests for Test Marketing," *Harvard Business Review,* vol. 39, no. 2 (March–April 1961), p. 74.

percent share of market is desired in the long run. An incorrect conclusion could easily be drawn.

The key to understanding what is happening in the test market lies in Table 12–4. This type of table is referred to as a "brand switching matrix." It tells us how many purchasers we retained from one period to the next, how many switched to other brands, and how many switched from other brands to our product. This is accomplished by collecting data from a consumer panel in the test market. Panel member diaries reveal the brands which they purchased in each period. Additional information can be collected from panel members to determine the reasons for their brand preferences. In the case of Electra, the outlook is not particularly good. At the intersection of the first column and first row, we note that only 12 percent of Electra buyers are repeat purchasers. This figure does not compare well with the range of 21 percent for Meadowlark to 25 percent for Gloria.

Furthermore, reading across the first row and then down the first column, we note that Electra is experiencing a net gain only from previous period purchasers of the private label. Further investigation (interviews) indicated that private label users tend to be price conscious and were temporarily attracted by special introductory offers which accompanied Electra's introduction. If the pattern revealed in the matrix continues, it is unlikely that Electra will be able to achieve the long-run market share objectives. Thus, a brief test market has helped the manufacturer of Electra avoid a potential failure by providing useful information on brand switching behavior.

Table 12–4
Table of switching and staying tendencies by consumers of various brands of oleomargarine

Reading across, you can see the percentage of Electra buyers who switched to other brands during the second period

Reading down, you can see the percentage of original buyers of other brands who switched to Electra during the second period

Buyers of these brands in the first period	Bought these brands in the second period							
	Electra	Gloria	Meadowlark	Aunt Mary's	B-R private label	All other	Did not buy in the period	Total
Electra	12%	5%	7%	4%	3%	28%	41%	100%
Gloria	5%	25%	3%	2%	2%	26%	37%	100%
Meadowlark	3%	2%	21%	5%	3%	26%	40%	100%
Aunt Mary's	2%	5%	1%	23%	4%	25%	40%	100%
B-R stores private label	4%	1%	3%	2%	22%	30%	38%	100%
All other	3%	5%	3%	4%	5%	23%	57%	100%
Did not buy in the period	5%	3%	4%	1%	2%	28%	57%	100%

Source: Benjamin Lipstein, "Tests for Test Marketing," *Harvard Business Review*, vol. 39, no. 2 (March–April 1961), p. 76.

Implement product commercialization

Ultimately, new products do enter the market. Since they will all experience the product life cycle, it is necessary to monitor each product's success in terms of company goals and objectives. In many companies the emphasis on new product development often causes management to overlook existing products until they become a problem. "Therefore, an organized approach is needed to periodically review all of the firm's products in order to identify those which are no longer earning revenue in proportion to the efforts and resources required to produce and sell them."[14] One approach to solving this problem is "A Product Review and Evaluation Subsystem Model called PRESS."[15]

PRESS is a particularly useful device for companies with a large number of products. It is these firms which frequently lose sight of the contribution of each product until certain individual items are clearly in the declining stage. To illustrate this approach, the following example involves 25 selected products in a furniture manufacturer's line. Two assumptions are made to simplify the illustration, but they are not necessary constraints of the PRESS model. First, it is assumed that "the available production factors can be utilized to produce any pattern in the line. Second, contribution margin has been selected as the primary criterion for comparing the value of the several products."[16]

Products are compared in the PRESS model in terms of the Selection Index Number (SIN). SIN is calculated for any particular product using the following formula:

$$SIN_i = \frac{CM_i/\Sigma CM_i}{FC_i/\Sigma FC_i} \times (CM_i/\Sigma CM_i)$$

Where:

SIN_i = Selection Index Number for product "i"
CM_i = Contribution Margin for product "i"
FC_i = Facilities Costs for product "i"
ΣCM_i = Summation of Contribution Margin of all products
ΣFC_i = Summation of Facilities Costs of all products[17]

With this formula, a product whose percentage of contribution is less than its percentage of resource utilization will receive an SIN value which is even less than the value which straight accounting analysis would have indicated. Similarly, a product whose percentage utiliza-

---

[14] Paul W. Hamelman and Edward M. Mazze, "Improving Product Abandonment Decisions," *Journal of Marketing*, vol. 36 (April 1972), p. 20, published by the American Marketing Association.

[15] Ibid.

[16] Ibid.

[17] Ibid.

tion of resources is less than its percentage contribution would receive an even higher SIN value than the straight accounting contribution would reflect.

To illustrate this concept with the furniture company example, refer first to Table 12–5 which contains the data necessary to calculate the contribution margin for each product. The first three columns show the unit variable cost for material, labor, and overhead. The fourth column is simply the total of these variable costs. The unit sales price and quantities sold in the most recent accounting period are shown in columns 5 and 6 respectively. With this data, it is possible to calculate SIN values for each of the 25 products. These values and the data required for their calculation are illustrated in Table 12–6. Note that the product model numbers in Table 12–6 are in decreasing order of SIN value.

The first column in Table 12–6 is the total contribution margin of the product. This is calculated by subtracting total unit variable costs from price, and multiplying by the number of units sold (see Table

Table 12–5
Variable costs, price, and unit sales for 25 furniture products

Product number	Unit material cost $	Unit labor cost $	Unit variable overhead $	Total variable cost $	Unit sales price $	Unit quantity sold
801	39.32	32.17	19.04	90.53	180	189
802	27.71	40.17	21.91	89.79	170	186
803	22.17	47.47	23.71	93.35	120	141
804	21.09	57.12	29.17	107.38	130	29
805	7.09	16.75	8.90	32.74	104	82
806	13.07	17.44	7.93	38.44	60	291
807	41.71	37.74	19.91	99.36	215	104
808	28.82	39.11	15.42	83.35	200	97
809	14.25	21.42	12.75	48.42	59	502
810	47.17	39.77	18.02	104.96	200	390
811	24.40	42.70	21.35	88.45	150	207
812	33.13	61.74	33.07	127.94	190	402
813	17.74	14.42	9.47	41.63	57	607
814	14.42	23.44	12.24	50.10	125	72
815	19.77	30.14	17.13	67.04	175	109
914	30.88	24.36	16.00	71.24	130	154
917	21.16	45.91	29.56	96.63	171	35
922	14.86	49.22	26.67	90.75	140	17
923	9.27	16.57	10.61	36.45	68	160
926	16.38	5.63	2.60	24.61	45	65
927	13.02	13.87	8.07	34.96	58	869
951	21.21	10.69	6.32	38.22	65	197
952	34.52	61.28	44.87	140.67	242	32
959	34.69	31.06	22.83	88.58	150	156
960	6.75	11.84	7.82	26.41	54	168

Adapted from Paul W. Hamelman and Edward M. Mazze, "Improving Product Abandonment Decisions," *Journal of Marketing*, vol. 36 (April 1972), pp. 22 and 23, published by the American Marketing Association.

Table 12–6
Selection index numbers for 25 furniture products

Product	Total contribution margin ($)	Percentage contribution margin	Cost of facilities utilization ($00's)	Percentage facilities utilization	SIN
810	37065.60	15.45	60.15	4.78	49.94
927	20021.80	8.35	22.16	1.76	39.56
812	24948.10	10.40	95.64	7.60	14.23
801	16909.80	7.05	52.19	4.15	11.98
813	9229.59	3.89	24.33	1.93	7.82
802	14919.10	6.22	62.77	4.99	7.75
815	11767.60	4.91	48.26	3.84	6.27
811	12740.90	5.31	65.27	5.19	5.44
807	12026.60	5.01	58.69	4.66	5.39
808	11315.10	4.72	55.25	4.39	5.07
914	9049.04	3.77	41.90	3.33	4.27
959	9581.52	3.99	55.62	4.42	3.61
951	5275.66	2.20	17.54	1.39	3.47
806	6273.96	2.62	25.59	2.03	3.36
805	5843.32	2.44	25.83	2.05	2.89
960	4635.12	1.93	20.00	1.59	2.35
923	5048.00	2.10	27.41	2.18	2.03
809	5311.16	2.21	34.53	2.74	1.79
814	5392.80	2.25	36.40	2.89	1.75
803	3757.65	1.57	71.73	5.70	0.43
926	1325.35	0.55	9.05	0.72	0.42
952	3242.56	1.35	107.88	8.57	0.21
917	2602.95	1.09	76.53	6.08	0.19
922	837.25	0.35	76.63	6.09	0.02
804	655.98	0.27	86.82	6.90	0.01
		100.00%		100.00%	

Source: Paul W. Hamelman and Edward M. Mazze, "Improving Product Abandonment Decisions," *Journal of Marketing*, vol. 36 (April 1972), p. 24, published by the American Marketing Association.

12–5). In the case of product no. 810, the calculation is as follows:

$$(200 - 104.96) \times 390 = 37065.60$$

The second column in Table 12–6 is the percentage of total contribution margin attributed to the individual product. Thus, product 810 contributed 15.45 percent of the total contribution margin for the 25 products. The third column indicates the allocation to each product of the cost of the facilities utilized to produce it. This is expressed as a percentage of total facilities utilization costs in column 4. The SIN value in column 5 is calculated using the percentage contribution margin and percentage facilities utilization costs in the formula presented earlier.

Notice that the last 6 products have SIN values below 1.00. This condition makes these products candidates for abandonment. It should be pointed out, however, that other factors may intervene to keep the product in the line. For example, the product may be particularly useful in creating goodwill, or it may be necessary to round out a line.

This simplified illustration of one model indicates the complexity of monitoring products through their life cycles. The PRESS model can also be used to analyze the effect of a change in price for a given product. Thus, if a product is not performing well, it may be possible to raise price, particularly if demand for that product is relatively inelastic. In any event, the primary concern of management during commercialization of a product is to insure its continuing contribution to the attainment of company goals and objectives. The PRESS model is one approach to gathering and utilizing information for this type of decision making.

Summary of research for product decisions

This section of the chapter has dealt with a select, but wide range, of information needs which arise during new product development. New product development can be viewed as a seven step process beginning with the generation of new ideas and culminating with the implementation of new product commercialization. The entire process involves a wide range of information needs and an equally diverse range of research techniques.

The first two steps of new product development involve idea generation and screening. Although information from consumers and competitors are valuable inputs, the opinions and judgments of experienced executives is nowhere more important in the process than here. The jury of executive opinion approach is particularly appropriate in the development of screening criteria.

Compared to final products, ideas come cheap. That is, literally hundreds of ideas may ultimately lead to but a few real products. In fact, beginning with idea screening, the objective of the process is to reduce the number of remaining alternatives until only those few products which best meet company objectives enter the market. The first step in this direction is *concept development*. At this step an attempt is made to further elaborate the idea into a concept which has meaning to consumers and can be related to other concepts and/or products. Concept development typically involves sophisticated consumer research and was illustrated in terms of a new rum drink concept in this chapter. The rum drink example involved locating relative positions of a variety of rum and nonrum drinks on two dimensions which were relevant to a particular market segment. Multidimensional scaling is a common measurement task in concept development.

Throughout the process, products should be evaluated in terms of financial feasibility. As the concept becomes more specific, forecasts of sales by market segment enable researchers to provide estimates of profitability. Internal secondary data are major sources for developing this information.

Product concepts which survive business analysis undergo a stage referred to as product development. At this step a prototype is developed, along with a brand, package, and other product features. Research to provide information at this stage can involve any of the various techniques described in this text. Product development was illustrated through the Chrysler turbine car project, Brown-Foreman's "Frost 8/80," and Gillette's "Trac II."

The final step preceding full scale commercialization is test marketing. Test markets provide a firm with an opportunity to evaluate a new product in the reality of the marketplace. Final adjustments in strategy can also be evaluated in tests. One of the problems associated with test markets is correctly interpreting market share trends. A means of resolving this problem, the brand switching matrix, was illustrated.

The final step of new product development is commercialization. Unfortunately, the focus of management on new products often causes existing products to be overlooked until they become problems. A model for continuously evaluating each member of a product line, PRESS, was used to illustrate information for improving product abandonment decisions.

SECTION B: RESEARCH FOR PRICING DECISIONS

The marketing mix variable which is perhaps most closely associated with the product is price. It is hard to imagine a product concept which does not carry some notion of its value to consumers and sellers. At the same time pricing decisions tend to be one of the most perplexing problems facing management. Although a wealth of pricing theory has been developed, particularly by economists, numerous difficulties are encountered in the application of those theories.

To the extent that it is possible to isolate pricing decisions, two broad areas can be delineated. First, business firms are faced with the problem of establishing pricing policies and strategies. These are the broad guidelines under which more specific pricing activities take place. Second, managers are faced with the actual task of determining specific prices. A number of approaches have been developed which are either cost oriented, market oriented, or a combination of the two. The remainder of the chapter is devoted to these two broad areas of pricing decisions and the information requirements associated with each.

Establishing pricing policies and strategies

Policy and strategy level decisions are influenced largely by the structure of the industry in which a firm competes and the firm's fixed commitments. That is, if a firm operates in an industry which is extremely competitive, price and other product features may be used to some strategic advantage in acquiring and maintaining market share. On the other hand, if the firm operates in an oligopolistic environment, the range in which price can vary may be minimal. The various traditional demand curves are illustrated in Figure 12–4.

Figure 12–4
Traditional demand curves, individual firms

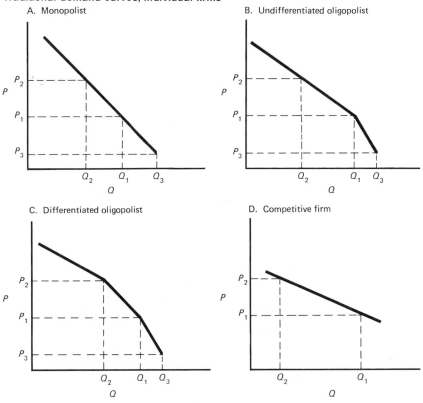

Research for this aspect of pricing decisions should provide the firm with an estimate of the demand curve which it faces for each of its products. If the demand curve is similar to the one in Figure 12–4A, the ratio of changes in quantity to changes in price is less than one, and the nature of demand in relation to price is inelastic. That is, an increase in price does not result in a particularly drastic decrease in quantity. Obviously, few firms will find themselves in this position (of monopoly) in our society. Those that do are frequently subject to price regulation by government agencies. Since they are well aware of this fact, analysis of the nature of price in the demand function for their products is of little use.

Firms which operate in industries characterized by few competitors should be concerned with the shape of demand curves for their products. They would face demand curves similar to the one in Figure 12–4B or the one in Figure 12–4C. The difference may appear minimal, but it is significant. Most oligopolies which are characterized by homogeneous products, such as steel and petroleum products, face the undifferentiated oligopolistic demand curve illustrated in Figure 12–4B. These firms have virtually no flexibility in manipulating price since price is elastic above that point and inelastic below it. Thus, an attempt to lower price would be a signal for competitors to match the price decrease, and the industry would suffer with lower profits. A price increase would result in a disproportionate loss in volume since competitors would still be offering the product at a lower price.

Most of the large consumer goods oligopolies in this country face demand curves similar to the one illustrated in Figure 12–4C. They are able to distinguish their product, through product differentiation or market segmentation, and create a price range within which they have monopolistic control in the marketplace. That range is indicated in Figure 12–4C between price $P1$ and price $P2$. The absolute demand for their specific product is not adequate to provide quantity increases disproportionately high to compensate for pricing decreases. Similarly, above price $P2$ consumers will seek satisfactory alternatives. A food processor, for example, might determine in a consumer survey that a new "natural" breakfast food appeals to a particular segment which is willing to pay a price somewhat higher than traditional breakfast cereals. Below a certain price, however, the firm would find that the pool of potential customers begins to decrease. Similarly, above a certain price, consumers are no longer willing to use the product given alternatives available on the market. Within the upper and lower ranges derived from this consumer-based information, the firm may seek to set a price which maximizes profit.

Finally, we encounter the traditional competitive environment in which demand is continuously elastic. This situation is illustrated in Figure 12–4D. Although there are relatively few markets which meet the criteria for this type of demand curve, some industries, such as fresh foods, face relatively lengthy ranges in which demand is elastic. Agricultural economists spend a considerable amount of time estimating the specific demand curves for these various products. For example, a complete study may be devoted to estimating the nature of the demand curve for apples in a particular region of the country. Econometric techniques are usually employed in which secondary data are analyzed using associative techniques, such as regression analysis.

Although research which provides insight into the nature of industry structure is an invaluable input for pricing policy and strategy decisions, most going concerns are even more concerned with their fixed commitments. These include, among others, fiscal plant operations, credit limits, fixed distribution systems, long-term supply contracts, and an available pool of labor. While the industry structure analysis deals largely with the factors affecting demand for the firm's product, fixed commitments have a tremendous impact on the cost structure within which the firm must achieve its goals.

Most of the research associated with fixed commitments involves internal secondary sources of data. The sources may include the balance sheet and other financial statements from which managers can determine the extent to which they have discretion in committing additional capital resources. Meeting a higher level of demand may require undesirable commitments of transportation and distribution facilities. Finally, uncontrollable external environmental factors, such as political and legal constraints, should be considered. Perhaps this area of decision making would best be illustrated by an example.

Assume that a major oil company investigates the industry structure and its fixed commitments and determines the following:

1. An analysis of the demand function for the subject product reveals an undifferentiated oligopoly [as illustrated in Figure 12–4B] in which the firm plays the role of price leader.
2. Analysis of industry data from trade sources indicates that the firm already has the largest market share, and competitors are attempting to capture larger shares through price competition.
3. The firm has the most extensive fixed facilities for distribution in the market and must maintain a high level of output to operate profitably.
4. The members of the marketing staff responsible for pricing have received a memorandum from the legal staff which indicates that a real contingency exists of government intervention and antitrust litigation if the firm appears to be enlarging its market position for this product.

Given this set of inputs, the corporate level marketing management team develops the following policies and strategies:

1. Prices for the product must be sufficiently competitive to insure a level of output consistent with minimal requirements for profitable operation of fixed facilities.

2. The firm will remain sufficiently competitive to protect its market share.
3. The firm will retain its role of price leader for price increases.
4. The firm will not act as the price leader for decreases, but will follow price decreases initiated by competitors (subject to 1 above).

Notice that information needs for pricing policy and strategy decisions can be extremely subjective. Furthermore, these decisions are usually closely related to other decision areas faced by management. Another excellent example of the dangers involved in relying too heavily on price as a strategy variable involves the A&P "WEO" strategy.

Long a leader in food retailing, A&P found itself in a stagnating position by the early 1970s.[18] Sales had remained relatively constant for the last half of the 1960s, and market share was declining. Table 12–7 illustrates the sales, income, and market share positions for A&P and its two largest competitors, Safeway and Kroger. Analyzing the industry structure and the environment for competition, A&P's top level management decided that the solution to their problem would be a new policy of discount pricing implemented through discount-store type competitive strategies. With almost reckless abandon, margins were drastically reduced on a large number of food items and the depth of product offering in the typical A&P store was reduced in preparation for the high volume low margin discount operation.

Unfortunately, in implementing this strategy A&P overlooked a number of critical variables which related more to their product than price. For example, A&P had been late in entering the supermarket/shopping center trend in food retailing. As a result, many of their remaining outlets were of the old free-standing grocery store type. They may have underestimated the financial strength and staying power of their competitors in all-out price competition. Furthermore, they failed to bring other aspects of their products up to competitive standards. For example, A&P stores were not particularly well kept, shelves were frequently out of stock, and customers were frequently faced with long check-out waiting lines. Finally, the drastic margin reductions implemented by A&P actually resulted in relatively small actual dollar reductions in the price of individual products. For example, a 10 percent reduction in the price of a canned vegetable might actually reduce the price to the customer by only 2¢.

Given the multitude of problems and a general failure to comprehend the entire scope of their competitive problems, A&P was not

---

[18] The A&P illustration is adapted from Robert F. Hartley, *Marketing Mistakes* (Columbus, Ohio: Grid, Inc., 1976), pp. 98–109.

Table 12–7
Comparative performance statistics for A&P, Safeway and Kroger

	A&P			Safeway			Kroger		
	Sales (000,000)	Income	Market share*	Sales (000,000)	Income	Market share	Sales (000,000)	Income	Market share
1963	$5,189	$57.49	20.9	$2,650	$44.82	10.7	$2,102	$22.08	8.5
1965	5,119	52.34	19.0	2,939	48.18	10.9	2,555	31.30	9.5
1966	5,475	56.24	18.8	3,345	59.75	11.4	2,660	29.38	9.1
1967	5,458	55.90	17.6	3,361	50.89	10.8	2,806	25.72	9.0
1968	5,436	45.25	15.8	3,686	55.06	10.7	3,161	34.00	9.2
1969	5,753	53.30	15.4	4,100	51.31	11.0	3,477	37.39	9.3
1970	5,664	50.13	13.1	4,860	68.89	11.2	3,736	39.77	8.6
1971	5,508	14.62	12.1	5,359	80.18	11.8	3,708	36.27	8.1

* Percentage of A&P sales to total grocery chain (11 or more units) sales.
Sources: Based on U.S. Dept. of Commerce reports, and Moody's. From Robert F. Hartley, *Marketing Mistakes*, (Columbus, Ohio: Grid, Inc., 1976), p. 102.

successful in achieving its goals through the discount strategy. In fact, the ultimate result was a disastrous effect on income. By 1974, A&P had fallen so far behind Safeway in total sales and income that it is unlikely the gap will be closed in the near future. Fortunately, A&P management learned a lesson well, and they have implemented a more comprehensive and successful competitive strategy in the wake of the WEO disaster.

Determining specific prices

The problem of setting actual prices generates much more specific information needs than policy and strategy decisions. The pricing process itself may be no more objective than policy and strategy decisions, but they tend to concentrate on narrower problems. Approaches to pricing can be grouped into four categories. These include cost-oriented pricing, market-oriented pricing, competition-oriented pricing, and combined cost and demand pricing. Each of these approaches is a different type of decision problem and leads to varying information requirements. Each one is discussed briefly in terms of the typical use of the approach and the type of information used in establishing a price.

Cost-oriented pricing. Cost-oriented approaches to pricing tend to be one of two types. The most common involves the use of markups or some type of predetermined percentage increase which is added to the cost of the product. The management problem in these cases is relatively simple, and the primary source of information is a standard percentage published either in a company guide book or some trade source. A grocer, for example, may purchase a case of canned vegetables for $7.20, or 30¢ per can. If the standard markup for that product is 15 percent, he simply adds $1.08 to the case cost to get $8.28, or 35¢ (rounded) per can. The cost of the product is information provided on invoice receipts, and the markup percentage is provided either by the company if the grocer is a member of a chain, or from a trade association publication if the grocer is independent.

Although the information involved in this type of pricing decision may seem overly simplified, the system is not without merit. The problem facing managers of certain types of businesses, such as retail food stores, is that they must price a very large number of items and change many of those prices frequently. The standard markup usually reflects historically profitable margins and provides a good guideline for pricing.

A somewhat more sophisticated approach to pricing is break-even analysis. The formula for calculating a break-even price is:

$$P = \frac{F + VQ}{Q}$$

Where

P = Break-even price
Q = Quantity
F = Fixed cost, and
V = Variable cost

The information required to utilize this formula is available from internal secondary sources. Specifically, the accounting information system (with appropriate reclassification for marketing information) provides the fixed and variable costs with which a schedule of break-even points can be derived. Assume, for example, that a firm has the following costs associated with a product:

F = $10,000
V = $1.00 per unit

Given these costs, a schedule of break-even prices can be calculated for various quantities as is illustrated in Table 12–8 and Figure 12–5.

Table 12–8
Sample break-even schedule

Fixed cost $(F) = \$10,000$
Variable cost $(V) = \$1.00$ per unit

$$p = \frac{F + VQ}{Q}$$

Quantity (Q)	Break-even price (P)
1,000	$11.00
2,000	6.00
3,000	4.33
4,000	3.50
5,000	3.00
6,000	2.67
7,000	2.43
8,000	2.25

Break-even pricing is a reasonable approach when there is a limit on the quantity which a firm can provide and particularly when a target return objective is sought. Assume, for example, that the firm with the costs illustrated in the previous example determines that it can provide no more than 10,000 units of the product in the next period of operation. Furthermore, the firm has set a target for profit of 20 percent above total costs. Referring again to internal accounting records and the marginal cost of production at near capacity levels, a new total cost curve is calculated. This new curve is illustrated in Figure 12–6. From the cost curve profile, management sets the desirable level of production at 80 percent of capacity, or 8,000 units. From the total cost curve in Figure 12–6, it is determined that the cost for

Figure 12–5
Break-even analysis

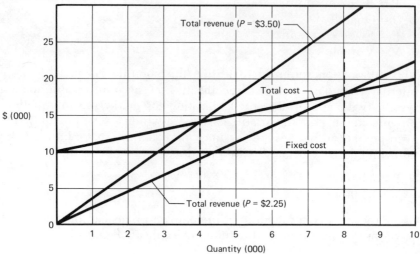

producing 8,000 units is $18,000. Twenty percent of $18,000 is $3,600. Adding this to the total cost at 8,000 units yields the point at that quantity through which the total revenue curve must pass. Finally, $21,600 divided by 8,000 units yields the price of $2.70 per unit. Thus, if 8,000 units are in fact produced and sold at $2.70 per unit, the $3,600 in profit would be realized. The obvious shortcoming of the break-

Figure 12–6
Break-even analysis for target return

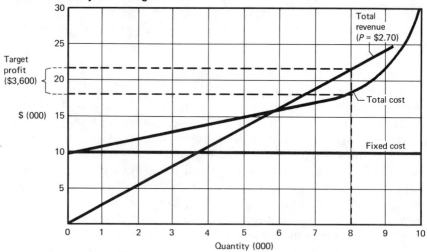

even approach to pricing is the absence of any information concerning the demand for the product at the desired price. It is assumed, that all of the units will be sold at the price which provides the desired return.

It would be necessary, therefore, to determine whether the desired price is in fact attractive to potential customers in the marketplace. If break-even pricing is to be used, it should be supplemented by additional information concerning customer perceptions of the relevant range of price for the product. The source of this information would most commonly be survey research, as well as a thorough review of pricing practices by competitors in the industry. In spite of their shortcomings, break-even pricing and target return pricing are very common business practices.

Market-oriented pricing. Frequently, managers are much more concerned with price-related information derived in the marketplace as an initial base for pricing decisions. This information is acquired from one or both of two sources, customers and/or competitors. Customer-based information provides estimates of the relationship between price and demand. Recall from the earlier discussion that firms in differentiated oligopolies are able to exercise some control over price within a relevant range. For these firms demand-oriented pricing is usually a matter of "price discrimination." Pricing which is based on competitive information can obviously rely on the going rate in the marketplace. A more difficult area of competitive pricing is competitive bidding. The problems and information requirements for each of the market-oriented pricing approaches are briefly illustrated in the following discussion.

The differentiated oligopolistic environment is created when a firm is able to discriminate on a profit basis, customer basis, location basis, or time basis. (Note that the term "discrimination" is not being used in the legal sense in this discussion. It refers rather to psychological or preference differences between customers which relate to different value sets for the same product.) For example, a television set in a simulated wood cabinet may be priced disproportionately higher than the same set in a plastic cabinet on the basis of the marginal difference in cost between the wood and plastic. Similarly, two people attending the same baseball game are willing to pay different prices depending upon their location, or proximity to the playing field.

Assume, for example, that a manufacturer produces his product in two versions, a regular model and a quality model.[19] Using past price and sales records, regression analysis was used to estimate the follow-

---

[19] This illustration of price discrimination is adapted from Philip Kotler, *Marketing Decision Making: A Model Building Approach* (New York: Holt, Rinehart and Winston, 1971), pp. 344–47.

ing demand functions for the two segments, and internal records have provided the following total revenue and cost equations:

$$\text{(Demand)}$$
$$Q_1 = 400 - 2P_1 \quad Q_2 = 150 - .5P_2$$

$$\text{(Revenue)}$$
$$R_1 = 200Q_1 - .5Q_1^2 \quad R_2 = 300Q_2 = 2Q_2^2$$

$$\text{(Cost)}$$
$$C = 10,000 + 2Q(Q_1 + Q_2)$$

where

Q_i = Quantity in segments i for $i = 1,2$;
P_i = Price in segments i for $i = 1,2$;
R_i = Total revenue in segment i for $i = 1,2$;
C = Total cost

Using the standard assumptions of the marginal analysis model, profits are maximized when marginal revenues in each segment equal marginal cost:

$$\frac{dR_1}{dQ_1} = \frac{dR_2}{dQ_2} = \frac{dC}{dQ}$$

or
$$200 - Q_1 = 300 - 4Q_2 = 20,$$

or
$$Q_1 = 180, \text{ and } Q_2 = 70.$$

Substituting Q_1 and Q_2 in the demand equations, we get:

$$P_1 = 110, \text{ and } P_2 = 160.$$

Finally, total profits would be:

$$Z = P_1Q_1 + P_2Q_2 - C(Q_1 + Q_2)$$
$$= (110)(180) + (160)(70) - (20)(250)$$
$$= 16,000.$$

Thus, if the seller sets the price for the regular model at $110 and the quality model at $160, he will sell 180 units and 70 units respectively to each segment at a total profit of $16,000.

It can be demonstrated that the seller cannot realize a higher profit by charging the two segments the same price. Starting with the same demand and cost functions, a uniform price for maximum profit is calculated as follows:

$$Q = Q_1 + Q_2 = 40C - 2P_1 + 150 - .5P_2$$
$$= 550 - 2.5P, \text{ the aggregate demand function}$$
$$Z = PQ - C$$
$$= P(550 - 2.5P) - [10,000 + (20)(550 - 2.5P)]$$
$$= -21,000 + 600P - 2.5P^2$$

Since profit is at a maximum when marginal profit is zero,

$$\frac{dZ}{dP} = 600 - 5P = 0$$
$$P = 120$$
and $$Z = 15,000$$

Price discrimination between the two segments provided an additional $1,000 in profit in this example. Therefore, firms who are faced with the prospect of price discrimination between segments must utilize both internal secondary sources of information (in order to develop appropriate cost functions) and demand analysis (to provide demand in the form of revenue functions).

Some firms, particularly smaller ones, are often faced with the dilemma of making pricing decisions when internal company records do not provide adequate cost information. This also applies to new firms, or firms which are entering a new area of business activity. In these cases, one of the best sources of information for pricing decisions is the pricing activity of competitors. As was the case with fixed industry margins, the assumption is that successful companies are selling products at prices which are attractive in the market and yield a profit. As additional information becomes available to the firm, more sophisticated pricing techniques can be employed.

Sometimes, relevant cost information is available, but the firm's primary concern is competitive reaction. This is particularly true of contract bidding. Models for competitive bidding can be quite complex. Since our purpose in this chapter is simply to illustrate the types of pricing problems which arise and the sources of information which enable managers to make good decisions, a simplified bidding model is illustrated below.

The basic model for competitive bidding treats the bid price as a variable which must usually exceed the seller's costs while remaining low enough to win the contract. The bids of competitors are not known, so a probability distribution is constructed for various bid prices. If a competitor has a known history of bidding, the probability distribution can be derived directly from that information. If the past behavior of competitors is not known, a probability distribution can be subjectively derived by assuming that competitors have similar costs. In Figure 12–7, for example, a bid of $25 has a 50 percent probability of being equal to or below the competitive bids. A higher bid, say $27, would contribute more profit but has a lower probability of winning.

The expected value of a given bid can be expressed as follows:

$$E(\text{Bid}) = (\text{Bid} - \text{Cost}) \times P(\text{Bid})$$

That is, the expected value of a bid is equal to the amount of the bid minus the estimated cost of fulfilling the contract times the probability

Figure 12-7
Probability distribution for winning at a bid price

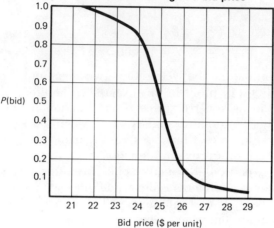

Bid price ($ per unit)

of winning with that bid. Expected values for the distribution in Figure 12-7 are listed in Table 12-9. The highest expected value ($1.70) is associated with a bid of $24.

The simple analysis described above is feasible only if certain conditions exist. One such condition is the initial assumption of a profit maximization objective. The cost of bidding is assumed to be negligible and has not affected the decision. Furthermore, in the simplest case, we assume that all bidders are known and that each bidder has the same costs. Finally, we would have to assume that no subjective preferences exist on the part of the contractor. That is, every company's probability of winning with a given bid is the same. Obviously, some combination of these constraints exist in most bidding situations, but the probability of all of them applying simultaneously is small. It is necessary, therefore, to acknowledge the implications associated with

Table 12-9
Expected value of a bid

Price	Price-cost ($22)	Probability of winning	E(bid)
$21	-$1	.99	-$ .99
22	0	.97	0.00
23	1	.94	.94
24	2	.85	1.70
25	3	.50	1.50
26	4	.15	.60
27	5	.06	.30
28	6	.05	.30
29	7	.04	.28

each condition if the model is to be a useful decision tool. Furthermore, the simple analysis described in this illustration is feasible only if certain conditions exist. For further information the reader should refer to the suggested readings at the end of the chapter.

Combining cost and demand.   At this point in most traditional discussions of pricing, reference would be made to marginal analysis. Simply put, marginal analysis is based on three assumptions: (1) the sole objective of a firm is to maximize profits, (2) profit is the difference between revenue and cost, and (3) demand and cost can be measured accurately for analysis. Given cost and revenue information, profit is maximized when marginal revenue equals marginal cost. That is, when the cost of producing a unit of output equals the marginal revenue added by placing that unit on the market, the level of output has been attained at which profits are maximized. As with earlier approaches to pricing, marginal analysis relies primarily upon internal secondary data and market surveys to provide the cost and demand information respectively.

The lack of attention devoted to techniques which combine demand estimates and internal cost information is not intended to deemphasize the importance of these approaches to pricing. Rather, they are relatively simple in their theoretical form, but extremely complex in their applied form. The development of marginal cost schedules requires extensive expense category definitions and policies concerning the handling of costs which many firms are reluctant to reveal. Similarly, demand estimates tend to be proprietary information for individual firms. Thus, it is difficult to provide a realistic illustration of this approach to pricing. Furthermore, it is seldom used as a sole approach or information base for price setting. Rather, marginal analysis may be used as an aid in combination with other information.

Additional comments on research for pricing

The treatment of pricing in this chapter has been deliberately simplified. Note, for example, that all of the techniques discussed are oriented to single product pricing. Furthermore, only the setting of base prices has been discussed. That is, the question of establishing discount schedules and other allowances has not been treated. These omissions are necessary given space limitations and an attempt to cover some relevant pricing topics well. One area, however, deserves some further elaboration. Managers often attempt to utilize consumer price perceptions when setting prices. That is, attempts to relate price and quality, the use of odd-ending pricing, and other strategies are not based upon economic or financial models but assume some psychological aspect of pricing.

Two areas in which price perception has been researched are price/quality relationships, and odd and even pricing. In the case of the former the assumption is that, within a relevant range, a higher price implies quality in a product. In the case of the latter, the theory suggests that a small fractional difference in price actually creates the impression of a nuch larger difference. For example, $1.97 would appear to be much less than $2.00. The typical approach used to study these theories is some kind of formal experiment. Since numerous experiments have failed to establish or refute the validity of these theories, it would be difficult to illustrate this type of research without citing numerous examples. The suggested readings at the end of the chapter include several references which illustrate this type of research in detail.

Summary of pricing research

As a decision variable, price is closely related to the product itself. Although it is often difficult to gain a competitive advantage through pricing strategy, it is easy to become noncompetitive through poor pricing practices. In this chapter, pricing decisions are treated in two broad categories: (1) setting price policies and (2) determining actual prices.

The most important factors bearing on price policy decisions are external environmental elements and internal constraints. Research for policy decisions, therefore, tends to rely heavily on studies of industry structure and examination of internal secondary data. This research reveals the nature of price as a competitive variable and constraints on the flexibility of pricing. Examples of an oil company and A&P were provided to illustrate the use of this type of information.

The problem of setting specific prices is one of the most perplexing problems facing marketing management. Approaches to this problem tend to be one of three types: (1) cost-oriented, (2) market-oriented, or (3) some combination of market and cost orientation. Each approach creates needs for different types of information.

Two approaches to cost-oriented pricing were illustrated. Perhaps the simplest pricing technique involves the use of markups. This type of pricing usually requires information from trade or company sources in order to determine appropriate markups over cost for each product. Thus, research for markup pricing focuses on secondary data sources, both internal and external.

Another cost-oriented approach is break-even analysis. If fixed and variable costs are known, a schedule of break-even prices and associated quantities can be calculated. Note, however, that the price/quantity schedule is not an estimated demand function. Rather, it represents combinations of price and quantity at which the firm will break even if the quantity is actually sold. In break-even analysis a price is usually selected at which a desired profit would be realized and a desired level of output capacity utilized. This target return approach was also illustrated in the earlier discussion.

Three types of market-oriented pricing were discussed. First, and simplest, is that of meeting competition. The research task becomes one of knowing what competitors are charging. This information is available from published external secondary sources, salesforce feedback, and observation. The problem of determining separate prices for differentiated products is considerably more complex. The illustration provided demonstrated the profit advantage of "price discrimination." This approach, however, requires estimates of both demand and cost functions. A single decision technique can thus require data from both consumer (or buyer) surveys and internal secondary sources.

The final illustration of market-oriented pricing involves competitive bidding. The most crucial input in determining a competitive bid is an estimate of the probability distribution of winning with a variety of prices. Given internal cost information, the profit associated with each price can be determined. Applying the probability distribution to profit calculations, the expected value of each bid price can then be determined. In even this simplified example, the research problem could involve an application of both jury of executive opinion (probability distribution) and internal secondary data (profit estimates).

The treatment of pricing decisions in this chapter is necessarily abbreviated. Since the combination of cost and market orientations usually involve theoretical marginal analyses, this approach is not illustrated. The reader is referred to suggested readings in economics listed at the end of the chapter. Other strategy related inputs which are not illustrated in the text involve customer perceptions of price.

DISCUSSION QUESTIONS

1. The president of Kinder Kom Company (producer and distributor of early age educational films) has been approached by several investor groups each interested in joint venture product development. Group A proposes to share with Kinder Kom in the development of a series of films on safety. The subjects would include bicycle safety, water sport safety, safety at home, and emergency first aid. These films would be aimed at the 9– to 12–year old age group and sold to schools, libraries, a variety of service agencies, and certain companies or trade groups.

   Group B has proposed the development of a series of science films for use in late elementary and intermediate grade level science instruction. Eight films are proposed featuring a variety of insects, wildlife, geography, and plant life. Although educational media centers constitute the major market, these films could also be sold to libraries.

Finally, group C has proposed a new concept for the distribution of popular literature. Specially designed racks would be placed in convenience outlets, such as supermarkets and drug stores. Publishers would contract for distribution of paperback editions directly through Kinder Kom/group C who would guarantee placement in a certain number of outlets. The retailer providing space and Kinder Kom/group C would receive commissions on gross sales for their respective services. Kinder Kom/group C would be responsible for inventory control and maintaining the displays. Finally, it was also suggested that the displays could contain rear screen projectors on which brief sound film loops could be played to highlight several of the currently popular books.

All three proposals are at the idea stage. The president of Kinder Kom is concerned that all three diverge from the firm's traditional products and exclusively school-oriented market. On the other hand, he recognizes a need for diversification to maintain continued growth. How should he go about evaluating the three ideas? What information is required, and how could it be obtained?

2. Mr. Owens, Marketing Manager for BOXT, Inc., is faced with the problem of establishing a price for a new product, a consumer electric appliance. BOXT is new to the consumer market having operated with only industrial products in the past. The new item is produced on an assembly line which has a capacity of 20,000 units per year. Each line requires an investment (equipment and start up costs) of $1 million. The costs associated with producing the product are:

Fixed cost:	$500,000/yr.
Variable costs:	$10/unit @ .75-1.00% capacity
	$12/unit @ .50-.74% capacity
	$15/unit @ below .50% capacity

Furthermore, the BOXT board of directors requires a 10 percent first year return on all new product investment dollars.

The product is available in varying levels of quality and with different features for retail prices ranging between $65 and $75 (inclusive). All distribution will be handled through distributors who sell to retailers. The combined margin for distributors and retailers is 40 percent of the retail price. The BOXT version of the product has average features and above average quality. Assuming that BOXT can only invest in one production line and that no additional information is available, what price should Mr. Owens recommend? What additional information would Mr. Owens need to make a more relevant decision, and how would he acquire that information?

SELECTED REFERENCES

Alford, Charles L. and Mason, J. B.   "Generating New Product Ideas," *Journal of Advertising Research*, vol. 15 (December 1975), pp. 27–32.

Banks, Seymour.   "The Relationship between Preference and Purchase of Brands." *Journal of Marketing*, vol. 15 (October 1950), p. 145–57.

Edelman, Franz.   "Art and Science of Competitive Bidding." *Harvard Business Review*, vol. 43 (July–August 1965), p. 53–66.

Green, Paul E.   "Bayesian Decision Theory in Pricing Strategy." *Journal of Marketing*, vol. 27 (January 1963), p. 5–14.

Monroe, Kent B.   "Buyers' Subjective Perceptions of Price." *Journal of Marketing Research*, vol. 10 (February 1973), p. 70–80.

Morgenroth, William M.   "A Method for Understanding Price Determinants." *Journal of Marketing Research*, vol. 1 (August 1964), p. 17–26.

Pessemier, Edgar A., and Root, H. Paul.   "The Dimensions of New Product Planning." *Journal of Marketing*, vol. 37 (January 1973), p. 10–18.

Richman, Barry M.   "A Rating Scale for Product Innovation." *Business Horizons*, vol. 5 (Summer 1962), p. 37–44.

Scheuing, Everhard E.   *New Product Management*. New York: The Dryden Press, 1974.

Walker, Arleigh W.   "How to Price Industrial Products." *Harvard Business Review*, vol. 45 (September–October 1967), p. 125–32.

Wentz, Walter B., and Eyrich, Gerald I.   *Marketing: Theory and Application*. New York: Harcourt, Brace and World, Inc., 1970, p. 235–89.

chapter

13

Research for distribution and promotion decisions

Decisions and information needs associated with distribution and promotion are more concerned with the management of organizations and activities than with the relatively conceptual nature of product and pricing decisions. Included in the area of distribution are channel structure, institutions (such as retailing management), physical distribution, and logistics. Promotion, sometimes referred to as marketing communications, includes advertising, personal selling, sales promotion, public relations, and publicity. This broad base of activity has resulted in significant managerial specialization. That is, advertising tends to be looked upon as a unique decision area rather than an integral component of promotion. Advertising, sales management, and other promotion decisions are often made in relative isolation. The same is true for channel design and physical distribution decisions. Thus, no convenient interrelated framework is available which provides a logical sequencing of the following discussion.

The coverage of illustrations in this chapter is necessarily limited to a small sample of selected aspects of these two broad decision areas. In the following sections, several research methodologies are illustrated in the context of channel structure and retail management. A subsequent section illustrates research in the areas of advertising, sales promotion, and sales management.

SECTION A: RESEARCH FOR DISTRIBUTION DECISIONS

The traditional view of marketing channels is taken from the perspective of the manufacturer in the case of consumer goods. Although the manufacturer is not always the primary force in a channel structure, it is convenient to think of one institution within the channel as the prevailing source of power. Since the purpose of this discussion is to illustrate research applications in channel decisions, a more thorough treatment of channel theory is left to other sources. The following discussion draws upon two illustrations of channel structure and conflict resolution which are not intended to represent all of their respective areas of decision making. In the first case, the classification of consumer goods is examined as a basis for channel structure. In the second, a case study involving a manufacturer of consumer durable goods is used to illustrate the type of research involved in identifying channel conflict and the means of conflict resolution. Illustrations of retail location strategy and a stock-out cost model are also presented.

Determining bases for channel design

For many years the classification of consumer goods has been considered as an important basis for determining channel structure. For example, a convenience good, such as razor blades, would require intensive distribution with several intermediaries in the channel. This would enable concentrated manufacturers to approach a widespread market through the successively increasing geographic coverage of each channel member, culminating in the retailer. Traditionally, the method of classifying good relied heavily on existing marketing practices associated with the same or similar products. Furthermore, products tended to be categorized as generically one type; razor blades would be classified as convenience goods only and require intensive distribution. If a large number of consumers consider razor blades as a specialty good, however, exclusive distribution might be more appropriate for that segment.

In a recent study an attempt was made to measure consumer goods classifications based directly upon the perceptions of consumers.[1] Since the definitions of the classifications imply consumer behavior, it is reasonable to classify any given product in terms of the consumer's point of view. Using this approach, a manufacturer can determine the classification which best fits his particular product concept without relying entirely on his intuitive feel for similar products on the market. The study involved a survey of consumers. The respondents were given a questionnaire and asked to respond to statements which would provide the researchers with the basis for classifying a series of products for each individual consumer. A given product could be clas-

---

[1] This illustration is adapted from Barnett Greenberg and Danny Bellenger, "The Classification of Consumer Goods: An Empirical Study," Research Monograph No. 56, School of Business Administration, Georgia State University, Atlanta, Ga., 1974.

sified as a convenience good for one respondent and as a specialty good for another.

Four factors were considered important for determining in what class the consumer viewed the product. These were potential needs for the product, intention to buy within the foreseeable future, willingness to shop, and brand preference. The series of questions used to provide this information is illustrated in Figure 13–1.

Figure 13–1
Questions used to determine classification of goods

a. Do you now or will you in the future have any potential use for
_____ ?   Yes _____   No _____

b. Are you likely to buy _____ within the next (time period specified)?   _____ Yes   _____ No
(If the answer to *(b)* is yes, please answer *(c), (d)* and *(e)*)

c. How much time and effort are you willing to spend shopping for this product? (Shopping includes all forms of information seeking, as well as in-store searching.)

Very   A large
little · _____ · _____ · _____ · _____ · _____ · _____ · amount
    1   2   3   4   5   6   7

(Check the number that indicates your willingness to shop.)

d. How much preference do you have for some specific brand of this product?

                                          Insist
                                       on one
          No   particular
preference · _____ · _____ · _____ · _____ · _____ · _____ · brand
      1   2   3   4   5   6   7

Source: Barnett A. Greenberg and Danny N. Bellenger, "The Classification of Consumer Goods: An Empirical Study," Research Monograph No. 56, School of Business Administration, Georgia State University, Atlanta, Georgia, 1974, p. 22.

Referring to Figure 13–1, the various combinations which would lead to a particular classification are described as follows:

If the person answered NO to *(a)* he was assumed to be "Not in the Market" for the given product. This is, of course, not a product class, but is essentially a screening device. If he answered YES to *(a)* but NO to *(b)* the product was classified as an unsought good for the consumer. A yes on both *(a)* and *(b)* means the product is either a convenience, shopping or specialty good. Questions *(c)* and *(d)* were used to determine the exact class. If the respondent circled 1–4 on question *(c)* the product was classified as a convenience good for that consumer. A 5–7 on *(c)* and a 1–4 on *(d)* was classified as a shopping good. A 5–7 on *(c)* and a 5–7 on *(d)* was classified as a specialty good. These are the operational definitions of the consumer perceived product class used in the study.[2]

The findings had some particularly interesting implications for distribution strategy. With the exception of razor blades and high-quality golf clubs, the responses of consumers led to classifications across the entire scale. The distributions for automobile tires and high-quality cameras are clearly illustrated in Figure 13–2 and Figure 13–3 respectively.

Figure 13–2
Consumers per product class for automobile tires

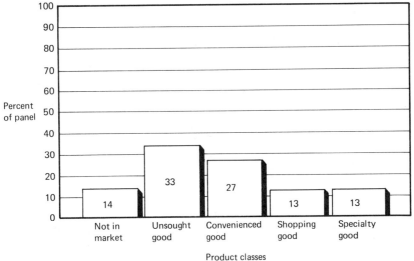

(N = 205)

Source: Barnett A. Greenberg and Danny N. Bellenger, "The Classification of Consumer Goods: An Empirical Study," Research Monograph No. 56, School of Business Administration, Georgia State University, Atlanta, Georgia, 1974, p. 21.

Traditionally, automobile tires were viewed as shopping goods. This classification would lead a manufacturer to adopt a "selective" policy in channel design for distribution through retail outlets with a particular emphasis on in-store promotion and personal selling. Figure 13–2, however, suggests that an equal number of consumers perceived automobile tires as specialty goods, while twice as many perceived them to be convenience goods. Thus, if a major brand manufacturer of automobile tires wanted full coverage of a market it would have to seek three different approaches to channel design. Obviously, these different classifications also imply the need for product differentiation.

[2] Ibid. p. 15–16.

Figure 13–3
Consumers per product class for high-quality camera (over $200)

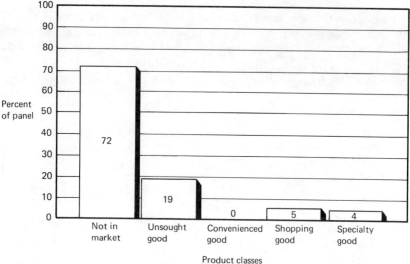

(*N* = 205)

Source: Barnett A. Greenberg and Danny N. Bellenger, "The Classification of Consumer Goods: An Empirical Study," Research Monograph No. 56, School of Business Administration, Georgia State University, Atlanta, Georgia, 1974, p. 22.

In Figure 13–3 we note that most of the consumers in the survey were not in the market for high-quality cameras. Of those who were, however, an almost equal number perceived the product to be a shopppng good as did those who perceived it to be a specialty good. Thus, a manufacturer of high-quality cameras could differentiate a product for more intensive distribution through multiple brands. This would allow the firm to maintain highly selective (exclusive) distribution for a specialty brand, while seeking additional market penetration through somewhat less selective distribution with a different brand. This study clearly demonstrates the possibility of additional market potential for manufacturers who have viewed their products in terms of only one consumer goods class.

Identifying channel conflict and sources of conflict resolution

Although the development of marketing channels for the distribution of products is an important decision area for management, a more common problem area concerns the effectiveness of existing channels. The subject of conflict and its resolution is of considerable interest to marketing managers. An interesting study of conflict by Rosenberg involves a three-level contractual marketing system for a specific branded product.[3] "The components of this channel system consist of the manufacturer, a set of distributors within a specific geographic region of the company's operations, and a set of dealers within that region.[4] The product will simply be referred to as Brand X, an expensive (about $500) household durable good. The subject of this particular study was restricted to the distribution of the product to consumers. Management was concerned with achieving effective and efficient channel performance through a minimization of intrachannel conflict.

The questionnaire used to gather information from channel members is described by the researcher as follows:

A field instrument, with several modifications for each class of organizations in the case study channel system, follows from the following research objectives: (1) to obtain attitudinal data on conflict issues; (2) to devise an operational measure of the intensity of conflict; and (3) to secure descriptions of overt conflict behavior. The questions to each channel segment are similar in content and format, since the instrument must satisfy both mail and personal interviewing requirements.

Three versions of the research instrument, one for each class of members, each contain two major sections: (1) two sets of conflict issues and (2) a conflict incidents reporting form. In the first section, two conflict issue sets for each organization are selected from the three sets available for all intrachannel dyads—manufacturer-distributors . . . , distributors-dealers . . . , and manufacturers-dealers. . . . (See Figure 13–4 for sample sets.) Each firm completed those two sets applicable to the dyads of which it is a member. The respondent can state his opinion, which he believes to be in his company's best interests, on a Likert-type scale of five choices: *strongly agree, agree, neutral, disagree, and strongly disagree.*

While the first major section of the instrument treats conflict issues which may be covert, the second contains an open-ended part in which the respondent is asked to recall three important disputes with the two reciprocal channel organizations. These descriptions are intended to spotlight overt episodes of conflict. A dispute is denoted as a complaint, discussion, or demand concerning an issue or problem about which the respondent became actively involved along with either of the other two firms. Descriptions of disputes, at best, include who participated, nature of disagreement, why it came about, and how it was or was not resolved. Along with the description of the incident, the tension level of the participants is recorded on a five-point scale: very high, high, medium, low, and very low. The tension level is designed to reflect the perceived magnitude of the disputed issue, and the emotional feelings generated through direct involvement.[5]

---

[3] This illustration is adapted from Larry J. Rosenberg, "An Empirical Examination of the Causes, Level, and Consequences of Conflict in a High Stake Distribution Channel," (dissertation, The Ohio State University, Columbus, Ohio, 1969).

[4] Ibid., p. 151.

[5] Ibid., pp. 46–50.

Figure 13–4
Sample items for three dyads in channel conflict questionnaire

Manufacturer-distributors issue set:

1. Manufacturer is dominant in the relationship between manufacturer and distributor and that is the way it should be.
2. As a part of the manufacturer's selling thrust, distributor does not want to sacrifice his independence and discretion over his own business.
3. When manufacturer is out of a specific product, distributor should not have to pay freight costs when the product is sent from another distributor.
4. Manufacturer should want to settle for a somewhat reduced profit if it means his distributors can obtain an increased profit figure.
5. Manufacturer has a significantly higher concentration of knowledge and experience in industry problems than does distributor.
6. Distributor should be entitled to higher quality discounts on very large orders.
7. Distributor is willing to compete vigorously to increase Brand X's share of market in distributor's territory.

Distributors-dealers issue set:

1. When dealer has a serious complaint, he has the right to go over the distributor's head and discuss the matter with manufacturer.
2. Dealer is not promotional-minded enough in his pursuit of business.
3. Distributor's net profit as a percent of sales of Brand X is higher than dealer's.
4. Dealer's complaints to distributor are caused by dealer's desire to be able to satisfy fully his customers.
5. When dealer returns a defective product, dealer should not have to incur any cost, like payment of handling charges.
6. In setting the minimum level of inventory to be carried by dealer, the dealer should make the final decision.
7. Distributor is inflexible in that he does things by the book with little regard for exceptions.
8. When dealer returns a defective part to obtain credit, he should not have to pay the bill for the replacement part when it is due.
9. Dealer is always pressuring distributor to do more for him, because dealer wants to avoid some responsibilities and the costs incurred when dealer performs them.
10. Distributor has the right to set sales quotas for dealer and to hold dealer accountable for meeting them.
11. The more distributor helps dealer run his business, the greater will be dealer's sales volume.

Manufacturer-dealers issue set:

1. If manufacturer is to be the leader in the industry, he should be constantly expanding his sales volume.
2. Where breakdowns can be traced to manufacturer's fault, dealer should receive both a labor and materials allowance from manufacturer.

Figure 13–4 (continued)

3. Items to dealer's advantage to add major sidelines to its business, rather than to concentrate fully on the primary product of Brand X.
4. Manufacturer should have detailed and timely information about his dealer's business.
5. Dealer sacrifices his identification and individuality when he joins manufacturer's distribution system.
6. When it is difficult to determine who was responsible for the product's breaking down, repair costs should be absorbed by manufacturer (who is best able to assume them).
7. Manufacturer's suggested accounting system for dealer should be used by all dealers.
8. Dealer's ability to install and service a Brand X unit for the customer is more important than manufacturer's ability to produce the best quality brand in the industry.
9. Dealer's showroom area is very well maintained for customer demonstrations.

The questionnaire was administered to key headquarters executives and members of a selected regional field office staff as a representative group for the manufacturer. Within the region, 11 of 14 distributors agreed to be interviewed. Finally, the questionnaire was sent to the 250 dealers who operated within the territories of the 11 distributors. Questionnaires were returned by 87 of those dealers for a 35 percent response rate. Only the results of the manufacturer distributor dyad will be illustrated in the interests of conserving space. Taking the 32 issues in the first part of the questionnaire and using the t-test for the differences between manufacturers' and distributors' responses, the researcher derived the information in Figure 13–4. Notice that the items selected for illustration in Table 13–1 for this dyad relate to the 10 conflict issues for which the t-test was significant at the .05 level. (The same holds true for the other dyads, although the results of the t-tests are not illustrated.) As expected, item 13 indicates that distributors felt that manufacturers should sacrifice profit somewhat if it meant increased profits for the distributor. Although this finding is to be expected, it is important to note the strength of the t-test and its position relative to the other conflict issues.

Recall that the second section of the questionnaire allowed each member of the dyad to indicate specific issues which had actually arisen as disputes. The results for this part of the questionnaire for the manufacturer-distributor dyad are illustrated in Table 13–2. Notice that product unavailability was regarded as the primary area of dispute both by the manufacturer and the distributors. The other areas of dispute ranked by level of tension are also illustrated in the table. The

Table 13–1
List of ten highest conflict issues between manufacturer and distributors

Rank	Item no.	Issue	t*
1	13	Manufacturer's profit expectations	4.8077†
2	29	Distributor's competitive vigor	3.6079†
3	16	Knowledge of industry problems	3.5720†
4	6	Distributor's payment of freight costs	2.5760†
5	3	Dominance of manufacturer	−2.5643†
6	18	Quantity discounts to distributor	2.2978†
7	5	Distributor's independence	2.1534†
8	19	Manufacturer's product shortages	−2.0381
9	32	Manufacturer's accounting system for distributor	1.9311
10	22	Share of dealer training	1.8707

* A positive sign indicates that distributors agreed with the item more than the manufacturer; a negative signifies that the manufacturer agreed more than distributors.
† Significant at .05 level (P = 2.080, df = 21).
Source: Larry J. Rosenberg, "An Empirical Examination of the Causes, Level, and Consequences of Conflict in a High Stake Distribution Channel," (dissertation, the Ohio State University, Columbus, Ohio, 1969), p. 87.

total information provided in this type of study enables the manufacturer, in this case the selector of the channel, to understand areas in which conflict arises, the intensity of conflict, and the specific activities which would reduce conflict. Although some contend that marketing channels are not managed as a total system, it is obvious that those firms interested in their vertical channel relationships would benefit from the type of research described here. The manufacturer might discover, for example, that improvements in inventory controls would result in increased sales and a reduction of conflict.

Retail location strategy

The two previous illustrations of research in the area of marketing channels emphasized the broad scope problems of total channel management. Some of the more common and better developed areas of decision making involve the problems of specific channel institutions. The most numerous of these institutions are the retailers.

Since the purpose of the retailer is to collect an assortment of goods and make them available to a relatively restricted geographic market, the location of the retailing establishment is of particular importance. The subject of the following example is the "Suburban Financial Corporation (fictitious name)."[6] As a holding company for a chain of sav-

---

[6] This illustration is adapted from C. Joseph Clawson, "Fitting Branch Locations, Performance Standards, and Marketing Strategies to Local Conditions," *Journal of Marketing*, vol. 38 (January 1974), pp. 8–14.

Table 13–2
Issues embodied in conflict incidents occurring in the manufacturer-distributors dyad

	Very high	High	Medium	Low	Very low	Total
	Tension level					

	Very high	High	Medium	Low	Very low	Total
Reported by manufacturer regarding distributors						
1. Equipment unavailability and allocation	2	3	1			6
2. Product quality and defects	1	2	2	1		6
3. Service problems by distributor's personnel	1	3				4
4. Ineffective communication—verbal and computer	1	1	1			3
5. Warranty administration			2			2
6. Distributor cash flow tightness				2		2
7. Documenting rebates and payments		1				1
8. Loss and damages in delivery		1				1
9. Competition with manufacturer's sister corporation		1				1
10. Documenting advertising expenditures		1				1
11. Weak market penetration by distributor		1				1
12. Violation of sales policy			1			1
13. Price protection policy			1			1
14. Incentive trip payment			1			1
15. Gaps in product line			1			1
Total	5	14	10	3	0	32
Reported by distributors regarding manufacturer						
1. Product unavailability	1	3	2			6
2. Inadequacy of new products	1	3	1			5
3. Ineffective communication for problem solving	1	2	1			4
4. Product quality and defects	2	1				3
5. Unavailability of special parts	2					2
6. Faulty sales forecasting	2					2
7. Pricing and bidding matters	1		1			2
8. Competition from manufacturer's sister corporation	1					1
9. Unmet rural distributors' needs			1			1
10. Damages due to packing				1		1
11. Off-season financing burden				1		1
Total	11	9	6	2	0	28

Source: Larry J. Rosenberg, "An Empirical Examination of the Causes, Level, and Consequences of Conflict in a High Stake Distribution Channel," (dissertation, The Ohio State University, 1969), p. 103.

ings and loan associations, SFC is concerned with its ability to pene-
trate the various market opportunities within a community. One of the
key strategy ingredients is the successful location of retail outlets
which offer the proper mix of financial services.

After studying the situation in the community of interest and previous research findings, SFC has identified one particular outcome of its
strategy decisions which is a particularly important performance criterion. The outcome is the "net savings gain" of each individual branch.
Also, three general blocks of variables which should lead to performance are population, competition, and branch characteristics. A total
of 24 variables were identified in these three areas which appear relevant to net savings gain. Including the dependent variable, a total of
25 variables are listed in Table 13–3 along with the units of measurement and mean values for those variables for the 26 branches involved
in this particular study. The data which was required to quantify the
variables was gathered from a number of sources including both internal and external secondary sources, and internal and external primary
sources. For example, variable X_2, renter-occupied dwellings, is obtained from census data. On the other hand, variable X_{23}, exterior attractiveness, is obtained by the jury of executive opinion. The procedure in the case of the latter was as follows:

Ratings of exterior attractiveness, interior decor, and parking adequacy for the
26 SFC branches were based on a consensus of executive researcher judgments. They ranged from a low rating of 1 to a high rating of 5.[7]

Notice that the preceding discussion reveals variables which were
"hypothesized," or developed through exploratory research. A method
of analysis was selected in this study which would help identify those
specific variables which are most relevant in determining net savings
gains at a particular branch. Specifically, the use of step-wise regression analysis was employed.[8] In the step-wise procedure variables are
brought into the analysis on the basis of incremental R^2. The summary
of results illustrated in Table 13–4 include the ten independent variables which increased R^2 by at least .01. They are listed in the same
order by which they entered the regression formula.

As illustrated in Table 13–4, the most significant variable in determining the net savings gain for an SFC branch is the average net gain

---

[7] Ibid., p. 10.

[8] The application of step-wise regression in this particular case is questioned in Mark
I. Alpert and Jon L. Bibb, "Fitting Branch Location, Performance Standards, and Marketing Strategies: A Clarification," *Journal of Marketing*, vol. 38 (April 1974), pp. 72–74.
Nevertheless, this illustration serves as a good example of a situation in which this
approach is useful.

Table 13–3
List of variables analyzed in regression study of 26 branches

		Units	Mean
Dependent variable			
X_1	Net savings gain, 12 months, in branch	$000	3,341
Population block (P)			
X_2	Renter-occupied dwellings	%	50.9
X_3	S—L savings per capita (total savings held in all local S&L facilities, divided by local population)	$	2,645
X_4	Income per capita	$	3,492
X_5	Median value of owner-occupied homes	$	30,247
X_6	Persons age 45–64	%	22.8
X_7	Persons age 65 and over	%	11.1
Competition block (C)			
X_8	Competing S&L facilities	No.	4.3
X_9	Population per S&L facility	No.	18,361
X_{10}	Commercial bank facilities	No.	10.5
X_{11}	Average net savings gain of local S&L competitors, 12 months	$000	2,970
X_{12}	Share of total local S&L savings held by local main and executive offices of competitors	%	27.2
X_{13}	Branch of Colossal S&L Association nearby	1 or 0	0.27
X_{14}	Total assets of competing S&L associations having local branches	$000,000	2,742
Branch block (B)			
X_{15}	Retail sales per year within one-half mile radius of SFC branch	$000,000	46.7
X_{16}	Branch inside formal shopping center	1 or 0	0.15
X_{17}	Branch opposite formal center	1 or 0	0.15
X_{18}	Branch approaching formal center	1 or 0	0.04
X_{19}	Branch in central business district	1 or 0	0.50
X_{20}	Branch in free-standing building	1 or 0	0.81
X_{21}	Age of branch	Years	13.1
X_{22}	Exterior attractiveness (rating)	1–5	3.3
X_{23}	Interior decor (rating)	1–5	3.8
X_{24}	Parking adequacy (rating)	1–5	3.6
X_{25}	Branch advertising and promotion cost	$000	23.3

Source: C. Joseph Clawson, "Fitting Branch Locations, Performance Standards, and Marketing Strategies to Local Conditions," *Journal of Marketing*, vol. 38 (January 1974), p. 10, published by the American Marketing Association.

by competitors in the same market area. This is reflected by the R^2 for variable X_{11} of .449. A negative coefficient, such as for variable X_{12}, means that the variable represents a detractor for SFC branch net savings gain. In the case of X_{12} the presence of main and executive offices of competitors in a branch area tends to lessen that branch's ability to perform in terms of net savings gain.

Assume that SFC is now contemplating opening branch #27 in the same major community. The formula from Table 13–4 is reproduced in Table 13–5 along with the values for the proposed branch and the

Table 13–4
Summary of major relationships revealed in formula for net savings gain

Variable number	Description*	Block	Regression coefficient	Initial increase in R*	Final t-value
X_{11}	Average net gain by competitors	C	0.708	.449	3.59
X_6	Age 45–64	P	147.191	.147	1.39
X_{22}	Exterior attractiveness	B	131.404	.106	3.25
X_4	Income per capita	P	1.142	.053	2.53
X_{25}	Local promotion	B	29.987	.029	2.54
X_{12}	Main and executive offices	C	−35.401	.036	−2.99
X_8	Population per S&L facility	C	0.087	.035	3.16
X_{15}	Retail sales	B	20.531	.028	2.30
X_2	Renters	P	−52.925	.019	−2.23
X_{18}	Approaching center	B	−2505.012	.013	−1.51
—	(Intercept)		−9342.863		

* Units are shown in Table 13–3.
Source: C. Joseph Clawson, "Fitting Locations, Performance Standards and Marketing Strategies to Local Conditions," *Journal of Marketing*, vol. 38 (January 1974), p. 11, published by the American Marketing Association.

estimated net savings gain for the branch. Given the variables which contribute to net savings gain, and the anticipated gain from the analysis, SFC can make a decision concerning the feasibility of proceeding with branch #27. It is important to note, however, that this analysis provides only a portion of the information required in a location decision. Other factors, such as local restrictions, the availability of desirable property, and short-term capital availability must also be considered. Nevertheless, any location decision which is made without the benefit of this type or some similar form of analysis carries an extremely high risk of failure.

Research for retail management: A stock-out cost model

One of the most perplexing problems facing the retailer is that of maintaining a sufficient inventory of each product to insure adequate customer service while, at the same time, minimizing costs. A number of models exist which deal with the question of reorder points, but the question of stock out cost is frequently treated in an unrealistic manner. An interesting study reported by Walter & Grabner represents an attempt "to explore a method of determining consumer reaction to

Table 13-5
Calculation of estimated net savings gain for any branch (illustrated for branch 27)

No.	Description	Regression coefficient*	Value for branch 27	Contribution to estimated net savings gain ($000) Branch 27†	All-branch average‡	Difference§
X_{11}	Avg. gain of competitors	0.708	$1,362	$ 964	$2,102	$-1,138
X_6	Age 45–64	147.191	25.6%	3,768	3,360	+ 408
X_{22}	Ext. attractiveness	1131.404	3	3,394	3,742	− 348
X_4	Income/cap.	1.142	$3,667	4,187	3,986	+ 201
X_{25}	Local prom.	29.987	$ 4	120	699	− 579
X_{12}	Main and exec. offices	−35.401	0	0	− 964	+ 964
X_9	Population per facil.	0.087	1,3751	1,196	1,590	− 394
X_{15}	Retail sales	20.531	$ 30	616	959	− 343
X_2	Renters	−52.925	32.2%	−1,704	−2,696	+ 992
X_{18}	Approaching center	−2505.012	0	0	− 96	+ 96
—	(Intercept)	−9342.863		−9,343	−9,343	0
	Estimated net savings gain ($000)			$3,198	$3,339	$− 141
	Actual net savings gain ($000)			3,304	3,339‖	− 35
	Residual (actual-estimated)			$ 106	0	+ 106

* From Table 13–4.
† Arrived at by multiplying first two columns of this table.
‡ Arrived at by multiplying first column of Table 13–5 by second column of Table 13–3.
§ Difference between branch 27 contribution and all-branch average contribution: advantage (+), disadvantage (−).
‖ Differs from $3341 in Table 13–3 due to rounding.
Source: C. Joseph Clawson, "Fitting Branch Locations, Performance Standards, and Marketing Strategies to Local Conditions," *Journal of Marketing*, Vol. 38 (January 1974), p. 12, published by the American Marketing Association.

retail stock out situations, and to demonstrate how varying responses can be translated into an economic cost to the retailer of being out of stock on any one particular item."[9]

The basic stock out model used in the study is illustrated in Figure 13–5. The model assumes that a customer intends to purchase a specific brand and a specific size and price item within that brand. Faced with an in-stock situation, the customer would simply proceed to purchase the item. Faced with an out-of-stock situation, the customer would proceed either to substitute at the same store, postpone the purchase until another visit, or visit another source. In the event of

---

[9] This illustration is adapted from C. K. Walter and John R. Grabner, "Stock-Out Cost Models: Empirical Tests in a Retail Situation," *Journal of Marketing*, vol. 39 (July 1975), pp. 56–60.

Figure 13–5
Basic stock-out model

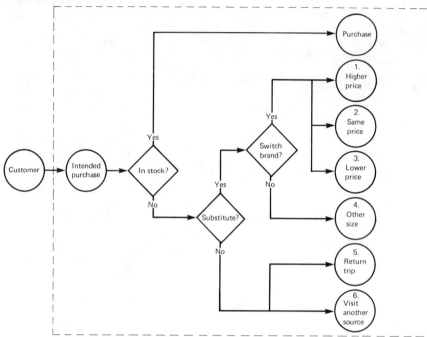

Source: C. K. Walter and John R. Grabner, "Stock Out Cost Models: Empirical Tests in a Retail Situation," *Journal of Marketing*, vol. 39 (July 1975), p. 57, published by the American Marketing Association.

substitution, the customer would either select another size in the same brand or switch brands.

"Each alternative has an economic consequence, which is measurable in terms of the revenue difference, RD, between the intended purchase and the actual purchase."[10] In the stock-out case the revenue difference for the retailer is zero if the brand switch to another item of the same price occurs. Similarly, the revenue difference over time is zero if the item is in stock and purchased on a return trip. The worst case is the complete loss of a sale in the event of no substitution and a visit to another source. Thus, the basic model for RD involves a simple calculation of the actual revenue differences between the intended purchase and actual purchase, times the probability of each occurrence. In the particular study reported by Walter and Grabner, two additional modifications are provided to account for lost consumption during the period of time that a customer waits for the product to be in

[10] Ibid., p. 57.

stock and to allow quantities other than single units in the purchase intentions. The general case revenue difference equation is:

$$RD = [(UA \cdot PA) - (UO \cdot PO) - (AU \cdot WT \cdot PA)]$$

Where:

UA = Units actually purchased
UO = Units desired by out of stock
PO = Price of out-of-stock item
PA = Price of item actually purchased
AU = Annual number of units of the item purchased under in-stock
         conditions
WT = Waiting time as a fraction of a year

In order to test the model, Walter and Grabner solicited the aid of the Ohio Department of Liquor Control. By using the state controlled liquor stores the researchers were able to make certain simplifying assumptions about the test. For the most part, price as a competitive tool and most promotional activities were eliminated from the market, since they are not allowed in the sale of liquor in Ohio. Stock outs do occur in the state controlled stores, however, and the product and retail distribution system did provide a realistic base for the test.

The data collection procedure was described as follows:

A questionnaire was designed to elicit customer reaction to stock out conditions. A total of 14,820 questionnaires were delivered to ten stores throughout Ohio for distribution to customers. The store cashier included a questionnaire and a postage-paid business reply envelope in the sack with each purchase made over a three-day weekend period. In most instances, the customer first encountered the questionnaire when he removed the bottles from the sack . . . This procedure was chosen to insure the privacy and anonymity of the customers, since they were considered to be particularly sensitive to questions pertaining to liquor products. Questionnaires in usable form were received from 1,433 respondents. . . .

Multiple-choice questions were used to ascertain customer's reactions to stockouts of the brand and size of the product they intended to purchase when they entered the store. Responses were tabulated to determine the relative frequency of the types of possible behavior included in the stockout model. Each respondent was also asked to supply information about the number of times per month he typically visited the liquor store.[11]

The results of the study can be viewed in terms of a basic model or as a repeated stockout model. The former case (basic model) for the Ohio study is illustrated in Table 13–6. The various alternatives facing

[11] Ibid., p. 58.

Table 13–6
Basic stock-out model parameters

Alternatives	Revenue difference ($)	Proba- bility	Expected value ($)
Higher price	+ .61	.026	+.02
Same price	.00	.591	.00
Lower price	− .61	.024	−.01
Other size*	−1.93	.193	−.37
Return trip†	−6.61	.025	−.17
Other source‡	−5.21	.141	−.73
Expected monetary cost/unit of unfilled demand			−$1.26

* Revenue difference is the weighted average price difference between fifths and pints of the top five brands, accounting for 22% of total liquor sales. *Source:* Cleveland Press, *Ohio Liquor Sales: 36th Annual Analysis* (Cleveland: Cleveland Press, 1970), p. ix.

† It was assumed that the desired item was available one week later. Median number purchased per year = 66. RD = $5.21 · 66 · 1/52.

‡ Revenue difference was the weighted average price of a fifth of a gallon bottle of each of the top five brands. *Source:* Cleveland Press, *Ohio Liquor Sales*, p. ix.

Source: C. K. Walter and John R. Grabner, "Stock-out Cost Models: Empirical Tests in a Retail Situation," *Journal of Marketing*, vol. 39 (July 1975), p. 58, published by the American Marketing Association.

a consumer in the event of a stock out are listed in the left hand column. The probabilities of the alternatives are "The relative frequencies with which each alternative was exercised, measured from the collected data . . ."[12] The average single stock-out cost of $1.26 is "the expected revenue difference between what would have been received by the store had the stock out not occurred and what was actually received from each customer who encountered a stock out."[13] If, for example, a particular product is sold at an average daily rate of ten units, the daily expected cost of being out-of-stock of that item would be $12.60, assuming that the stockout persisted through an entire day.

To test the case of a repeated stockout model, "The questionnaire also asks the respondent what he would do on his next shopping trip if a desired item had been out of stock on his two previous trips."[14] The results for the repeated model appear in Table 13–7. Notice that the average expected monetary cost of being out of stock several times is $2.49 for the retail store only. That is, the Ohio Department of Liquor Control would have an expected loss of 41 cents when consumers change the item requested to a lower priced item or substitute a different size. The $2.08 expected monetary loss for selecting a different

[12] Ibid.
[13] Ibid.
[14] Ibid., p. 59.

Table 13–7
Repeated stock-out model parameters

Decisions	Proba-bility*	Revenue difference		Proba-bility	Expected value ($)
		RD($)	wt. RD($)		
Change item requested:					
Higher price	.027	· + .61 =	+ .02		
Same price	.790	· .00 =	.00		
Lower price	.040	· − .61 =	− .02		
Other size	.143	· −1.93 =	− .28		
			− .28	· .246 =	− .07
Request special order			+ .50†	· .029 =	+ .01
Select different store			−5.21	· .399 =	− 2.08
Do not change item requested:					
Substitute:					
Higher price	.031	· + .61 =	+ .02		
Same price	.607	· .00 =	.00		
Lower price	.037	· − .61 =	− .02		
Other size	.204	· −1.93 =	− .39		
No substitute:					
Return trip	.034	· −6.61 =	− .22		
Other store	.087	· −5.21 =	− .45		
			−1.06	· .326 =	− .35
Expected monetary cost/unit of unfilled demand					−$2.49

* The figures in this column are the probabilities that a specific action within one purchase alternative will be taken. For example, 24.6% of the respondents indicated that they would change the item requested if repeated stockouts were encountered. Of these, 79.0% indicated that they would request, or select, an item in the same price range as the one they originally desired.

† A special-order charge of $.50 per bottle was assumed. This charge is added revenue for the store.

Source: C. K. Walter and John R. Grabner, "Stock-out Cost Models: Empirical Tests in a Retail Situation," *Journal of Marketing*, vol. 39 (July 1975), p. 60, published by the American Marketing Association.

store would lead the consumer to another store controlled by the department. Obviously, in the case of most retail stores the total loss would be relevant.

Given a method such as the one just described for calculating the cost of being out of stock, a retailer can proceed to evaluate alternative reorder systems which would minimize the total cost of being out of stock by including consideration of the costs and investment associated with additional inventory. This type of information need is extremely complex and typically involves data collected from a wide variety of sources. The reader may pursue this subject by consulting the list of suggested readings at the end of the chapter.

Summary of research for distribution decisions

Management decisions in the area of distribution are concerned with placing products where the customer wants to buy them. This broad area of decision making encompasses a variety of decision sub-areas and research problems. The three general areas of investigation illustrated in this chapter include: (1) channel design, (2) channel conflict, (3) retail location, and (4) retail inventory management. These illustrations do not cover all of their respective topics, and space limitations prohibit the inclusion of additional topics such as physical distribution, transportation, and nonretail intermediaries.

While experts might classify automobile tires as shopping goods, survey responses indicated a significant proportion of consumers treating tires as convenience, shopping, and specialty goods. A manufacturer could use this information to adopt a multiple channel strategy in order to service each classification segment. Similar findings dispell the notion that high quality cameras are exclusively specialty goods. This study illustrates the potential influence of a consumer behavior survey on channel design decisions.

One of the major areas of concern to channel members is the inevitable conflicts that arise when different levels of the channel operate at cross purposes. In this illustration a consumer durable good manufacturer, its distributors, and their dealers were studied to identify conflict issues and their sources in the three possible channel dyads. This study is particularly interesting in that an attempt was made to provide the manufacturer with a comprehensive examination of conflict in the entire distribution channel. Information of this type is often restricted to a study of isolated conflict incidents.

The largest number of institutions in the marketing channel is at the retail level. Of particular importance to the channel is the location of retail firms. The illustration here involved a savings and loan association with numerous branch offices in a metropolitan market area. Previous studies identified population, competition, and branch office variables as determinants of branch "net savings gains." Within these variable categories, 24 independent variables were defined. The relationship between those variables and net savings gain was estimated through the application of linear step-wise regression analysis. The resulting equation could then be used to estimate net savings gain for proposed branch locations. This approach to location analysis is but one of many involving a wide range of analytical techniques.

Of the managerial problems facing retailers, inventory control is both important and perplexing. The cost of being out of stock is a variable which must be considered in developing reorder policies. This illustration concerns the application of a stock-out model which accounts for the alternative courses of action taken by retailers. In the setting of a state controlled liquor distribution system, the study provided probabilities for alternative consumer responses to stock-outs. By applying these probabilities to the known consequences of each response, the expected cost of being out of stock is determined. This cost information was then available as an input in the development of an inventory control system.

SECTION B: RESEARCH FOR PROMOTION DECISIONS

Research for management decisions in the area of marketing promotion tends to be concentrated in the areas of advertising, sales management, and sales promotion. Within the area of advertising, numerous studies are conducted concerning copy strategy, copy testing, media allocation, media strategy, and advertising effectiveness. Sales management decisions frequently require research inputs on such topics as compensation, motivation and sales territory allocation. Experiments are often conducted to determine the usefulness of such sales promotion techniques as in-store demonstrations and premiums. Illustrations of research for advertising, sales management, and sales promotion decisions are provided in the remainder of this section.

Advertising research

Since advertising is basically a communication process, much of the research in advertising deals with the ability of advertisements to get through to consumers. One study in which researchers were concerned with evaluating commercials involved a refinement of the jury of executive opinion method of forecasting. Specifically, this study was concerned with predicting recall for television commercials.[15] That is, how many viewers recall the commercial within a 24-hour period? The firm was particularly interested in developing a method which would produce a quantified rating.

As was the case with the previous example, this study began with an exhaustive search of previous research findings. "The raw data for the review exercise were obtained from day-after recall studies of TV commercials"[16] Researchers who were experienced in both advertising research techniques and advertising analyzed the previous studies. This analysis produced the following results:

The analysis revealed certain basic elements of communication that correlated with high-scoring, well-remembered copy. Prominent to the point of excluding all others were four key elements: pictorial value, empathy, interest, and clarity.

---

[15] This illustration is adapted from Terry P. Haller, "Predicting Recall of TV Commercials," *Journal of Advertising Research*, vol. 12 (October 1972), pp. 43–45.

[16] Ibid., p. 44.

Pictorial value was found by judging to what extent the picture assisted the sound track in getting the copy message across.

Empathy concerned the degree to which the message spoke to the viewer personally.

Interest (or stopping power) was hard to define, but it was equated with how well the commercial resisted boring the viewer (this is the most subjective of the four elements and requires a tremendous effort in the direction of pure objectivity).

Clarity was the ability of the commercial to speak straight rather than to imply, to avoid talking in riddles, and to leave nothing to the viewer's need to form a conclusion.[17]

A total value for an average commercial was designated as 20. Similarly, the value for a very good, but not excellent, commercial was designated as 40. Thus, each element is assigned an index value of 10 for an above average commercial. Equally distributed index scores for a very good commercial are illustrated in Figure 13–6A.

FIGURE 13–6
Sample index values for commercial (cml.) ratings

A. Equally distributed scores

	Pictorial	Empathy	Interest	Clarity	Total recall
Imaginary commercial	10	10	10	10	= 40

B. Average commercial

	Pictorial	Empathy	Interest	Clarity	Total recall
Test commercial 1	3	6	5	9	= 23

C. Very good/excellent commercial

	Pictorial	Empathy	Interest	Clarity	Total recall
Test commercial 2	12	9	9	13	= 43

Adapted from Terry P. Haller, "Predicting Recall of TV Commercials," *Journal of Advertising Research,* vol. 12 (October 1972), p. 44–45.

Now assume that experts have viewed a test commercial several times and found it to be "remarkably clear, of average interest, fairly good in generating empathy, and very bad in making the video reinforce the audio."[18] The evaluation for such a commercial is illustrated in Figure 13–6B. The total recall index of 23 would indicate an average commercial. It should be pointed out that the total recall index

[17] Ibid.

[18] Ibid., p. 45.

could exceed 40. "So it is possible to come across a commercial that is so good on, say, pictorial value and clarity" that you would end up with ratings such as those illustrated in Figure 13–6C.[19]

The firm has used this technique a number of times and found their recall predictions to be extremely close to the day-after recall tests. It should be pointed out again, however, that "to be able to do this well, you had to have a fair amount of experience in copy research; say, two years at the supervisory level."[20] In the implementation of the technique, several people each independently rate the commercial, and their diagnoses are averaged to determine a final index rating.

Another major area of advertising research involves media selection. Decisions must be made concerning the type of medium, such as print or broadcast, as well as specific media, such as one or more magazines or television stations. In one particular case a chain of discount department stores in a major metropolitan area was interested in the use of direct mail advertising.[21] Management wanted to know who was receiving, reading, and being influenced by a small catalog. They also needed to know what proportion of their customers were purchasing items as a result of the advertising and what new business it attracted.

The catalog was a small booklet with a glossy cover and newsprint pages. The theme of the campaign was fighting higher prices, and roughly three fourths of the advertised items were on sale at reduced prices. A wide variety of items (210 in all) were advertised including clothing, groceries, hardware, tires, jewelry, and shoes. The booklets were addressed to "occupant" and mailed to 291,435 residents in the metro area. An attempt was made to avoid the very high and very low income groups.

To evaluate the booklet, in-store interviews were conducted over a three-day period (shortly after the mailing) in each of the seven stores. Approximately 200 interviews were conducted at each location yielding 1,405 usable responses. The sample was biased somewhat toward home owners, younger shoppers, women, and whites. Nevertheless, the sample was considered adequately representative of the chain's market.

The three key questions asked relative to the booklet were:

Did you receive this book in the mail recently? (A copy of the book was shown)
Did you read or look through the book?

---

[19] Ibid.

[20] Ibid.

[21] Danny N. Bellenger and Jack R. Pingry, "Direct Mail Advertising at the Retail Store Level," *Journal of Advertising Research* vol. 17 (June 1977), pp. 35–39.

Did you come to this store to buy something you saw advertised in the book? (They were also asked to specify the item)[22]

The sequence in which key variables were analyzed and the frequencies for those variables are illustrated in Figure 13–7. Notice that of the respondents who were buying something they read about in the booklet 73.4 percent were frequent customers, and 24.8 were not. Thus, 7.1 percent of the total sample were making purchases which might be considered (in part) additional business attributable to the booklet.

Tables 13–8 and 13–9 are profiles of "readers" and "buyers," respectively. This information helped the chain management determine the nature of the market influenced by the direct mail campaign. Another profile of those receiving the booklet revealed a bias toward homeowners, whites and frequent shoppers. Those biases may simply reflect deliberate income constraints in the sampling procedure or imperfections in the handling of mail at apartment complexes. Table 13–8 reveals several characteristics of respondents who took the time to read the booklet. These include age, sex, and shopping frequency. Similarly, home ownership and sex were distinguishing variables in the buyer profile in Table 13–9.

As a result of this study, the chain management proceeded to develop a more refined direct mail strategy. Product mix in the booklet was biased somewhat toward females and home owners. Similar research was then planned to determine if the changes resulted in improved performance. An estimate of the value of additional business could also be obtained by comparing the results with a similar study of television and newspaper advertising. In this manner media selection decisions can be based on more objective criteria.

A final illustration of advertising research deals with the question of message repetition. That is, how often must a particular advertising message be repeated to achieve effectiveness? This early study involved Oscar Mayer & Company, a major producer of packaged meat products.[23]

During the 1963 baseball season, Oscar Mayer & Company sponsored 162 Milwaukee Brave radio broadcasts at a total cost of $80,000, with a 38-station lineup covering 800,000 radio homes. During the last week of the season 1,200 completed telephone interviews were made, 200 in each of 6 Wisconsin cities. Respondents were asked how many of the games they had heard, who spon-

---

[22] Ibid.

[23] This illustration is adapted from Dik Warren Twedt, "How Can the Advertising Dollar Work Harder?" *Journal of Marketing*, vol. 29 (April 1965), pp. 60–62, published by the American Marketing Association.

Figure 13–7
Summary of key variables

Of the total sample of 1,405,
100 or 7.1% were shoppers who
had bought something they saw
advertised in the booklet and
had not shopped there within
the last two weeks.

Table 13-8
Reader profile

Characteristics	Categories	Read booklet	Did not read booklet	N
Residence	Apartment	86.3%	13.7%	241
	House	87.0	13.0	667
	Other	96.2	3.8	26
Have children	Yes	87.1	12.9	533
	No	87.0	13.0	401
Age	Under 18	84.4	15.6	32
	18–25	91.2	8.8	217
	26–35	89.0	11.0	228
	36–45	81.2	18.8	202
	46–55	83.6	16.4	140
	56–65	88.6	11.4	79
	Over 65	93.5	6.5	31
Sex	Male	78.7	21.3	216
	Female	89.6	10.4	718
Race	White	87.5	12.5	830
	Black	83.7	16.3	104
Shopped here within last 2 weeks	Yes	89.4	10.6	696
	No	79.8	20.2	223
	Don't know	86.7	13.3	15

	Chi-square	DF	Level of significance
Residence versus Read/Not read	2.03	2	.3617
Have children versus Read/Not read	.01	1	.9295
Age versus Read/Not read	13.31	6	.0384
Sex versus Read/Not read	16.39	1	.0001
Race versus Read/Not read	.88	1	.3485
Shopped here within last 2 weeks versus Read/Not read	13.65	2	.0011

Source: Danny N. Bellenger and Jack R. Pingry, "Direct Mail Advertising at the Retail Store Level," reprinted from the *Journal of Advertising Research.* © Copyright 1977, by the Advertising Research Foundation.

sored the games, what brands of wieners they bought most often, and how many pounds of wieners they had used the last 30 days.[24]

The results of the study are illustrated in Figure 13–8.

In Figure 13–8, the dotted line represents the percentage of respondents who indicated Oscar Mayer as the brand they purchased. The solid line indicates the percent of respondents who identified Oscar Mayer as the sponsor of the Braves broadcasts. Notice that the percentage of respondents who purchased Oscar Mayer remains un-

---

[24] Ibid., p. 61.

Table 13-9
Buyer profile

Characteristics	Categories	Buying based on booklet	Buying not based on booklet	N
Residence	Apartment	50.6	49.4	241
	House	40.6	59.4	667
	Other	38.5	61.5	26
Have children	Yes	45.2	54.8	533
	No	40.4	59.6	401
Age	Under 18	25.0	75.0	32
	18–25	42.4	57.6	217
	26–35	47.8	52.2	228
	36–45	44.1	55.9	202
	46–55	45.0	55.0	140
	56–65	34.2	65.8	79
	Over 65	48.4	51.6	31
Sex	Male	34.7	65.3	216
	Female	45.7	54.3	718
Race	White	43.7	56.3	830
	Black	38.5	61.5	104
Shopped here within last 2 weeks	Yes	42.5	57.5	696
	No	44.8	55.2	223
	Don't know	46.7	53.3	15

	Chi-square	DF	Level of significance
Residence versus Buy/Not buy	7.45	2	.0242
Have children versus Buy/Not buy	1.97	1	.1602
Age versus Buy/Not buy	9.53	6	.1457
Sex versus Buy/Not buy	7.69	1	.0056
Race versus Buy/Not buy	.84	1	.3583
Shopped here within last 2 weeks versus Buy/Not buy	.45	2	.8002

Source: Danny N. Bellenger and Jack R. Pingry, "Direct Mail Advertising at the Retail Store Level," reprinted from the *Journal of Advertising Research.* © Copyright 1977, by the Advertising Research Foundation.

changed for those respondents who heard fewer than 20 broadcasts. The figure shows that:

Identification of Oscar Mayer as a sponsor of the Milwaukee Braves radio broadcasts rose steadily with the number of times respondents said they had heard the games. But looking at the top line in the chart, advertising seems to have had little effect on brand purchased, until respondents had at least 15 exposures to Oscar Mayer commercials.

In other words, two things have been established: (1) the media vehicle is appropriate for advertising wieners; (2) the advertising, after it reaches a critical exposure point, has a measurable effect on brand purchase.[25]

---

[25] Ibid., pp. 61–62.

Figure 13–8
Oscar Mayer brand purchase

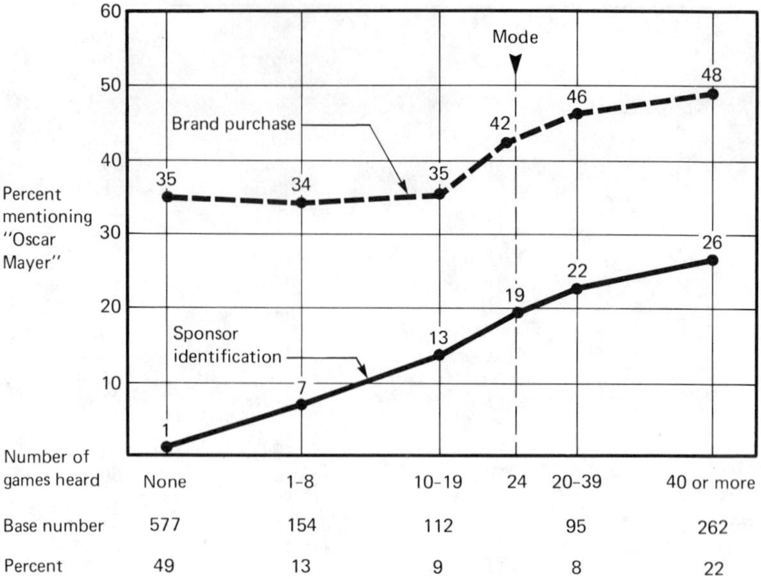

Number of games heard	None	1-8	10-19	24	20-39	40 or more
Base number	577	154	112		95	262
Percent	49	13	9		8	22

Source: Dik Warren Twedt, "How Can the Advertising Dollar Work Harder?" *Journal of Marketing*, vol. 29 (April 1965), p. 61, published by the American Marketing Association.

Coupled with numerous earlier studies, this study lent credence to the idea that numerous repetitions of media commercials for consumer goods are required before an effect is determined. In this particular case, the researcher proceeded to establish that the return on the advertising investment was in fact acceptable. This may not always be the case, however, so it is not sufficient to merely determine the number of repetitions at which an effect is felt. A complete study must also include the economic feasibility of achieving that level of repetition.

Sales promotion research

Sales promotion involves the use of premiums, in-store displays, special events, and other forms of promotion which fall somewhere between advertising and personal selling. Much of the research in this area of promotion tends to be quite similar to the research used in advertising.

One particular example of a study concerning in-store displays, however, seems worthy of note since it involves the observational method of data collection. This particular study concerned the use of white consumers' responses to black models in in-store display materials.[26] The study tested three hypotheses:

H1: There are differences in the sales responses of white consumers to promotional materials utilizing (1) all white models, (2) all black models, or (3) black and white models (integrated).

H2: A greater proportion of male white consumers than female white consumers will purchase products that utilize promotional materials containing black models.

H3: A greater proportion of 'younger' white consumers than 'older' white consumers will purchase products that utilize promotional materials containing black models.[27]

The experimental treatments involved the use of in-aisle displays. The displays were life size figures of two female models holding a banner which displayed the brand of a product. In one treatment, both models were white; in another, one was white and one was black; and in the third treatment, both were black. The product selected for the experiment was bars of soap. The selection of this product was based on previous research findings which had "suggested that the type of product being promoted may be an important variable in determining market response to black models. Specifically, Stafford, Birdwell, and Van Tassell hypothesized a more adverse reaction to black models when the product being promoted was 'personal' rather than 'nonpersonal'". . .[28] This study was conducted in Phoenix, Arizona with the cooperation of a supermarket chain. A description of the supermarkets and population follows:

Three supermarkets were selected to serve as experimental units in this study. In the selection, an effort was made to insure homogeneity both in the stores and in the socioeconomic characteristics of the trade areas they served. For purposes of this study, the trading area of each of the supermarkets was defined as the census tract within which the supermarket was located. Ninety-seven percent of the people living in these areas were white, and there was a relatively even distribution between those heads of household who were under 50 and those who were 50 and over. The areas were relatively affluent, with a median household income of $12,000 and a median of 13 years of education among household heads.[29]

---

[26] This illustration is adapted from Ronald F. Bush, Robert F. Gwinner, and Paul J. Solomon, "White Consumer Sales Response to Black Models," *Journal of Marketing*, vol. 38 (April 1974), pp. 25–29.

[27] Ibid., p. 26.

[28] Ibid., p. 27.

[29] Ibid.

The duration of the experiment was one shopping week. The three displays were rotated daily between the supermarkets. Thus, each appeared in each supermarket twice during the study. The Latin square experimental design used to evaluate the results is illustrated in Table 13–10. Notice that this design allows the researchers to evaluate the results "with respect to the three conditions of model's race, shopping days, and the 'store effect' among the three experimental supermarkets."[30]

Table 13–10
A double Latin square design for testing the effects of models' race on the sales of bath soap.

Super-markets	Days of the shopping week					
	Mon-day	Tues-day	Wednes-day	Thurs-day	Fri-day	Satur-day
A	I	W	B	I	W	B
B	W	B	I	W	B	I
C	B	I	W	B	I	W
	Square 1			Square 2		

Note: Treatment conditions: (randomly assigned)
　　W = White model display
　　B = Black model display
　　I = Integrated model display

Source: Ronald F. Bush, Robert F. Gwinner, and Paul J. Solomon, "White Consumer Sales Response to Black Models," *Journal of Marketing*, vol. 38 (April 1974), p. 27, published by the American Marketing Association.

Observers were placed inconspicuously in positions where they would be able to record consumer purchases of the displayed product. Each day of the experiment observers recorded consumer activity for six hours. The six hours were selected at random from the normal twelve daily operating hours of the stores. Each observer used the following procedure:

. . . As each white consumer walked into the defined area surrounding the display, the observers recorded whether or not he or she purchased the experimental product. Also, the sex and age ('older' or 'younger') of the shoppers were recorded. Black shoppers' responses, though very few in number, were recorded separately.[31]

---

[30] Ibid.
[31] Ibid.

One of the shortcomings of the observational method of data collection is the difficulty of quantifying certain variables, such as age. In this study, observers were trained and tested concerning their ability to distinguish between individuals who are 46 and over versus those who are 45 or under. Although this is at best a gross measure of age difference, it was consistent with the objectives of the research and feasible given proper instructions to the observers.

In all, 13,443 white consumers were observed during the experiment. Table 13–11 illustrates the results of analysis of variance

Table 13–11
Results of analysis of variance of the effect of models' race on the sales of bath soap

Source of variation	Sum of squares	Degrees of freedom	Mean squares	F-ratio[a]
Between Latin squares.....	8.71	1	8.71	3.27
Stores	.33	2	.17	<1
Stores by squares	4.34	2	2.17	<1
Days within square	6.20	4	1.55	<1
Treatments	1.12	2	.56	<1
Error	15.98	6	2.66	
Total....................	36.68	17		

[a] .05 level for treatments is 5.14.

Source: Ronald F. Bush, Robert F. Gwinner, and Paul J. Solomon, "White Consumer Sales Response to Black Models," *Journal of Marketing*, vol. 38 (April 1974), p. 28, published by the American Marketing Association.

applied to the experimental design. Notice that none of the tests prove significant. That is, no differences were observed between the frequency of purchase for white consumers regardless of the treatment effect or in terms of conditions of the experiment. Further analysis utilizing chi-square test showed no significant difference between age or sex categories. Thus, all three hypotheses were rejected. Although this single study cannot be considered adequate evidence on the question of model's race for in-store displays, it lends additional evidence to the same findings in other studies which treat different aspects of the question. In this manner, key issues in the design of promotional displays can be resolved.

Research for sales management and personal selling

Research associated with personal selling activities can be divided into two broad categories. First, questions arise concerning the actual methods of selling used by salespeople. Much of this research is similar to that used in advertising, but we are now dealing with interpersonal communication as opposed to mass communication. The second broad area of research involves the management of personal selling. Research of this type assists managers in making decisions concerning sales territory assignments, compensation plans, sales force motivation, and other personnel decisions. Although the amount of research of the first type is rather limited, an example has been selected for illustration. Most of the available material, however, illustrates the managerial type of decision making.

An interesting topic which has been the subject of research in the area of selling techniques is that of structured versus flexible sales presentations.[32] Actually, the researcher in this particular study conceived of a continuum of presentations including the following five designs:

Fully automated—Sound movies, slides, or film strips dominate the presentation. The salesman's participation consists of setting up the projector, answering simple questions, and/or writing up the order. Many audio-visual systems are available.

Semiautomated—The salesman reads the presentation from copy printed on flip charts, read-off binders, promotional broadsides, or brochures. He adds his own comments when necessary.

Memorized—The salesman delivers a company prepared message that he has memorized. Supplementary visual aids may not be used.

Organized—The salesman is allowed complete flexibility of wording; however, he does not follow a company pattern, check list, or outline. Visual aids are optional.

Unstructured—The salesman is on his own to describe the product any way he sees fit. Generally, the presentation varies from prospect to prospect.[33]

Notice that the first three of these designs are highly structured, while the last one contains virtually no structure. The fourth one, organized presentation, "draws heavily from both the sales person and the firm."

In a review of the sales presentation objectives for a number of firms, the researcher identified the eight following objectives:

1. Conserve the prospect's time.
2. Tell the complete story.
3. Deliver an accurate, authoritative, and ethical message.
4. Persuade the prospect.
5. Anticipate objections before they occur.
6. Facilitate training of salesmen.
7. Increase the salesman's self-confidence.
8. Facilitate supervision of salesmen.[34]

---

[32] This illustration is adapted from Marvin A. Jolson, "Should the Sales Presentation Be 'Fresh' or 'Canned'?" *Business Horizons*, vol. 16 (October 1973), pp. 81–88. Copyright, 1976 by the Foundation for the School of Business at Indiana University. Reprinted by permission.

[33] Ibid., p. 81.

[34] Ibid., p. 82.

The researcher further pointed out that "These objectives may be subdivided in terms of the requirements of the prospect (Objectives 1, 2, 3), the company (Objectives 4, 5, 6), and the sales force (Objectives 7, 8)."[35] The study involved a questionnaire which was mailed to sales executives. They were asked to rate the five presentation designs in terms of their effectiveness in obtaining the eight objectives. The respondents were asked to rate each design on a five-point scale from highly effective to not effective. Respondents were also asked "to indicate the percentage of sales presentations currently delivered by each method in his firm. Respondents were requested to specify the predominant type of customer served, annual corporate sales volume, and the firm's average unit sale in dollars."[36] The sample of top field sales executives in 147 organizations listed in the *Sales/Marketing Executives* of Baltimore and Washington was selected for the study. "After one follow-up letter, 86 replies were received of which 75 (or 51 percent) were usable."[37]

The method of analysis used in the study was described as follows:

Each respondent's effectiveness score was converted to an original rank for each presentation method/objective combination. The Friedman test statistic Xr was computed and checked for statistical significance in order to determine the ranking of perceived effectiveness of the presentation modes in accomplishing the various sales objectives.

Subsequent to the test of overall scatter achieved by the Friedman test, the Wilcoxon-Wilcox test was used to compare individual pairs of presentation methods as rated by all 75 firms. In analyzing the most frequently used sales presentation modes, the chi-square statistic was used. This procedure was not used to compare current presentation method preferences by target customer, annual sales volume, and average unit sale, since a large number of categories (cells) contained low expected frequencies and combining of categories was not desirable.[38]

Although the organized and unstructured designs were clearly the most popular, "Nearly 80 percent of the sampled firms use more than a single of type of sales presentation structure."[39] The results of the test of effectiveness are illustrated in Table 13–12. Although a number of findings resulted from the study, it is particularly interesting to note that the organized approach was considered most effective by sales executives in seven of the eight objective categories. Furthermore, both the memorized and unstructured approaches rated poorly in al-

---

[35] Ibid.

[36] Ibid.

[37] Ibid.

[38] Ibid., p. 83.

[39] Ibid.

Table 13–12
Rankings by sales executives of effectiveness of alternative sales presentations
(all firms: $N = 75$)

Objective	Fully auto- mated	Semi- auto- mated	Memo- rized	Orga- nized	Un- struc- tured	χ_r^2	Sig- nifi- cance level*
Conserves the prospect's time	3	2‡	5	1†	4	13.7	<.01
Tells the complete story	2§	3§	4	1†	5	20.0	<.001
Delivers an accurate, authoritative and ethical message	1†	2†	4	3†	5	57.1	<.001
Persuades the prospect	4	3§	5	1‖	2†	78.2	<.001
Anticipates objections before they occur	3‡	2	5	1‖	4	14.2	<.01
Facilitates training of salesmen	3†	2†	5	1†	4	28.3	<.001
Increases salesman's self-confidence	4	2**	5	1#	3#	23.5	<.001
Facilitates supervision of salesmen	3	2	4	1‖	5	11.3	<.05

* Calculated by the Friedman test (df = 4) to evaluate observed divergence among column sums.
† More effective than methods ranked 4 and 5 at .01 level of significance (Wilcoxon-Wilcox test).
For details of the Wilcoxon-Wilcox test see Frank Wilcoxon and Roberta Wilcox, *Some Rapid Approximate Statistical Procedures* (Pearl River, N.Y.: Lederle Laboratories, 1964), p. 11. The author is indebted to R. J. Senter of the University of Cincinnati for his assistance in applying this method.
‡ More effective than method ranked at 5 at .05 level of significance (Wilcoxon-Wilcox test).
§ More effective than methods ranked 4 and 5 at .05 and .01 levels of significance, respectively (Wilcoxon-Wilcox test).
‖ More effective than methods ranked 3, 4, and 5 at .01 level of significance (Wilcoxon-Wilcox test).
More effective than methods ranked 2 through 5 at .01 level of significance (Wilcoxon-Wilcox test).
** More effective than method ranked 5 at .01 level of significance (Wilcoxon-Wilcox test).
Source: Marvin A. Jolson, "Should the Sales Presentation Be 'Fresh' or 'Canned'?" *Business Horizons*, vol. 16 (October 1973), p. 85. Copyright, 1976 by the Foundation for the School of Business at Indiana University. Reprinted by permission.

most every case with the notable exception of persuasibility. The organized and unstructured approaches rated highest in this category. The findings suggest that sales presentations should be well organized in order to be effective.

Another study in the sales area was particularly relevant to the issue of marketing information. The researcher was concerned with the use of sales force feedback as a means of acquiring information about competitive activity.[40] Two firms with large national sales organizations agreed to cooperate in the study. The firms agreed to the following conditions:

1. Each firm would provide several units of a simulated "new" product that could be used at the discretion of the research team. These units had to be totally new to all of the firm's salesmen, and any identifying corporate seals or trademarks was necessary because the same products were to be placed in the field with actual customers of each firm, who in turn showed the "new" product to the salesman when he called, representing it as the new product development of a competitor.

2. Each firm agreed to cooperate with the research team and permit monitoring of all incoming communications from the salesmen to their sales managers for a period of three months after the salesman was initially exposed to the "new" product. . . . While the research team did not *personally* monitor all communications, the secretarial staffs of each firm were trained to achieve this objective.

3. Each firm selected had to have previously instituted into its sales training program a specific emphasis upon the value of feedback from the field sales force. . . .

4. Lastly, it was necessary for each participating firm to suggest customer accounts that would in turn pass on the information to their salesmen. The research team stressed with the account the anonymity feature . . . plus the fact that since a university research team would be monitoring the feedback, no negative sanctions would be applied to nonreporting salesmen.[41]

Table 13–13
Summary of findings

	Corp. X	Corp. Y
Number of sales territories	46	24
Number of salesmen providing feedback	5	4
Percentage of total sales force reporting "new" product	10.9%	16.7%

Source: Dan H. Robertson, "Sales Force Feedback on Competitor's Activity," *Journal of Marketing*, vol. 38 (April 1974), p. 71.

The findings of the report are illustrated in Table 13-13, and the results of extensive debriefing interviews with salesmen from each firm are illustrated in Table 13–14.

In spite of the emphasis placed on sales force feedback by both of the participating firms, only 10.9 percent of the salesmen in Corpora-

---

[40] This illustration is adapted from Dan H. Robertson, "Sales Force Feedback on Competitor's Activity." *Journal of Marketing*, vol. 38 (April 1974), pp. 69–71, published by the American Marketing Association.

[41] Ibid., p. 70.

Table 13–14
Salesmen's reasons for noncommunication

	Corp. X	Corp. Y
"Management doesn't use it anyway"	35%	29%
"Too busy with other activities"	28	42
"Not important enough to report"	20	8
All other reasons combined	17	21
	100%	100%

Source: Dan H. Robertson, "Sales Force Feedback on Competitor's Activity," *Journal of Marketing*, vol. 38 (April 1974), p. 71, published by the American Marketing Association.

tion X and 16.7 percent of the salesmen in Corporation Y actually provided feedback on the competitor's new product. Furthermore, management learned from the debriefing interviews that salesmen did not receive any particular motivation for reporting on this type of activity. Obviously, management found itself a long way from achieving the following goals:

The modern salesman, in other words, not only communicates the company's story to customers but also feeds back customer reaction to the company. He is a vital link both in the communication and marketing processes. [42]

Another major decision area facing sales management executives is that of sales-force motivation. Although compensation is obviously a major factor in motivating a salesman, a considerable amount of attention is devoted to nonfinancial incentives. In one particular study the researchers were concerned with the relationship between job satisfaction and various types of nonfinancial incentives. [43] Drawing on previous research and sales management literature, the researchers decided to use three types of nonfinancial incentives; status pay, privilege pay, and power pay. Each of these is defined as follows:

Status pay is defined as public acknowledgement of the value that management places upon an individual; the attention the manager calls to the outstanding characteristics and achievements of the individual. Privilege pay is the freedom to interact with him. Individuals frequently feel that being able to talk freely with their boss is a genuine privilege. Power pay is the reward given an employee by making his job more important in the organization. This usually is accomplished by giving the individual more responsibility and at the same time by letting him know management feels that his performance is of critical importance to the firm. [44]

---

[42] Dan H. Robertson, "Sales Force Feedback on Competitors' Activities," *Journal of Marketing,* April 1974, pp. 69–71.

[43] This illustration is adapted from Henry O. Pruden, William H. Cunningham and Wilke D. English, "Nonfinancial Incentives for Salesmen," *Journal of Marketing,* vol. 36. (October 1972), pp. 55–59.

[44] Ibid., p. 55.

The researchers defined the purpose of the study and the hypotheses to be tested as follows:

This (study) examines the relationship between job satisfaction and the amount of nonfinancial incentives which salesmen feel they receive from management. In general, it is proposed that salesmen's job satisfaction increases as their perceived level of nonfinancial incentives increase. Three specific hypotheses are tested in this study: (1) The more the salesmen's needs for nonfinancial incentives are fulfilled, the more satisfied the salesmen are; (2) The lower the nonfinancial need deficiency, the higher the satisfaction of salesmen; (3) The more important the nonfinancial incentives are to salesmen, the more satisfied the salesmen are.[45]

The approach used was a questionnaire survey of salesmen who worked for a large West Coast lumber company. Of the firm's 300 salesmen, 126 were randomly selected and received the questionnaire. One hundred salesmen completed and returned the questionnaire. The statements used to measure the nonfinancial incentives and job satisfaction are illustrated in Table 13–15. The exact form of the test is described as follows:

For each test item the respondents were asked to answer the following questions on a six-point scale:

1. How much is there now?
   (minimum) .... (maximum)
2. How much should there be?
   (minimum) .... (maximum)
3. How important is this to me?
   (minimum) .... (maximum)

The first question represents the subject's need fulfillment for nonfinancial incentives with the higher, absolute score assumed to indicate greater need fulfillment. Need deficiency for nonfinancial incentives was measured by the relationship between the first question ("How much there is") and the second question ("How much there should be"). Need deficiency becomes greater as the absolute difference between "how much there should be" less "how much there is" increases. The third question was a measure of how important nonfinancial incentives are to salesmen.[46]

The salesmen indicated their agreement or disagreement with the job satisfaction statements on a six-point Likert type scale from "definitely yes" to "definitely no."

The correlation between job satisfaction and nonfinancial incentives was tested using Spearman's rank order correlation. The results of these tests are illustrated in Table 13–16. The table is presented with three columns, each representing one of the three types of nonfinancial need

[45] Ibid.

[46] Ibid., p. 56.

Table 13–15
Test items for nonfinancial incentives and job satisfaction

Nonfinancial incentives	*Test items*
Status pay	1. My boss is careful to make well known to me and to others the things that I am able to do better than other people.
Privilege pay	1. My boss places value on my professional and technical opinion and really wants me to freely express my opinions about operating problems.
	2. The frequency with which I am on a man-to-man basis with my boss, rather than on a superior-subordinate basis.
Power pay	1. The customer accounts in my territory are under my exclusive jurisdiction. In a sense, they are considered as "belonging to me." No one else from my company would call on these accounts without notifying me beforehand.
	2. The number and variety of products I carry.
	3. The number of customer accounts which I have.
	4. The amount of influence I have on decisions about the granting of credit to my customers.
	5. The amount of influence I have on decisions concerning delivery time of products to my customers.
	6. The amount of influence I have on a decision about the type and number of products to offer my customers.
	7. The amount of influence I have on a decision concerning the price to charge a customer.

Job satisfaction

1. Do you feel promotion opportunities are wider in jobs other than yours?
2. Do you feel it is easy to demonstrate ability and initiative in your job as in others?
3. Would you advise a friend looking for a new job to take one similar to yours?
4. Do you think there is as much a feeling of security in your job as in others?

Adapted from: Henry O. Pruden, William H. Cunningham and Wilke D. English, "Nonfinancial Incentives for Salesmen," *Journal of Marketing*, vol. 36 (October 1972), p. 56, published by the American Marketing Association.

fulfillment described earlier. A positive correlation in Table 13–16 means there is a direct relationship between job satisfaction and nonfinancial incentive. For example, highly satisfied salesmen perceived that they received more privilege pay. This is reflected in Table 13–16 by the positive correlation of .19 in the Column A portion of the privilege pay row. Furthermore, this correlation is statistically significant at the .06 level.

The general relationship between job satisfaction and nonfinancial incentives are well summarized in the last row of the table. Referring to the first hypothesis, we might conclude from Column A that the proposition can be accepted. That is, the more a salesman's need for nonfinancial incentives is satisfied, the more the salesman is satisfied with his job. Likewise, the significant negative correlation in Column B would lead us to accept the second hypothesis. That is, if nonfinancial incentives are provided, higher job satisfaction is associated with a relatively low level of need deficiency. The insignificant correlation in

Table 13–16
Need fulfillment, need deficiencies, and need importance

Nonfinancial incentives	A Need fulfillment n = 100	B Need deficiencies n = 100	C Need importance n = 100
Privilege pay			
rho	.19	−.13	.13
p	<.06	NS	NS
Status pay			
rho	.08	−.22	.01
p	NS	<.03	NS
Power pay			
rho	.25	−.23	.20
p	<.02	<.03	<.06
Combined nonfinancial incentives			
rho	.24	−.31	.12
p	<.02	<.01	NS

Source: Henry O. Pruden, William H. Cunningham, and Silke D. English, "Nonfinancial Incentives for Salesmen," *Journal of Marketing*, vol. 36 (October 1972), p. 57, published by the American Marketing Association.

Column C, however, would lead us to reject the third hypothesis. This does not necessarily imply that job satisfaction is not related to a level of importance salesman place on financial incentives. "Rather this indicates that the same degree of importance is attached to nonfinancial rewards irrespective of the subject's degree of job satisfaction."[47]

Summary of research for promotion decisions

The subject of marketing promotion encompasses advertising, personal selling, sales promotion, publicity, and public relations. The first three topics tend to be of more immediate relevance to marketing managers involved in product promotion. Selected examples of research in each of these decision areas were presented in this chapter.

The first of three illustrations of advertising research involved the development of measurement scales for evaluating television commercials. This illustration of measurement research involved the development of an index which could be used to predict recall for television commercials. The study relied on a jury of executive opinion, both in the development and implementation stages.

The second illustration involved research for a media selection decision. A chain of discount department stores used in-store interviews to determine profiles of customers who had received and read a direct

---

[47] Ibid., p. 58.

mail advertisement, as well as who was influenced by it. The third advertising research illustration concerned the issue of repetition. Households in a municipality were surveyed to determine their awareness of the sponsor of the local major league baseball broadcasts. They were also questioned regarding brand preferences and purchase of the sponsored product.

The illustration of sales promotion research involved white customer response to the use of black models for in-store displays. Although previous research suggested that no effect would be observed, this study is of particular interest as an example of the observational technique of data collection.

The research illustrations pertaining to selling emphasized sales management information needs. One exception is a study which addressed the issue of structured versus flexible sales presentations. One study specifically related to information needs concerned sales force feedback on competitive activity. The salesmen had been trained to report on competitions' activities, but analysis of feedback revealed few reports of a "new" product. Further analysis indicated a general lack of confidence on the part of salesmen in the actual use of the reports. The final illustration dealt with nonfinancial incentives for salesmen. Salesmen responded to questions regarding the adequacy of several types of nonfinancial rewards and job satisfaction. Analysis of the responses indicated that nonfinancial incentives were related to job satisfaction. The level of correlation also suggested that nonfinancial incentives were only a portion of the total sources of influence leading to job satisfaction.

DISCUSSION QUESTIONS

1. Assume that you are faced with a decision concerning the expansion of a sporting goods company. The firm's original retail store was located in the downtown area of a major city which is the hub of a large metropolitan area. Since then, the firm has opened two additional stores in suburban shopping centers. Encouraged by the performance of the newer stores, the company's president has asked you to find another location. What information would you need in order to reach such a decision and how would you go about obtaining it?

2. A firm has sought to expand for several years through acquisition. Generally these acquisitions have involved advanced technology businesses, particularly firms involved in some way with the production of electronic products. One such firm produced a product which is used as an input for a manufacturer of certain electronic components. The parent company purchased the production facilities from the former owners, but retained the original management on a contract to market the product. The parent firm became quite concerned with the sales performance of the subsidiary and questions arose regarding the management contract. Specifically, the

parent company executives felt that the marketing strategy which was being implemented through the sales force was outdated and failed to account for recent advances in technology which were being utilized by competitors and buyers. Assume that you have been asked by the president of the parent firm to investigate the situation and report to him whether he should consider breaking off from the management contract and building an in-house sales force. What information would be needed to make such a decision and how would you get it?

3. A group of creative individuals has developed a new adult game which involves the use of strategy to win political offices. Hand made sets of the game have been used to test it in use, and the results are very positive. The group has secured the necessary legal rights and has found a number of toy reps who are interested in selling the game to wholesalers and retailers. Several members of the group are concerned, however, that the game will not sell well at the retail level without some form of promotion. Assume that you are a consultant and that the group has approached you with this problem. What information would you suggest gathering and how; to allow the group to develop and implement a promotional strategy?

SELECTED REFERENCES

Applebaum, William. "Methods for Determining Store Trade Areas, Market Penetration, and Potential Sales," *Journal of Marketing Research*, vol. 3 (May 1966), pp. 127–41.

Cravens, David W.; Woodruff, Robert B.; and Stamper, Joe C. "An Analytical Approach for Evaluating Sales Territory Performance," *Journal of Marketing* vol. 36 (January 1972), pp. 31–37.

Hauk, J. G. "Research in Personal Selling." in G. Schwartz (ed.), *Science in Marketing*, New York: John Wiley and Sons, Inc., 1965, pp. 213–49.

Huff, David L. "Defining and Estimating a Trading Area." *Journal of Marketing*, vol. 28 (July 1964), pp. 34–38.

Katz, Elihu. "The Two-Step Flow of Communication." *Public Opinion Quarterly*, vol. 21 (Spring 1957), pp. 61–78.

Mayer, David, and Greenberg, Herbert M. "What Makes a Good Salesman?" *Harvard Business Review*, vol. 42 (July–August 1964), pp. 119–25.

Palda, Kristian S. *The Measurement of Cumulative Advertising Effect*. Englewood Cliffs, N.J.: Prentice-Hall, Inc., 1964.

Ray, Michael L., and Wilke, William L. "Fear: The Potential of an Appeal Neglected by Marketing." *Journal of Marketing*, vol. 34 (January 1970), pp. 55–56.

Seipel, Carl-Magnus. "Premiums—Forgotten by Theory." *Journal of Marketing*, vol. 35 (April 1971), pp. 26–31.

Sweeney, Daniel J. "Improving the Profitability of Retail Merchandising Decisions." *Journal of Marketing*, vol. 37 (January 1973), pp. 60–68.

chapter

14

The marketing information management system

WHAT IS AN INFORMATION MANAGEMENT SYSTEM?

Definition

A marketing information management system can be defined as a structure designed to implement the research process. As such, it includes all personnel, equipment, and procedures developed to produce information for managerial decision making. The purpose of the system or structure is to perform certain functions necessary in carrying out the research process. Research, as previously defined, is used broadly to include all information-generating activities. The ultimate purpose of the information is to improve the decisions made by the managers receiving the information. The functions involved in carrying out the research process are collecting data, processing the data to transform it into useful information, and transmitting the information to the manager.

An illustration of how one of the pioneers in this area developed his information system may be helpful in understanding the concept. The development of information systems at Pillsbury from 1956 to 1966 was described by Mr. Terrance Hanold, executive vice president, Finance and Planning, as follows:

> From 1956 to 1961, the bulk of our efforts were directed at the immediate savings which systems staff could realize from reflowing paperwork and at the further savings more slowly obtainable from substituting primary data pro-

cessing equipment for clerical procedures. These efforts centered on the primary accounting levels in the central and branch office areas where paper flourished, where the targets were clusters of people employing the lowest routine skills, and where the savings were directly demonstrable.

While they seemed hectic and adventurous at the time because of the novelty of the systematic approach and the drastic dislocations of personnel which their rigorous application always seems to threaten (without quite accomplishing), in retrospect they were halcyon days when we lived with clearly quantified ideas and produced crisply measurable results.

This was the period of simple substitution, when we replaced one method of doing things with another and better method, but the frame of things remained essentially unscathed.

Overlapping the latter end of this five-year period and continuing in the five-year span that followed (1961-1966) was the trend toward consolidation of identical operations into fewer locations.

So long as the orders, invoices, and accounts receivable are processed by clerical routines, it seems to make little difference whether they are concentrated or dispersed, and tradition held that they were best done in intimate relation to the field sales force and in proper subordination to the branch sales manager. But the expense of data processing equipment and the necessity of its optimum use made plain the economics of more limited geographic locations, so we gradually shrank our grocery products branch accounting offices from 33 to 4. And when the advent of our first computer made it possible in 1960, to a single location in Minneapolis.

After our transfer to [our first computer] a centrally operated GE–225 computer in 1962, we made parallel consolidations at Minneapolis of our field sales accounting operations in our refrigerated and flour milling products divisions as well.

The order-invoice cycle is the operation critical to any total systems treatment of our main business areas. The programming of this cycle has been repeated, laborious, and continuous. It was achieved in primitive style as we moved from manual to automatic data processing in more advanced form when we changed to our first computer; in far more comprehensive shape as we moved to the GE–225; and is being expanded again as we have transferred this summer [1966] to a large-scale GE–635 [a time-sharing system with 92 remote terminals]. Experience, experiment, and discovery are forever disclosing new potentials for information, analysis, decision, and control as logical by-products of the process. And more of these values came properly within our reach until central processing was fully attained.

But the progress of this primary consolidation of a few operations brought more than enhanced informational and analytical capabilities in its train. It also started a current of fundamental shifts in the management structure of which the meanings are only beginning to be perceived. One immediate result was the removal of a very large administrative function from the branch sales manager, and of a very large administrative supervisory job from his superiors. Another result was to relieve the information flow of the frequent and varying modifications which branch managers habitually had given to the data before transmitting it to the divisional office.

With the addition of a Datanet–30 communications computer to our Minneapolis center, an effort of like character began in our plants and mills, and is just now coming to completion. Only original entry data of materials received, of ingredients processed, and of shipments initiated is recorded at these points, and then as a rule only in a form sufficient for transmission to the computer center. All inventory, payroll, costing, scheduling, and other accounting and control procedures are maintained by the central electronic apparatus with such informational returns to the plant office as operations may require.

Again, the administrative load of the plant manager is lightened, and his concentration on production and engineering matters is encouraged.

Noting the disappearance of several echelons in the chain of command, we discovered the compacting effect on organization of more advanced computer programming, and because of the length and vertical reach which this advance gave managers, the executive level found itself much nearer the field of action than it had formerly been.

Next, computer disciplines began to infiltrate areas in which the judgments of specialists and technicians had enjoyed unfettered play—those of nutrition, formulation, traffic, quality control, procurement, and many others. In these enclaves, where the tangled threads of decision embraced many factors and infinite interrelations between them, which prevented either adequate direction of evaluation by conventional methods, linear programming techniques are providing both guides to decision and measurements for review.[1]

Dimensions of the information management system

Before going into a detailed discussion of the nature of an information management system, some of the general identifiable dimensions of a typical system should be understood. These dimensions permit different systems to be described, compared, and contrasted on a common basis even when each marketing manager has unique information requirements and unique perspective of both the environment and of the firm. In this context the following dimensions are significant:

1. Management access.
2. Information recency.
3. Information aggregation.
4. Analytical sophistication.
5. System authority.[2]

---

[1] Terrance Hanold, "Management by Perception," *Information Systems Review*, vol. 1, (1966), pp. 6–7.

[2] Arnold E. Amstutz, "Market-Oriented Management Systems: The Current Status," *Journal of Marketing Research*, November 1969, pp. 481–83.

Management access.   The first dimension of evaluation measures the time lapse between management's request for certain information and receipt of the desired report or display. Measurements along this dimension range from several months for manual compilation of extensive statistics, to fractions of a second for on-line computer access, to information in primary storage.

Information recency.   Information recency refers to the time lapse between the occurrence of an event in the environment and inclusion of data describing that event in the system. This may range from several weeks for certain market developments to a few hours or minutes for automated inventory control.

Information aggregation.   Information aggregation describes the detail with which information is maintained in the systems data bank. Inventory control systems in which information on product components or subassemblies is maintained at the item level represent relatively disaggregate (micro) data maintenance, while industry market share statistics (developed through trade associations) represent highly aggregate (macro) measures.

Analytical sophistication.   Analytical sophistication represents the complexity of models or statistical procedures encompassed by the system. Several levels of sophistication are possible within an information management system. At the lowest level of analytical sophistication, the computer retrieves a specified record and displays the information it contains. The second level involves aggregation, gathering numbers from one or more records to produce a total or subtotal. At a higher level the system may perform arithmetic averaging or compute differences. The fourth level, introduces classification schemes through which data are aggregated within subsets or conditionally segmented. At the next level, statistical techniques are used to develop extrapolations from historic data, statistical best estimates, analyses of variances, or trend estimates. Macro process models may be used at the sixth level to relate multiple factors in the management environment to current or expected future conditions. At the higher levels of analytic sophistication, micro analytical behavioral models are encountered. These behavioral simulations may be used to produce an artificial environment paralleling the real world environment monitored by the information network.

System authority.   The final dimension of evaluation, authority delegated to the system, is closely associated with analytic sophistication. Management is more willing to delegate authority to sophisticated systems and conversely, as management places greater demands on an information management system, a greater level of analytic sophistication is required.

THE NEED FOR INFORMATION MANAGEMENT SYSTEMS

Marketing information flows

The system approach to marketing management is a way of viewing and analyzing a marketing organization so that the manager can improve the performance of the major marketing activities. A systems analyst or manager in attempting to group major marketing management activities should consider (1) the general area that the decision concerns, (2) the time dimension of the decision process, and (3) similar requirements for information in the decision process.[3] Using these criteria marketing management can be grouped into the decision areas of market analysis and formulating the marketing mix.

The system must be able to trace all information flows associated with these management activities and with the decision-making processes involved, regardless of the organizational boundaries that must be penetrated. The network of information flows that is outlined for each group of management activities forms the basis of the information management system. The focus of the information system activities is on the generation and management of the necessary information flows. If the system is to be an effective information network, it must deal with all major information flows. An information flow is essentially the movement of data from its source to the manager and includes the processing of data to convert it into usable information. In considering methods of getting timely and accurate information to the marketing manager, the two major information flows must be considered. These are marketing intelligence and the internal information flow.

Marketing intelligence is the flow of information from the environment to points within the firm. This information comes from such sources as wholesalers, competitors, customers, and the government whose actions affect pricing, advertising, and other marketing management decisions. Marketing intelligence is a term used to encompass raw data, statistics, inferences, opinions, impressions, and rumors from outside the firm. The idea of marketing intelligence is borrowed from the military. "The high level military decision maker is usually far removed from the battlefield and therefore is totally dependent upon secondhand information in directing the battle;"[4] thus, he uses hunches and rumors as well as hard facts. The marketing manager is in a similar position; he is fighting for sales in the market place with allies such as suppliers, channel members, and complementary producers

---

[3] See Thomas R. Prince, *Information Systems for Management Planning and Control.* (Homewood, Ill.: Richard D. Irwin, Inc., 1975).

[4] Philip Kotler, "A Design for the Firm's Nerve Center," *Business Horizons,* vol. 9, no. 3, p. 66.

Figure 14–1
Marketing information flows

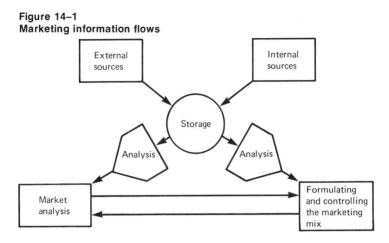

against the competitive enemies. Action is also constrained by the external environment within which operations must be conducted. Information from outside the firm is essential in effectively conducting the essential managerial activities.

The second flow is the internal marketing information flow which consists of the flow between relay points within the firm. This includes the marketing intelligence after it has entered the firm. The internal flow is comprised of downward, upward, and horizontal flows. The downward flow consists of communications from top management to subordinates. The upward flow is made up of "grapevine" as well as requisitioned information moving from the lower levels of the organization toward the top. The horizontal flow consists of information passed between employees on the same level.

These marketing information flows are shown in Figure 14–1. The flows are initiated with the collection of data from internal and external sources. Internal sources are within the firm and provide such data as performance reports and decision rules. External sources, outside of the firm, provide data relating to the customers, markets, the competitive situation, and environmental constraints. Data from these sources typically flow into some type of storage network. The data may then be analyzed by the application of model or statistical techniques before transmission to the manager engaged in some specific type of decision making. These transmissions form a flow of information to the managers responsible for conducting each of the marketing management activities involved in market analysis and formulating and controlling the marketing mix. The types of data collected and the nature of the flows and analysis depend on the needs of marketing managers in conducting these activities.

Problems in management of information flows

Several factors have worked to inhibit the development of well-managed, integrated information systems.[5] First, marketing information needs have usually been satisfied on a piecemeal basis by using data sources and reports designed for other management purposes, such as financial reporting, production control, and accounting. This "hand-me-down" method sometimes looks like an economical way to solve continuing marketing information problems. Basic information needs go unfulfilled, however, since important aspects of customer identification, cost allocations, and external market conditions cannot be captured unless special provisions are made for doing so.

Secondly, EDP techniques have been successfully applied first where dollar savings or operating advantages have been easily recognized; accounting, inventory control, order entry, and production scheduling usually get top priority. The benefits of better information for the marketing function are difficult to quantify in dollars and cents.

Finally, the concepts behind a marketing information management system may be misinterpreted by senior executives. At one extreme, they may expect such systems to deliver the answers to the most difficult kinds of questions—the effectiveness of advertising and promotion, for example. At the other extreme, the systems approach may be dismissed as just another sales reporting scheme. Neither concept is correct.

The lack of an effective information management system can lead to many problems. Three such problems which may arise with an unmanaged or poorly managed information management system are:

1. *Information disappearance.* A salesman obtaining information about a competitor's activities may forget to relay the data, may not know who should receive the data inside the organization, or may purposely suppress the information for personal reasons.
2. *Information delay.* Marketing intelligence and internal information may take longer than necessary to travel from the original relay points through the handling system to the decision makers. Thus decisions may be delayed and lose their effect or may be made without sufficient information which can lead to poor decisions.
3. *Information distortion.* Data may be changed or misinterpreted in the process of being encoded, transmitted, processed, and decoded. This can result in a poor managerial decision even when accurate data is being gathered at the collection level.[6]

---

[5] Neil Doppelt, "Down-to-Earth Marketing Information Systems," *Management Adviser,* (September–October 1971).

[6] Kotler, "A Design for the Firm's Nerve Center," *Business Horizons,* p. 64.

These problems may arise when a marketing department has an inefficient or unplanned information system. Additional problems may be generated, of an equally serious nature, if a narrow view of information flows is adopted. The narrow model for a traditional information system is a closed network covering all of the major information flows within the business organization. The network supporting such a closed system contains both vertical and horizontal flows. The characteristics of a closed system suggests that the organization is situated in a constant type of environment and that the management process can be conducted in a specified manner. This viewpoint suggests that within the time frame of one planning cycle, management does not intend to respond or react to changes in the raw materials markets, the external environment, the finished goods market, or actions by competitors.

The implication of a closed network is that the overall business system does not need to react or respond to external changes; and that the nature of business activity is such that all phases of the planning process can be completed before any of the activities in the time period covered by the plan begin. This means that the control process begins only after the planning process (strategic and management) has been completed and that management control seeks conformance of activity to the plan. All aspects of the planning process must be performed within the time frame of the cycle. Once the complete planning process has been performed, the process cannot be repeated during the time frame of the cycle. This means that based on changes in the environment under conditions of a traditional information management system, it is not possible to quickly change the assignment of resources or personnel for purposes accomplishing a new order of identified tasks.

A more realistic approach is to view planning and control as continuous and overlapping operations. Time requirements for information vary considerably: at one extreme, information may be required continuously (for management control) and at the other extreme some information is needed only once (for strategic planning). To meet the needs of effective management, the general model for a marketing information management system must be open.[7] It must cover all major information flows within a marketing organization and between the marketing organization and its environment. It must also be flexible regarding the time requirement for obtaining and processing information.

---

[7] Prince, *Information Systems for Management Planning.*

The need for an information management system

There is a need for a set of procedures to diagnose and solve the basic informational problems arising in the management of an organization. The information management system provides a systematic method for accomplishing this task. The systems analyst (should attempt) to identify, observe, analyze, and specify the requirements for information (for the management) activities throughout the business organization, to determine the sources of data, and to match the information requirements with the appropriate data sources by employing some of the current management science tools and techniques.[8]

The aim is to establish the ideal system that is compatible with the major management requirements in the existing unique environment of a particular business firm. In one firm the ideal system may make use of computer equipment, communication facilities, and operations research techniques; however, in another firm, limited use may be made of these items. The need is to develop a unique system in each organization that is appropriate for the unique conditions in that organization. This ideal system for a given organization should attempt to balance the most timely, the most efficient, and the most economical arrangement of information flows for that organization. Thus, management will have better information for particular management activities and can establish control devices for dealing with recurring types of problems on an exceptions basis.

Functions performed by the information management system

In order for the total information system to operate effectively, certain basic functions must be performed. These functions may be grouped into three sets:

1. Data collection
2. Data processing
3. Information transmitting[9]

Data collection. The first step in data collection is a careful specification of pertinent data needed by management in each phase of the management process. This should be provided by the information audit. A data search should then be conducted to locate the sources of the necessary data. Data may be available in journals, gov-

---

[8] Ibid.

[9] Kotler, "A Design for the Firm's Nerve Center," *Business Horizons*, pp. 71–73.

ernment publications, internal reports or other secondary sources. These should be used whenever possible in order to reduce cost and increase the efficiency of the system. When secondary sources are not available, primary data must be collected or purchased. Procedures should be developed in securing relevant data, and screening to filter out unimportant material. The system must also be able to retrieve stored information from the data bank in order to produce periodic reports and form a basis for various types of analysis.

Data processing. A second important function is that of data processing. The data processing function includes the elements of storage, manipulation, and movement of data. Systems may be organized in various ways to accomplish this function. A centralized system is one in which all of the processing is performed by an organization clearing house of information. All data collecting and processing within the organization is done by a centralized system, where data is stored and used to prepare the required reports. A decentralized system involves several rather autonomous parts serving functional departments or suborganizations within the enterprise. Each of these gathers its own data, produces reports as needed by the department it is serving, and stores data accordingly. Another form of system is a distribution-oriented one whose operations emphasize the transmission of information to managerial stations throughout the organization. The opposite is the storage-oriented system which is more concerned with the efficient storage of data than with its transmission to information users in the managerial system. Retrieving information from such a unit may require an excessive amount of effort on the part of the manager who needs the information. "An information (. . . storage unit) is considered small by authorities . . . if it has access to 50,000 or less records. A record is an amount of information pertinent to something or somebody about which the organization needs information."[10] Units that store and have available up to 1 million records are usually considered to be medium sized, and large systems contain over 1 million records at any one time.

Most information systems include data-retrieval and document-retrieval procedures which aid in the processing function. Data-retrieval procedures take many different types of data, kept in storage devices, and manipulate them in such a way that a desired report can be produced, usually involving mathematical calculations. Document-retrieving procedures are able to produce a given document upon request but with little or no manipulation of data. This type of procedure

---

[10] Richard W. Brightman, *Information Systems for Modern Management*, (New York: The Macmillan Co., 1971), p. 22.

sometimes makes use of microfilm and other recording techniques that use miniatured reproduction in order to store documents and records.

Almost every system uses both manual and automated techniques in getting its work done. It is possible to develop a system that is entirely manual in which all of the storage, manipulation, and movement of data is accomplished without the use of any automated devices. This is usually seen only in very small businesses. The degree to which a system should be automated depends upon the speed with which the data must be processed, the amount of data to be processed and stored, and the value of the information to the manager as compared to the costs of automating the system.

The key aspect of processing is the manipulation of data in such a way as to transform it into useful information. This manipulation is carried out by the application of various statistical techniques and models to the raw data. The appropriate techniques and models vary with the managerial activity under consideration. The selection of analytical techniques was discussed in earlier chapters.

In terms of computer procedures the most common data processing techniques are those that make great use of batch, or sequential processing techniques. A batch technique is one which gathers and saves all transactions affecting a file of data, and after a certain period of time or after a specified number of transactions have been accumulated, the file is updated making use of the transactions that have been collected to that point. Real-time systems do not gather transactions for processing at some later time, but process each transaction as it occurs.[11]

Information transmitting.   The third function of the marketing information management system is to deliver needed information to the manager and aid him in using the information. The manager needs the information either in the form of periodic reports or special project data, depending upon whether the decision under consideration is strategic or managerial. In addition, he may need a research specialist to help him interpret the information delivered to him. Help may also be required in formulating problems and specifying the types of information needed. Finally, the manager may find computer program assistance of value. Specialists in the computer field can help the decision maker in understanding the computer and the kind of things it can do. These various types of technical assistance should enhance the manager's ability to secure and use information to make accurate and timely decisions.

---

[11] For additional information on data processing, see Brightman, *Information Systems for Modern Management*.

A FRAMEWORK FOR THE INFORMATION
MANAGEMENT SYSTEM

Basic components

Five basic elements or components are key functional parts of the typical information management system. These components perform the necessary functions of the system and include: the data collection procedures, data bank, statistical bank, model bank, and display unit. Figure 14–2 shows the procedural and data flows through the system. This flow is initiated by questions arising in the management process. These questions which may relate to either market analysis or formulation of the marketing mix were collected by a unit designed to handle the interface between the system and the managers. Such a mechanism is usually referred to as a display unit.

These managerial questions are the basis for determining data requirements for the system. The output of the system should be information designed to aid the manager in answering questions related to the decisions he must make. Data may be needed to answer questions of a major nature which arise only occasionally as in the case of strategic decisions or to answer questions which arise on a regular basis as in the case of management decisions. After the data requirements have been established, the question should be asked, "Are the data in the data bank?" In many cases, data which has already been collected for some other purpose can be used in answering new questions. If this is the case, the precollected data should be used to avoid the cost of duplication. With management decision data requirements standard collection procedures can be established to collect and feed data into the data bank. In the case of strategic decision data needs, the question must be asked—Are standard data (collected for operational questions) sufficient? If the answer is yes, the data will be generated through standard collection procedures. If the answer is no, a second question must be answered—Should we buy information or design our own research?

If the decision is to design research, data collection procedures must be selected to collect and feed data to the data bank. The method for using the system's analytical capabilities must also be determined and programmed into the analytical bank. If the decision is to buy, the purchased data flows either into the data bank or the analytical section. Data may then flow from the data bank directly to the display units or to the analytical unit for processing. Processing may take place in either the statistical bank or the model bank. Data may pass to both of these banks in order to complete the processing.

Figure 14–2
General model of a marketing information management system

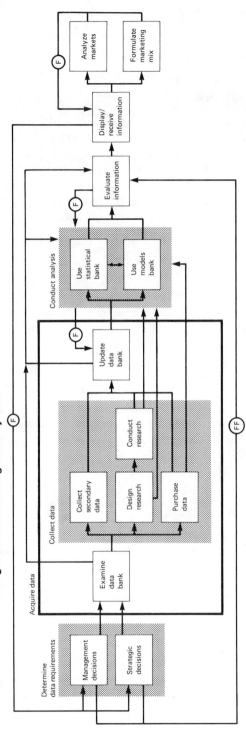

After the information is processed, it may flow back to the data bank for storage or to the display unit. From the display unit, information goes to the manager to answer specific questions which aid him in the decision-making process.

Data collection procedures.   Data collection procedures consist of all methods of gathering relevant data. Such data might originate at numerous sources, and the collection procedure should be varied depending on the source and type of data needed. Typical data classified by source include the following:

1. Secondary data: Internally generated (sales records, cost-price data, advertising expenditures, etc.)
2. Secondary data: Externally generated (economic data, legal regulations, Nielsen Retail Index, competitors' product data, etc.)
3. Primary data: From qualitative approaches (this is subjective data basically in the form of hypotheses generated by focus group interviews, depth interviews or projective techniques).
4. Primary data: From quantitative approaches.
    a. Survey Data (sales surveys, consumer characteristics and buying behavior, competitive price and distribution analysis, etc.)
    b. Experimental data (awareness tests, price sensitivity tests, sales promotion effectiveness, etc.).
    c. Simulation data (data generated by simulation models).

Methods for collecting data were examined in Chapters 5–6. Procedures for determining information and data needs were outlined in Chapters 3 and 5.

Data bank.   The data bank serves as a memory unit for the system.[12] It holds the sum total of past information available to the organization. Such information is a vital input into the management process. In order to facilitate the storage and handling of this information, an attempt should be made to classify and index information along relevant management dimensions (in the case of marketing management these dimensions are market analysis and formulating the marketing mix). Some data cannot be placed in any one area and must thus be stored in a common unit.

Since the volume of data in any one area of the data bank may be quite large, an attempt should be made to compress information. This data compression may be achieved by filtering out insignificant information, aggregation of data and/or conversion of data into probabilistic terms.

Statistical bank.   The statistical bank should contain those techniques needed for the statistical manipulation of data. These may in-

---

[12] See James C. Emery, *Organizational Planning and Control Systems: Theory and Technology* (New York: The Macmillan Co., 1969), pp. 39–58.

clude several basic procedures such as cross-classification, chi-square analysis, and regression. Statistical techniques may be used for several different purposes including description, building tailor-made models, and setting the parameters of generalized models. These techniques, because of their broad applications, are not normally segmented by decision dimensions but form a general statistical bank. Basic statistical techniques and their uses were dealt with in Chapter 9.

Model bank. A model may be defined as "a simplified representation of the relevant aspects of an actual system or process."[13] Many types of models are of use in marketing management, and most of them are symbolic in nature. Some of these models have been discussed in earlier chapters.

In many decision situations, marketing models such as transportation models, the product life cycle model, break-even models, media selection models, and numerous others can be very useful if the models' parameters can be established. These models can be segmented by management activity and selected models used to analyze data for specific types of marketing decisions.

Display unit. The display unit is the point of interface between the information mechanism and the manager.[14] It receives and routes questions from the manager and provides him with the informational outputs of the system. The display unit should provide aid in the utilization of the information. The format for the presentation of information is dependent upon the nature of the problem and the sophistication of the system. Whenever possible, data should be presented in simplified tables and/or graphs for ease of interpretation and use by the manager. Research reporting was discussed in Chapter 10.

The information management system as it relates to the research process

The information management system is a structure within the organization designed to carry out the research process. Its basic components work to accomplish the functions required of the system. The data collection procedures perform the data collection function; the data bank, statistical bank, and models bank work together to perform the data processing function; and finally, the display unit performs the information transmission function. When these functions are carried out effectively the research process of generating information can be accomplished. Thus a flow of information is provided to the decision

---

[13] James H. Donnelly, Jr. and John M. Ivancevich, *Analysis for Marketing Decisions* (Richard D. Irwin, Inc.: Homewood, Ill., 1970), p. 13.

[14] Emery, *Organization Planning and Control Systems*, p. 62.

makers within the organization. This relationship is shown in Figure 14–3.

Figure 14–3
Summary of the system/process relationship

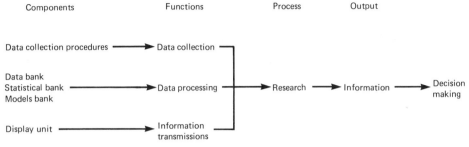

| Components | Functions | Process | Output |

BUILDING A MARKETING INFORMATION MANAGEMENT SYSTEM

The modern marketing information management system is capable of providing valuable information for the marketing manager.[15] Yet certain questions pertaining to the information management system seem to perplex those who are willing to build such a system in their companies. Some of the important questions raised by marketing managers are:

1. What development strategy should be followed?
2. Should the attempt be to build a total system in one move or in stages?
3. What should be the major characteristics of the system?
4. How much should be spent on developing and operating the system?
5. What kind of behavioral problems are likely to arise in the development process?

The following discussion is not exhaustive but rather is intended to provide some general guidelines and working hypotheses that are worthy of consideration when building an information management system.

Reading the organization

The starting point in development of an effective and efficient system should be a review and appraisal of the entire marketing organiza-

---

[15] Parts of this discussion were adapted from D. F. Cox and R. F. Good, "How to Build a Marketing Information System," *Harvard Business Review*, May–June 1967, pp. 145–54.

tion and the policies that direct it. As one marketing executive pointed out, "We realized we couldn't develop a marketing control system until we had clearly and sharply defined the responsibilities of our marketing managers . . . (the purpose of the) system was to measure their performance against plans, we had to specify precisely what each man was accountable for." This statement holds for the development of any type of information network and its subparts. In fact, the specification of who is responsible for what automatically determines many of the characteristics of the decision-making process and thereby, many of the dimensions of the information management system.

Organizing for development

Management must next decide how to organize the development activities. Cox and Good observed that this is a much more complex problem than might be assumed. Sophisticated systems require the coordinated efforts of many departments and individuals including top management, marketing management, system designers, programmers, computer equipment experts and suppliers. The contribution of each group depends on its specialized talents and interests in the system. As an example, programmers cannot define the marketing manager's information needs and managers usually cannot program. It is virtually impossible to find one person within an organization with sufficient knowledge of the organization and expertise in technical areas to accomplish all facets of the development of a desirable system. Therefore, the question to be answered is who should be responsible for design, planning, and development? The approaches which have been tried to solve the problems of organization and leadership can be characterized under the following categories:

1. *Clean piece of paper approach.* This involves drawing a new organizational chart. The idea procedure is to abolish the traditional information gathering and processing departments and establish a new management information department.
2. *Committee approach.* Under this approach some companies have established marketing information committees. They are designed as vehicles for communicating points of view and for joint learning and sharing in the experience of developing the information network. They should create shared awareness of compatibility and coordination problems and of the need and means to resolve them.
3. *Low level approach.* Some companies, on the other hand, have assigned the task of development to a junior member of the mar-

keting research department, often as a part time assignment. This reflects a total lack of understanding of the difficulty of the task. The low level approach is the least satisfactory of the typical approaches.

4. *Information coordination approach.* Finally, some companies while retaining traditional departmental boundaries, have appointed a top level executive to the post of information coordinator. His job is to bring together the necessary resources (human and physical) to develop an effective and efficient information network. Such a coordinator is sometimes called a director of marketing systems. This approach has the advantage of leadership with sufficient authority to get things done within the organizational framework. The information coordinator approach has met with considerable success in the business community.

How sophisticated should the system be?

The level of sophistication of the system must now be decided. This decision should be based on a review of the information needs of the management process and the cost of meeting those needs. To develop and use effectively some of the more sophisticated models and statistical techniques the managers must be able to: define specific information needs; develop analytical approaches (statistical and model); make explicit their decision-making procedures; and be able to interpret and use sophisticated information. One of the characteristics of more advanced systems is automation of certain aspects of the marketing management process through the use of decision rules. It is essential to make the process explicit before such advanced procedures can be used.

The key to the decision on the degree of sophistication is system-manager balance. It is necessary to maintain a balance between management sophistication and the complexity of analytical techniques employed in the information management system. The fact is that information quality can be upgraded much more rapidly than management quality. It is relatively easy to throw the management system out of balance by installing procedures which are too sophisticated for the managers. A more positive approach is to develop a master plan for upgrading the system gradually over several years so that management has sufficient time to adjust to the changes.

Is it desirable to build a complete system in one move?

While an attempt to develop a highly sophisticated, total marketing information management system at the outset has a high probability of failure, it is desirable to develop a complete framework in one move. This will generate a more integrated structure than a fragmentary approach. Additional sophisticated procedures can then be developed and instituted within the overall framework at a rate which will allow management to fully absorb and utilize them.

Micro specifications

Apart from decisions on the general characteristics of the system to be used, the micro specifications must be determined. In addition to the type of system to be developed, other important considerations are the nature of the data bank, the form and the method of data displays, and computer selection:

1. *The micro data bank.* In designing the data bank, it is important to provide for common denominators in different sets of data so that the full analytical potential of the system can be realized. This means that such elements as the geographic, time, and responsibility boundaries of different types of data must be compatible to permit meaningful comparisons.
2. *Data display.* Developing an effective system includes resolving the questions of what information should be presented, how it should be presented, and to whom it should be made available? One important aspect of these questions is the degree of manager-system interaction desired. At the extreme of "distance" managers receive information in the form of regular reports. With somewhat closer but not complete interaction, the manager can make special requests for information from the data bank. At the extreme of "closeness," the manager can obtain almost instantaneous computer response with a time-sharing or on-line system. Given the current state of the art, regular reports supplemented with special request procedures appears to be the most practical arrangement.
3. *Computer selection.* The computer requirements for the information management system will depend on the system's performance specifications and the decision management has made on each of the preceding design problems. While technical help is usually necessary in the decisions on hardware, management has the responsibility for making certain that the equipment chosen will meet the system needs both at the time of installation and in the future when the system becomes larger as well as more sophisticated. In this respect the system designer should recognize that the managers will learn many new ways to use the computer as they become more experienced in the use of the new procedures and thus room for expansion is essential.

Cost and value

It is extremely difficult to generalize about how much an advanced information management system will cost or how much it will be worth. Usually, there is little increase in data collection costs since most companies already collect much of the raw data required. Cost increases result mainly from increased requirements for data storage and transforming the raw data into useful information. The difficulty in determining past development cost arises from the fact that many companies lack accounting arrangements (such as interdepartmental billing) which would allow them to keep track of the total cost of the manpower contributing to the program.

Usually computer-based information systems, such as those used for accounting, have been justified on the grounds that they reduce personnel and other administrative costs. Advanced marketing information management systems could be justified on the basis of cost reductions, but a more meaningful justification is improved marketing management. Determining how much the new information will increase marketing effectiveness is again a difficult task. The involvement of management in developing overall specifications, in terms of the management needs for information, should help in making an estimate of the total system benefits.

Potential behavioral problems in developing the information management system

Individuals have a natural tendency to resist change; thus unfavorable behavioral consequences often accompany the introduction of a sophisticated information system.[16] In order to minimize such unfavorable consequences the manager must not only recognize that such problems are likely to arise, but must also understand the basic factors underlying such behavior:

1. *Changes in the formal organizational structure.* Most organizations have definite departmental boundaries and divisions of formal responsibility. Changes in these boundaries and divisions often occur in connection with the introduction of a new information system, and as these formal lines of responsibility are violated resistance becomes inevitable.
2. *Changes in the informal structure.* The informal relationships which develop within any organization may be highly complex and of importance to the individuals involved. Informational and social ties develop; breaking such relationships can generate adverse reactions.

---

[16] See W. Dickson and John K. Simmons, "The Behavioral Side of MIS," *Business Horizons,* (August 1970), pp. 59–71.

3. *Personal characteristics.* Personal characteristics and back-ground of the particular individuals affect their behavior toward new developments. Younger people with fewer years of service tend to be less opposed to change than older people with more years of service. Besides this, many people see the computer as the most recent intrusion of the machine into man's domain and to them it represents a danger to their status and perhaps their job.

4. *Managerial climate.* The members of an organization are more likely to respond favorably to a proposed change if the managerial climate maintains open communications and permits all griev-ances to be heard. The method used by management to introduce change is another significant variable affecting its likelihood of success.

These and other underlying factors may generate various forms of dysfunctional behavior. Usually such dysfunctional behavior takes one or more of three forms depending upon the individual's position within the organization.

1. *Aggression.* Aggressive behavior represents an attack intended to injure the object causing the problem. The most dramatic aggres-sion toward the system occurs as sabotage (when people attempt to destroy the system's components). A less dramatic but more common form of aggression occurs when people attempt to "beat the system."

2. *Projection.* Projection exists when people blame the system for causing difficulties that are in fact caused by something else. In many instances the system may be blamed for failings actually caused by too rapid an implementation or the incompetence of the individuals involved.

3. *Avoidance.* People may defend themselves by withdrawing from the frustrating situation. In the area of management utilization this behavior often takes the form of ignoring the system output. This is particularly the case when the system does not totally fulfill infor-mation needs.

The manager must attempt to minimize dysfunctional behavior. To do this, special attention should be given to the following:

1. *Proper atmosphere.* Critical aspects are the attitudes of both management and any affected employee, organizational cohesive-ness, and organizational culture. The attitude of top management should be one of full support for the system. There should also be open lines of communication between different levels of man-agement, between management and employees, and between line and staff employees.

2. *Participation.* Which items will be included, what information
    will be given to whom, and possible job modifications are the
    important considerations. The specialists must not dominate the
    installation; more responsibility should be given to the operating
    managers than has often been the case. An attempt should be
    made to achieve harmony between individual and organizational
    goals.

3. *Clarity of the system.* The purpose and characteristics of the
    system should be as clear as possible to those who have direct
    contact with it. This means that the nature and detail of a system
    must be fully explored and discussed with those affected before,
    during, and after installation. Another factor of importance is
    minimizing initial system errors. Frequent mistakes can delay or
    even completely undermine a potentially good system.

4. *Plan scope.* The fact that a computer has the ability to do some-
    thing does not necessarily mean that the computer should do it.
    Attention should be paid to the possible need to deliberately ex-
    pand the scope of activities for the individual within a computer-
    controlled system resulting in a calculated inefficiency that can
    save the humanity within the system.

5. *New challenges.* New challenges may be opened up by the in-
    stallation of a sophisticated system. A look should be taken at what
    management and employees ought to be doing that is more impor-
    tant and satisfying than what they did before. The manager should
    discover and emphasize these new challenges in discussions with
    individuals at all levels.

6. *Re-examine performance evaluation.* There will likely have to
    be a shift from rewards based on individual accomplishments to
    rewards based on group achievements if integrated programs are
    to be useful.

7. *User orientation.* The design of the system must fulfill the needs
    of the user if he is to be satisfied with the output. Otherwise he is
    compelled to maintain his own system which defeats the basic
    purpose of the installation. The system should be carefully
    developed so as not to overwhelm the user with a large volume of
    output which the user either cannot understand or cannot use ef-
    fectively. This is why user orientation is the *key factor* in attempt-
    ing to minimize dysfunctional behavior.

SUMMARY

Marketing managers are faced with increasingly complex problem
situations. The development of sophisticated marketing information
management systems is a logical response to the increased information

needs generated by these problems. Thus, it seems reasonable to suppose that business will continue to implement advanced information systems and that the successful manager of the future needs to be able to understand and operate efficiently within such an environment.

The information management system within an organization is the machinery (procedures, personnel, and equipment) set up to do research. Research in this context means any type of information production activity. Information is, of course, a vital ingredient in the decision making of marketing management. To carry out the research process and insure an orderly flow of information within the firm, the system must perform three basic functions: data collection, data processing, and information transmission. Most systems have five components designed to accomplish these functions: data collection procedures to collect data; a data bank, statistical bank, and models bank to process data; and a display unit to transmit information to the managers. These components form the functional parts of the system. Its inputs are raw data and its outputs are information for decision making.

A careful reading of the organization is the key to building an effective information management system. To work well, the system must be user-oriented; it must serve the needs of the decision makers. The building process should thus start with a careful information audit which locates the relevant decisions, who makes each decision, and what information is needed.

DISCUSSION QUESTIONS

1. What is a marketing information management system? What are its components and functions?

2. Discuss the relationship between marketing research, marketing management, and the marketing information management system.

3. Discuss the advantages and disadvantages of alternative strategies for building information management systems.

4. What specific types of behavioral problems may result in the development of a sophisticated information management system and how can these problems be avoided?

5. Suppose that you are a sales manager for a large insurance company. You are responsible for the selection, training, supervision, and control of twenty salesmen. What types of information might be needed for the decisions involved in this job? How might an information management system be designed to handle these needs?

6. You are responsible for new product development for a men's leisure clothing manufacturer. What types of information would you need? How could the information management system be structured to meet your needs?

SELECTED REFERENCES

Alter, Steven L. "How Effective Managers Use Information Systems." *Harvard Business Review*, November–December 1976, pp. 97–104.

Barnett, Arnold. "Preparing Management for MIS." *Journal of Systems Management.* January 1972, pp. 40–43.

Buzzell, Robert D.; Cox, Donald F.; and Brown, Rex V. *Marketing Research and Information Systems*. New York: McGraw-Hill Book Company, 1969, pp. 697–713.

Cox, D. F., and Good, R. E. "How to Build a MIS." *Harvard Business Review*, May–June 1967, pp. 145–54.

Derman, Irwin H. "Do You 'MIS' Understand?" *Business Horizons*, October 1972, pp. 55–64.

Dickson, W., and Simmons, J. K. "The Behavioral Side of MIS." *Business Horizons*, August 1970, pp. 59–71.

Gibson, Lawrence D., et al. "An Evolutionary Approach to Marketing Information Systems." *Journal of Marketing*, April 1973, pp. 2–6.

Head, Robert V. *Manager's Guide to Management Information Systems*. American Management Association, 1969, pp. 1–36, 99–121.

Kotler, Philip. "A Design for the Firm's Nerve Center." *Business Horizons*, Fall 1966, pp. 63–74.

Zani, William M. "A Blueprint for MIS." *Harvard Business Review*, November–December 1970, pp. 95–100.

Cases for part three

13

Pomona Products Company*

Last July, the officers of the Pomona Products Company met to discuss the company's possible introduction of its line of southern vegetables into the New York market. The focus of the meeting was the strategy to be used for the introduction. They were particularly interested in the possible methods of promoting the products and in the channels of distribution to be used in distributing the southern vegetables.

COMPANY BACKGROUND

Pomona Products Company traces its beginnings to 1911, when a young man, George Riegel, saw a can of Spanish pimientos on a grocery shelf in Griffin, Georgia. (A pimiento is a red sweet pepper often used as a garnish, stuffing for green olives, or in relishes and salads.) He and his brother and father were commercial vegetable growers on a

---

* This case was prepared by Kenneth L. Bernhardt and John S. Wright, Georgia State University.

farm near Griffin, and together they had worked on improving the quality of vegetable crops, particularly peppers. Through the American Consul in Spain the Riegels secured six ounces of pimiento seed and in 1912 grew enough plants to set out 1½ acres of pimiento plants on the Riegel farm.

Attempts to sell the pimientos on the fresh market met with no success because of the extreme toughness of the pimiento skins. George Riegel recalled that his interest in pimientos had stemmed from the canned Spanish product, so he decided to attempt the canning process himself. Skins were removed by immersing the pimientos in a lye solution, and after cleaning they were canned with salt and vinegar. The use of lye proved so tedious that the help of the Spanish Consul was again sought, and he reported that the skins in Spain were removed by roasting the pimientos for several minutes in a hot oven and wiping off charred skins with clean cloths.

The roasting operation proved far more satisfactory and by 1913 Mark Riegel perfected a mechanical roaster. It consisted of a coke-burning tunnel of fire brick, through which the cored pimientos passed, each placed over a steel spike fastened to an endless chain. The charred skins were them removed by sprinkler washers and brushes, with the final cleaning done by hand.

Finding the new roaster satisfactory, the Riegels continued their research on canning pimientos in a small shed on a farm near Pomona, Georgia, a few miles from Griffin. During the summer of 1914 they put up a small pack of pimientos in this little plant and the H. V. Kell Wholesale Grocery Company of Griffin marketed the entire pack.

An executive who was associated with the wholesaler became interested in the new pimiento cannery after his success in selling the first can of pimientos. He offered to provide financing for two additional roasters and a plant, to be built on his farm. Plans were made and the Pomona Products Company's first plant was built and equipped. The plant was an extremely large food processing facility relative to the standards of that day.

Pimientos were first canned in the new plant in 1916 and sold under the Sunshine brand name. The total crop that year came from 75 acres, all located in Spalding County, of which Griffin is the county seat.

In 1920, the company was sold and the plant was moved several miles to Griffin where gas was available to provide fuel for the huge roasting ovens which charred the skins so they could be removed from the pimientos.

In spite of the problems faced by a new company processing a new product, Pomona Products Company grew and prospered. There were bleak years—when the pimiento crop was too short to produce a profitable pack. But the bad years were outnumbered by the good years and pimiento volume climbed steadily. Pomona's success led to the entry of other canners in the pimiento field, and over the years as many as 18 or 20 firms were in the business at one time. Growing of pimientos by farmers, once limited entirely to Georgia, now extends into several adjoining states and California.

To reduce its dependency on a single product, Pomona began processing and packing a number of southern fruits and vegetables which were also marketed under the Sunshine brand name. Currently, about 20 different fruits and vegetables are processed and canned including turnip greens, green beans, pickled peaches, potatoes, squash, rutabagas, and several varieties of peas and beans.

In 1955, Pomona Products Company became a subsidiary of Stokely-Van Camp, Inc., of Indianapolis, Indiana. The Pomona Division is operated with a large degree of independence, but the relationship has given the firm greater resources for expanding their business. Stokely-Van Camp 1961 sales were $197 million. Sales for the Pomona Products Company were approximately $5 million in 1961.

BACKGROUND ON THE PRODUCT LINE

The Pomona product line could be categorized into the following groups of products:

1. Pimientos.
2. Green beans.
3. Greens—turnip greens, collard greens, mustard greens, etc.
4. Potatoes.
5. Miscellaneous southern vegetables—field peas, squash, rutabagas, etc.
6. Pickled peaches.

A list of products sold by Pomona, together with the share of company sales, is presented in Table 1.

Data on the total market for the individual products was difficult to compile because the trade association, the National Canners Association, included most of Pomona's products in the "Miscellaneous Vegetables" category, which contained a wide variety of unrelated products. The director of marketing for Pomona estimated that the company had about 35 percent of the pimiento market, about one third of the leafy greens market, and less than one percent of the total market for green beans and Irish potatoes.

The product line contained a number of products which are very seasonal in nature. Table 2 contains a seasonal shipping index by month for the company's three major product types.

Table 1
Pomona Products Company—Sales breakdown by products (this year)

Commodity	Total case sales	% of total
Pimientos	642,633	35.3%
Turnip greens	297,076	16.3
Green beans	204,924	11.3
Pork and beans	175,766	9.6
Pickled peaches	110,284	6.0
Collard greens	60,709	3.3
White potatoes	58,049	3.2
Beans and potatoes	51,761	2.8
Blackeyed peas	42,925	2.3
Mustard greens	30,902	1.7
Squash	30,248	1.7
Field peas	29,189	1.6
Spinach	24,534	1.3
Rutabagas	23,044	1.3
Mixed greens	12,758	.7
Boiled peanuts	11,467	.6
Lady peas	6,910	.3
Kale	5,597	.3
White acre peas	3,259	.2
Kidney beans	2,413	.1
Green and shelled beans	1,772	.1
Total	1,826,210	100.0%

Table 2
Seasonal shipping index for Pomona Products (retail size pimientos, greens and green beans)

	Pimientos	Greens	Green beans
Average month	100	100	100
June	87	63	64
July	98	60	56
August	148	102	95
September	82	128	93
October	125	137	122
November	57	70	83
December	82	72	68
January	134	142	132
February	94	152	132
March	94	72	149
April	91	81	83
May	113	114	78

In addition to being concentrated in several seasons, the sales were concentrated by geographic area. Approximately 70 percent of Pomona's sales came from five states—Georgia, Texas, Florida, North Carolina, and Alabama. Table 3 shows the sales breakdown by state.

Table 4 contains an analysis by product, of Pomona's strengths and weaknesses together with comments on the company's competitive position. Table 5 presents information on each of the company's major competitors for pimientos and for southern vegetables.

Table 3
Pomona Products sales by state,
top 10 states

State	Percent of total sales
1. Georgia	25%
2. Texas	16*
3. Florida	14
4. N. Carolina	7
5. Alabama	7
6. S. Carolina	4
7. Tennessee	3
8. Mississippi	2
9. Virginia	2
10. Illinois	1
Other states	19
	100%

* 90 percent of sales in Texas are pimientos.

POMONA PRODUCTS' MARKETING STRATEGY

The company defined its customers as retail and institutional grocery distributors and food manufacturers in the United States (excluding New Mexico, Arizona, Nevada, California, Oregon, Washington and Alaska). Pimientos were marketed nationally, with the above exceptions, and the line of southern vegetables were marketed from Washington, D.C. to San Antonio. The products were not marketed on the west coast because there was a strong competitor located there. With the high shipping costs, the price Pomona would have to charge would be too high for strong consumer acceptance.

Pomona's customers purchased regularly and frequently, usually at least once per month. Chains and large wholesalers purchased more often averaging twice per month. A typical chain would sell about 300 cases per year per store. No exclusive franchises were awarded, and all distributors were considered potential customers.

A network of about 70 food brokers was used as the company's sales organization. Pomona's principal competitors also used food brokers

Table 4
Analysis of Pomona Products Company (PPC) market position

In terms of strengths and weaknesses in sales, product, manufacturing and marketing we rate our market position by category as follows: (+ = strength, − = weakness, 0 = no special strength or weakness)

Category	Sales	Product	Manufac-turing	Mar-keting	Overall
1. Pimientos	+	+	+	0	+
2. Greens	+	+	+	0	+
3. Spinach	−	0	+	0	0
4. Green beans	−	−	+	0	−
5. Green beans w/potatoes	+	+	+	0	+
6. Irish potatoes	−	0	−	0	−
7. Miscellaneous seasonal vegetables	+	+		0	+
8. Pickled peaches	+	+	+	+	++
9. Nonseasonal vegetables	−	−	−	0	−

Most products suffer from a "commodity" image in the minds of retail and wholesale customers, and probably consumers. There are no apparent or significant differences in product quality or packaging or most items compared to major competition. Specific exceptions are turnip greens with diced turnips, green beans with potatoes and pickled peaches. These specialty or combination items enjoy "brand" status and are among our leading volume and profit producers.

PPC is an unquestioned leader in the domestic pimiento industry.

PPC is probably the largest processor of leafy greens excluding spinach in the United States.

PPC has an exclusive product in pickled peaches, distinctive from spiced peaches. This item is extremely strong in the Southeast.

PPC was the first canner of turnip greens with diced turnips and has achieved strong distribution for the product.

Green beans with potatoes have responded to special sales effort in recent years and are in a fairly strong position.

In miscellaneous seasonal vegetables, rutabagas enjoy a unique position. Distribution is very good and volume is steadily increasing.

except for the National Biscuit Company, which had company salesmen in some areas. The brokers were paid 3 percent of sales.

Pricing of pimientos was generally competitive, but stable. Vegetable prices varied more, but differences usually reflected freight advantages. Pomona's prices were competitive with major competition on pimientos, greens, green beans, other seasonal items, and nonseasonal products.

Very little advertising was done by Pomona or its competitors. Most of the promotion budget went into trade allowances. Several times a

Table 5
Pomona Products competition

I. *Pimientos*

A. *National Biscuit Company*, Special Products Division, Woodbury, Ga. Dromedary brand. NBC is probably largest domestic pimiento processor. National distribution. Strong franchise, sound pricing. An industry leader. Marketing headquarters in NYC.

B. *Cherokee Products Co.*, Haddock, Ga. "O'Sage" brand and buyer's label. Strong regional competitor. Strength in SE especially with Winn Dixie. Spotty distribution outside SE (NYC and Pacific Coast). A price follower.

C. *King Pharr Canning Operations, Inc.*, Cullman, Ala. "King Pharr" and "Miss America" brands and buyer's label. Third or fourth largest SE processor. Follows industry pricing but makes exceptions through advertising rebates, promotion agreements, etc. A boat rocker.

D. *Besco Products Co.*, Zebulon, Ga. "Miss Georgia" brand. Small packer. Price follower.

E. *Monticello Canning Co.*, Crossville, Tenn. "Betty Ann" brand. Small packer. Follows industry pricing. Strong in Nashville and Chicago.

F. *Heublein, Inc.*, Coastal Valley Canning Co. Division, Oxnard, Cal. "Ortega" brand. Largest Pacific coast packer. Distribution generally west of Rocky Mountains and Houston. Marketing decisions made in East by Heublein.

II. *Southern Vegetables*

A. *Bush Bros.*, Dandridge, Tenn. "Bush's Best" and "Showboat" brands. A strong, multiline, reputable competitor. Very strong in green beans, greens, and dry packs. Stable pricing. Good trade reputation. Primary distribution in South and Midwest.

B. *King Pharr Canning Operations, Inc.*, a multiline packer. Erratic pricing. Does not have a high quality image with trade.

C. *HLH Products, Inc.*, Dallas, Texas (plant in Sanford, Florida). Full line packer of green beans, greens dry packs. Price cutter and dealers not known as a quality packer.

D. *Miscellaneous other canners* include *Steel Canning Co.*, Springdale, Ark.; *Allen Canning Co.*, Siloam Springs, Ark., *Besco Products Co.*; *Cherokee Products Co.* These are competitors on one or two items but not the full line of our products. The Arkansas packers are strong, low price competition on greens outside the SE.

year an allowance of 50 cents per case would be offered on a few of the products.

The margins on the product line were approximately 20 percent for the retailer, 5 percent for the wholesaler and 3 percent for the broker.

The average case sales price to wholesalers and chains was $3.10 per case which is equivalent to approximately 17 cents per average can to the consumer.

Pomona Products Company had a reputation with the trade as a company with good to high quality products, excellent service, flexible promotions, and fair pricing. The company's brokers were well accepted by nearly all customers, and Pomona was considered a leader in the southern canning industry. The Sunshine brand label was used on all the company's products and private labels were utilized by a few of Pomona's customers.

The company had not conducted any research to determine the characteristics of the end consumers of their products. It was felt, however, that a significant proportion of the buyers were blacks, and the products sold well in predominantly black areas.

THE DECISION CONCERNING ENTRY INTO THE NEW YORK MARKET

In the spring, Mr. Ted Groth, who had been handling the company's sales for many years in the New York area, switched broker organizations and joined the Aris Brokerage Company. Pomona's sales in the New York market had been primarily pimiento sales, with only a small number of cases of southern vegetables. The new broker firm had a young, aggressive management who recognized the potential for the rest of the Pomona line in the New York market. Pimiento sales last year were approximately 7,000 cases and the new brokerage firm felt that with the addition of the line of southern vegetables they could sell at least 50,000 cases a year within a short period of time. There were more southern blacks in New York, for example, than were in the state of Georgia. There had been a large migration of people from the South into New York and other northern markets in the past two decades, and the executives felt that they would be very receptive to the Sunshine line of products. The key question was how to introduce the products into the market.

The brokerage firm prepared the list of grocery store distribution shown in Table 6. There were a large number of chains in the New York market and the 32 chains on that list account for only two thirds of the food store volume in the area. Several of the Pomona and Aris executives felt that they should start with the A&P chain, try to get distribution in their stores, establish a successful sales record, and then seek distribution from the other chains. Other executives wanted to seek immediate distribution from as many chains as possible.

Another issue concerned which stores of a particular chain should stock the line of products. Should only the outlets in predominantely

Table 6
Grocery store distribution—New York area stores

Chain	Number of stores in area	Percent of area volume
A&P	447	12.5
Bohack	175	5.5
Pathmark	28	5.1
Walkbaum	78	5.0
Hills	57	4.7
Grand Union	107	3.9
Shoprite/Foodarama	50	3.1
Daitch Shopwell	90	3.0
First National	73	2.8
Key Food Stores	139	2.6
Food Fair	58	2.6
Met Foods*	996	2.4
King Kullen	43	2.3
Associated Food Stores*	200	1.6
Gristede	108	1.4
Dan's Supreme	19	.8
Bozzuto*	107	.8
Royal Farms	21	.7
Sloan's	23	.7
Durso	11	.7
Handell	15	.6
Krasdale Foods*	900	.5
E&B	8	.5
Mid Eastern Coop	12	.5
Trunz	56	.4
Faith Supermarkets	5	.4
7-Eleven	30	.4
D'Agostino Brothers	12	.4
Fedco Foods	14	.4
Pick Quick	11	.4
Food Pageant	8	.3
Meat's & Treats	10	.3
		67.3%

* Voluntary chain.

black areas sell the products, or should Pomona strive for side distribution in the market?

The executives also wondered what promotional effort should be undertaken. Table 7 contains a list of the various newspapers and radio stations available in the New York market, together with advertising rates. The company's gross margin was only about 25 percent of sales, so they wondered what promotional budget they could afford.

Although no canned southern vegetables were available in the market, frozen southern vegetables were. The executives felt that their pricing and margins would have to be the same as in other areas of the country to enable retailers to sell the products at a price competitive with the frozen products.

Table 7
Media rates for New York area

	Rate	Circulation
Radio stations (daytime rate, one minute announcement)		
WABC	$ 80	
WADO*	30	
WCBS	150	
WEVD	60	
WHN	100	
WHOM	40	
WINS	90	
WJRZ	45	
WLIB	22	
WMCA	60	
WNBC	125	
WNCN	20	
WNEW	125	
WNJR†	22	
WOR	165	
WPAT	70	
WPOW	16	
WQXR	42	
WRFM	27	
WTFM	25	
WVNJ	40	
WWRL	20	
Newspapers (one 70 column inch ad—approx. 1,000 lines)		
El Diario De Nueva York‡	650	60,269
Herald Tribune	1,670	373,508
La Prensa‡	350	33,282
Journal American	1,900	625,631
Mirror	2,000	851,928
News	4,060	1,952,404
Post	1,700	320,149
Times	2,500	754,225
World Telegram & Sun	1,850	460,833

* Black and Spanish programming.
† All black programming.
‡ Spanish language paper.

There would be virtually no additional fixed costs associated with the entry into the New York market. There was excess plant capacity for production, and the company had a warehouse in New York for pimientos, and there was plenty of space available for additional storage. Shipping costs would be about 50 cents per case, but this would be charged to the customers and passed on to the final consumers.

The marketing decisions had to be made soon to insure that the plans could be executed before the slow end-of-the-year season. If they were to enter the New York market, a total program would have to be developed in the next month.

case
14

National Bank of
Georgia—Sheffield Branch*

In 1973, the National Bank of Georgia (NBG) received approval from the Comptroller of Currency to open a branch office in the Sheffield Building. The Sheffield office became NBG's 24th branch (including the main office) and provided a potential source of continued rapid growth. The branch is a separate unit of NBG and acts as a full service bank, offering complete personal and commercial banking services. One aspect of the facility, however, became a matter of concern to NBG's vice president for branch operations:

> . . . The location of the . . . branch does not permit drive-in facilities as a part of the branch itself. Owners of the building, however, have granted permission to locate a remote drive-in facility on property now used for surface parking for tenants and customers of the buildings. Establishment of remote drive-in facilities will be determined by cost and technical feasibility.

The presence of a drive-in facility would expand the potential market for the branch, and the issue therefore warranted serious consideration. The decision involves essentially three alternatives: (1) do nothing; that is, operate without a drive-in facility; (2) build a remote manned facility; or (3) build a remote video facility. Although the branch opened in 1974, the vice president for branch operations was not ready to make a decision regarding drive-in facilities. He postponed the decision for the time being. A number of factors were considered in an attempt to reach a decision. These include: (1) the history and policies of NBG, (2) the target market for the branch, (3) and the economic implications of each alternative.

THE NATIONAL BANK OF GEORGIA

Founded in 1911 under a state charter as the Morris Plan Bank of Georgia, NBG in 1973 was the fifth largest bank in Atlanta and sixth

---

* This case was prepared by Barnett A. Greenberg, Georgia State University.

largest in Georgia. From its inception the bank had been "a financial institution that offered its services and resources to the average man . . . the man who had nothing with which to secure his credit but a steady job and his good character." Consistent with its personal banking orientation, the bank had a number of innovations to its credit. These included installment loans in 1911, automobile loans in 1923, and free personalized checks in 1955.

NBG's first branch was opened in 1949 to "carry banking to the people." Although the number of branches grew over the years, the bank remained relatively small with assets of only $43.6 million at the end of 1960. That year, however, marked the beginning of an era of unprecedented growth for the institution. During 1960 and 1961, NBG became a member of the Federal Reserve System, a member of the Atlanta Clearing House Association, opened three new branches (bringing the total to eight), and moved into a new 31-story building. The year 1961 was also significant as the bank organized a full-service trust department.

In 1965, the Bank of Georgia became the National Bank of Georgia upon receiving the first national charter awarded in Georgia in 56 years. Success in the decade of the 1960s is evidenced by the 260 percent increase in assets (see Table 1). The outlook for the 1970s appeared equally bright and received a particular boost from a new branch banking law. The new law permitted NBG to expand countywide in Fulton and Dekalb counties, while the previous law restricted branching to city limits. (Atlanta city limits lie in both Fulton and Dekalb counties.) NBG responded immediately by opening five new branches. The total number of branches increased from 12 in 1969 to 24 (including the Sheffield Building) in 1974.

The bank's heavy reliance on personal banking services made the branches a particularly important source of growth. As with its other branches, the Sheffield office serves a rather specific target market and provides growth largely through new personal, small business, and professional accounts.

THE SHEFFIELD BRANCH

A detailed description of the market area for the Sheffield branch is provided in the Appendix. The description was written by a consultant for NBG and contains information on the population, income, housing and geography of the market. The consultant specifically noted the potential for drive-in facilities given the flow of traffic and projected market growth.

The primary purpose of the Sheffield branch is to serve the tenants (medical practices) of the Sheffield Building, the nearby Piedmont

Table 1
Selected financial information and number of branches ($000)

	1950	1955	1960	1962	1964	1966	1968	1970	1971	1972	1973
Resources											
Loans and discounts	$ 7,936	$15,103	$24,771	$32,339	$41,795	$56,676	$ 73,496	$ 76,878	$ 97,383	$134,441	$147,224
Other	6,746	12,793	18,823	24,211	35,002	41,772	64,741	80,213	92,937	107,520	105,489
Total	14,682	27,896	43,594	56,550	76,797	98,448	138,237	157,091	190,320	241,961	252,713
Liabilities											
Deposits	13,038	24,933	36,793	48,726	66,274	86,173	121,963	137,729	165,328	213,452	216,800
Other	1,544	2,963	6,801	7,824	10,523	12,275	16,274	19,362	24,992	28,509	35,913
Total	14,682	27,896	43,594	56,550	76,797	98,448	138,237	157,091	190,320	241,961	252,713
Net income*	143	161	290	314	484	629	802	1,049	1,020	1,095	1,281
Number of branches†	3	4	8	8	9	11	12	17	20	22	23

Note: All figures are year end.
* Net income is before securities transactions.
† Includes main office.

Professional Building, and the staff and employees of the Piedmont Hospital. The following excerpt from the branch application summarizes its intended purpose:

The proposed branch will be located in a commercial building whose tenants are primarily medical doctors and related professional businesses. It is adjacent to the Piedmont Hospital which in its complex includes the new Piedmont Professional Building and a nurses training facility. Medical doctors in the Sheffield Building, Piedmont Professional Building and staff of Piedmont Hospital are estimated at 630. Employees of the medical doctors in the Professional Building and auxiliary personnel of the hospital are estimated at 1,600. Estimated number of nurses, including special duty nurses at Piedmont Hospital, is 600. In addition to the existing market from the medical profession, it is anticipated the Piedmont Hospital will have a major expansion of facilities within the next two years which upon completion would add 100 to 150 beds.

In addition to the market represented by the medical profession, the service area also includes numerous small commercial businesses fronting on Peachtree Street convenient to the proposed new branch. The service area also includes a residential population mix of individual residences in the medium-high income range and medium income range as well as several major apartment complexes and high rise apartments.

The primary purpose of the branch will be to develop the banking relationships of the medical profession and auxiliary personnel in the professional buildings and hospital area. This is a highly specialized market but one in which the National Bank of Georgia has considerable experience. This market, therefore, represents the primary purpose for the proposed branch.

DEPOSIT AND LOAN ESTIMATES

It is estimated that The National Bank of Georgia now has approximately $300,000 in deposits and $250,000 in loans derived from the areas to be serviced by the proposed branch office. We estimate that the deposits of this new facility would be approximately $1,200,000 at the end of the first year's operation and $3,000,000 at the end of the third year's operation. Estimates of loans outstanding for the facility would be $1,000,000 at the end of the first year's operation and $2,500,000 at the end of the third year's operation.

The above estimates are based on the experience of NBG with other new branch offices and our knowledge of this particular location and its potential.

SERVICE TO EXISTING BUSINESS

The location of the proposed branch strategically places it as the most convenient branch bank to Piedmont Hospital and professional buildings located within the complex area. The primary commercial development in the service area is in the .5 mile area south of the proposed branch. Since three of other four major Atlanta banks are located in this portion of the proposed service area, it represents a strong competitive market. The area north of the proposed branch has office buildings and commercial establishments at lesser density; however, it is in this area that future commercial development is anticipated. This development would place a proposed branch to best advantage for convenience within the area.

STAFFING OF THE FACILITY

The branch will be fully staffed in keeping with the projected market. The staff would consist of manager, assistant manager, secretary, and three paying and receiving tellers. The secretary would also serve as new accounts clerk and vault custodian.

PROFIT AND LOSS PROJECTIONS

The following is a breakdown of estimated earnings and expenses for each of the first three years of operations of proposed new branch:

	First year	Second year	Third year
Income:			
Loans	$ 45,000	$126,000	$193,000
Investments	–0–	15,000	22,500
Service charges	13,000	29,000	40,000
Total Income	$ 58,000	$170,000	$255,500
Expenses:			
Interest on time deposits	$ 24,000	$ 54,000	$ 72,000
Salaries and employee expense	62,000	66,600	71,450
Occupancy expense	18,160	18,160	18,160
Other operating expense	15,000	16,500	22,100
Total Expenses	$119,160	$155,260	$183,710
Operating profit or (loss)................	($ 61,160)	$ 14,740	$ 71,790

RELATED INFORMATION

The banking area for the proposed branch will be on the ground floor lobby of an existing seven-story office building. The official name for the building is "Sheffield Building" and its primary tenants are medical doctors. The proposed branch will contain 2,270 square feet of net usable space. Service areas of the branch are located within the building and therefore do not have to be provided separately. In addition to the 2,270 square feet for the proposed branch, the lessor has granted NBG the right and option to lease an additional 900 square feet of space immediately adjacent to the premises by granting NBG the right to exercise the option to lease within six months prior to the expiration of leases of present or future tenants. It is customary that office space not be granted for a lease period over three to five years. Said option shall continue for the period of the primary lease and renewals thereof.

Separate negotiations are required for acquiring space to locate a drive-in facility. The location to be considered is owned by the lessors of the proposed branch but is subleased for parking lot purposes until November 1974. Upon reversion to the lessors, it is contemplated that the property will be developed. The lessors have agreed to negotiate a second lease to permit location of a remote drive-in facility compatible with plans of development. Since drive-in facilities are desirable although not critical to the proposed branch, feasibility studies on the remote drive-in are being deferred since the expense does not appear to be warranted without first having received approval to establish a branch.

Drive-in facilities

Physical constraints at the Sheffield branch would require a *remote* drive-in facility. That is, the drive-in stations would be separate from, and out of sight of the branch office. NBG must therefore choose from two types of drive-in stations: (1) a traditional face-to-face manned unit or (2) a remote control unit operated with televised communication between the customer and a teller in the branch office. Since there is room for one or two drive-in lanes, three options are available:

1. A single customer lane served by a single remote facility. This amounts to a one-to-one relationship between teller and customer.
2. Two customer lanes served by one teller. This is accomplished through a combination of manned and remote stations or a single video unit for two remote controlled stations.
3. Two customer lanes served by two tellers through either manned or remote control equipment.

Manned drive-in stations. A manned remote station is a "minibank" in which a teller carries out all normal transactions on a face-to-face basis with customers. In other words, this type of facility is a regular bank teller's station which is housed in its own building. The building must have its own climate control, comfort facilities, and security systems making it a rather expensive structure on a square-foot basis. With one manned station, however, the second station can be remote control and operated by the drive-in teller. This configuration is less expensive than two manned stations both in terms of construction and operating costs. On the other hand, when both stations are occupied simultaneously by customers, the single teller is hard pressed to provide competitive service. Nevertheless, financial data for the various remote manned station options are included in Table 2. The information was submitted by both The Mosler Safe Company and Diebold, Inc. (Banks/Systems Division).

Remote control stations. Remote control drive-in stations rely on television cameras and monitors for visual and auditory communication between customer and teller. The transaction is transported in a "carrier" through pneumatic tubing with terminals at the teller and customer stations. NBG has received information from both Mosler and Diebold on remote pneumatic equipment (see Table 3).

Pneumatic systems are further classified as either "loose carrier" or "captive carrier." In the case of the former the carrier is removed from

Table 2
Selected information about remote manned drive-in teller stations

		Purchase price*	Site prepara- tion†	Approxi- mate average trans- action time	Approximate net addition to branch operating expenses‡
I.	One teller/ One customer lane				
	Diebold	$ 8,520	$10,000	2 min.	$10,940/yr.
	Mosler	8,289	10,000	2 min.	10,940/yr.
II.	One teller/ Two customer lanes (loose carrier only for pneumatic unit)				
	Diebold	18,670	16,500	2.4 min.	12,680/yr.
	Mosler	18,489	16,500	2.4 min.	12,680/yr.
III.	Two tellers/ Two customer lanes				
	Diebold	17,040	20,000	2 min.	21,880/yr.
	Mosler	16,578	20,000	2 min.	21,880/yr.

   * The manned station comes in a unit which is installed in a building provided by the customer. Prices effective in August 1974. Unit includes bay-type window w/long skirt. II includes a non-video pneumatic unit.

   † The customer must prepare the site, provide the foundation, pave the drive, provide electrical, plumbing, and other hookups, etc. Actual installation is provided by the seller.

   ‡ Teller's salary and benefits account for most of the added expense. Figures exclude depreciation, but include utilities and maintenance.

the terminal by the customer or teller to load or unload a transaction. In a captive carrier system, the carrier remains in the terminal. Transactions are loaded and unloaded through a door in the terminal which is actually part of the carrier. As noted in Table 3, the captive carrier systems are more expensive, the higher price reflecting the more automated and complex nature of the equipment. In recent years Diebold has held the lead for captive carrier systems through technical and operational superiority. Mosler, however, has been able to claim superior loose carrier units. Thus, Diebold has tended to push its captive carrier system, while Mosler has emphasized loose carriers. As of the summer of 1974, however, both manufacturers were claiming competitive lines.

The primary advantage of remote pneumatic drive-in stations is security. That is, neither bank personnel nor cash need be located outside the branch office. Further savings can be realized in reduced personnel expense since the same tellers inside the branch can handle walk-in and drive-in customers. Among the systems the captive carrier reduces the number of movements required in a total transaction by 25 percent. The loose carrier, however, is mechanically less complex and

Table 3
Selected information about remote controlled drive-in teller stations

	Purchase price†	Site preparation	Approximate average transaction time	Approximate net addition to branch operating expenses‡
One teller terminal/				
One customer terminal				
Diebold				
Captive carrier	$27,650	$ 9,000	3 min.	$2,200/yr.
Loose carrier	25,500	9,000	4 min.	2,200/yr.
Mosler				
Captive carrier	28,400	9,000	3 min.	2,200/yr.
Loose carrier	25,250	9,000	4 min.	2,200/yr.
One teller terminal/				
Two customer terminals				
Diebold				
Captive carrier	47,250	15,000	3.5 min.	3,800/yr.
Loose carrier	43,450	15,000	4.5 min.	3,800/yr.
Mosler				
Captive carrier	49,500	15,000	3.5 min.	3,800/yr.
Loose carrier	42,450	15,000	4.5 min.	3,800/yr.
Two teller terminals/				
Two customer terminals*				
Diebold				
Captive carrier	53,250	15,000	3 min.	4,000/yr.
Loose carrier	49,450	15,000	4 min.	4,000/yr.
Mosler				
Captive carrier	55,150	15,000	3 min.	4,000/yr.
Loose carrier	48,450	15,000	4 min.	4,000/yr.

  * One teller can serve either lane. When both lanes are occupied, a second teller operates the second terminal.

  † Prices effective in August, 1974.

  ‡ Assumes no net addition of tellers to branch. Figures exclude depreciation, but include utilities, rent, and maintenance.

easier to maintain. Although transaction movements are greater, the loose carrier takes the transaction into the customer's car where it cannot be blown away or dropped on the ground.

1975 DEADLINE

NBG's vice president for branch operations must decide before 1975 whether the Sheffield branch should have drive-in facilities. The lease on the parking deck beside the branch will be renegotiated during the first quarter of 1975. This will be the only near term opportunity for several years to acquire use of some of that property. The facilities can only be justified, however, if they generate enough new accounts to be profitable.

The vice president has called in a consultant to help with the decision. He explained that no two branches are alike, but drive-in business is usually low cost demand-account transactions. Thus, profit from these facilities (as a percentage of total deposits) is as much as double that of the bank's overall deposit account transactions. He further noted that the branch was justified on the basis of its existing market in the nearby professional and commercial buildings. Drive-in facilities could only be justified if they generate incremental business and profits.

Finally, the vice president noted that space and design limitations have rendered competitors' drive-in facilities relatively ineffective. As in the case of NBG's Sheffield branch, other branches were built in existing office structures. Rarely was a convenient traffic flow inherent in those situations.

The consultant gathered up the available information and agreed to return in two weeks with a preliminary recommendation. The consultant also suggested that the bank request presentations from both Mosler and Diebold.

APPENDIX

EXCERPTS FROM MARKET DESCRIPTION FOR SHIEFFIELD BUILDING BRANCH

Population and income

The population of Atlanta during the last three census is:

1970*	1960*	1950†
496,973	487,455	437,785

* Population figures for entire city, including that portion in Dekalb County.

† 1950 figure is revised to reflect the 1960 population within the current boundaries of the city.

Estimate of service area population

The service area consists of census tracts 91, 93, and a portion of 95, all of Fulton County. Total 1970 population for these three tracts was 18,479. Only the southeastern quadrant of tract 95 is within the service area. Adjusting the census figures to conform more closely with the market yields a 1970 service area population of 14,167. Using revised estimates provided by the Atlanta Regional Commission, the 1973 service area population drops to 13,333. It should be noted that this drop does not necessarily reflect a significant trend of residential abandonment. To the contrary, population should remain rather stable in the short-term and increase steadily after 1974. The density of population is typically greatest in residential areas close to Peachtree Road, becoming less dense as the distance from Peachtree Road increases.

The service area extends from the proposed branch location approximately 1.4 miles north; 1.0 mile east; 0.6 mile west; and 0.8 mile south (see map in Exhibit A–1). There is no apparent extension of the market area due to the north-south linearity of development and traffic flow. Any extended boundary would overlap with other service areas to the north and south. Poor east-west access precludes expansion further out from Peachtree Road.

Income in the service area

Household incomes averages $20,600, $16,900, and $34,200 in tracts 91, 93, and 95 respectively in 1970. Visual observation of the service area portion of tract 95 suggests a lower average income for those households. Current average incomes probably run in the $18,000 to $25,000 range. Overall, household incomes are higher than the average for Atlanta and will probably remain so.

THE RESIDENTIAL ENVIRONMENT

Present

The portion of the service area which lies south of Peachtree Creek is included in an area designated by the Atlanta Planning Department as the Northside Parkway Area (NP). That portion of the service area which lies above Peachtree Creek constitutes the southwest corner of the planning area designated North Buckhead (NB).

. . . .

Although structural conditions are excellent in both NP and NB, isolated areas of deterioration were cited in the Atlanta Planning Department's report "Planning Atlanta: 1970." Some of that deterioration existed in the service area. It is anticipated, however, that the conversion of property in the area to higher yield uses will eliminate the problem entirely. The conversion will involve both medium to high density housing and commercial projects.

Overall, housing densities are higher in the service area than is common of NP and NB in general. Older, but well maintained houses on relatively small lots, as well as a concentration of some of the areas'

Exhibit A–1

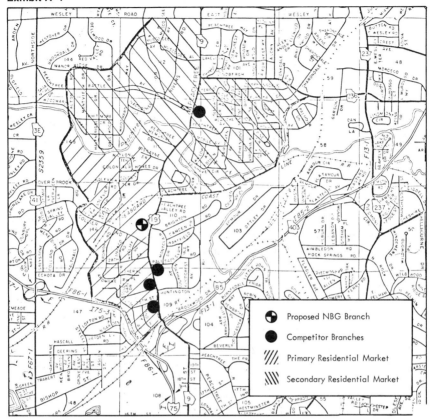

Legend:
- Proposed NBG Branch
- Competitor Branches
- Primary Residential Market
- Secondary Residential Market

multifamily units contribute to the residential density. The area is known for the cohesiveness of its home owners. This sense of community insures stability and the maintenance of quality in the low density residential portions of the service area.

Future

Future intended land use, as projected in "Planning Atlanta: 1970," reflects little change in residential portions of the service area. Conversion of some existing low density areas to higher density use is inevitable. Furthermore, some of the land along the Peachtree Road commercial strip will go to high density housing. One such project will add 200 apartments in a high-rise structure on the west side of Peachtree Road just below the Seaboard Coast Line tracks. Overall, the area's strategic location serves to protect property values and suggests continued improvement. Population growth will be slow, but steady as lower density residential land use yields to higher density conversion.

THE COMMERCIAL ENVIRONMENT

Industrial activity in Northside Parkway (NP) and North Buckhead (NB) is negligible. The small current industrial land use is located in two isolated pockets west of Peachtree Road and at a few points along railroad right-of-way. The bulk of commercial activity is service oriented and consists of small retail businesses, professional services, and Piedmont Hospital.

. . . .

North of the proposed branch site, on the east side of Peachtree Road, and below the Seaboard Railroad, are two large buildings, the Bankers Fidelity Life Insurance Company and the Darlington Apartments. Both are high rise structures offering high commercial and residential density. The tenant population of the office building is approximately 250. The apartments contain 600 efficiency and one-bedroom units and at least 10 retail merchant and service businesses. South of the apartments (on the east side of Peachtree Road) is a string of small businesses including a restaurant, grocery store, and several smaller shops. Within this group is a building owned by Carrier Air Conditioning. This building has over 24,000 square feet and is staffed with 50 employees.

South of Collier Road both sides of Peachtree Road are lined with a mix of small retail establishments, a number of low rise office buildings, and several community oriented facilities (Scottish Rite Temple, Jewish Community Center, and Atlanta Jewish Welfare Federation). The competition for banking services in the commercial community south of Collier Road is definitely more intense than that to the north. There are no bank facilities between Collier Road and Peachtree Battle Avenue.

Future

The plan for the service area indicates a solid commercial strip along both sides of Peachtree Road. The only exceptions are Piedmont Hospital and public property west of Peachtree Road between Peachtree Battle Avenue and Peachtree Creek. The portion of this strip north of the proposed branch site appears to be due for extensive redevelopment. There is room for several low- to high-rise structures. No appreciable increase in industrial activity is anticipated within the service area. The land immediately east of the southeastern border of the service area (along the Southern Railroad) should see some increase in industrial activity. That area is known as the Armour Industrial Park and is separated from the service area by the grade topography of the railroad right-of-way. Activity within the park should have little impact on the service area.

TRAFFIC AND TRANSPORTATION

Only one major artery runs through the service area, Peachtree Road. Furthermore, the other closeby arteries, Piedmont Avenue and Northside Drive, run parallel to Peachtree Road (north-side). Principle east-west access is provided by Collier Road and Peachtree Battle Avenue to the west and Lindbergh Drive and I–85 to the east. This particular situation has both desirable and undesirable features. On the positive side the lack of through streets has helped preserve the low density housing communities in the service area. With no improvement in sight, these communities should remain stable for some time.

On the negative side is the extreme concentration of commercial and high density residential development along Peachtree Road. Every new development in the area necessarily worsens the traffic problem on Peachtree Road. Again, no street improvement activities are projected for the service area. This congestion problem may eventually force some action. It is not apparent at this time whether the Rapid Transit plan will adequately alleviate the situation.

Of specific interest for the proposed branch is the traffic pattern at Collier Road and Peachtree Road. For a number of service area residents, Collier Road to Peachtree Road is the only convenient access to a wide range of commercial services. (The area is illustrated on map.) Thus, a natural traffic flow to the proposed site (using a Collier Road entrance) is available for a drive-in facility. A similar, but more competitive situation exists for Peachtree Road traffic southbound from Peachtree Battle Avenue, Lindbergh Drive, and Peachtree Hills Avenue. Access to the site for northbound traffic is at best limited.

SUMMARY

The service area for the proposed Sheffield Building branch is a stable, high quality residential and commercial community. Although not as dynamic as certain other areas in metropolitan Atlanta, the service area will experience steady growth in population and commercial activity. Much of the commercial growth will occur along Peachtree Road north of the proposed site. Banking competition there is light.

Traffic flow in the service area is definitely strong at the Collier Road/ Peachtree Road intersection. Much of the potential residential market could be serviced at this location through drive-in facilities. This would all be in addition to the base of business provided by the tenants of the Sheffield Building and adjacent medical offices and facilities.

case
15

Smith Chemical Company*

Since 1961 Smith Chemical has been located in Chase City, West Virginia, a city of 44,000. As communities and companies through the country developed a greater awareness of air pollution, Smith Chemical too became concerned about the extent to which its plant was causing odors to settle on the city's residents.

The company's management decided in 1966 to install pollution control devices. Since then, additional equipment has been incorporated into the initial devices. These efforts to control air pollution, while effective, did not completely eliminate the odor problem, and Chase City residents (with their heightened sensitivity to pollution) became disturbed by what they thought was a failure to correct the problem. Property owners insisted to the company's management that the odors were offensive and unbearable. They contended that the pollution was causing a decline in the value of their property. In addition, there was personal discomfort, which was manifested in eyes smarting.

A small group of property owners developed a petition requesting Smith Chemical to eliminate the odor. The petition was signed by more than 1,200 property owners in Chase City and was presented to the Smith management. The central thrust of the petition was that

* Case in *Marketing Decision Making: Analytic Framework and Cases* by William F. O'Dell, Andrew C. Ruppel, and Robert H. Trent (Cincinnati, Ohio: South-Western Publishing Co., 1976), pp. 251–56.

Smith Chemical had not yet solved the pollution problem and they demanded immediate corrective action.

The company management was sympathetic to the feelings of the community's residents. They pointed out to the group's leader that since 1966 they had been adding to their pollution control equipment. They stressed that they thought they had gone as far as they could without adopting a completely new manufacturing process, which, from a cost point of view, would be prohibitive. They had no desire to move out of the community, they stated, but continued insistence might cause them to do so. This comment received considerable coverage in the Chase City newspaper, and charges and counter-charges developed.

Smith Chemical did not wish to move from the community. In fact the management was of the private opinion that the pollution problem was being overstated by the highly vocal group that presented the petition. They therefore decided to conduct a telephone survey to measure the attitudes of the Chase City population to determine just how serious the problem was in the eyes of the community. The survey was designed to measure among other things:

Level of awareness of odors in the air.

Degree of concern about odors.

Description of odors.

Identity of sources of odors.

Frequency of noticing odors.

The resident locations of all petitioners were plotted on a map of Chase City. The vast majority lived in a broad area west of the Smith plant, which was located on the eastern edge of the city. The survey itself was conducted among petitioners and nonpetitioners. An analysis of the data revealed that there were virtually no differences between the signers and nonsigners. Thus, the data were combined.

The questionnaire did not reveal to interviewees that air pollution was the principal subject of the survey nor was Smith Chemical identified as the sponsor. The pollution questions were intermingled with questions on a variety of other subjects, such as property taxes, busing, law and order, education, and other local issues. The sample size was 514, divided equally among men and women of property-owning families.

An important finding is shown in Table 1. Of eight local issues, air pollution ranked sixth in terms of the respondents being "very concerned" about the particular issue. A total of 44 percent were "very concerned" about air pollution, in contrast to 76 percent being similarly concerned about property taxes. Education, law and order, streets

Table 1
Property owners' concern for community issues

					Local issues			
Level of concern	Property taxes	Education/ schools	Law and order	Streets and roads	Sewage treatment	Air pollution	Zoning	Parks/ recreation
Very concerned	76%	60%	62%	61%	60%	44%	25%	26%
Somewhat concerned	13	26	22	25	21	24	21	29
Slightly concerned	6	10	10	7	11	20	20	24
Not at all concerned	5	4	6	7	8	12	34	21
Total	100%	100%	100%	100%	100%	100%	100%	100%
Number of respondents	514							

and roads, and sewage treatment all were of greater concern to the property owners of the city than was the air pollution issue.

Another question asked of respondents related to which one of eight community issues was considered to be the most serious problem for property owners. The findings are shown in Table 2.

Table 2
Most serious community problems

Community problem	Percentage of property owners holding this viewpoint
Property taxes	33
Education/schools	28
Law and order	21
Streets and roads	5
Sewage treatment	5
Air pollution	5
Zoning	2
Parks/recreational facilities	1
Total	100
Total sample	514

Respondents were also read several statements pertaining to the Chase City community. On each statement they were asked the extent of their agreement or disagreement. As shown in Table 3, nearly half the population agreed with the statement, "Air pollution is not a problem in Chase City." Better than three out of four disagreed with the statement, "Industries that pollute the air should be closed down even if it means putting people out of work." And three out of four property owners feel that Chase City should do all it can to attract new industry to the city.

Table 3
Property owners' agreement with statements regarding local issues

	Statements and sequence in which they were read			
	(1)	*(2)*	*(3)*	*(4)*
	Chase City has fewer problems than other cities of its size	*Chase City should do all it can to attract new industry*	*Air pollution is not a problem in Chase City*	*Industries that pollute should be closed down*
Level of agreement				
Definitely agree	13%	74%	22%	8%
Tend to agree	32	15	23	14
Tend to disagree	37	6	28	28
Definitely disagree	18	5	27	50
Total	100%	100%	100%	100%
Number of respondents	514			

Property owners were also asked about their reactions to several types of pollution such as noise, water, and odor from sewage treatments as well as from industrial plants. While industrial air pollution was recognized as a serious problem in terms of the extent to which property owners thought the pollution "unreasonable to the degree that it interferes with life or property" (see Table 4).

Table 4
Degree to which property owners feel they are affected by various types of pollution

	Noise pollution	Order from sewage treatment	Water pollution	Order from industrial plants
Respondents aware of this type of pollution said:	22%	33%	41%	63%
The pollution is reasonable, although it may be annoying	9	12	10	26
The pollution is unreasonable, but not an interference with life or property	8	14	20	24
The pollution is unreasonable to the degree that it interferes with life and property	5	7	11	13
Respondents not aware of this type of pollution	78	67	59	37
Total	100%	100%	100%	100%
Number of respondents	514			

The complete report contained additional data, but for the most part it did not pertain to the overall attitudes of the Chase City property owners. These additional data related to such subjects as:

Frequency of noticing odors

Time of day odors are most noticeable

Type of day when odors are most noticeable

Season when odors are most noticeable

Descriptions of odors

Frequency of odor compared to last year

Smith Chemical's management, after reviewing the complete report, set aside a full morning to determine their next move. The company's president told those in attendance at the meeting that, if necessary, they would continue in session for the full day and that all persons invited to the meeting should plan their schedules accordingly.

case
16
Synthetic Quartz*

INTRODUCTION

In the early 1970s Dr. Edgar French and two colleagues were interested in the possibility of starting a company to grow synthetic piezoelectric quartz. Dr. French was employed at the time by Precision Communications Corporation, a large advanced technology firm involved in a wide range of electronic communications products. He had worked for a number of years in areas where he was exposed to the use of quartz crystals in a wide range of time and frequency standards and communications products. Although recent cutbacks in government spending had temporarily dampened the growth trend of the communications industry, French felt that the long-term outlook for communications products, and thus quartz crystals, was promising.

French had noticed that all of the domestic growers of synthetic quartz bars (from which crystals were produced) were located in the Mid-west and East. Although there were a number of firms who processed the quartz bars into crystal wafers, and an even greater number of firms using the crystals in other products, there were only a handful of firms in the business of growing the quartz bars. Given their expertise in the use of the product, French felt that he and his colleagues might be able to successfully enter the business and capture a share of the market. Having little more than this intuitive feel for the situation, French turned to two sources of information to get a better idea of the industry situation. First, he looked at the technical literature to gain a more thorough understanding of the background and nature of the production of synthetic quartz bars. Second, he retained the services of a consultant to get a more detailed estimate of the size of the market for synthetic quartz bars and the operating costs and capital requirements associated with the business.

---

* This case was prepared by Barnett A. Greenberg, Georgia State University.

HISTORY OF CULTURED QUARTZ

In the electronic world quartz is very important. It is the only material with which the highly accurate standards of frequency and time can be obtained that are necessary for telephone systems, data networks, and satellites. Its importance depends on its piezoelectric property: When subjected to mechanical stress, quartz produces electricity; when subjected to a voltage, it produces mechanical displacement.

Quartz crystals, properly cut and shaped into thin wafers are used as precision oscillators and highly selective wave filters. Such crystals, each cut vibrates at a particular frequency called the residence frequency, can vibrate at frequencies ranging from 400 cycles to 125 megacycles. Some quartz oscillators can remain accurate to 1 second for about 32 years.

Although quartz is abundant in the earth's crust, only a small percentage is suitable for electronic use. The largest and most numerous deposits of suitable quartz are found in Brazil, usually in hard-to-reach places. This situation is complicated further because, to avoid damage, crystals which are usually several inches in diameter must be hand mined. Then flaws must be removed before the crystal can be cut and fabricated in use for electronic circuits.[1]

This points out a critical element in the background of the development of cultured quartz. Although considerable controversy remains over the uncertainties associated with the purchase of natural quartz from Brazil, the need for a replacement for natural quartz after the second world war was increasingly an economic matter. Due to uncertainties in the delivery of natural quartz, quartz users found themselves accumulating large stock piles of raw material. Furthermore, the cutting of natural quartz resulted in considerable waste. This occurred in spite of the inspection in selecting quartz prior to shipment. Since quartz is purchased by the pound, it is imperative to use only those pieces of quartz which have maximum useful areas for cutting.

This problem became particularly acute for Western Electric, the manufacturing arm of the Bell system.

It has been estimated that only 6 percent of the total quartz found in Brazil is of suitable quality and size to be shipped to Western Electric for consideration. Because of the poor quality of natural quartz Western Electric has an agreement with the importers which permits the company to inspect stones prior to purchase; hence, at Western Electric the natural quartz is inspected and approximately 30 percent of the crystals are returned to the supplier as unsatisfactory. When it is considered that 20–25 thousand pounds of quartz are purchased each year, inspection and sorting involve considerable labor.

The Western Electric standard cost of natural quartz is $30 per pound, exclusive of handling and inspection. Of the quartz stones accepted only

---

[1] "Synthetic Quartz Equals Performance of Natural Crystals," *Chemistry* (November 1967).

40–60 percent of each stone is usable for the production of crystal units; a total of 90 percent of the quartz is lost, both as dust during sawing and lapping operations and also as scrap because of the previously mentioned imperfections in the stones and because the irregularity of the shape of the natural stone does not conform to the dimensions of quartz plates.

Thus, in the final quartz plates the cost of the quartz alone is about $1,500 per pound, or about $94 per ounce.

Also, there is the expense of carrying the two-year's inventory of natural quartz, valued at $1,200,000 which is necessitated by the instability of the foreign supply.[2]

Interruptions in the supply of natural quartz during World War II resulted in pilot projects for the production of cultured quartz by Bell Laboratories. By the mid 1950s, Bell Laboratories had developed the technique sufficiently advanced to warrant a parallel program at Western Electric for the development of production scale equipment. Although technological advances since that time have increased the capacity of a single production unit, the process has remained essentially the same.

The vessel in which quartz is grown is referred to an autoclave. An autoclave is a long tube which is designed to withhold tremendous pressures (30,000 pounds per square inch) and maintains specific temperatures at different points along the tube. An illustration of an early autoclave is provided in Exhibit 1. To grow a culture, quartz nutrients or small pieces of quartz which cannot be used to produce crystals, are lowered to the bottom of the autoclave. A rack is then lowered into the top of the autoclave from which seed crystals are hung. Temperature and pressure are then used to dissolve the nutrient and create a saturated environment around the seed crystals. By carefully regulating temperatures the new crystal will begin to grow around the seed. The size, shape, and mounting of the seed will determine the characteristics of the quartz bar which is grown. Also, large quartz bars require considerably longer growth cycles than smaller bars.

A typical autoclave in the early 1970s had an interior diameter of nine inches and a length of nine feet. Technological advances in the areas of alloy development and pressure containment at high temperatures promised larger autoclaves in the near future. Facilities for producing quartz tended to be capital intensive, as opposed to labor intensive. That is, labor is only required for loading and unloading the autoclaves. Once loaded, an autoclave operates automatically for at least 30 days (the minimum growth cycle for usable quartz). Birth cycles should be staggered since the power required to start up a

---

[2] Richard A. Sullivan, "Growing Quartz Crystals," (journal unidentified) (April 1959), p. 4.

Exhibit 1
Typical early production autoclave

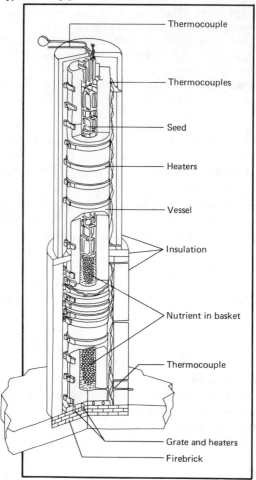

- Thermocouple
- Thermocouples
- Seed
- Heaters
- Vessel
- Insulation
- Nutrient in basket
- Thermocouple
- Grate and heaters
- Firebrick

production cycle is significantly higher than that required to maintain it. A variety of hoisting equipment is also required for handling the heavy head of the autoclave, nutrient baskets, seed racks, and the movement of autoclaves for repair.

CULTURED QUARTZ

Cultured quartz is grown in bars which generally resemble the illustration in Exhibit 2. This illustration is the common "Y" bar which constituted the bulk of cultured quartz production in the early 1970s.

Exhibit 2
Growth zones and dimensions of a cultured quartz bar grown on a Z cut seed

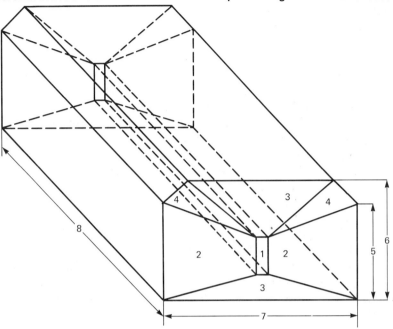

Key:
1. Seed
2. Z-growth
3. X-growth
4. B-growth
5. Base, face height
6. Height
7. Width
8. Length

These bars are grown from Z-cut seed, or seeds which are cut from the Z-growth region of a bar. Specifications for a bar include "handedness" and "orientation." These are both technical characteristics which relate to the manner in which the bar is to be cut and the applications of wafers cut from the bar.

The physical dimensions of a bar include length, width, height, gross height, basal face height, and weight. The length is essentially the length of the seed. The width is measured across the regions of Z-growth, while height is measured across the X-growth (see Exhibit 2). Height is either gross height, the maximum direction through the region of X-growth, or basal base height, the height of the Z-growth region. Weight is measured in pounds with typical Y-bars ranging from a few ounces each to several pounds each.

As of 1970, there were basically two types of bars being produced. The common Y-bar illustrated in Exhibit 2 grew from a relatively thin seed and promoted growth in both the Z and X dimensions. Another type of bar, the type with which Western Electric was most interested, grew from a much larger Z cut seed and produced a much larger area of pure Z-growth. Some quartz growers also offered a feature known as "lumbering." Lumbering was essentially a cutting process in which the regions of X and Z growth were reduced to provide maximum concentration of Z-growth. For certain applications lumbering reduced the amount of effort required for producing wafers from the bar. Obviously, lumbered bars sold for approximately twice the price per pound as nonlumbered bars.

While technology in the area of production tended toward emphasis increasing the capacity of autoclaves, product development technology emphasized improved quality and expanded applications for cultured quartz. Quality was essentially a matter of producing quartz which exhibited no impurities, as well as quartz with "Q" values approaching those of natural quartz. The Q value indicated the efficiency of the quartz piezoelectric property. The addition of lithium nitrate to the growing solution of the autoclave produces cultured quartz with a wide range of Q values which equal that of natural quartz.

. . . However, the electronic grade cultured product generally has a slightly lower Q than natural quartz. While this has not been detrimental in most applications, it can be noticeable in high precision design to requiring the higher Q of those operated at temperature extremes.

Crystals can be produced over a frequency range of roughly 1,000 Hz to 200 MHz. There are certain practical limitations to the use of crystals at the lower and upper extremes of this range. While a crystal can be produced at 1,000 Hz, it is generally more practical to use a higher frequency crystal and divide the desired frequency as a 1,000 Hz unit is difficult to manufacture and package and does not optimally utilize the raw material.

Similarly, frequencies in the high end of the range can best be achieved by using lower frequency crystals and multiplying the output. While 225 MHz can be reached by a ninth overtone crystal, circuit design problems inherent using such a device usually call for some alternative. Devices in the 100 kHz to 150 MHz range are easy to produce and offer a favorable degree of reliability, stability, and price.[3]

Thus, culture quartz crystals were technically competitive with natural quartz for a wide range of applications, but advances were needed for applications which involved extremely high or extremely low frequencies and extremely high or extremely low operating temperatures.

---

[3] Daryl Kemper and Lawrence Rosine, "Quartz Crystals for Frequency Control," *Electro-Technology* (June 1969), p. 43.

THE MARKET FOR UNCUT CULTURED QUARTZ

Although hundreds of firms produced quartz crystal components for use in communications and time frequency equipment, relatively few firms purchased quartz uncut. That is, a small number of firms purchased uncut quartz and cut "blanks" for use in the production of the actual crystal units. In all, those firms probably numbered less than 50 in 1970. Publicly available documents, such as proceedings of symposia on electronics and communications, as well as trade periodicals, provided ample sources from which to construct a list of potential purchasers of quartz (see Exhibit 3). These lists include many foreign purchasers.

Exhibit 4 is a composite of statistics from the Bureau of Mines. These figures illustrate the long-term trends through the late 1960s for quartz consumption and the mix of natural and synthetic quartz used. Overall, these statistics point out the trend toward increased use of synthetic quartz which is replacing natural quartz applications and providing increased productivity in the number of units produced per pound.

Annual purchases of uncut quartz by individual firms ranged from several hundred pound to over 20,000 pounds. Firms purchasing over 1,000 pounds of quartz a year were considered to be major customers by their suppliers. As of 1970, there were probably not more than 20 to 25 major users of synthetic quartz. The largest known single user was Western Electric, and they produced quartz to meet their own needs. Furthermore, Western Electric sold very little quartz in the open market. Other major users included Collins Radio, CTS KNIGHTS, Electronic Research, and Motorola.

As is the case with many technical industrial products, quartz tended to be homogeneous given the same specifications from any manufacturer. Manufacturers were able to distinguish themselves by offering technical services, prompt delivery, and special features, such as lumbering and high Q. Price had been a particularly strong competitive tool in the soft market of the late 1960s. Fast-growth, 30-to-45 day Y-bars were selling for $15 to $18 a pound. Nevertheless, continued growth for cultured quartz would be dependent upon more firms using it to replace synthetic quartz. Thus, technical services was becoming one of the most important areas on which a quartz grower could differentiate himself from competitors.

CONSULTANT'S REPORT

The consultant retained by Mr. French confirmed the general nature of the market and current trends in the demand for quartz. He added, however, detailed information concerning the capital require-

Exhibit 3
Sample list of quartz users

Company	LF < 1 MHz	HF > 1 MHz		Oscillators		Crystal filters		Circle number for data
	Non-AT cut	AT-cut solder-seal cans	Precision glass, cold weld	VCXO	TCXO	Conventional	Monolithic	
Accutronics, Inc.	●			●	●			451
American Crystal Co.		●	●					452
Anderson Electronics, Inc.		●				●		453
Austron, Inc.	Oven-controlled crystal oscillators							454
Bliley Electric Co.	●	●	●	●	●	●		455
Bomar Crystal Co.		●	●					456
CTS Knights, Inc.	●	●	●	●	●		●	457
Clark Crystal Corp.	●	●	●					458
Collins Radio Co.	●	●	●		●		●	459
Crystal Products, Inc.	●	●						460
Crystek Div. of Whitehall Electronics Corp.	●	●						461
Damon Engineering, Inc.				●		●	●	462
Eldson Electronic Co.	●	●						463
Electra/Midland Corp.	●	●	●	●	●	●		464
Electronic Crystals Corp.	●	●	●					465
Electronics Div. of Bulova Watch Co.	●	●	●	●	●	●	●	466
Electronic Research Co.	●	●	●	●	●	●	●	467
Erie Frequency Control	●	●	●	●	●	●		468
Filtech Corp.		●				●		469
Greenray Industries, Inc.				●	●			470
P. R. Hoffman Co.	Unmounted blanks only							471
Newport Beach Div. of Hughes Aircraft Co.	●	●	●	●	●	●		472
Industrial Crystal Corp.		●	●	●				473
International Crystal Mfg. Co.	●	●	●		●			474
M-tron Industries Inc.		●	●					475
McCoy Electronics Co.	●	●	●	●	●	●	●	476
Microsonics Div. of Sangamo Electric						●	●	477
Monitor Products Co.	●	●	●	●		●		478
Motorola C & E, Inc.		●	●	●	●	●	●	479
R. E. Nebel Laboratory		●	●	●	●			480
Northern Engineering Labs, Inc.	●	●	●	●	●			481
Petersen Radio Co.	●	●	●					482
Philips Electronics Ind., Ltd.	●	●	●					483
Piezo Crystal Co.	●	●	●		●	●	●	484
Piezoelectric Div. of Clevite Corp.	●	●	●		●	●		485
Precision Crystal Lab. Div. of Olympic General Corp.	●	●						486
Reeves-Hoffman Div. of Dynamics Corp. of America	●	●	●	●	●	●	●	487
Sentry Mfg.	●	●	●	●				488
Tedford Crystal Labs., Inc.	●	●		●	●	●	●	489
T. M. C. Systems (Ariz.), Inc.	●	●		●	●	●	●	490
Torotel, Inc.	●	●	●	●	●	●		491
TRW Electronics Group	●	●	●					492
TRW Crystal Plant	●	●	●					493
Tyco Crystal Products Group	●	●	●			●	●	494
Valpey Fisher Corp.	●	●	●	●	●		●	495

Source: Daryl Kemper and Lawrence Rosine, "Quartz Crystals for Frequency Control," *Electro-Technology,* (June 1969), p. 49.

Exhibit 4
Selected statistics on quartz consumption

Year	Consumption of all quartz for producing piezoelectric units (000 pounds)	Piezo-electric units produced (000s)	Units per pound of quartz consumed	Estimate of natural quartz consumption (000 pounds)	Synthetic quartz consumption (000 pounds)
1955	134	4,090	30.5	—	—
1956	162	5,390	33.3	—	—
1957	182	5,787	31.8	—	—
1958	158	5,510	34.9	157.6	0.38
1959	210	6,820	32.5	206.1	3.9
1960	230	8,712	37.9	225.4	4.6
1961	188	6,444	34.3	181.5	6.5
1962	291	11,787	40.5	278.0	13.0
1963	325	13,614	41.9	307.0	18.0
1964	344	17,920	52.1	314.0	34.9
1965	315	17,832	56.6	265.0	50.6
1966	363	27,463	75.5	283.4	79.6
1967	332	23,340	70.5	229.3	102.6
Average annual percent increase/(decrease)					
1958–1963	15.5%	19.9%	3.8%	14.3%	47.0%
1964–1967	0.5%	14.5%	13.9%	(7.6%)	55.0%

Source: Bureau of Mines.

ments and operating resource requirements for a firm in the quartz growing business. The key component of the process, the autoclave, cost approximately $25,000 installed. The typical nine-inch by nine-foot autoclave would produce approximately 300 pounds of quartz in a single production run. With good quality control, 90 to 95 percent of that yield would be marketable. Assuming that an average production cycle was 45 days, a single autoclave will produce a total of 2,400 pounds of quartz in a year of which 2,200 to 2,300 would be marketable.

It is necessary to buy a number of autoclaves since one out of every five production runs would have to be devoted to growing quartz for seed crystals. Furthermore, occasional experimental runs are necessary to continuously develop competitive products and improve the production process itself. Finally, plans should be made to load no more than one autoclave in a 24-hour period. As mentioned earlier, this allows efficient utilization of electrical power. This poses no serious problem since a relatively small facility could plan to load no more than one autoclave in any given week.

It is not uncommon in this industry for autoclaves and their enclosures to account for one half of a firm's fixed assets. Similarly, over one half of current assets can be easily tied up in raw materials and finished goods inventory. Since the ability of a firm to meet delivery schedules is an important competitive tool, and since orders can range from a few pounds to a thousand pounds or more, a sizable stock should be maintained.

The consultant provided estimates on an operation involving ten autoclaves. This would allow a new firm to devote a considerable amount of its production to seed runs and experimentation. Seven autoclaves devoted full time production runs would provide adequate capacity for annual sales up to 12,000 pounds or 13,000 pounds. Starting on a small scale would also allow the grower to add larger more efficient autoclaves as they become available and sales increase. Assuming first year sales to be 10,000 pounds at an average net price of $15 per pound, the consultant felt that the operation would earn $30,000 before taxes. The expected breakdown of major expense categories:

Depreciation—25 percent Direct product cost—35 percent Selling expenses—20 percent General and administrative expenses—20 percent

EDWIN FRENCH'S DILEMMA

Dr. French feels that he can be successful in the quartz business. He has a background of experience both in the use of quartz and in dealing with quartz growers. He has felt for some time that there is an opportunity for a bright, aggressive, technically competent entrepreneur to gain the competitive foothold by providing superior service to the quartz users. He is troubled, however, by the fact that none of the information which he has received to date takes into consideration old established loyalties between suppliers and customers and the noticeable decrease in the rate of total quartz consumption. His colleagues are exerting pressure to pursue the venture, but he feels that additional information is required before an intelligent decision can be reached.

QUESTION

What information should he seek and how could it be obtained?

case
17
Bender Mattress Company*

The Bender Mattress Company of Los Angeles, California, manufactured mattresses, box springs, convertible sofas, and some furniture. The greatest portion of its business was in mattresses and box springs, under the brand name Restful. It sold to retail stores in Southern California and the territory up to but not including San Francisco.

The major concern of the company was to increase unit sales. In this industry, according to Bender executives, prices are predetermined by competition, particularly in national companies, and average costs are approximately constant throughout the significant volume range. Thus, increased profits become a function of increased volume, which, in turn, is dependent largely upon the effectiveness of marketing efforts.

Of Restful's annual advertising budget of $400,000, 60 percent was being spent to sponsor the weather forecast on the 11 P.M. newscast on Tuesday, Thursday, and Sunday over Channel 4; 24 percent in cooperative newspaper advertising; and 16 percent on point-of-sale material. This media plan had been in effect for three years.

For Downy, a competing brand, the total amount and breakdown of advertising were estimated to be approximately the same. The Nighttime Company, in contrast, was spending about as much but concentrating it on cooperative advertising in newspapers. Restful and Downy were the only two brands using TV.

Bender commissioned a research agency to test the effectiveness of its advertising program, for a fee of $5,000. Questionnaires were mailed to a sample of 6,000 family units in the Los Angeles metropolitan area selected at random; and 999 usable returns were received. Some of the resulting tabulations follow in Exhibits 1 through 6.

---

* Case in *Cases in Marketing Management* by Edward C. Bursk and Stephen A. Greyser, 2d ed. (Englewood Cliffs, N.J.: Prentice-Hall, Inc., 1975), pp. 12–18.

Exhibit 1
Brand decision—All respondents

Decision on brand to purchase made by:

Husband	9%
Wife	27
Both	46
Do not remember	7
No response	11
Total..............................	100%

Exhibit 2
Brand recognition—All respondents

Brand name

Night-time	90%
Restful....................	88
Downy	87
Bye-Bye	82
Californian	65
Posture-plus	34
Sleep-Rest	25
Angelic	16
Moonlight.................	10
Other	12
No response	3

Exhibit 3
Shopping habits—All respondents

Number of stores shopped

One	33%
More than one	57
Do not remember; no response	10
Total..............................	100%

Furniture bought with mattress

Bedroom set	23%
Springs and bed	16
Springs	28
Purchased mattress only	28
Other and no response	5
	100%

Type of store in which mattress was purchased

Department	31%
Furniture	36
Discount	4
Sleep shop	3
Other and no response	26
Total..............................	100%

Exhibit 4
Brand preferences

A. Pre-purchase preferences—All respondents

Restful	7%
Bye-Bye	2
Downy	6
Night-time	10
Californian	2
All other	8
No preference	65
	100%

B. Brand purchased and brand preferred—Respondents with prepurchase preference

Prepurchase brand preference

Brand purchased	Restful	Bye-Bye	Downy	Night-time	Californian	All others
Restful	77%	—	—	6%	—	—
Bye-Bye	—	82%	—	1	—	—
Downy	2	6	83%	—	—	5%
Night-time	12	6	—	82	—	3
Californian	2	—	2	1	82%	1
All others	2	6	6	6	12	84
Do not remember	5	—	9	4	6	7
Total	100%	100%	100%	100%	100%	100%

Exhibit 4 (continued)

C. Recall of advertising—All respondents

Source of advertising	Recalled mattress advertising		Recalled brand advertised						Brand not recalled or not related to source	Total
	Yes	No	Restful	Bye-Bye	Downy	Night-time	Californian	All others		
Radio	16%	84%	2%	1%	2%	2%	*	*	9%	16%
TV	76	24	26	8	31	4	1	*	6	76
Newspapers	48	52	6	2	4	6	1	3	26	48
Magazines	44	56	5	3	3	9	2	*	22	44
Billboards	15	85	1	1	1	1	1	*	10	15

* Less than 1 percent.

D. Recent and nonrecent purchases by prepurchase brand preference—TV viewers only

Prepurchase brand preference	Recent purchasers		Nonrecent purchasers	
	Number	Percent	Number	Percent
Restful	23	28	27	19
Bye-Bye	3	4	10	7
Downy	18	21	21	15
Night-time	15	18	43	31
Californian	3	4	12	8
All others	21	25	28	20
Total	83	100	141	100

Exhibit 5 Relative importance of factors affecting selection of brand by brand purchased—All respondents

Factors and relative importance	Restful	Downy	Night-time	Bye-Bye	Californian	All others	Do not remember and no response	Total all brands
Salesman's suggestion								
Very important	24%	16%	18%	22%	21%	22%	14%	19%
Important	22	23	19	29	28	23	21	22
Not important	24	30	29	18	21	24	21	25
No response	30	31	34	31	30	31	44	34
Total	100%	100%	100%	100%	100%	100%	100%	100%
Advertising								
Very important	19%	24%	13%	6%	10%	8%	8%	12%
Important	27	28	21	20	14	16	13	19
Not important	23	18	28	29	30	36	31	29
No response	31	30	28	45	46	40	48	40
Total	100%	100%	100%	100%	100%	100%	100%	100%
Previous experience								
Very important	35%	23%	39%	35%	30%	30%	14%	28%
Important	14	21	13	16	9	12	9	13
Not important	18	20	20	16	21	23	27	22
No response	33	36	28	33	40	35	50	37
Total	100%	100%	100%	100%	100%	100%	100%	100%
Special discount								
Very important	17%	16%	13%	29%	30%	18%	13%	17%
Important	20	15	9	11	14	12	16	13
Not important	25	27	32	25	23	30	20	27
No response	38	42	46	35	33	40	51	43
Total	100%	100%	100%	100%	100%	100%	100%	100%
Advertised sale								
Very important	12%	26%	11%	14%	14%	17%	16%	16%
Important	10	19	9	12	4	9	13	11
Not important	37	30	35	35	39	36	25	33
No response	41	25	45	29	44	38	46	40
Total	100%	100%	100%	100%	100%	100%	100%	100%

Exhibit 6
Factors related to selection of store where purchased—All respondents

	Relative importance				
Factors	Very important	Important	Not important	No response	Total
Location of store	14%	16%	33%	37%	100%
Reputation of store	54	19	4	23	100
Generally shop there	20	12	29	39	100
Store advertising	9	15	32	44	100
Special price	31	17	18	34	100
Store salesman	13	13	31	43	100

QUESTIONS

What can the Bender management learn from the tabulations as to the effect of various factors on the purchase of the brand of mattress? Should it make any changes in its promotional mix?

---

case
18

Pantry Pride versus Acme: A comparison shopping test*

Pantry Pride is a series of supermarkets owned by Food Fair Stores, Inc. In 1975, Food Fair management became concerned about the impact of an advertising campaign by one of their competitors in the Philadelphia market (Acme/Super Saver). The campaign involved heavy use of media (radio, TV, and newspapers) to communicate the message that Acme had lower prices. The gist of the TV commercials was to portray an Acme shopper being intercepted after she had checked out of the supermarket. She was asked to go to another store of her choice and duplicate her Acme order. She was then filmed returning from the other store with her purchases. The totals were compared

_____
* This case was prepared by Danny N. Bellenger and Barnett A. Greenberg, Georgia State University.

and the Acme shopper invariably claimed that she saved anywhere from pennies to many dollars by shopping at Acme. A typical Acme ad is shown in Exhibit 1.

Exhibit 1
Typical Acme ad (copy only)

Mrs. Bea Drier

After she had checked out her Acme/Super Saver order, Mrs. Bea Drier was asked to go to another store of her choice, that same day, and, at our expense, duplicate her Acme/Super Saver order—item for item, pound for pound. She agreed and when she returned from the other store with the identical purchases, the two totals were compared. Mrs. Drier had saved $1.37 at Acme/Super Saver.

Super savings every day...you're going to like it here!

Management felt that an unfair impression was being communicated to the consumer, thus they commissioned Chilton Research Services to do a price comparison test between Pantry Pride and Acme. The nature and findings of that study were as follows:

STUDY PROCEDURES

Data collection

This study was conducted between 9 a.m. Monday, October 13, 1975 and 6 p.m. Wednesday, October 15, 1975 in the following stores:

	Pantry Pride	*Acme*
# 37	Aramingo & Castor Avenue	Aramingo & Westmoreland
# 53	522 City Line Avenue	7600 City Line and Narbeth, PA
#106	Wayne, PA	Wayne, PA
#109	6601 Roosevelt Blvd.	Magee & Harbison
#400	Moorestown, NJ	Moorestown, NJ

Prior to going to the stores all interviewers were personally briefed by Chilton Research Services field supervisors and given detailed written instructions (see Appendix).

In the case of the City Line Pantry Pride store, the interviewers were originally instructed to take all shoppers to the Acme at 7600 City Line. However, on Monday morning, October 13, 1975, it became apparent that the designated Acme was out of stock on a majority of the items that the shoppers had purchased at Pantry Pride. It was, therefore, decided to take the shoppers to the next nearest Acme which was located in Narbeth, PA. Chilton Research Services recommended this change to avoid biasing the study in favor of Pantry Pride.

The procedures followed at each store were as follows:

1. At each sample Pantry Pride store, the respondents were approached by the Chilton interviewers *as they were ready to check out*.
2. The selected respondent was asked to participate in the study and checked for qualification and demographic characteristics. No employee or relative of an employee of Food Fair Stores, Inc. or Pantry Pride was allowed to participate in the study.
3. If the respondent qualified, she was then taken to a special checkout counter where the cashier rang up each item and called out the item, price, and if necessary, the weight and price per pound. The Chilton interviewer wrote down each item as it was called out by the checker.
4. The Chilton interviewer then took the respondent to the nearby Acme and duplicated the order exactly. In those cases where a Pantry Pride brand was purchased, the comparable Acme brand was also purchased. This is the only time substitution was allowed.
5. At the Acme store, the interviewer recorded each item purchased by the shopper, its price and, if necessary, its weight and price per pound.
6. After checking the order out of the Acme, the respondent was taken back to the Pantry Pride store and given a $25 gift certificate for her cooperation.
7. The Acme order was marked for identification and brought to the Radnor office of Chilton Research Services for checking.

Analysis

As the Acme orders were received at Chilton Research Services, they were grouped by respondent. All orders and forms were then checked in the following manner.

1. The prices of the Pantry Pride purchases recorded on the shopping list were checked, item by item against the cashier tape from the store, and any discrepancies noted.
2. All Acme purchases were checked against the shopping list and the Acme cashiers tape, and any discrepancies noted.
3. The amount spent at both stores prior to coupon deductions and taxes was determined and recorded.
4. The cost of all items that were purchased at Pantry Pride but could not be purchased at Acme was deducted from the Pantry Pride total. This procedure, if anything, biased the results in favor of Acme since a large number of respondents purchased sales items at Pantry Pride, but could not obtain these items at Acme. Therefore, the item was deleted from the study.
5. The cost of all items in which the incorrect brand, size, or weight was purchased at Acme was deducted from both the Pantry Pride and Acme totals.
6. In order to be absolutely fair to Acme, all respondents were given credit if the item was purchased, for the store coupons they could have used. This credit was based on the advertisements for both stores that appeared in the *Sunday Inquirer* of October 12, 1975. The specific items for which coupon credit was given are as follows:

Pantry Pride

Mrs. Filberts Soft Golden Margarine (1 lb bowl) .... 07¢
Right Guard Anti-Perspirant Deodorant (5 oz can) .... 20¢
Cheerios Cereal (10 oz package) .... 08¢
Dishwasher All Detergent (Auto. Dishwasher) (3 lb 2 oz package).............. 20¢
Wizard Air Freshner (9 oz can) .... 10¢
Dial Bath Soap (4–5 oz bars) .... 24¢
Buitoni Frozen Cheese Ravioli (15 oz pkg.) .... 10¢
Seamist Pine Oil Cleaner (1 pt. 8 oz bottle) .... 10¢
Promise Margarine (1 lb package) .... 12¢
Gold Medal Flour (10 lb bag) .... 20¢

Acme

Lancaster or Farmdale Franks (1 lb pkg.) .... 20¢
Purina Asst. Varieties Cat Food (5–6 oz can) .... 35¢
Revlon Milk Plus 6 (8 oz bottle) .... 30¢
Revlon Hi-Dri Roll On Deodorant (2½ oz pkg.) .... 25¢
Jergens Lotion (10 oz bottle) .... 30¢
Digel Mint Flavor (100 tablets or 12 oz) .... 50¢
Correctol Laxative Tablets (pkg. of 30) .... 30¢
Promise Margarine (1 lb pkg.) .... 12¢
Mrs. Filberts Soft Corn Oil Margarine (2–8 oz cups) .... 10¢
Ideal Cheese (Blue or Monterey Jack Pre-cut) .... 15¢
Total Cereal (12 oz box) .... 08¢
Betty Crocker Ready to Spread Frosting (16. 5 oz can) .... 10¢
Salada Tea Bags (pkg. of 100) .... 35¢
Glad Plastic Wrap (100 sq ft roll) .... 10¢
Final Touch Fabric Softener (33 oz bottle) .... 20¢
White Potatoes (10 lb or 20 lb pkg.) .... 30¢

7. In the case of meat, produce, and delicatessen, the Acme cost was adjusted to the weight purchased at Pantry Pride by multiplying the Pantry Pride weight by the Acme cost per pound. This ensures the absolute comparability of both orders.
8. The calculations for each store were recorded on the appropriate forms, double checked and tabulated by Chilton Resarch Services.

General

A total of 100 interviews were obtained. These interviews were grouped as follows:

27 with respondents spending $10 to $19

27 with respondents spending $20 to $29
18 with respondents spending $30 to $39
28 with respondents spending $40 or more

18 at store #37
20 at store #53
20 at store #106
22 at store #109
20 at store #400

All food purchased at the Acme stores was donated by Food Fair Stores, Inc. to the Roger Greaves School for the Blind at 118 South Valley Road, Paoli, PA.

FINDINGS

Table 1
Number and percent of shoppers saving money at each supermarket chain, Philadelphia area

Saved money at:	Number	Percent
Pantry Pride	73	73%
Acme	25	25
No difference	2	2
Base	(100)	(100)

Table 2
Number and percent of shoppers saving money at each supermarket chain by size of order, Philadelphia area

Size of order	Number	Percent
$10 to $19		
Pantry Pride	20	74.1%
Acme	5	18.5
No difference	2	7.4
Base	(27)	(27)
$20 to $29		
Pantry Pride	20	74.1%
Acme	7	25.9
Base	(27)	(27)
$30 to $39		
Pantry Pride	14	77.7%
Acme	4	22.2
Base	(18)	(18)
$40 to $60		
Pantry Pride	19	67.9%
Acme	9	32.1
Base	(28)	(28)

Table 3
Number and percent of shoppers saving money at each supermarket chain by specific Pantry Pride stores, Philadelphia area

53 and City Line	Number	Percent
Pantry Pride	15	75.0%
Acme	4	20.0
No difference	1	5.0
Base	(20)	(20)
Roosevelt Blvd.		
Pantry Pride	18	81.8%
Acme	3	13.6
No difference	1	4.5
Base	(22)	(22)
Castor and Cottman		
Pantry Pride	14	77.8
Acme	4	22.2
Base	(18)	(18)
Wayne, PA.		
Pantry Pride	14	70.0%
Acme	6	30.0
Base	(20)	(20)
Moorestown, NJ		
Pantry Pride	13	65.0%
Acme	7	35.0
Base	(20)	(20)

Table 4
Number and percent of shoppers saving $1 or more at each supermarket chain, Philadelphia area

Saved $1 or more at:	Number	Percent
Pantry Pride	19	19.0%
Acme	4	4.0%
Saved less than $1 at either store	77	77.0%
Base	(100)	(100)

Table 5
Actual counts of amount saved by shopping at each store, Philadelphia area

Size of order	Pantry Pride	Acme	No difference
$10 to $19	0.22	0.34	1
	1.45	0.24	
	0.36	1.15	2
	0.29	0.12	
	0.66	0.12	
	0.81		
	0.28		
	0.07		
	0.21		
	0.23		
	0.58		
	0.03		
	0.98		
	0.57		
	0.58		
	1.49		
	2.06		
	2.58		
	0.30		
	1.68		
$20 to $29	0.03	0.31	
	1.17	0.52	
	0.47	0.36	
	0.02	0.17	
	1.89	0.09	
	0.56	0.69	
	0.05	0.47	
	3.05		
	1.65		
	0.19		
	1.16		
	0.14		
	0.08		
	0.59		
	0.59		
	0.80		
	0.12		

Table 5 *(continued)*

Size of order	*Pantry Pride*	*Acme*	*No difference*
	0.68		
	0.11		
	1.28		
$30 to $39	0.52	0.04	
	0.18	0.73	
	0.45	1.43	
	0.41	0.95	
	0.03		
	0.13		
	0.35		
	0.75		
	0.38		
	6.47		
	0.48		
	0.48		
	1.61		
	1.25		
$40 to $60	0.71	1.64	
	0.19	0.39	
	0.14	0.38	
	1.39	1.67	
	0.89	0.33	
	2.50	0.55	
	0.88	0.33	
	0.12	0.51	
	0.72	0.36	
	0.13		
	0.66		
	0.68		
	0.64		
	1.63		
	0.71		
	1.37		
	0.63		
	0.35		
	1.48		

MANAGEMENT ACTIONS

Based on the results of the study, management decided to launch an advertising campaign to counter Acme. A typical ad from the campaign is shown in Exhibit 2.

Exhibit 2
Pantry Pride counter ad (copy only)

Q. Do Those Ladies on TV Really Save All That Money by Shopping at Acme?
A. Not If They Shop At Pantry Pride First!

According to a study done last week by one of the nation's top research firms, Chilton Research Services, they'd save more if they shopped at Pantry Pride.

"On Monday, Tuesday & Wednesday of last week, 100 shoppers were selected at random in Pantry Pride stores and asked to duplicate their Pantry Pride orders in an Acme store—'item for item, pound for pound'.

"*The Result:* 73 of the 100 shoppers— almost three out of four—saved money by shopping at Pantry Pride."

Research conducted and results certified by CHILTON RESEARCH SERVICES

Bruce Z. Bortner
Director, Survey Research

At Pantry Pride You Win Because We Don't Play Games.

QUESTIONS

1. Discuss the managerial use of this research.
2. Evaluate the methodology used in the study.
3. What alternative approaches do you suggest?

APPENDIX

Radnor, Pennsylvania 19089
215-687-8200

DATE: October 10, 1975

TO: All Interviewers   FROM: Ruth Finkel, Field Supervisor

SUBJECT: Instructions for Shopping Study #8973

We have made arrangements to have a special cashier ring up and check out your respondent's order. In this way, we hope to make your job easier and eliminate cashier mistakes and interviewer mistakes. We realize that by approaching the respondent prior to her check-out, it will be more difficult to fill your quota groups exactly. The store manager will aid you by telling you approximately how much an order should come to by looking at the baskets. He has had enough experience to be able to total the costs at an eye's glance. The quota per store is 20 shoppings and broken down as follows:

$10–$19—5 shoppings

$20–$29—5 shoppings

$30–$39—5 shoppings

$40–$60—5 shoppings

At the Pantry Pride store, you will be recording each item purchased as the cashier is checking it out. You will use one line on the form for each ring of the register. At the Acme store, you will record on the line opposite the product purchased at Pantry Pride the price marked on the item or shelf as you go through the store with your respondent.

The same exact items must be purchased at the Acme store. If at the Acme store they do not have the same exact item, do not purchase anything, i.e. brand must match brand and size must match size. (Exception: Pantry Pride brand versus Ideal brand. Covered in later instructions). The most difficult ones to do this with are items from meat and produce. The following items should help you in your decision making:

In produce, if you have a prepackaged item, you must purchase the same item prepackaged, i.e., if you buy prepackaged three to a package tomatoes in Pantry Pride, you must buy prepackaged three to a package tomatoes in Acme. If you buy loose mushrooms in Pantry Pride, you must buy loose mushrooms in Acme. With meat, you must buy the same exact cut of meat, i.e., if you buy chicken halves with backbone, you must buy chicken halves with backbone in Acme. You may have to buy more than one package to equal the quantity that was purchased at Pantry Pride, i.e., if respondent purchased one container of chicken halves with backbone which equal three pounds, you may have to purchase two 1½ pound containers of chicken halves with backbone in order to equal the weight. Take your time in doing your shopping and be sure to get the correct brands and correct quantity. It doesn't hurt the study nor is there any effect on you if the other store doesn't have the same exact item.

INTERVIEWING OPERATING PROCEDURES

Selection of respondent—As the respondent comes up to the check-out lanes in the front of the store, you will approach respondent, explain study and ask her cooperation.

Complete the one page questionnaire—Be very sure that you do not take any one who works for or has a relative that works for Food Fair or Pantry Pride.

Have respondent sign release form.

Take respondent to special check-out counter to have her groceries checked-out as she normally would.

At special check-out counter cashier will tell you all the information which you will need to fill in your forms. As she is ringing up each item, she will tell you what the brand name is, what the product is, the size and the price. If it is produce which must be weighed, she will tell you how much each item weighs, the price per pound and total cost. As she is doing this, you will be recording all the specific information on your shopping list.

At this time, you should have your shopping list completed, listing all items which were purchased by the respondent.

You will now take the respondent and your shopping list to the nearest Acme store listed on your sheet. You will duplicate her exact order which she purchased in Pantry Pride.

Go around with respondent as she purchases each item. Be sure that each item is the same brand and the same exact size as indicated on your shopping list.

Note: For items that are Pantry Pride brand, the respondent must get the comparable Acme brand (Ideal). If the same exact size is not available, do not purchase any brand. No substitutes. If the same brand is not available, do not purchase anything. No substitutes.

As the respondent puts each item into the shopping cart, you are to be checking the following things:

a. If possible, a price is stamped on the item (except produce).
b. It is the same brand as purchased in Pantry Pride (except for store brand).
c. It is the same size as purchased in Pantry Pride.

Note: In the case of meats, produce, and Deli, you are to come to the closest weight possible that was purchased in Pantry Pride. If the respondent purchased a pre-bagged package of apples she must purchase one pre-bagged package of apples in Acme. You may not substitute loose items for bagged items and vice versa.

Take respondent to check-out counter. Let her bag as you watch cashier ring up order. Be certain cashier rings up correct amount for each customer.

When cashier weighs the produce ask her for the exact weight and cost. Then record this on the special produce sheet which you have been provided. If cashier is going too fast for you tell her to slow down. Act as if you are the customer.

Pay for order and be sure you obtain your cashier register receipt.

Take respondent back to original Pantry Pride store.

a. Have her sign Acme receipt. Also have her sign Pantry Pride receipt.

b. Give her back the groceries.

c. Give her her gift certificate

Attach shopping list and cashier register receipts to questionnaire.

Take meats and ice cream out of bags and cut off complete label or flap containing price.

Give these items to Pantry Pride store manager. Put labels into envelope and put back into Acme shopping bag for this respondent.

Make sure that Acme order is stored away and that respondents names are on all packages in dark printing.

Get another respondent and begin again.

SHOPPING LIST

As you can see we have given you two separate sheets for your shopping list. One sheet is for your Groceries, and the second is for your Meat and Produce. This is because we need more detailed information for meat and produce.

First, let's talk about the Grocery list column for column.

At the top lefthand corner is a place for you to record the Pantry Pride address. On the righthand side is space for you to record the address of the Acme store. Then there is room to record the name of the respondent.

We have divided the sheet into one-half Pantry Pride and one-half Acme. This should make your shopping and recording easier.

Brand: You are to record the brand name of each product that the respondent purchased (i.e., Del Monte, Kellogg's, Pantry Pride, Abbott's, Dairy Maid, etc.)

Product: Record a full description of the item. You must be able to tell exactly what was purchased at Pantry Pride when you are at the Acme store (i.e., canned green peas, (Frozen Green Peas), Rice Krispies, 4-ply toilet paper, vanilla ice cream, sour cream with chives).

Weight (Size): All you have to do here is record the actual weight which is on the product (i.e., 7.5 oz., 18 oz., 3½ oz., 4 rolls).

Note: If a customer buys 3 cans of Campbell's Tomato soup @ .15 and the cashier rings up .45, this is what would be entered on one line. On the other hand, if the cashier rings up each can separately at .15 each, use 3 lines as indicated below:

Campbell's Canned Tomato Soup	10 oz.	1	.15
Campbell's Canned Tomato Soup	10 oz.	1	.15
Campbell's Canned Tomato Soup	10 oz.	1	.15

YOU MUST HAVE A SEPARATE LINE FOR EACH CASH REGISTER RING!

Now, we come to the Acme side of the list.

Brand, product and weight (size): Even though the brand, product, weight (size) should be exactly the same, we still want you to record this information from the product which you are purchasing at Acme. The only change in brand should be from Pantry Pride to Ideal, otherwise it should be exactly the same or do not purchase the item.

Listed Price: Record the price stamped on the item or listed on shelf. That is:

.22
.35
1.60
2 for. 39

Quantity: Must be the same as in the Pantry Pride store.

Check if not available: Place a check in this column to indicate that for whatever reason (wrong size, wrong brand, etc.) you did not purchase the product.

The next columns are of Office Use Only, and you will not record anything in it.

Produce and meat

The top of the sheet is filled in exactly as before.

Brand: Very often with produce and meat there is not a brand name. Therefore, you would just record Pantry Pride. Be careful, however, because there are items which have brand names. For example, there may be just regular packaged chicken or it may be a manufacturer's brand such as Purdue. Oranges could be just "no brand" types or they could be Sunkist oranges. What you purchase in one store must be purchased in the other exactly.

Product: As before, you must record exactly what is purchased, i.e., navel oranges, baking potatoes, seedless white grapes, chicken breasts with back, regular ground chuck, pork loin roast, rib lamb chops, boiled imported ham, lean corn beef, etc.

Weight: On items such as meat and poultry there is usually a label on it which states the price per pound, how much the meat actually weighs and total cost. From this label you are to take the actual weight and record it in this column.

Note: When the label reads 3.07, that is 3.07 lbs., *not* 3 lbs., 7 oz.

With produce, most of it will be weighed and priced at the cashier counter. The cashier will tell you exactly what it weighs. You will record the weight (3 lbs. 7 oz.) in this column. (At Pantry Pride the cashier will tell you this.)

Loose or prebagged: Some produce is loose and the respondent will pick the ones she wants and then it must be weighed. Other produce is prepackaged and already weighed; i.e., apples can come loose and then must be weighed to get the price, or they may come in a prepacked bag that is marked 3 lbs. Check the appropriate column for each item.

Note: If respondent bought prepackaged apples at Pantry Pride, she must purchase prepackaged (NOT LOOSE) apples at Acme.

Price per pound: Record the actual price per pound for the product. For meat and poultry it should be on the label. For produce the cashier will have to tell you what it is.

Cost to customer: The total price that each item cost the customer.

Now we are on the Acme side! You will record everything the same way as you did on the Pantry Pride side. Be careful when you are trying to duplicate weight. For meat items you may have to buy two packages to equal the weight that was purchased at Pantry Pride. We have given you enough space in the columns so you can fit the package weight in the one block.

If a product is not available, check the "not available" column.

At Acme you are to ask the cashier or weigher for the actual weight of each product.

IF CASHIER IS GOING TOO FAST, TELL HER TO SLOW DOWN!

INDEXES

Author Index

Subject index

This book has been set in 10 and 9 point Caledonia, leaded 2 points. Part numbers and titles and chapter titles are 20 point Helvetic Bold. Chapter numbers are 20 point Helvetica Bold and 48 point Caslon 540. The size of the type page is 27 by 45½ picas.